FAMILY LAW

FAMILY LAW

Third Edition

Anne Griffiths, LLB, PhD
Professor of Law at the University of Edinburgh

John M. Fotheringham, LLB, WS
BTO Solicitors, Edinburgh & Glasgow

Frankie McCarthy, LLB, PhD
Lecturer in Private Law at the University of Glasgow

Previous edition by

Lillian Edwards, LL.B., LL.M., M.Sc.
Professor of Law at the University of Strathclyde

and

Anne Griffiths, LLB, PhD
Professor of Law at the University of Edinburgh

SWEET & MAXWELL

 THOMSON REUTERS

First edition published 1997
Second edition published 2006
Third edition published 2013

Published in 2013 by W. Green & Son Limited
21 Alva Street
Edinburgh EH2 4PS

Typeset by Servis Filmsetting Ltd, Stockport, Cheshire

Printed and bound by CPI Group (UK) Ltd, Croydon, CR0 4YY

No natural forests were destroyed to make this product;
only farmed timber was used and replanted.

A CIP catalogue record of this book is available from the British Library.

ISBN 978-0-414-01846-4

Thomson Reuters and the Thomson Reuters logo are trademarks of
Thomson Reuters.

© Thomson Reuters (Professional) UK Limited 2013

PREFACE

It is seven years since the second edition of *Family Law* was published. As always with family law there have been many changes.

Greater recognition has been given to the diversity of family forms currently found in Scotland. The Human Fertilisation and Embryology Act 2008, which has come into force since the last edition, extends the notion of parenthood in cases involving assisted reproduction to cover civil partners and unmarried, same-sex couples, in addition to recognising that one parent alone may be sufficient for a family. Proposed legislation enabling same-sex couples to marry, set out in the Marriage and Civil Partnership (Scotland) Bill, is currently under Parliamentary consideration and seems likely to pass into law. The legislation on financial claims following the end of a cohabiting relationship, newly minted at the time of the second edition of this text, has given rise to a number of important cases, cementing non-marital cohabitation as another significant family form in Scotland.

A broad approach to support and appropriate intervention in the lives of children continues to be developed. *Getting It Right for Every Child* (GIRFEC) marked a shift in Governmental policy focus towards early, proactive intervention, the details of which are fleshed out in the *National Guidance for Child Protection in Scotland* (2010). Major legislative reform has already occurred in this area by way of the Children's Hearings (Scotland) Act 2011, which addresses human rights concerns raised in challenges to the previous system, as well as bringing about changes to the organisational structure of children's panels. The 2011 Act creates a new national panel for children's panel members and a new national panel for safeguarders. It updates and introduces new grounds for referral and makes changes to the definition of who qualifies as a "relevant person", along with altering rules relating to confidentiality and disclosure, and legal representation through legal aid to be administered through the Scottish Legal Aid Board. Further changes in this area seem likely to result from the Children and Young People Bill, a legislative embodiment of the principles and values of GIRFEC, which is currently the subject of Parliamentary consultation and debate.

A further important legislative reform in relation to children and parents since the second edition of this text is the Adoption and Children (Scotland) Act 2007. The Act aims to strike a better balance between the rights of birth parents, adoptive parents and children by introducing permanence orders which allow for greater stability for the child and the adoptive family, whilst enabling continuing contact with the birth parent where appropriate. Whether the Act strikes the balance it seeks remains in question, however. The legislation has already been the subject of a Supreme Court decision in *ANS and DCS v ML* [2012] UKSC 30, concerning the human rights compliance of the provisions dispensing with (birth) parental consent to adoption in certain circumstances. The court found in favour of the Act on this occasion. It may be that further challenges will follow.

In the area of prevention of and protection from abuse, the Forced Marriage, etc (Protection and Jurisdiction) (Scotland) Act 2011 has been introduced to address abusive practices in which individuals are forced to marry under duress from family members or others. The legislation creates the "forced marriage protection order" which interdicts threatening conduct designed to coerce a person into entering a marriage, and provides the court with additional powers to move a vulnerable person to a place of safety. Reforms to the Protection from Harassment Act 1997 have also been introduced by the Criminal Justice Licensing (Scotland) Act 2010 and the Domestic Abuse (Scotland) Act 2011, making it easier for individuals to obtain non-harassment orders against offenders, including criminal sanctions

We have taken the decision to omit discussion of welfare benefits from this edition of the text. The sharp distinction between the former benefits system and the new universal benefit to be introduced under the Welfare Reform Act 2012, coupled with the uncertainty surrounding assessment of eligibility for the new benefit and its operation in practice, led us to conclude that meaningful consideration of the provisions at the time of writing was not possible. Nevertheless it has been necessary to include discussion of the major reforms to the statutory child support system which are coming into force just at the time of publication. Their precise effect can only be guessed at.

Since the second edition of *Family Law* the authorial team has undergone some changes. John Fotheringham and Frankie McCarthy have come on board adding new energy and insights to the production of the third edition. Lilian Edwards, a former author, has left the team to focus on information technology law and we would like to thank her for all her past contributions and to wish her all the best in her chosen field of research.

Many people have assisted us in bringing this volume to fruition and we would like to thank David Nichols, Katy MacFarlane, Louise Johnson, Kate Spencer and our colleagues at W. Green for all their help and support, without which this edition might never have become a reality.

The law is stated as at the end of May 2013. However, it has been possible to include later developments in places.

Anne Griffiths
John Fotheringham
Frankie McCarthy

August, 2013

CONTENTS

TABLE OF CASES

TABLE OF STATUTES

TABLE OF SCOTTISH STATUTES

TABLE OF STATUTORY INSTRUMENTS

TABLE OF SCOTTISH STATUTORY INSTRUMENTS

TABLE OF CONVENTIONS AND EUROPEAN REGULATIONS

CHAPTER 1
LEGAL PERSONALITY AND FAMILY RELATIONS

This book is about the law of Scotland relating to families. The first question that is logically raised by this statement is what we mean by a family. Unfortunately, there is no simple answer to this question. Although the stereotypical media image of the family may be of the "nuclear family", consisting of a married couple and two to three children, in reality family forms are widely disparate. A "family" may be comprised of adults in a married or cohabiting relationship, with or without children; couples who once shared such a relationship but are now divorced or separated but still have connections, possibly via their children; a single parent with a child or children; or multifarious other groupings made up of persons who have biological or social connections, including blood relations such as grandparents and also step relations.   **1–01**

Not only is there diversity in the form that families take but it is quite possible for a person to be a member of more than one family at any given moment in time. So, for example, where a child has parents who split up, and each subsequently forms a new relationship, that child may be considered a member of both the new resulting families. It is important to accept that families are not static, but tend to progress through a life cycle; so, for example, the cohabiting couple without children may marry in time, have children who will become adults in due course and who, like their parents, may start their own family. The rights, duties, and obligations that exist between such persons, and their relationship with state agencies and institutions, such as courts and local authorities, are family law; the subject of this book.   **1–02**

The legal regulation of families thus revolves around relationships between "natural persons" who have certain legal rights and are subject to certain legal duties. This raises the important question of when a "person" technically comes into existence in law; that is, when legal personality begins, for according to Scots law, all living human beings have legal personality.[1] The concept of legal personality is fundamental to the operation of the legal systems in the United Kingdom.   **1–03**

Only legal persons have standing in the courts and access to the legal process, are able to hold and enforce legal rights, and can be sued and thus be held subject to legal duties. The category of legal persons is not confined to "natural" living persons but extends also to other entities endowed with legal personality: referred to as "artificial" or "juristic" persons. Juristic persons cover a whole range of bodies,[2] including those incorporated by or   **1–04**

---

[1] *Knight v Wedderburn* (1778) Mor. 14545.

[2] See Gloag and Henderson, *The Law of Scotland*, 12th edn (Edinburgh: W.Green, 2012) (hereafter "Gloag and Henderson"), Ch.47, pp.994–1000; N. MacCormick, "General Legal

under statute,[3] or by Royal Charter,[4] or through custom and usage.[5] As the focus of this book is on the legal relationships between natural persons, as members of a family, we will restrict ourselves in this chapter to examining legal personality with respect to natural persons.

1–05   Just as families experience a life cycle, so do natural persons, who progress from birth to death, through childhood, adolescence, adulthood and old age. In the next seven chapters we will examine the legal problems associated with children. Subsequent chapters will deal with the regulation of adult domestic relationships. In this chapter we will be principally concerned with an area that has been the subject of intense debate over the years, namely the legal status of the unborn child or fetus, and, in particular, the issue of when legal personality commences. While this is too large an area to be covered in depth, we shall highlight important issues such as civil liability for ante-natal injury and negligence, criminal acts affecting the unborn child, and, in particular, abortion, and consider what the law in these areas says about the status of the unborn child in Scots law.

Commencement of Legal Personality

The General Rule

1–06   The general rule is that legal personality and the attendant rights commence at birth. A certificate of live birth is lodged with the appropriate registrar who issues a birth certificate.[6] Prior to birth, the fetus or unborn child has no legal rights and Scots law upholds the proposition put forward in *Re F*[7] that, "The fetus cannot . . . have any right of its own at least until it is born and has a separate existence from the mother".[8]

1–07   It was held in *Re F* that the court had no power to ward an unborn child. In reaching this decision the court observed that if there were such a power it would give rise to a conflict of interest between the mother and the child.

1–08   Attempts have been made to challenge this view, most notably in the recent case of *Vo v France*[9] which went all the way to the European Court of Human Rights.

Concepts" in *Stair Memorial Encyclopaedia of the Laws of Scotland* (hereafter "*Stair Encyclopaedia*"), Reissue (2008), paras 41–44.

[3] e.g. limited companies under the Companies Act 2006 or the Law Society of Scotland under the Solicitors (Scotland) Acts of 1949 and 1980.

[4] e.g. the Royal Bank of Scotland or the BBC.

[5] e.g. the Faculty of Advocates or the W.S. Society.

[6] Registration of Births, Deaths and Marriages (Scotland) Act 1965 ss.13–20 and SI 1997/2348.

[7] *Re F* [1988] 2 All E.R. 193.

[8] *Re F* [1988] 2 All E.R. 193, per May L.J. at 195. See also the Scottish case of *Kelly v Kelly*, 1997 S.L.T. (2nd Div) 896.

[9] *Vo v France* (2005) 40 E.H.R.R. 12.

Vo v France[10]

In this case a Vietnamese women, Mrs Thi-Nho Vo, attended a hospital in Lyon for a routine ante-natal appointment. There was another Vietnamese outpatient there whose name was also Vo and who was in attendance to have a contraceptive coil removed. Due to a lack of language skills, the medical staff had difficulty understanding the women with the result that there was a mix up and Mrs Thi-Nhos Vo's fetus's amniotic sac was penetrated, eventually resulting in the death of the fetus.

1–09

Mrs Vo raised a case against the doctor under the French Criminal Code for the offence of unintentional homicide. She opted to do this rather than pursue a civil remedy because she considered such a remedy was incapable of securing judicial acknowledgement of the homicide of her child. The issue for the court in this case was whether or not a fetus aged 20–21 weeks was a "human person" or "another" within the meaning of the French Criminal Code.

1–10

The court of first instance held that—at 21 weeks of gestation—the fetus had not been viable, and therefore was not a human person. The Cour d'Appel, however, said that viability was an indefinite and uncertain concept and "reverted to the concept of 'the beginning of life'".[11] The case was referred to the European Court of Human Rights where the central question before the Court was whether the absence of a criminal remedy within the French legal system to punish the unintentional destruction of a fetus constituted a failure on the part of the state to protect by law the right to life within the meaning of Art.2 of the European Convention on Human Rights and Fundamental Freedoms.[12]

1–11

Mrs Vo argued that:

1–12

- it was now "scientifically proven" that all life begins at fertilisation;
- that the term "everyone" in Art.2 that provides that "Everyone's right to life shall be protected by law" was to be taken as referring to human beings rather than persons possessing legal personality;
- that subject to the exception provided in the law on abortion, French law guaranteed all human beings the right to life from conception;
- that the availability of abortion did not exonerate the State from its duty to protect the unborn child under the terms of Art.2.

In response, the French Government argued that Art.2 could not be intended to apply to the fetus (and that this must be so because the Article would otherwise be contrary to domestic legislation of those states that had enacted enabling legislation on abortion). In support of this claim it was argued that states other than France allowed terminations beyond 20-weeks gestation and that it would be paradoxical for states to have a margin of

1–13

---

[10] *Vo v France* (2005) 40 E.H.R.R. 12.
[11] J.K. Mason and G. Laurie, *Law and Medical Ethics*, 8th edn (Oxford: Oxford University Press, 2011), para.9.85.
[12] For fuller discussion of the issues see J.K. Mason, "What's in a name?: The vagaries of Vo v France" (2005) 17 CFLQ 97.

appreciation that excluded a protection of the fetus in the context of abortion without having a similar margin when a pregnancy was terminated as a result of unintentional negligence.

European Court's Ruling

1–14   The European Court asserted that it was still an unsettled question of what constitutes the "beginning" of "everyone's right to life" in the context of Art.2. So far, the issue had only been raised in the context of abortion, and the Court was reluctant to expound on this, noting that the question of when the right of life begins comes within the margin of appreciation that is attributed to individual states. In this situation, it was impossible to answer the question of whether or not the unborn child was a person for the purposes of Art.2 of the European Convention in the abstract. Moreover, there was no call to decide whether or not "the abrupt end of the applicant's pregnancy" fell within the scope of Art.2 in so far as there had been no failure on the part of France to comply with the requirements relating to the preservation of life in the public health sphere, that is, in relation to the law on abortion.

1–15   The Court then went on to debate the reverse side of Art.2—that is the duty of the state to take appropriate steps to enable other interested parties to establish liability and obtain compensation for a death, including one associated with either the public or private provision of medical services. The Court held that this obligation was satisfied "if the legal system affords victims a remedy in the civil courts, either alone or in conjunction with a remedy in the criminal courts, enabling any liability of the doctors concerned to be established and civil redress through damages". In this case Mrs Vo had opted not to pursue a civil remedy (which was now time barred). In any event, the Court held that even if Art.2 had applied to a fetus, there had been no legal procedural failure to provide the applicant with an effective remedy and thus no violation of Art.2.

In *A, B and C v Ireland*,[13] the Grand Chamber affirmed its decision in *Vo*. It reasserted its view that, given differing definitions of the beginning of life, states could legitimately have different positions as to the limits on lawful abortion.[14]

The Nasciturus Exception

1–16   So far, attempts to attribute legal personality to a fetus before birth have been unsuccessful. However, this general rule is subject to modification in certain circumstances, by virtue of the legal fiction referred to as the nasciturus rule,[15] which is applied where it would benefit the child to make such

---

[13] *A, B and C v Ireland* (2011) 53 E.H.R.R. 13.

[14] *A, B and C v Ireland* (2011) 53 E.H.R.R. 13 at 237.

[15] Derived from the Latin maxim, *nasciturus pro jam nato habetur quando agitur de ejus commodo*. See Walker, *Principles of Scottish Private Law*, 4th edn (Oxford: Oxford University Press, 1988), Vol.1, p.205. See also R. Paisley, "The succession rights of the unborn child", 2006 Edin. L. R. 28.

a modification.[16] The nasciturus rule provides that, so long as that child is subsequently born alive, an unborn child can be regarded as being capable of having rights at a prenatal time, where that would be to his or her advantage. This fiction was first applied in the context of succession, to enable a child born posthumously to have a right of inheritance in a deceased parent's estate. The general rule for succession is that only those heirs who are alive and legal persons at the time of the deceased's death have a right to succeed to the deceased's estate.[17] Thus, if a father leaves a share of his estate to his children, a child still in utero at the time of his death strictly does not qualify to share in the estate. However, the nasciturus rule would enable such a child to share in the deceased father's estate by setting up the legal fiction that he or she should be deemed to have been born and to have become a legal person by the date of that father's death for the purposes of succession rights. Note that the rule only operates where its application will be to the child's direct advantage.[18]

The nasciturus rule has been extended beyond the context of succession. **1–17** For example, in *Cohen v Shaw*[19] the court held that a child born after the death of his father—who had been negligently killed in a road accident by a third party—was entitled to sue for damages. Under the legislation then in force, the right to sue was only conferred on a relative,[20] defined to include a person who "was a child of the deceased".[21] The judge saw no reason to limit the application of the rule to succession cases.[22]

CIVIL ACTIONS RELATING TO ANTE-NATAL INJURY OR NEGLIGENCE

The Right to Sue in Respect of Ante-natal Injury: General Principles

Does the fact that legal personality does not commence until birth mean **1–18** that a child (or his or her parents) cannot sue for injuries sustained *by the child* before birth as a result of another's negligence? This matter came to particular legal prominence in the 1970s after a large number of women, who had taken the drug Thalidomide during their pregnancies, gave birth to children with severe physical deformities. Injury to the fetuses those women were carrying had arguably occurred as a result of the negligent acts of the manufacturers of Thalidomide. The English Law Commission concluded that

---

[16] Stair notes that "in all things ending in favour of the unborn, they are accounted as born", *The Institutions of the Law of Scotland*, III. v. 50 (Walker (ed.), 1981).

[17] Subject to the rules on deferred vesting in testamentary gifts, e.g. where a legacy is to vest subsequent to a liferent.

[18] *Elliot v Joicey*, 1935 S.C. (H.L.) 57.

[19] *Cohen v Shaw*, 1992 S.L.T. 1022.

[20] Damages (Scotland) Act 1976 s.1. See now the Damages (Scotland) Act 2011 s.4 and see also paras 10–15 to 10–17.

[21] Damages (Scotland) Act 1976 Sch.1, para.1(b). See now the Damages (Scotland) Act 2011 s.14.

[22] There is a body of opinion, however, which doubts that the rule, which originated in Roman law, was intended for use outside the realm of property and succession: see Norrie, "Liability for Injuries Caused Before Birth", 1992 S.L.T. 65 at 68; Rodger, "Case and Comment; Report of the Scottish Law Commission on Ante-Natal Injury", 1974 J.R. 83.

English law was so uncertain in this area that there should be legislation.[23] This took the form of the Congenital Disabilities (Civil Liability) Act 1976, which provides in ss.1(1) and (3) that anyone responsible for an "occurrence" affecting either parent of a child, or the child himself, which causes that child to be born disabled, will be answerable to the child if he or she was or would have been liable in tort to the parent.[24] This applies whether or not actual injury was caused to the parent. The Scottish Law Commission (hereafter "SLC") however, took the view that legislation was unnecessary in Scotland as there was no bar at common law to a person recovering damages for ante-natal injuries resulting from another's negligence.[25] The child once born alive is a legal person and has a right to sue in respect of personal injury, whether or not the act causing the injury occurred before or after *conception*. In the view of the SLC, parents also have a right to sue in respect of ante-natal injury to their unborn child. In Scotland, therefore, no legislation was passed and the matter has been left to be clarified by case law.

Case Law Under the Damages (Scotland) Act 1976

1–19   In Scotland, two cases, *Hamilton v Fife Health Board*[26] and *McWilliams v Lord Advocate*,[27] have dealt with the issue of liability for ante-natal injury. In both these cases the parents of babies who died shortly after birth[28] sought damages in the form of a loss of society[29] award under the Damages (Scotland) Act 1976 s.1. The parents alleged negligence by medical personnel, prior to the birth of their children, which resulted in their children's deaths after birth, caused by the injuries sustained ante-natally. The parents' claims were based on s.1(1) of the 1976 Act which provides that:

> "Where a *person* dies in consequence of *personal injuries sustained by him* as the result of an act or omission of another person . . . then . . . the person liable to pay those damages . . . shall also be liable to pay damages in accordance with this section to any relative of the deceased". [Emphasis added.]

1–20   The key issue at stake in these cases was whether or not it was necessary for there to be a legal person in existence at the time that the injuries were "sustained by him". The judges in the Outer House adopted different interpretations of the statute. In *Hamilton*, Lord Prosser reiterated the general legal rule that prior to being born, a child is not a "person" in legal terms. In his view, then, the "child had quite simply lacked the status of being a person

---

23 *Report on Injuries to Unborn Children*, Law Com. No.60, Cmnd.5709 (1974).
24 For a fuller commentary, see Mason, *Medico-Legal Aspects of Reproduction and Parenthood*, 2nd edn (Aldershot: Dartmouth, 1998), Ch.6.
25 Liability for Ante-natal Injury, Scot. Law Com. No.30, Cmnd.5371 (1973).
26 *Hamilton v Fife Health Board*, 1992 S.L.T. 1026 (O.H.), and 1993 S.L.T. 624 (Ex. Div.).
27 *McWilliams v Lord Advocate*, 1992 S.L.T. 1045.
28 In *Hamilton* the child died three days after birth and in *McWilliams*, after six weeks.
29 Damages (Scotland) Act 1976 s.1(4) enables a relative to claim damages by way of compensation for the loss of the benefits a relative might have expected to derive from a deceased's society as well as for grief and sorrow caused by the deceased's death.

when the injuries were sustained",[30] and so could not be said to have died "in consequence of personal injuries sustained by him".[31] The nasciturus rule had no application here, because it was not the child who was suing for damages and thereby benefiting directly from the action, but the parents. As we saw above, the nasciturus rule can only be invoked where it is directly to the benefit of the child.

In *McWilliams*,[32] however, Lord Morton took another view, namely, that **1–21** it was not necessary to rely on the nasciturus rule, a legal fiction:

> "to give a child who is born alive a title to sue for injuries sustained in utero and . . . if a child dies after being born alive and the death is caused by injuries sustained in utero the parents of that child have a title to sue for damages for the death of that child".[33]

In his opinion, the fact that the injury caused by the negligent act was inflicted **1–22** on a victim who was then in utero and therefore not yet a legal person, was not a bar to a subsequent right of reparation when that unborn child was later born alive. In other words, in His Lordship's view the act which causes injury and the sustaining of injury by a legal person need not occur simultaneously.

When *Hamilton* was subsequently appealed to the Inner House[34] it was by **1–23** and large the approach of Lord Morton in *McWilliams* which was upheld. The Inner House held that in order to sue for damages there must be both *injuria* (wrongful act) and *damnum* (loss). It noted that:

> "An unborn person, a fetus, is not a person in the eyes of the law—at least in relation to the law of civil remedies—and there can be no liability to pay damages to a fetus, even although the fetus has sustained injuries resulting from a negligent act or omission".

But that

> "once the fetus ceases on birth to be a fetus and becomes a person there is a concurrence of injuria and damnum and the newly born child has a right to sue the person whose breach of duty has resulted in the child's loss. The coming into existence of that right to sue does not depend upon the application of any fiction".[35]

The Damages (Scotland) Act 2011

The 1976 Act has now been repealed and replaced by the Damages **1–24** (Scotland) Act 2011. Section 4(3)(b) of the 2011 Act is in substantially similar terms to s.1(4) of the 1976 Act. It therefore presumably remains possible in Scotland for parents to sue under the 2011 Act for injuries sustained by their

---

[30] *Hamilton v Fife Health Board*, 1992 S.L.T. 1026 at 1028.
[31] *Hamilton v Fife Health Board*, 1992 S.L.T. 1026.
[32] *McWilliams v Lord Advocate*, 1992 S.L.T. 1045.
[33] *McWilliams v Lord Advocate*, 1992 S.L.T. 1045 at 1048.
[34] *Hamilton v Fife Health Board*, 1993 S.L.T. 624.
[35] *Hamilton v Fife Health Board*, 1993 S.L.T. 624, *per* Lord McCluskey at 629.

child before birth as a result of the negligence of a third party, as long as the child is subsequently born alive.[36] It also seems now to be accepted even in England and Wales that the child him or herself, if born alive, can sue third parties at common law in respect of ante-natal injury.[37]

Child's Right to Sue Parents for Ante-natal Negligence

1–25   So far, we have considered cases involving children who have suffered ante-natal injury as a result of the negligent acts of third parties other than the mother. But can a child sue his or her mother where ante-natal injury has occurred as a result of their negligence (or, indeed, deliberate act)? The kind of situation where this might arise is where the mother has abused drugs or alcohol during pregnancy with resulting injury to the child in the womb. In theory there is no special reason why a child should not be able to sue a parent in respect of ante-natal injury. However, the courts might well refuse such claims on the basis of public policy as undermining the stability of the family. It is also difficult in such cases to establish that the child's infirmities were wholly or even mainly caused by the ante-natal negligence of the mother, and not by other factors affecting the child before and during birth. In England, s.1(1) of the Congenital Disabilities (Civil Liability) Act 1976 makes it clear that a child cannot sue his or her mother for fetal neglect.[38] There is, however, no equivalent legislative guidance in Scotland.

1–26   Although negligent acts by a mother affecting her unborn child may not as yet clearly allow a claim for damages by the child once born, such acts are not wholly without legal consequence. Ante-natal parental negligence may be grounds for invoking the powers of the local authority and the courts to remove the child from the care of the parents to that of the state. Under the Children (Scotland) Act 1995, Pt II (see Chs 7 and 8), a fetus, not being a person in law, cannot be made the subject of legal action but the child subsequently born can be. The situation is similar in England. In *D (a minor) v Berkshire County Council*,[39] the mother of a child was a registered drug addict during her pregnancy, and continued to take drugs after the birth. Her child was born suffering from withdrawal symptoms so acute that it had to be kept in intensive care for several weeks after birth. The House of Lords[40] held that in deciding whether or not to make a care order under the Children and Young Persons Act 1969, which would enable the local authority to remove the child from the mother's care as soon as it was born, a court was required to consider whether there was any continuing impairment, neglect or ill-treatment of the child at the time immediately prior to the initiation of care proceedings. So, a court when considering the welfare of a child is entitled to look to the past, including to events before that child was born, in order to assess whether there might be problems that are likely to continue to

---

[36] The 1976 Act was amended by the Damages (Scotland) Act 1993 subsequent to the decision in *Hamilton*. The changes made do not, however, affect the ratio of that case.
[37] See English case of *Burton v Islington Health Authority* [1992] 3 All E.R. 833.
[38] Although see s.2 which provides that a pregnant woman driving a motor vehicle is under a duty to take care for her unborn child.
[39] *D (a minor) v Berkshire County Council* [1987] 1 All E.R. 20.
[40] *D (a minor) v Berkshire County Council* [1987] 1 All E.R. 20 at 33.

affect the child's development in the future. In Scotland, although there is no equivalent case law, there seems no reason why a local authority might not obtain, inter alia, a child protection order[41] to remove a newly-born infant to a place of safety if there was evidence either that the child was already suffering "significant harm" or if not removed from the family home would be likely to do so, and that the making of such an order was necessary to prevent such harm occurring.[42]

Parents' Rights to Sue for Wrongful Pregnancy and Wrongful Birth

In some cases, pregnancy and birth may give rise to parents suing health carers and, vicariously, health authorities on the grounds of "wrongful pregnancy" or "wrongful birth". A claim for damages on the ground of "wrongful pregnancy"[43] relates to an unplanned pregnancy which has occurred as the result of another's negligence. The term "wrongful conception" is sometimes used, however, as pregnancy without implantation causes no injury, the former phrase is to be preferred. A duty of care is owed by a doctor to a person who consults him or her about sterilisation or contraception. In particular, a duty is owed to both sexual partners if they come together to a doctor seeking an agreed limitation of fertility. A failure with respect to duty of care can be attributable either to:

1–27

- incompetent clinical expertise; or to
- inadequate explanation of the shortcomings of the procedure, in particular, as to the inherent possibility that conception might still occur after treatment due purely to the vagaries of nature.

A claim for damages on the ground of "wrongful birth" however, arises where the parents of a child who has been born disabled raise an action in negligence against a doctor or genetic counsellor who has failed either to:

1–28

- advise them of the risk of illness in their child(ren) prior to birth; or to
- carry out, and interpret correctly, appropriate diagnostic procedures which would have disclosed abnormality in the fetus.

In such a situation the health carer owes the parents a duty of care, which if breached, may result in the parents contending that they have been deprived of the opportunity to terminate the pregnancy as a result of which they are now faced with caring for a disabled child.

---

[41] From a court, by virtue of the powers in the Children (Scotland) Act 1995 s.57.

[42] See further Chs 7 and 8. Another option might be to refer the newborn child to the children's hearing on the ground that he or she was suffering from lack of parental care (Children (Scotland) Act 1995 s.52(2)(c)).

[43] J.K. Mason and G. Laurie, *Law and Medical Ethics* (2011) at para.10.01 prefer to use the term 'uncovenanted pregnancy' which was first used by Kennedy J. in *Richardson v LRC Products Ltd* (2001) 59 BMLR 185 to cover this situation. Their reasoning is that they consider it undesirable to refer to a child who has come to be accepted as an "unwanted" child when what is really at stake is the fact that an unexpected happening, which was not-contemplated by the parties, namely a pregnancy, has occurred.

1–29   In assessing whether negligence has occurred in either of these cases, what
constitutes a breach of a duty of care is largely governed by the principle
laid down in *Bolam v Friern Hospital Management Committee*[44] that a doctor's action will not be held to be negligent if it conforms to a practice which
would have been adopted by a responsible body of medical opinion. There
are a number of cases establishing parameters of parents' right to sue in these
circumstances that cover two heads of liability, being:

- those that derive from pregnancy itself, including damages for pain and
  suffering of gestation and childbirth, and loss of earning, plus additional
  expenses resulting from pregnancy and convalescence; and
- those relating to maintenance and upkeep of the child.

The question to be resolved is whether damages for upkeep of an uncovenanted[45] child should ever be awarded, and if so, whether the condition of
the child or its mother should affect the quantum?

1–30   A conflict arises here because it has been widely argued that where a
healthy child is born this must always be regarded as a blessing and should
never be regarded as a matter for compensation. This was the view taken
by the judge in *Udale v Bloomsbury Area Health Authority*.[46] In this case
the doctor negligently performed a sterilisation operation. As a result, an
unwanted pregnancy occurred. The judge held that damages under the first
head, that is for pain and suffering along with loss of earnings following a
negligently performed operation were recoverable. However an award to
cover the cost of bringing up the child was firmly rejected on the grounds that
the joy of having a child and the benefits it brought in terms of love should
be offset against any inconvenience and financial disadvantage resulting from
its birth.

1–31   This view was criticised in the later case of *Emeh v Kensington Area Health
Authority*[47] which also involved negligent sterilisation of a woman who gave
birth to a congenitally abnormal child. In this case the Court of Appeal
awarded damages not only for pain and suffering and loss of earnings prior
to birth but also for loss of future earnings, maintenance for the child up to
trial and in the future, and for the plaintiff's future loss of amenity including
the extra care that the child would require and the cost of rearing the child.
Importantly it was held that damages would be awarded whether or not
the child had been disabled. It rejected the objections against such recovery
voiced in *Udale* and held that the fact that the women's pregnancy in this case
was discovered in time for her to opt for an abortion did not limit her right
to damages. A similar approach was adopted in *Thake v Maurice*[48] which
attempted to lay to rest the distinction between entitlement to damages for

---

[44] *Bolam v Friern Hospital Management Committee* [1957] 2 All E.R. 118. Note: popular usage
is reference to 'Bolam', however in Scotland the principle was established in *Hunter v Hanley*,
1955 S.C. 200.
[45] J.K. Mason and G. Laurie, *Law and Medical Ethics* (2011) at para.10.01.
[46] *Udale v Bloomsbury Area Health Authority* [1983] 2 All E.R. 522.
[47] *Emeh v Kensington Area Health Authority* [1984] 3 All E.R. 1044.
[48] *Thake v Maurice* [1986] 1 All E.R. 479.

pain and suffering and those representing the cost of the child's upbringing. The plea that the parents' damages should be cancelled out or reduced by their joy at the birth of a healthy baby was expressly dismissed. As a result, subsequent English cases came to cover damages under both heads of liability and, in some cases, even incorporating the costs of private education when that seemed appropriate[49] up until the House of Lords decision in *McFarlane v Tayside Health Board*,[50] that is.

The Scottish position

Prior to *McFarlane*, the case of *Allan v Greater Glasgow Health Board*[51]   **1–32**
accepted the proposition in Scots law that the unexpected birth of a healthy child due to another's negligence could give rise to damages. It held that there were no grounds in principle or policy to prevent an award of damages for the upbringing of a child born in such circumstances. However, the House of Lords decision in *McFarlane v Tayside Health Board*[52] has overturned established authority in this area and limited what is recoverable in *both* cases of wrongful pregnancy and wrongful birth.

McFarlane v Tayside Health Board[53]

The pursuers were a married couple with four children who decided that   **1–33**
as they did not want any more children, the husband would undergo a vasectomy. The operation was performed by a surgeon employed by the defenders (the Health Board). When the husband later submitted sperm samples to the hospital for analysis he was informed by the surgeon that his sperm counts were negative and that contraceptive measures were no longer necessary. The pursuers acted on the advice received but to their surprise the wife became pregnant and, after a normal pregnancy and labour, gave birth to a healthy child whom the parents loved and cared for as an integral part of their family. They raised an action for damages against the Health Board on the grounds that that they had suffered loss as a result of the Board's negligence and claiming damages:

- for the physical discomfort suffered by the wife from her pregnancy, confinement and delivery (*mother's claim*); as well as
- for the financial costs of caring for and bringing up the child (*the parents' claim*—one of patrimonial loss).

At first instance, the Lord Ordinary, Lord Gill, held that: **1–34**

- that normal, even if undesired, pregnancy and labour could not amount to personal injuries, or even if they could, they were injuries for which no damage was recoverable;

---

[49] *Allen v Bloomsbury Health Authority* [1993] 1 All E.R. 651.
[50] *McFarlane v Tayside Health Board* [2000] S.C.L.R. (HL) 105; [2000] 2 A.C. 59.
[51] *Allan v Greater Glasgow Health Board* (1998) S.L.T. 580.
[52] *McFarlane v Tayside Health Board* [2000] S.C.L.R. (HL) 105; [2000] 2 A.C. 59.
[53] *McFarlane v Tayside Health Board* [2000] S.C.L.R. (HL) 105; [2000] 2 A.C. 59.

- that the benefits of parenthood transcended any loses which the parents might have suffered.

He also expressed sympathy with the defender's argument that public policy considerations militated against allowing such an action to be brought.

1–35   Lord Gill's views, however, were rejected by the Inner House who held that

- the issue was not whether the effect of pregnancy/childbirth could be described as personal injury but whether or not they represented *damnum* (loss). Material prejudice suffered by a pursuer could be recognised as such a loss and was experienced by the wife;
- the fact that the pursuers chose to keep the child did not disrupt or break the chain of causation, namely that the defenders' negligence had caused loss;
- that the extra expenditure which the pursuers would incur in the case of the child (even if part of the normal parent/child relationship) was a loss for which they could seek compensation; and finally
- that even if the birth of a child brought about the benefits of parenthood (which could not always be said to be the case), there was no principle in Scots law that recognised that such intangible benefits had to be set off against patrimonial loss.

1–36   The decision by the Inner House was very much in line with earlier rulings by the English Court of Appeal but it was overturned by the House of Lords on appeal. While the majority of the Law Lords accepted that under normal delictual principles there was liability, they held that the claim for maintenance costs for the child represented a claim for pure economic loss which imposed additional considerations that were not met in this case. As a result, no damages under this head could be awarded. While their decision was unanimous, the Law Lords' reasons for reaching it varied. The majority[54] based their decision on the grounds that where economic loss was concerned, a claim had to meet the test of fairness laid down in *Caparo Industries Plc v Dickman*.[55] This requires a closer link between the act and the damage than the concept of "forseeability" alone provides. For, over and above the required relationship of "neighbourhood" or "proximity" between a person owing a duty and person to whom it is owed, there exists the question of whether it is "fair, just and reasonable" for the law to impose a duty. It was held that this test had not been met in *McFarlane*. Other objections were put forward by individual judges. Lord Steyn, for example, incorporated considerations of distributive justice that indicated that the law did not permit the parents of a healthy but unwanted child to claim the cost of its upbringing from a health authority or doctor in the circumstances of the case.[56] Lord Clyde, on the other hand, expressed the view that to relieve the parents of the financial obligations of caring for their child went beyond proportional-

---

[54] Lord Slynn of Hadley, Lord Steyn and Lord Hope of Craighead.
[55] *Caparo Industries Plc v Dickman* [1990] 2 A.C. 605.
[56] *McFarlane v Tayside Health Board* [2000] 2 A.C. 59 at 80A–E.

ity between the wrongdoing and the loss suffered[57]; while Lord Millett was of the opinion that the law regarded the birth of a healthy, normal baby as a blessing and not as a detriment with the advantages and disadvantages of parenthood being so inextricably bound together that the benefits should be regarded as outweighing any loss.[58]

However, since pregnancy was a type of "physical damage", the plaintiffs were allowed to recover for all loses that flowed directly from the pregnancy, including special damages for extra medical expenses, clothing and loss of earnings.[59] In reaching their decision the House of Lords rejected the argument that the claimants were under a duty to mitigate loss by having an abortion or putting the child up for adoption. It is noteworthy that "the mother's claim" has never been disputed in subsequent litigation.   **1–37**

Macfarlane was followed by the High Court of Ireland in *Byrne v Ryan*.[60] Other jurisdictions have not necessarily adopted the *McFarlane* approach to the "parental" claim.[61] In Australia, for example, in the case of *Cattanach v Melchior*[62] a High Court of seven judges expressly declined to follow *McFarlane* and held that a claim for maintenance expenses for a child was competent. While the decisions in the two cases appear to be diametrically opposed, they may be reconciled on the basis that the common denominator in the House of Lords decision in *McFarlane* is an appeal to justice, fairness and reasonableness based on the *Caparo* case, a case which does not feature in the Australian jurisprudence of tort law. It is important to note that *McFarlane* is a case involving damages with respect to the upkeep of a *healthy* child.[63] Two of the Law Lords, Lord Steyn and Lord Clyde, raised the possibility of a different outcome if the child were found to be disabled. Subsequent case law dealing with uncovenanted pregnancy and wrongful birth has struggled to deal with the issue of how far the ruling in *McFarlane* extends.   **1–38**

Wrongful Birth

How far the ruling in *McFarlane* extends is especially pertinent in cases dealing with damages for wrongful birth where, due to the negligence of the doctor/genetic counsellor or other health carers,[64] parents are not afforded   **1–39**

---

[57] *McFarlane v Tayside Health Board* [2000] 2 A.C. 59 at 105F–H and 106A.
[58] *McFarlane v Tayside Health Board* [2000] 2 A.C. 59 at 111D–F and 113H–114A–D.
[59] Lord Clyde, while having no difficulty in allowing the claim for *solatium* because "the pain which she [second pursuer] suffered through the carrying of an unwanted child seems to me to be reasonably a subject for compensation" (at 100A), nonetheless dissented from allowing a claim for loss of earnings by the mother and "for additional costs in caring for, feeding and clothing and maintaining the child, and the expenses of the layette" (at 106D).
[60] *Byrne v Ryan* [2007] High Court of Ireland (IEHC) 207.
[61] For a comparative survey, see M. Hogg, "Damages for Wrongful Birth", 2010 1(2) J. Eur.Tort L. 156.
[62] *Cattanach v Melchior* [2003] HCA 38.
[63] For discussion of the case see J.K. Mason, "Unwanted Pregnancy: A Case of Retroversion?", 2000 Edin L.R. 191; J. Thomson, "Abandoning the Law of Delict? *McFarlane v Tayside Health Board* in the House of Lords", 2000 S.L.T. (News) 43; L. Sutherland, "The Blessing of the Unplanned Pregnancy—*McFarlane* in the House of Lords", 2000 Reparation L.B. 33–5.
[64] In a substantial number of cases the error is either made within a laboratory or by a radiographer who failed to detect evidence of abnormality during tests which are primarily those

the opportunity of aborting the fetus with the result that a disabled child is born. What damages, if any, are recoverable in this situation? Prior to the House of Lords decision in *McFarlane* it appeared that damages extending to full recovery for the child's upkeep were recoverable. In *Anderson v Forth Valley Health Board*,[65] the pursuers were a married couple who had two sons born with muscular dystrophy which is a genetically inherited disease. They sued the health board for negligence on the grounds that in the light of their medical history they should have been referred to genetic counselling and if they had been, the genetic disorder would have been discovered and they would have opted for termination of the pregnancy. In the Outer House, Lord Nimmo Smith, applying the ordinary principles of delict, held that:

- there was no reason why the defenders should not have owed a duty of care to *both* pursuers in the provision of medical services;
- the purpose of the Abortion Act was to prevent events harmful to pursuers which ought to have been within contemplation of defenders and which, if they had used reasonable care, would not have happened;
- in the birth of a child, the pursuers had suffered personal injuries in respect of which they could claim for *solatium* and *patrimonial* loss;
- it cannot be said that birth of a child always outweighs any adverse consequences. Additional costs to parents associated with the children's disabilities were recoverable and did not cease on a child reaching the age of majority.[66] This was because a claim for care costs arose from the natural bond between parent and child which did not end on the child attaining majority but would continue throughout the child's life.

1–40 For these reasons the judge permitted a proof-before-answer to take place because entitlement to damages in these circumstances was essentially a jury question. This approach to damages was followed in *McLelland v Glasgow Health Board*.[67] The pursuers in this case had a son born with Down's Syndrome. They sued the Greater Glasgow Health Board on the basis that it had negligently failed to diagnose the child's condition at a stage when the pregnancy could have been terminated. They maintained that had the condition been properly diagnosed, they would have had the pregnancy terminated and would have attempted to have had healthy children. In this case the defenders argued that:

- the father had not suffered "personal injury" and so could not recover *solatium* for his emotional distress; and that
- since the pursuers, in any event, would have sought to have healthy chil-

---

routinely carried out as part of the ante-natal care of a pregnant woman, although some are offered to women over a certain age or whose family history indicates it would be appropriate. See, for example, *Farraj v King's Healthcare NHS Trust* [2009] EWCA Civ 1203, which concerned the respective liabilities of the laboratory and the NHS trust.

[65] *Anderson v Forth Valley Health Board*, 1998 S.L.T. 588.

[66] Note that the parents only sought to recover the additional costs associated with the children's disability which Lord Nimmo Smith was prepared to allow in principle, provided such costs were reasonable.

[67] *McLelland v Glasgow Health Board*, 1998 S.C.L.R. 1081.

dren—for whose upbringing they would have been responsible—they could not recover the ordinary costs of caring for the child, even though the defenders might be responsible for the extra cost of caring for a Down's Syndrome child.

However, their arguments were unsuccessful and Lord MacFadyn in the Outer House held 1–41

- that the mother was entitled to *solatium* covering the physical consequences to her of continuing with the pregnancy beyond the date when it would have been terminated, including the pain and suffering of the Caesarean delivery;
- that failure to provide information had caused a) severe shock and distress on discovery that the child was affected by Down's syndrome, and b) in the longer term, this failure had increased stress in bringing up and caring for the child and that for these reasons *both* pursuers were entitled to claim *solatium* for this distress[68]; and that
- the pursuers were entitled to damages in respect of expenditure which they had incurred and were likely to incur with respect to the child's future maintenance.

In this case, Lord MacFadyn did not limit damages to the extra costs associated with bringing up a disabled child, nor did he accept that the costs incurred should be offset against the costs that the pursuers would have willingly incurred with respect to a healthy child. On this issue he asked the question 1–42

"whether the basic cost of bringing up a handicapped child can be equated with the equivalent cost of bringing up a normal healthy child ... it is not the amount but the nature of the expenditure, that is in issue ... is the cost of bringing up a healthy child 'spent on an identical purpose, in pari materia with the costs of [the handicapped child]'? I find myself unable to accept that that question must be answered in the affirmative. Of course I accept that the extra costs of bringing up the handicapped child are dealt with elsewhere in the claim and are recoverable. But it does not seem to me to follow that spending money on bringing up a handicapped child who has been born as a result of the defenders' negligence is in substance the same thing as spending money on bringing up a healthy child who would have been born at some later date if the negligent omission had not taken place ... the cost of bringing up [G] [the handicapped child] is something which has been forced on them by the defenders' negligence. It would in my view be wrong to deny the pursuers recovery of the latter, forced, unwanted expense on the ground that, but for the negligence, they would probably have spent a similar amount of money in willingly incurring the former expense".[69]

---

[68] This was the first time that a father was awarded damages for *solatium* on the basis of the shock and distress that he had suffered.
[69] *McLelland v Glasgow Health Board*, 1998 S.C.L.R. 1081 at 1094.

1–43   However, by the time the case was referred to the Inner House in 2001, the House of Lords had given their judgment in *McFarlane v Tayside Health Board*.[70] As a result of that decision, the Inner House[71] only awarded damages for *solatium*, rejecting any claim for the child's maintenance on the basis that it did not meet the *Caparo* test, that is, that it was not fair, just and reasonable to award damages even though the child had Down's syndrome.[72] Since then, there have been a number of English cases grappling with this issue which highlight significant divergences of opinion as to how to quantify the parents' claim.

Rand v East Dorset Health Authority[73]

1–44   In *Rand*, flawed ante-natal screening failed to detect that a fetus had Down's syndrome and so the parents were denied the opportunity to terminate what had been a desired pregnancy. The claimants argued that they were now burdened with the cost of bringing up a disabled child that they would not have wanted. They sought the full costs of bringing up the child, plus additional damages to cover the special needs of the disabled child. Part of the losses claimed included loss of profit as a result of being forced to give up the family business which had had to be sold prematurely.

1–45   The court held that the existence of the Abortion Act 1967 introduced a duty of care on the part of the Health Authority (defenders) to take steps to ensure the proper exercise of their duty under the Act. The very existence of the Act was sufficient to impose liability on the defenders for the financial consequences of failing to draw to the claimants' attention the fact that Mrs Rand might have been carrying a disabled child. However, the parents had suffered no personal injury and the claim was effectively for pure economic loss and as a result a claim for the full cost of the maintenance and upkeep of the child was not sustainable.[74] However, losses related to the *disability* were recoverable and were not limited in time to the child reaching the age of 18.

So, the claim for past expenditure on therapies and equipment, and for likely future costs on these items was successful, but claims for private education and accommodation of the child failed. Mrs Rand, however, was entitled to general damages for pain and suffering and for what she had suffered during her third pregnancy,[75] and both claimants could recover damages for the loss of amenity they sustained in caring for their child, with the attendant consequences upon their private life.

1–46   Importantly, the judge distinguished "wrongful birth" cases from "wrongful pregnancy" cases on the basis that in the former the parents were com-

---

[70] *McFarlane v Tayside Health Board* [2000] S.C.L.R. (HL) 105; [2000] 2 A.C. 59.

[71] *McLelland v Glasgow Health Board*, 2001 S.L.T. 446.

[72] This was not a unanimous decision; Lord Morrison dissented.

[73] *Rand v East Dorset Health Authority* (2000) 56 BMLR 39.

[74] The judge's reasoning here was that to allow the full cost of maintenance, as was the case in *Salih v Enfield Health Authority* [1991] 3 All E.R. 400, CA, would be going too far because "It led him [the judge] to attribute no value to a handicapped life, where the facts established the contrary".

[75] Note: Mrs Rand had had a third child in order to prove to herself and others that she could have a normal child.

mitted to having a child, and that this affected not only general damages, but also what economic loss might be imposed on the defendant. As a result he found that the parents had a legally maintainable claim based upon the extended *Hedley Byrne*[76] principle for the financial consequences flowing from the child's disability, rather than from the fact of her existence. At the end of the day, Mr and Mrs Rand could only recover such losses as they had actually sustained and might reasonably sustain in the future. This included the loss of profits from the family business, suffered as a result of the claimants' giving up work to enable the mother to act as the child's primary carer. However, in determining these losses the judge held that:

> "Their [parents'] own means, as opposed to [K]'s [the handicapped child's] needs, are determinative of this issue. In my judgment this must follow as a matter of law from the categorisation of the claim as a claim for pure economic loss. I recognise that this will inevitably give rise to wealthy parents being in a position to obtain higher awards than parents of poor or modest means but this is a regular and accepted consequence in claims for damages".[77]

A similar decision was reached in *Hardman v Amin*,[78] although a different approach was adopted in relation to quantum. In this case a General Practitioner failed to diagnose or test for rubella in a pregnant woman who gave birth to a very seriously disabled child, one who would never be capable of employment or of living independently and who would require constant care and supervision well into adult life. In reaching its decision the court considered the remit of *McFarlane* and concluded that it did not affect the law as it related to the wrongful birth of *disabled* children. It categorised the claim for the child's maintenance as representing one for pure economic loss which called for the adoption of the test in *Caparo*—that liability was established if damage was foreseeable, if there was a relationship of proximity, and if it was just and reasonable to make an award.[79] Having regard to the principles of distributive justice, as defined by Lord Steyn in *McFarlane*,[80] it was said,

1–47

> "if the commuters on the London Underground were asked who should bear the costs of bringing up [D] [the handicapped child] a substantial majority would say the expense should fall on the wrongdoer".[81]

In this case it was held that the requirements posed by *Caparo* were met and it was fair, just and reasonable to make an award. However, the award would

1–48

---

[76] *Hedley Byrne & Co v Heller & Partners Ltd* [1964] A.C. 465. This case pertains to the existence of a duty to prevent economic loss in situations where the defendant in giving advice or information was fully aware of the nature of the 'transaction' which the plaintiff had in contemplation and knew the plaintiff would rely on that advice or information in deciding whether or not to engage in a 'transaction' in contemplation.

[77] *Rand v East Dorset Health Authority* (2000) 56 BMLR 39 at 58.

[78] *Hardman v Amin* (2000) 59 BMLR 58.

[79] *Caparo Industries Plc v Dickman* [1990] 2 A.C. 605.

[80] *McFarlane v Tayside Health Board* [2000] 2 A.C. 59 at 82–83.

[81] *Hardman v Amin* (2000) 59 BMLR 58 at 72.

not go beyond reasonable restitution, that is, damages for extra costs associated with providing for the child's special needs and care related to his disability.[82] However, when it came to assessing quantum, this was not to be limited to the parents means but based on the child's needs on the grounds that

> "categorisation of a claim as one for economic loss identifies the criteria to be satisfied before a duty and its scope are established, but has nothing to do with the quantification of damages once a breach of duty is shown to have resulted in loss of a type which the defendant was under a duty to avoid".[83]

He was of the view, that to limit damages to what the claimant could afford, would not provide proper compensation as the claimant would not, as far as was possible, be restored to the position she would have been in but for the breach.

1–49   Thus in cases of "wrongful birth" where parents sue for loss of their legal right to terminate a pregnancy due to fetal abnormalities, the trial courts have adhered to the pre-*McFarlane* authorities holding the Health Authority responsible for maintenance costs. *Rand* and *Hardman* acknowledged the impact of *McFarlane* by allowing claims only for costs related to special needs. However, in the case of *Lee v Taunton and Somerset NHS Trust*,[84] the court declined to limit liability to the additional costs associated with disability, which in this case involved a child being born with spina bifida due to the defendants negligent ante-natal screening. In *Lee*, when considering *McFarlane*, Toulson J. noted that

> "[it] presents no obstacle to the present claim. I do not believe that it would be right for the law to deem the birth of a disabled child to be a blessing, in all circumstances and regardless of the extent of the child's disabilities; or to regard the responsibility for the care of such a child as so enriching in the ordinary nature of things that it would be unjust for a parent to recover the cost from a negligent doctor on whose skill that parent had properly relied to prevent the situation".[85]

1–50   As for *Rand*, in his view the judge in that case had accepted the health authority's argument that the claimant could only recover damages in respect of such economic loss which was proved to raise from the child's disability, rather than from the fact of her existence. Toulson J. himself, however, perceived of the matter in a different light, namely that

> "[G] [the handicapped child], was incapable of being born *other than* severely disabled. That being so, to try to separate the consequences of [G]'s existence and [G]'s disabled existence is metaphysically impossible

---

[82] The judge noted that the imposition of damages here would not be invidious or morally offensive to Daniel as the purpose of distinguishing Daniel from a healthy child was merely to quantify the additional costs caused by his disabilities (and not to question the value of his existence).

[83] *Hardman v Amin* (2000) 59 BMLR 58 at 74.

[84] *Lee v Taunton and Somerset NHS Trust* [2001] 1 F.L.R. 419.

[85] *Lee v Taunton and Somerset NHS Trust* [2001] 1 F.L.R. 419 at 430E–F.

and practically unreal. If [G]'s birth was not a deemed blessing, I cannot see a barrier to Mrs Lee recovering the full costs of his maintenance, *except for* the important fact that she was wanting to bear a healthy child. If following a termination of her pregnancy with [G], she had continued with her attempts and had been successful, she would have incurred the costs of bring up a healthy child in any event".[86]

As to the question of quantification of damages, he agreed with the decision **1–51** in *Hardman* that this should be judged on the basis of the *child's* needs and not the parents' means. He took the view that

> "if [G] were able to bring a claim, his loss would be defined by his need. But those needs are inextricably linked with Mrs Lee's needs, since she bears the burden of attempting to cater for his needs. I do not accept that her loss is defined by her means rather than by her reasonable needs".[87]

Wrongful Pregnancy Resulting in Disabled Child

So far, we have been examining cases involving wrongful pregnancy and **1–52** wrongful birth but what is the position post-*McFarlane* in a combined case of wrongful pregnancy where a child is born disabled? This is the situation left open by *McFarlane* which therefore merits special attention. In *Parkinson v St James and Sea Croft University Hospital NHS Trust*[88] a doctor negligently performed a sterilisation operation on the claimant who conceived a 5th child 10 months later. She went to see a consultant at the hospital who warned her that the child might be born with a disability but she chose not to have her pregnancy terminated. The child was eventually born with disabilities—being autistic—however, such disability was not immediately recognisable at birth. The judge at first instance awarded costs of providing for the child's special needs and care relating to his disability, but not for the basic costs of his maintenance. This was upheld by the Court of Appeal who held that the costs of providing for the disabled child's specialist needs and care, where the loss flowed forseeably from an unwanted conception which was caused by negligence on the part of a doctor, were recoverable. It was held that the birth of a child with congenital abnormalities was a foreseeable consequence of the surgeon's careless failure to properly carry out a sterilisation operation.[89] There was no difficulty, in principle, in accepting the proposition that the surgeon should be deemed to have assumed responsibility for the foreseeable and disastrous economic consequences of performing his services negligently where the purpose of the operation was to prevent a woman from conceiving any more children, including children with congenital abnormalities. However, damages would be limited to the special upbringing costs associated with

---

[86] *Lee v Taunton and Somerset NHS Trust* [2001] 1 F.L.R. 419 at 432B–C.
[87] *Lee v Taunton and Somerset NHS Trust* [2001] 1 F.L.R. 419 at 433B.
[88] *Parkinson v St James and Sea Croft University Hospital NHS Trust* [2001] 3 All E.R. 97.
[89] For fuller consideration of the post-*McFarlane* cases see J.K. Mason, "Wrongful Pregnancy. Wrongful Birth and Wrongful Terminology" (2002) 6 Edin L.R. 46.

rearing a child with a serious disability, as that would, according to Lord Justice Brooks, reflect an award that was fair, just and reasonable. In reaching his decision he noted that, if the principles of distributive justice were called in aid, ordinary people would consider it to be fair for the law to make an award in such a case, provided it was limited to the extra expenses associated with bringing up a child with a significant disability. What constituted a significant disability would have to be decided on a case-by-case basis in line with the definitions used by local authorities for the purposes of providing services under the Children Act 1989. Although it would not include minor defects or inconveniences, the expression would certainly stretch to include disabilities of the mind, including severe behavioural disabilities, as well as physical disabilities.

1–53   The reasoning underpinning Lord Justice Brooks' decision in this case does nothing to undermine the House of Lord's decision in *McFarlane*. However, Lady Justice Hale's reasoning provides an alternative perspective. Her opinion was premised on the assumption that to cause a woman to become pregnant against her will is an invasion of her bodily right to integrity.[90] She then enlarged on this, listing some of the consequences of that fundamental invasion which, because they should never have happened, remained invasive despite the fact that they derived from a natural process. They include profound physiological and psychological changes during pregnancy and for some time thereafter which are accompanied by a severe curtailment of personal autonomy so that "one's life is no longer just one's own".[91] The process of giving birth is "rightly termed labour" and the hard work does not stop after pregnancy. She observed that in this case, unlike most personal injury cases,

> "the care is provided by the very person who has been wronged and the legal obligation to provide it is the direct and foreseeable consequence of that wrong. It is, perhaps, an indication of the reluctance of the common law to recognise the cost of care to the carer that claims for wrongful conception and birth of healthy children have not previously been analysed in this way . . . the law has found it much easier to focus on the associated financial costs".[92]

1–54   Her opinion is clearly supportive of the Inner House in *McFarlane*.

In reaching her decision she pointed out that a majority of the House of Lords had accepted that, on normal principles, the McFarlanes' claim would have been allowable. The ultimately decisive concept of an equilibrium between the benefits of a child and its costs is open to challenge, and she thought it limited the damages that would otherwise have been recoverable on normal principles. This being the case, there was no reason or need to take

---

[90] *Parkinson v St James and Sea Croft University Hospital NHS Trust* [2001] 3 All E.R. 97 at 114g.

[91] *Parkinson v St James and Sea Croft University Hospital NHS Trust* [2001] 3 All E.R. 97 at 116b.

[92] *Parkinson v St James and Sea Croft University Hospital NHS Trust* [2001] 3 All E.R. 97 at 117e–f.

the limitation any further than it was taken in *McFarlane* which took account of the ordinary costs of the ordinary child. This approach, she concluded, "treats a disabled child as having exactly the same worth as a non disabled child . . . It simply acknowledges that the costs are more".[93] The trouble with Lady Hale's analysis is that, as Mason and Laurie point out,[94] it can be applied almost verbatim to the wrongful pregnancy terminating in the birth of a normal child. In other words her arguments not only justify the award of damages in the event of the birth of a disabled child but it opens the way for a review of the *McFarlane* case. For in her view, the costs of bringing up a child do not amount to "pure" economic loss, but should rather be characterised as the economic loss consequent on the incursion on the woman's autonomy by becoming pregnant or remaining pregnant against her will. Such reasoning implies that Lady Justice Hale would have concluded such costs to be recoverable, as she points out that all of the maintenance costs are part and parcel of the caring responsibility which flows as a direct consequence of the invasion of the women's rights, being the conception following from the negligent medical care.

What the House of Lords would have made of such arguments has never **1–55** been put to the test, as permission to appeal this case was refused. Currently, therefore, *Parkinson* remains the law in this area and the unanswered question where the child born is disabled—left open by the House of Lords in *McFarlane*—is answered.

Wrongful Pregnancy Resulting in Disabled Parent Giving Birth to a Healthy Child

Another variant on the issue of disability arose in *Rees v Darlington* **1–56** *Memorial Hospital NHS Trust*.[95] In this case the claimant was a woman with a genetic condition which left her visually impaired and who wished to be sterilised. The consultant to whom she was referred knew her reasons for wanting the operation, including her belief that her eyesight would prevent her from looking after children properly. Unfortunately, the sterilisation operation was carried out negligently and the claimant gave birth to a healthy child. She sued for damages. The judge at first instance[96] ruled against the claim for damages for the upkeep of the child, consistent with the House of Lords decision in *McFarlane*, on the grounds that able-bodied parents could not recover damages for the cost of bringing up a healthy child, although the mother was entitled to damages for the pain, inconvenience and experience of pregnancy and childbirth.

On appeal, however, the Court of Appeal held that she was entitled to **1–57** recover the "extra" costs of bringing up her child which she would incur as a result of her disability. The reasoning of the majority centred on the fact that there was an important difference between able-bodied and disabled parents.

---

[93] *Parkinson v St James and Sea Croft University Hospital NHS Trust* [2001] 3 All E.R. 97 at 123g.
[94] J.K. Mason and G. Laurie, *Law and Medical Ethics* (2011), para.10.27.
[95] *Rees v Darlington Memorial Hospital NHS Trust* [2004] 1 A.C. 309
[96] Unreported trial judgment delivered March 9, 2001.

Able-bodied parents had the capacity to care for and bring up a child themselves, but disabled parents would need assistance in so doing.[97] Therefore, just as the extra costs involved in discharging parental responsibility towards a disabled child could be recovered, so also should the additional costs incurred by a disabled parent bringing up a healthy child. In receiving compensation for those extra costs, the claimant was not being over-compensated but was being put in the same position as an able-bodied person. There was nothing unfair, unjust or unreasonable in holding that a surgeon should assume a greater responsibility for the consequences of a failed sterilisation when he knows of the mother's disability and that this was the reason she wished to avoid having a child. The majority of the judges noted that in *McFarlane* their Lordships (with the possible exception of Lord Slynn) did not address the problem of the disabled child or that of a disabled mother. On this basis, they viewed *Rees* as being a legitimate extension of Parkinson's case and noted that disabled persons are a category of the public whom the law increasingly recognises as requiring special considerations, pointing to the Disability Discrimination Act 1995 as an important legislative landmark.

1–58   Lord Justice Waller, however, dissented from the majority opinion. He argued that on normal principles, the claim for damages for bringing up a healthy child as a result of the negligence of a surgeon would succeed.[98] It was only disallowed when the test of whether it is just, fair and reasonable was applied. He took issue with the decision in *Parkinson* on the grounds that, applying normal principles, recovery would be competent in both situations. However, in applying the just, fair and reasonable test, the court allowed recovery of the extra costs of looking after a disabled child, while disallowing recovery for the costs of looking after a healthy child. He questioned how fair it is to allow recovery, where others who would recover under normal principles are denied it. He considered an example of a lady who has four children and who does not wish to have a fifth. Having a fifth would cause a crisis in health terms, unless help in caring for the child was available. Due to *McFarlane*, she cannot recover the costs of caring for the child which might alleviate the crisis. But, he argued, the need to avoid a breakdown in her health is no different from the need of someone already with a disability and indeed her need might be greater depending on the degree of disability. He posited the question, "Does she, or ordinary people, look favourably on the law not allowing her to recover but allowing someone who is disabled to recover?"[99] For these reasons he would not have allowed recovery for the extra costs of bringing up the child incurred through the mother's disability.

---

[97] In her article entitled "Misconceptions about Wrongful Conception", 2002 M.L.R. 883, L.C.H. Hoyana attacks this reasoning, particularly Lady Justice Hale's exposition of 'deemed equilibrium' that justifies excluding the case from the remit of *McFarlane* on the basis that a disabled parent 'necessarily' will have greater difficulty in discharging her childcare responsibilities, as being discriminatory (at pp.900–901). She points to the pitfalls of associating disability with incapacity and questions the premise that the visually impaired cannot develop coping mechanisms but must rely upon third parties to supply their children's care needs which, she argues, not only perpetuates but deepens "the stigmatisation of the disabled" (at p.901).

[98] The core of his opinion is to be found at (2002) 65 BMLR 117 at [52]–[55].

[99] (2002) 65 BMLR 117 at [53].

When the case went on appeal to the House of Lords, it unanimously **1–59** affirmed *McFarlane* on the basis that it would be improper to reverse a decision of the House within such a short period of four years. The majority of their Lordships in a court of seven judges, went on to hold that damages to cover the costs of bringing up the child were not recoverable, and would not be available even though additional child-rearing costs were incurred as a result of the claimant's disability. Argument rested on whether, on the one hand, it was disability in *either* the child or the parent which dictated exceptional costs in bringing up the child—and hence attracted recompense—or whether the overriding factor was normality in the *resultant child*. It was the latter view that prevailed with the result that the appeal was successful in having the damages claim for the child's upkeep dismissed.

Nonetheless, their Lordships accepted that *McFarlane* represented an **1–60** exception to the normal rules of tort (delict), thus raising concerns that justice, at least, was not being seen to be done. Lord Bingham expressed the view:

> "I question the fairness of a rule which denies the victim of a legal wrong any recompense at all beyond an award immediately related to the unwanted pregnancy and birth."[100]

He proposed, and the majority of his colleagues supported his view, that there should be recognition that the parent of a child born after a vasectomy or sterilisation that had been performed negligently was the victim of a legal wrong. In recognition of this a conventional award of £15,000 should be made to mark the injury that had been suffered and loss of freedom to limit family size and that this award should be added to the award of damages made for pregnancy and birth in wrongful conception cases in general. It was stressed, in making this award, that it was not compensatory. This raises the question of what then it is there to represent? Mason[101] argues that it amounts to recognition of a new head of damages, that is, a breach of autonomy or interference with the right to plan one's life as one wishes.

The House of Lords judgment in *Rees* was not unanimous, there were **1–61** three dissenting judgments. Lord Steyn[102] took the view that special consideration should be given to the serious disability of a mother who wanted to avoid having a child by undergoing a sterilisation operation. In his opinion the injustice of denying such a seriously disabled mother the somewhat limited remedy of damages to cover the extra costs caused by her disability outweighed other policy consideration. He also stated that there was no United Kingdom authority to support the award of a conventional sum. Lord Hope[103] took the view that the fact that the child's parent was seriously disabled put her into a different category from able-bodied parents, and provided a ground for distinguishing the *McFarlane* case. It would be fair,

---

[100] *Rees v Darlington Memorial Hospital NHS Trust* [2004] 1 A.C. 309 at 317.
[101] J.K. Mason, "From Dundee to Darlington: An End to the *McFarlane* Line?", 2004 Judicial Review 365, p.385.
[102] *Rees v Darlington Memorial Hospital NHS Trust* [2004] 1 A.C. 309 at 319–328.
[103] *Rees v Darlington Memorial Hospital NHS Trust* [2004] 1 A.C. 309 at 328–336.

just and reasonable to hold that such extra costs as could be attributed to the disability were within the scope of the duty of care owed by the trust, and were recoverable. He also took the view that the splitting up of the claim into two parts in order to allow recovery of one part by means of a conventional sum and deny recovery of the other was contrary to principle. Finally, in Lord Hutton's opinion,[104] the *McFarlane* case did not bar the mother from recovering damages in this case.

Wrongful Pregnancy Resulting in Miscarriage or Stillbirth

1–62   In England, it has also been held that, on the basis of *Macfarlane*, damages will also be available where a wrongful pregnancy results in a miscarriage or stillbirth. In *Less v Hussain*,[105] negligent medical advice had been given as to the risks associated with pregnancy. It was accepted that, if causation had been established, the claimant would have been able to recover for the pain and suffering associated with her pregnancy and all losses flowing from the death of her child during the pregnancy.[106] The damages available in *Rees* for loss of autonomy[107] were, however, thought to represent the "real as opposed to theoretical"[108] losses that would be incurred in actually bringing up a child. They were therefore not available where the wrongful pregnancy had not resulted in such losses.

Legal Options

1–63   What are the legal options raised by such cases of wrongful pregnancy and wrongful birth?

- Damages should never be awarded.
- Damages should always be awarded.
- The blessing of parenthood should be offset against the economic loss and the damages adjusted accordingly.
- A distinction should be made between a healthy and disabled child.
- If such a distinction is made, damages should be recovered (a) for full cost of maintaining disabled child or (b) only for the extra costs associated with the child's disability.

How Law Now Stands

1–64   As the law currently stands, no damages may be awarded for the upkeep and maintenance costs of a healthy, uncovenanted child. The rule is modified in so far as a conventional award is proffered in recognition of the wrong done to a woman's autonomy by denying her the chance to exercise reproductive choice. The persistence of the Court of Appeal ruling in *Parkinson*, however, means that recompense in tort/delict is available for the excess costs

---

[104] *Rees v Darlington Memorial Hospital NHS Trust* [2004] 1 A.C. 309 at 336–343.
[105] *Less v Hussain* [2012] EWHC 3513 (QB).
[106] *Less v Hussain* [2012] EWHC 3513 (QB) at 175–176.
[107] See *Rees v Darlington Memorial Hospital NHS Trust* [2004] 1 A.C. 309 at 349.
[108] *Less v Hussain* [2012] EWHC 3513 at 180.

imposed by any disability in the resultant child. This raises the question that if there should be another case like that of *Parkinson*, will both damages for excess upbringing costs for a disabled child *and* a conventional award be given, or will one replace the other? It remains to be seen how the law will develop.

Wrongful Life Actions—A Child's Claim

So far we have been discussing the parents' right to sue for damages in respect of "wrongful pregnancy" or "wrongful birth". We now turn to a further area which remains controversial and which concerns a child's claim for so-called "wrongful life". This is a claim by a congenitally-disabled child that, through the negligence of a third party, his or her parents were not afforded the opportunity to terminate the pregnancy. The "wrongful life" claim may arise where medical tests have been negligently interpreted or carried out, resulting in failure to detect abnormalities in the fetus and where, if the parents had been properly informed, they would have sought an abortion. The conditions are, therefore, similar to those in which damages are sought for "wrongful birth"—indeed where an action for wrongful life is brought, it is customary for both to be brought together. The wrongful life action is, however, crucially different from the "wrongful birth" action in that in the latter case it is alleged that a duty was owed to the parent(s) which was not fulfilled, resulting in the unwanted birth of a child. In the "wrongful life" action, by contrast, the child him or herself brings the action (through the parents suing on the child's behalf), pleading that the defender owed a duty of care towards the child, and claiming damages on the basis that had the third party not been negligent in fulfilment of that duty, the child would not have been born at all and so forced to suffer a debilitated life. Essentially the child is saying, "I would have been better off never having existed than living this life; and but for your negligence, I would not have lived; so I deserve compensation from you."

The conceptual problems surrounding the "wrongful life" action can be examined by looking at the leading English case of *McKay v Essex Area Health Authority*.[109] Here a pregnant woman, who had been in contact with the rubella virus, took medical advice as to whether this would have any effect on her unborn child. Through the alleged negligence of the health authority in conducting tests, she failed to receive the correct information that the fetus might well have been affected by the virus. The child was subsequently born severely handicapped. The mother initiated a number of claims including a "wrongful life" claim on behalf of the child on the basis that as a result of the health authority's negligence, the child had entered into life with highly debilitating injuries.

The Court of Appeal was not prepared to recognise the claim by the child of damages for wrongful life.[110] The court held that a doctor clearly owes the fetus a duty not to injure it. However, in this case, the injuries which

1–65

1–66

1–67

---

[109] *McKay v Essex Area Health Authority* [1982] 2 All E.R. 771. See also the Australian case of *Harriton v Stephens* [2004] NSWCA 93.

[110] There is of course no reason why a mother in such circumstances should not have a legal

the fetus experienced were not caused by the doctor's negligence, but by the rubella virus. To uphold a duty of care in these circumstances would amount to placing the doctor under a legal obligation to abort the fetus. The court was concerned as to whether this could ever be legal. To impose such an obligation

"would mean regarding the life of a handicapped child as not only less valuable than the life of a normal child, but so much less valuable that it was not worth preserving, and it would even mean that a doctor would be obliged to pay damages to a child infected with rubella before birth who was in fact born with some mercifully trivial abnormality. These are the consequences of the necessary basic assumption that a child has a right to be born whole or not at all, not to be born unless it can be born perfect or 'normal', whatever that may mean".[111]

1–68   The Court of Appeal thus held that a claim for wrongful life would be contrary to public policy as a violation of the sanctity of human life. Not only that, but it would be impossible to evaluate the damages claimed because this would necessarily involve comparing the value of existence in a physically-challenged state with non-existence.[112] Furthermore, if the medical profession were to be held liable for damages in these circumstances, doctors might in turn be encouraged to put pressure on their patients to abort in any case where there might be a risk (however small) of fetal impairment. For these reasons the court upheld the view that:

"The only way in which a child injured in the womb can be compensated in damages is by measuring what it has lost, which is the difference between the value of life as a whole and healthy normal child and the value of its life as an injured child".[113]

As the doctor and health authority were not responsible for the injury that the child in fact suffered, and as they were under no legal duty to the fetus to terminate its existence, the child's action for damages for wrongful life was dismissed.

1–69   Since the time of the facts on which the decision in *McKay* was founded, the Congenital Disabilities (Civil Liability) Act 1976 came into effect in England, and now arguably rules out any right by a child to sue for damages in respect of "wrongful life".[114] However, as the 1976 Act does not apply

---

claim to damages in respect of the negligent failure to advise her that she might wish to choose an abortion discussed at para.1–28 above.

[111] *McKay v Essex Area Health Authority* [1982] 2 All E.R. 771, *per* Stephenson L.J. at p.781.

[112] See Teff, "The Action for 'Wrongful Life' in England and the United States" (1985) 34 I.C.L.Q. 423 for the counter view that there is nothing to prevent us from assigning values to both life and non-existence and then calculating damages accordingly. For a rebuttal see Norrie, "Wrongful Life in Scots Law; No Right, No Remedy", 1990 J.R. 205 at pp.217–223.

[113] *McKay v Essex Area Health Authority* [1982] 2 All E.R. 771, *per* Stephenson L.J. at 781.

[114] Under s.1(2)(b) and *per* Ackner L.J. in *McKay* [1982] 2 All E.R. 771 at 785–786. See, however, for a contrary view, Fortin, "Is The Wrongful Life Action Really Dead?" (1987) J.S.W.L. 306. Further, s.1(2A) which was inserted by s.44 of the Human Fertilisation and Embryology Act

to Scotland, here the matter is still governed by common law. In the event that an action for wrongful life should be raised in Scotland, the *McKay* case would be highly persuasive although not binding on a Scottish court. Nonetheless, given the tendency of courts on both sides of the border to follow one another's decisions in this area it is unlikely that such a claim would be successful.[115]

In *Harriton v Stephens*,[116] the High Court of Australia also found that the nature of the damage alleged in a wrongful life action was not such as to found a duty of care. A comparison between a life with disabilities and non-existence was not possible.[117] In the words of Crennan J, "Life with disabilities, like life, is not actionable".[118] **1–70**

A different approach was adopted in France, which became the first European jurisdiction to allow a wrongful life action in what is referred as the *Perruche* case.[119] As in *McKay*, a mother became infected with the rubella virus but due to her doctor's negligence she was not counselled about the risk to the fetus or the risk of a disabled child being born. Had the mother been apprised of the risk she would have terminated the pregnancy. The parents sued for damages based on breach of contract and the court of first instance not only held both the physician and the laboratory liable for damages, but also found them liable to the child for the loss caused by his disability.[120] On appeal, the Cour d'Appel however followed precedent and, while confirming the decision in favour of Mme Perruche, overturned the award of damages to the child. Eventually, the case was referred to a full chamber of the Cour de Cassation which found in favour of the child's claim to compensation. The ruling caused a furore in France, even going so far as to prompt the medical profession to go on strike. As a result, emergency legislation was passed to rectify the situation. The law adopted by the French Senate in 2002 was to the effect that in such a situation, parents of a child born with a disability can claim compensation for harm suffered by them but *not* for expenses attributable to the child's being disabled (which would be covered by social services). In passing this legislation the French **1–71**

1990 allows for an action by a disabled infant when the disability is attributable to wrongful acts or omissions. As Mason and Laurie state (*Law and Medical Ethics* (2011)), this seems indistinguishable from an action for wrongful life. For a critical assessment of the current law, see R. Scott, "Reconsidering 'wrongful life' in England after thirty years: legislative mistakes and unjustifiable anomalies", 2013 72(1) C.L.J. 115.

[115] Mason and Laurie, above, who argues that it is inequitable that the child have no remedy in respect of, e.g. negligent genetic counselling, and suggests that one way forward may be to regard the action as one where damages are sought for "diminished life" rather than for "wrongful life". Note, an action for "wrongful life" is not admissible in Australia or Canada and only in three US States as it is usually prevented either by statute or by common law.

[116] *Harriton v Stephens* [2006] HCA 15. For commentary, see Mason and Laurie, *Law and Medical Ethics* (2011) at paras 10.61–10.64.

[117] Mason and Laurie, *Law and Medical Ethics* (2011) at para.252.

[118] Mason and Laurie, *Law and Medical Ethics* (2011) at para.277.

[119] "X c Mutuelle d'Assurance du Corps Sanitaire Francais et a" (2000) J.C.O. 2293. For discussion of the details and analysis see T. Callus, "'Wrongful Life' a la Francaise" (2001) 5 Med Law Internat 117; T. Wier, "The Unwanted Child" (2002) 6 Edin L.R. 244; A. Morris and A. Sentier, "To Be or Not To Be: Is That The Question? Wrongful Life and Misconception" (2003) 11 Med. L.R. 167.

[120] Tribunal de Grande Instance, Evry, January 13, 1992.

government considerably narrowed the scope for a damages claim by out-lawing damages for the general upkeep of an uncovananted child regardless of whether s/he is healthy or disabled.[121]

Criminal Law and Fetal Rights

1–72   Until now we have been considering issues raised in the *civil* law of neg-ligence relating to the unborn child. The status of the unborn child also, however, creates difficulties within the criminal law. One problem is whether causing the death of a child while it is, as yet, not a legal person can be regarded as murder or culpable homicide. In *McCluskey v HM Advocate*,[122] a man was charged with causing death by reckless driving. By his negligence he caused an accident in which a pregnant woman was injured, who then gave birth prema-turely. The child was delivered alive, but died shortly thereafter. The accused defended himself on the basis that he had not caused "the death of another person" as required by s.1 of the Road Traffic Act 1972, as this could only refer to a person who was independently alive at the time that the act of reckless driving took place. Since that did not include the child who died, who was in utero at the date of the accident, the charge could not be sustained. On appeal, the High Court of Justiciary rejected this interpretation of the statute, and held that "there is no authority in the law of Scotland to the effect that a relevant charge of culpable homicide would not lie"[123] where death was caused by inju-ries inflicted before birth, as long as that person was born alive before dying as a result of the injuries. In other words, there is no crime of killing a fetus which is never subsequently born in Scots law ("feticide"), only of murder of a legal person by infliction of injuries sustained before live birth. This approach, which protects the interests of the fetus, but only after it has been born alive and achieved legal personality, is consonant with the approach taken in the civil cases examined above. It does, however, have the perhaps paradoxical result that legally it is more culpable to injure a child in the womb so he is later born impaired, than it is to kill him prior to delivery by the mother.

1–73   The English Court of Appeal has taken a similar approach to that of the Court of Appeal in *Attorney General's Reference (No.3 of 1994)*.[124] In this case, the respondent stabbed his girlfriend, in the knowledge that she was pregnant with their child. The knife penetrated the fetus, and one month later, the girlfriend gave birth to a grossly premature daughter who subse-quently died from a lung condition which was unconnected with the knife-wound, but resulted directly from the premature birth. The respondent was charged with the murder of the child but was acquitted on the grounds that there was no offence.

1–74   The Attorney-General sought a ruling from the Court of Appeal on whether murder or manslaughter could be committed where unlawful injury was deliberately inflicted on either a child in utero, or on a mother

---

[121] For a full discussion of the *Perruche* case, see P. Lewis, "The necessary implications of wrong-ful life claims: lessons from France" (2005) 12 Euro J. Hlth Law 135.

[122] *McCluskey v HM Advocate*, 1989 S.L.T. (Notes) 175.

[123] *McCluskey v HM Advocate*, 1989 S.L.T. (Notes) 175 at 176.

[124] *Attorney General's Reference (No.3 of 1994)* [1996] 2 All E.R. 10.

carrying a child in utero, in circumstances where the child was subsequently born alive but died thereafter, and where the injuries inflicted while in utero caused or contributed substantially to the child's death. First, the court held that causing injury to the fetus can be murder or manslaughter, provided the fetus is subsequently born; and secondly, that the statutory provision in question did not require that the person who died should be a person in being at the time the act causing the death was perpetrated.[125] Thereafter, the case went to the House of Lords which ruled out feticide absolutely.[126]

ABORTION

The cases discussed above lead us naturally to the controversial topic of abortion and its treatment in the criminal law. Abortion can be described unemotively as the elective termination of pregnancy. In the United Kingdom, abortion is dealt with on a statutory basis in the Abortion Act 1967 (hereafter "the 1967 Act"), as amended by s.37 of the Human Fertilisation and Embryology Act 1990 (hereafter "the HFEA 1990"). Prior to the 1967 Act, abortion was a crime at common law in Scotland, and in England under the Offences Against the Person Act of 1861, ss.58 and 59, although in both jurisdictions defences were available.[127] The Infant Life (Preservation) Act 1929 also introduced the crime (in English law only) of "child destruction", that is, causing the death of a child capable of being born alive before it has an existence independent of its mother. Prima facie, a fetus is capable of being born alive if it is 28 weeks old.[128]   **1–75**

The 1967 Act did not decriminalise abortion; instead it set out the circumstances in which a termination of pregnancy would not be unlawful and provided a number of statutory defences available to doctors to protect themselves from prosecution. Where an abortion is not carried out in a way authorised by the 1967 Act, it will still be unlawful, and the parties involved will be liable to prosecution. In practice, the effect is that the United Kingdom now enjoys a relatively liberal regime of access to lawful abortion; but nothing in the law gives a pregnant woman a *right* to an abortion, as is the case in jurisdictions such as the United States and Canada, where abortion, at least within the first trimester,[129] is seen as part of a woman's constitutional right to "privacy" in the sense of control of her own body.[130] It is important   **1–76**

---

[125] The court also held that the requisite intent required for a charge of murder was an intention to kill or cause really serious bodily injury to the mother, since the fetus was regarded as being an integral part of the mother prior to birth, i.e. the English doctrine of "transferred malice" applied.

[126] Note however that in England the murder of a fetus might be charged as an offence of "child destruction" under the Infant Life (Preservation) Act 1929, if the fetus was over 28 weeks old or "capable of being born alive".

[127] See *R. v Bourne* [1939] 1 K.B. 687.

[128] Infant Life (Preservation) Act 1929 s.1(2).

[129] See para.1–79.

[130] See especially *Roe v Wade*, 93 S Ct 705 (1973) (United States); *R v Morgenthaler* [1988] 1 S.C.R. 30 (Canada).

to realise when discussing the impact of abortion law on the legal status of the fetus, that the provisions of the 1967 Act are structured neither to protect the rights of women, nor of the unborn child, but to safeguard doctors and patients from prosecution under the criminal law. However, importantly, it removed the likelihood of women seeking "back street" abortions at great risk to their mental and physical health.

The Abortion Act 1967

1–77   Under the 1967 Act, s.1(1),[131] an abortion may be carried out without breaching the criminal law if two conditions are met. First, the pregnancy must be terminated by a registered medical practitioner. Secondly, normally two registered medical practitioners must have formed the opinion, prior to termination, and in good faith, that one of four conditions laid down in s.1(1) is met.

1–78   The first ground upon which an abortion may be justified is where,

> "the continuance of the pregnancy would involve risk, greater than if the pregnancy were terminated, of injury to the physical or mental health of the pregnant woman or any existing children of her family" (s.1(1)(a)).

This involves what are often referred to as "social" conditions justifying abortion. Section 1(1)(a) is by far the most common ground under which abortion is performed in the United Kingdom. In determining whether a ground exists under s.1(1)(a), doctors may take into account the pregnant woman's "actual or reasonably foreseeable environment".[132] An abortion carried out under this ground must be performed before the pregnancy exceeds its 24th week.[133]

1–79   The other grounds for abortion found in s.1(1) are not subject to a time-limit. These are:

- that the termination is necessary to prevent grave permanent injury to the physical or mental health of the pregnant woman[134];
- that the continuance of the pregnancy would involve risk to the life of the pregnant woman, greater than if the pregnancy were terminated[135];
- or that there is substantial risk that if the child were born it would suffer from such physical or mental abnormalities as to be seriously handicapped.[136]

---

[131] Which has been significantly amended by the Human Fertilisation and Embryology Act 1990 s.37.

[132] Abortion Act 1967 s.1(2) (which, for these purposes, is unaffected by the Still-Birth (Definition) Act 1992).

[133] This time-limit was inserted by s.37(4) of the HFEA 1990 and brings Scots and English law into line on this point. Section 37(4) also inserted the proviso in s.5(1) of the 1967 Act that no doctor performing a lawful abortion under the 1967 Act commits a crime under the Infant Life Preservation Act 1929. This removed the fear in England that lawfully aborting a fetus under the 1967 Act, which then proved to be capable of a live birth, might still be charged as a criminal offence under the 1929 Act. Practical problems may arise in ascertaining when a pregnancy begins. Medical practice appears to favour measuring the duration of pregnancy from the first day of the woman's last period.

[134] Abortion Act 1967 s.1(1)(b).

[135] Abortion Act 1967 s.1(1)(c).

[136] Abortion Act 1967 s.1(1)(d).

Only one medical opinion is required where a registered medical practitioner is of the opinion, formed in good faith, that the termination is immediately necessary to save the life of, or to prevent grave permanent injury to the physical or mental health of a pregnant woman.[137] However, as noted above, the majority of abortions that are performed are based on the s.1(1)(a) ground to which this proviso does not apply.

In relation to all grounds, it is interesting to note that it is the forming of the opinion in good faith by the requisite number of doctors that a s.1(1) ground exists that renders the abortion lawful—not the objective existence of the ground. It is thus extremely unlikely that a court will ever declare an abortion to have been illegally carried out in retrospect.[138] In all cases where an abortion is authorised it must be carried out in a NHS hospital or in places approved for the purpose by the Minister of Health or Secretary of State.[139] The latter proviso allows for abortions to be performed privately and for a fee.[140]

1–80

Abortion and Fetal Interests

As noted above, abortion is seen in many jurisdictions, notably the United States and Canada, as an issue of basic legal rights where the health, welfare and wishes of the mother must be balanced with the rights and interests of the unborn child. In the United States, for example, the Supreme Court has recognised that during the first trimester the woman has a largely unfettered right to abortion. However, during the second trimester, as the fetus develops, so do its interests, and during the third trimester the state has a compelling interest to intervene and protect the life of the fetus—though not to the detriment of the life of the woman.[141] In the United Kingdom, by contrast, abortion law tends to avoid the fetal/maternal rights debate by treating the whole issue as one which is primarily a matter for the medical profession, as long as they act in good faith. Just as the Abortion Act 1967 does not give a right to a woman to have an abortion, it also says nothing about the rights of the fetus. However, it is true that the issue of abortion does colour other decisions the courts make about the rights of the unborn child, since any attempt to give legal status or rights as a person to the fetus must inevitably generate conflicts with the laws that allow women access to legal abortion.[142] In some cases, third parties such as the father of the child, have sought to represent and defend the interests of the unborn child faced with abortion at the request of the mother.[143] In general, however, these attempts to extend fetal rights have been resisted by the courts.

1–81

---

[137] Abortion Act 1967 s.1(4).
[138] Only one reported case seems to exist where this was held: *R. v Smith* [1973] 1 W.L.R. 1510.
[139] Abortion Act 1967 s.1(3).
[140] Further, the Human Fertilisation and Embryology Act 1990 introduced s.1(3A) to the 1967 Act which relaxed the location rules for "medical" abortions—by use of antiprogesterones.
[141] See *Roe v Wade*, 93 S Ct 705 (1973) (United States) in n.20, above.
[142] As, e.g. in Ireland where abortion is, in principle, illegal because the right of the fetus to life is enshrined in the Constitution. See, for further examination of the conflicts this engenders, *Att Gen v X* (1992) 15 BMLR 104. However, abortions under limited circumstances will be allowed where there is a threat to the life of the mother in the Republic of Ireland under the Protection of Life During Pregnancy Act 2013.
[143] e.g. see *Kelly v Kelly*, 1997 S.L.T. (2nd Div) 896.

1–82   In the leading English case of *Paton v BPAS Trustees*,[144] a woman was granted a medical certificate stating there were grounds for an abortion. Her husband applied for an injunction to restrain her from having the abortion without his consent. The court held that since an unborn child had no rights of its own, and a father had no rights at common law over a child born outside of marriage, the husband's right to apply for an injunction had to be based on his status as a husband. As the courts had never exercised jurisdiction to control personal relationships within marriage, and the husband had no right to be consulted under the 1967 Abortion Act, the court held that the husband had no rights in law, either to prevent his wife from having the abortion, or to stop the doctors from carrying it out.

1–83   The husband then took his case before the European Commission on Human Rights as *Paton v UK*,[145] on two grounds. First, that United Kingdom legislation violated the unborn child's right to life under Art.2 of the Convention of Human Rights; and secondly, that it constituted an unjustified interference with the applicant's right to respect for family life contained in Art.8.[146] Article 2 states that "Everyone's right to life shall be protected by law". The Commission ruled that this provision was subject to an implied limitation justifying termination of pregnancy in its early stages in order to protect the life and health of the woman at that stage. On this basis, it ruled that an abortion of a 10-week old fetus under British law to protect the physical or mental health of a pregnant woman was not in breach of Art.2. In its reasoning, the Commission observed that

> "The 'life' of the fetus is intimately connected with, and cannot be regarded in isolation from, the life of the pregnant woman. If Article 2 were held to cover the fetus and its protection under this Article were, in the absence of any express limitation, seen as absolute, an abortion would have to be considered as prohibited even where the continuance of the pregnancy would involve a serious risk to the life of the pregnant woman. This would mean that the 'unborn life' of the fetus would be regarded as being of a higher value than the life of the pregnant woman".[147]

1–84   The applicant husband was no more successful in his claim that failure to consult the father over an abortion amounted to denial of respect for family life. The Commission ruled that in so far as abortion interfered with the applicant's right to respect for family life, it was justified under Art.8(2) as being necessary for protection of the rights of the mother. It noted that

> "any interpretation of the husband's and potential father's right, under Article 8 of the Convention, to respect for his private and family life, as regards an abortion which his wife intends to have performed on her,

---

[144] *Paton v BPAS Trustees* [1979] 1 Q.B. 276.

[145] *Paton v UK* [1981] 3 E.H.R.R. 408.

[146] For a more detailed discussion of these Articles and the Commission's interpretation of them, see Harris, O'Boyle and Warbrick, *The Law of the European Convention on Human Rights* (London: Butterworth, 1995).

[147] Harris, O'Boyle and Warbrick, *The Law of the European Convention on Human Rights*, at para.19, p.415.

must first of all take into account the right of the pregnant woman, being the person primarily concerned in the pregnancy and its continuation or termination, to respect for her private life . . . in the present case the Commission, having regard to the right of the pregnant woman, does not find that the husband's and potential father's right to respect for his private and family life can be interpreted so widely as to embrace such procedural rights as claimed by the applicant, i.e. a right to be consulted, or a right to make applications, about an abortion which his wife intends to have performed on her".[148]

Although the father in *Paton* was unsuccessful, the Commission in their ruling have left open the controversial question of whether the European Convention on Human Rights affords any protection at all to the unborn child, such as a right to life subject to certain implied limitations, such as were found to exist in *Paton*.[149] What *Paton* certainly does establish is that Art.2 does not recognise an absolute right to life belonging to the unborn child.[150] It remains open for discussion whether the Commission would have been more interested in ascribing a (possibly limited) right to life to a more mature fetus which was, for example, "capable of being born alive".[151] **1–85**

In Scotland, the father in the case of *Kelly v Kelly*[152] attempted to interdict his wife from terminating her pregnancy on the ground that what was contemplated was an actionable wrong and that any wrongful action sustained by a child in utero was actionable at the instance of the child acting through his parent or guardian. His argument was that any actionable wrong was a wrong capable of prevention by interdict and that a wrong which could be interdicted was not confined to a wrong causing injury only but included a wrong resulting in the death of the child. He contended that the effect of the Abortion Act was merely to decriminalise abortion in certain circumstances and that it had no effect in regard to civil liability for abortion as a wrong. The Inner House, however, rejected his claim on the basis that while a child had a right of action in respect of an injury caused by actions before his or her birth, an injury to the fetus was not actionable before birth. The court held that, **1–86**

> "The fatal flaw in the pursuer's argument was that of treating the fetus as a person with rights. In particular there was no law to the effect that the fetus had the right to remain where it was, in the womb. So long as there was an unborn fetus there was no legal persona which was separate from that of the mother; and hence no wrong done to the fetus as such".[153]

---

[148] Harris, O'Boyle and Warbrick, *The Law of the European Convention on Human Rights*, at para.27, pp.416–417.

[149] [1981] E.H.R.R. 408.

[150] Harris, O'Boyle and Warbrick, *The Law of the European Convention on Human Rights*, at para.23, p.416.

[151] See *C v S* [1987] 1 All E.R. 1230 where a father unsuccessfully argued, in circumstances similar to *Paton*, that an abortion should be prevented because the fetus was capable of being born alive and it was therefore possible that an abortion would be a crime under the Infant Life Preservation Act 1929.

[152] *Kelly v Kelly*, 1997 S.L.T. 896.

[153] *Kelly v Kelly*, 1997 S.L.T. 896 at 899K.

1–87   It is, however, important to note from our earlier discussions that while the fetus is not a person in law and thus has no rights, that does not mean to say that it has no legally protected interests. As our earlier discussions have shown it has been established that injury to the fetus is injury to a person if the fetus is subsequently born alive.[154] But, as Mason and Laurie observe, "this is essentially protection of the neonate"[155]; it remains the case that "recognition of the fetus *itself* has been steadfastly opposed".[156]

OVERVIEW

1–88   As we have seen from the statute and case law examined above, the consensus of the civil and criminal law in both Scotland and England is that the unborn child is not a legal person and has no standing in law. However, if the child survives to be born alive, he or she becomes a legal person with legal rights like anyone else, and may, for example, make civil claims in negligence in respect of ante-natal injury. With regards to abortion, the unborn child is in theory given the protection of the criminal law, but in practice the decision as to whether abortion is justified and lawful under the 1967 Act is one left to the good faith of the medical profession; the 1967 Act gives neither the fetus nor the husband or partner of the mother rights to oppose or restrain the abortion.

1–89   For a brief time there did appear to be some support for fetal rights in a number of English cases concerning pregnant women who refuse to consent to Caesarean sections. In *Re S*,[157] for example, the court exercised its inherent jurisdiction to authorise the carrying out of an emergency Caesarean section against the wishes of the mother, on the basis that the operation was vital to protect not only her own life but also that of the unborn child. The decision in *Re S* was taken on an emergency basis and was followed in two further High Court cases.[158] However, this approach was firmly quashed in the Court of Appeal decision in *Re MB*[159] where the court stressed that persons of full age and sound mind cannot be treated against their will. It made it clear that where a person is competent, that is of sound mind, s/he can refuse medical treatment for any reasons, whether rational, irrational or even on the basis

---

[154] See paras 1–16 to 1–17.

[155] Mason and Laurie, *Law and Medical Ethics* (2011), p.3, para.5.6.

[156] Mason and Laurie, *Law and Medical Ethics* (2011). See also the decision of the European Court of Human Rights in *Vo v France* (2004) 79 BMLR 71 (discussed at paras 1–09 *et seq*), which held that there was no European Consensus on the nature and status of the embryo and/or fetus although they were beginning to receive some protection in the light of scientific progress. It noted that: "At best, it may be regarded as common ground between states that the embryo/fetus belongs to the human race. The potentiality of that being and its capacity to become a person—enjoying protection under the civil law, moreover, in many states, such as France, in the content of inheritance and gifts and also in the United Kingdom . . . require protection in the name of human dignity, without making it a 'person' with the 'right to life' for the purposes of Article 2" (at 106).

[157] *Re S* [1992] 4 All E.R. 671

[158] See *Norfolk and Norwich Healthcare (NHS) Trust v W* [1996] 2 F.L.R. 613 and *Tameside and Glossop Acute Services Trust v CH (a patient)* (1996) 34 BMLR 175.

[159] *Re MB (an adult: medical treatment)* [1997] 38 BMLR 175.

of no reason at all. The only situation where non-voluntary treatment may arise, is when the patient is incapable of giving consent and when treatment is in the patient's best interests. However, where a competent pregnant woman decides to refuse treatment, there is no jurisdiction to declare medical intervention as being lawful, even although this may result in the death or serious handicap of her baby.[160]

In this particular case, the woman was declared incompetent because it was **1–90** established that it was her fear of needles which led her to refuse treatment to which she would otherwise have consented. This decision reinforced the cardinal rule in medicine that patients of full mental competence have the right to refuse consent to medical treatment, and have that refusal respected, even if that choice is not in their own welfare and may even result in their death.[161] It is only where a person is incompetent, that the court may addresses the question of whether or not treatment is in that patient's best interests, a view endorsed in a subsequent Court of Appeal decision in *St George's Healthcare NHS Trust v S (Guidelines)*; *R v Collins, Ex p. S (No.2)*[162] that went so far as to issue guidance for healthcare professionals who are faced with deciding whether or not a patient is competent to grant consent to or refuse treatment.[163]

In the next chapter, we examine the capacity of children to enter into legal transactions, and how this affects their parents and other third parties.

---

[160] For an attempt to strengthen the legal position of the fetus through a human rights analysis of the issues see G.T. Laurie, "Medical Law and Human Rights: Passing the Parcel Back to the Profession" in *Human Rights and Scots Law: Comparative Perspectives on the Incorporation of the ECHR* (Oxford: Hart Publishing, 2002).

[161] See *Re T (adult: refusal of medical treatment)* [1992] 4 All E.R. 649 and *Airedale NHS Trust v Bland* [1993] A.C. 789.

[162] *R v Collins, Ex p. S (No.2)* [1998] 3 All E.R. 673.

[163] For discussion of the issues surrounding enforced caesareans and the case law see, H. Lim, "Caesareans and Cyborg's", 1999 Feminist Legal Studies 7 at pp.133–173; A. Morris, "Once Upon a Time in a Hospital . . . The Cautionary Tale of *St. George's Health Care NHS Trust v S.R.V. Collins and Others Ex Parte*" [1998] 3 All E.R. 673, 1999 Feminist Legal Studies 7 at pp.75–84; R. Scott, "Maternal Duties Toward the Unborn? Soundings from the Law of Tort", 2000 8 Med. L.R. 1–68.

CHAPTER 2
THE CHILD AND LEGAL CAPACITY

INTRODUCTION: PERSONALITY, RIGHT-HOLDING AND CAPACITY

2–01   As we have seen in Ch.1, a child acquires legal personality at the moment of birth.[1] This is the first step towards the child's acquisition of the full legal standing of an adult. On birth, a child will also hold certain rights, including human rights[2] and, in the private law context, the right to own property.[3] However, he cannot do anything to enforce those rights, such as take a case to court complaining of a violation of his rights, or write a will disposing of his property. In other words, at birth a child has passive legal capacity to be the object or holder of rights, but not active legal capacity to transfer, enforce or otherwise interact with those rights. As we will see, those actions must be taken on his behalf by a parent or another person entitled to act as his legal representative.

2–02   As the child grows, he gradually acquires greater legal rights and powers. Sometimes he will attain a new right by virtue of having reached a certain age: for example, at age 12, a child has the capacity to make a valid will.[4] In other cases, he will acquire the right by virtue of having reached a certain level of maturity in the eyes of a relevant adult: for example, a child can consent to medical treatment if, in the eyes of his doctor, he is sufficiently mature to understand the nature and consequences of that treatment.[5] At the age of 16, a child acquires full legal capacity,[6] and at 18 is recognised to have attained the age of majority.[7]

2–03   In this chapter, we shall examine the legal position of children as influenced by the development of international children's rights, before going on to consider in more depth the legal capacity of children of different ages along with related duties and responsibilities.

---

[1] For discussion of the problems associated with ascribing legal personality to a foetus prior to its being born alive, see Ch.1.

[2] See further paras 2–06 et seq., and the Human Rights Act 1998, incorporating the European Convention on Human Rights (ECHR) into UK law.

[3] See Erskine, i. 6.53.

[4] Age of Legal Capacity (Scotland) Act 1991 s.2(2), discussed at para.2–22 below.

[5] Age of Legal Capacity (Scotland) Act 1991 s.2(4), discussed at paras 2–24 to 2–32 below.

[6] Age of Legal Capacity (Scotland) Act 1991 s.1(1).

[7] Age of Majority (Scotland) Act 1969 s.1

CONCEPTIONS OF CHILDHOOD

The idea that children are in some way a fundamentally different species to **2–04**
adults is not an inherent one, but one, it has been argued, which is culturally
constituted. There have been different conceptions of childhood during different periods of history, in different societies, and in different groups within
society. One highly influential treatise argues that in medieval European
society there was no conception of childhood at all.[8] Children were merely
miniature adults, and were neither separated from, nor protected from, the
adult world in the way that is customary now. Significantly, there was no
attempt to segregate them from adult sexual behaviour, nor to punish them
differently to adult offenders. Works such as these were founded upon in
the late 1960s and 1970s by "children's liberationists", who argued that
the status of minority was oppressive by its very existence.[9] The liberation-
ist position, developed primarily by US scholars, was that children should
hold all the same legal rights and capacities as adults, including the rights to
drive and engage in sexual activity. This was set in opposition to outdated
Victorian models of childhood, where children were seen as possessions of
their parents, devoid of autonomy until the age of majority. Present-day
writers tend to advocate a more moderate conception, where children are
considered entitled to a greater degree of protection than adults, but within
a context that supports and encourages the development of their ability to
make autonomous, independent choices as appropriate to their age and
maturity.[10] Eekelaar proposes a model of dynamic self-determinism, where
the best interests of the child are promoted within a framework which allows
the growing child increasing participation in the determination of those
interests.[11]

It is clear that it is our particular societal conception of how children are **2–05**
different from adults, what differences are significant, and consequently how
and when childhood should give way to adulthood, that informs our view of
how the law should restrict, protect and empower children.[12] For example,
in some non-Western cultures, play is not clearly distinguished from work,
nor is work something which replaces play at a certain level of maturity. All
members of the community would usually undertake some work suited to
their sizes and capabilities from very early years. In Western society, there is
generally a clear demarcation between work and non-work activities for children. Paid work is considered inappropriate for very young children and so
the hours and conditions of children's work are strictly regulated. Of course,
no society's conception of childhood is fixed. As our ideas about children
continue to evolve, so too will our ideas of what rights they should have, what
legal capacity, and what protection they need.

---

[8] Aries, *Centuries of Childhood* (Vintage Books, 1962).
[9] See generally R. Farson, *Birthrights* (Collier McMillan, 1974) and J. Holt, *Escape from Childhood: The Needs and Rights of Childhood* (EP Dutton, 1974).
[10] For general discussion, see S. Fredman and S. Spencer, *Age as an Equality Issue* (Hart, 2003).
[11] J. Eekelaar, "The Interests of the Child and the Child's Wishes: the Role of Dynamic Self-Determinism" (1994) 8(1) Int. J.L.P.F. 42.
[12] Freeman, *The Rights and Wrongs of Children* (Pinter Pub Ltd, 1983), Ch.1.

CHILDREN AND INTERNATIONAL HUMAN RIGHTS STANDARDS[13]

2–06   One of the key drivers towards a changing legal conception of children in
Scots law in the last 25 years has been the increasing regard given to international human rights standards, in particular the European Convention
on Human Rights (ECHR) and the UN Convention on the Rights of the
Child (UNCRC).[14] The European Convention provides basic guarantees
of civil and political rights for all citizens, including children. It has been
incorporated into domestic law through the Human Rights Act 1998, which
provides that legislation must be given effect in a Convention-compliant
manner if possible,[15] and that non-compliant legislation will be ultra vires
the Holyrood Parliament,[16] or subject to a fast-track amendment procedure
in Westminster.[17] Any act or omission by a public authority which is incompatible with the Convention is unlawful.[18] Any individual who believes his
human rights have been breached by the state may raise an action to that
effect in the domestic courts, with a right of appeal leading all the way to the
European Court of Human Rights in Strasbourg.[19]

2–07   The UNCRC, by contrast, has no court with specific jurisdiction to hear
complaints of violations. Nor is it possible to raise such complaints in the
UK courts, since the UNCRC has not been incorporated into domestic
law. Instead, the UNCRC is enforced principally by the obligation on states
parties to submit reports on compliance to a central UN Committee on the
Rights of the Child every five years.[20] The Committee scrutinises the reports
and issues "Concluding Observations" which include criticisms where the
state has failed to comply fully with its obligations under the Convention.[21]

---

[13] See further literature on the UNCRC and ECHR from a Scottish child law angle, L. Edwards,
"Incorporation of the European Convention on Human Rights: what will it mean for
Scotland's children?" in *Human Rights and Scots Law* (Oxford: Boyle *et al.* (eds), Hart
Publishing, 2002); K. Norrie, "The Rights of Children", 2004 J.R. 55; A. Cleland and
E. Sutherland, *Childrens' Rights in Scotland*, 3rd edn (Edinburgh: W.Green, 2009); A. Cleland,
"Children's Voices" in *Family Dynamics: Contemporary Issues in Family Law* (J. Scoular
(ed.), Butterworths, 2001); K. Marshall, *Children's Rights in the Balance: the Participation-
Protection Debate* (The Stationery Office, 1997); K. Tisdall, *The Children (Sc) Act 1995,
Developing Policy and Law for Scotland's Children* (The Stationery Office, 1997).

[14] Adopted November 28, 1989 (28 International Legal Materials 1448), and ratified by the
United Kingdom on December 16, 1991.

[15] Human Rights Act 1998 s.3(1).

[16] Scotland Act 1998 s.29(1).

[17] Human Rights Act 1998 s.4, s.10 and Sched.2.

[18] Human Rights Act 1998 s.6(1).

[19] A detailed account of the history and current place of Convention rights in Scots law can
be found in R. Reed and J. Murdoch, *A Guide to Human Rights Law in Scotland*, 3rd edn
(Bloomsbury Professional, 2011), Chs 1–2.

[20] UNCRC, art.44(1). For a fuller account of enforcement procedures, see C. Hamilton,
"Children's rights and the role of the UN Committee on the Rights of the Child: underly-
ing structures for states in implementing the Convention on the Rights of the Child" 2010
(March) *International Family Law* 31.

[21] Reports by States Parties and subsequent Concluding Observations by the Committee from
around 1999 onwards can be found, somewhat confusingly, on the UNHCR website at *http://
www.unhcr.org/cgi-bin/texis/vtx/refworld/rwmain?page=publisher&skip=0&publisher=CRC*
[accessed August 5, 2013]. Older Reports can be found via the UN Treaty Body database at
http://www.unhchr.ch/tbs/doc.nsf [accessed August 5, 2013].

Significant concerns have been raised in connection with this enforcement model, not least because the critical observations of the Committee in response to previous UK reports[22] have led only exceptionally to changes in the law.[23] The position in Scotland is further complicated by the fact that the United Kingdom as a whole is the state party to the UNCRC, and so reports to the Committee tend to focus on English law with Scottish provisions somewhat "tacked on" where they differ.

In recent years, the Scottish Government has taken a series of steps designed to improve compliance with its obligations under the UNCRC and in the area of children's rights more generally. In 2003, the office of Children's Commissioner for Scotland was created by statute.[24] The Commissioner has a general responsibility to promote and safeguard the rights of children and young people,[25] backed up by various specific obligations including the requirement to consult with children and young people[26] and to produce an annual report detailing the work of the Commissioner in the previous year, highlighting areas of concern in relation to human rights compliance.[27] In 2009, following the Concluding Observations by the UN Committee on the UK report in 2007,[28] the Scottish Government published an action plan for children's rights entitled *Do The Right Thing*.[29] The action plan identified 21 areas for priority action in response to the Committee's observations, ranging from general issues such as the promotion of children's rights within the Government to more particular concerns such as the treatment of 16 and 17 year olds in the youth justice system. A progress report on the action plan was issued in May 2012.[30]   **2–08**

Perhaps most significantly to date, in September 2011 the Government announced plans to create a duty on Scottish Ministers to have due regard to the UNCRC when exercising any of their functions. Following a period of consultation in the summer of 2012,[31] the Children and Young People   **2–09**

---

[22] There have been three UK reports to date, in 1994, 1999 and 2007. Concluding Observations in response were published by the Committee in 1995, 2002 and 2008. The next report is due to be submitted in January 2014.

[23] For a general discussion, see J.P. Grant, "Monitoring and Enforcing Children's Human Rights" in A. Cleland and E. Sutherland (eds), *Children's Rights in Scotland*, 3rd edn (Edinburgh: W. Green, 2009).

[24] Commissioner for Children and Young People (Scotland) Act 2003.

[25] Commissioner for Children and Young People (Scotland) Act 2003 s.4

[26] Commissioner for Children and Young People (Scotland) Act 2003 s.6

[27] Commissioner for Children and Young People (Scotland) Act 2003 s.10. The reports are available on the Commissioner's website at *http://www.sccyp.org.uk/reports-publications/annual accountsandreports* [accessed August 5, 2103].

[28] The UK Report is available at *http://www.unhcr.org/refworld/pdfid/4806162b2.pdf* [accessed August 5, 2013.). The Scottish contribution to that document was made available by the Scottish Government in its *Report on the Implementation of the UN Convention on the Rights of the Child in Scotland 1999–2007* (2007) available at *http://www.scotland.gov.uk/ Publications/2007/07/30114126/0* [accessed August 5, 2013].

[29] *Do the Right Thing: for people who work with children or work on their behalf* (2009) available at *http://www.scotland.gov.uk/Publications/2009/08/27111754/25* [accessed August 5, 2013].

[30] *Do the Right Thing—a progress report on our response to the 2008 concluding observations from the UN Committee on the Rights of the Child* (2012) available at *http://www.scotland.gov.uk/ Publications/2012/05/3593* [accessed August 5, 2013].

[31] *Consultation on Rights of Children and Young People Bill* (2011), available at *http://www. scotland.gov.uk/Publications/2011/09/07110058/0* [accessed August 5, 2013].

Bill was introduced into Parliament in April 2013.[32] The Bill provides for a duty of due regard to the UNCRC to be implemented across the public sector, together with additional duties on the Government to promote and raise awareness of children's rights. Additionally, the powers of the Children's Commissioner are to be extended to allow investigations on behalf of individual children and young people. It seems the Government has no plans at present to place the UNCRC on a wholly statutory footing, despite apparent support for that approach amongst the respondents to the consultation.

2–10   To what extent has this increased focus on human rights actually improved the position of children in Scotland? It is possible to point to a number of specific legislative changes which can be attributed to our human rights obligations. One high profile example is the incorporation into domestic legislation of the child's right to an education,[33] set out in articles 28 and 29 of the UNCRC. Various provisions supporting the right of a child to participate in decisions affecting his life can be found in recent Scottish statutes.[34] Changes have been made to the treatment of children within the criminal justice system with a view to improving the protection of vulnerable children.[35] Numerous further examples could be cited. It is fair to say that children's rights are having an impact.

2–11   However, some words of caution on the impact of children's rights should also be included here. Questions remain as to the value of a human rights framework as a basis for improving the lives of children.[36] Assigning rights to children brings into sharp relief the tension which exists between the need to protect children from the responsibilities of the adult world and the desire to enable children to participate in the decisions which affect their lives. Infant children cannot exercise rights in any practical sense, and even older children may not have the resources required to meaningfully assert their rights, for example, in the courts. Additionally, it is unclear how well the rights of children can be balanced against the rights of parents. The focus of human rights instruments is on preventing oppression by the state, but for children, rights violations are more likely to be carried out by parents or other carers, and this conundrum is not easy to resolve. More broadly, it is questionable whether the individualistic language of rights makes sense at all in a context like family law, where relationships, rather than individuals, are the focus.

2–12   From a practical perspective, it cannot be asserted that human rights standards have guaranteed a particular quality of life for Scottish children. The Concluding Observations of the UN Committee on the Rights of the

---

[32] The Bill and accompanying documents are available at *http://www.scottish.parliament.uk/ parliamentarybusiness/Bills/62233.aspx* [accessed August 5, 2013].

[33] Standards in Scotland's Schools, etc. Act 2000 s.1.

[34] Examples include Children (Scotland) Act 1995 ss.6 and 11(7)(b); Standards in Scotland's Schools etc Act 2000 s.2(2); Adoption and Children (Scotland) Act 2007 s.32; Children's Hearings (Scotland) Act 2011 s.27.

[35] Criminal Justice (Scotland) Act 2003 ss.51 and 53; Criminal Procedure (Scotland) Act 1995 s.41A.

[36] There is a huge literature in this area. A useful starting point with abundant reference to further reading is S. Choudhry and J. Herring, *European Human Rights and Family Law* (Hart, 2010), pp.127–138.

Child in 2008[37] laid out a damning indictment of the United Kingdom's performance in implementing the guarantees of the UNCRC. Child poverty levels, and associated malnutrition, homelessness, pregnancy and suicide rates for children, remained unacceptably high despite Governmental efforts. Child asylum seekers were being detained along with adults and denied basic due process rights. Rates of exclusion of children from schools, and thus denial of education rights, though improving, were still far too high. Minority children, particularly travellers and those with disabilities, suffered entrenched discrimination. Family violence, abuse and neglect of children within families were alarmingly prevalent, and no national strategy for intervention or recovery was in place. A third of soldiers in the United Kingdom were recruited, deliberately, from the ranks of the under 18s. Many of these problems cannot be resolved by family law alone, but progress in the implementation of children's rights should not be used to obscure the entrenched difficulties that children in our society continue to face.

MINORS AND PUPILS: HISTORICAL DEVELOPMENT OF SCOTS LAW CONCEPTION OF CHILDREN

Although the age of majority in Scotland is set out in statute as 18,[38] Scots law has traditionally recognised that the development from child to adult happens incrementally. In a framework adapted from Roman law principles, children were divided into *pupils* and *minors*. Pupillarity lasted from birth until the age of 12 for a girl and from birth until the age of 14 for a boy. (The distinction reflected different ages for attaining puberty.) Girls over the age of 12 but under 18, and boys over the age of 14 but under 18, were in minority.[39] This historical background sharply distinguishes the development of the Scots treatment of the capacity of children from English law where, in strict principle, a child still moves straight from being an infant to an adult at the age of 18, rights and capacities under the age of 18 being conferred only by a patchwork of exceptions under statute and common law.[40] **2–13**

At common law, the rules as to the capacity of pupils and minors to enter various legal transactions, and especially contracts, were highly complex.[41] In general, a pupil child had no active legal capacity.[42] Instead, in all legal transactions, the guardian of the pupil, known as a tutor, acted for the **2–14**

---

[37] The Concluding Observations are available at *http://www.unhcr.org/refworld/pdfid/4906d1d72. pdf* [accessed August 5, 2013.)

[38] Age of Majority (Scotland) Act 1969 s.1. Before that date, following Roman law, minority originally lasted until the age of 25. This was reduced to 21 and then to 18.

[39] Erskine, i.7.1.

[40] See Bainham, *Children—The Modern Law*, 3rd edn (Longman Law, 2005), p.19. However, this view of English children is now severely compromised by the rights of mature minors that were recognised in *Gillick v West Norfolk and Wisbech Area Health Authority* [1986] 1 A.C. 112 (see paras 2–24 to 2–32).

[41] See, for a full account, Wilkinson and Norrie, *The Law Relating to Parent and Child in Scotland*, 2nd edn (Edinburgh: W. Green, 1999) (hereafter "Wilkinson and Norrie"), Ch.1.

[42] Erskine, i.6.2, i.7.33 gives minor exceptions to this rule.

child, giving any necessary legal consent. Thus, any contracts a pupil child purported to make on his or her own were void. However, as stated above, there was nothing to stop a pupil being the passive recipient of rights, so that a pupil was capable of, inter alia, owning and inheriting property. A minor child, on the other hand, had, in principle, almost the equivalent of adult legal capacity, but could only exercise it with the *concurrence* of his or her guardian, known as a curator. Thus, a contract made by a minor with the consent of the curator would be legally valid—any other contract would be void. There were numerous exceptions to this rule, by which a minor could sometimes enter legal transactions on his or her own. Furthermore, three classes of minors also had extensive capacity to act on their own without a curator: minor children who had no curator, e.g. orphans; minors who had married; and minors who had left home and taken up an independent exist-ence (a state known as forisfamiliation).[43] For both pupils and minors, the guardian, whether known as tutor or curator, was the person with parental rights, normally the parent or parents.[44] Minors who made valid contracts either with the consent of their curators or on their own under one of the exceptional regimes, also had an advantage under the law in that they could sometimes have the contract later declared void if they had been taken advan-tage of due to their youth and inexperience (this was known as the remedy of minority and lesion).

2–15   The law on the capacity of children was radically transformed by the Age of Legal Capacity (Scotland) Act 1991,[45] which introduced for most legal purposes a different categorisation of children according to whether they are above or below the age of 16. The older framework of pupils and minors no longer has effect in so far as it conflicts with the 1991 Act.[46]

2–16   The 1991 Act was introduced in response to many perceived problems with the old law.[47] The law was highly complex, with more exceptions than unqualified rules.[48] It was largely drawn from the institutional writers and very old case law and was thus somewhat obscure and uncertain, and untailored to the needs of modern society. Because it was inappropriate to the modern world it was, in many respects, largely ignored. There was, in particular, a strong feeling that the ages of 12 and 14 were not especially significant for modern Scottish children and that the distinction between the sexes was not defensible. Because of the arbitrariness of the rules in modern society it was felt the law was at times over-protective and yet sometimes did not go far enough. Given all this, the Scottish Law Commission decided that comprehensive reform would be preferable to mere "tinkering with the rules".

---

[43] Erskine, i.6.53.

[44] For the rules on who has parental responsibilities and rights, see Ch.3.

[45] Hereafter "the 1991 Act". It came into force on September 25, 1991.

[46] 1991 Act s.1(4).

[47] See, generally, *Report on the Legal Capacity and Responsibility of Minors and Pupils*, Scot. Law Com. No.110 (1987).

[48] For a critique of whether the 1991 Act in fact succeeded in simplifying the law, or merely introduced its own new set of complexities, see Thomson, "Minor's Rights—Some Minor Changes?", 1989 J.L.S.S. 335.

THE AGE OF LEGAL CAPACITY (SCOTLAND) ACT 1991

The basic framework of the 1991 Act is that children under the age of 16 **2–17** have, in principle, no capacity to enter into any transaction, while children over 16 have, in principle, full legal capacity.[49] A "transaction" is given a wide interpretation by s.9 of the Act to include any transaction having legal effect, which includes, notably, the making of contracts, but also expressly includes unilateral transactions, such as making a promise, giving a legal consent to medical treatment, appointing a trustee, and the raising or defending of civil proceedings in court. The age of 16 was selected as significant because it reflected "an important social reality".[50] At 16, a child can marry; can leave school; can take up full-time employment and so become independently economically active; can embark on full-time higher education and so begin to pursue a career. To set the age of capacity, as previously, at 12 or 14 was to ignore the fact that young persons of those ages are rarely involved in significant independent legal transactions and are often still deemed to be in need of parental guidance; while to set it at 18 (the age of majority and the age at which significant public law rights arise, such as, primarily, the right to vote) was to ignore the substantial leap into the adult world which the age of 16 represents and would have radically curtailed the existing powers of minor children without good cause. The conclusion of the Scottish Law Commission was that the age of 16 represented a realistic dividing line between those who needed special protection on account of immaturity and those who did not.[51]

The Child Under 16

Section 1(1)(a) of the 1991 Act states that a person under 16 years of age **2–18** has no legal capacity to enter any transaction. A child under 16 is therefore in the same position as a pupil under the old law; any transaction he or she seeks to enter will be void.[52] As with a pupil under the old law, capacity must be supplied for the child by his or her parent or legal representative, who performs legal functions on the child's behalf. The law on guardianship and legal representation[53] will be examined more closely elsewhere. For present purposes it is enough to state that the legal representatives of a child are the persons with parental responsibilities and rights in respect of that child under the Children (Scotland) Act 1995. Parental responsibilities and rights are automatically granted to (i) the mother of the child,[54] (ii) the father if married to the mother at conception or subsequently,[55] failing which if registered as

---

[49] 1991 Act s.1.
[50] *Report on the Legal Capacity and Responsibility of Minors and Pupils*, Scot. Law Com. No.110 (1987), para 3.19.
[51] *Report on the Legal Capacity and Responsibility of Minors and Pupils*, Scot. Law Com. No.110 (1987), para 3.5.
[52] 1991 Act s.2(5).
[53] The law on legal representation and guardianship was reformed shortly after the 1991 Act came into operation by the Children (Scotland) Act 1995 ss.7–10; see paras 6–10 to 6–14.
[54] Children (Scotland) Act 1995 s.3(1)(a)
[55] Children (Scotland) Act 1995 s.3(1)(b)(i)

the father in a United Kingdom register of births, deaths and marriages,[56] or (iii) the second female parent of the child[57] if in civil partnership with the mother,[58] failing which if registered as a parent in a United Kingdom register of births, deaths and marriages.[59] It is possible for other parties (such as a step-parent or grandparent) to apply for parental rights including guardianship, or for a guardian to be appointed in the event of the natural parents' death.[60] However, the incapacity of under-16 children is subject to some significant exceptions.

Exceptions to the General Rule

s.2(1) A person under the age of 16 years shall have legal capacity to enter into a transaction—(a) of a kind commonly entered into by persons of his age and circumstances, and(b) on terms which are not unreasonable.[61]

2–19   This exception is intended to deal with the reality that children of all ages regularly engage in a range of economic activities. Children buy goods such as food and clothes, pay for journeys on public transport, download apps and so on. Contracts of this type would be void under the general principle of s.1(1)(a) if no further provision was made. Although this would often make little difference in a standard cash transaction, it could be crucial to securing rights under consumer protection legislation that a valid contract was made. For example, the purchaser of a defective CD player has rights in respect of quality and fitness for purpose under the Sale of Goods Act 1979[62] which he would not have if the contract was void.

2–20   The aim of the provision then, is to recognise the validity of everyday, common transactions of children of differing ages and circumstances. The test is designed to be factual, rather than legally prescriptive. "Everyday" transactions, it is recognised, differ widely in different geographical areas, different social classes and at different ages. A seven-year-old may commonly buy sweets; a twelve-year-old may buy mobile phone credit. The provision avoids setting any normative test, such as what is a reasonable or necessary transaction for a child. It is also capable of changing with the times. In 1783, it was accepted that a young gentleman had capacity to buy lengths of red silk for himself for clothing but not as a gift for his lady friend, as the former but not the latter purchase was regarded as a "necessary".[63] Nowadays, probably neither contract would be regarded as a transaction "of a kind commonly entered" unless it could be subsumed into the more general transaction of purchasing clothing.

2–21   Finally, note that even if the transaction is of a kind commonly entered

---

[56] Children (Scotland) Act 1995 s.3(1)(b)(ii)
[57] This legal status is acquired by the non-gestational mother where a same sex female couple has received licensed assisted reproductive treatment: see Human Fertilisation and Embryology Act 2008 ss.42–44 discussed at paras 3–79 to 3–82 below.
[58] Children (Scotland) Act 1995 s.3(1)(c).
[59] Children (Scotland) Act 1995 s.3(1)(d).
[60] Children (Scotland) Act 1995 ss.7 and 11; see also para.6–10.
[61] 1991 Act s.2(1).
[62] Sale of Goods Act 1979 s.14.
[63] *Scoffier v Read* (1783) Mor.8936.

into, it will still be void if it is entered into on *unreasonable terms*. This is intended to protect a child under 16 from making an extortionate bargain and being held to it.

s.2(2) A person of or over the age of 12 years shall have testamentary capacity, including legal capacity to exercise by testamentary writing any power of appointment.[64]

Testamentary capacity is the power to make a will determining what is to **2–22** happen to the testator's property on his death. Power of appointment is the capacity to name a person who shall have discretion to distribute property on the testator's behalf after his death, where the testator does not wish to make express provision in the will. It seem that any child who dies before the age of 12 must die intestate (without leaving a valid will) since it is established that no parent or guardian can make a will for a child.[65]

s.2(3) A person of or over the age of 12 years shall have legal capacity to consent to the making of an adoption order in relation to him.[66]

An adoption order cannot be made in respect of a child of 12 or older **2–23** without his consent.[67] The same rule applies in respect of a permanence order,[68] discussed further at para.6–21 below.

s.2(4) A person under the age of 16 shall have legal capacity to consent on his own behalf to any surgical, medical or dental procedure or treatment where, in the opinion of a qualified medical practitioner attending him, he is capable of understanding the nature and possible consequences of the procedure or treatment.[69]

The power to consent to medical treatment in respect of children is an **2–24** aspect of the parental responsibility (and accompanying right) to act as a child's legal representative.[70] Historically, it seems to have been the position throughout the United Kingdom[71] that a child had no say in a decision of this sort. However, the position was altered by the landmark case of *Gillick v West Norfolk and Wisbech Area Health Authority*.[72]

Victoria Gillick applied to the English courts for determination on whether **2–25** a notice issued by the Department of Health and Social Security was lawful. The notice advised doctors that while it was desirable when persons under 16

---

[64] 1991 Act s.2(2).
[65] *Rintoul's Trs v Rintoul*, 1949 S.C. 297.
[66] 1991 Act s.2(3).
[67] Adoption and Children (Scotland) Act 2007 s.32
[68] Adoption and Children (Scotland) Act 2007 ss.84(1) and (2).
[69] 1991 Act s.2(4).
[70] Children (Scotland) Act 1995 ss.1(1)(d) and 2(1)(d).
[71] The position in Scotland was less certain than in England, where the rule was enshrined in the Family Law Reform Act s.8. See Norrie, "The *Gillick* Case and Parental Rights in Scots Law", 1985 S.L.T. (News) 157 for a strong argument in favour of the independent capacity of minors before *Gillick*; see Thomson for a rebuttal, "The *Gillick* Case and Parental Rights in Scots Law: Another View", 1985 S.L.T. (News) 223.
[72] *Gillick v West Norfolk and Wisbech Area Health Authority* [1986] 1 A.C. 112.

sought contraceptive advice and treatment for their parents to be informed and consulted, nevertheless, in exceptional circumstances, the doctor might treat the child alone so long as he did so in good faith and with regard to the child's best interests. Mrs Gillick argued that this advice was legally wrong, claiming (inter alia) that, in English law, a child over 16 only had a right to consent to medical treatment by virtue of statute and a child under 16 had no common law right to give such a consent. Hence it was argued that the only person who could give such a consent was the parent or guardian by virtue of their parental rights, and so a doctor would be acting illegally if he treated a child without the consent (and by implication, the knowledge) of a parent or guardian.

2–26 The Court of Appeal agreed that a child under 16 did not have the right to consent without parental approval. However, in the House of Lords by a narrow margin of three to two, the decision was reversed. It was held that children under 16 could, exceptionally, consent to receiving contraceptive treatment, and by extension all other forms of medical procedure, *provided* they had reached a certain degree of maturity and understanding. However, the exact criteria for becoming (as it has since become known) "*Gillick*-competent" were left a matter of some controversy. Lord Fraser emphasised, along with other factors, that a doctor should only regard a child as competent if the treatment requested was in that child's best interests. Lord Scarman, on the other hand, required that for a child to be competent he or she should not only understand the nature of the medical treatment but also have sufficient maturity to understand what was involved, including moral and family questions and the risks to health and emotional stability.

2–27 *Gillick*, while technically not of binding authority in Scotland, is highly persuasive as a decision of the House of Lords, and has also received much favourable comment from academic writers.[73] It encapsulates a societal shift away from the belief that children are objects of property in the power of their parents—a view enshrined in many Victorian cases—to the belief that children are to be nurtured by their parents towards eventual autonomy and that parental rights exist to facilitate the welfare of the child.

2–28 It is clear that s.2(4) of the 1991 Act essentially puts the kernel of the decision in *Gillick* on a statutory basis for Scotland. In particular, the provision appears to lean towards Lord Scarman's rather than Lord Fraser's conception of "*Gillick*-competence", speaking as it does of the "nature" and the "consequences" of the medical treatment in question. There is, deliberately, no requirement made in the section for the doctor to establish that the treatment is in the child's best interests. The Scottish Law Commission, after extensive consultation on this point, came to the conclusion that if a child was deemed to have sufficient maturity then it should not matter if the treatment was for his or her benefit or not.[74] The implication is that if the child is found to be competent, then, like an adult, the child has a right to take risks or make wrong choices, and the willingness to take the consequences of those risks and choices. A question remains as to whether the jurisdiction of the

---

[73] See, for example, Norrie, "*Gillick* again: the House of Lords decides", 1986 S.L.T. 69.

[74] *Report on the Legal Capacity and Responsibility of Minors and Pupils*, Scot. Law Com. No.110 (1987), paras 3.61–3.77.

court could be invoked to prevent a competent child making a bad choice. The court has power to make orders in respect of specific issues connected to the exercise of parental responsibilities and rights. Where a child is Gillick-competent, one argument posits that parental responsibilities and rights are no longer applicable, which would deny the jurisdiction of the court here. However, by letter of statute, parental responsibilities and rights continue until the child reaches 16, which can be interpreted to mean the court's jurisdiction subsists until that time.[75]

In practice, the issue of the best interests of the child is not wholly removed **2–29** from the equation. In most cases, a doctor will be asked to sanction treatment which is unequivocally therapeutic. If the treatment is not unequivocally in the best interests, e.g. cosmetic surgery or tissue donation,[76] then part of the doctor's task in assessing maturity will be to consider why the child wishes to undergo this treatment and whether they have thought the risks and the advantages through. It is unlikely, for example, that a 14-year-old seeking cosmetic surgery in order to attain a more gracious nose is displaying a high level of maturity. On the other hand, a child of a similar age seeking to have his or her nose pierced arguably has a lower hurdle to surmount to prove competency since the procedure in question is less permanent and involves less risk (e.g. no general anaesthetic[77]). In the paradigm case of contraception, where there may be no consensus between child and parents on whether contraceptive treatment is in the child's best interests, the doctor must assess if, say, a girl of 14 has considered and balanced the health and emotional risks of under-age sexual intercourse, and the disruption to family harmony, with the advantages of contraceptive protection. In many ways, this is not dissimilar from an assessment of whether treatment is in her best interests, although it is, in principle at least, a less paternalistic approach.[78]

Section 2(4) does not just empower minor children approaching full **2–30** adulthood, but reflects the gradated nature of child development. So, a very young child of perhaps five or six can give a valid consent to the school nurse

---

[75] By application to the court under s.11 of the Children (Scotland) Act 1995 (see Ch.4). At common law, an adult has the right to make a decision to refuse medical treatment even if this has fatal consequences; but see the highly exceptional case of *Re S* [19921 4 All E.R. 671, where the Caesarean section of an adult woman was authorised by the English High Court, apparently in the interests of the foetus. See discussion in Ch.1.

[76] Particularly acute issues about non-therapeutic consent can arise when a child is asked, for good medical practice reasons, to donate, e.g. bone marrow or a kidney, to a sibling or other relative. In England the matter falls under the Family Law Reform Act 1969 s.8, and authorities on this are conflicting; the matter is addressed in Annex E of the HFEA Law and Ethics Committee Guidance on Consent to Medical Treatment, ELC (06/04).

[77] In fact, there is medical evidence that the very common practice of *ear* piercing is rather more risky than most people think: see "Ear Piercing and Children's Rights" (1994) 308 B.M.J. 1636. Oddly perhaps, Scots (and UK) law requires parental consent to tattooing under the age of 18 (Tattooing of Minors Act 1969 s.1) but has no such rule concerning other piercings of any kind: in practice however most shops seem to operate a policy of no piercing without parental consent for those under the age of 16, or sometimes 18. The Scottish Executive consulted on this matter in 2001 (*Regulation of Skin Piercing* (Scottish Executive, 2001)) but no legislation resulted. See *Stair Encyclopaedia, Child and Family Law (Reissue)* (Butterworths, 2004), para.273.

[78] See de Cruz, "Parents, Doctors and Children: the *Gillick* Case and Beyond" (1987) J.S.W.L. 93 for a cogent argument that the "welfare" approach of Lord Fraser and the "capacity" approach of Lord Scarman are not so far removed from each other.

bandaging his cut knee, a fairly unambiguously therapeutic procedure. The most difficult scenario, perhaps, is where a child has fluctuating capacity, able to act with full maturity on some occasions but on other occasions being rash or irresponsible. While such fluctuations in behaviour are perhaps not atypical of the adolescent child, the major difficulty is likely to arise in relation to children with mental health conditions such as bipolar disorder. In England, it has been established that where a child fluctuates between rational and irrational periods, then the child cannot be regarded as "*Gillick*-competent" even if during a rational period they appear able to act with sufficient maturity.[79] Per Sir Thomas Bingham M.R.: "*Gillick*-competence is a developmental concept and will not be lost or acquired on a day to day or week to week basis."[80]

2–31   Section 2(4) establishes then, that a child who meets the test of understanding may give a valid consent to a medical procedure, and by implication, following *Gillick*, that his parent or parents do not have a right of veto in respect of that consent, even, arguably, where the child is not acting in his or her own best interests. This, however, leaves two important questions open: first, what happens if the child *refuses* consent but the parent(s) are willing or insistent on *providing* a consent? In this case, there is a clash between the parent's right to provide a consent to medical treatment, which is an aspect of the right and responsibility to act as the child's legal representative, and the capacity of the child to withhold consent. Secondly, if a child is sufficiently mature to give a competent consent, then can a *court*, rather than a parent, overrule that child's wishes and, if so, in what circumstances?

2–32   There are no answers to these questions to be found in the 1991 Act. These are questions which are intimately concerned with the issue of whether children have autonomous rights, and how their rights interact with the rights and responsibilities of their parents and of the state. We therefore consider these issues further in Ch.4.[81]

s.2(4A) A person under the age of 16 years shall have legal capacity to instruct a solicitor, in connection with any civil matter, where that person has a general understanding of what it means to do so; and without prejudice to the generality of this subsection a person twelve years of age or more shall be presumed to be of sufficient age and maturity to have such an understanding.

2–33   Where a child under 16 has capacity to instruct a solicitor, he also has capacity to sue or defend a civil action.[82] The statute does not apply to capacity in respect of criminal proceedings.[83] A child without capacity would again be represented by a person holding parental responsibilities and rights in respect of him.[84]

---

[79] *Re R (A Minor)* [1991] 4 All E.R. 177.
[80] *Northampton Health Authority v Official Solicitor* [1994] F.L.R. 162, at p.168. It is interesting to compare this with the approach traditionally taken under Scottish contract law, that a person may be *capax* during lucid intervals, even where there is fluctuating capacity.
[81] See paras 4–25 to 4–40.
[82] 1991 Act s.2(4B).
[83] 1991 Act s.2(4C).
[84] Children (Scotland) Act 1995 ss.1(1)(d) and 2(1)(d).

In most circumstances, this is a satisfactory state of affairs. For example, **2–34** it is routine for parents to sue for damages on behalf of their children; thus, where one parent has been killed in an accident, it is commonplace for the surviving spouse to sue for damages in respect of the death on his own behalf and also that of the children of the marriage.[85]

But what if the child wishes to raise an action which his parent or guard- **2–35** ian does not condone, or more importantly, what if the child wishes to sue his own parent? [86] The capacity afforded by s.2(4A) is important in such circumstances. Understanding of legal matters is presumed at age 12, but there is nothing to prevent a younger child from proving he has sufficient understanding for capacity to arise. A child with s.2(4A) capacity may still be represented by his parent provided he consents.[87] Where a child does not have capacity, and his interests conflict with those of his parent, the court may appoint a curator *ad litem* to represent him.[88]

In practice, giving children capacity to sue their parents (or other persons) **2–36** is of little value unless access to legal aid by children is also ensured. The Legal Aid Board accept that a child aged 12 or over, instructing a solicitor without parental assistance, may apply for civil legal aid or legal advice and assistance, conditional only on the solicitor instructed enclosing a letter confirming that he has satisfied himself that the child does indeed have a general understanding of what it means to instruct a solicitor (the s.2(4A) test). For a child under 12, the procedure is the same except that the Board reserves the right to query any such letter, for example if the child appears unreasonably young.[89]

It is noteworthy that s.2(4A) makes no statement about who is to under- **2–37** take the job of assessing if a child has the "general understanding" required to gain capacity to litigate. The Legal Aid Board practice note seems to assume that it is the solicitors on the "coal face" who will assess a child's capacity when they come seeking legal advice and representation, and in practice this is what does indeed happen in Scotland.[90] In England, however, where a similar law has been passed, the job of assessment of capacity has in some cases been assumed by judges, some of whom have shown hostility to

---

[85] See, e.g. *Scott v Occidental Petroleum (Caledonia) Ltd*, 1990 S.L.T. 882.

[86] One of the most publicised of a number of recent English cases in which children have gone to the courts was that of an 11-year-old girl who successfully obtained a court order allowing her to live with her former foster parents (*The Times*, November 6, 1992). Conversely, in *Re T (A Minor)* [1993] 3 W.L.R. 602, a 13-year-old girl petitioned the court to allow her to remove herself from her adoptive parents and instead to grant a residence order in favour of her paternal aunt.

[87] 1991 Act s.15(6).

[88] 1991 Act s1.(3)(f).

[89] See SLAB Children's Legal Assistance Handbook, Part III, para2.17, available at *http://www. slab.org.uk/providers/handbooks/Childrens-Handbook* [accessed August 5, 2013]. The legal foundation of the right to apply for legal aid under the age of 16 is now to be found in the Legal Aid (Scotland) Act 1986, s.29, due to be repealed and replaced by the new ss.28B–28S introduced by the Children's Hearings (Scotland) Act 2011, s.191. Section 29(4) of the 1986 Act does apply a welfare test, namely that "it is in the interests of the child that legal aid be made available". The new s.28D(3) requires legal aid to be "in the *best* interests of the child" (emphasis added).

[90] See also the guidance to lawyers in the Law Society of Scotland's Child Protection and Representation Principles for Children's Lawyers, launched November 2005.

the independent representation of children.[91] In Scotland, there are as yet no reported cases where judges have intervened to declare a child is not of sufficient capacity to instruct a lawyer.[92] However, occasional judicial hostility to the entry of children into the process can be detected in the reported cases. In *Henderson v Henderson*,[93] the concern of the sheriff was the increased drain on the legal aid fund caused by additional parties to an action, particularly where (as in this case) the child's views coincided with those of her mother. In *B v B*,[94] Sheriff Principal Bowen refused a 12-year-old child leave to enter the process in respect of an action concerning contact arrangements for himself and his sister on the basis of the markedly more paternalistic concern that it would not be fair or in his best interests to subject him to pressures of the litigation, in addition to which it was not clear that he could give instructions of anything other than a restricted nature.[95] It is arguable whether this decision gave proper weight to the child's right to participate in judicial proceedings affecting his interests.[96]

2–38   It is also important to note that a child under 16 retains the ability to be the passive holder of rights, although he may not have capacity to raise an action in relation to those rights.[97] For example, a child of three may own money which is held in a bank account in his name. However, the contract with the bank can only be made by his guardian, who supplies capacity, and only the guardian will have capacity to make withdrawals until the child reaches competency. This principle is well illustrated by the case of *Huggins v Huggins*[98] in which it was held competent at common law to make payments of aliment direct to a pupil child, and that the tax consequences of this transaction should be determined on the basis of the child's income and exemptions, not the mother's. However, it was recognised that the administration of the money would still have to be handled by the mother since the child had no active capacity and hence the funds had to be paid straight to the mother.

---

[91] See, e.g. *Re H* [1994] All E.R. 762.

[92] It is worth noting however *H v H*, 2000 G.W.D. 11–376, where a 13-and-a-half-year-old child with attention deficit disorder, Asperger's syndrome and Tourette's syndrome was allowed not only to give evidence but to be sisted as a party to an action for contact raised by his stepfather. The question of whether he was of an "age and maturity" to join as a party appears to have been spoken to by the bringing of evidence from health professionals. This appears to be the first reported civil Scottish case since the 1995 Act in which the competence of a child to give views and be a party has been assessed by anyone other than his or her solicitor and (implicitly) the presiding judge. See further also F. Raitt, "Judicial discretion and methods of ascertaining the views of a child" (2004) 16 CFLQ 151, especially at 156.

[93] *Henderson v Henderson*, 1997 Fam L.R. 120.

[94] *B v B*, 2011 S.L.T. (Sh. Ct) 225.

[95] The case was complicated by the fact the child had previously been represented by a curator, in whom he had lost confidence part way through the proof after five days of evidence had been heard. The Sheriff Principal was understandably influenced by the fact that, had the child been permitted to enter the process in his own right, the witnesses would likely have had to be recalled for fresh cross-examination and the proof further delayed.

[96] But see *Fourman v Fourman*, 1998 Fam. L.R. 98, where the sheriff commented positively on the appropriateness of a 14-year-old child's decision to join the action as party minuter, with independent legal representation.

[97] 1991 Act s.1(3)(e).

[98] *Huggins v Huggins*, 1981 S.L.T. 179.

The Child Aged 16–18: "Young Persons"

Children aged 16 or over have full legal capacity to enter into any legal **2–39** transaction.[99] They are not subject to the control of a parent or guardian[100] as parental rights terminate when the child reaches 16.[101] They are therefore free to choose their own residence, make any contracts they please, instigate and defend legal proceedings, pick their own religion and so forth.

However, this does not mean that children over 16 but under 18, the full **2–40** age of majority, are not still regarded as in need of some degree of special care and protection. In the law's eyes, they are almost, but not quite, adults. The law recognises this in several not wholly consistent ways. For example, under the Children (Scotland) Act 1995, local authorities have extensive duties to promote the welfare of children until they reach the age of 18.[102] Similarly, in principle, the children's hearings system deals only with children under the age of 16 who are in need of compulsory measures of care; but if the child has already been placed under the supervision of the hearing they may stay within the system until they reach the age of 18.[103] Those who fall into this ambiguous band between age 16 and age 18 are perhaps best described as "young persons"[104] rather than children.

The 1991 Act attempts to protect young persons by providing under s.3 **2–41** that any transaction entered into by a person over 16 but under 18 may be set aside if it is a "prejudicial transaction". The young person may make an application to the courts for the setting aside of such a transaction at any time until he reaches the age of 21.[105] If a transaction is set aside then parties should be returned to the position they were in prior to the transaction. In other words, if the prejudicial transaction was a sale to the young person of a car at an exorbitant price, the car should be returned to the seller and the purchase price to the young person. If it is not possible to return parties to the position they were in prior to the transaction—for example, because the car has been destroyed—it is thought under general principles of the common law of obligations that setting aside may not be possible.[106]

A prejudicial transaction is one which: (a) an adult, exercising reasonable **2–42** prudence, would not have entered into in the circumstances of the applicant at the time of entering the transaction; and (b) has caused or is likely to cause substantial prejudice to the applicant.[107] This is an interesting test. Essentially the court is asked to consider if a particular young person in particular circumstances (a subjective test) would have entered a particular transaction if they had been a reasonable adult (an objective test). The intent is to provide a remedy in respect of transactions which are not only prejudicial but actively unreasonable or unfair. Suppose we imagine the case of a 17-year-old child

---

[99] 1991 Act s.1(1)(a).
[100] 1991 Act s.5(2).
[101] 1991 Act s.5(2) and Children (Scotland) Act 1995, s.2(7).
[102] 1995 Act ss.22 and 93(2).
[103] 1995 Act ss.54 and 93(2)(b).
[104] This terminology is not found in the legislation.
[105] 1991 Act s.3(4).
[106] *Boyd & Forrest v Glasgow and South-Western Railway Company*, 1915 S.C. (HL) 20.
[107] 1991 Act s.3(2).

who, unable to find work or receive benefits, takes out a loan. It can be argued that the reasonably prudent adult in these circumstances would do the same thing—therefore the transaction will not be set aside even though the transaction is certainly prejudicial since there will be interest payments to be met. However, now suppose the loan is made at an exorbitant interest rate. We can now safely assume that the reasonably prudent adult would not enter the contract and so the application to set aside should succeed.

2–43   The effect of s.3 then, is that all transactions of young persons are potentially voidable. Several exceptions to the rule are set out at s.3(2). The exercise of testamentary capacity,[108] consent to adoption,[109] participation in civil legal proceedings[110] or consent to surgical, medical or dental treatment[111] are all excluded from the prejudicial transaction regime, in line with the provisions on capacity of minors in s.2.[112] Additionally, transactions may not be set aside if made in the course of the applicant's trade, business or profession,[113] nor if the other party was induced to enter the transaction by the young person's fraudulent misrepresentation as to his age or any other material fact.[114]

2–44   The Act also makes provision for ratification of transactions entered into by young persons. A ratified transaction cannot be set aside under s.3, and may be a practical solution where an adult wishes to transact reasonably with a young person but is put off by the lingering possibility that the transaction may be set aside at any time until the young person turns 21. On reaching the age of 18, the young person has the power to ratify any transaction he entered into whilst 16 or 17.[115] Alternatively, parties may apply to the court for ratification *in advance* of a transaction taking place. The court will ratify if it is satisfied that the transaction is not prejudicial. It is not clear why this should not be possible retrospectively.[116]

OTHER ASPECTS OF CAPACITY

2–45   The 1991 Act is now the principal guide to matters of capacity in private law but it is not the whole story. Other aspects of capacity remain to be determined by common law or other statutory provisions.

Delictual Liability[117]

2–46   Liability in delict arises where a person, through a breach in duty, causes harm to another person or their property. The most important head of delictual liability is negligence. Liability in negligence arises where a person owes a duty

---

[108] 1991 Act s.3(3)(a) and (b).
[109] 1991 Act s.3(3)(c).
[110] 1991 Act s.3(3)(d).
[111] 1991 Act s.3(3)(e).
[112] Discussed at paras 2–19 to 2–38 above.
[113] 1991 Act s.3(3)(f).
[114] 1991 Act s.3(3)(g).
[115] 1991 Act s.3(3)(h).
[116] 1991 Act s.4.
[117] The 1991 Act explicitly does *not* deal with delictual liability of children: s.1(3)(c).

of reasonable care to another and fails to fulfil this duty, with resulting loss or damage.[118] In Scots law, there is a remarkable dearth of authority as to how old a child has to be before he can be said to be responsible for his own delictual acts. It seems, however, that a child of any age can be liable in delict if he is old enough to form an intention to do wrong or to appreciate what he ought not to do. The test, as Erskine says,[119] is to do with the exercise of reason, and is not based on any specific age. Since young children are rarely rich or insured against liability, few are likely to be sued directly, but Scots law has recognised in several cases that very young children can be found to have contributed through their own negligence to damage caused them by another party's fault.[120]

In most cases where damage results from the careless actions of a child, the party damaged is likely to be more interested in suing the parents than the child, since they are more likely to have access to resources. In principle, children are not to be regarded as owned by their parents, like animals, and therefore parents are not automatically liable for the delicts of their children. However, in practice, parents or others who have physical custody or care of children may be liable in negligence if they fail to take reasonable care to supervise or attend the children. Here it seems reasonable to recall the concepts of the gradual maturing of children under the age of 16 of which we have spoken earlier. If a child is mature enough to be able to make independent choices, then he is also sufficiently mature to take the financial consequences of his actions. As parental rights diminish, so should parental duties of supervision. This principled argument is, however, unlikely to be of much comfort to the third party who has suffered loss. **2–47**

The capacity of children to sue for damages in delict is an aspect of capacity to litigate generally.[121] Awards of damages made to children by courts are now protected by s.13 of the Children (Scotland) Act 1995, under which such order can be made relating to the payment and management of the sum for the child as the court thinks fit.[122] A child of any age can give an adequate discharge for damages paid to him if the court has directed under s.13(2) that the damages should be paid directly to the child and not the parent(s) or anyone else (s.13(3)). **2–48**

Giving Evidence

There is no fixed age at which a child acquires capacity to be a witness in either civil or criminal proceedings. According to the test laid down in *Rees v Lowe*,[123] a child becomes a competent witness when a judge is satisfied that the child knows the difference between truth and lies and appreciates the duty to tell the truth. The judge should investigate to satisfy himself as to a young child's capacity and should administer the oath or admonish the witness to tell the truth. **2–49**

---

[118] See generally J. Thomson, *Delictual Liability*, 4th edn (Edinburgh: Tottel, 2009), Chs 3–6.

[119] Erskine, i.1.63 and see Smith, "The Age of Innocence" (1975) 49 Tulane Law Review 311.

[120] See, e.g. *McKinnell v White*, 1971 S.L.T. (Notes) 61; *MacDonald's Tutor v Macleod*, 1995 G.W.D. 28–1498 (6-year-old guilty of contributory negligence).

[121] See paras 2–33 to 2–38.

[122] See discussion in Ch.5.

[123] *Rees v Lowe*, 1990 S.L.T. 507.

2-50   The evidence of very young children may be crucial in the increasing
number of cases concerning child abuse and neglect. In *Rees* itself, the
witness in question was a three-year-old girl. For such witnesses, the giving
of evidence in open court may be, at best, a traumatic affair and, at worst, an
impossibility.[124]

2-51   At common law, judges have a discretion to take steps to put children
at ease and may, for example, remove wigs and gowns, take evidence from
children in the well of the court rather than in the witness box and permit a
supportive relative to be nearby.[125] In policy terms however the best solution
is still for the child not to have to appear in court at all. Hearsay accounts of
evidence are increasingly admissible in both civil and criminal proceedings.[126]
Could a recording of a child's evidence in relation to, say, sexual abuse be
used in order to spare the child giving direct testimony in court?[127] A difficulty
was identified with this approach in a series of civil cases in the late 1990s.[128]
Only the evidence of a child competent in the *Rees* sense could be admissible
in court. This included hearsay evidence. How could the competence of such
a child be ascertained? Only through judicial investigation, meaning the child
would be required to come to court after all simply to establish competence
for the hearsay evidence to be admissible.

2-52   This catch-22 was resolved by the wide-ranging reforms of the Vulnerable
Witnesses Act 2004.[129] This legislation applies not just to children, but to
witnesses who are vulnerable due to age or infirmity, and also those who are
in danger of intimidation. Under the Act, any person under the age of 16 is
regarded as a "vulnerable witness"[130] and there are special provisions that
relate specifically to child witnesses.[131]

2-53   Anyone citing a child witness in a civil case must give notice to allow for
appropriate arrangements to be made.[132] The notice should also indicate
which of the "special measures" are likely to be the most appropriate.[133]
Standard "special measures" are to be the use of live TV links, the use of a

---

124 See further, *Children as Witnesses* (Dent and Flin (eds), Wiley, 1992) and Spencer and Flin,
   The Evidence of Children: The Law and the Psychology, 2nd edn (Blackstone Press, 1993).
125 See High Court of Justiciary Practice Note No.2 of 2005 (Child Witnesses: Discretionary
   Powers).
126 Civil Evidence Act 1988 s.2(1); Criminal Procedure (Scotland) Act 1995 s.259.
127 See further, Kearney, "The Evidence of Children: the Scottish Dimension" in Spencer (ed.),
   Childrens' Evidence in Legal Proceedings (J.R. Spencer, 1990).
128 *F v Kennedy (No.1)*, 1993 S.L.T. 1277. See also *L v L*, 1996 S.C.L.R. 11; *Sanderson v
   McManus*, 1997 S.C. (H.L.) 55; *AR v Reporter for Aberdeen Local Authority*, 1999 Fam. L.R.
   20 and *T v T*, 2000 S.C.L.R. 1057 which substantially altered the position prior to the sweeping amendments of the Vulnerable Witnesses Act 2004 which represent the current law.
129 The Act was preceded by SLC Discussion Paper No.75 and SLC Report No.125, "Evidence
   of Children and Other Vulnerable Witnesses" and *Vital Voices: helping Vulnerable
   Witnesses Give Evidence* (Scottish Executive, 2002). See also *Guidance on the Questioning
   of Children in Court* (Scottish Executive, 2003) available at *http://www.scotland.gov.uk/
   Publications/2003/09/18264/27015* [accessed February 15, 2013].
130 Other types of "vulnerable witnesses" are defined at s.11 of the 2004 Act. Here we deal only
   with the rules as they affect children.
131 Vulnerable Witnesses (Scotland) Act 2004 s.11. A "child witness" is defined by s.11(1)(a) as a
   child under 16.
132 Vulnerable Witnesses (Scotland) Act 2004 s.12(2).
133 Vulnerable Witnesses (Scotland) Act 2004 s.12(2)(a).

screen, and the use of a supporter for the child.[134] Other special measures which may be authorized may include the taking of evidence by a commissioner on oath, and giving evidence in chief by means of a prior statement made earlier being lodged in evidence. Notably, for such evidence, there is no need for the witness to adopt the statement or speak to it in court. A court where a child witness is to give evidence must either authorise the "special measures" or specifically make an order that these are not necessary.[135] The latter course of action should only be adopted where the risk of prejudice substantially outweighs the risk of harm to the child.[136] The law expressly states that evidence is not inadmissible solely because the witness does not understand the nature of the duty of a witness to give truthful evidence, or the difference between truth and lies.[137] Such matters will simply become part of the job of the judge or jury, as appropriate, to assess, when they come to decide what credence and weight to give the evidence of a child witness.

In respect of criminal cases, the 2004 Act made extensive amendments to parts of the Criminal Procedure (Scotland) Act 1995. Similar "special measures" to those available in civil proceedings are also to be available to vulnerable witnesses in the criminal courts.[138] In addition, a party intending to cite a child witness in criminal proceedings must lodge a "child witness notice" with the court 14 days before the trial diet specifying which, if any, of the special measures they consider to be appropriate.[139] There is a presumption that a child under 12 need not give evidence in person where the offence(s) charged are murder, culpable homicide, and certain sexual offences along with several other prescribed offences.[140] This presumption is only displaced if the accused can show that its operation would prejudice his case significantly and that risk of prejudice must "*significantly outweigh*" the risk of prejudice to the child's interests by presumption being rebutted.[141] There is no analogous provision in civil proceedings. As in civil proceedings, however, the need to test the competency of the child before they give direct evidence is abolished for criminal trials.[142]   **2–54**

Documentary Witnesses

A child cannot act as a documentary witness. A child must be over the age of 16 before he or she can competently witness a deed.[143]   **2–55**

---

[134] Vulnerable Witnesses (Scotland) Act 2004 s.18.
[135] Vulnerable Witnesses (Scotland) Act 2004 s.12(1).
[136] Vulnerable Witnesses (Scotland) Act 2004 s.12(4).
[137] Vulnerable Witnesses (Scotland) Act 2004 s.24.
[138] Criminal Procedure (Scotland) Act 1995 s.271H, as inserted by the Vulnerable Witnesses (Scotland) Act 2004 s.1.
[139] Criminal Procedure (Scotland) Act 1995 s.271A as inserted by the Vulnerable Witnesses (Scotland) Act 2004 s.1.
[140] Criminal Procedure (Scotland) Act 1995 s.271B as inserted by the Vulnerable Witnesses (Scotland) Act 2004 s.1.
[141] Criminal Procedure (Scotland) Act 1995 s.271B(3) as inserted by the Vulnerable Witnesses (Scotland) Act 2004 s.1.
[142] Vulnerable Witnesses (Scotland) Act 2004 s.24.
[143] Requirements of Writing (Scotland) Act 1995 s.3(4)(c)(ii).

Criminal Liability

2–56   Children can be held responsible for criminal acts at the age of eight.[144] However, a child under the age of 12 cannot be prosecuted for an offence, and no person can be prosecuted for offences committed whilst under the age of 12.[145] Except in the case of very serious crimes, a child under 16 will not be prosecuted in the criminal courts but will be referred to the children's hearing as in need of compulsory measures of supervision. Prosecution is only to be made on the instructions of the Lord Advocate, or at his instance.[146]

WHO IS A CHILD?

2–57   In the first chapter we posed the question, who is a legal person? In this chapter, we have conspicuously failed to ask, or to give an answer to the question, who is a child? At the beginning of this chapter, we spoke of the idea that each society at any point in time has a different conception of the nature of childhood. A further refinement of this concept is that there are different *dimensions* of childhood—in other words, that we describe certain persons as children in certain contexts but not in others, according to social ideas of what activities are more or less reserved for adulthood.

2–58   As we have seen, in terms of capacity to take part in transactions in the sphere of private law, the law's clearest demarcation is between those under and over the age of 16. Yet, for many purposes, this clear dividing line must be compromised and, in particular, young persons within the bracket from age 16 up to age 18 live in a halfway house between the rights and responsibilities of full adulthood and the protection of childhood. Below the age of 16, we encounter the still less well-defined status of "mature minor" or "*Gillick*-competent" minor, a status which is of increasing importance in both case law and statute.[147]

2–59   The law often regards children as developing, immature, inexperienced or vulnerable creatures on the way to adulthood. It deals with this in diverse ways. As we have already seen, and will see, responsibilities are primarily put on parents to protect their children. Where they fail, the state may intervene.

---

[144] Criminal Procedure (Scotland) Act 1995 s.41. Criminal responsibility is specifically not affected by the 1991 Act: s.1(3)(c).

[145] Criminal Procedure (Scotland) Act 1995 s.41A, inserted by the Criminal Justice and Licensing (Scotland) Act 2010 s.52. Prior to the introduction of this legislation, concern as to whether the low age of criminal responsibility in Scotland complied with international human rights obligations led the Scottish Law Commission to produce a Report on the Age of Criminal Responsibility (Scot. Law Com. No.185, 2001). Its recommendation was that the "gateway" age of criminal responsibility should be abolished. Children would legally be capable of criminal behaviour at *any* age, but would only be prosecuted in the adult criminal justice system in exceptional circumstances. This recommendation was not taken forward by the Government.

[146] Criminal Procedure (Scotland) Act 1995 s.42.

[147] In England, the Children Act 1989 makes many important concessions to the rights of children depending on their age and understanding. In Scotland, the Children (Scotland) Act 1995 also places emphasis on giving children rights to be consulted dependent on age and maturity, but usually with a presumption this maturity is attained at age 12.

However, in addition, age limits are often imposed for particular protective purposes within various statutes.[148] A young person cannot obtain a driving licence until he is aged 17,[149] buy alcohol till he is 18,[150] nor acquire a heavy goods vehicle licence for lorries over 7.5 tonnes until he is 21.[151] On the other hand, the law allows children to take on a limited amount of paid employment from the age of 13.[152] These are areas where the law has not left matters to the discretion of individual parents or carers. We find more ambiguity when we look at the age up to which the law expects parents to be responsible for maintaining their children. Under the Child Support Act 1991, parents are normally under an obligation to aliment their children only until the age of 16;[153] although the earlier Scots law on aliment continues to apply and in some cases allows children to obtain aliment up to the age of 25.[154] It becomes obvious that we cannot simply define a child as someone under 16, or even someone who has a right to be supported by his or her parents, or to whom parents or guardians owe parental responsibilities.

Potentially the most important protections a child has may come in the future from the international guarantees found in the ECHR and perhaps eventually even more so in the UN Convention on the Rights of the Child, which defines a child as a human being below the age of 18.[155] The most positive view, then, may be to see a child not as a person with special vulnerability but with special rights. We take this up in Chs 4 and 5. For now, though, we turn to our third crucial question: who is a parent?   **2–60**

---

[148] The 1991 Act provides that specific statutory age limits are unaffected by the general principles of the Act: s.1(3)(d).

[149] Road Traffic Act 1988 s.101.

[150] Licensing (Scotland) Act 2005 ss.102–110.

[151] Road Traffic Act 1988 s.101.

[152] Subject to small exceptions allowing light employment by parents at an earlier age. See *Stair Encyclopaedia*, para.269, n.6.

[153] Child Support Act 1991 s.55.

[154] See Family Law (Scotland) Act 1985 s.1(5) and Child Support Act 1991 s.55. For further explanation of these complex rules see Ch.5.

[155] ECHR Art.1.

CHAPTER 3

CHILDREN AND PARENTS

3–01 A child's first legal relationship is with his or her parent or parents. At one time, the law's major concern in regulating the status of children was whether their parents were married to each other. The question of illegitimacy was the first topic to be dealt with in the section of Erskine's *Institute* dealing with relationships between parent and child[1] and in the first major textbook on Scottish child law, Fraser on *Parent and Child*.[2] Nowadays, the topic of illegitimacy has virtually been expunged from Scottish family law and the law is at pains to treat all types of children equally, regardless of the marital status of their parents.[3] Instead, the focus of the law is on the legal consequences of the relationship between parent and child, how that relationship is constituted and proven and how that relationship alters with time.[4]

3–02 An essential starting point to any consideration of the law relating to children and parents is to decide who is a parent. This is no longer the relatively simple task it once was. Advances in reproductive technology have compelled us to think as a society about who should be allowed or assisted to become parents. A distinction can now be made between "traditional" parents, who can conceive (in the case of the mother) or impregnate (in the case of the father) without the use of medical assistance or technology, and so-called "artificial" or "assisted" parenthood, in which the link between genetic parenthood and social or gestational parenthood may be broken. Changes in social norms, particularly the growth in cohabitation outside marriage and the increasing birth rate of children outwith marriage, compel us to think about whom we *want* to be regarded as a parent, or alternatively, what the consequences of parenthood should be. In this chapter, we will not only be categorising different types of parent, but asking why these classifications have been adopted. First, in order to give this exercise a purpose, we must briefly assess the legal consequences of parenthood, especially in terms of parental responsibilities and rights.

---

[1] Erskine, VI. 2. 49.

[2] Fraser, *A Treatise on the Law of Scotland Relative to Parent and Child*, 3rd edn (Edinburgh: W. Green, 1906), p.1. Wilkinson and Norrie now take a similar approach to the text at hand in separating the issue of legitimacy from the main discussion of parentage and its effects.

[3] See Ch.5 for more detail.

[4] Hoggett and Pearl summed up this process of legal development with admirable simplicity: "Once upon a time it was the child of unmarried parents who was thought to be the problem. Now the law tries to treat the child himself just like any others but still distinguishes between different sorts of parent." (*The Family, Law and Society: Cases and Materials*, 3rd edn (Butterworths, 2002), p.443.)

THE LEGAL CONSEQUENCES OF PARENTHOOD

The question "who is a parent?" is an important one to ask in a variety of   **3–03**
circumstances. Perhaps the two most important effects of parentage from the
private law point of view are

- that parentage is an important prerequisite to establishing parental
  responsibilities and rights; and
- that a parent is responsible for the financial support of his or her children.

The second of these topics will be dealt with in depth in Ch.5, which is   **3–04**
concerned with the rights of the child. The topic of parental responsibilities
and rights will be dealt with at length in Ch.4. These are not, of course, the
only legal effects associated with parentage. In succession law, for example,
children and parents have rights in each other's estates and so determination
of parentage may be vital to establish the distribution of an estate. Children
have indefeasible rights, known as legal rights, in the moveable portion of
their parents' estate at common law[5]; statutory rights may also be claimed
in the free estate where a parent dies in a state of total or partial intestacy.[6]
Similarly, if a child dies intestate without a spouse or children of his own,
then his parent or parents will have a claim to either all or half of the child's
free estate, depending on whether the child leaves any surviving siblings.[7] The
establishment of the relationship of parent and child may also be important
in public law contexts, notably social security law and immigration law.

For the moment, however, we shall look at to whom Scots law awards   **3–05**
parental responsibilities and rights ("PRRs"). The law on this is now to be
found in the Children (Scotland) Act 1995 (hereafter "the 1995 Act"). It is
crucial to observe that Scots law has never drawn an automatic link between
the establishment of status as a parent and the award of parental rights. This
remains so today, although there is now as much emphasis on the *responsibilities* owed by parents to their children as what rights they have over them.
What is included within PRRs is discussed in depth in Ch.4, but basically a
parent with PRRs has all the powers necessary to promote and safeguard the
welfare of the child, to provide appropriate direction and to represent the child
in law.[8] All PRRs, with one exception, terminate when the child reaches 16.[9]

---

[5] See para.5–82.
[6] See Succession (Scotland) Act 1964 s.2(1)(a). If a parent dies intestate and leaving no surviving
spouse then the combined effect of rights to *legitim* and to free estate is that the children (or issue)
between them take the whole estate. A review of the law of succession was carried out by the
Scottish Law Commission, see S.L.C. *Report on Succession* No.215 (2009). For discussion see Reid
"From the Cradle to the Grave: Politics, Families and Inheritance Law" (2008) 12 *Edin LR* 391.
[7] See Succession (Scotland) Act 1964 s.2(1)(b) and (d). If there are no siblings, the parent or
parents take the whole free estate between them; if there are siblings, the siblings take half and the
parents take half. For a full discussion of the modern law of intestate succession and legal rights
see M. Meston, *The Succession (Scotland) Act 1964*, 5th edn (Edinburgh: W. Green, 2002) and
Macdonald, *Succession*, 3rd edn (Edinburgh: W. Green, 2001), Ch.4. For current figures applying to intestate succession see the Prior Rights of Surviving Spouse and Civil Partner (Scotland)
Order 2011 (SSI 2011/436).
[8] 1995 Act ss.1 and 2.
[9] 1995 Act ss.1(2)(a) and 2(7). The exception is the duty to provide guidance to the child in s.1(1)
(b)(ii) which continues until the child reaches 18.

AUTOMATIC PARENTAL RESPONSIBILITIES AND RIGHTS ("PRRs")

3–06   According to the 1995 Act s.3(1)(a), a child's mother automatically has PRRs in respect of her child irrespective of whether or not she is married to the child's father. By contrast, s.3(1)(b) of the 1995 Act originally gave a child's father automatic PRRs only if he was: "married to the mother at the time of the child's conception or subsequently". As we shall see below, there are now other ways for a father not married to the mother to acquire PRRs automatically. PRRs acquired by virtue of marriage subsist, however, even if the marriage is later found to be voidable.[10] If the marriage is void, but both parties believed in good faith that the purported marriage was valid (whether by error of fact or law), then the father still acquires parental rights under s.3(1)(b).[11]

3–07   So, for example, imagine that John and Jane live together for a year. Jane becomes pregnant by John and gives birth to Jimmy. The couple decide to marry. John acquires PRRs over Jimmy by virtue of, and from the moment of, the marriage, since it has occurred "subsequently" to the conception. If John and Jane now divorce, in principle John's PRRs are unaffected. If *no* award of PRRs is made by the court, then John and Jane will continue to share joint PRRs in respect of Jimmy even after their marriage has been dissolved. However, the court *may* make an order in respect of any children of the marriage which may have the effect of removing some or all of the father's (or mother's) parental rights.[12]

3–08   There is no practical difficulty about the concept that both John and Jane can exercise parental rights. By s.2(2) of the 1995 Act, where two or more persons have any parental right, either can exercise it without the consent of the other (or others). So, for example, Jane can sign a consent form for Jimmy to be given an injection by the school nurse, as an aspect of her parental right to give a legal consent to medical procedures in respect of her child. There is no need for her to consult with John, nor does he have a right to veto her.[13] However, if John is unhappy with her decision he can apply to the court for a "specific issue order" which will allow the court to decide this particular question on the basis of the welfare of the child.[14]

3–09   Section 3(1)(b) thus leaves all other parties without automatic PRRs. In respect of two groups, grandparents and step-parents, this has become a point of controversy. In both cases, there are arguments for and against the granting of automatic PRRs, or at least some rights, e.g. an automatic right to contact, and this is discussed further below. Parties such as step-parents, grandparents and other relatives can however acquire PRRs using a s.11 court order.

---

[10] 1995 Act s.3(2)(a). Since the only ground on which a marriage is voidable is the incurable impotence of one of the parties, there are unlikely to be many fathers taking advantage of this subsection.

[11] 1995 Act s.3(2)(b).

[12] Though, as we shall see, the court's preferred starting point will be to make no award—see Ch.4. Prior to the advent of the 1995 Act awards of exclusive custody to the mother were made in some 90% of Scottish divorces: see S. Morris, S. Gibson and A. Platt, *Untying the Knot: Characteristics of Divorce in Scotland* (Scottish Office, 1993).

[13] Jane should, however, "have regard" to John's views if she is making a "major decision" concerning parental responsibilities or rights: 1995 Act s.6(1).

[14] 1995 Act s.11(2)(e) and (7). See paras 4–48 to 4–50 and paras 4–63 to 4–65.

Unmarried Fathers

Historically, Scots law discouraged any legal connection between parent 3–10
and child which sprang from a relation outside marriage, so much so that
an illegitimate child was said to be *filius nullius*, nobody's child, unconnected
in law to both father and mother. While never an entirely true description,[15]
the legislative reform of illegitimacy has removed any differences in the legal
relationship of a mother to her child born within or outwith marriage.[16]

Until the Family Law Act 2006, an unmarried father had no automatic 3–11
parental rights under any circumstances. This was justified by the Scottish
Law Commission in 1984[17] on the basis that (i) to give automatic full rights
to unmarried fathers would give rights to fathers even where the child had
resulted from a casual liaison or even rape; (ii) many such fathers did not
have a continuing relationship with their illegitimate children; (iii) mothers
who were not married to the fathers of their children might feel that they
were subject to interference and harassment by fathers in the upbringing of
the child, and this might cause distress or offence especially where the mother
had struggled to bring up the child alone without financial support from the
father; and (iv) if fathers were to have automatic rights, they would have
to be involved in proceedings relating to the child such as adoption, recep-
tion into care, etc. which might unnecessarily protract and complicate such
proceedings.

However, denial of automatic PRRs to unmarried fathers became increas- 3–12
ingly hard to justify as a result of a number of social, cultural and legal
changes. The nature of child bearing outside of marriage has changed considerably since the early 1980s. 51% of children are now born outside wedlock,[18]
and while the number of births within marriage is declining, the number
outside marriage is increasing. Furthermore, of those children born out of
wedlock, most were registered as the child of both parents and in a substantial majority of *these* cases the registration is not only joint, but the parents
are listed as at the same address, i.e. one presumes, cohabiting.[19]

These demographics lent support to claims by unmarried fathers to rights 3–13
through the mid to late 1990s because they established that in a large number
of families, children were being denied the benefit of two parents with legal
responsibilities and rights simply because their parents had not entered the
institution of marriage. Many children born out of wedlock were clearly not

---

[15] See Wilkinson and Norrie, para.1.39, who describe it as "inadequate, and in some degree
an inept" description. For example, neither father nor mother of an illegitimate child had at
common law the right to be its guardian, but the mother had the prima facie right to custody
unless a court order was made in favour of someone else. Both father and mother owed the
illegitimate child a duty of aliment. It was only in the field of succession that at common law
the child had no relationship at all with either father or mother.

[16] See now 1995 Act s.3(1)(a), as discussed above.

[17] *Report on Illegitimacy*, Scot. Law Com. No.82, para.2.5.

[18] Registrar General for Scotland, *Scotland's Population 2011* (Annual Review), p.23. The report
notes that this figure has remained constant over the last few years and may be compared with
43.3% of births registered 10 years earlier and 29.1% recorded for 1991.

[19] Only 5.3% of births were registered in the mother's name alone suggesting that "babies [are]
born to unmarried partners who are in a stable relationship" (Registrar General for Scotland,
Annual Report 2011, p.23).

the products of a casual liaison but intended to be the joint responsibility of a settled couple. There has also been a re-assessment of the social role of the father, with a shift from "the stereotyped image of the unmarried father as a social deviant"[20] to the idea that unmarried fathers have something positive to add to the upbringing of their child, an idea reinforced generally by wider acceptance of ideals of joint parenting and shared childcare by the so-called "new father".[21] The early 2000s saw growing pressure from organisations such as Families Need Fathers for more concern to be shown for the rights and needs of fathers.

3–14   Finally, changes in the law of human rights have lent strength to the unmarried father's position. The ECHR, Art.8(1), which guarantees respect for family life, is now incorporated into United Kingdom law by virtue of the Human Rights Act 1998 and Strasbourg jurisprudence indicates a need for the state to take more positive steps to ensure rights for all fathers.[22] The steps taken under the Child Support Act 1991 to enforce the duty on unmarried fathers to pay for the support of their children also, cynically perhaps, lead to a greater demand for corresponding rights to go with duties of maintenance. Factors such as these influenced the Scottish Law Commission in 1992 to reverse its previous position and assert that "the law discriminates against children born outside marriage by denying them a father with the normal responsibilities and rights".[23] They recommended that both parents should have automatic PRRs.[24]

3–15   Giving *all* unmarried fathers full automatic rights was however not the only, nor necessarily the optimum, solution. The demographic figures reveal that some unmarried fathers are likely to be in responsible and stable relationships; others will not be. At the furthest extreme, what the Scottish Law Commission described in 1992 as the "phantom" of the rapist father[25] cannot be dismissed lightly. Many feel that it would be immoral to give a man automatic parental rights in respect of children fathered by his rape, even if in practice he would never be in a position to exercise them.[26] Both the Scottish and English Law Commissions have in the past agreed that the attempt to

---

[20] Eekelaar, "Second Thoughts on Illegitimacy Reform" (1985) 15 Family Law 261.

[21] The reality of the contribution of fathers to childcare has, however, been questioned (Bainham, "When is a Parent Not a Parent? Reflections on the Unmarried Father and his Child in English Law" (1988) 3 Int. Jnl of Law and the Family 208), in an article that is otherwise stridently in favour of rights for unmarried fathers.

[22] Bainham, Bainham, "When is a Parent Not a Parent? Reflections on the Unmarried Father and his Child in English Law" (1988) 3 Int. Jnl of Law and the Family 208. No specific decisions of the European Court of Human Rights have so far actually required states to give full PRRs to all unmarried fathers. However, see, inter alia, *Marckx v Belgium*, ECHR, Series A, No. 31, 18 Y.B. 248, which enjoins states to act in a manner calculated to allow ties between near relatives to develop normally; *McMichael v U.K.*, ECHR, February 24,1995, had an important influence in Scots law in encouraging the Government to have greater concern for the rights of unmarried fathers within the children's hearing system: see further Ch.8; *Soderback v Sweden* [1999] 1 F.L.R. 250 where the European Court held that the adoption of a child against the wishes of his natural father was a breach of his Art.8 right to respect for family life.

[23] *Report on Family Law*, Scot. Law Com. No.135 (1992), para.2.44.

[24] *Report on Family Law*, Scot. Law Com. No.135 (1992), para.2.50.

[25] *Report on Family Law*, Scot. Law Com. No.135 (1992), para.2.47.

[26] See Bainham, "When is a Parent Not a Parent? Reflections on the Unmarried Father and his

distinguish "meritorious" from "unmeritorious" fathers, or cohabiting from non-cohabiting fathers, when awarding PRRs, is impractical.

The 1995 Act, s.4 compromised by giving unmarried fathers the chance to   **3–16** acquire PRRs, not automatically, but as a result of agreement between the father and mother of the child, either at, or subsequent to, the child's birth. The advantage of this scheme was that rights could not be given to the father against the wishes of the mother, thus reducing the chances of interference and harassment; and, in the nature of things, such agreements were likely to be entered into only by stable couples. A similar model was adopted in contemporaneous English legislation.[27] Under s.4 of the 1995 Act, the child's mother and unmarried father may agree that, from the date of the agreement, the father shall have all the rights and responsibilities of a married father. The agreement must be made in prescribed form[28] and registered in the Books of Council and Session and, once made, is irrevocable. The agreement must be for the transfer of *all* parental rights and responsibilities: it is therefore a condition of s.4 that the mother must not have been deprived of any parental rights by the courts. The problem however, is that in practice, as in England, it turned out that very few unmarried couples chose to use s.4: the anecdotal evidence suggests that couples do not think to make such agreements while their relationship is still harmonious, and cannot reach agreement once it deteriorates. As a result, the Family Law (Scotland) Act 2006 ("FLSA 2006") adopted a more radical approach.

The FLSA 2006[29] amended s.3(1)(b) of the 1995 Act so that fathers after   **3–17** the 4th May 2006 also acquire automatic PRRs where, although not married to the mother, the father is registered as the child's father under any of the United Kingdom's Acts enabling registration of births, deaths and marriages. Since joint registration requires joint consent by father and mother, this has the advantage of still excluding the father whose mother is opposed to the sharing of PRRs with the father. The provision is not retrospective.[30] Some commentators have suggested that the period immediately after the birth during which the birth must be registered, is an undesirable time during which to ask a woman to decide if she wishes to share parental responsibilities with the father. She is likely to be exhausted, over-burdened, and possibly medically depressed, and it may well be difficult for her to appreciate that registering a birth jointly now has more far-reaching implications than it had in the past. However the new provision brought Scotland into line with England,[31] allowing for consistency across the border in issues concerning status and right. It is also possible—though perhaps unusual—for the child to be registered solely by the mother within the post-birth time limit, and the father's name added later, in which case automatic PRRs would flow from

---

Child in English Law" (1988) 3 Int. Jnl of Law and the Family 208, and Thomson, "Parental Rights and Responsibilities", 1996 S.L.G. 19.

[27] See the Children Act 1989 s.4 as amended by the Adoption and Children Act 2002 s.111.

[28] A statutory form was published for making these agreements under s.4 of the 1995 Act in the Parental Responsibilities and Rights Agreements (Scotland) Regulations 1996 (SI 1996/2549).

[29] FLSA 2006 s.23.

[30] FLSA 2006 s.23(4).

[31] This provision has been the law in England since December 1, 2003. See the Children Act 1989 s.4 as amended by the Adoption and Children Act 2002.

that time of registration, so long as that was after the 2006 Act amendments came into force.[32] While a person with PRR's may not abdicate their responsibilities, they may arrange for some or all of them to be fulfilled or exercised by another person on his or her behalf.[33]

Section 11 Applications for Parental Responsibilities and Rights ("PRRs")

3–18   Under s.11 of the 1995 Act, any person without PRRs but claiming interest may make an application to the court for an order in relation to parental responsibilities, rights, guardianship or the administration of a child's property.[34] On such application, the court may make such order as it sees fit, but in particular it may make one of a number of orders specified in s.11(2) including a residence, contact or specific issue order. In deciding whether to grant the order applied for, the court shall: (a) regard the welfare of the child involved as a paramount consideration; and (b) shall not make any order unless satisfied that to do so will be better for the child than making no order at all.[35] In other words, the court must be convinced it is better to alter the status quo than to leave it alone. Before making such an order, the court is also instructed to take account of the views of the child concerned, having regard to his age and maturity; a child of 12 or more is presumed to be old enough to form a reasonable view.[36]

3–19   Section 11 can thus be used by step-parents[37] and other persons such as unmarried fathers still lacking automatic rights[38] to apply for PRRs. It is also possible for a child's parent to prospectively transfer PRRs by nominating a person in writing as the guardian of that child, to act after the death of the nominating parent.[39] So a mother might appoint her new husband, or the unmarried father of her child, the guardian of her child after her death. The parent making the appointment must make it in writing and sign it, and must at the time of his or her death have been the legal representative of the child.

3–20   It is interesting to briefly move from the popular acceptance of automatic rights for (at least some) unmarried fathers, to the more equivocal status of step-parents. Given the prevalence of divorce and re-marriage it is apparent that the step-family population is large and expanding. In the past, most step-families formed after the death of one parent; now most step-families are the result of re-marriage following divorce. Families may contain a mixture of children from the current relationship with children from one or more previous relationships involving either current partner. (Such families are

---

[32] Confirmed in the Justice 1 Committee Private Briefing Paper on the Family (Scotland) Bill, supplementary note to oral hearing on March 15, 2005.

[33] 1995 Act s.3(5).

[34] As long as they have not previously been divested of parental rights. See s.11(3)(a)(i) and para.4–40.

[35] 1995 Act s.11(7)(a).

[36] 1995 Act s.11(7)(b) and (10).

[37] Prior to the 1995 Act such applications could be made under s.3 of the Law Reform (Parent and Child) (Scotland) Act 1986. See *Bangham v Bangham*, 1992 G.W.D. 12–96 (step-father unsuccessfully applied for custody).

[38] See, inter alia, *Sloss v Taylor*, 1989 S.C.L.R. 407 (unmarried father successfully applied for custody); *Stewart v Monaghan*, 1993 Fam. L.B. 2–5.

[39] 1995 Act s.7. See Ch.6 for a full discussion of guardianship.

sometimes known as "reconstituted" or "blended" families.) Step-parents may informally regard their stepchildren as an integral part of their family unit, but due to their lack of a genetic link, they have no official status and no more rights in respect of these children than any other de facto carer.[40] Many worry about their lack of formal status and how they will manage if the blood parent dies first, leaving them de facto but not *de iure* in charge of children. It is of course possible for stepparents to apply for parental responsibilities under s.11. However, cases decided prior to the 1995 Act showed that the attitude of the courts in Scotland is not favourable to step-parents who attempt to compete for rights with natural parents or even natural relatives of a child. In *Bangham v Bangham*,[41] for example, a stepfather sought custody of his stepson, aged 12, who had been accepted into the family on his marriage to the mother over eight years before. The mother contested custody. It was held that since the son remained in contact with his natural father, an award of custody to the stepfather was not appropriate. He was, however, allowed access.

In *Breingan v Jamieson*,[42] a stepfather was advised his case was too weak   **3–21** even to attempt to dispute the custody of the child of his wife by her former husband, after his wife's untimely death. Instead, custody was fought out between the former husband and the maternal relatives (who won). This categorisation of the stepfather as a poor substitute for a "real", genetic father seems particularly invidious since if a stepfather has accepted his stepchild as a "child of the family" then he is liable to aliment him in the same way as a natural parent would be.[43] Even since the 1995 Act, there seems to have been little shift in this perception of step-parents as a "poor second choice" to blood parents.[44]

Other options are available to step-parents seeking rights. The most   **3–22** popular option for stepfathers is probably to seek rights by adopting the stepchild jointly with the natural mother. This has problems of its own which are discussed further in Ch.6. More radically, it has been suggested that step-parents should be able to acquire rights without going to court, either through some sort of automatic sharing of rights possessed by the natural parent to whom they are married, or by agreement with the natural parent or parents.[45] Many of the same arguments can apply, as have been discussed in the context of the unmarried father. In its consultation document, *Family Matters*,[46] the Scottish Executive suggested in 2004 that step-parents might

---

[40] See paras 6–08 to 6–09.

[41] *Bangham v Bangham*, 1992 G.W.D. 23–1296.

[42] *Breingan v Jamieson*, 1993 S.L.T. 186.

[43] Family Law (Scotland) Act 1985 s.1(1)(d). However step-parents are not liable to support their stepchildren under the scheme of the Child Support Act 1991.

[44] See evidence from Stepfamily Scotland to Justice 1 Committee Report on the Family (Scotland) Bill, paras 162 *et seq*. It was suggested however that parents can delegate (though not abdicate) PRRs to third parties under s.3(5) of the 1995 Act (though it was also acknowledged that this was little used); furthermore, as noted at para.3–19 above, a step-parent can be named as testamentary guardian by the natural parent.

[45] See J. Masson, "Old Families Into New: a Status for Step-parents" in *The State, the Law and the Family* (Freeman (ed.), Tavistock Publications, 1984).

[46] *Family Matters*, Scottish Executive, 2004.

be able to make an agreement with a natural parent to share parental responsibilities and rights, in a style akin to s.4 of the 1995 Act. The details of such a scheme proved intractably difficult to resolve between all parties, however. Should the making of an agreement require the consent of the other natural parents in all cases? Should one parent who is the sole parent with PRRs (say, a mother not married to the natural father, and not jointly registered as parents) be able to confer such rights on her new partner, *without* the consent of the other natural parent? Should the agreement be terminable by mutual agreement (important given the high rate of second marriage breakdown) or should it only be revocable by a court, or should it be terminable by unilateral notice of the natural parent with PRRs? What happens in the event of third or fourth re-marriages? What if someone involved in such an agreement *ceases* to be a step-parent, because they divorce the natural parent or are divorced? Such manifold possibilities seemed to threaten a chaos of multiple agreements and frequent court applications. StepFamily Scotland suggested that an agreement be available only to a step-parent who had lived with the family for over two years. In the end however, the proposal was shelved from the FLSA 2006.[47]

WHO IS A PARENT?

3–23 So far, we have established that although the law will not award parental rights to every genetic parent, the establishment of parentage is a first prerequisite. In this section, we will first consider who is a "traditional" parent and how parentage, and in particular, paternity, can be proven. The principal statute in this area is the Law Reform (Parent and Child) (Scotland) Act 1986 ("the 1986 Act"). We will go on to consider the new reproductive technologies and what problems they raise in the legal interpretation of who is a mother and who is a father.

Maternity

3–24 At common law, there was no dispute that the legal mother was the person who gave birth to a child.[48] Motherhood was seen as certain by comparison to the possible uncertainty surrounding paternity.[49] Due to the public nature of pregnancy and birth, doubt infrequently arises which requires proof of the maternity of a child. Conceivably, mix-ups in hospital administrative arrangements may occur, in which case an action to prove maternity might be raised in the shape of a declarator of parentage under s.7 of the 1986 Act. In *Douglas v Duke of Hamilton*,[50] the pursuer sought to prove that he was the son of Lady Jane Douglas and hence the heir to substantial estates.

---

[47] In England, however, step-parent agreements were indeed introduced by the Adoption and Children Act 2002 s.112.
[48] And this status of maternity persists even where an assigned gender of male has been adopted by a mother under the Gender Recognition Act 2004: see s.12.
[49] See the maxim from Justinian's *Digest* (D. II, 4, 5): "*mater semper certa est etiamsi vulgo conceperit*" (the mother is always certain even if the son has been conceived in promiscuity).
[50] *Douglas v Duke of Hamilton* (1769) 2 Pat. 143.

Difficulties arose both because Lady Jane had married in secret at an age well past normal child-bearing years for the time—48 years old—and her pregnancy and delivery had been shrouded in secrecy, observed only by servants and had taken place abroad to avoid the knowledge of her brother. The mother had died before the date of the action. After evidence was brought both as to the mother's capacity to give birth at that age, and as to the gentleness and tenderness she showed her child, it was held the evidence established a presumption that the pursuer was her child which the defender was unable to rebut.

Paternity

Proof of paternity has always represented a problem since wherever more than one man has had sexual access to the mother during the period surrounding the date of conception there is potential uncertainty. Thus the law has developed a number of techniques to assist in establishing paternity. It is important to note that until the advent of the new reproductive techniques there was never any doubt that the father of a child was the genetic father, i.e. the person whose sperm fertilised the egg of the mother.[51] As we have seen above, someone who merely takes the social role of father such as a step-parent or new partner of the mother has not been regarded legally as a father. Because of this, until scientific tests were developed based on analysis of blood or body tissue, approaches to proving paternity had to rely on inferring proof of the genetic link from circumstantial evidence. **3–25**

Proof of Paternity: Presumptions

Because of the inherent uncertainty attached to paternity, and social approval of legitimate birth, the law has always presumed certain persons to be fathers until proven otherwise. This is done by the device of legal presumptions. All legal presumptions of paternity are now found within s.5 of the 1986 Act. A person who has the benefit of such a legal presumption will be regarded in law as the father and anyone seeking to rebut this will have to prove the contrary on a balance of probabilities,[52] i.e. the normal civil standard. **3–26**

Presumption Arising by Virtue of Marriage

The most important s.5 presumption is found in s.5(1)(a) and states that a man shall be presumed to be the father of a child "if he was married to the mother of the child at any time in the period beginning with the conception and ending with the birth of the child". **3–27**

For this purpose, a void, voidable or irregular marriage will have the same effect as a valid and regular marriage.[53]

---

[51] As in n.64 above, it should be noted that status as a father is not disturbed if that person adopts an assigned gender as a woman under the Gender Recognition Act 2004: see s.12.

[52] 1986 Act s.5(4).

[53] 1986 Act s.5(2). If a woman married Mr A, then bigamously went through a marriage ceremony with Mr B, then it follows logically that both Messrs A and B would have the benefit of a s.5(1)(a) presumption, since it arises from the void second marriage as well as the

3–28   This is a statutory re-enactment of the common-law presumption that *pater est quem nuptiae demonstrant*, i.e. "the father is shown by the marriage" or the mother's husband is presumed to be the father of a child born during the marriage. Section 5(1)(a) is more extensive than the common law presumption, however, in that it presumes that a man is the father of the child if he marries the mother at any time before the child is born.[54]

3–29   The s.5(1)(a) presumption can be rebutted on the balance of probabilities. This is an important alteration from the common law presumption which could only be rebutted by evidence beyond reasonable doubt. This was because a finding that the presumption was rebutted was equivalent to a finding that a married woman had had intercourse with a man not her husband, i.e. had committed adultery, which was at one time a criminal offence. A successful rebuttal of the presumption also implied that the child was illegitimate, a finding the courts have historically been reluctant to make. However, now that the legal disabilities associated with, and the whole status of, illegitimacy, have been removed from Scots law[55] there is no reason not to use the normal civil standard of proof. Given that it was virtually impossible in pre-1986 Act cases to rebut the *pater est* presumption unless the husband had had almost no possibility of access at the approximate time of conception,[56] common law cases are poor guides to the modern law on what sort of evidence is necessary to rebut the presumption on the balance of probabilities.

3–30   In any case, as we will see below, the use of scientific tests to establish paternity has now made it possible in most paternity cases to give a virtually definitive rather than probabilistic answer to who the father is. Consequently, standard of proof sufficient to rebut the presumption is no longer the major issue it once was.[57] Instead, the focus of argument has shifted to whether it is in the interests of the various parties, and especially the child, to allow the use of these tests, and what inferences should be drawn from them if they are used: we will come back to these points below.[58]

3–31   It is important to realise that s.5(1)(a) does not operate where a child is both conceived and born before the mother enters a marriage. Hence, where a couple cohabit and the woman has a child, the male partner will not be

---

valid first one. In such a case, a literal reading would suggest the two presumptions would cancel each other out. One suspects that in practice the claim of the legal husband would be preferred.

[54] At common law, a man was not legally presumed to be the father if he married a pregnant woman, only if the child was born during the duration of the marriage. However, there was a presumption of fact (not law) that where there had been an "avowed and open courtship" of a man by a woman who subsequently fell pregnant, and he then subsequently married her, that he was the father (*Gardner v Gardner* (1876) 3 R. 695).

[55] See Ch.5.

[56] See, e.g. *Ramsay v Ramsay's Curator ad litem*, 1986 S.L.T. 590, the last case decided prior to the coming into force of the 1986 Act in which it was stated that "nothing less than completely satisfactory evidence can be sufficient".

[57] Few paternity cases have been reported since the 1986 Act came into force which have not turned upon scientific tests, and in even fewer has evidence been lead to rebut a s.5(1)(a) presumption; see, however, *Campbell v Grossart*, 1988 G.W.D. 24–1004, where the s.5(1)(a) presumption of paternity of the husband was not rebutted by the child pursuer.

[58] See paras 3–51 to 3–56.

presumed father under s.5(1)(a) even if they subsequently marry. No legal presumption arises simply because a man is cohabiting or associating with a woman at a time when she conceives or gives birth.

Presumption Arising by Acknowledgment and Registration

However, the law does implicitly pay some recognition to the type of case where the father of a child, although not married to the mother, can be clearly identified from the circumstances of the parents. **3-32**

Section 5(1)(b) of the 1986 Act provides that a man shall be presumed to be the father of a child if: (i) both he and the mother have acknowledged that he is the father; and (ii) he has been registered as such in the appropriate Register of Births, Deaths and Marriages.[59] Normally, both of these requirements will be combined in one in the shape of the declarations the parents must make before a man who is not the husband can be registered as the father of a child. It is, of course, possible for these steps to be taken at a time when the mother is still legally married to another man. In such a case, where a man already has the benefit of the s.5(1)(a) presumption, s.5(1)(b) does not operate; hence, in such a situation the only man who gains the benefit of a presumption of paternity is the husband (or ex-husband) and there is no possibility of conflict. **3-33**

Section 5(1)(b) is clearly intended to extend the benefit of the presumption of parentage to cohabiting couples but it is important to note that legally its scope is quite different. The presumption is based not on evidence of co-residence but on joint acknowledgment and registration. Generally, an unmarried father can only be registered as such if he makes a joint request with the mother, which requires her assent and his presence at the registry office.[60] Thus, even if a couple are cohabiting, the father may not be registered through the mother's hostility to the idea, his indifference or general inconvenience. Even so, a very high number of births involve joint registration.[61] **3-34**

As with s.5(1)(a), this presumption can be rebutted by evidence on the balance of probabilities. **3-35**

Presumption from Prior Decree of Declarator of Parentage

If a judicial finding that X is the father of a particular child is made in an action for decree of declarator of parentage,[62] then it gives rise to a legal presumption that X is father whenever the issue is raised in the future.[63] This presumption takes precedence over any other presumption arising from marriage or registration or a prior court decree. **3-36**

---

[59] Note that this is in line with the familiar rule that a man's name on the birth certificate does not prove he is father, but there is *a presumption* that he is father.

[60] Registration of Births, Deaths and Marriages (Scotland) Act 1965 s.18. It is possible for either a mother or father acting alone to register the child born out of wedlock as the child of a particular father by taking along statutory declarations by both the mother and the man in question that he is the father of the child; but in practice such types of registration are numerically small.

[61] Only 5.3% of births to unmarried parents involve registration in the mother's name alone (Registrar General for Scotland, *Scotland's Population 2011* (Annual Review), p.23).

[62] 1986 Act s.7.

[63] 1986 Act s.5(3).

Proof of Paternity: Scientific and Other Evidence

3–37   If the presumptions above do not apply or if the facts of paternity are nonetheless disputed, then the matter must be resolved by evidence. The question
of paternity may be resolved by raising an action for decree of declarator of
parentage or non-parentage[64] or may arise as an incidental question within
other proceedings such as an action for divorce, aliment, or parental rights or
responsibilities.[65] The standard of proof in proceedings to establish or deny
parentage is the normal civil standard of the balance of probabilities.

Scientific Tests: Blood Groups and DNA Profiles

3–38   The most useful evidence in modern paternity proceedings is undoubtedly
that gathered from scientific tests, such as blood tests or "DNA profiling".
These tests attempt to discern if a man, or one of several men, is the genetic
father of the child in question. Originally, the attitude of Scots law to the
use of blood tests was hostile. Blood tests work on the well-known basis
that a person's blood has characteristics which distinguish it from the blood
of other people. Typically, blood types fall into the groups O, A, B or AB,
although there are many more subtle classifications. Since the genes responsible for these blood types are inherited from parents, an analysis can be done
comparing the blood of the child and both parents. Such a blood group analysis is not well suited to establishing paternity, however, because in principle
it provides only an exclusionary result, i.e. it can establish that a man could
not be the father but not conclusively that he must be (since there are many
persons who share a single blood group typing). Thus, the consequence of
blood group testing in a paternity case may be that a child is proven to have
no known father, and if a presumption of paternity of the husband is rebutted, then he will no longer be presumed to be the child's father. Given these
factors, and also the fact that early blood tests were invasive and relatively
unreliable, the Scottish courts took the view early on that no-one should be
compellable by the courts to undergo tests, or to give consent for anyone else
to do so.[66] It was held in *Whitehall v Whitehall*[67] that to subject a person to
a blood test against their will would be to force them to undergo a surgical
operation against their will, albeit a minor one, and so would constitute an
"unwarrantable invasion of private rights".

3–39   As blood testing became more refined, however, the lack of a power to
order the taking the blood samples became less justifiable. Judicial opposi-

---

[64] 1986 Act s.7.
[65] 1986 Act s.7(5). Only declarators of parentage or non-parentage can be sought; decorators
of legitimacy, illegitimacy and legitimation were abolished by the Family Law (Scotland) Act
2006 s.21(2). The declarator can be raised in the Sheriff Court or Court of Session if any of the
child or alleged or presumed parent was domiciled in Scotland, or habitually resident for one
year or born in Scotland or the sheriffdom, as appropriate. A "presumed" parent is one with
the benefit of a presumption of parentage under s.5 of the 1986 Act. Declarator can be asked
for independently or as an ancillary order in other relevant proceedings (s.7(5)). It is possible
to seek declarator after the child has died: s.7(2)(c).
[66] We refer here, of course, to civil proceedings only.
[67] *Whitehall v Whitehall*, 1958 S.C. 252. See also *Imre v Mitchell*, 1958 S.C. 439.

tion to the use of blood tests had declined[68] but courts were still constrained by the principle in *Whitehall*. The debate was brought to a head by the commercial availability of a new type of scientific test known as DNA testing or DNA finger-printing. DNA is genetic material found in all human body tissue, not just blood that can be taken from hair or a swab from inside the mouth making it a much less invasive procedure than taking blood. A sample of body tissue from a human body can be processed to produce a DNA profile, which is a pattern of bands resembling the bar-code found widely on supermarket goods. A DNA profile is highly individual, unlike a blood group, hence the comparison to fingerprints. By comparing DNA profiles from a child, the mother and one or more possible fathers, it is possible to say with an extremely high degree of probability—verging on certainty[69]—that a certain person positively is the father of a particular child. Thus, a positive as opposed to an exclusionary result can be derived. Since DNA tests can be done using any bodily tissue, such as hair or nails, rather than just blood, they are a less invasive procedure than blood tests, particularly for young children.

Clearly, DNA evidence, freely available in paternity cases, could contribute a great deal in terms of a speedy, reliable and cheap means to determine the action. However, initially it remained open to the parties to refuse to give a sample. In *Torrie v Turner*[70] the Inner House held that the principle in *Whitehall* applied to DNA testing. Lord Mayfield reluctantly conceded that the law had not changed because of the advent of a conclusive method of testing such as DNA testing. The matter might have gone to the House of Lords had legislation not intervened.   **3–40**

The Law Reform (Miscellaneous Provisions) (Scotland) Act 1990 s.70(1)(a) now makes it plain that in any civil proceedings, the court may request a party[71] to proceedings to provide a sample of blood, or other body fluid, or of body tissue, for the purpose of blood or DNA tests. The use of the word "may" makes it clear that the court has a discretion whether to choose to make such a request and will not do so in every paternity case. The court may make this request either on the application of one of the parties, or of their own volition.   **3–41**

However, the civil liberties argument, which was so strong in the early history of blood test cases, has not been entirely abandoned. If a request is made, and the party it is addressed to does not comply, then they will   **3–42**

---

[68] See, e.g. *Docherty v McGlynn*, 1983 S.L.T. 645; *Allardyce v Johnston*, 1979 S.L.T. (Sh. Ct) 54.

[69] It was said in *Torrie v Turner*, 1990 S.L.T. 718 that DNA evidence as to paternity was "beyond statistical doubt" (Lord Mayfield at 719L). However, in criminal proceedings where a prosecution will fail if a reasonable doubt as to guilt is raised, there have been attempts to rebut the accuracy of particular instances of DNA testing: see MacDonald, "DNA profiling—Less Than the Whole Truth?", 1990 S.L.T. (News) 285.

[70] *Torrie v Turner*, 1990 S.L.T. 718.

[71] A party under s.70 includes an executor, even if this is someone other than a relative, such as a solicitor (*Mackay v Murphy*, 1995 S.L.T. (Sh. Ct.) 30, in which the sheriff commented "It may be difficult but one should eventually be able to get blood out of a solicitor"). It does not however include a curator *ad litem* appointed to an adult incapax defender in a paternity action: see *Cameron v Carr*, 1997 S.C.L.R. (Notes) 1165. However the sheriff in that case ingeniously suggested that instead, in such a case, the court could supply consent to the taking of a sample under s.6(3) of the Law Reform (Parent and Child) (Scotland) Act 1986 (see para.3–45 below).

not under the present law be physically compelled to undergo tests, nor be rendered in contempt of court, which could result in imprisonment pending compliance, as both of these were felt to be unacceptable sanctions in civil proceedings.[72] Instead, following the model of parallel English legislation,[73] if a party to whom a request has been made does not comply, then the court may draw such adverse inference, if any, as seems appropriate, taking into account the subject matter of the proceedings.[74]

Consent on Behalf of a Child

3–43   Section 70 also deals with the case where consent to the taking of a sample must be given on behalf of a child. As we saw in Ch.2, a child under 16 has no capacity in theory to give a consent to any legal transaction,[75] including a consent to the taking of a blood or body tissue sample for the purpose of paternity tests. However by s.2(4) of the Age of Legal Capacity (Scotland) Act 1991, a child may have capacity to consent to giving a sample if they are "capable of understanding the nature and possible consequences of the procedure", in the opinion of a qualified medical practitioner. There will, therefore, be two classes of children: those who are capable of understanding the nature and consequences of giving a blood or DNA sample for the purpose of determining parentage; and those who are not. Under s.70(1)(a), a request may be made to a child in the first class to provide a sample if they are a party to the proceedings.[76] It is hard to see though what adverse inference can usefully be drawn if a child refuses to give a sample, as he may be as much in the dark about his origins as anyone else.

3–44   However, if it is desired to take a sample from a child in the second class, i.e. a non-competent child, then legal consent must be given by a person who has power to supply that consent. If such a person is unwilling to assist by providing consent to taking a sample, then under s.70(1)(b) of the Law Reform (Miscellaneous Provisions) (Scotland) Act 1990 the court can request them to do so.[77] As with any other s.70 request, if consent is not then given, an adverse inference may be drawn if appropriate.

3–45   Who then has power to give a legal consent to the taking of a sample on behalf of an incompetent child? By s.6(2) of the Law Reform (Parent and Child) (Scotland) Act 1986, any person having parental responsibility for a child under 16, or care and control of such a child, may give consent.[78] If no

---

[72] See *Blood Group Tests, DNA and Related Matters*, Scot. Law Com. Discussion Paper No.80 (1988) and subsequent report (Scot. Law Com. No.120 (1989)).

[73] Family Law Reform Act 1987, Pt III; prior to this legislative change English law also forbade the court to order a person to undergo blood tests (*S v S* [1972] A.C. 24).

[74] 1990 Act s.70(2). This resolves doubt as to whether the court had power to draw adverse inferences at common law: see *Docherty v McGlynn*, 1983 S.L.T. 645 (n.84); *cf.* Lord Mayfield in *Torrie v Turner*, 1990 S.L.T. 718 who felt such a power had to be provided by Parliament.

[75] Age of Legal Capacity (Scotland) Act 1991 s.1(1)(a) and 9(d). See Ch.2 for a fuller discussion of children's capacity.

[76] They may well not be. For the child's right to be given notice of proceedings concerning him or her, see para.4–58.

[77] Again, so long as they are a party to the proceedings.

[78] This is probably an extension of the common law position prior to the 1986 Act under which the right to give a legal consent to the taking of a sample was an aspect of the parental right

such person exists, or if such a person exists but it is not reasonably practicable to obtain a consent from him, or he is unwilling to accept the responsibility of giving or withholding consent, then the court may give that consent.[79] If the court supplies a consent in one of these circumstances, then it must first be satisfied that the taking of the sample would not be detrimental to the child's health; it is very unlikely this will be the case with modern DNA testing, which need not involve the collection of blood. Note that there is no inherent overriding power in the court to give a consent on behalf of a child just because the person with parental responsibility does not *wish* to supply this evidence. Instead, the correct procedure when consent is refused is to ask the court to make a s.70(1)(b) request, and if this is refused, to draw the appropriate adverse inference.

A difficult chicken-and-egg problem arises where presumptive fathers enter actions to assert or deny their own paternity. A married man is presumed to be the father of his child by s.5(1)(a) (so long as the child was either conceived or born during the course of the marriage) and is also therefore presumed to have parental responsibility and rights by virtue of s.3(1)(b) of the 1995 Act. Should such a presumptive father be able to give a consent for a sample to be taken from the child in question, if his own paternity is what is actually in dispute? **3–46**

This problem arose in the leading Inner House case of *Docherty v McGlynn*.[80] Here, the mother of a child had died before the action was raised. At the date of her child's conception and birth, the mother was married to McGlynn, who was therefore the presumptive father by virtue of marriage. However, the mother had left the father and taken up living with her lover, Docherty, before the birth of the child. Docherty raised an action of declarator to establish that he was the father of her child and not McGlynn. He had de facto care of the child, and he had also been registered as the child's father at its birth. McGlynn sought to defend his paternity using blood test evidence. The principal issue in the case was whether McGlynn, as the presumptive father had the right to give a legal consent to the taking of a sample for blood tests from the child. If not, this evidence would be unavailable. **3–47**

It was held that the presumptive father retained the right to give a legal consent in respect of a child unless and until that presumption was rebutted by contrary proof. A mere challenge to that paternity did not in any way deprive such a father of the right to exercise his rights and powers. In fact, a presumptive father is required to go on fulfilling his parental responsibilities unless and until the presumption of paternity is rebutted. **3–48**

In *Docherty*, the presumptive father was attempting to uphold his own presumed paternity. But what if (as will more often be the case) he had been attempting to *disprove* it? It was suggested obiter by Lord Emslie in **3–49**

---

of guardianship only. A curator *ad litem* appointed to safeguard the interests of a child in paternity litigation cannot give consent on behalf of the child: *Docherty v McGlynn*, 1983 S.L.T. 645 at 647.

[79] 1986 Act s.6(3).

[80] *Docherty v McGlynn*, 1983 S.L.T. 645.

Docherty,[81] commenting on the case of *Imre v Mitchell*,[82] that a husband seeking to deny the paternity of a child born to his wife, cannot rely on his own right to consent to the taking of blood samples from that child. Lord Cameron was concerned, that the child's interests might be prejudiced, since the effect of a successful challenge by a husband denying paternity would be to render the child illegitimate, which was still a stigma that might cause pain and distress. It has been argued forcefully[83] since *Docherty* that the legislative and social stigma of illegitimacy have been so reduced since 1983 that it is no longer a justification for restricting access to blood tests. However, the matter remains unresolved, notwithstanding the changes in the law, in *Smith v Greenhill*.[84] It can only be definitively said that *Docherty* stands as authority for the proposition that a presumptive father has a right to give a consent to blood or DNA tests on his child, so long as he is seeking to uphold not deny his paternity.[85] Now that the status of illegitimacy has been entirely abolished however,[86] it is hard to see a court taking this line of reasoning seriously.

3–50   It is submitted in any case that the question of how the outcome of blood or DNA tests may affect the welfare of the child is one that should be considered only after the question has been settled of whether a legal consent to the taking of the sample exists. There is no requirement under s.6 that a person with parental responsibilities must take into account the welfare of the child when deciding whether to give or withhold consent, let alone regard it as paramount. Such a requirement would be unworkable since the interests of adult parties involved in actions either to deny or affirm parentage are very different from the interests of the children involved. The paradigm paternity action, for example, is probably one in which a man denies he is the father of a particular child in order to avoid financial responsibility. The father's interest is not in the welfare of the child but in his own financial affairs. A paternity action is not an action relating to parental responsibilities or rights[87] (although decisions about parental rights may flow from it) and so the welfare of the child is not the paramount consideration. On the other hand, the court does and should maintain an interest in the welfare of the child in paternity proceedings. They have an undoubted power in the exercise of their protective jurisdiction to exclude evidence derived from blood or DNA tests where to admit it would be against the interests of the child.[88] However, this power is separable from the issue of who can give a legal consent. It is in essence a question of discretionary exclusion of evidence.

---

[81] *Docherty v McGlynn*, 1983 S.L.T. 645 at 647.
[82] *Imre v Mitchell*, 1958 S.L.T. 57.
[83] See J. Thomson, *Family Law in Scotland*, 4th edn (2002), p.180.
[84] *Smith v Greenhill*, 1993 S.C.L.R. 776, *per* Sheriff Craik at 777C.
[85] In *Petrie v Petrie*, 1993 S.C.L.R. 392 (discussed below at para.3–52) a husband, seeking to rebut the presumption of paternity, asked the court to make a s.70 request to his wife to give her consent to the taking of a sample from the third child of their marriage. If there was certainty that a presumptive father could give such a consent to *disprove* his own paternity, there would have been no reason for him to make such a request.
[86] Family Law (Scotland) Act 2006 s.21.
[87] See *Soutar v Kilroe*, 1994 S.C.L.R. 757.
[88] See *Docherty v McGlynn*, 1983 S.L.T. 645, especially *per* Lord Cameron at 650.

Making a s.70 Request

Two further questions arise from the 1990 legislation. First, given the court **3–51** has a discretion to make a request to a party[89] to provide a DNA sample under s.70, when will they exercise that discretion? Secondly, if a request is made and the party refuses to comply, what "adverse inferences", if any, are likely to be drawn? Similar issues of policy are raised in both cases.

In *Petrie v Petrie*[90] a husband sought to deny paternity of the third child **3–52** of his wife in the course of their divorce proceedings. He asked the court to request his wife to consent to the taking of a sample of blood from their daughter under s.70. The wife argued that no request should be made, on the grounds, inter alia, that: (i) the request if granted might result in the child being found to be illegitimate; and (ii) the husband should not be allowed to seek to rebut his own presumed paternity on grounds of "mere suspicion". Rejecting the wife's arguments, the court held that if it were to refuse to make a request for a DNA sample, it would be blinding itself to a clear and relevant piece of evidence. The father already had doubts about paternity and it was better for these to be resolved than for the presumption of paternity to be preserved artificially. It would always be in the interests of the parties and usually in the interests of the child for the truth to be ascertained.

The argument in *Petrie* is fundamentally about whether it is always best for **3–53** the truth about parentage to be known or whether there are circumstances in which it may be best for it not to be revealed, or at least, not explored. In *Docherty*[91] the First Division were conscious that a "difficult and delicate" balance had to be struck between the desirability of achieving truth through litigation, which requires that the best evidence should be available, and the preservation of the interests of the child. On the whole though, they were convinced that the interests of the child are usually best met by establishing certainty rather than by withholding the truth.[92] Lord Emslie remarked that "The very worst that could happen to this child is that she may be left in a state of uncertainty upon a matter of vital importance in her life".

But what if there is good reason to believe that the child's interests will **3–54** not be best met by revealing the truth? Thomson suggests that it is no longer a good enough reason to obstruct the truth about paternity emerging that a child who was presumed legitimate may be rendered illegitimate. On the other hand, he suggests that exceptional circumstances might justify this, such as that the child might be revealed as the product of an incestuous relationship.[93] In ordinary life, what seems of great concern is not revelations

---

[89] Note that the person making the request may in respect of a "party to the proceedings" is not restricted to the alleged parent. In *Mackay v Mackay*, 1995 S.L.T. (Sh. Ct) 30 it was held to cover a deceased's executrix where the mother of child sought a declarator that a soldier who was killed before her child was born was the father of the child. It does not, however, cover a curator ad litem for a potential parent where, for example, the defender is mentally ill, as in the case of *Cameron v Carr's Curator Ad Litem* (also known as *Cameron v Carr No.1*), 1998 S.L.T. (Sh. Ct) 22.

[90] *Petrie v Petrie*, 1993 S.C.L.R. 391.

[91] At this time the court had no statutory power to request blood or DNA samples.

[92] In constructing this balance the First Division drew upon the English House of Lords case of *S v S* [1972] A.C. 24.

[93] J. Thomson, *Family Law in Scotland*, 4th edn (2002), p.180.

about the history of the child's origins but how the disclosure of paternity is likely to affect their present day-to-day care. In *Docherty*, however the facts about paternity turned out, the child was guaranteed a loving father. In *Petrie*, the parents were in any case already at the divorce courts. In *Smith v Greenhill*,[94] however, disclosures about paternity threatened the child's security within an established family unit. In this case, Mrs Greenhill had had an affair of uncertain length with Smith, but had throughout the affair remained living with and (it was proven) having sexual relations with her husband, by whom she already had two children. Mrs Greenhill conceived another child who was registered as the child of her husband, who was also the presumptive father by s.5(1)(a) of the 1986 Act. Smith sought to establish his paternity of the child so he could apply for access rights. The wife wanted nothing to do with Smith by this stage. The court agreed to make a request for a DNA sample to be taken from Mrs Greenhill but she refused to comply. The question then arose as to what adverse inference should be drawn by the court. The court chose *only* to infer that Mrs Greenhill had not been telling the whole truth about the extent and duration of her relationship with Smith. This, on the facts, was not enough to rebut the husband's presumption of paternity and so Smith lost the case. On appeal, the decision was upheld but it was admitted that if there had been no husband in the picture with a presumption of paternity, a more damning inference might have been drawn.

3–55   *Smith* resembles the English Court of Appeal case of *Re F*[95] in which the facts were very similar. The child in that case was being brought up as the child of the mother and her husband and the court agreed that it would do the child no good to allow the mother's former lover access to DNA tests to prove his paternity. Balcombe L.J. said that:

> "Anything that may disturb . . . the stability of that family unit within which [the child] has lived since her birth is likely to be detrimental to [her] welfare".

But this, again, is not the whole story. In recent years, the need of a child to know the truth about his or her genetic origins and, if necessary, to explore them, has been stressed in the adoption context.[96] If such a psychological need exists, it should apply equally here. Knowing who one's true father is does not *necessarily* mean that the relationship with a social father need be prejudiced.[97] If the child's welfare is to be explored when deciding whether to make a s.70 request, or what adverse inferences should be drawn, then the long-term psychological welfare as well as the short-term material welfare should be considered.[98]

3–56   *Smith* also establishes that the court is not bound to draw any adverse inference when a s.70 request is not complied with if it feels it is not appropri-

---

[94] *Smith v Greenhill*, 1993 S.C.L.R. 944.

[95] *Re F* [1993] F.L.R. 598.

[96] See Tresiliotis, *In Search of Origins: the Experience of Adopted People* (1973) and para.6.70. The need to know one's genetic heritage is also recognised to a limited extent in relation to children born via egg or sperm donation: see paras 3.97–3.98.

[97] Of course it may do: see, e.g. *Watson v Watson*, 1994 S.C.L.R. 1097.

[98] See further, pursuing this argument Fortin, "*Re F*: the Gooseberry Bush Approach" (1994) 57 M.L.R. 296.

ate to do so.[99] This might arise, for example, where a person refuses to give a sample of blood, because of religious scruples, fear of contracting HIV infection or needle phobia. Since DNA tests do not usually require the taking of blood, however, these are unlikely scenarios.

Other Evidence

If, for some reason, DNA or blood test evidence is not available then it may still be necessary to use other types of more circumstantial evidence to try to establish paternity. In the past, evidence was often lead to try to establish that the pursuer could not have been the father because around the estimated date of conception he did not have sexual access to the mother of the child. These claims are based on establishing that if the pursuer had been the father, then given his dates of access, the gestation period of the child would have been either abnormally short or abnormally long. Because of the very high standard of proof required in the past to rebut the presumption of paternity, the courts have allowed some extremely unlikely periods of gestation as possible. In *Preston-Jones v Preston-Jones*,[100] for example, the court was willing to believe that a child was the legitimate child of the husband even though this implied a gestation period of either 360 days or 186 days and the child had the appearance of an ordinary full-term baby. It is unlikely a modern court would accept such a story given the change to proof on the balance of probabilities.[101] **3–57**

Many other facts will be relevant evidence in a paternity dispute. In the past, evidence has been lead as to the mother's opportunity to have sexual relations with other men, her actings around the time of conception, the opinions of friends and relatives, and so forth. The naming of a father on the birth certificate of a child is of evidential use but is in no way conclusive as the certificate is a record of birth not parentage. It is not significant where a woman has an equal chance of conceiving by either of two men that one is her regular boyfriend or partner.[102] **3–58**

ASSISTED PARENTHOOD

We turn now to the question of assisted parenthood and the law. It is useful here to survey briefly what types of treatments for infertility are available and what kind of major legal issues arise.[103] We will then examine three **3–59**

---

[99] *Smith v Greenhill*, 1993 S.C.L.R. 944, *per* Sheriff Principal Nicholson at 948B.

[100] *Preston-Jones v Preston-Jones*, 1951 A.C. 391. See also *Currie v Currie*, 1950 S.C. 10.

[101] A modern case in which abnormal gestation period evidence was used is *Wilson v Currie*, 1991 G.W.D. 14–872; 300 days accepted as not impossibly long.

[102] *Robertson v Hutchison*, 1935 S.C. 708, where the mother had sex in one night with both her boyfriend and another man. No finding of paternity could be made. Of course if one had been her husband, then because of the presumption of paternity he would have been found to be the father.

[103] There is a vast literature about the legal and ethical implications of the new reproductive techniques. As an introduction see Mason and Laurie, *Mason and McCall-Smith's Law and Medical Ethics*, 8th edn (Oxford University Press, 2010). See also G. Douglas, *Law, Fertility and Reproduction* (London: Sweet & Maxwell, 1991); *Legal Issues in Human Reproduction* (Mclean (ed.), 1989); *Law Reform and Human Reproduction* (Mclean (ed.), 1992); McCandless

general issues: how do the new techniques affect the definitions of who is a legal parent; what kinds of person should have access to parentage via these treatments; and what rights do children produced by these techniques have to discover their genetic origins? The legal regulation of assisted parenthood is contained in the Human Fertilisation and Embryology Act 1990 (hereafter "the HFEA 1990") and in the HFEA 2008.[104] The 2008 Act has allowed for parental responsibilities and rights to be extended to those qualifying as parents under ss.42 and 43 of the Human Fertilisation and Embryology Act 2008, discussed below.[105] This Act introduces a new concept of parenthood for a mother's female partner in certain circumstances, as well as extending the notion of parenthood in cases involving assisted reproduction to cover civil partners and unmarried, same sex couples.

Artificial Insemination

3–60   Artificial insemination involves the injection into a woman of sperm collected from a male donor. A woman may be artificially inseminated with the sperm of her husband or partner as a treatment where, for example, infertility derives from the man's low sperm count. This type of treatment (known as artificial insemination by husband[106] or AIH) is merely a mechanical variation on natural insemination and as such has few legal implications.[107] On the other hand, if a man cannot produce sperm or if his sperm cannot successfully fertilise his wife or partner, then artificial insemination by donor (AID[108]) may be the answer.[109] AID was originally a controversial method of treatment in the context of use by, primarily, married couples, since the use of third-party donor semen was seen as akin to adultery. However, it was established in *MacLennan v MacLennan*[110] that AID could not be regarded as adultery since that required a sexual act involving penetration of the female

and Sheldon, "The Human Fertilisation and Embryology Act 2008 and The Tenacity of the Sexual Family Form (2010) 73(2) *Modern Law Review* 175; Zanghellini "Lesbian and Gay Parents and Reproductive Technologies: The 2008 Australian and UK Reforms" (2010) 18 *Feminist legal Studies* 227.

[104] This impetus for legislation in the form of the HFEA 2008 was primarily to ensure that the regulation of assisted reproduction and embryo research was fully up to date with scientific advancements and social attitudes to them. It amends many of the provisions of the 1990 Act but the main features of the existing model of regulation are retained. For an overview of reform see Fenton, Heenan and Rees "Finally fit for the purpose? The Human Fertilization and Embryology Act 2008" (2010) 32(3) *Journal of Social Welfare & Family Law* 275. The Act received Royal Assent on 13 November 2008 and most of its provisions came into effect on October 1, 2009.

[105] 1995 Act s.3(1)(c) and (d).

[106] Artificial insemination treatment may be sought by unmarried couples but the acronym is a useful one.

[107] AIH can raise issues when it is used as a means to try and select in advance the sex of a child. Such approaches are currently not wholly perfected but already raise issues of eugenics, medical ethics and abortion as family planning. See Mason and Laurie, *Mason and McCall-Smith's Law and Medical Ethics*, 8th edn (2010), p.258.

[108] An increasingly common alternative term for this is DI (Donor Insemination) which avoids confusion with Auto Immune Deficiency Syndrome (AIDS).

[109] Couples may hedge their bets by attempting treatment using insemination with sperm from husband and donor (AIHD). This may be regarded for legal purposes as equivalent to AID.

[110] *MacLennan v MacLennan*, 1958 S.C. 105.

by the male organ. The use of AID by a married woman without the consent of her husband will however probably constitute unreasonable behaviour and therefore be grounds for divorce.[111]

AID has been available as an NHS treatment since 1968 and since that time **3–61** has become morally uncontroversial but has nevertheless remained shrouded in secrecy. Male infertility has been regarded as a stigma and something to be hidden. Sperm donations have traditionally been made by anonymous donors (though this is changing—see below) and in many or most cases in the past, the husband or other "social" father has been falsely registered as the father on the birth certificate rather than the genetic donor (for obvious reasons it is hard to give statistics). The main legal problem arising out of AID is who should be regarded as the father of the child—the "social" father or the sperm donor? This problem was addressed in the HFEA 1990 and is now dealt with under s.41 of the 2008 Act, discussed at para.3–77 below.

In vitro Fertilisation

AID is a relatively cheap and painless technique and has been in use since **3–62** at least 1884. Treatment for female infertility is generally more difficult and has arrived much more recently on the scene. *In vitro* fertilisation (IVF) is a form of treatment for female infertility in which the human egg (or ovum) is fertilised outside of the womb, in a Petri dish, and then re-implanted. Where a woman has blocked fallopian tubes, for example, the removal of one of her own eggs, fertilising it with her husband's sperm, and implanting it back into the womb will be a way to avoid the physical blockage. This is akin to AIH in creating no real problems as to legal parentage.[112] On the other hand, it may be that the woman cannot produce eggs to be implanted, or that her ovaries have been removed as cancerous. In cases like these, egg or ovum donation from another woman may be the answer. The egg donated may be fertilised with sperm of the husband or regular partner of the woman who is being treated, and the fertilised egg or embryo created re-implanted into the infertile woman's womb. The result of this ovum donation is that the woman who bears the child—the "gestational mother"—is a different person from the woman who supplied the genetic material—the "genetic mother". It is possible in this kind of scenario that the husband or partner of the woman undergoing treatment may also be infertile, in which case ovum donation may be combined with the use of third-party donated sperm. Here the embryo implanted is composed of genetic material entirely from donors other than the couple seeking to have a baby at the end of the day. (This is sometimes known as embryo donation or transfer.) In this case we effectively combine the problems of parentage of AID with those of ovum donation.[113]

IVF, unlike AID, has never been regarded at any stage of its development as **3–63** an inherently immoral or stigmatised practice. However, as we shall see below, the legal regulation of IVF is affected by the social context in which it is used.

---

[111] Divorce (Scotland) Act 1976 s.1(2)(b).
[112] This was the treatment used to create the original "test tube baby", Louise Brown, in 1978.
[113] This may sound like a remote possibility. However, it has been estimated this might apply to as many as one in every 100 marriages where children are sought.

Surrogacy

3-64   Surrogacy is in many ways an odd companion to the two techniques discussed above, since it is neither a medical technique to combat physical infertility, nor does it require any kind of essential technology, nor is it particularly new. However, the perceived need to regulate surrogacy arrangements has had an important inter-relationship with the regulation of other infertility techniques. Surrogacy is as old as the Bible, which furnishes a good example of its use. When Rachel could not give Jacob, her husband, a child, he had intercourse with her handmaid and by that means acquired two sons.[114] Jacob had no option but to resort to natural intercourse, but the techniques of AID, and, in particular, ovum donation, have made surrogacy a much more attractive option in the last decade or so.

3-65   If a couple (the "commissioning parents") wish to commission a child from a surrogate mother, then it is possible that the surrogate may be inseminated by the commissioning husband using AID, thus avoiding natural intercourse. It is also possible for the commissioning mother to donate an egg, which can be fertilised with the sperm of the commissioning husband, and the resulting embryo implanted into the surrogate mother. Such an exercise in total surrogacy has been evocatively labelled "womb-leasing" and though it is medically identical as a technique to embryo donation discussed above, it raises very different issues of policy, since it is not the gestating mother but the commissioning mother who intends to be the social parent.

3-66   Both these enhancements to old-fashioned surrogacy have made it a growth area, especially in the USA. However, even in the United Kingdom, reportedly 157 children had been born as of 1996 via surrogacy with the help of one non-commercial surrogacy agency, Childlessness Overcome Through Surrogacy (COTS). Surrogacy can be seen as an effective treatment for the infertility of women who cannot bear a child to term, e.g. because they have had a hysterectomy. In the United Kingdom, however, the governmental attitude to surrogacy has oscillated between panic, hostility and indifference. There are a great many complicated arguments surrounding the morality or otherwise of surrogacy.[115] Surrogacy is seen as ethically dubious because it tends to involve a commercial relationship between would-be parents and the mother of a child. Surrogacy is sometimes seen as akin to adoption, and a commercial surrogacy contract as akin to babyselling, which is outlawed in most countries out of concern for the welfare of the child. Looking at the welfare of the surrogate mother, surrogacy is seen as exploitative, especially as research reveals that many surrogates are on low incomes or unemployed.[116]

3-67   On the other hand, surrogacy can be seen as empowering women by giving them an alternative wage-earning capacity. In many ways, these arguments parallel the debate about female prostitution. Finally, when surrogacy agree-

---

[114] Genesis 30:1–6.

[115] There is another body of literature focusing specifically on surrogacy. In addition to the sources above, see especially the Warnock Report which laid the ground work for the HFEA 1990: *Report of the Committee of Inquiry into Human Fertilisation and Embryology*, Cmnd.9314 (1984), Ch.8.

[116] Parker, "Motivation of Surrogate Mothers: Initial Findings" (1983) 140 American Journal of Psychiatry 117.

ments go wrong the practical difficulties can be enormous. In the nature of such agreements there is a risk that the surrogate will decide to keep the child (or try to) and then issues such as parentage, parental rights and responsibility and financial support will have to be adjudicated in the court.

In the United Kingdom, legislation was passed to prohibit the arrange-   **3–68** ment of a surrogacy contract on a commercial basis in the Surrogacy Arrangements Act 1985,[117] long before other infertility techniques were dealt with in the HFEA 1990. This was an emergency measure resulting from a "moral panic" following Britain's first widely publicised court case involving a surrogate mother and a commissioning couple.[118] Non-commercial surrogacy, however, remains legal. Since then it is fair to say that the government has chosen to maintain a rather distrustful distance from surrogacy which it has neither encouraged nor totally suppressed. Recent years have, however, perhaps seen institutional opposition to surrogacy services softening and in 1998, surrogacy was reportedly available for free in one third of NHS clinics.[119] The HFEA 1990 s.36, substituting s.1A into the 1985 Act, tidied up one problem left unattended to by the 1985 Act by declaring that a surrogacy contract should be unenforceable. Thus there is no possibility that commissioning parents can seek a remedy in contract to force an unwilling surrogate to hand a baby over. On the other hand, it means that neither contracting party can rely on the terms of the agreement they have entered into, which may not be to the benefit of anybody, including the child. It has been suggested that

> "surrogacy is better policed by a scheme in which the legal system recognises and enforces surrogacy contracts, rather than one in which they are left limbo-dancing in the twilight of social disapproval and legal vacillation."[120]

One solution might be some system whereby the courts must approve a surrogacy contract before it is entered into, rather like their vetting of an arranged adoption before making an adoption order. Certainly surrogate motherhood and any associated contractual obligations will always be a minefield, as demonstrated in the United Kingdom by the "Internet Twins" case, where a broken contract left two new born babies in a protracted legal limbo between the United Kingdom and California, to much public disquiet.[121]

In 1998, Professor Margaret Brazier conducted a comprehensive review of   **3–69**

---

[117] The Act expressly provides that the surrogate mother herself and the commissioning parents do not commit a criminal offence; e.g. it is the agency, lawyer or doctor who specifically make money from arranging or assisting in surrogacy that the Act criminalises.

[118] *Re C (a minor)* [1985] F.L.R. 846 (perhaps better known as the "Kim Cotton" case.) The moral outrage was caused not only by the fact of surrogate motherhood and the fact that the surrogacy was arranged by a branch of a commercial US agency, but by Ms Cotton's intention to sell her story for money.

[119] See M. Brazier, *Surrogacy: Review of Current Arrangements for Payment and Regulation*, Cm.4068 (1998). HFEA Code of Practice, 6th edn (2003), para.3.17 explicitly allows surrogacy in HFEA licensed clinics.

[120] Morgan, "Who to Be or Not to Be: the Surrogacy Story" (1985) 49 M.L.R. 358.

[121] *W v H (child abduction: surrogacy)* [2002] 2 F.L.R. 252.

United Kingdom surrogacy regulation.[122] The main conclusions were: first, that payments to surrogate mothers should cover only "genuine expenses" associated with pregnancy. "Additional" payments would be prohibited and courts would lose the power to authorise questionable expenses retrospectively; secondly, surrogacy clinics would be required to register with an agency run by the relevant Department of Health and would, like HFEA clinics, be subject to a Code of Practice; thirdly, the non-enforceability of surrogacy contracts[123] and the ban on advertising surrogacy services introduced in the 1985 Act should continue. It may be asked however if there is a point to encouraging people to negotiate in advance as to what items of expenditure will be payable expenses, if the agreement reached cannot subsequently be enforced? Finally, the report recommended the creation of a new consolidated Surrogacy Act. These recommendations were largely rubber-stamped in the comprehensive HFEA 1990 review commenced in 2005.

ASSISTED REPRODUCTION AND LEGAL PARENTHOOD

Married Couples—Maternity

3–70   Earlier we noted that at common law there was no difficulty in assuming that the genetic mother was also the person who gave birth to the child. However, ovum and embryo donation techniques open up a choice as to who is the "true" mother between the gestational mother and the genetic mother. The Warnock Committee, considering this issue, consciously based their recommendation as to who should be the legal mother on a model based on egg donation to a woman who wished to bear and bring up a child, rather than on egg donation to a surrogate mother.[124] They therefore recommended that when a child is born to a woman following the placing in her of an egg or embryo, then the woman giving birth should be treated for all purposes as the mother of that child. This was implemented in s.27(1) of the HFEA 1990 and is now contained in s.33(1) of the 2008 Act. This conclusive preference for the gestational mother as the legal mother can be justified on the basis that the bonding which takes place during nine months of pregnancy is the essential basis of motherhood. However, it is a radical diversion from the previous default assumption for genetic parenthood.[125] Section 33(1) provides that "the woman who is carrying or has carried a child as a result of the placing in her of an embryo or of sperm and eggs, *and no other woman* (own italics) is to be treated as a mother of the child". This is the case unless a child is subsequently adopted or parenthood is transferred through a parental order.

---

[122] M. Brazier, *Surrogacy: Review of Current Arrangements for Payment and Regulation*, Cm.4068 (1998).

[123] 1985 Act s.1A.

[124] See Warnock Report, *Report of the Committee of Inquiry into Human Fertilisation and Embryology*, Cmnd.9314 (1984) (above, n. 10), para.8.19.

[125] Nor is it an uncontroversial or universal choice. In California, e.g. the Supreme Court has gone the other way and the genetic mother has been recognised as legal mother on the basis that she had the *intention* to become the parent, unlike the surrogate (see *Johnson v Calvert* (1993) 5 Cal 4th 84). This opens up the intriguing prospect of an international private law of parentage.

The provision, however, does not apply to any title, coat of arms, honour or dignity transmissible on death.[126] For these rather limited purposes, genetic parenthood is all that counts.

Paternity

As discussed above, the new techniques open up a choice as to who should be father as well as mother. At common law, in cases of AID, or AID combined with IVF, the genetic father, i.e. the sperm donor, was the legal father. This meant that although invariably of unknown identity, he could theoretically be held liable for maintenance of any children (and there might be several) who had been produced using his sperm. On the other hand, the person who intended, and was indeed often desperate, to play the role of the father was the husband or partner of the woman who had been inseminated. As we have seen, he would often be willing to perjure himself to register the child falsely as his own genetic child. The Warnock Committee, considering the paradigm case of a married couple undergoing AID treatment[127] to conceive a child, were unanimously agreed that the AID child should be treated in law as the child of the mother and her husband where they had both consented to treatment.

3–71

The HFEA 1990 went further than the Warnock proposals in extending this deemed paternity not only to husband but also to unmarried partners undergoing AID or associated treatment together. The basic provision previously contained in s.28(2) and now contained in s.35 of the 2008 Act provides that a husband, whose wife conceives after the donation of sperm, or implantation of an embryo created with donated sperm, is to be treated as the father of the child *unless* it is shown that he did not consent to the treatment. In other words, there is a rebuttable presumption that the husband consents to treatment. The husband is to be treated as the father for all purposes except for minor exceptions relating to succession to titles, coats of arms, etc.[128] This solves the problem of false birth registration as "all purposes" must surely imply the right to register as the legal father.[129] The presumption of the husband's consent is reasonable given that it is routine in clinics to secure the consent of the husband before embarking on treatment.

3–72

Unmarried Heterosexual Couples

Receiving "treatment services . . . together"

The 1990 Act also, however, extended treatment to unmarried, heterosexual couples who sought treatment together under s.28(3). The phraseology used has, however, given rise to considerable difficulty. First, could

3–73

---

[126] HFEA 2008 s.48(8).
[127] Warnock Report, *Report of the Committee of Inquiry into Human Fertilisation and Embryology*, Cmnd.9314 (1984), para.4.17.
[128] HFEA 2008 s.48(8).
[129] Although when this provision was being debated in the House of Lords, Lord Denning remarked that he was unhappy about the statutory encouragement of perjury. It is still possible under the Act for a child to discover something about his or her true genetic heritage: see paras 3–101 to 3–102.

"treatment services" be said to be "provided for her [the mother] and a man together" where the man plays no actual physical role in the fertilisation process at all? This is true of any case where the sperm of a donor is used for either AID or the creation of an embryo which is then implanted in the woman. In *Re Q (Parental Order)*[130] an English court found that s.28(3) did not extend to cases of this nature. Fortunately this was overruled in *U v W*[131] where the court found that if a doctor was responding to a request for treatment from a woman and a man as a couple, then on the facts, they might still qualify under s.28(3) even though there was no actual physical participation by the man. Secondly, what if an unmarried couple begin fertility treatment together, but by the time of actual conception or birth they have split up? This was the scenario in the English House of Lords case of *Re R (A Child) (IVF: Paternity of Child)*.[132] B, the intended mother, entered treatment services with her partner D, who signed the required consent form for treatment. D and B then split up, but B continued treatment without him, unknown to D and the hospital. With some difficulty, their Lordships held that although the couple had indeed been receiving treatment together at the time of the original consent, they were not by the time of the eventual birth, and so D was not deemed the father by s.28(3). Clearly though, this decision was to some extent influenced by the court's dislike of B's deception.

3–74   Finally, have a couple consented to "treatment services . . . together" where there is a major mix up in the treatment (and hence the baby) delivered? In the remarkable case of *Leeds Teaching Hospitals NHS Trust v Mr and Mrs A*[133] Mr and Mrs A, a white couple, went to the fertility clinic for IVF treatment having spent years unsuccessfully trying for a baby. So, unfortunately, at the same time did Mr and Mrs B, who were black. When twin babies were born to Mrs A, she noticed they were clearly of mixed race. It became apparent after DNA tests that Mr B's sperm had been injected by mistake into Mrs A's egg, which, when fertilised, had been re-implanted into Mrs A's uterus. The legal question, then, was who was the father? The court accepted that s.28(2) could not operate to deem Mr A the legal father, even though he was married to Mrs A, because he had not consented to a "treatment" of Mrs A being impregnated by Mr B. Fundamental error had vitiated his consent. This left the outside possibility of invoking s.28(3) to make Mr A the legal father. However, the same error also, the court held, "vitiate[d] the whole concept of 'treatment together' for the purposes of the 1990 Act." Accordingly, s.28(3) cannot operate to deem a man the father if his consent to being treated together with the mother is void through fundamental error.[134]

---

[130] *Re Q (Parental Order)* [1996] 1 F.L.R. 369.
[131] *U v W* [1997] 2 F.L.R. 282.
[132] *Re R (A Child) (IVF: Paternity of Child)* [2005] 2 A.C. 621.
[133] *Leeds Teaching Hospitals NHS Trust v Mr and Mrs A* [2003] EWHC 259 (QB).
[134] Interestingly, the court nonetheless were prepared to contemplate awarding parental rights of residence to Mr and Mrs A, the intended "social" parents, even though the genetic and legal father of the child remained Mr B, as s.28(6) also did not operate to remove the paternity of the "sperm donor" in these circumstances of error. See further Norrie, "Paternity and Reproductive Technology", 2002 S.L.P.Q. 232.

Replacement of "receiving treatment services. . . together" with contractual provision

The provisions of the 1990 Act, which enabled an unmarried man to be the   **3–75**
father of a donor-conceived child if he is "treated together" with the mother
in a licensed clinic, have been replaced by ss.36 and 37 of the 2008 Act.[135]
These provisions attempt to deal with the problems arising from the wording
"receiving treatment services . . . together" by eliminating this phraseology,
and creating a specific procedure that is to be followed based on contract and
the forms it must take. The new provisions require the couple to be treated in
a UK licensed clinic, as before to ensure there is clear evidence of the parents'
intention about fatherhood. However for the man to be the father, the couple
must each have given notice of consent to him being treated as the father at
the time the embryo or gametes were placed in the woman or she was artificially inseminated.[136] Neither of them must have subsequently withdrawn
consent. The woman to be treated must not have given consent to another
man or woman being treated as the child's parent. The notices of consent
must be presented to the "person responsible" at the clinic. The requirement
for written notice is waived if any of the parties involved is unable to sign up
because of illness, injury or physical disability.

After the transfer of gametes or embryo neither the man nor the woman   **3–76**
can withdraw their consent. Section 36 extends deemed paternity to the case
where an unmarried couple are being treated together. This achieves the
result that a man who is not married to his partner and is not the genetic
father of her child is nonetheless conclusively deemed to be its father.[137]
This at the time of the passing of the HFEA 1990 was a surprisingly strong
vindication of social parenthood; it can now be seen as in line with recent
moves towards extending the rights attached to marital status to cohabiting
couples. Of course, since he is unmarried the father will still not have any
parental rights over the child unless he is jointly registered as the father of the
child,[138] or makes an agreement under s.4 of the 1995 Act, or seeks a court
order.[139]

In this process the sperm donor is removed from the legal picture entirely.   **3–77**

---

[135] Note that the couple must not fall within the forbidden degrees of relationship as defined in s.58(2) of the HFEA 2008 that includes parents and children, siblings and uncles or aunts and their nephew or nieces. Close relatives of this kind may not jointly be treated as a child's parents.

[136] For the notice to be valid the parties must not fall within the prohibited degrees of relationship defined in s.58(2).

[137] Section 38(1) provides that, where a person is treated as a child's father under ss.35 and 36, no other person is to be treated as the father. Note, however, that ss.35 and 36 do not affect the common law presumption that a child is the legitimate child of the parties to a marriage. So, for example, if a woman marries between the conception of the donor-conceived child and its birth, it will be presumed that her new husband is the father of the child, even if the agreed fatherhood conditions were satisfied in relation to a different man at the time when the gametes or embryo were transferred. However, the presumption may be rebutted by evidence showing that the husband is not the child's father in which case the provisions of s.36 would apply and the man in respect of whom the agreed fatherhood conditions were satisfied would be the child's father.

[138] Children (Scotland) Act 1995 s.3(1)(b).

[139] Children (Scotland) Act 1995 s.11.

By s.41 of the 2008 Act he is not to be treated as the father of the child.[140] Thus, the genetic link is broken entirely, at least as long as the sperm donor has given an effective written consent to bring him within the regulatory framework of the Act.[141] If the mother has been treated without the consent of a male partner, therefore the resulting child will be legally fatherless. If the sperm donation was made on a "DIY" basis, however,[142] s.41 does not apply and the sperm donor will remain the legal father.[143] This is intended to discourage informal sperm donation outwith the licensing controls of the Human Fertilisation and Embryology Authority (hereafter "the HFEA"), which licenses and supervises all clinics that provide infertility treatment under the Act.

3–78   What if a husband avoids the deeming provision of s.35(1)(b) by proving that he did *not* consent to the treatment of his wife by AID? It seems logical that the normal presumption of genetic paternity by virtue of *marriage* under s.5(1)(a) of the 1986 Act would still persist. So a husband will normally be presumed the father under this provision even if he had refused to consent to the treatment. However, it will not be hard for the husband to rebut the presumption in this situation as he will be able to lead the evidence of artificial insemination and prior infertility, which will prima facie disprove the genetic link.[144]

Same Sex Couples—Civil Partners

3–79   One of the important reforms brought about by the 2008 Act is the introduction of a new concept of parenthood for a mother's female partner in certain circumstances, making equivalent provision to that for opposite sex couples. It also makes provision for parenthood in respect of children born after a surrogacy arrangement which is intended to put same sex couples and unmarried opposite sex couples in the same position as married couples. Thus although the Act's new provisions provide same sex couples with a route to legal parenthood this is predicated upon a heterosexual, two-parent model of the family.

Woman in civil partnership at time of treatment

3–80   Section 42 of the 2008 Act makes provision that is not found in the 1990 Act for the position of civil partners to be brought into line with that of married couples. It does this by providing that, where a woman gives birth to a child conceived as a result of the placing in her of sperm and eggs or donor

---

[140] See also HFEA 2008 s.38(1) which provides that if a husband or partner is deemed father under ss.35 or 36 then no-one else is to be treated as the father of the child.

[141] HFEA 2008 Sch. 3, para.5.

[142] e.g. where a male friend is recruited to assist a lesbian or lesbian couple to conceive outwith any clinic or doctor's surgery.

[143] The unmarried father's position may be contrasted with that of a husband for whom legal fatherhood is preserved where a child is conceived through the use of donor sperm whether the treatment was licensed on unlicensed. So, while DIY inseminations do effect the legal position of an unmarried father, they do not effect a husband's legal position with regard to fatherhood provided the conception was not achieved through sexual intercourse.

[144] He might also use DNA testing as discussed above to rebut the s.5(1)(a) presumption.

insemination (anywhere in the world),[145] her civil partner will automatically be treated as "a parent" of the child, unless the civil partner did not consent to the mother's treatment.[146] While the terminology differs from that applied to married couples the legal provisions have the same effect, apart from the fact that the gender neutral terminology here refers to "a parent". A woman recognised as a parent by virtue of s.42 acquires PRRs under s.3(1)(c) of the Children (Scotland) Act 1995.

Female Parenthood Conditions

Just as the 1990 Act made provision for unmarried heterosexual couples, so the 2008 Act makes provision for same sex female couples who are not civil partners under ss.43 and 44. This is similar to the provision made for opposite-sex, unmarried couples under ss.36 and 37. Where one of the women has a child as a result of donor insemination or IVF in a UK licensed clinic,[147] and the couple have current notices of consent in place at the time of treatment, then the mother's partner will be a legal parent.[148] As with opposite-sex couples, the provisions about withdrawing consent and providing information to the other party apply. Notice must be in writing and signed by the person giving consent.[149] However, if either of the parties involved is unable to sign because of illness, injury or physical disability the requirement for a signature will be waived. Once again, for notice to be valid the parties must not fall within the prohibited degrees of relationship.[150]   **3–81**

In certain cases, the provisions of ss.42 and 43 will not affect who is to be considered the parent of the child, as for example, in the case of a child that has been adopted, or where there is a marriage, in which case the child is presumed to be the legitimate child of the married couple.[151] However this presumption can be rebutted, for example, by DNA evidence.   **3–82**

Male Civil Partners and Same Sex Couples

Constructing legal parenthood for male civil partners or same sex couples is more complex, given that a man cannot give birth to a child under current reproductive conditions. This means that a third party will need to become involved to fulfil the role of a gestational mother. This involves a surrogacy arrangement. In this situation the gestational mother can nominate one of the men to be the father under s.37 of the 2008 Act dealing with agreed fatherhood conditions. Where these are met he will be the legal father of the child.[152] This leaves the male partner of the father, however, with no legal relationship to the child because, as the law currently stands, only two   **3–83**

---

[145] Who is treated as the mother under s.33 of HFEA 2008.
[146] HFEA 2008 s.42(1). Note that this recognition of legal parenthood covers the use of both licensed and unlicensed or self-arranged insemination.
[147] Unlike the case of civil partners, where treatment is unlicensed the conditions for female parenthood will not be met, resulting in the sperm donor becoming the child's other legal parent.
[148] See s.3(1)(d) of 1995 Act conferring PRR's on her if she is registered as a parent of the child.
[149] HFEA 2008 s.44.
[150] For example, a mother and daughter, or two sisters would fall within the prohibited degrees.
[151] HFEA 2008 s.45.
[152] HFEA 2008 s.38(1).

parents are recognised and in this situation, the surrogate who gives birth will qualify as the mother, regardless of whether she has any genetic connection with the child.[153] Thus, the position of women in a same sex relationship is somewhat different from that of men. This is because in the case of the former, one woman can be the mother and the other can be the other legal parent by virtue of being the mother's civil partner, or through compliance with the agreed female parenthood conditions. This is not possible where men in a same sex couple are concerned, leaving one member of the couple without any legal connection to the child. This situation can also arise with a heterosexual couple, where the woman in the couple is not the birth mother and a third party has been engaged as a surrogate. An attempt has been made to deal with this situation through parental order under s.54 of the 2008 Act, discussed at para.3–91 below.

The Surrogacy Dimension

3–84   We have seen above that the status provisions of the HFEA 1990, now contained in the 2008 Act, were drafted in an attempt to solve the problems of maternity and paternity associated with AID and IVF. In particular, it was assumed that the couple receiving infertility treatment were the couple who intended to become parents and bring up the child. However, in the surrogacy situation, these assumptions are false. In a case of total surrogacy, applying the HFEA 2008, the legal mother of the child is deemed to be the surrogate mother, as she is the one who bears the child and gives birth[154] and, if the surrogate mother is married at the date of treatment, then her husband will be deemed to be the legal father of the child[155] unless he can prove that he did not consent to the insemination or to the IVF treatment. In many cases of surrogacy it will be impossible for him to prove this lack of consent, or he may well have actually consented.

3–85   These are not the results one would expect.[156] They are only explicable if regarded as a way other than criminal sanctions by which the law attempts to discourage people from entering non-commercial surrogacy agreements. After all, the whole aim of surrogacy is that the commissioning parents should have their own legal child at the end of the day. Potential surrogate parents may think twice when they are advised they will not automatically be treated as the legal parents of their surrogate offspring. Prior to the HFEA 1990, the commissioning father who was the sperm donor would have been the legal as well as the genetic father. However since then, under s.28(6) of the 1990 Act and now s.41(1) of the 2008 Act, he entirely loses his legal status as father.

3–86   There are, nonetheless, approaches surrogate parents can take to try to obtain parental responsibilities and rights, and at best, full status as legal

---

[153] This is made clear by HFEA 2008 s.33(1) and by s.47 that provides that a woman is not to be treated as a parent of a child merely because of egg donation.

[154] HFEA 2008 s.33.

[155] HFEA 2008 s.35(1).

[156] These undesirable results in the surrogacy situation were pointed out in an early paper: Montgomery, "Assisted Reproduction after the Family Law Reform Act 1987" (1988) Family Law 23.

parents in relation to their surrogate children. It is possible, for example, to apply for a residence order under s.11 of the 1995 Act. However, such an application will, of course, be regulated by the welfare of the child. In the few reported United Kingdom cases on residence disputes between surrogate mothers and commissioning parents, the courts have generally inclined towards the view that a child is better off with the natural, gestational parent where a maternal bond has already formed. In *Re P*,[157] for example, the surrogate mother declined to hand over twin babies to a married professional couple, having been inseminated by the husband; she subsequently won custody. The court, significantly, placed a higher value on the preservation of the maternal bond that had formed than on the material advantages the commissioning couple could offer.

On the other hand, in the only Scottish surrogate mother case to date, **3-87** *C v S*,[158] the sheriff awarded custody to the commissioning parents rather than the gestational mother, principally on the grounds that the year-old child had (pursuant to the contract) been living with the commissioning parents since birth and was a near stranger to the natural mother. The Inner House reversed the sheriff by making an adoption order rather than a custody order, but still found it in the child's welfare to reside permanently with the commissioning parents. It is hard to imagine a case in which the United Kingdom courts would prefer the claim of the commissioning couple to that of a surrogate mother who had retained possession of her child after birth.

Even where both commissioning parents and surrogate mother agree that **3-88** the arrangement should go ahead as planned, merely awarding parental responsibilities and rights to the commissioning couple is not the ideal solution. For one thing, parental rights terminate at 16; furthermore, the rights extend to upbringing but the rights holder is still not a legal *parent*, which has legal consequences for, inter alia, succession, nationality and domicile.

If commissioning parents wish to become full legal parents, the obvious **3-89** legal avenue is adoption. However, this option is even more difficult than acquiring parental rights. Adoption not only requires a court order but will usually involve the commissioning parents to undertake the lengthy process of vetting that all prospective adoptive parents must pass through. Furthermore the question of whether a surrogacy arrangement is equivalent to baby-buying may rear its head. Section 72 of the Adoption and Children (Scotland) Act 2007[159] prohibits adoptive parents from making any payment in consideration for the adoption of a child, although such a payment may be permitted if it falls within the remit of excepted payments under s.73. In *Re an Adoption Application (Surrogacy)*,[160] the commissioning parents Mr and Mrs A made a payment of £5,000 (cut down from an original agreement for £10,000) to a surrogate mother who gave up her job to have the child. When Mr and Mrs A applied for an adoption order, the court had to consider whether this payment contravened the law. Latey J. held that the mother had

---

[157] *Re P* [1987] 2 F.L.R. 421.
[158] *C v S*, 1996 S.L.T. 1387.
[159] This was previously prohibited under s.51 of the Adoption (Scotland) Act 1978.
[160] *Re an Adoption Application (Surrogacy)* [1987] 2 All E.R. 826. The case concerned the equivalent provision in the English Adoption Act 1976.

not been primarily motivated by financial considerations and that there was nothing commercial about this adoption.

3–90   It seems that payments for loss of earnings and expenses can safely be made to a surrogate, and then retrospectively authorised by the court, but anything on top akin to a fee will risk prejudicing any adoption. What exactly can be got away with as "expenses" remains controversial.[161] In *C v S*, discussed above, involving the old legislation under the HFEA 1990, the commissioning parents were refused an adoption order at first instance, because they had paid the surrogate £8,000. The sheriff regarded this as far more than could truly be justified as expenses, since the surrogate was unemployed with no prospect of work. On appeal to the Inner House, however, the Lord President found that even if the money was an illegal payment, it had been made to secure a parental order[162] not as consideration for an *adoption*. There was therefore no contravention of the statutory provision.[163] This seems an artificial distinction justifiable only on the facts of the case. To make it easier for the court to deal with this question of expenses and their effect on the adoption process the Adoption and Children (Scotland) Act 2007 now provides that, even where applicants have made or accepted payments prohibited by s.72 of that Act, a court can still make an adoption order in their favour.

Parental Orders

3–91   The legal position in which a commissioning couple found themselves was highlighted by the case of *Re W (minors)*,[164] which involved a surrogate mother bearing a child conceived by means of embryo transfer, that is, a child who had no genetic relation to the surrogate at all. Although there was no dispute between the surrogate and the commissioning parents, the local authority intervened and sought guidance from the courts as to who was the legal mother.[165] This prompted legislation in the form of s.30 of the HFEA 1990 that allowed such parents to apply within six months of the surrogate child's birth for a *parental order*. The effect of a parental order is to treat the child as the child of the applicant parties for all legal purposes. It is effectively equivalent to an adoption order without the need to go through the adoption process.[166] Under the current provision relating to parental orders, contained in s.54 of the HFEA 2008,[167] the category of persons who may apply for such order has been extended beyond married couples to civil partners and "two persons who are living as partners in an enduring family relationship and are

---

[161] In adoption cases, sums of £8,000 or more paid to the child's natural mother have been authorised while sums as low as £1,000 have been declared illegal, depending on the circumstances.

[162] Under s.30 of the 1990 Act.

[163] Contained in s.51 of the 1990 Act.

[164] *Re W (minors)* [1991] 1 F.L.R. 385.

[165] Since this was prior to the passing of the HFEA 1990 in Parliament, s.27 had of course not yet cleared this point up.

[166] See further the Parental Orders (Human Fertilisation and Embryology) (Scotland) Regulations 1994 (SI 1994/2804).

[167] In order to give effect to s.54, new regulations in the form of the Human Fertilisation and Embryology (Parental Order) Regulations 2010 have come into effect, replacing the Parental Orders (Human Fertilisation and Embryology) Regulations 1994.

not within the prohibited degrees of relationship to each other". Numerous conditions must be satisfied before a court can grant a s. 54 order. Both the applicants must be aged eighteen or over[168] and must make an application within six months of the birth of the child[169] whose home must be with the applicants.[170] In addition, the surrogate mother must consent freely to the making of the order; so must her husband or partner if he is the legal father of the child by virtue of s.35 or s.36 of the 2008 Act.[171] This consent is not effective if given within six weeks of the child's birth.[172] Most importantly, the court must be satisfied that no money has changed hands other than expenses reasonably incurred.[173] Where these conditions are fulfilled it is exceptional for such an order to be refused.[174]

"Intentional" Parentage

A different approach than that of treating surrogacy as a kind of post-natal adoption is possible. In the case of *Johnson v Calvert*,[175] the Californian Supreme Court was asked to rule on whether a genetic commissioning mother or a surrogate gestational mother was the legal mother. The court decided in favour of the genetic mother, but not for that reason. Instead, they held that it was the woman who *intended* to bring about the birth of a child she intended to raise as her own who should be treated as the legal mother. This concept of "intentional" parentage would produce what might be called the "right" result in both surrogacy and conventional assisted reproduction cases. This radical approach has not yet provided a foundation for legislative change in the UK and it remains to be seen whether it will be taken up in future approaches to reform in this area.[176]

3–92

Regulating Access to Assisted Reproduction

In most Western democratic countries there are no legal obstacles to becoming a parent by natural means. If natural parents fail to look after their children adequately they may be removed by the state; but concepts such as the licensing of natural parents, or restrictions for the sake of population control,[177] are regarded as an unwarranted intrusion into personal privacy. When children are born as a result of reproductive technology, however, the ground shifts. On the one hand, here is an opportunity to regulate access to parentage without the need for an abhorrent invasion and monitoring of

3–93

---

[168] HFEA 2008 s.54(5).
[169] HFEA 2008 s.54(3).
[170] HFEA 2008 s.54(4).
[171] HFEA 2008 s.54(6).
[172] HFEA 2008 s.54(7).
[173] HFEA 2008 s.54(8).
[174] See Mason and Laurie, *Mason and McCall-Smith's Law and Medical Ethics*, 8th edn (2010), p.287.
[175] *Johnson v Calvert* (1993) 5 Cal 4th 84.
[176] For a proposed framework for change on these lines see Callus, "A new parenthood paradigm for twenty-first century family law in England and Wales?" (2012) 32 *Legal Studies* 347.
[177] China's one-family one-child policy is probably the best known example of this kind of regulation.

ordinary family life and sexual relations. On the other hand, it can be asked why infertile would-be parents should be regulated when any other person, however unfit for parenting, can have a child without passing tests. The debate turns on whether assisted reproduction is seen more as akin to natural childbirth or to adoption, but is complicated by the fact that artificial pro-creation is in general a considerably more expensive business than the natural kind. If the state is putting resources into assisted reproduction then arguably it has a stake financially in making sure the children are born to adequate homes, so that it does not end up meeting the costs of their care—in addition, of course, to its protective interest in the welfare of future children.

3–94 One type of restriction on access to IVF treatment which undoubtedly already operates is economic. Not all NHS clinics offer IVF and without NHS support, such treatment is prohibitively expensive for many couples, particularly as the success rate (i.e. the live birth rate) is low and therefore multiple attempts are not unusual. Plans do exist to offer three free cycles of IVF on the NHS to all who wish it but this is still an aspiration rather than a reality.[178] The costs of surrogacy are less easy to quantify[179] but there is some evidence that it is often a way for infertile middle-class couples to acquire babies carried to term by working-class or unemployed women.

3–95 An obvious goal of regulation is to protect the welfare of as yet uncon-ceived children. What criteria for suitable parents this indicates is highly con-troversial. Clinics providing treatment under the HFEA 2008 (and previously under the 1990 Act) are licensed by the Human Fertilisation and Embryology Authority. As a condition of that license they must comply with guidelines provided in a Code of Practice.[180] Under the 1990 Act a woman was not to be provided with infertility treatment including AID and IVF unless account has been taken of the welfare of any child that may be born as a result of the treatment.[181] This expressly required a consideration of "the need of that child for a father".[182] In an earlier HFEA Code of Practice, centres were enjoined to take account of this factor but were also directed to consider if there was someone within the mother's family or social circle who was willing to share responsibility for the child's needs.[183] Clinical practice varied in applying these broader guidelines and when the legislation was being updated an opportunity was taken to bring the Act into line with changing social and family norms in order to "recognise the wider range of people who seek and receive assisted reproductive services in the 21st century".[184] For it was acknowledged that the original formulation of s.13(5) favoured a het-erosexual couple to the exclusion of single and same-sex parents. As a result

---

[178] According to Mason and Laurie, *Mason and McCall-Smith's Law and Medical Ethics*, 8th edn (2010), who note that "currently only nine of the 151 Primary Care Trusts in England meet the standard", p.271.

[179] According to press reports in April 1996, the first NHS-funded birth to a surrogate mother via ovum donation occurred in 1994. The cost to the public was around £5,000.

[180] Currently contained in the 8th edn (last revised April 2012) available on *www.hfea.gov.uk* [accessed February 20, 2013].

[181] 1990 Act s.13(5).

[182] 1990 Act s.13(5).

[183] HFEA Code of Practice, 6th edn (2003), Pt 3, especially paras 3.13–3.15.

[184] House of Commons Science and Technology Committee 2005, Ev 195, para 21.

s.13(5) of the 1990 Act was amended by the 2008 Act, deleting the reference to consider the need for a father, and substituting it with a requirement to consider the child's need for "supportive parenting".[185]

Under the Eighth Code of Practice guidance is given as follows: **3–96**

Supportive parenting is a commitment to the health, well being and development of the child. It is presumed that all prospective parents will be supportive parents, in the absence of any reasonable cause for concern that any child who may be born, or any other child, may be at risk of significant harm or neglect. Where centres have concern as to whether this commitment exists, they may wish to take account of wider family and social networks within which the child will be raised.[186]

Other factors which may be taken into account include the medical and **3–97** social history of each patient and their partner,[187] along with any factors that are likely to give rise to significant harm or neglect to any child who may be born, or to any existing child of the family, including past or current circumstances that may lead to serious physical or psychological harm.[188] When reaching a decision about treatment parties are entitled to a fair assessment that must be done in a non-discriminatory manner. This means there can be no discrimination on the grounds of gender, race, disability, sexual orientation, religious belief or age.[189] Where parties seeking treatment wish to pre-select the sex of the child for social reasons this is prohibited.[190] Embryos, however, may be tested and pre-implementation diagnosis (PGD) may be permitted in certain limited circumstances, for example where sex selection is essential for the birth of a healthy child (e.g. where a genetic disease is transmissible only to male children),[191] or for the creation of a healthy "saviour sibling" (a child who can, e.g. donate tissue to cure a sibling with an inherited genetic disease).[192] The latter was subject to judicial review in the *Hashmi* case[193] which went to the Court of Appeal where the Master of the Rolls concluded that IVF treatment that includes PGD constituted "treatment for the purpose of assisting women to bear children" irrespective of the purpose of the PGD.[194] In recent years cases have arisen with regard to the positive selection of embryos with known genetic defects. Savulescu, for example, refers

---

[185] For a discussion of the history and amendments to s.13(5) see McCandless and Sheldon "No Father Required"? The Welfare Assessment in the Human Fertilisation and Embryology Act 2008" (2010) 18 *Feminist Legal Studies* 201.

[186] HFEA Code of Practice, 6th edn (2003), para.8.11.

[187] HFEA Code of Practice, 6th edn (2003), para.8.9.

[188] See paras 8.10–12 that list factors such as previous convictions or child protection issues, drug or alcohol abuse, or violence or serious discord in the family environment.

[189] HFEA Code of Practice, 6th edn (2003), para.8.7.

[190] 1990 Act Sch.2 as amended sets out activities that may be licensed under the Act. Section 1ZA lists the circumstances under which embryos may be tested through pre-implantation diagnosis and these doe not include sex selection for social purposes. See also, Code of Practice, 8th edn, para. 10D.

[191] 1990 Act Sch.2, s.1ZA(1)(b) and (c).

[192] 1990 Act Sch.2, s.1ZA(1)(d).

[193] *R (on application of Quintavelle on behalf of Comment on Reproductive Ethics) v HFEA Authority* [2003] 2 All E.R. 105.

[194] *R (on application of Quintavelle on behalf of Comment on Reproductive Ethics) v HFEA Authority* [2003] 3 All E.R. 257. The 1990 Act has now been amended to provide for this under Sch.2, s.1ZA(1)(d).

to a lesbian couple suffering from congenital deafness who sought to acquire a child through IVF with a similar disability.[195] Amendments made to the 1990 Act[196] now make it clear that embryos that are known to have a gene or chromosomal abnormality that involves a significant risk that a person with that abnormality will develop a serious physical or mental disability must *not* be preferred to those that are not known to have such an abnormality.

3–98   Where an applicant is turned down for treatment can the matter be reviewed by the courts? In the case of *R v Ethical Committee of St Mary's Hospital ex parte Harriott*,[197] a woman sought judicial review of the decision of the hospital ethical committee and consultant not to accept her for IVF treatment. She had in fact been rejected because of her criminal record for prostitution and brothel-keeping. Significantly, her (unsuccessful) application for review was based on the claim that the hospital had treated her unfairly by not revealing they had already rejected her as an unfit parent for some 14 months. Her counsel made no attempt to attack the substantive policies of the hospital concerning IVF candidates. Such an attack would only seem possible if the hospital selection policy was discriminatory to a group, not an individual, e.g. if a clinic refused to treat any black or Jewish patients.

Assisted Reproduction after Death of, or Separation from, Partner

3–99   Yet another set of difficult questions revolve around whether the state should assist, or even allow, a woman to have children by their partner even after his death. This issue was raised to great public concern by the difficult case of Mrs Diane Blood.[198] Mrs Blood obtained a sample of her husband's sperm while he was on his death-bed, in a coma, and thus without his consent. Although there was anecdotal evidence that the two had always planned to have children, there was no written consent to storage of Mr Blood's gametes prior to insemination, as required by the HFEA 1990. In the end Mrs Blood won her case, but only under EC law on freedom of movement of goods and services, which required the United Kingdom clinic to allow the transmission of the sperm sample to a foreign clinic which was prepared to carry out the post-death insemination treatment.[199] In the light of a review[200] Parliament enacted the Human Fertilisation and Embryology (Deceased Fathers) Act 2003. This has since been repealed but its terms are incorporated in the 2008 Act.[201] These provisions allow for a man to be registered posthumously as the father of a child[202] provided certain conditions are met, the most important

---

[195] J. Savulescu, "Deaf lesbians, 'designer disability' and the future of medicine" (2002) *BMJ*, Vol.325, p.771.

[196] See s.13(9) and (10) inserted by s.14(4) of the HFEA 2008.

[197] *R v Ethical Committee of St Mary's Hospital ex parte Harriott* (1988) 18 Fam. Law 165.

[198] *R v Human Fertilisation and Embryology Authority, ex p Blood* [1997] 2 All E.R. 687.

[199] [1997] 2 All E.R. 687. In the end Mrs Blood had two children posthumously using the sperm of Mr Blood, both conceived via fertility treatment in Belgium.

[200] SAM McLean *Review of the Common Law Provisions Relating to the Removal of Gametes and of the Consent Provisions in the Human Fertilisation and Embryology Act 1990* (1998).

[201] HFEA 2008 ss.39–41.

[202] This is case whether or not the man's own sperm or donor sperm is used in the treatment. Note the separate provisions here for posthumous genetic fatherhood and posthumous non-genetic fatherhood contained in ss.39 and 40.

of which is that consents he consents to this in writing. Such registration, however, is merely a recognition of paternity and has no legal force with regard to other issues such as succession or nationality. Section 46 of the 2008 Act makes similar provision for the registration of a deceased same sex partner or intended female parent as a child's parent. Thus the 2008 Act provides comprehensively for a woman to continue with treatment after the death of her husband, male partner, female civil partner and female same-sex partner.[203] While these provisions are to be welcomed they do not alter the situation raised by the Blood case where the man is unable to consent in writing to the use of his sperm.

Another problematic situation is exemplified in the case of *Evans*. This case **3–100** concerned a woman who had created stored embryos with her male partner via treatment in HFEA clinics, but who had then separated from the partner, who in turn had then withdrawn consent to storage and subsequent uses of the embryos. The principle of the law here is that in essence a man cannot be forced to become a father against his will. In Evans' case however this was a particularly hard situation as she subsequently had cancer and lost any other chance of having children. Her argument that the HFEA rules were thus in breach of her right to respect for family life under Art.8 of the ECHR, was, however, rightly, if harshly, rejected by the United Kingdom courts[204] and eventually, by the European Court of Human Rights.[205] The furore surrounding the case of Mrs Evans led to some amendments to the conditions governing modification and withdrawal of consent to the use of gametes and embryos.[206] They do not resolve the issue as they only provide more time for the gamete donors who are in dispute to achieve a reconciliation, by allowing the embryos to be stored for a further twelve months after withdrawal of consent. Mason and Laurie have argued for greater reform in this area. They point out that within the spectrum of assisted reproduction it is far more difficult for a woman to produce eggs than for a man to produce sperm. Given these disparities in biological contribution to reproduction, they propose that there should be legislation introducing a 'right to management' that would be vested in the proposed woman recipient.[207] While this might place financial liability on the man for the subsequent child this could handled by legislation granting a man wishing to opt out the same legal immunity that is accorded to a sperm donor.

Children and their Genetic Heritage

As noted above, AID has in the past been typically a procedure cloaked **3–101** in secrecy. Egg donors are also usually anonymous unless they are family members. Although donors involved in licensed treatment can no longer be held financially responsible for their offspring[208] there are other reasons why

---

[203] The Act does not address the position where the surviving prospective parent is male.
[204] *Evans v Amicus Health Care Ltd* [2004] 3 All E.R. 1025; [2004] EWCA (Civ) 727. See further SAM McLean, "Creating postmortem pregnancies: A UK perspective" [1999] Juridical Review 323.
[205] *Evans v UK*, European Court of Human Rights, App. No.6339/05, March 7, 2006.
[206] Sch.3, para 4 and 4A.
[207] Mason and Laurie, *Mason and McCall-Smith's Law and Medical Ethics*, 8th edn (2010), p.281.
[208] See para.3–77.

anonymity is desirable. The Warnock Report took the view that anonymity of third-party donors was not only a matter of good practice but protected all concerned from emotional difficulties and, crucially, ensured a plentiful supply of donors.[209] However, occasions may arise where some knowledge of genetic history is desirable for medical reasons, e.g. where a couple plan to marry and fear that they may be incestuously related, or where they wish to check against the possibility of reinforcement of a genetically transmitted disease. Section 31 of the HFEA 1990 thus provided that a child born as a result of treatment services might, on attaining 18, seek non-identifying information of this type from a register kept by the HFEA to be prescribed by regulations. A person under 18 but over 16 who is about to marry can also apply for information.

3–102   In the adoption context there has been general acknowledgment that children who have been removed from their birth families may feel a need to know something about their heritage. The adoption legislation now facilitates this need.[210] If the children of AID and IVF feel the same need to investigate their origins, they have in the past probably been frustrated by what they can obtain from the register, which usually provides access only to basic medical and genetic information, and not the names or personal identifying details of donors unless they choose to supply these. Mason and McCall-Smith have argued in the past[211] that the children of assisted reproduction, unlike adopted children, need never question their maternity nor their paternity, since there will be nothing to indicate anyone other than their parents was involved in their conception judging by the birth certificate or circumstances of birth. However this view has not won the day. In *Rose v Secretary of State for Health*,[212] s.31 was successfully challenged as insufficient on the ground that it potentially infringed the right to identity, which forms part of Art.8 of the ECHR. Accordingly, new regulations were passed which will in future ensure that the children of donated eggs and/or sperm will be able to find out the name, date and place of birth, appearance and last known address of their genetic parents.[213]

The revised 1990 Act now contains extensive provisions for exchange of information between the Authority, the donor and the applicant. While the age at which a donor-conceived person can access identifying information about their genetic parents remains the age of eighteen, now people aged 16 can access non-identifying information at the discretion of the HFEA.[214] They may also request information about half-siblings born as a result of

---

[209] Warnock Report, para.3.03. A survey in 1994 of sperm donors found that 63% would not have donated sperm if their identity was to be made available to resulting children when they reached 18 (HFEA 3rd Annual Report (1994), para.6.1).

[210] Adoption and Children (Scotland) Act 2007 s.38.

[211] See Mason and McCall-Smith, *Mason and McCall-Smith's Law and Medical Ethics*, 7th edn (2005), pp.86–87.

[212] *R. (on the application of Rose and another) v Secretary of State for Health* [2002] 2 F.L.R. 962; (2002) 69 BMLR 83.

[213] HFEA (Disclosure of Donor Information) Regulations 2004 (SI 2004/1511). These regulations are prospective only and so will only apply to children who reach 18 in 2023, i.e. 18 years after the Regulations came into force on April 1, 2005.

[214] HFEA 1990 s.31ZA.

donor treatment.[215] Such persons may also wish to know if they are related to the person they not only intend to marry but also with whom they intend to form a civil partnership or establish an intimate relationship.[216]At the same time, the donor is entitled to know anonymously that inquiries are being made[217] and should he wish to know, he must be informed as to the number, sex and age (but not the identity) of any children born as a result of his donation.[218] In order to facilitate disclosure the HFEA may keep a voluntary contact register for those seeking information about a person to whom they are genetically related.[219] In all these cases disclosure can only be legal if the applicant has been offered counselling.

FUTURE REFORM: BEYOND THE TWO PARENT MODEL?

This chapter has shown us that the question "who is a parent?" is not a simple one, just as in the last chapter we similarly found there was no single definition of a child. There are a multiplicity of different types of parents in the modern world—genetic or "natural" parents, "assisted" parents, surrogate parents, step-parents and social parents—but the law attempts to sort them out by rigid rules into two simple classes: parents and non-parents. As we have seen, these rules are often, inevitably, inconsistent: for example, "licensed" sperm donors are genetic parents but not legal parents, while the husband of a woman receiving AID treatment is a legal parent, though not a genetic one. Despite changes in the law that have extended parenthood to same sex couples there is still an adherence to a two parent model that embraces 'parental dimorphism' in the form of one mother plus one father or female parent[220] who should notionally be involved in a sexual relationship.[221] While the reality of children's lives has brought the model of parenthood based on the heterosexual couple into question nonetheless it continues to frame understandings of parenthood. For although same sex couples now come within its remit, there is still a focus on two parents, only one of whom can be a mother with the other being a father or other female parent.[222] An opportunity was lost to create a new model of parenthood that would not

3–103

---

215 HFEA 1990 s.31ZA(2)(b). But note that this does not include the legal children of the donor. There are also provisions or inter-sibling disclosure of a relationship under s.31ZE.

216 HFEA 1990 s.31ZB(2).

217 HFEA 1990 s.31ZC.

218 HFEA 1990 s.31ZD(3).

219 HFEA 1990 s.31ZF.

220 McCandless and Sheldon "The Human Fertilisation and Embryology Act (2008) and the Tenacity of the Sexual Family Form" (2010) 73(2) *M.L.R.* 175 at p.188.

221 As Wallbank has observed the HFEA 2008 can be "understood as a means of anchoring the same-sex family and regulating women's reproductive power to the heterosexual two-parent tradition". See Walbank, "Channelling the messiness of diverse family lives: resisting the calls to order and de-centring the hetero-normative family"(2010) 32(4) *Journal of Social Welfare and Family Law* 353 at p.365.

222 For a critique of this approach to reform and failure to embrace the possibilities offered by reproductive technologies to radically rethink the nature of parenthood see McCandless and Sheldon above, and Fox "The Human Fertilisation and Embryology Act 2008: Tinkering at the Margins" (2009) 17 *Feminist Legal Studies* 333.

only recognise the social importance of the biological parentage link but that would reserve legal status for those who are the intentional parents who carry out its functions,[223] What this model would involve is de-legalising parentage (formed through the biological link) in favour of privileging parenthood that would constitute "a legally recognised relationship formed from the intention "to parent, ie to care for and look after the child".[224] Under this model both elements would be recorded on the birth certificate so that it would reveal the functional (intentional) parents as well as the biological parents (the sperm and/or egg donor).[225] In many cases these would be one and the same, but for those where this is not the case it provides for recognition that may go beyond the two parent model to embrace multiple parenting.[226] While Scots law has so far been resistant to this, such recognition might well help to deal more equitably with the kind of problems that arise when it comes to the kind of claims that are made with regard to children and the exercise of parental responsibilities and rights that are discussed in the following chapters.[227]

---

[223] See Callus, "A new parenthood paradigm for twenty-first century family law in England and Wales?" (2011) 32(3) *Legal Studies* 347.

[224] Callus, "A new parenthood paradigm for twenty-first century family law in England and Wales?" (2011) 32(3) *Legal Studies* 347 at p.359.

[225] It is argued that basing parental responsibility on intention is the only way in which the interests of lesbian and parents and their children can be adequately protected. See Zanghellini "Lesbian and Gay Parents and Reproductive Technologies: The 2008 Australian and UK Reforms" (2010) 18 *Feminist Legal Studies* 227.

[226] It might also provide a better model for dealing with transgender parentage, for example the case where a transgender man who undergoes gender reassignment but retains the ability to gestate a pregnancy which he undertakes because of his wife's inability to do so. He gives birth to a daughter. How does the law treat such a man who gives birth when it comes to parenthood? For a discussion of this case see McCandless and Sheldon, n.103 above, at pp.201–203.

[227] See Griffiths, "Reconceiving Families and the Ties that Bind: A More Inclusive Approach?", pp.71–103 in J. Scoular (ed.) (2001) *Family Dynamics: Contemporary Issues in Scots Family Law*.

CHAPTER 4

PARENTAL RESPONSIBILITIES AND RIGHTS

In the last two chapters we spoke of the relationship between a child and **4–01** his or her parents as the child's first legal relationship. We have looked at how the law decides who is a child, and who is a parent, for various legal purposes. We have seen to which parents the law gives automatic parental responsibility and rights ("PRRs"), and which are excluded. In this chapter we will discuss the different ways in which the law describes the *relationship* between parents and children: how the law deals with conflict between the rights of parents and the wishes of children, and how the courts resolve disputes about the parent-child relationship. How can children move from being objects of concern to autonomous individuals with their own rights and duties? Should parents be free to bring up their children as they please? In this chapter we will be looking in detail at Pt 1 of the Children (Scotland) Act 1995 (hereafter "the 1995 Act).[1] In the next chapter, specific aspects of parental responsibility and children's rights in Scots law will be examined. Any discussion of parental responsibility must start with some appreciation of the different models for the relationship between parent and child which have been dominant at different stages of the development of Scots family law.[2]

PARENTAL POWER

In Roman law, the father of the household or *paterfamilias* had absolute **4–02** power over his children, whom he could deal with as he wished, even having the power of life or death. This idea of *patria potestas* in somewhat diminished form was received into Scots law and was still found in Stair's time as can be seen from this quote from his Institutes: "The obligation of children towards their parents consists mainly in their obedience to them."[3]

However, by the latter part of the nineteenth century it was clear that **4–03** the *patria potestas* was subject in some circumstances to the control and intervention by the courts. Fraser wrote that where the court was satisfied that

---

[1] Pt 1 of the 1995 Act came into force on November 1, 1996.
[2] For a comparable study of the development of English law, see the seminal article, Eekelaar, "The Emergence of Children's Rights" (1986) 6 O.J.L.S. 161.
[3] *Stair Encyclopaedia*, i. 5.8. For the justification of this and the rest of Stair's views on the matter, based on Higher Authority, see also i.5.1.

"the government of a father is vicious or immoral, or calculated to engender irreligious or atheistical opinions, or that the treatment of the child is cruel, harsh and oppressive, they have an undoubted jurisdiction to interfere for the benefit of the child".[4]

It has been argued that what was being protected at the time was not so much the interests of the child as of society. For example, the protection of children from harsh or oppressive treatment may have been aimed at maximising the labour pool at a time of frantic industrialisation. The protection of the child from "atheistical" fathers may have been intended to safeguard the dominant religious attitudes of the day.[5] Nonetheless, these kinds of decisions by courts to intervene in the custodial rights of fathers are clearly the end of absolute parental rights, and the beginning of what is today enshrined as the "welfare principle".

PARENTAL RIGHTS AND THE WELFARE PRINCIPLE

4–04 It is one of the fundamental tenets of modern child law that parents do not have absolute rights but are only entitled to exercise their rights in the interests of the child. This idea first entered the statute book in 1886,[6] when the courts were instructed when dealing with issues of custody or access to have regard to the welfare of the child concerned. In 1925,[7] the welfare of the child was declared to be the paramount consideration in these kind of disputes. In 1986, the Law Reform (Parent and Child) (Scotland) Act declared with great generality that in any proceedings relating to parental rights, the court should regard the welfare of the child as paramount, a provision now restated in similar terms in the Children (Scotland) Act 1995 s.11(7). Furthermore, s.2(1) of the 1995 Act enacts, for the first time explicitly, that parents only have rights in order to fulfil their parental responsibilities.[8] Responsibilities must be carried out in the interests of the child, so far as this is practicable.[9]

4–05 Even laws which seem on the face of them not wholly at one with the welfare principle, can be reconstructed to fit this mould. For example, Scots parents historically had the right to "reasonably chastise" their children.[10] In more modern terms this was interpreted to mean that parents have the right to hit their children, but only to the extent that the punishment is in the children's best interests and fulfils a parental responsibility, e.g. to provide direction and guidance to the child.[11] If a dispute arose as to whether the parents were misapplying discipline, the court had to decide if the parents were

---

[4] Fraser, *Parent and Child*, 2nd edn (1866).
[5] See on this Eekelaar, "The Emergence of Children's Rights" (1986) 6 O.J.L.S. 161 at pp.162–163.
[6] Guardianship of Infants Act 1886.
[7] Guardianship of Infants Act 1925.
[8] For a more detailed historical sketch see *Stair Encyclopaedia*, Vol.10, paras 1274–1280.
[9] 1995 Act s.1(1). See also infra 4–12, fn.26 for dictum of Lord Fraser of Tullybelton.
[10] Children and Young Persons (Scotland) Act 1937 s.12(7).
[11] 1995 Act s.1(1)(b).

putting the welfare of the child first in making their child-rearing decisions.[12] This illustrates one of the biggest problems that arise when one tries to apply the "best interests" standard: who should decide what it means? The parent (who will maintain that the child needs to learn certain correct behaviour)? Or the child (who will almost certainly not want to be hit)? Or the courts (who may feel by "average" societal standards these particular parents are over-strict disciplinarians)? And is the welfare principle really the only appropriate standard here?

The "welfare principle" protects children from parental excess or caprice **4–06** but it leaves them subject to what Freeman has called "liberal paternalism".[13] This is basically the once uncontroversial idea that parents know better than children do what is good for the latter. If parents are supposed to exercise their rights in the interests of the child, this usually translates as the parents deciding what choices are best for the child concerned. An alternative approach is to adopt "substituted judgment" in which the parents, when deciding what is best for the welfare of the child, do not decide on the basis of what *they* think is good for the child, but consider what the *child* would have felt to be best for him *if he were an adult.* The matter is of general importance and is not restricted to the issue of corporal punishment. The importance of the welfare principle was emphasised in the English case of *Re B (a child)*[14] and there is little doubt that the Court would adopt the same stance in a Scottish appeal. The Court at first instance took the view that a child who had lived with his grandparent for years should nevertheless be moved to the care of the father because he would be a 'good enough parent'. The Court of Appeal agreed, but the Supreme Court did not, saying that there was no room for the concept of the 'good enough' parent and that the welfare of the child was and remained the paramount consideration, trumping any claim based on the biological link.

In reality, choices parents make for their children tend to be examined only **4–07** when they come under the scrutiny of the courts, usually at the instigation of a third party such as social work or the police. In *Re D (Sterilisation),*[15] for example, an educational psychologist brought to the attention of the English courts the planned sterilisation of an 11-year-old girl suffering from Sotos Syndrome, which had impaired her intellectual development. Since the right to consent to medical procedures is an aspect of parental rights, and the child's mother had consented, the operation appeared prima facie to be legitimate. However, Heilbron J. held that the procedure was not in the girl's best interests. Sterilisation should not be undertaken lightly since it would irrevocably remove the girl's basic right to reproduce. On the particular facts of this case, the girl was likely at some future date to be able to make an informed choice about whether sterilisation was appropriate, and might have the intellectual capacity to marry. The mother had consented to the operation because she herself was afraid her daughter would become pregnant and have an "abnormal" child; these were her own fears rather

---

[12] The law has now further restricted any right of reasonable chastisement following significant case law in the European Court of Human Rights: see further below and para.5–11 and 5–14.

[13] Freeman, *The Rights and Wrongs of Children* (1983).

[14] *B (a Child),* UK SC 5.

[15] *Re D (Sterilisation)* (1976) Fam. 185.

than a true consideration of the child's own future welfare and wishes. Since Heilbron J. specially noted that the child might one day look back and feel frustration and resentment that she was sterilised without her consent at such a young age, it is fair to consider this a case where "substituted judgment" was employed.

4–08   In *Re B (A Minor) (Wardship: Sterilisation)*,[16] by contrast, no such consideration of the child's future capacity to choose was possible. Here, the court was asked to decide if the sterilisation of "Jeannette", a 17-year-old girl with very limited intellectual development, was legitimate. Again, both her mother and the doctors concerned supported the operation. Jeannette was of far more limited mental capacity than the girl in *Re D*. Although she was sexually aware, it was unlikely she would ever be able to make a causal link between sexual intercourse and pregnancy. She could not be placed on any effective contraceptive regime. If she became pregnant, all options of termination, natural or Caesarean delivery would be extremely traumatic and possibly dangerous for her, and she was unlikely to be able to care for or enjoy looking after the child. In these circumstances, the House of Lords found sterilisation was in her best interests. Lord Templeman in particular emphasised that this decision was not for the social good but was exclusively made as in Jeannette's own interests:

> "I desire to emphasise once again that this case is not about sterilisation for social purposes; it is not about eugenics; it is not about the convenience of those whose task it is to care for the ward or the anxieties of her family; and it involves no general principle of public policy. It is about what is in the best interests of this unfortunate young woman and how best she can be given the protection which is essential to her future well-being so that she may lead as full a life as her intellectual capacity allows".[17]

Note that in determining Jeanette's welfare, Lord Templeman's emphasis was wholly on what was necessary to *protect* her; there is no reference to what she might have wanted had she had the mental capacity to express her views now or in the future.

4–09   In both these cases, although the legal issue was whether the parent was giving a consent to treatment that was in the welfare of the child, the final decision was truly made by the court. In fact one of the dicta made by the House of Lords in *Re B* was that in future all such decisions to sterilise children of limited mental capacity must be confirmed by the courts.[18] The welfare principle implicitly restricts parental autonomy, and it is one of the continuing tensions in child law how far parents—or families—should be entitled to bring up their children as they see fit, and how far they should

---

[16] *Re B (A Minor) (Wardship: Sterilisation)* [1988] A.C. 199.

[17] *Re B (A Minor) (Wardship: Sterilisation)* [1988] A.C. 199, per Lord Templeman at p.212-C.

[18] *Practice Note, Official Solicitor Sterilisation* [1993] 3 All E.R. 222. See, e.g. *Re F* [1990] 2 A.C. 1. In Scotland, power has been granted by the court to a tutor-dative to consent to the sterilisation of a mentally incapable adult on the best interests principle: *L v L's Curator ad Litem*, 1997 S.L.T. 167.

be restricted by the state and by societal standards to which they may not personally accede.

These tensions can be seen very clearly in a Scottish medical consent case, **4–10** *Finlayson Petr.*[19] Here, a child of nine suffered from severe haemophilia. His parents refused to consent to the child receiving transfusions of the blood product "Factor VIII", partly because of fear he would contract AIDS and partly because they preferred homeopathic remedies. The case was referred to the Children's Hearing who found that although the parents were genuinely concerned for the child's well-being, they were not objectively acting in the best interests of the child. This enabled a finding to be made that the child was in need of compulsory measures of care due to lack of parental care,[20] and allowed the Hearing to impose conditions relating to the child's treatment. Effectively, the parents' view of correct parenting was overturned. Similarly, parental refusal to consent to treatment for their children on conscientious religious grounds has been overridden by the courts.[21]

Clearly, the greatest damage is done to parental autonomy, and the bitter- **4–11** est conflicts caused, when children are forcibly removed into care. The degree of autonomy given to parents tends to be as much a political as a moral choice.[22] Following a number of child abuse scandals[23] in which social work authorities were seen as exercising unreasonable power to the detriment of both parents and children, extensive changes have been made to childcare legislation both in Scotland and England,[24] in a bid to restate the balance between parental autonomy and state power to intervene. We consider this further in Chs 7 and 8.

If parental rights are always subject to the welfare principle, can they really **4–12** be called "rights" at all? They are certainly not rights in the same sense as rights to property, or contractual rights, which impose correlative duties on a defined person or persons, and sanctions if those duties are not met.[25] In *F v Wirral Metropolitan Borough Council*,[26] a mother voluntarily placed her two children in the care of the local authority. Some months later, the local authority decided to compulsorily assume parental rights over the children with a

[19] *Finlayson Petr*, 1989 S.C.L.R. 601.
[20] Social Work (Scotland) Act 1968 s.32(2)(c); now see s.52(1)(c) of 1995 Act.
[21] e.g. *Re E (A Minor) (Wardship: Medical Treatment)* [1993] 1 F.L.R. 386. At levels of life or death however, religious views often remain involved if not decisive in controversial cases. See, e.g. *NHS Trust v MB* [2000] EWHC 507 (Fam) in which the court upheld the decision of parents taken on conscientious religious grounds that the life of thier infant child (who was born severely physically handicapped, but not in a coma or persistent vegetative state) should be preserved by medical intervention such as ventilation, even though the view of doctors was that the child's quality of life was so poor he should be allowed to die. The decision was taken exclusively on a "best interests of the child" analysis, not on the basis of any argument based on right to respect for family and private life under Art.8 of the ECHR.
[22] See Adler, *Taking Juvenile Justice Seriously* (1985), Ch.3.
[23] See, inter alia, *Report of the Inquiry into Child Abuse in Cleveland* ("the Butler-Sloss Report"), Cm.412; *Report of the Inquiry into the Removal of Children from Orkney in February 1991* ("the Clyde Report"); *Report of the Inquiry into Child Care Policies in Fife* ("the Kearney Report").
[24] Children (Scotland) Act 1995 Pt II; Children Act 1989.
[25] In Hohfeldian terms, parental "rights" are not claim-rights but more akin to privileges or even duties. See for discussion of this Eekelaar, "What Are Parental Rights?" (1973) 89 L.Q.R. 210; Dickens, "The Modern Function and Limits of Parental Rights" (1981) 97 L.Q.R. 462.
[26] *F. v Wirral Metropolitan Borough Council* [1991] Fam. 69.

view to placing them for adoption. All this was done legitimately in accordance with the statutory childcare code. The mother, lacking any other remedy, sued the local authority for damages for their interference with her parental right to enjoy the company of her children. The Court of Appeal rejected her claim. Parental rights were not absolute rights but more akin to privileges or claims, derived from parental duty and existing only for the protection of the child. Since the local authority has statutory duties imposed on it to protect the welfare of children, it might well have to interfere with the privilege or right of a parent to the society of his or her child. It would be inconsistent with both the welfare principle and childcare legislation if the authority were found to be liable in damages in a civil action for fulfilling its statutory duties. Hence no common law action lay for interference with parental rights.[27]

4–13   This does not mean that parents have no remedies at all. If, for example, their wishes concerning the medical treatment of their young child were being ignored, they could apply to the courts for, say, a specific issue order under s.11 of the 1995 Act.[28] But such an order, like their "right" itself, would be conditional on the parent's preferred choice of medical treatment being in the child's best interests.

4–14   Another important way in which parental rights differ from conventional property rights is that they cannot voluntarily be relinquished, sold or abdicated.[29] However, it is legitimate to arrange to *delegate* responsibility to someone else, e.g. a friend, relative or baby-sitter,[30] although liability for failure of duty will still lie with the parent or parents.[31] It is competent, and sometimes very useful, to have a Deed of Arrangement under s.3(5) whereby a parent with full parental responsibilities and rights specifically delegates those responsibilities and rights to another person who regularly has the practical care of the child. Such a document, especially if registered in the |Books of Council and Session and extracted, can convince minor officials, medical receptionists and the like, that the person with the actual care of the child is entitled to consent, as a parent, on the child's behalf.

PARENTAL RESPONSIBILITIES AND RIGHTS

4–15   If parental rights, as we have seen, exist only to enable parents to fulfil their parental responsibilities, then the whole concept of rights becomes subservient to, if not quite subsumed by, the idea of *responsibilities*. This is very much the approach taken by the 1995 Act, which for the first time in Scots legislative history lay out a list of parental duties in its first section. It is surely significant that parental responsibilities appear in s.1 of the Act, with parental rights at s2. The latter are subordinate to the former.

---

[27] A Scottish Outer House case, *McKeen v Chief Constable, Lothian and Borders Police*, 1994 S.L.T. 93 appears implicitly to follow the same reasoning as *Wirral*.
[28] See para.4–48, below.
[29] 1995 Act s.3(5).
[30] See *Scott v Occidental Petroleum (Caledonia) Ltd*, 1990 S.L.T. 882 (decided at common law) where it was agreed a mother's responsibility for administering a child's property could be delegated to a judicial factor but not completely transferred to trustees.
[31] 1995 Act s.3(6).

Parents have in relation to their children the responsibility: **4–16**

(a) to safeguard and promote the child's health, development and welfare;
(b) to provide, in a manner appropriate to the stage of development of the child—
  (i) direction;
  (ii) guidance
  to the child;
(c) if the child is not living with the parent, to maintain personal relations and direct contact with the child on a regular basis; and
(d) to act as the child's legal representative.[32]

These responsibilities last until the child reaches 16, with the exception of   **4–17**
s.1(1)(b)(ii) which persists until the child is 18.[33] A parent now has the right:

(a) to have the child living with him or otherwise to regulate the child's residence;
(b) to control, direct or guide, in a manner appropriate to the stage of development of the child, the child's upbringing;
(c) if the child is not living with him, to maintain personal relations and contact with the child on a regular basis; and
(d) to act as the child's legal representative.[34]

It is evident that the new responsibilities of s.1 are intimately related to the rights of s.2. This is only natural as the rights are endowed to enable parents to fulfil their duties. The duty on the non-residential parent to maintain personal relations and regular contact with his child in s.1(1)(c), for example, is enabled by the *right* to contact in s.2(1)(c). The right is not a free-standing right and will not be supported by the Court unless it is in the interests of the child. Thus, if a child resides with his mother in Dumfries and the non-resident father lives in Aberdeen, he may correctly say that because he has a responsibility to maintain contact, he also has a right to do so. If he demands to exercise that right by way of residential contact every second night, he will not succeed in Court because such an arrangement would clearly not be in the child's best interests. A parental right should be interpreted as a parental power—a power to discharge a responsibility rather than a right to be exercised at the unencumbered will of the right holder.

The list of rights in s.2 is comprehensive, superseding any analogous rights   **4–18**
previously enjoyed by parents at common law.[35] What was known as the right of "custody" prior to the 1995 Act has been split neatly into its two aspects: first, the right to regulate the physical residence of the child; and secondly, the more general right to determine every aspect of the child's upbringing. This will include such matters as the right to determine how and where the child

---

[32] 1995 Act s.1(2).
[33] 1995 Act s.1(2).
[34] 1995 Act s.2(1).
[35] 1995 Act s.2(5). *Statutory* rights given to parents, e.g. the right to register the name of the child at birth, are unaffected.

is educated, what religion the child is raised in, how the child's leisure time is spent, what clothes the child wears, with whom he or she associates and a myriad other matters. Not every aspect of "upbringing" however may be regarded as a matter of parental right.[36]

4–19   If a parent does not share a home with his or her child then he or she has the right to maintain contact with that child, a right similar to the pre-1995 right of "access". Such a right might be exercised by visits to, or at, the main place of residence of the child or elsewhere, or by periods in which the child temporarily resides with the non-residential parent, e.g. at weekends, during school holidays. The right to act as the child's legal representative covers acts such as the giving of a legal consent, the representation of the child in litigation and the administration of the child's property, all of which were previously seen as elements of the parental rights of guardianship. Since a legal consent may be required for a wide range of activities such as having a surgical procedure or joining a club or association, there may well be some overlap between the right to direct the child's upbringing and the right of legal representation. We consider some of these aspects of parental responsibility in more detail at paras 5–22 *et seq.*

4–20   All parental *rights* terminate at age 16.[37] This is consistent with the policy of the Age of Legal Capacity (Scotland) Act 1991 that children attain full legal capacity at the age of 16.[38] Yet, even young persons over 16 may benefit during the transient stage between childhood and adulthood of 16 to 18 from parental *guidance* as opposed to control. For this reason, parents are still legally *responsible* for the guidance of their children to the age of 18 although they have no formal right to make choices for them.[39]

4–21   Does the move from talk of parental rights to responsibilities signify a real sea-change in Scots law towards child-centeredness or just a change of terminology? The 1995 Act attempts to give the concept of responsibility teeth by making it plain that children have title to sue parents who fail to fulfil their parental duties.[40] Furthermore, children need no longer be represented by their parents in such litigation, nor by a curator *ad litem* whose principal duty is to the court, but are recognised as having independent capacity to instruct solicitors so long as they are capable of understanding the nature and consequences of such an act.[41] Although doubtless Parliament did not envisage this would cause gangs of disgruntled children to rush out and serve writs on their slovenly parents, it is a valuable remedy. Children might, for example, sue errant divorced fathers who failed to exercise their duty of contact regularly (although it is doubtful how useful a remedy the court could provide). More

---

[36] e.g. in *Flett v Flett*, 1994 S.C.L.R. 189 it was originally held in Scots law that the giving of children's surnames was not a matter of PRRs but merely custom and practice. This was later reconsidered: see Ch.5, para.5.22.

[37] 1995 Act s.2(7).

[38] 1991 Act s.1. See Ch.2.

[39] See *Report on Family Law*, Scot. Law Com. No.135 (1992), paras 2.7–2.13. It was also suggested that persons under 18 were owed such guidance in terms of the UNCRC which defines children as persons under 18.

[40] 1995 Act s.1(3) but see also cases cited at para.4–43.

[41] 1991 Act s.4A, inserted by 1995 Act Sch.1, para.44. See further on a child's capacity to litigate independently, paras 2–38 to 2–44.

seriously, they might sue parents for damages in respect of sexual or physical abuse. However, the courts will probably be unwilling to find a parent negligently rather than deliberately in breach of parental duties. Consider comments made by the Court of Appeal in the English case of *Surtees v Kingston-Upon-Thames Borough Council*[42] in which foster parents were sued for negligently allowing a child in their care to be scalded while bathing:

> "There are very real public policy considerations to be taken into account if the conflicts inherent in legal proceedings are to be brought into family relationships . . . We should be slow to characterise as negligent the care which ordinary loving and careful mothers are able to give to individual children, given the rough-and-tumble of home life".

Having said all this, it is going too far to propose that the parental responsibilities of s.1 should be regarded as giving independent rights to children.

CHILDREN'S RIGHTS[43]

The 1995 Act is arguably not concerned with children's rights, though we **4–22** may note that the parental responsibilities are largely derived from the United Nations Convention on the Rights of the Child which was ratified by the UK on December 16, 1991. As we have seen, it clearly states that parental rights exist only in order to further the interests of children and not the interests of parents. However, this is not the same as saying the Act gives *children* rights. An example helps to illustrate this. In the case of *Finlayson Petr*, discussed above, the parents' view of how best to fulfil their parental duties was rejected by the courts in the interest of the child involved. Essentially, the parental right to decide was replaced by the right of the courts to decide. At no point in the case was the opinion of the child himself, a 9-year-old boy, canvassed as to whether he supported his parents' views on medical treatment; and whatever his wishes were, they would not legally have decided the issue (though they might have contributed to the court's view of what his best interests were). He had no *right* to decide his medical treatment but was subject to the desire of his parents, themselves subject to the restraint of the welfare principle.

Similarly, in divorce cases, where there is disagreement between parents as **4–23** to post-divorce arrangements for children, the court is instructed to decide which parent shall have the child living with them, and any issue of contact, on the basis that the welfare of the child is paramount but *having regard* to

---

[42] *Surtees v Kingston-Upon-Thames Borough Council* [1991] 2 F.L.R. 559.
[43] There is a large body of literature on the nature of children's rights which it is outwith the scope of this book to deal with in detail, A useful collection is *The Ideologies of Children's Rights* (Freeman and Veerman (eds), 1992); see also the essays in 5 *International Journal of Law and the Family* (1991), and *Children's Rights in Scotland* (Cleland and Sutherland (eds), 3rd edn (2009)). See also the extensive discussion on the inter-relationship of children's rights in domestic law and international human rights standards below and at paras 2–06 *et seq.* above.

the views of the child.[44] In such cases, it is not unusual for the court to hear the wishes of the child but these wishes will not bind the Court. The justification is that children, depending on their age and maturity, do not always know what is best for them. In *Fowler v Fowler*,[45] for example, a pre-1995 Act custody case where the views of the child concerned were put forward in evidence, Lord Stott said:

> "I am fully conscious of the fact that that while in questions of custody the interest of the child is the paramount consideration it cannot be assumed that a child's interests necessarily coincide with her wishes."

He subsequently went on to consider whether or not the child's views had been unduly influenced by pressure from one or both parents, before accepting them. This paternalistic attitude is perfectly acceptable in accord with the welfare principle under the 1995 Act but does not accord children *rights* in the divorce process.[46]

4–24   There are many definitions of rights but what they tend to have in common is the idea that a right must be respected by those against whom it can be said to operate. If the right is flouted then the rightholder can use the rules and agents of the legal system to protect and assert it. Feinberg states that:

> "Rights are not mere gifts or favours, motivated by love or pity, for which gratitude is the sole fitting response. A right is something a man can stand on, something that can be demanded and insisted upon without embarrassment or shame."[47]

Adults can vindicate their right to ownership of their own property in the courts. They can ask a court to restore their right to freedom if they are imprisoned for no legal cause. Children may be able to sue their parents to fulfil their PRRs under the 1995 Act but they cannot, within that Act's schema, ask the court to uphold their right, say, to live with their father rather than their mother *unless* they can convince the court this is in their best interests. Effectively, this means, in the strict sense, the child does not have the right of freedom of residence in the same sense as an adult does. Of course a child may simply refuse to stay with the allotted parent and run away; he or she retains de facto power, depending on age. But this is not the same as having legal rights.[48]

---

[44] 1995 Act s.11(7)(a) and (b).

[45] *Fowler v Fowler*, 1981 S.L.T. (Notes) 9. See also *Russell v Russell*, 1991 S.C.L.R. 429 and para.4–87 below.

[46] For further consideration of the wishes of the child in residence and contact orders see para.4–87.

[47] Feinberg, *Social Philosophy* (1973), pp.58–59.

[48] Kathleen Marshall makes this point strongly, stating that if children's rights in decision making are not recognised, they will subvert parental attempts to control them (Marshall, "Rights and Responsibilities in the Family", unpublished paper available from Scottish Child Law Centre, 1993).

DOMESTIC CHILDREN'S RIGHTS AND THE INFLUENCE OF INTERNATIONAL HUMAN RIGHTS STANDARDS

In recent years, however, as discussed above at paras 2–05 *et seq.*, the land- **4–25**
scape of children's rights has shifted radically as a result of greater awareness
of international human rights standards, both in the form of general human
rights instruments and those tailored directly for children. In Ch.2, we discussed how the incorporation of the European Convention on Human Rights
(the "ECHR") into United Kingdom domestic law in the Human Rights Act
1998 provides basic guarantees of fundamental civil and political rights to all
United Kingdom citizens, which are now directly enforceable in *all* United
Kingdom courts (not just final courts of appeal after exhaustion of other
remedies, or at the European Court of Human Rights in Strasbourg). For the
first time therefore, children (although not mentioned as a particular subset
of citizens empowered by the ECHR) can at least in theory make claims for
enforcement of their private law rights in United Kingdom domestic courts,
without necessarily having those claims mediated by the "best interests"
principle. (Perhaps, more unfortunately, the same is also true for claims made
by parents in respect of their rights *over* children.[49]) This has the potential
to revolutionise the effectiveness of child rights, and we have already seen
considerable change in the law as a direct result of challenges made under
the ECHR. Corporal punishment of children, for example, was banned from
local authority schools as a result of a Strasbourg ECHR case, *Campbell
and Cosans v UK*[50] and more recently, the parental "right of chastisement"
discussed at para.4–05 above was abolished as a result of the Strasbourg case
of *A v UK*.[51] Parental rights to discipline children physically remain, but in
extremely attenuated form.

The UN Convention on the Rights of Children ("UNCRC"), arguably **4–26**
the most influential and authoritative source of rights for children in modern
law as discussed in Ch.2, is, meanwhile, not a source of Scots or United
Kingdom law, having not yet been incorporated. It is thus merely persuasive
in Scots courts. However it is often cited in Scottish child law cases and was
one of the leading influences on the drafting of the 1995 Act. Furthermore
the Government of the United Kingdom is under an international obligation
to bring its domestic law into line with the minimum standards set by the
Convention and must periodically supply reports on its progress in meeting
this obligation. At the time of writing the Scottish Government's Children
and Young People (Scotland) Bill is being considered in Parliament. The Bill
purports to reflect in domestic law the role of UNCRC in influencing the
design and delivery of services and to put duties on ministers.

One right asserted in the UN Convention has particular significance for **4–27**
private law rights and is implementable without the need for comprehensive economic programmes: the right of the child to be consulted in Art.12.

---

[49] However the Scottish courts have so far successfully attempted to resist incursion into the
welfare principle by the "rights based discourse" of the ECHR. See Ch.2 generally on adoption and human rights.
[50] *Campbell and Cosans v UK* 1982 4 E.H.R.R. 293.
[51] *A v UK* [1998] EHRLR 82; [1999] 27 E.H.R.R. 611. See further Ch.5 at paras 5–11 *et seq.*

Article 12 states that:

> "1. States parties shall assure to the child who is capable of forming his or her own views the right to express those views freely in all matters affecting the child, the views of the child being given due weight in accordance with the age and maturity of the child.
> 2. For this purpose, the child shall, in particular, be provided the opportunity to be heard in any judicial or administrative proceedings affecting the child, either directly or through a representative or an appropriate body, in a manner consistent with the procedural rules of national law".

It is this right, the right to be heard and thus to participate in decisions, rather than to actually make or take control of decisions, which is unequivocally protected and recognised by the Children (Scotland) Act. Section 11(7)(b) of the 1995 Act provides that when a court is making any order relevant to parental responsibilities or rights then it shall have regard so far as practicable to the views (if he or she wishes to express them) of the child concerned, taking account of his or her age and maturity. Furthermore, a child aged 12 or more is presumed to be sufficiently mature to form a view.[52] In practice the Scottish Courts have been willing to take into account the views of very much younger children in s11 cases. The criterion is the age and maturity of the child rather than the chronological age.[53] The extent to which the views of a very young child will be taken into account will depend also to some extent on the nature of the matter in dispute. Although this is newly stated in statute, it is nothing very novel in the law of Scotland. As we have seen above in *Fowler*, the courts have always been prepared to consider the views of the child concerned as one of the factors relevant to making a decision about custody or access (now residence and contact). However, this has never compelled them to accept the views of children as decisive and s.11(7)(b) does nothing to alter this.

4–28   What is more radical is the provision in s.6(1) of the 1995 Act that where *any person* makes a "major decision" relating to parental responsibility or rights then they shall have regard as far as practicable to the views of the child.[54] Again, this is subject to the child's age and maturity and a 12-year-old child is presumed sufficiently mature to form a view. In theory, this affects every serious decision made by a parent. For example, parents who are divorcing often execute minutes of agreements which make detailed arrangements as to with whom the children should reside and what contact arrangements should be made for the non-residential parent. Such agreements are subject to the scrutiny of the court during the divorce process to see whether they are in the welfare of the child, but are usually rubber stamped. Parents must in theory consult their children of sufficient age and maturity before making such agreements. What sanctions are there for non-consultation? Presumably

---

[52] 1995 Act s.11(10).

[53] See *Shields*, 2002 S.L.T. 579.

[54] They should also take account of the views of any other person with parental responsibilities and rights. The difficulties of deciding what is a 'major decision' within the meaning of teh Act were discussed in *Clayton v Clayton*, 1995 G.W.D. 18-1000.

the court could refuse to accept the provisions of the minute if there was inadequate evidence of consultation. In most parental decisions however, the courts are not directly involved, e.g. if parents choose to move the household, without consultation, from Edinburgh to Lerwick, and in such circumstances it is hard to see what practical legal remedy there could be even if the children went so far as to sue the parents for their failure in duty of consultation. The Act also specifically provides that lack of consultation cannot be grounds for challenging a transaction entered into by a third party in good faith, e.g. if a parent acting as legal representative sold a 12-year-old child's house to a bona fide third party without the child's knowledge or consent then the child could not have that sale reduced.[55] There was considerable scepticism at the time that s.6 was passed that its effect would be symbolic only, and many years on it is still unclear if parental consultation is embedded in practice as well as theory. A pilot study by the Scottish Executive in 2002 found that there were still problems with respect to hearing the "voice of the child": social barriers to child representation and participation in legal proceedings still remained (see also Ch.2); children have difficulties accessing the information necessary to participate (though the Internet may have partly ameliorated this since); and gender differences exist, with boys finding it less easy than girls to talk to their families. More training for legal and other professionals would also help children to participate in decisions.[56] The very existence of ss.4 and 4A of the Children (Scotland) Act 1995 flies in the face of any apparent duty to take the views of a child affected by the deed. There is no practical test, before registration of an agreement under either section, that the child has even been informed, far less consulted, by its parents.[57]

Can it be said then that the 1995 Act does not only protect children but also gives them significant rights? The right of consultation found in ss.11 and 6 is a far cry from the kind of children's rights espoused by radical child liberationists. Writers such as Richard Parson and John Holt have argued for the equal treatment of children under the law, which they take to mean having equal rights like adults to work for money, vote and take a full part in political affairs, travel and live away from home, control (or abandon) their own education, handle their own financial affairs, engage in sexual relations legal between consenting adults and generally run their own lives in a self-determining fashion. They argue that age is as suspect and discriminatory a reason to withhold rights as race or gender once were, that some children exceed some adults in cognitive ability, and that in any case, adults are not tested on their cognitive capacities before they are allowed to vote, work, etc. As Parson has put it, "The only people in our society who are incarcerated against their will are criminals, the mentally ill and children in schools".[58] **4–29**

There is little sympathy for this kind of extreme advocacy of children's **4–30**

---

[55] 1995 Act.6(2).

[56] See Marshall, Tisdall, Cleland at al., *"Voice of the Child" Under the Children (Scotland) Act 1995: Giving Due Regard to Children's Views In All Matters That Affect Them, Parts 1 and 2* (Scottish Executive Central Research Unit, 2002).

[57] The matter is addressed in *M Petrs*, 2010 S.L.T. 587 and *M v G*, 2010 G.W.D. 17–339 and in Wilkinson & Norrie, 3rd edn, para.6.12.

[58] Parson, *Birthrights* (1978), p.96.

rights in Scots law and for good reason. The corollary of rights is responsibility, and if we are to give children these kind of rights of self-determination then we are also logically giving them responsibility for their own survival,[59] and the power not only to run but also to wreck their own lives. Freeman, for example, justifies compulsory education of children and restrictions on child employment, because if children are not forcibly given the opportunity to gain an education then they will not be able to maximise their future development and realise their potential for a future as a rationally autonomous person. He argues persuasively that the ideas of child rights and child protection are not so opposed as has been presented thus far, and that respect for the personality of children can be expressed by protection consonant with their age and maturity, as well as respect for their independent capacity.[60] Another way to say this perhaps is that one of the rights of children should be a right to a childhood.[61]

4–31   The right to consultation can be regarded in this context then as a kind of compromise between child protection and child autonomy: it gives children the chance to participate in and influence decisions affecting them, but it does not allow them through immaturity or inexperience to jeopardise their own future. While parents and children have roughly harmonious goals, this seems a viable solution. But we must turn now to examining how serious conflict between the wishes of parents, and children as they approach adulthood, is handled by the law.

CONFLICT BETWEEN CHILDREN AND PARENTS

4–32   In the discussion so far we have talked, for simplicity, of children as if they were all of the same kind. But it is of course apparent that children vary considerably in their maturity and capacity to understand and thus to make their own choices. In particular, adolescent children approaching the age of 16 and full capacity have a special claim to have their choices given weight. They are also more likely to find themselves in conflict with parents than younger children as an inevitable part of the process of growing up, and particularly, reaching sexual maturity. Above, we noted that by s.2(7) of the 1995 Act, parental rights extend until the child reaches 16. Thus it seemed that children to this age have no independent rights to make their own choices, but are subject to the rights of parents, who are themselves responsible for exercising these rights in accordance with the welfare principle.

4–33   This model does not fit well with the current international appreciation for the rights of children, nor with the idea that children are of steadily growing capacity throughout their childhood. Scots law historically recognised the emerging capacity of older children by dividing persons below the age of majority into pupils, who had little or no active legal capacity, and minors,

---

[59] Bainham, for example, points out that if children are emancipated from parental rights and responsibility, it seems hard to justify why parents should be under an obligation to pay maintenance (1994 J.S.W.L. 552).
[60] Freeman, *The Rights and Wrongs of Children* (1983), Ch.2.
[61] Freeman, *The Rights and Wrongs of Children* (1983), p.3.

who were still subject to the control of their parents or guardians in relation to their property, but were free to make their own decisions concerning their person. However, this distinction was removed by the Age of Legal Capacity (Scotland) Act 1991, which states in s.1 that children under 16 in principle have no legal capacity to enter any juristic transaction (subject to some important exceptions) while children over 16 have essentially full adult legal capacity.[62]

However, this is not the end of the story for children under 16. In Ch.2, **4–34** we considered in detail the case of *Gillick v West Norfolk and Wisbech Area Health Authority*,[63] an English case but one which has been accepted as highly influential in Scots law. Here the House of Lords held that, exceptionally, children under 16 have the right to give their own consent to medical treatment, provided they have attained a degree of maturity and understanding sufficient to appreciate the risks and advantages of the treatment proposed; a standard that has since become known as "*Gillick*-competence". There was, however, dissention between Lords Fraser and Scarman as to whether a child could only be regarded as "*Gillick*-competent" if he or she were acting in his or her best interests. Lord Scarman held that competence involves only "sufficient understanding and intelligence" which would mean competent children would be free, like adults, to make mistakes as well as wise choices in their own welfare.

It is clearly the ratio of *Gillick* that, if a child is found to be *Gillick*- **4–35** competent, not only does he or she have the right to consent, but also a parent cannot exercise any right of veto. So a girl of 15 who is found to be *Gillick*-competent can go on the Pill without having to get the consent of her parent, and even if the parent finds out and opposes this course, this will have no legal effect.[64] Lord Scarman in a key dictum put it as

> "parental right *yields* to the child's right to make his own decisions where he reaches a sufficient understanding and intelligence to be capable of making up his own mind on the matter requiring decision".[65] [Emphasis added.]

On the face of it, this seems to imply quite plainly that where a child is competent to consent, parental rights terminate. Thus, if a competent child refused to consent, the parent's right to consent would have terminated and so no-one could consent to the procedure: hence the child would have an effective right to refuse any procedure.

However, English cases subsequent to *Gillick* have interpreted it quite **4–36** differently. In *Re R (A Minor)*[66] a girl aged 15 years and 10 months suffered from severe mental health problems including psychotic episodes. The

---

[62] Discussed in detail in Ch.2.
[63] *Gillick v West Norfolk and Wisbech Area Health Authority* [1985] 3 All E.R. 402. See Ch.2.
[64] However, it must be noted that both Lords Scarman and Fraser felt that a doctor was under a duty to try *to persuade* the child to consult with parents.
[65] *Gillick v West Norfolk and Wisbech Area Health Authority* [1985] 3 All E.R. 402, per Lord Scarman at 422a.
[66] *Re R (A Minor)* [1991] 4 All E.R. 177. See also *Re W* [1992] 4 All E.R. 62.

question arose as to whether the local authority, who had assumed parental rights from her natural parents, could consent to psychiatric treatment, including the administration of drugs, even if R herself *refused* to consent. R was found in the course of proceedings not to be "*Gillick*-competent" due to the fluctuating nature of her mental capacity, but Lord Donaldson chose anyway to discuss how the issue would have been resolved, if she had been so competent. He found that even if R had the right to consent, the *parent's* right to consent did not totally disappear but was simply no longer able to defeat any consent given by the child. Thus, even if the child *refused* to give a consent, there was nothing to stop the parent supplying it. Lord Donaldson chose to regard both the child and the parents as "keyholders": both parents and child hold a "key"—the right to consent to treatment—but if one does not choose to "unlock the door", that is, give consent, this did not mean another keyholder cannot. Thus, even if R refused to take anti-psychotic drugs, the local authority could still give consent for them to be given.

4–37   In Scotland, as we saw in Ch.2, the kernel of *Gillick* was put on a statutory basis in s.2(4) of the 1991 Act, which provides that children under 16 can consent on their own behalf to any surgical, medical or dental procedure where, in the opinion of a qualified medical practitioner, they are capable of understanding the nature and possible consequences of the procedure or treatment. No Scottish case has yet authoritatively decided if the right to "consent" of s.2(4) includes the right to refuse consent[67] and in this absence of authority *Re R* must thus be regarded as persuasive. This would be bad news indeed for children's rights in Scotland, as it appears to sanction the possibility of mature and competent children being subjected against their wishes to drug treatment, compulsory hospitalisation, and possibly even abortion or surgical procedures such as the removal of organs for donation. In *Houston*[68] Sheriff McGowan found that a mother did not have the right to give a consent to detention of her 15-year-old son, when the son himself, who, it was conceded, was competent under s.2(4), was refusing consent. In his view "the patient [was] competent and entitled to decide not to accept the medical treatment prescribed for him. That refusal is not overridden by the consent given by the mother". These remarks, though strongly asserted, do however appear to be obiter and therefore not binding on future courts.

It is arguable that s.15(5) prevents a parent from granting consent to treatment where the competent child has refused it though the terms of the subsection refer to 'transactions' rather than to treatment.

4–38   Most Scottish commentators, such as Wilkinson and Norrie, have, however, taken the view that *Re R* and *Re W* do not represent the law of Scotland and that the right to consent does include the right to refuse consent.[69] Current NHS guidance notes to doctors in Scotland also recommend

---

[67] In *V v F*, 1991 S.C.L.R. 225, Sheriff Poole found parents had the right to consent to the treatment of a 15-year-old girl for depression, even in spite of her own refusal to accept treatment (hospitalisation). However, the case was decided prior to s.2(4) coming into force, and it is difficult to tell from the report if the girl in question was regarded as "*Gillick*-competent" or without legal capacity to consent; hence it is of little value as a precedent.

[68] *Houston*, 1996 S.C.L.R. 943.

[69] See Wilkinson and Norrie, 2nd edn, para.8.50; L. Edwards, "The right to consent and the right to refuse" [1993] Jur Rev 52.

that the refusal of treatment by "competent young people" under 16 "must be respected".[70]

This leaves one final concern: do the *courts* have the right to override the wishes of the *Gillick*-competent child? To this the answer is almost certainly yes,[71] so long as the child is under the age of 16 the court retains the right to make an order "in relation to (a) parental responsibilities [and] (b) parental rights".[72] We examine the criteria the courts will apply when deciding whether to make a s.11 order in the next section.

4–39

Section 2(4) of the 1991 Act deals only with medical treatment, as does the *ratio of Gillick*. However, there seems no good policy reason why mature minors approaching the age of 16 should not be able to make their own choices in other areas which would previously have been dealt with solely by parents by virtue of their parental rights. For example, children who are mature enough to understand the nature and consequences of their choices should be able to make their own choice of religion, even if it is not clearly in their welfare, e.g. a religion which encourages the giving away of all one's property, or forbids the use of modern medicine, despite parental opposition. Similarly competent children should be able to determine their own residence. These were rights which once accrued to a Scots child at a predetermined age of minority (12 for a girl, 14 for a boy) but which are better seen now as arising from a certain degree of cognitive capacity and emotional maturity rather than mere attainment of age. As with the right to consent to medical treatment, if a child is competent to consent then the parent's right to determine the issue should terminate.

4–40

Court Orders

The courts may become involved with the relationship between children and parents for a number of reasons. As we have seen, outside agencies, such as hospitals, may apply to the courts to establish if parents are exercising their rights in the welfare of the child concerned. Children themselves may invoke the jurisdiction of the court in order to assert their own rights or to challenge parental discretion. It is not uncommon for a person with no PRRs, such as an unmarried father, step-parent or grandparent to apply to the court for full PRRs or some aspect thereof (e.g. rights of contact with the child). Most commonly, however, the courts will be invoked because of a conflict of wishes between two persons who both have PRRs. This conflict most frequently arises in the context of divorce.

4–41

---

[70] *A Good Practice Guide on Consent for Health Professionals in NHS Scotland (Scottish Executive Health Dept 2006)*. See especially Ch.2 of the Guide.

[71] In England, it was established in *Re W* (above) that the courts could override the wishes of a child until the age of 18 by virtue of their inherent protective jurisdiction. In Scotland, it seems highly unlikely the child over 16 but under 18 could be subjected to the authority of the court, even via the *nobile officium*, since the whole scheme of modern child law is that the child over 16 is *sui juris. Sed quaere* Lord Hope's comments in *Law Hospital NHS Trust v Lord Advocate*, 1996 S.L.T. 848.

[72] 1995 Act s.11(1). Logically, it could be asserted that once the child is competent, the issue is no longer one of *parental* rights and therefore the court has no jurisdiction. However, the court is likely to regard the issue as one falling into their competence since parental rights and responsibilities under ss.1 and 2 last prima facie until the child is 16.

Applications for Parental Responsibility and Rights

4–42   Under s.11 of the 1995 Act, an application can be made to the court in relation to parental responsibilities, parental rights, guardianship or the administration of the child's property. Such an application can be made by:

(a) persons who already have parental responsibilities or rights, such as, typically, married parents;

(b) persons who have never had parental responsibilities or rights but claim an "interest"[73]; and

(c) the child[74] him or herself.

(d) persons who have lost parental responsibilities and rights in respect of the child for a reason other than one mentioned in s11(4) [footnote: The r4easons which exclude an entitlement to apply for a parental responsibilities and rights order are that the parent's former responsibilities and rights have been extinguished by an adoption order or by an order in terms of s30(9) of HFEA 1990 or by transfer of responsibilities and rights to a local authority.

Who qualifies as a person who "claims an interest" in relation to s.11? Obvious candidates include unmarried fathers without automatic PRRs, grandparents and siblings of the child concerned, who may be seeking contact, perhaps if the child has been adopted by new parents who have no desire to maintain contact between the newly adopted child and the natural relatives.[75] In *F v F*,[76] Lord Hope took a general liberal approach to the question of interest. His attitude was that the requirement of a claim of interest "was not intended to restrict the category of [applicants] with results which could in some cases be contrary to the best interests of the child". It would seem that not only blood relatives and carers, but also anyone with a connection to, or interest in, the welfare of the child, such as a friend, teacher, doctor, health visitor, etc. can claim the requisite "interest".[77]

4–43   Controversy has also arisen in relation to title to sue in s.11 applications for contact by children under 16. As noted above, s.11(5) clearly contemplates that s.11 applications might be made by children themselves, as well as their parents, or other holders of PRRs, so long as they could claim "interest". Yet in *D v H*,[78a] it was held by Sheriff Principal Bowen, on rather technical grounds,[79] that a 15-and-a-half-year-old boy was not entitled to seek an order

---

[73]   1995 Act s.11(3)(a)(i) and (ii).

[74]   1995 Act s.11(5). For a child's right to instruct a solicitor and raise an action in his or her own name, see paras 2–39 to 2–44.

[75]   A sister in this position was held to have "interest" in *AB v M*, 1988 S.L.T. 652 (decided in relation to s.3 of the Law Reform (Parent and Child) (Scotland) Act 1986).

[76]   1991 S.L.T. 357 (again, decided in relation to s.3 of the 1986 Act). See also *M v Lothian Regional Council*, 1989 S.L.T. 426.

[77]   A restrictive approach to title and "interest" was however applied to a same-sex partner in *X v Y* (2002) Fam. L.R. 58 (see para.4–76 below). It is submitted this case was wrongly decided. A preferable authority can be found at *E v E*, 2004 Fam. L.R. 115.

[78a]   *D v H*, 2004 S.L.T. (Sh. Ct) 73. For further discussion see 2004 Fam. L.B. 71.

[79]   The basic argument is that s.11(2)(b) of the 1995 Act only allows the court to impose responsibilities and rights on persons who are "at least 16 years of age" (or a parent of the child in

under s.11(2)(d) for contact with his 14-year-old sister. The policy argument underlying is that since parental rights are given to persons to further the exercise of parental responsibilities, the Act did not contemplate parental rights being granted to persons under 16 who cannot fulfil such responsibilities. Not only does this run against the longstanding policy of Scots law that a liberal attitude to title to sue in family actions should be adopted (see para.4–40 above) but it also seems to fly in the face of the 1995 Act's general empowering attitude towards children's rights in general, and children's rights of independent litigation in particular. *D v H* was distinguished (though not over-ruled) in the Dundee Sheriff Court case of *E v E*.[80] The key distinction asserted was that the pursuer in *E v E* had a better case on the merits than the boy in *D v H* and therefore should not be denied the opportunity to pursue his case. The sheriff took note also however of the rights of the child under both the ECHR and the UNCRC and declared, correctly, that Parliament must be presumed to have legislated in accordance with these Conventions and that the important factor was, therefore, the best interests of the child. The sheriff's view is supported in Wilkinson & Norrie, 3rd edn, 8.11.

An application can be made under s.11 either as an independent action, or **4-44** as an ancillary issue to divorce proceedings.[81] The action can be raised in the sheriff court or the Court of Session. In independent applications, the Court of Session has jurisdiction if the child is habitually resident in Scotland at the date of the application, or is present in Scotland and not habitually resident in any other part of the United Kingdom.[82] It also has an emergency jurisdiction to hear the case if the child is present in Scotland and at the date of the application it is necessary for the protection of the child to make an order immediately.[83] The appropriate sheriff court has concurrent jurisdiction on the same basis with the additional proviso that the child be habitually resident, or present (as appropriate) in the sheriffdom.[84] In relation to s.11 applications specifically relating to the administration of the child's property, the Court of Session has jurisdiction if the child's property is situated in Scotland or the child is habitually resident in Scotland; the sheriff court has jurisdiction if the property is situated, or the child is habitually resident in, the sheriffdom.[85] Where a s.11 application is made relating to the guardianship of the child, jurisdiction is based on the child's habitual residence in Scotland or as appropriate, the sheriffdom.[86]

---

question). Section 11(2)(d), which allows the making specifically of a contact order, has no such restriction. The order in *D v H* was sought under s.11(2)(d) exclusively, but the Sheriff Principal accepted that contact orders are all sub-sets of orders imposing PRRs made under s.11(2)(b).

[80] *E v E*, 2004 Fam. L.R. 115.

[81] 1995 Act s.11(1) and (1A) as amended by European Communities (Matrimonial Jurisdiction and Judgments) (Scotland) Regulations 2001 and then by European Communities (Matrimonial and Parental Responsibility Jurisdiction and Judgments) (Scotland) Regulations 2005. See Ch.14 for background to the divorce process and ancillary actions, and jurisdiction to raise them.

[82] Family Law Act 1986 ss.9(a) and 10(a).

[83] Family Law Act 1986 s.12.

[84] Family Law Act 1986 ss.9(b), 10(b) and 12.

[85] 1995 Act s.14(1) and (2).

[86] Family Law Act 1986 s.16.

4–45   All the above is now, perhaps unfortunately, subject to mandatory European rules of jurisdiction, known as Brussels II *bis*,[87] governing all Member States of the EU. Decisions about jurisdiction between different parts of the UK still fall under the rules of the Family Law Act 1986. In most domestic cases involving parents and children exclusively Scottish habitually resident, the new rules are likely to make little difference. But in cases involving a foreign element, these rules may be very significant.

4–46   The Regulation covers cases involving "parental responsibility" whether or not the action is connected to an action of divorce, judicial separation or nullity. So actions for say, contact or residence, in relation to children of an unmarried couple, or stepchildren, are included.[88] "Parental responsibility" includes rights of custody and access, guardianship, actions to do with the child's person or property, fostering and the protection of the child. It does not however cover parentage, adoption, the name of the child, maintenance (aliment), trusts or succession.[89] In general, under Art.8 of Brussels II *bis*, the courts of a Member State have jurisdiction if the child is habitually resident[90] in that Member State at the time the court is seised. However under Art.9, if the child moves lawfully[91] (i.e. not by means of abduction or retention) to another EU Member State, the courts of his former habitual residence retain jurisdiction in relation only to variation of access or contact rights for three months. (This rule applies only if the holder of access/contact rights remains in the former state and there is no agreement ("prorogation") for a new jurisdiction to be in charge of the matter.) Parties can agree on a new jurisdiction to hear disputes relating to parental responsibility so long as this is in the welfare of the child.[92] If a court cannot be identified from the above rules to hear an action for parental responsibility, the court where the child is present shall have jurisdiction.[93] This also applies to refugee and internationally-displaced children. In exceptional cases, a court can transfer a child case to a court it regards as better placed to hear the case.[94]

---

[87] EC Council Regulation No 2201/2003 which came into force with direct effect in the UK (and throughout the EU) on March 1, 2005. It repealed the previous Brussels II Regulation No 1347/2000. For clarity, Brussels II *bis* is also incorporated into Scots law by the European Communities (Matrimonial and Parental Responsibility Jurisdiction and Judgments) (Scotland) Regulations (SSI 2005/42). Reg.5 of the 2005 Regulations expressly applies the EC rules to ss.9, 11 and 13 of the Children (Scotland) Act 1995. The amendments only apply to actions commenced after March 1, 2005.

[88] Art.1(1), Brussels II *bis*.

[89] Art.1(2) and (3), Brussels II *bis*.

[90] "Habitual residence" is not defined in the Regulation. Instead, it is to be interpreted according to the case law of the court where the matter arises (Art.66). Accordingly in Scotland, existing Scottish case law on "habitual residence" is relevant.

[91] If the child moves *unlawfully*, i.e. as a result of removal or retention in breach of custody rights acquired by law or by court order or by agreement, then the rules as to when the court may accept jurisdiction are different, and somewhat similar to those in the Hague Convention on the International Abduction of Children 1980, though stricter: see Arts 2(11) and 10 and 11. However Brussels II *bis* takes precedence over Hague for EU Member States: see Art.66. The question of child abduction, and the problems it rises in relation to jurisdiction, recognition and enforcement of judgments relating to parental responsibilities and rights, are beyond the scope of this text.

[92] Art.12, Brussels II *bis*.

[93] Art.13, Brussels II *bis*.

[94] Art.15, Brussels II *bis*.

In actions for divorce, judicial separation or declarator of nullity of marriage, the court not only has jurisdiction but also the obligation to consider whether it is necessary for them to make a s.11 order in relation to any child of the family under the age of 16.[95] In other words, if the court felt it necessary it might, for example, make an order that a child reside with a third party, if neither parent seemed a suitable carer given the evidence presented during the divorce hearing. In exceptional cases, the court can postpone granting the decree of divorce (or other decree) until it has given further consideration to the case, if it feels this is desirable in the interests of the child.[96] It might wish to seek more information in the form of independent reports on the welfare of the child, or hear evidence from the child him- or herself.[97] The court's other option in such cases is to refer the child to the children's hearings system, specifying that a particular ground of referral has been found to be established. In such circumstances, the Principal Reporter retains a discretion to decide if a hearing should be convened, depending on whether he feels the child is in need of compulsory measures of supervision.[98]

4-47

Types of s.11 Order

Section 11(1) provides that the court can be asked to make any order it thinks fit in relation to parental responsibilities or rights, guardianship or the administration of the child's property. As well as this general power, some particular "named" s.11 orders can be sought. These include:

4-48

A *residence order*,[99] which regulates with whom a child under 16 is to live. A parent with a residence order may thus choose to look after the child at home, or decide the child should live elsewhere, e.g. with a relative during the holidays. The order can specify that a child resides with different people during specified periods. For example, the child might live with the mother during term and the father during school holidays. A contact order (see below) could regulate each parent's right to contact during their non-residential period;

A *contact order*,[100] which regulates the arrangements for maintaining personal relations and direct contact with a child under 16. The order can specify that this may be exercised by personally at a supervised venue such as a local authority contact centre, at the home of the non-residential parent, or elsewhere; or via letter, telephone, email, etc. It might also make provisions as to time periods or that leave that to agreement[101];

---

[95] 1995 Act s.12(1) and (3). A "child of the family" includes any child of *both* the parties getting divorced, or any other child who has been *treated by both parties* as a child of their family (other than a foster child placed by a local authority or a voluntary organisation): s.12(4).

[96] 1995 Act s.12(2).

[97] See below, paras 4–55 to 4–59.

[98] 1995 Act ss.12(1) and 54. See further, Ch.8.

[99] 1995 Act s.11(2)(c).

[100] 1995 Act s.11(2)(d).

[101] There is clearly a cross-over between applying for a residence order and applying for a contact order which involves a certain amount of residence, e.g. overnight stays. *McBain v McIntyre*, 1996 S.C.L.R. (Notes) 181 illustrates how seeking the wrong order can cause problems and gives some guidance.

A *specific issue order*,[102] which regulates any specific issue which has arisen, or may arise, in relation to parental responsibility, rights, guardianship or the administration of a child's property. A typical example where this may be useful is where, after divorce, the parents continue to share parental responsibility and rights but the child lives with the mother, who gives consent to the school nurse to vaccinate the child for rubella. Since either parent can exercise a parental right without the consent of the other,[103] legally only a court order can interfere with a decision of the mother. The father can dispute the mother's decision, by asking the court to resolve this specific issue. Similar applications might be made in respect of one parent's decision about the child's education, religious upbringing, residence in the United Kingdom or leisure. In *G v G*[104] the mother sought a specific issue order that the daughter attend a private fee-paying boarding school at the father's alimentary expense. On appeal the father successfully defeated the claim, on the grounds that there was no reason as yet to disturb the status quo under which the girl was attending an excellent day school. An alternative order in such circumstances would be:

- An *interdict prohibiting the taking of a particular step*[105] in fulfilment of parental responsibility or rights. Taking the scenario above again, the father could dispute the mother's decision to consent to vaccination by asking the court to interdict the step she had taken. In such cases, the decision of the court will primarily rest on the welfare principle, not the wishes of either parent;
- An order *depriving* a parent of parental responsibility or rights.[106] This would be the appropriate order to seek if, for example, it was desired to entirely remove a parent's rights, e.g. the right of a father to deal with a child's property where he had proved financially corrupt or incompetent;
- An order *imposing* upon a person parental rights or responsibilities.[107] This would most typically be used where a person *without* automatic responsibility and rights, such as a grandparent, sought rights in relation to a child. As discussed in para.4–42, such orders cannot be imposed on a person under 16 unless they are the parent of the child in question;
- An order appointing or removing a person as a *guardian* of the child.[108]
- An order in respect of a *proposed relocation* of a child to another jurisdiction without the consent of the other parent.

Section 11 also contemplates the making of a number of orders specifically relating to the management of a child's property, which are discussed in more detail at paras 5–29 to 5–31. Any reference in s.11 to an order includes a reference to an interim order, or any order varying or discharging an order.

---

[102] 1995 Act s.11(2)(e).
[103] 1995 Act s.2(2).
[104] *G v G*, 2000 (59) Fam. L.B. 5.
[105] 1995 Act s.11(2)(f).
[106] 1995 Act s.11(2)(a). See also *AY v MM*, 2012 G.W.D. 33–674 which has been subject to negative comment in Wilkinson & Norrie, 3rd edn, para.8.09.
[107] 1995 Act s.11(2)(b).
[108] 1995 Act s.11(2)(h). See below, Ch.6.

CRITERIA FOR MAKING A S.11 ORDER

There are three basic principles under s.11(7) which the court is instructed to **4–49**
bear in mind when making any s.11 order.

The Welfare of the Child is Paramount

The welfare or "best interests" principle has been the paramount consider- **4–50**
ation of the court in cases relating to parental rights (and now, responsibility)
since the Guardianship of Infants Act 1925. What is meant by the "welfare
of the child" is a classic problem of linguistic open texture. Hundreds if not
thousands of reported cases have turned on the interpretation of this phrase.
Below we will discuss how the welfare principle has been construed in existing
case law.

*The court should not make any order unless it considers it better than making
no order at all*

This has been called the *minimum intervention principle*,[109] and implements **4–51**
an important part of the general philosophy of the Children (Scotland) Act,
namely that courts should not interfere unnecessarily with the arrangements
reached by a parent, or parents. (As we will see in Ch.7, courts are instructed
to take a similar approach in relation to the making of orders taking children
into local authority care.) Prior to the 1995 Act, it was common and indeed
often virtually automatic for courts to award sole custody to one or other
parent, whether this was by the agreement of the parents or, less frequently,
after a disputed proof.[110] Although custody was only one of several parental rights held jointly by married parents, such a sole custody award was
often perceived as effectively removing the non-custodial parent from any
involvement with, or responsibility for, the child's life. Divorce was seen as
a carve-up, in which the winner gained custody, and the loser, if they were
lucky, took access rights as a consolation prize.

The SLC recognised this as an unsatisfactory state of affairs, and preferred **4–52**
when reconsidering the law to reinforce the notion that "a child will continue
to have two parents after separation or divorce who share responsibility
for his/her upbringing".[111] Under the 1995 Act, not only is the terminology of sole custody dispensed with, but joint responsibility is actively promoted. Since married parents automatically share PRRs prior to divorce,
the minimum intervention principle implies that an award of sole PRRs to
one parent on divorce—the nearest equivalent of the former "sole custody"
award—must be positively justified by the party seeking it as better than no
award. The Act thus effectively implements a presumption that joint parental
responsibility will be the norm after divorce. If parents are seen as owing
responsibilities to their children, rather than as having rights, then it should

---

[109] Nome, *Children (Scotland) Act 1995*, 2nd edn (2004).
[110] In 90% of ordinary divorce actions involving children in 1991, an award of sole custody to
one or other parent was made (92% to mother, 7% to father): Morris, Gibson and Platts,
Untying the Knot: Characteristics of Divorce in Scotland (1993).
[111] *Report on Family Law*, Scot. Law Com. No.135 (1992), para.2.29.

rarely be in the interests of the child to deprive one parent unnecessarily of such responsibility.[112]

4–53   One result of the minimum intervention principle, at least initially, was that it discouraged the award by the courts of shared PRRs to unmarried couples whether cohabiting or not. Unmarried fathers with no automatic parental rights, it was thought, had the onus of proof against them and thus had to show the court by positive evidence of some kind that it was better to make an order in their favour than to leave the legal status quo as it stood. In a number of post-1995 Act cases, argument on this point dominated the case more than the actual merits. The perceived difficulties raised for unmarried fathers would, in any case, have been severely diminished by the granting of automatic PRRs to many or most unmarried fathers by the Family Law (Scotland) Act 2006 (see para.3–18). However since these provisions are not retrospective, it is fortunate the courts have also chosen to clarify the issue. The notion of an onus of proof for parties without existing PRRs was dispelled in the Inner House case of *White v White*.[113] In a stirring judgment, Lord McCluskey[114] made it plain that:

> "Nowhere in the 1995 Act do I find a provision that, in arriving at a decision in relation to contact between a father and his daughter, the paramount consideration shall be the onus of proof".[115]

Lord Rodger further clarified the law. If onus was no longer an issue, then on what basis was the court to make a s.11 order? Quite simply the court must "consider all the relevant material and decide what would be conducive to the child's welfare." Or even more simply, the decision in *White* returns the law to the basic principle that the welfare of the child is paramount and should be assessed on the balance of probabilities, on what evidence is available, independent of any question of presumptions and onuses.

4–54   Along with the minimum intervention principle, comes the idea that any order made under s.11 should have the *minimum effect necessary* to achieve its purpose. Section 11(11) states that any order shall have the effect of depriving a parent of rights and responsibilities only so far as expressly stated and only to the extent necessary to give effect to the order. This has important implications again for post divorce or separation arrangements. If during divorce proceedings, one parent applies for and gets a residence order in relation to a child, then, unless expressly stated to do so, this order should not deprive the other parent of any of his or her rights and responsibilities under ss.1 and 2 (except, obviously, the right to determine the child's residence).[116] Thus, it

---

[112] A notable pre-1995 Act case in which the sheriff accepted this argument and thus refused to make any order for custody for either party is *Potter v Potter*, 1993 S.L.T. (Sh. Ct) 51. See also *Ross v Ross*, 1997 S.L.T. (Sh. Ct) 51 (decided under pre 1995 Act rules), but *cf McNeill v McNeill* (1997) Fam. L.B. 30–7.

[113] *White v White*, 2001 S.L.T. 485 (IH).

[114] Effectively also therefore, on this point, reversing the decision from which he had previously dissented in the Inner House in *Sanderson v McManus*, 1995 S.C.L.R. 902 (I.H.), discussed below at paras 4–100 to 4–101.

[115] *White v White*, 2001 S.L.T. 485 at 493L–494A.

[116] Note, however, that if the person in favour of whom a residence order is made does not have

is not in any way equivalent to the "carve-up" described above which was the common result of the old law. Where one parent truly wishes to remove the other parent from having any involvement with or responsibility for the child's life, they will have to seek an order explicitly depriving that parent of all rights and responsibilities. The court will then have to decide if such an order is appropriate on the basis of the s.11 criteria. In the pre-1995 Act case of *Clayton v Clayton*,[117] the father of the child was a 72-year-old professor of genetics and the mother, with whom the child lived, a Ph.D. student some 30 years his junior. The father, who was notably cantankerous and strong-willed, sought constantly by virtue of his joint parental rights to question and undermine the mother's decisions about the child, in relation to health and leisure as well as education. The court agreed to award sole custody to the mother on the grounds that the father's constant interference was undermining her confidence as a single parent, and this was not in the welfare of the child. It is submitted that a similar decision would now be made to award PRRs solely to the mother.

The court shall, as far as possible, have regard to the views of the child, taking into account the child's age and maturity

A child aged 12 or more is presumed to be sufficiently mature to form **4–55** a view, without prejudice to the possibility of a child under that age being sufficiently mature.[118] As discussed above, this provision formally meets the requirements of Art.12 of the UNCRC which states that children have a right to be heard in any judicial proceedings affecting them. It is necessary to consider however: (i) how children are to be given an opportunity to indicate they wish to express their views; and (ii) by what method they can then effectively communicate their views.

Prior to the 1995 Act, disputes as to parental rights, especially in the context **4–56** of divorce, were largely seen as disputes between adults in which children were the objects of the process, not participants. Parents, not children, were the parties to the action.[119] The vast majority of divorces are undefended and involve only affidavit evidence, and even in those that are defended on issues relating to parental rights, only a very small fraction involve the hearing of oral evidence.[120] Furthermore, in around a quarter of divorces, disputes between parties, including disputes over the children, are settled by means of a joint minute of agreement negotiated between parties and presented to the courts very much as *a fait accompli*.[121] Thus, it is illusory to imagine that the

---

all the parental rights and responsibilities of ss.1 and 2 then they shall have them all while the order is in force (s.11(12)).

[117] *Clayton v Clayton*, 1996 G.W.D. 18–1000.

[118] 1995 Act s.11(10).

[119] A child could, in theory, join the action as a party minuter. However, in practice this was virtually unheard of.

[120] In 1991, 79% of ordinary divorce actions were undefended and proved be means of affidavit evidence only, and 19% were defended and proved by affidavit only. Only 2% of actions involved the hearing of oral evidence. See Morris, Gibson and Platts, *Untying the Knot: Characteristics of Divorce in Scotland* (1993).

[121] See Wasoff, McGucken and Edwards, *Mutual Consent: Written Agreements in Family Law* (Scottish Office, Central Research Unit, 1997). "Joint minutes of agreement" are agreements

courts frequently hear direct evidence of the views of children. A more realistic summary is that the courts usually accept the arrangements of parents unless these are the subject of dispute, or there is other evidence at hand, from parties such as a social worker, psychologist or advocate, which attracts more detailed inspection. Moreover, the courts increasingly attempt to encourage parents to agree on arrangements for their children, if necessary by referring them to mediation.[122] There are no guarantees that children will be given a voice in mediation, nor that their interests will be paramount. Children are also sometimes seen as too vulnerable to be involved in the brutality of divorce mediation. However attempts are being made by mediation practitioners to involve children more in such mediation, as required by their right of consultation under s.6 of the 1995 Act.[123]

4–57 The views of children are thus most often supplied to the courts indirectly via affidavit evidence produced by the competing parties, via partisan lay or expert witnesses such as educational psychologists, or at best via independent reports. The court has the power to order an independent report, usually compiled by a solicitor, advocate or social worker,[124] and a sheriff may choose to hear direct oral evidence from a child, although, again, in the past this has been the exception rather than the rule. The Rules of Court governing procedure in family actions were reformed after the 1995 Act[125] in an attempt to give children a better opportunity to participate in legal processes affecting their welfare—in particular, the divorce of their parents.

4–58 First, in any action affecting a child under 16, that child must receive intimation of the action, via a form written in "child-friendly" language, which provides brief details of the action and invites the child to inform the sheriff if he or she has views he or she wishes to express.[126] The sheriff has discretion to postpone or dispense with intimation, e.g. where the child

---

lodged with the court to which the court interpones its authority. In 1990 they featured in 20% of ordinary Scottish divorce actions. Separating parents also often make "minutes of agreement" which are simple contracts about the separation arrangements not forming part of a court process. Around 70% of minutes and joint minutes made by parties with children contain arrangements between parties as to who the children should live with. Minutes would be presented as part of the documentary evidence the court sees, and would rarely be questioned in an undefended divorce. See further, Ch.15.

[122] See Ordinary Cause Rules 1993 (hereafter "OCR"), 33.22.

[123] It is difficult to find out how many children actively participate in the mediation of their parent's divorce or separation. The Family Mediation Scotland Annual Review 2005 gives no clues, but does indicate that 71% of the children "involved in" their mediations are under 12 and therefore do not prima facie have s.6 rights. The website of CALM, the association of solicitor-mediators in Scotland, gives no such figures.

[124] The court can order such reports either under common-law powers or by virtue of the Matrimonial Proceedings (Children) Act 1958 s.11.

[125] Act of Sederunt (Family Proceedings in the Sheriff Court) 1996 (SI 1996/2167).

[126] OCR 33.7 (as amended) and Form F9. Rules of the Court of Session 1994 (hereafter "RCS"), 49.23. If the child concerned is too young to understand or might be upset or traumatised by being told about the action then as an alternative, r.33.33(7) provides that the pursuer can crave that intimation be dispensed with, and averments justifying dispensation must be included in the initial writ along with the crave. If neither intimation nor crave for dispensation is included in the writ then it is faulty: see *Gallacher v Gallacher*, 1997 S.C.L.R. (Notes) 174.

is too young to understand the issues. Secondly, the sheriff is given a wide discretion to take such steps as he or she sees necessary to ascertain the views of the child.[127] This attempts to meet difficult problems associated with asking children to give evidence in court. Children are easily intimidated by the prospect of giving oral evidence in a courtroom, yet sheriffs have felt uneasy in the past about speaking to children in their chambers, as such private communications do not have the status of proven evidence.[128] Furthermore, children will often be unwilling to publicly give evidence preferring one parent to the other. An important provision in the rules allows a sheriff to record the views of a child, as expressed by the child him or herself or a third party, or in writing supplied by the child, and seal those views as confidential in the court process.[129] Sheriffs may however *choose* not to seal evidence as confidential for reasons discussed in the next paragraph.

One of the main problems for children expressing their views is acknowledged to be that without guarantees of confidentiality they may not be able to speak freely, either directly to a court as party[130] or witness, via affidavits, or through a third party such as a curator *ad litem*. Children, especially younger and more vulnerable children, often do not wish to be seen as taking the side of one parent against the other. Sometimes children will be afraid of admitting what they feel or know if there is a risk of a parent finding out afterwards, e.g. where they are making allegations of physical or sexual abuse. They may be physically scared of one or other parent. For this reason, it is often said that confidentiality is an essential part of giving children a voice in legal proceedings. **4–59**

In *Dosoo v Dosoo*[131] two children, aged 14 and 12, were interviewed by the sheriff and contributed their views on contact to a report which had been ordered by the court. This report partially contributed to the father being denied contact. The children asked that their views remain confidential. The father asked for disclosure of the children's views (asking, in fact, for the envelope to be unsealed) and arguing that to refuse to do so would be a breach of his rights to a fair hearing and respect for his right of family life, under Arts 6 and 8 of the ECHR. The Sheriff however held that she was *not* required to reveal the record to the father. The children were clearly afraid of the repercussions if their father read what they had said. The sheriff went on to observe as a general rule **4–60**

> "that for a child to be able to express his views 'freely' he must be able to feel confident in privacy if he so wishes, and the court should respect that privacy except in very compelling circumstances."

---

[127] OCR 33.19(2). RCS 33.27A.
[128] *MacDonald v MacDonald*, 1985 S.L.T. 244.
[129] OCR 33.20.
[130] See for example *Henderson v Henderson*, 1997 Fam. L.R. 120, discussed above at para.2–37. Although the child in question, a 10-year-old girl, did successfully win the right to join the case as a party with her own independent representation, she was unable to speak in confidence to the judge about her father having contact with herself.
[131] *Dosoo v Dosoo*, 1999 S.L.T. (Sh. Ct) 86; 1999 S.C.L.R. (Notes) 905.

This approach also respected the children's rights to a voice in proceedings under Art.12 of the UNCRC.

4–61 *Dosoo* was reconsidered in *McGrath v McGrath*.[132] In *McGrath* the child wished to express her views to the sheriff via her curator *ad litem* but for them not to be revealed to her parents. The father asked for disclosure, but lost at first instance. On appeal, the Sheriff Principal attempted to balance the interest of the father, in disclosure of the case against him as part of natural justice, with the interest of the child in confidentiality and free expression, drawing on the English House of Lords case of *Re D*[133] and the European Court of Human Rights case of *McMichael v UK*.[134] In *Re D*, the House of Lords had declared that to decide such issues the court must go through a three-part test:

(i) determine whether disclosure of the material would involve a real possibility of significant harm to the child;
(ii) if it *would* involve such a risk, consider whether the overall interests of the child would benefit from non disclosure; and
(iii) finally, if satisfied the interests of the child pointed to non-disclosure, then that consideration had to be *weighed against* the interests of the parent or other party in disclosure.

The outcome was that, unlike in *Dosoo*, in *McGrath* the father won a rehearing. Sheriff Principal Bowen noted ruefully that:

"The practicalities involved in reconciling the right to a fair hearing and a child's right to express his views are thus of immense difficulty. They can best be resolved in my view by having regard to the principles set out by Lord Mustill [in *Re D*, above]".

4–62 One point not canvassed in *Dosoo* and *McGrath* is the right of *the child* to a fair hearing under Art.6 of the ECHR, which, it could be argued, is prejudiced if confidentiality of submissions cannot be guaranteed. But since *McGrath*, the matter of confidentiality seems to have reached an uneasy solution. The Sheriff in *Onyenyin v Onyenyin*[135] considered the question, concluding that the welfare of the child was a relevant factor but not the paramount consideration in deciding whether or not the views of the child should be kept confidential. The argument seems sound, but it does make it difficult for solicitors to advise young clients about the confidentiality of any views which the young client may wish to express. Certainly, no guarantee can be given. Until the matter is definitively addressed in the Inner House, we can say only that *McGrath* probably represents the law of Scotland.

---

[132] *McGrath v McGrath*, 1999 S.L.T. (Sh. Ct) 90; 1999 S.C.L.R. (Notes) 1121.
[133] *Re D* [1995] 4 All E.R. 385.
[134] *McMichael v UK* [1995] 20 E.H.R.R. 205.
[135] *Onyenyin v Onyenyin*, 1999 G.W.D. 38–1836.

Welfare

When making a residence order, the paramount concern of the court is the   **4–63**
welfare of the child. Innumerable factors can be taken as affecting the child's
welfare, amongst which only the most prominent are the physical and emotional welfare of the child, the age and sex of the child, the characteristics of
the parents or other applicants including their moral, material, spiritual and
sexual nature, the relationship of the child with others sharing a proposed
residential household, the psychological security of the child and so forth.
Interpreting the welfare principle has been described rather imprecisely in the
House of Lords as,

> "a process whereby, when all the relevant facts, relationships, claims
> and wishes of parents, risks, choices and other circumstances are taken
> into account and weighed, the course to be followed will be that which
> is most in the interests of the child's welfare as that term now has to be
> understood."[136]

In England, courts are assisted by a statutory checklist of factors to take into   **4–64**
account when making an order under the Children Act 1989. No such checklist occurs in the 1995 Act, but there is help in the case law relating to custody
and access under the older law as well as in post-1995 cases. Thịese older
authorites must be treated with caution for a number of reasons. First, these
decisions were based solely on the welfare principle, while s.11 applications
must also be decided with reference to the minimum intervention principle
and the wishes of the child concerned, and so a different balancing of factors
may result. Secondly, and more importantly, however, a decision on custody
prior to 1995 was, as we have seen, factually if not legally, often equivalent
to a comprehensive disposal of the child to one parent, not simply a decision
on where the child should reside. Thus many factors which the court has
sometimes regarded as extremely significant in deciding custody, such as the
child's moral welfare or one parent's sexuality, may be regarded as less so
when making a residence order, where the non-residential parent continues
in law to play an important role in the child's life.

Another caveat that is true of all authority in this area is that each case   **4–65**
is not properly a precedent but simply an example. No case turning on the
welfare principle can ever have a truly determinate outcome, at least within
a conventional doctrinal analysis.[137] The welfare principle ideally demands
a comprehensive approach in which all the disparate factors that may be

---

[136] *J v C* [1970] A.C. 668, *per* Lord MacDermott at 710–711.
[137] See Lord Jauncey in *Brixey v Lynas*, 1996 S.L.T. 908 which was concerned with whether a
maternal preference exists in respect of a child of tender years: "[This case] raises no question
of legal principle and is devoid of merit" (at 909B). For a discussion of how decisions about
children based on the welfare principle can be made potentially predictable by reference to a
non-doctrinal feminist analysis, see Edwards, "Modelling Law Using a Feminist Theoretical
Perspective" (1995) 4 Law, Computers and Artificial Intelligence 95. It is important to consider long term factors too: see *Senna-Cheribbo v Ward*, 1999 S.C. 328.

relevant are identified, studied and balanced. The courts have thus firmly declared that there is no pre-eminent right of a mother to be the "natural custodier" of her child. Even to suggest so would be to subvert the proper test of the child's best interests.[138] Nor is there a pre-eminent right of a natural or biological parent to be preferred to a non-parent if the latter can provide overall the better environment.[139] Similarly, a foreign decree can never simply be accepted by a Scottish court as determining the issue of residence even if it has been issued by a court of competent jurisdiction who have conducted a satisfactory enquiry into the facts.[140] The welfare principle must be the court's first concern, and the order of the foreign court, though deserving of "grave consideration", cannot prevent the domestic court from reaching a different conclusion if necessary.[141] Finally, it is clearly a breach of the welfare principle to prefer the "innocent" party in a divorce to the "guilty" one,[142] (at least if on that ground alone) and in any case this distinction is now meaningless in divorces granted on grounds of non-cohabitation. The courts will always prefer, in any given case, to apply the tests in s.11(7) of the 1995 Act than to be unduly influenced by reported authorities in superficially similar cases.

Status Quo

4–66   One way of short-cutting the Herculean task of balancing all the factors in a case is to adopt a shorthand method. The Scottish courts have developed such an approach in their use of what has become known as the status quo principle. When a couple with children split up, there is often a reasonable space of time before any (non-interim) application relating to parental rights and responsibility is adjudicated by the courts. This is obviously particularly true in the context of no-fault divorce. During this time, some settled arrangement will usually arise for the care of the child; in the majority of cases, for example, de facto care is assumed by the mother. The courts will often actively choose to preserve this existing arrangement, known as the status quo, since it can be relatively easily ascertained if the existing situation is in the child's welfare or not. It is more difficult for the courts to guess on inadequate evidence what other arrangement might be better for the child.

---

[138] See *Dance v Archibald*, 1989 G.W.D. 13–535, *per* Lord Cameron of Lochbroom; *Mooney v Mooney*, 1987 G.W.D. 3–80; *Whitecross v Whitecross*, 1977 S.L.T. 225.

[139] *Breingan v Jamieson*, 1993 S.L.T. 186, although *cf.* Lord Morison's comments in *Clark v Clark*, 1987 G.W.D. 35–1240.

[140] *Sinclair v Sinclair*, 1988 S.L.T. 87; *Campins v Campins*, 1978 S.L.T. (Notes) 41. Although this principle is now rather undermined in the interests of expediency by the Hague and Europe Conventions on Child Abduction (see note below).

[141] The prospects for undeterred forum shopping this seems to open up are restricted by the provisions of the Child Abduction and Custody Act 1985, which implements two international conventions on child abduction for the UK. Although outwith the scope of this book, the net effect is, broadly, that cases arriving in the Scottish courts and involving children habitually resident in a Convention signatory country are not investigated on the merits and instead the child is returned to that country for the case to be adjudicated, unless there are very good reasons not to return the child. See also *Calleja v Calleja*, 1996 S.C.L.R. (Notes) 963 in which the Inner House applied broadly these same rules to a case concerning a country not signatory to these conventions (Malta).

[142] *Hume v Hume*, 1926 S.C. 1008, in which the court asserted a presumption still existed in favour of the spouse innocent of matrimonial fault, is now universally understood to be overruled.

Thus a working, if not necessarily optimum, arrangement can be safely rubber-stamped by the court. In addition, there is psychological evidence that continuity of relationships is important to children post-divorce, which the courts appear to have implicitly adopted judging from their frequent references to stability as a major positive aspect of childcare arrangements.[143]

In *Breingan v Jamieson*[144] the mother of a seven-year-old girl tragically **4–67** died young. The daughter's custody[145] was subsequently disputed by, on the one hand, her father, who had lost custody of the child some years earlier on his divorce from the mother, and on the other, the maternal aunt, who had looked after the child since the mother's death along with other maternal relatives. Lord MacLean found that although the child had a good relationship with her father and his new wife, and there was no reason they could not supply her with a home, nevertheless, to remove her "to a totally different environment would be disruptive of her settled, happy life and detrimental to her best interests". This trumped the claim of the father which was "based effectively upon his role as the child's natural or biological parent".

In recent years, the Scottish courts have tended not to reverse the status **4–68** quo. Although the principle can only ever assist in interpreting the welfare principle, and cannot replace it, it can fairly be said that there is a presumption that the preservation of the status quo is in the child's best interests.[146] This is true even when it is arrived at by means other than consensus. In *Black v Black*,[147] a wife left her husband, along with the two sons of the marriage, because of his "social drinking" and went to stay with her father in England. Later, the husband took the sons back to the former family home in Scotland on an access visit and refused to return them. About a year later, he sued for custody. At first instance, custody was awarded to the mother. On appeal to the sheriff-principal it was held that, despite the disadvantages of the father's lifestyle—which included excessive encouragement of football to the detriment of traditional education, as well as habitual imbibing—the welfare of the boys was favoured by "the security of the life which they have with their father in familiar surroundings, with friends and at a school they know and like".[148] The sheriff-principal went on to add, in response to the claim that the status quo was being given undue weight, that "the fact that the status quo is not a paramount consideration does not mean that it is an unimportant one".[149] In the remarkable case of *Sherwin v Trumayne*[150] an unmarried father abducted his very young son from the mother, in breach of the Irish

---

[143] Goldstein, Freud and Solnit, *Beyond the Best Interests of the Child* (1973) is regarded as the most influential text promoting this theory. See also Wallerstein and Kelly, *Surviving the Break-Up: How Children and Parents Cope With Divorce* (1980).

[144] *Breingan v Jamieson*, 1993 S.L.T. 186.

[145] The words "custody" and "access" are used in relation to cases heard prior to November 1, 1996 when the Children (Scotland) Act 1995 Pt I, came into force, although, under that Act those words have been rendered meaningless.

[146] See *Hannah v Hannah*, 1971 S.L.T. (Notes) 42; *Breingan v Jamieson*, 1993 S.L.T. 186, above; *Brixey v Lynas*, 1996 S.L.T. 908, above, and cases discussed, below.

[147] *Black v Black*, 1990 S.L.T. (Sh. Ct) 42.

[148] *Black v Black*, 1990 S.L.T. (Sh. Ct) 42 at 461.

[149] *Black v Black*, 1990 S.L.T. (Sh. Ct) 42 at 46J.

[150] *Sherwin v Trumayne*, 1992 G.W.D. 29–1681.

custody order she held, and cared for him alone for over a year before applying for custody in Scotland. Despite the circumstances, the judge was not prepared to reverse the status quo and rejected claims that his decision was a "kidnapper's charter". The test was the welfare of the child, not that of either competing party.[151]

It appears then that some fairly negative factor or combination of factors is required before the courts will reverse an otherwise apparently stable and beneficial status quo situation. In *Kyle v Stewart*,[152] for example, a mother entrusted her child to her sister shortly before taking a fatal overdose. Although the sister then looked after the child, the natural father was subsequently awarded custody. The main negative factors seem to have been the sister's immaturity and the fact that she was already herself an unmarried mother.[153] Many of the cases cited below turn, explicitly or otherwise, on whether some negative aspect of the status quo is sufficient to persuade the courts to make an award altering it.

Although commentators have discussed the status quo principle, it is not truly a principle at all, but merely an observation that if one of the competing proposals can be shown to have been successful over a significant period of time then that is a factor (not a principle) giving that proposal an advantage over a contrary proposal which has not been tried.

Parental Care, Behaviour and Lifestyle

4–69   Since a parent with residence will be the primary carer for a child, it is of vital importance that an order should not be made in favour of a parent who will do damage to the child's mental or physical welfare. Violent behaviour, aggression and bad temper,[154] severe drunkenness and alcoholism,[155] or a history of child neglect on the part of a parent will thus, as one might imagine, be negative indicators, unless they are past problems which are highly unlikely to revive.[156] A residential parent must be able to supply the child with the essentials of life including food, clothes, lodging and emotional sustenance.[157] Either poverty, unemployment, or physical or mental disability may impede a parent in his or her ability to supply some or all of these, but frequently such disadvantages can be ameliorated by the availability of welfare benefits and social work support. In the past, the Scottish courts have generally taken the approach that disparities in financial means between

---

[151] See also *Basinski v Basinski*, 1993 G.W.D. 8–533. The court will not usually, however, decide on the merits if a child has been abducted in breach of a court order from a foreign country, or in breach of foreign custody rights—see further above.

[152] *Kyle v Stewart*, 1989 G.W.D. 14–580.

[153] See also *Hastie v Hastie*, 1985 S.L.T. 146.

[154] *Geddes v Geddes*, 1987 G.W.D. 11–349

[155] In *Shearer v Shearer*, 2004 G.W.D. 38–773, the court granted residence to a working father in preference to the mother, who though a full-time carer, had a history of drinking.

[156] In *Early v Early*, 1989 S.L.T. 114; 1990 S.L.T. 221, the father had two prior convictions for child neglect and had drunk heavily in the past, but was now seen as a reformed character and was awarded custody (albeit in competition with a lesbian mother). See also *R v M*, 2011 G.W.D. 1–33 in respect of past violence with a continuing effect.

[157] In *Shishodia v Shishodia*, 1995 G.W.D. 17–926 a father lost custody, inter alia, because he sent a boy child out on several occasions wearing female clothing.

two competing parents can be settled by an appropriate award of aliment, and that consequently, the emotional support and stability a household can offer should be regarded as more important than material advantages.[158] An unemployed father who can be a full-time carer might therefore be preferred to a working mother.[159] However, since the advent of the Child Support Act 1991, aliment for children is no longer at the discretion of the court assessing residence, and child support is quantified using a standard inflexible formula in all but exceptional cases.[160] This may have made it more acceptable to the courts to take cognisance of financial matters. In *Brixey v Lynas*,[161] the dispute was between a father from an affluent middle-class background and a mother from a discernibly less privileged background. The sheriff in award-ing custody to the father commented that "I have . . . come to the view that I should not deprive the child of the advantages which the accident of her paternity make available to her".[162] Although his award was later reversed, on this point he was expressly affirmed by the Inner House, who found that the advantages of background and environment were relevant. On the other hand, those advantages could not be decisive, and other considerations such as the long-term future of the child and her emotional security should hold sway.

Abuse

A particular problem in Scottish society is the prevalence of domestic vio- **4–70**
lence, particularly by men against female partners. It can be argued in theory that violence against a *partner* does not necessarily impact upon any *child* of the household, but empirical evidence has shown that the indirect effects on children of growing up in a climate of domestic abuse are deleterious even where the child is not physically harmed.[163] Furthermore violence against a partner can be a sign that children of the household are also being abused or potentially at risk.

How should such violence be taken into account when making a s.11 **4–71**
order? On the one hand it can be argued that a violent partner may still be a loving and non-violent one. On the other hand, the welfare of the child is, research shows, most closely connected to the welfare of the primary carer,

---

[158] *Geddes v Geddes*, 1987 G.W.D. 11–349.
[159] *Sloss v Taylor*, 1989 S.C.L.R. 407.
[160] See Ch.5. Although an award of financial provision under s.9(1)(c) of the Family Law (Scotland) Act 1985 can be made in order to share fairly the economic burden of caring for a child after divorce, the extent of any claim under that provision is probably restricted to such expenses as after-school clubs, etc.: see *M v S*, CSOH 125, 2008 SLT 871. This was an Outer House cohabitation case, but it derived its argument from an analogy with s.9(1)(c) of the 1985 Act A similar award can now be made under the Family Law (Scotland) Act 2006 where unmarried parents separate, and under the Civil Partnership Act 2004, where same sex partners terminate their civil partnership.
[161] *Brixey v Lynas*, 1994 S.L.T. 847, appealed to House of Lords, 1996 S.L.T. 908. This point was not, however, argued on appeal.
[162] *Brixey v Lynas*, 1994 S.L.T. 847 at 849. Both father and mother were unemployed.
[163] See M. Hester, "Domestic violence and child contact arrangements in England and Denmark 1996" and M. Kaye, "Domestic Violence, residence and contact" (1996) 8 Child and Family Law Quarterly 285.

for whom an award of contact with a violent ex-partner may mean continuing risk of abuse and terror. In countries like New Zealand, rules have been adopted that if there is evidence of domestic violence which seems to affect the child, there is a presumption of no contact between the violent parent and the child. In Scotland a more flexible solution was adopted in the Family Law (Scotland) Act 2006[164]: the court, when making any s.11 order, must have regard to the need to protect a child from abuse or the risk of abuse which affects or might affect the child; and also to the ability of the abuser to care for or meet the needs of the child. The court must also consider the effect any abuse might have on the primary carer. "Abuse" is defined widely to include violence, harassment, threatening conduct and any other conduct giving rise to physical or mental injury, fear, alarm or distress.[165] Psychological as well as physical abuse is thus clearly included. Abuse may also be aimed at a parent or other person, e.g. a sibling, as well as at the child, and includes "domestic abuse". "Conduct" includes both speech, and presence in a specified place or area.[166] So simply coming up to a mother in a shopping centre, or outside a school, given a history of abuse, could, it seems, be regarded as "abuse" if it caused that mother fear or distress. The Court of Session had to look at this issue in *S v J*,[167] in which there was behaviour on the part of the father, who sought contact, which could easily be criticised. [I think a line or two of detail on the facts here would make this case a more useful reference.] Although the case was unsatisfactory due to the lack of credibility of several of the witnesses, the Court was prepared to weigh the importance of the child's contact with the father more heavily than other factors

4–72   Finally, it is provided in s.11(7D) of the 1995 Act that the court shall also decide if it would be appropriate to make a s.11 order where that order involves two or more relevant parties having to co-operate with each other.[168] "Relevant parties" here includes anyone with PRRs and any parent of the child.[169] So, for example, if a father with a history of violence sought joint PRRs, or overnight contact two days a week (say), this would involve co-operation with the mother, and the court would have to take into account how feasible this was, given the background of abuse.

Arguably these rules add little new to Scots law. Courts have generally regarded evidence of domestic abuse or violence as relevant, [170] and the minimum intervention principle should already have operated to cause the court to stop and think before making any s.11 order that would be unworkable due to non-cooperation. However, the symbolic aim of the provisions, to highlight the need to think about the indirect and direct effects of domestic abuse in residence and contact disputes, is laudable.

---

[164] FLSA 2006 s.24, inserting s.11(7A)–(7B) into the Children (Scotland) Act 1995.

[165] FLSA 2006, inserting s.11(7C) into the 1995 Act.

[166] FLSA 2006.

[167] *S v J*, 2012 CSOH 49.

[168] Actually, in theory, cooperation is never needed in the exercise of any parental right according to s.2(2) of the 1995 Act. However, the non-pedantic meaning of the new sub-section is clear.

[169] FLSA 2006, s.24 inserting s.11(7D)–(7E) into the 1995 Act.

[170] See, e.g. *Haggerty v Woodrow*, 2005 G.W.D. 35–654, a pre-FLSA 2006 case.

Sexuality

The thorniest problems perhaps arise in relation to parental sexuality. **4–73**
The liberal and pluralistic values which generally prevail in current Scottish
society in strict theory indicate that the courts should only be interested in
the sexual preferences of parents in so far as they affect the child's welfare,
e.g. if a parent has violent tendencies. In practice, however, the courts have
in the past seemed willing to listen to evidence that it may in some indirect
way be bad for the child to be brought up by a non-heterosexual parent, most
notably the argument that such a child may be stigmatised in their peer group
by having same sex parents. In the first Scottish case on same sex parenting,
Early v Early,[171] the mother, who had recently begun cohabiting in a lesbian
relationship, sought custody of her third child, a boy aged 10. Although the
mother had the benefit of the status quo, custody was given to the father.
Lord Davidson accepted expert testimony that the lack of a male role model
in the child's life might lead to long-term problems, that there could be problems with teasing and stigmatisation at school, and, in general, there might
be "unusual difficulties". This approach was affirmed by the Inner House.
What is clearly objectionable about this decision is not that it implicitly
prefers an upbringing in an opposite sex household to a same sex one—which
is at root a value-oriented stance which can neither be approved nor vilified
on an objective basis[172]—but that the court overtly based its judgement on
stereotyped expert evidence about the risks for any child of growing up in
any lesbian household[173] rather than on a consideration of the happiness and
future of this particular child.

Following *Early*, a number of Scottish cases have taken less stereotyped judicial approach towards same sex parenting, including *Meredith v
Meredith*,[174] and *Hill v Hill*.[175]

Radical change came however in 1997 in the shape of *T Petr*,[176] an adop- **4–74**
tion case, in which the Inner House found that there was no reason in *principle* why an adoption order should not be made in favour of an unmarried

---

[171] *Early v Early*,1989 S.L.T. 114, affirmed by Inner House at 1990 S.L.T. 221.
[172] The English Court of Appeal, e.g. took it as unnecessary to prove that a opposite sex household is better for a child than a same sex one in *C v C* [1991] F.L.R. 223; Glidewell L.J. stating:
"I regard it as axiomatic that the ideal environment for the upbringing of a child is the home
of loving and sensible parents, her father and her mother. When the marriage between father
and mother is at an end that ideal cannot be attained. When the court is called upon to decide
which of the two possible alternatives is then preferable for the child's welfare, its task is to
choose the alternative which comes closest to that ideal." See comment in Boyd, "What Is a
Normal Family?" (1992) 55 M.L.R. 269.
[173] In *Early*, the mother's sexuality was not public knowledge, and therefore the risks of peer-
group hostility low, but this factor seems to have been disregarded. Generic evidence could as
well have been introduced denying that risks exist for children raised in lesbian households:
see, e.g. Tasker and Golombok, "Children Raised By Lesbian Mothers", 1991 Family Law
184, whose research found no discernible stigmatisation of children of lesbian mothers compared to a sample of children of single heterosexual mothers.
[174] *Meredith v Meredith*, 1994 G.W.D. 19–1150.
[175] *Hill v Hill*, 1991 S.L.T. 189.
[176] *T Petr*, 1997 S.L.T. 724. *T Petr* was also followed in England in *In Re W (a Minor) (Adoption:
Homosexual Adopter)* [1997] 3 All E.R. 620, a case dealing with an adoption application by a
lesbian woman cohabiting with another lesbian.

gay applicant, who in practice would bring up the child along with his long-standing male partner. At first instance, Lord Gill refused to grant the adoption order, even though the couple had been fostering the child for some 18 months, the social work department supported the petition and the mother did not object. His reason was that the risks of same sex parenting had not been properly explored. However, Lord Hope in the Inner House made it plain that nothing in the adoption legislation, with its emphasis on the welfare principle, suggested that it was a "fundamental objection to an adoption" that the applicant was living in a same sex relationship. It would be wrong to adopt any "hard and fast" rule,[177] or generalisation as to the attitude the courts should adopt towards non-heterosexual parents, as this in itself would be contrary to the assessment based on all circumstances demanded by the welfare principle. Although these comments were made in the context of adoption, they have proven very influential in areas such as residence and contact.[178]

4–75   Same sex parenting is an area which has perhaps transformed less as a result of shifting views in Scotland, and more as a result of international human rights pressures against discrimination. In particular, the ECHR has had a deciding influence, both pre- and post-incorporation. Since the English House of Lords case of *Fitzpatrick v Sterling House Association*[179] it has been generally accepted that same sex partners can claim the benefit of the right to respect for their family life under Art.8 of the ECHR, as well as the right not to be discriminated against. But of course, such rights have to be balanced against other considerations and it cannot be predicted how any particular case concerning same sex parenting will be addressed by the courts. Commentators such as Norrie[180] have declared that the ECHR has made discrimination in child law against a parent on grounds of sexuality illegal forthwith,[181] and that *Early* is unequivocally overruled. Norrie cites the ECHR case of *da Silva Mouta v Portugal*[182] in which the Strasbourg court held that discrimination based on a person's sexual orientation may constitute a breach of Art.14. The facts of the case were that a divorced father had his claim for a residence order rejected by the Portuguese courts on the basis that he was now living in a same sex relationship which did not provide a healthy environment for the social and moral development of the child. The European Court held that there had been no reasonable proportional-

---

[177] These comments were adopted with approval from the speech of Lord Kilbrandon in the English House of Lords case of *Re D (Adoption: Parent's Consent)* [1977] A.C. 602 at 641g–642b.

[178] See further Ch. 6, and Norrie, 1996 S.L.T. (News) 321.

[179] *Fitzpatrick v Sterling House Association* [2001] A.C. 27. This case actually concerned whether the same sex partner of a deceased had the right to succeed to his tenancy under statute as a member of his family.

[180] Norrie, 2000 5(2) S.P.L.Q. 169. Wilkinson & Norrie, 3rd edn, paras 9.34 et seq.

[181] But see *per contra* the ECHR case of *Frette v France* [2003] 2 F.L.R. 9, noted briefly at (2002) Fam. L.B. 58–6. See also Hogg, "Attitudes to Sexual Identity and Practice" in *Human Rights and Scots Law* (Boyle *et al* (eds) (Oxford: Hart Publishing, 2003); Dempsey, "Same Sex Couples in Scots Law, Part 1" (SCOLAG, October 2002), pp.181–183. The trend of the policy of the Court is illustrated by *X v Austria* Appl. 19010/2007, February 2013 "Differences based solely on considerations of sexual orientation are unacceptable under the Convention".

[182] *da Silva Mouta v Portugal*, 2001 Fam. L.R. 2.

ity between the objective of the court order (to uphold the welfare of the child) and the means used to achieve it (discrimination on grounds of sexual orientation) and thus the father's rights had been violated.

However much influence the ECHR has, problematic decisions are still **4–76** likely to arise in Scotland. The case of *X v Y*[183] raised a number of controversial issues. A gay man who agreed to become a sperm donor so that a lesbian couple could have a child was promised "heaps of contact" after the birth of the child. In fact the lesbian couple tried to exclude him from the baby's life. The court found him entitled to parental responsibilities and rights, but refused to regard the mother's partner, who had provided most of the practical care of the child, as having a relevant interest.

X v Y is however likely to be an anomalous case.[184] Given the arrival of **4–77** the Civil Partnership Act 2004,[185] which gives same sex partners who choose to enter civil partnerships rights almost identical to married persons, the Adoption (Scotland) Act 2007 which explicitly allows a gay couple to adopt as a couple, and the Scottish Government's intention, at the time of writing, to allow same sex marriages, it seems that Scots law is moving towards removal of discrimination in family law on grounds of sexuality.

Other types of parental sexual conduct, such as adultery or promiscuity, **4–78** will not now be seen as necessarily affecting the welfare of the child. The Scottish courts have sometimes seemed unwilling to believe that a single man can care for a child without the support of a woman, be it mother, sister, cohabitant, nanny or new wife.[186] It can be significant that one parent is willing to keep all the children of a family together,[187] though this need not always hold, for example, if the children themselves wish to live with different parents or, because of age or separation, have never developed relationships inter se.[188] The courts will not generally look favourably on a parent who continues to have such an embittered relationship with a former partner that he or she will not contemplate allowing that partner contact should they be granted residence: under the 1995 Act contact is now a responsibility of each parent, for the benefit of the child, and not a privilege which can be casually restricted. Of course in some exceptional circumstances, such as emigration to a new and prosperous future, it may be in the child's welfare to reside with one parent, even though this effectively cuts off contact with the other parent.[189]

---

[183] *X v Y* (2002) Fam. L.R. 58. And see L. Edwards, "Glasgow Kisses and Parental Wishes: *X v Y*" (2003) 7 Edin. L.R. 101.

[184] Indeed, only a few weeks after *X v Y* hit the press, a similar case (unreported, but see *Scotland on Sunday*, April 7, 2002) was decided in Edinburgh Sheriff Court. A lesbian couple both sought parental rights and responsibilities in respect of each other's biological child. Sheriff McPartlin granted this decree, which was supported by the natural father of one of the children. There seems to have been no issue raised concerning title to sue.

[185] See further Ch.9.

[186] In *Hogarth v Hogarth*, 1991 G.W.D. 30–1771, custody turned on the respective merits of the nannies employed by the father and the mother. In *Brixey v Lynas*, 1996 S.L.T. 908, the sheriff made it clear his award was as much to the father's family as the father himself.

[187] *Early v Early*, 1989 S.L.T. 114; 1990 S.L.T. 221.

[188] *Johnson v Johnson*, 1972 S.L.T. (Notes) 15. See also *Aberdeenshire Council Petrs*, 2004 G.W.D. 23–495 (an adoption case involving separation of siblings).

[189] See further paras 4–84 *et seq.* below.

Religion

4–79   The courts will look not only at sexual behaviour but at other aspects of the moral environment in which the parent proposes to raise the child. Traditionally it was said that the Scottish courts were interested in children being exposed to some kind of religious upbringing, as opposed to a wholly atheist upbringing, but were unconcerned about the merits of one religion over another.[190] In modern times this view has been based on two cases from the 1950s: *McClements v McClements*[191] and *McKay v McKay*.[192] In *McClements*, a father who was a convinced atheist failed to obtain a custody order on the grounds that the child ought not to be denied the opportunity of being brought up in a religious faith. In *McKay*, the father was not only a self-admitted atheist but also a communist. He was granted custody, but only on condition that his own mother, who shared childcare duties, undertook to bring the child up with a religious education. Lord Clyde, awarding custody to the father in these circumstances, made the much-quoted remark that:

> "Since the paramount consideration in custody cases is the welfare of the child, it would be almost impossible for a court in Scotland to award the custody to an atheist . . . For atheism and the child's welfare are almost mutually exclusive".[193]

4–80   In practice, in almost all modern cases, religion is not argued as a determining factor and the court does not inquire into it before granting decree of divorce.[194] Hence, even if these opinions still have any force of authority they have largely been bypassed. Wilkinson and Norrie argue that these cases never laid down a rule of law as such and that exposure to a narrow bigoted religious view may be as detrimental to the child's welfare as a militant and uncompromising atheism.[195] Certainly, recent cases in both Scotland and England have been more concerned with the potentially harmful effects of some non-mainstream religions than with the benefits of a religious upbringing. In *McKechnie v McKechnie*,[196] the court refused to award joint PRRs to the father of a child who was a Jehovah's Witness, because, inter alia, this would have given the father parental rights in respect of the child's medical treatment, whose welfare might be prejudiced should he need medical treatment such as a blood transfusion.[197] In modern English cases, courts have expressed concern about the effects of fringe or cult-like religions such as

---

[190] *McNaught v McNaught*, 1955 S.L.T. (Sh. Ct) 9. See also Thomson, *Family Law*, 4th edn (2002), p.227.
[191] *McClements v McClements*, 1958 S.C. 286.
[192] *McKay v McKay*, 1957 S.L.T. (Notes) 17.
[193] *McKay v McKay*, 1957 S.L.T. (Notes) 17.
[194] A relatively recent exception was *Baretdji v Baretdji*, 1985 S.L.T. 126.
[195] See Wilkinson and Norrie, 3rd edn, paras 9.35*et seq*.
[196] *McKechnie v McKechnie*, 1990 S.L.T. (Sh. Ct) 75.
[197] This reasoning is in fact hard to understand since even if the father refused consent to treatment, the mother would be able to supply it: 1995 Act s.2(2).

the Church of Scientology ("immoral and socially obnoxious"[198]) and the Exclusive Brethren ("harsh and restrictive"[199]).

Issues of religious observation have not frequently come before the Scottish **4–81** Courts in recent years, but when they do arise they can be central to the matter in dispute between the parties, as we see in *L v M*[200] and *S v S*.[201] It is clear, though that neither a religion nor a lifestyle should be presumed to be harmful to the welfare of the child without evidence. *KS v TS* was a Sheriff Court authority, but may be more than usually persuasive due to the particular Sheriff involved. A non-practising Christian woman and an intermittently practising Muslim man married in Egypt, returning later to live in Fife. Three children were born before the couple separated. The father, whose religious observance had intensified by the time of the proof, insisted that it was his religious duty to bring up the children as Muslims and that any attempt by the now-practising mother to teach the children about Christianity would only confuse them. The sheriff cited with approval the comments of the High Court in the English case of *Re N*,[202] in which the court affirmed, inter alia, that where both parents follow different religions and these religions are both socially acceptable, the child should have the opportunity to learn about and experience both religions. Furthermore, religious freedom, it must be remembered, is guaranteed by the ECHR.[203] In almost all cases, as we have seen, a residence order will leave the responsibilities and rights of the other parent untouched and he or she will therefore be fully able, to give the child an opportunity to know of and participate in lifestyles and credos other than those practised by the residential parent.

As always, the welfare test is paramount, regardless of the strongly held **4–82** views of either parent that his or her religion should have priority based on its inherent merit.

Race

The first reported case in the Scottish courts on the factor of race in rela- **4–83** tion to residence orders was *Osborne v Matthan*.[204] The child in question, F, was raised for her first eighteen months by her black Jamaican mother, Matthan, in Jamaica. Matthan then came to live in London where she worked as a dealer in illegal drugs. Her daughter was often looked after by her next door neighbour, Osborne, a white woman. Eventually Matthan was convicted of drug dealing and jailed for three years. During this time she asked Osborne rather than any of her own family to look after F temporarily. On her release from jail in late 1996, Osborne petitioned for custody[205] of

---

[198] *Re B and G (Minors)* [1985] F.L.R. 134, per Latey J. at 157.
[199] *Hewison v Hewison* (1977) 7 Family Law 207. See also *Re R (A Minor) (Residence: Religion)* [1993] 2 F.L.R. 163.
[200] *L v M*, 2012 G.W.D. 2–27.
[201] *S v S*, 2012 Fam. L.R. 148.
[202] *Re N*, 2011 EWHC 3737(Fam).
[203] See Art.9 of the ECHR and *Hoffman v Austria* (1994) 17 E.H.R.R. 293.
[204] *Osborne v Matthan*, 1997 S.L.T. 811 (Sheriff Court); 1998 S.C. 682; 1998 S.L.T. 1264 (Inner House). See also *AH and PH, Petitioners*, 1997 Fam. L.R. 84, an adoption case involving a transracial placement; *Perendes v Sim*, 1998 S.L.T. (Notes) (Scottish woman and Greek Cypriot father).
[205] This was a case based on pre-1995 Act law.

the child. Matthan, who faced deportation to Jamaica, was permitted to stay in the country to defend. Sheriff Wheatley, surveying the mother's history of unrepentant criminal activity came to a first conclusion that,

> "there could be no reason whatsoever in this case for supporting the defender's claim to have custody of her child returned to her but for the question of race. The pursuer and her family are white; the defender and her children are black."

He then accepted expert evidence that, ideally

> "[a child] should be brought up within its own racial and cultural identity, with pride in its identity and the appropriate and consequent measure of self esteem. To deprive a child of this was to risk serious advantage."

In the circumstances of this case, the choice was between making a transracial placement or uprooting the child from what was "undoubtedly" a warm and loving environment. Furthermore as the mother was to be deported to Jamaica, F would simultaneously be removed from her familiar home and from the only country and culture she had ever known to one wholly alien. Custody was granted to Osborne but with three caveats designed to secure the child's future welfare. The defender mother was to continue to be allowed to play as major a part in Fiona's life as circumstances would permit. Fiona was to be given every assistance in future to visit or even to go to live with her mother eventually. In the meantime, Osborne was to comply with advice and guidance from social work authorities, etc. on how the child's ethnic and cultural identity might appropriately be secured. The decision was upheld on appeal to the Inner House.

Relocation and Residence/Contact

4-84   Another problem that has become pressing in modern times is how to deal with the situation where the parent with primary care wishes to emigrate, and the other parent argues this will mean he (or she) will be unable to maintain contact. Section 2(3) of the Children (Scotland) Act 1995 provides that no person is allowed to remove a child from his habitual residence in the United Kingdom without the consent of any other party with rights (whether or not a parent). Hence relocation issues often come to the courts either in residence disputes and/or as specific issue orders. Should the wishes of the caring parent be sacrificed to the welfare of the child? Indeed can the welfare of the child be separated from the welfare of the primary carer? Traditionally, the courts have allowed the parent who is the primary carer to emigrate with their children.[206] However, in *SM v CM*[207] the Inner House took the opportunity to clarify matters. The Court said that there was a dual burden on the pursuer,

---

[206] See, e.g. *Borland v Borland*, 1990 G.W.D. 33–1883 (mother taking children to Crete with new Greek partner, father remaining in Scotland).
[207] *SM v CM*, 2012 S.L.T. 428.

first to show that the proposed relocation was in the best interests of the child and secondly to show that making a specific issue order was better than making no order at all. The paramountcy of the welfare of the child in the Scottish cases is in contrast to the position in England where the mother's psychological well-being following refusal has been a weighty factor, though even this is changing.[208]

Another important factor in recent relocation cases is the views of the **4-85** child(ren) involved. In *Fourman*, the eldest child, a boy of 10, joined the action as party minuter to express his wish to go on seeing both his parents and for the children to stay together, and his views and those of his siblings were clearly influential. In *Shields v Shields*[209] (discussed further at para.4-94) the views of the nine-year-old boy in question, once elicited, proved decisive in preventing his mother from seeking leave to emigrate. In *M v M*,[210] however, emigration was allowed, at least partly because the oldest of three children, age 12, supported her mother's desire to move to the USA.

Relocation is not always a matter of crossing international boundaries, **4-86** so s.2(3) does not always come into play. In *P v M*[211] the mother wished to relocate to Northern Ireland in order to further her relationship with another man. The children had a close and loving relationship with the father in Scotland and had close relationships with paternal relatives here. The court did not allow relocation.

The court did allow relocation in *B v D*.[212] In that case the child's interests **4-87** and welfare were strongly iodentified with those of the mother who had an extensive church and family network of support in Canada where she wished to live with the child. Less weight was given to the child's relationship with the father because, due to her young age, she was unlikely to miss him or his family acutely. There were averments of verbal and physical abuse by the father. The mother had had to involve the CSA in order to force the father to provide financial support.

Plainly, every case will turn on its own facts and the court will apply the **4-88** criterion of the best interests of the child, distinguishing those interests, where appropriate, from the interests of the resident parent.[213] Even if the court allows relocation, the other parent can seek an order to maintain contact by phone calls, letters and visits, including residential contact.[214]

The Child's Age and Sex

Children of different ages have different needs, particularly at two stages— **4-89** infancy and adolescence—and this may be a factor which the court finds relevant. At one time the Scottish courts probably acceded to a doctrine that children of "tender years" were better placed with their mother than their

---

[208] *K v K*, 2011 EWCA Civ 793.
[209] *Shields v Shields*, 2002 S.L.T. 579.
[210] *M v M*, 2000 Fam. L.R. 84.
[211] *P v M*, 2012 G.W.D. 26–549.
[212] *B v D*, 2012 GWD 14–285.
[213] *C v M*, G.W.D. 9–170.
[214] See *Borland v Borland*, 1990 G.W.D. 33–1883.

father.[215] Until recently it was thought, *pace* the odd judicial comment,[216] that no such presumption now existed in Scots law. However, in *Brixey v Lynas*,[217] the House of Lords found that custody of a female child who was 14 months at the date of the original proof but nearly four years old by the time the case reached the Lords, should be awarded to her mother. On the facts this was an understandable decision on the familiar status quo principle, since by that time the child had been in the care of the mother for around three and a half years, while the father had only had sole care for the two or three months prior to that period. However, the decision of the Inner House, who reversed the original award to the father made at sheriff-court level, was explicitly made on the basis that "during his or her infancy, the child's need for the mother is stronger than the need for a father".[218] This appeared to raise the ghost of the rule of maternal preference. The House of Lords affirmed the decision, but were at pains to stress that they were in no way laying down any type of legal principle or presumption.[219]

4-90   This begs the question: when is a presumption not a presumption? According to Lord Jauncey

"Nature has endowed men and women with very different attributes and it so happens that mothers are generally better fitted than fathers to provide for the needs of very young children. This is no more discriminatory than the fact that only women can give birth."[220]

And later

"the advantage to a very young child of being with its mother is a consideration which *must* be taken into account in deciding where lie its best interests in custody proceedings."[221]

These look remarkably like assertions that unless there is evidence to the contrary, a mother will be deemed better at caring for a young child than a father: something that is commonly known in law as a presumption. It is of course still open to fathers to prove on the facts of a particular case, that the best interests of the child lie with them, and this will be particularly plausible if they are already satisfactorily caring for the child and have established a status quo.[222] On the other hand, a mother of a young child

---

[215] *McLean v McLean*, 1947 S.C. 79.
[216] e.g. "In general it is in the best interests of a female child of tender years to be in the custody of her own mother", per Lord Marnoch in *Lewis v Lewis*, 1992 G.W.D. 27–1524.
[217] *Brixey v Lynas*, 1996 S.L.T. 908.
[218] *Brixey v Lynas*, 1994 S.L.T. 847 at 849, Lord Morison having quoted from Wilkinson and Norrie, 1st edn, p.211.
[219] *Brixey v Lynas*, 1996 S.L.T. 908.
[220] *Brixey v Lynas*, 1996 S.L.T. 908 at 911E–E.
[221] *Brixey v Lynas*, 1996 S.L.T. 908 at 911K–L.
[222] This was the case in *Whitecross v Whitecross*, 1977 S.L.T. 225 (boy aged almost two); *Sherwin v Trumayne*, 1992 G.W.D. 29–1681 (girl aged two); and *Cowen v Brown*, 1991 G.W.D. 29–1718 (girl aged three). In all three cases the father retained custody.

with the status quo will find her position doubly strengthened. This result has been criticised as sexually discriminatory[223]: but it arguably contains a kernel of common sense.[224] It is disappointing though, to see a decision, like *Early*,[225] on an individual child made on the basis of a general stereotype.

In *PAD v AAB*[226] the sheriff found in favour of the mother's crave for residence, saying: "Although there is no presumption in favour of as mother, I do consider that the young age of the child is a relevant factor".　　**4–91**

There is no general presumption in favour of a mother in any given case. If a very young child is being breast-fed then that may be a factor—and a strong one—in favour of residence with the mother, but it is not a presumption in law that a breast-feeding mother should always have residence. The facts of the case will determine the result and, as a matter of social observation, most young children spend most of their time with their mothers. This is really a part of the status quo factor rather than any independent factor to do with the age and sex of the child. It has been suggested that when approaching adolescence a male child needs the care of his father if there is no male figure within the household and that this may be a relevant consideration for residence.[227] There seems no reason, however, why a male role-model or mentor cannot be found outside the residential household, e.g. through contact with the father.　　**4–92**

The Views of the Child

The courts are now explicitly instructed to have regard to the views of the child.[228] In pre-1995 Act case law, as discussed above, children did not have any right to be heard, but the courts, when presented with the views of children, would give them some regard, especially where the child had reached minority. Under the 1995 Act, s.11(7)(b), the courts must actively give children an opportunity to express their views and will presume a child over the age of 12 to be mature enough to do so.[229] However the courts' paramount concern remains the welfare of the child. Historically, the Scottish courts have taken the attitude that children do not always know what is best for them: in the words of Lord Stott quoted above, "it cannot by any means be　　**4–93**

---

[223] Sutherland, "Mother Knows Best", 1994 S.L.T. (News) 375; her criticism was vigorously rejected by Lord Jauncey in the House of Lords. See further, Edwards, "Mother Still Knows Best", 1996 Fam. L.B. 23–5.

[224] French, *Guardian*, July 8, 1996, suggests that a presumption in favour of the mother is justified since statistically, most physical and sexual abuse of children is male- perpetrated. This, of course, sets up a contrary stereotype.

[225] *Early v Early*, 1989 S.L.T. 114; 1990 S.L.T. 221.

[226] *PAD v AAB*, 2011 WL 806791.

[227] *Early v Early*, 1989 S.L.T. 114; 1990 S.L.T. 221.

[228] 1995 Act s.11(7).

[229] Children under 12 frequently do however give evidence of their views. Younger children can have their views presented effectively by being interviewed by the sheriff in court or in chambers, by writing notes, or via a curator *ad litem*. In *Fairbairn v Fairbairn*, 1998 G.W.D. 23–1148 the views of children as young as seven and five, elicited by a curator, contributed towards a decision to transfer residence from the father to the mother.

assumed that a child's interests necessarily coincide with her wishes".[230] The evidence of children has also been regarded with some suspicion, since young children may be "coached" or pressurised into speaking for or against a parent. Awareness of the UNCRC and particularly Art.12 and its promotion of the "voice of the child" has however more recently lead to considerable weight being placed on the views of children, especially, though not exclusively, mature children aged 12 or over. In *Smith v Woodhead*,[231] for example, a 12-year-old boy's wish to live with his grandmother rather than his mother was held to be of "considerable" and eventually, decisive, significance, even though it was based on the erroneous belief that his mother no longer wanted him.

4–94   *Shields v Shields*[232] goes further by emphasising that it is not just the right of children to speak, but also the *duty of the court* to *hear* them. The dispute concerned a mother who wished to take her son, D, to Australia, against the wishes of her ex-husband. At the beginning of the case, D was aged seven and a half. The parties and sheriff agreed that intimation to D should be dispensed with. By the time the sheriff issued decree, in favour of the mother, the child was aged over nine. The father appealed unsuccessfully to the sheriff principal, who in refusing the appeal nevertheless noted his surprise that the child had never been asked what *his* views were on going to Australia. The father appealed again to the Inner House, this time successfully. A number of points were emphasised. First, even if everyone had initially agreed to dispense with the views of the child, that did not exonerate the court from its duty to provide the child with the opportunity to speak. Secondly, that duty was *continuing*, so even if the child was too young to consult at the start of proceedings, he should still have been asked if he wanted to state views later on. Indeed, the sheriff had a duty to ascertain the wishes of the child *at the time the order was made*, according to the wording of s.11(7). At that time, the child was nine and should definitely have been consulted. In general, Lord Marnoch stated,

> "so far as according a child the opportunity to make known his views, the only proper and relevant test is one of practicability".

In *Shields* itself, when it became plain the boy would express unwillingness to move to Australia, rather than restart the case with a new Sheriff Court hearing, the mother abandoned the case.[233]

---

[230] *Fowler v Fowler*, 1981 S.L.T. (Notes) 9.

[231] *Smith v Woodhead*, 1996 G.W.D. 10–533.

[232] *Shields v Shields*, 2002 S.L.T. 579.

[233] There may have been some retrenchment from the high standard of duty demanded of the court in *Shields*: see *G v G*, 2003 Fam. L.R. (Notes) 118 and *C v McM*, 2005 Fam. L.R. 21. (Where *Shields* was distinguished by the Sheriff Principal, on the grounds that the child in question had been given two opportunities to speak in the past, via interviews with social workers acting as reporters to the court. There was said to be no obligation on the court to give the child an opportunity to express a view more than once.)

CONTACT ORDERS

Contact is an increasingly fraught issue, for a number of reasons. First, it **4–95** should be remembered that in most divorces, the mother of a child, and the father who is or has been married to that mother, already have both the responsibility and the right of contact under ss.1 and 2 of the 1995 Act, if they do not have the child living with them. Since the Family Law (Scotland) Act 2006 has come into force, most unmarried fathers too have had automatic rights of contact. These rights are not in principle terminated on divorce. In most cases, therefore, that an application for a court order for contact will only be made where the parents are actively hostile to each other, often with a history of the parent with interim care impeding contact, since the details of contact can otherwise be settled by agreement.[234] The 1995 Act seeks to promote contact as primarily a responsibility owed by a parent to the child. In practice though, parents may well think of contact as their own "right", an aspect of their due as parents, and therefore something that can be traded in against other rights, such as property rights. It is possible that the incorporation of the ECHR and its "right to respect for family life" under Art.8 may also have added to this perception. See also the speech of Lord Fraser of Tullybelton in the *Gillick* case, above.a

All of these factors have meant that the relatively few contested applica- **4–96** tions for contact have tended to be hard-fought, embittered and increasingly legally complex. As a result, the even fewer reported cases around which discussion about contact tends to be structured in legal textbooks, are only the thinnest, least representative and most pathological end of the wedge, involving couples who have intransigently refused to reach agreement, and fathers who often have specific problems in gaining contact because of, e.g. their violent relationship with the mother or the mother's wish to remove the father from the child's life because of her own difficult relationship with him rather than because of any harm that she believes will befall the child during contact. To these cases, the courts will, undoubtedly, apply the s.11 criteria. Many of the reported cases cited above in relation to residence will be applicable *mutatis mutandis* in discerning what is in the welfare of the child. However, it must be remembered that for most of the children of divorce and separation in Scotland, contact will be settled by agreement rather than in court, and in such cases it is hard to know if the s.11 criteria are being applied. Similar issues may arise when contact disputes are referred to mediation.

Until the mid-eighties several bitter disputes turned upon the question of **4–97** whether a father has an inherent right to maintain contact with his child, or whether it is necessary for him to prove to a court that his contact with the child will positively be of benefit to him or her. Until the case of *Porchetta v Porchetta*,[235] it was largely assumed in the courts that contact with a

---

[234] An award of access was made in only 15% of ordinary divorce actions in 1991: Morris, Gibson and Platts, *Untying the Knot* (Scottish Office, CRU, 1993); compare to a figure of around 90% for custody orders. Of course some applications for access will have been made outside divorce actions, e.g. by unmarried fathers.

[235] *Porchetta v Porchetta*, 1986 S.L.T. 105.

biological father was inherently desirable[236] unless strong evidence was produced to the contrary, e.g. the father was violent towards the child, or might abduct the child if given the opportunity.[237] In *Porchetta*, however, Lord Dunpark recognised that, given the paramount interest of the welfare of the child, a father cannot have an absolute right to contact. The father in *Porchetta* had had virtually no contact with his 18-month-old son since his birth, and the mother was adamantly opposed to the resumption of contact. In the circumstances, there was "not a shred of evidence"[238] to suggest that this would be in the best interests of the child. The court made no award of access.

4–98   In *Russell v Russell*,[239] Sheriff Gordon identified the *Porchetta* approach as demanding that "it is for the parent seeking access to show, and indeed satisfy the court, that it will be in the interests of the child."[240] The onus in seeking contact lies with the applicant, then, to prove he or she has something positive to bring to the child, that is, something more than the simple fact of a biological link to the child. So, where a father has little or no relationship with his child, or where his contact causes great distress to the child, he will find this onus impossible to shift.

4–99   The *Porchetta* approach was, arguably, implemented by the 1995 Act in the form of the minimum intervention principle, which states that a s.11 order should not be made unless it is better that an order be made than that no order be made at all. This appeared at first blush to put the onus on an applicant father to bring some evidence, of some kind, to justify the making of a contact order by proving it is in the best interests of the child. Where this proved most controversial was in the borderline cases, often involving fathers not married to the mother of the child, who may have had little or no contact with the child, and who had little positive evidence they were a beneficial presence in the life of the child other than the sheer fact that they were the genetic or natural father of the child. How much weight should the courts give to this blood connection *per se*?

4–100   In the leading case of *Sanderson v McManus*,[241] a natural father, without PRRs, sought access. There was disputed hearsay evidence that the father had once assaulted his child on a contact visit. Against this was asserted the intrinsic value of the natural parent-child relationship. The father had made weekly visits to the child at a contact centre until these were terminated by the sheriff. The Inner House by a 2:1 majority found that a parent had no "right" to access and that the onus of proof to demonstrate access was in the welfare of the child was on the father, an onus he had not in the circumstances discharged. He was therefore denied access. More notable than the decision of the majority, however, is the ferociously dissenting judgement of Lord McCluskey, who declared that the courts should preserve contact

---

[236] See, e.g. *Blance v Blance*, 1978 S.L.T. 74; *Brannigan v Brannigan*, 1979 S.L.T. (Notes) 73.
[237] *Puddinu v Puddinu*, 1987 G.W.D.4–105.
[238] *Porchetta v Porchetta*, 1986 S.L.T. 105 at 106.
[239] *Russell v Russell*, 1991 S.C.L.R. (Notes) 429; see also the English House of Lords case of *Re KD (A Minor)* [1988] 1 All E.R. 577, denying any absolute right of a *mother* to access.
[240] *Russell v Russell*, 1991 S.C.L.R. (Notes) 429 at 430F.
[241] *Sanderson v McManus*, 1996 S.L.T. 745; 1995 S.C.L.R. 902.

between a natural father and his child unless there were very strong reasons to the contrary: essentially endorsing the *pre-Porchetta* state of affairs. This was because the parent-child link was,

> "a natural link, the importance of which is felt instinctively; it is a deep and abiding theme in literature, both sacred and profane, and in social and political history. It is a link which is properly understood to have value quite independently of any supposed 'right' in a parent to obtain from a court of law an order allowing 'access' to his or her child".[242]

Lord McCluskey's worries were taken account of in the subsequent Inner **4–101** House decision in *White v White*.[243] As noted earlier, the Inner House in *White* swept away any belief that a person without existing parental rights had any special onus to overcome in seeking them. Instead it reinstated the welfare principle, correctly, as the paramount concern of the court. On the matter of the value to be given to Lord McCluskey's "natural link", Lord Rodger, giving the lead judgement, firstly approved the much quoted statement of Lord Hope in *Sanderson v McManus* in the House of Lords that "it may normally be assumed that the child will benefit from continued contact with the natural parent". This was true in all cases involving fathers, whether they had existing PRRs or not. This was not, he went on to say, any kind of "presumption" or "assumption" but merely "a working hypothesis born of human experience". Thus the court is entitled to take account of the value of a child having contact with his father, without any need for this to be proven in evidence, e.g. by bringing the evidence of a child psychologist. However there remains, it seems, no "presumption" that a father should have contact with his child, though the courts will lean towards assuming this is usually a good thing.

Contact Orders and the Child's Wishes

In disputes over contact, it is almost impossible to disentangle the question **4–102** of respect for the wishes of the child from the issues of objective welfare and father's rights. In the not atypical event of hostility and bitterness between the parents after they break up, it is difficult to separate out the true attitude of the child towards contact from the feelings of both the warring parents. A parent with residence may influence the child to reject the other parent or to accept a new cohabitant as a replacement. Most likely, the child will not be certain of his or her own wishes. The practice of the Scottish courts is similarly variable. At one time, they were prepared to grant a father an order for contact even if the children had expressed a wish not to see him, if it seemed that the child's attitude was being mediated by the hostility or new arrangements of the mother. In *Cosh v Cosh*,[244] for example, it was said that the unwillingness of the children to see their father was neither "genuine"

---

[242] *Sanderson v McManus*, 1996 S.L.T. 750 at 752 D–E. Affirmed House of Lords, 1997 S.L.T. 629.
[243] See para.4–53, above.
[244] *Cosh v Cosh*, 1979 S.L.T. (Notes) 72.

nor "reasonable". In *Blance v Blance*,[245] it was even said to be the duty of the parent with residence to encourage and persuade the child to comply with the court order for contact, by all means short of physical compulsion.[246] However, in cases like *Russell*,[247] above, the court has become more willing to recognise that if a child becomes distressed and upset whenever contact is attempted then it cannot be in his or her best interests to enforce it against the child's will, even where distress is partly inspired by the attitude of the residential parent.[248] The problem here is that the statute gives the courts no guidance on whether they are to prefer the current or future welfare of the child, the latter of which may be better met by continuing contact even at the cost of current tears. It must be doubted furthermore if approaches such as those in *Blance*[249] square with the duty of the court under s.11 to have regard, as far as practicable, to the wishes of the child. It is often said that contact decisions in difficult cases like these are better made using mediation services rather than in a courtroom; yet as we have pointed out above, mediation may not be the best place for the child's wishes to be heard, nor does it tend to be effective in long-running embedded disputes.[250]

Enforcement

4–103   Finally, what if a parent obtains a contact order but the parent with residence will not comply?[251] In that case, as a final resort, the frustrated parent can enrol a motion that the party with residence be declared in contempt of court, a common law offence which can be punished by fine or imprisonment. This can also be used as a sanction where the party with the contact order breaches it, e.g. by repeatedly returning the child after the prescribed time.[252] The problem, with such a "stick" is that it will rarely be in the child's best interests for the primary carer to be sent to jail.[253] An alternative canvassed in

---

[245] *Blance v Blance*, 1978 S.L.T. 74.

[246] See also *Brannigan*, 1979 S.L.T. (Notes) 73; *Joffre v Joffre*, 1992 G.W.D. 27–1522; *Collins v Collins*, 1993 G.W.D. 5–245.

[247] *Russell v Russell*, 1991 S.C.L.R. (Notes) 429.

[248] See also *Cower v Cower*, 1969 S.L.T. (Notes) 78; *Cuthbertson v Cuthbertson*, 1993 G.W.D. 32–2020.

[249] *Blance v Blance*, 1978 S.L.T. 74, per Lord Stewart: "The best interests of the child may inevitably involve some temporary upset and the whole purpose of the court awarding access would be frustrated if the effective decision were to be handed over to the child" (1978 S.L.T. 74 at 75).

[250] One survey found that around 70% of disputes on contact resolved through mediation terminated with agreement of some kind: Jones, *Family Conciliation in Scotland* (Scottish Office, 1990). But this does not take into account the fact that between two-thirds and four-fifths of parties who bring a dispute to mediation do not find it is appropriate or practicable and withdraw from mediation.

[251] As discussed at para.4–45, international child abduction disputes arising from abuse of contact rights are outwith the scope of this book. Note, however, that the UK government may in future join the Council of Europe Convention on Contact Concerning Children (see Consultation Paper, Scottish Executive, 2005).

[252] *Johnston v Johnston*, 1996 S.L.T. 499. Since contempt of court is a criminal offence, proof of allegations must be beyond reasonable doubt.

[253] Although jail may not be necessary—see *Hunter v Hunter*, 1998 Fam. L.B. 33–5, where the mother refused access by the father to his daughter and was fined £100 for contempt. See also *M v S*, 2011 S.L.T. 918: a more extreme case in which a mother was imprisoned for three

$G v G^{254}$ is to reverse the award in force and, say, give residence to the father away from an obstructive mother. Of course this approach, too, does not necessarily place the child's interests first. The court in $M v S^{255}$ emphasised that it was a relevant, but not paramount, consideration that a custodial sentence would separate a child from its primary carer.

THE WELFARE PRINCIPLE: FINAL THOUGHTS

Much of this chapter has been taken up with consideration of the nature of **4–104** the welfare principle and how Scots law uses it both as a check on parental power, and as a criterion for dealing with disputes between parents which arrive at the courts. It is worth considering though, if the best interests of the child *are*, or *should*, always be the paramount consideration. We have already noted several times the potential and actual clashes between parents claiming rights under the ECHR, especially Art.8 which governs right to respect for family and private life, and the welfare principle. There are also areas of domestic law clearly affecting the vital interests of children where the welfare of the child is not paramount.

When making an exclusion order under the Matrimonial Homes Act 1981, **4–105** for example, the child's welfare is relevant but in no way overriding,[256] even though children are profoundly affected by domestic violence taking place in their household. Instead, the balance the court is instructed to strike is primarily between the property rights of the entitled spouse and the risk to the health of the non-entitled spouse. Similarly, when the court considers whether to return a child to its place of habitual residence under the child abduction conventions, the welfare principle does not apply, since otherwise the purpose of the legislation would be defeated[257]: instead the courts are only concerned if return will bring a "grave risk" to the child, or in limited cases, where the mature child objects to removal.[258] Perhaps the most important example comes from the Child Support Act 1991, considered in the next chapter, where a child support officer need only have "regard" to the welfare of the child when making a maintenance assessment.[259] Such assessments can be made even when the overall effect is negative for the child, for example, where an absent father is no longer financially able to visit the child.

---

months for failure to comply appropriately; and *Butterworth Scottish Family Law Service*, C 689.
[254] *G v G*, 1999 Fam. L.R. 30.
[255] *M v S*, 2011 S.L.T. 918.
[256] Matrimonial Homes (Family Protection) (Scotland) Act 1981, s.4(2). See further Ch.11.
[257] See *Dickson v Dickson*, 1990 S.C.L.R. 692.
[258] See further Anton, *Private International Law*, 3rd edn (Edinburgh: W. Green, 2011).
[259] Child Support Act 1991 s.2. It has been cynically suggested that the White Paper preceding the introduction of the 1991 Act, *Children Come First*, Cm.1263 (1990) might have been better titled *Taxpayer Comes First*.

CHAPTER 5

PARENTAL RESPONSIBILITIES AND RIGHTS II

5–01 In the last chapter we looked at the basic framework of Pt 1 of the Children (Scotland) Act 1995 (hereafter "the 1995 Act") and examined the principles to be applied by the Scottish Courts in making "contact" and "residence" orders in cases of parental dispute. In this chapter, we will look in more detail at some key examples of parental responsibilities and rights, and children's rights, including a child's right to financial support under the Child Support Act 1991. It should be stressed that this coverage cannot be comprehensive.

PARENTAL RESPONSIBILITIES AND RIGHTS

5–02 As we saw in Ch.4, under s.1 of the 1995 Act, a parent has the responsibility:

(a) to safeguard and promote the child's health, development and welfare;
(b) to provide, in a manner appropriate to the stage of development of the child—
  (i) direction, and
  (ii) guidance to the child;
(c) if the child is not living with the parent, to maintain personal relations and direct contact with the child on a regular basis; and
(d) to act as the child's legal representative.[1]

5–03 Under s.2 of the Act, parents are given correlative rights in order to allow them to fulfil these responsibilities. These include the right to regulate the child's residence; the right to "control, direct or guide" the child's upbringing in a way appropriate to that child's stage of development; the right to maintain contact with the child if not living in the same household; and the right to act as legal representative. As seen in the last chapter, these rights are not absolute, like property rights, but instead can only be exercised if to do so is in the interests of the child[2]; and, if necessary, the courts can be invoked to clarify what the child's best interests involve by means of a s.11 order.

5–04 The parental rights and responsibilities contained within the 1995 Act do not easily map onto the well-grooved categories of parental rights described in textbooks before 1995. Without attempting to be exhaustive, parents will now be legally responsible for: choices relating to the child's health,

---

[1] 1995 Act ss. 1(1) and 2(1). See also *Hay v Hay*, 2000 S.L.T. (Sh. Ct) 95.
[2] See above, paras 4–39 *et seq.*

education, training, and discipline; moral, physical, psychological and spiritual development; as well as the administration of the child's property and litigation on behalf of the child.

Health and Welfare

A parent has a duty to "safeguard and promote" a child's health. This duty   5–05
is enabled by the right of a parent as legal representative to give the consent which is required by law for any medical treatment.[3] The right to make choices about a child's healthcare is thus primarily an aspect of the right of legal representation.

This right is controlled in two ways. First, a parent cannot give consent   5–06
to treatment on behalf of a child unless to do so would be in the child's best interest. We discussed this in detail at paras 4–07 to 4–10. Secondly, the law now recognises that a child of sufficient maturity has the right to give a medical consent on his or her own behalf.[4] As we saw in Ch.4, this generates thorny issues as to whether the right of the child to consent should supplant or merely run in parallel to the right of the parent. It is submitted that in Scots law, once a child is deemed competent to consent under s.2(4) of the Age of Legal Capacity (Scotland) Act 1991, the right of the parent to consent flies away. Thus, if a child is competent, a parent cannot give a consent even if the child is refusing consent to treatment which might be objectively in his or her best interests.[5]

For many years it has been a criminal offence for a parent to fail to provide proper health care. Such a failure can contravene the Children and Young Persons (Scotland) Act 1937 s.12 and may justify referral to the Children's Hearing.

How can a parent's duty to promote health and physical welfare be   5–07
enforced? As we have seen, children have title to sue parents in respect of their parental responsibilities.[6] However, neglected or abused children are rarely in the best position to initiate legal proceedings, or may simply be too young. Children can, of course, sue their parents in delict for breach of duty when they have reached adulthood: but since such cases must be raised within three years of either the cause of the action, or of the date at which the child ceases to be under legal disability by reason of non-age[7] (whichever is later),

---

[3] Except in limited circumstances, e.g. where the patient is unconscious and treatment is necessary: see Mason and McCall-Smith, pp.218 *et seq*. See also the English case of *Re B* [1981] 1 W.L.R. 1421, in which parents unsuccessfully sought to refuse treatment for their child. The Court held that they had failed to show that the child's interests would have been better served by death. The Inner House came to a different decision on the facts in *Law Hospital NHS Trust v Lord Advocate*, 1996 S.C.L.R. 491.

[4] Age of Legal Capacity (Scotland) Act 1991 s.2(4).

[5] See the full discussion at paras 4–32 *et seq*.

[6] 1995 Act s.1(3); *Young v Rankine*, 1934 S.C. 499.

[7] Prescription and Limitation (Scotland) Act 1973 s.17(2) and (3). It is submitted that all children have three years to sue from attaining the age of 16 (Age of Legal Capacity (Scotland) Act 1991 s.1(1)), notwithstanding the exception in s.2(4B) inserted by the Children (Scotland) Act 1995 Sch.4, para.53, which allows a child to raise civil proceedings in his or her own name as soon as he or she has sufficient understanding. See concession to this effect by all sides in *Cameron v Stenhouse*, 1998 G.W.D. 24–1230.

the action may well be time-barred, unless the court is willing to extend the triennium period on equitable grounds.[8] Limitation of actions is a particularly difficult issue in relation to actions in respect of child abuse, especially sexual abuse, where the child may not have been conscious that there was legal redress for the harm, or indeed that they had been abused at all, until many years later. Memories of abuse are often buried or repressed, and may only resurface in therapy. In *Stubbings v Webb*,[9] an English case, the Court of Appeal was prepared to count the triennium as running from the date when the plaintiff, aged 30, became *aware* that there was a causal link between her long-term emotional problems and the abuse she had suffered as a child. However, on appeal the House of Lords reversed this decision, Lord Griffiths stating that he "would have the greatest difficulty in accepting that a woman who knows that she has been raped does not know that she has suffered a significant injury".[10] This restrictive approach, has not been adopted in recent Scottish cases. In *W v Glasgow City Council*[11] the pursuer, who averred that she had suffered abuse while in local authority care some years previously, claimed that she had been able to put the injuries (which were minor) behind her and had suffered no ill-effects until years later when forced to confront them when she was contacted by police. A similar course was adopted by the Court in *G v Glasgow City Council*,[12] in which the injuries were more serious. In each of these cases the court was prepared to exercise its discretion in terms of s.19A of the 1973 Act.

5–08   The major aim of the law, however, must be to prevent abuse, not award compensation after it has happened. The state enforces parental duty in various ways. Neglect, ill-treatment or the infliction of unnecessary suffering or injury to the health of a child meet with criminal sanctions.[13] More commonly, a child who appears to be in need of care, or suffering from abuse will be referred to the Children's Hearings System as in need of compulsory measures of supervision.[14] If a ground of referral is proven or accepted, then the child can be made the subject of a supervision order within the parental home, or if absolutely necessary, removed into care on a transient or permanent basis.[15]

Physical Punishment of Children

5–09   In most cases of neglect or abuse, if the facts are proven, the parents will have no defence. However, one major area of controversy concerns the traditional right of the parent (or parent-substitute, such as a school teacher) to discipline or chastise the child. Scots law traditionally allowed parents the right to discipline their children by hitting them, so long as the punishment

---

[8] 1973 Act s.19A.

[9] *Stubbings v Webb* [1991] 3 All E.R. 949 (C.A.); [1993] 2 W.L.R. 120 (H.L.).

[10] [1993] 2 W.L.R. 120 at 126.

[11] *W v Glasgow City Council*, 2011 S.C. 15.

[12] *G v Glasgow City Council*, 2011 S.C. 1.

[13] See para.5–11 below.

[14] See 1995 Act s.52(2). It is a ground of referral, e.g. that a child is likely to suffer unnecessarily due to lack of parental care (s.52(2)(c)(i)).

[15] See further Chs 7 and 8, below.

remained "reasonable"; however, where the punishment was unreasonable, disproportionate to the child's age and unruliness, or appeared to have simply been dealt out as retribution for bad behaviour without any "educational" element, then it became an abuse of parental responsibility, and could still be sanctioned, either by criminal[16] or child protection[17] routes.

Considerable pressure was placed on the government from groups such as EPOCH (End Physical Punishment of Children) to make all physical punishment of children automatically illegal. Many European countries, in line with Art.19(1) of the UNCRC, which requires Member States to protect children from all forms of physical violence, have already completely banned corporal punishment of children.[18] In *Campbell and Cosans v United Kingdom*,[19] the European Court of Human Rights found that corporal punishment of a child in school was not necessarily either "inhuman" or "degrading" treatment and so was not contrary to Art.3 of the ECHR. However the Strasbourg court did find that individual parents had a right to require the school not to hit their children as part of their right to have their children educated according to their religious and philosophical convictions.[20] Faced with a scenario in which some children in a school could be caned while others could not, the government gave in and banned corporal punishment in schools entirely.[21]   **5–10**

This still left the major question of whether parents themselves were allowed to hit their own children. The Scottish Law Commission proposed as far back as 1992 that parents should not have the right to hit a child with an object, such as a stick or belt, or to hit a child in a way that would cause injury or to cause discomfort lasting more than a very short time.[22] These proposals however remained politically impossible to implement until matters were brought to a head by an English ECHR case, *A v UK*.[23] In this case, a child was viciously beaten by his stepfather acting *in loco parentis*. The case was prosecuted as criminal assault, but the defence of reasonable chastisement was accepted by a jury. When taken to the European Court of Human Rights, the United Kingdom was found guilty of a violation of Art.3 of the ECHR ("no one shall be subjected to torture or to inhuman or degrading treatment or punishment") and placed under a duty to reform its law of assault so that such cases could not recur.   **5–11**

---

[16] Under s.12 of the Children and Young Persons (Scotland) Act 1937, now repealed. See *Peebles v Macphail*, 1989 S.C.C.R. 410 (incensed mother slapped two-year-old child once, knocking him over); *cf. Guest v Annan*, 1988 S.C.C.R. 275 (father smacking eight-year-old in fit of anger found to have no criminal *mens rea*); *G v Templeton*, 1998 S.C.L.R. 180; *D v Irvine*, 2005 Fam. L.R. 94.

[17] *B v Harris*, 1990 S.L.T. 208; *Kennedy v A*, 1993 S.L.T. 1134.

[18] e.g. Sweden, Finland, Denmark, Norway, Austria and Cyprus.

[19] *Campbell and Cosans v United Kingdom* (1982) 4 E.H.R.R. 293.

[20] See Art.2 of First Protocol to ECHR.

[21] See now the Standards in Scotland's Schools Etc (Scotland) Act s.16. The ban was initially only in the public sector but was extended to schools in the private sector in 1998 by the Education (Scotland) Act 1980 s.48A(1A) as amended by Education Act 1983 ss.293 and 294, which explicitly banned "inhuman or degrading treatment". But see UK Children's Commissioners' *Report to the UN Committee on the rights of the Child* (2008), p.14.

[22] *Report on Family Law*, Scot. Law Com. No.135 (1992), paras 2.67 *et seq.*

[23] *A v UK* [1998] EHRLR 82; [1999] 27 E.H.R.R. 611.

5–12   Consultation took place in both England and Scotland[24] and the result for Scotland was the changes ushered in by the Criminal Justice (Scotland) Act 2003, s.51. "Smacking" is still not banned entirely, even, as suggested in draft, in relation to very young children. The defence of reasonable chastisement is also retained even if the words *per se* are removed from the legal vocabulary,[25] and replaced by a detailed checklist which strongly resembled the SLC's 1992 proposals, only ten years on. In deciding if corporal punishment was justified as an aspect of "parental right", or if not, was a criminal assault, a court must have regard to the nature of the punishment, its duration and frequency, any effect on the child, and the child's age and personal characteristics. Blows to the head, shaking and hitting using an implement are rebuttably presumed to be non-justifiable assaults. Even if the level of severity of the chastisement does not breach that standard, it must be reasonable and be directed towards the discharge of parental responsibility.

5–13   In 2007 The Scottish Executive, in its report on compliance with the UN Convention on the Rights of the Child said that there had been no reported cases under s51.

Religious Upbringing

5–14   A parent has the right to determine in what religion a child should be brought up as part of the right to "control, direct and guide" the child's upbringing under s.1. Where there is disagreement between parents about the religious upbringing of the child, the court may be asked to adjudicate, e.g. if asked to consider religion as a factor when making a residence, contact, specific issue or other s.11 order. As we saw in Ch.4, the court's concern will be the objective welfare of the child, not the relative spiritual merits of different religions.[26]

5–15   The law may also, occasionally, have to intervene in the religious upbringing of a child even where there is no inter-parental conflict. In extreme circumstances, religious practices which are regarded as harmful to children may be treated as criminal.[27] In lesser circumstances, it is also possible that the child may be referred to the Children's Hearings System,[28] or otherwise taken under the protection of the local social work department.

5–16   If a child does come under the care or supervision of the local authority as a "looked after" child[29] then the authority must have regard to the child's reli-

---

[24] See for Scotland, the Consultation Paper *Physical Punishment of Children in Scotland* (Scottish Executive, February 2000). See also research carried out by the Central Research Unit, Anderson, Murray and Brownlie, *Disciplining Children: Research with Parents* (Scottish Executive, 2002).

[25] Children and Young Persons (Scotland) Act 1937 s.12(7), is repealed; however note that s.12(1) concerning child neglect continues. See, e.g. *L v Stott*, 2002 G.W.D. 35–1163.

[26] See recently *M v C*, 2002 S.L.T. (Sh. Ct) 82 (father objecting to Roman Catholic mother sending child to catechism classes after school).

[27] Female circumcision is the main example: Prohibition of Female Circumcision Act 1985; see also discussion of criminal sanctions for child abuse and neglect, para.5.11, above. Circumcision of male infants, a recognised practice in the Jewish and other faiths, is regarded as comparatively minor and has no special regulation.

[28] *Finlayson, Petr*, 1989 S.C.L.R. 601.

[29] See Ch.7.

gious persuasion, racial origin and cultural and linguistic background when making any decision about the child.[30] In particular, if it is decided to apply for an adoption or permanence order in respect of the child, then, even if the consent of the parent or parents has been dispensed with, courts and adoption agencies must still have regard for, inter alia, the child's religious persuasion.[31] It could, for example, be made the condition of an adoption order that the child be brought up in or at least be informed about, say, the Muslim religion.[32] It should be noted that the statutory duty is to have regard to the *child's* religion not the *parent's*. It is submitted that following *Gillick*, a child of sufficient maturity and understanding has the right to choose his or her own religion and this right should be respected by a local authority.[33] All education authorities are under a duty to provide for religious instruction and religious observance in schools.[34] The syllabus, according to guidelines laid down by the Scottish Office Department of Education, should focus on Christianity as the main religious tradition in Scotland but should also take account of the teachings of other religions. However, s.9 of the Education (Scotland) Act 1980 provides a "conscience" clause which allows any parent to withdraw a child from religious instruction or observance at school if they so desire.

An interesting point raised in the House of Lords case *R. (on the application of Williamson) v Secretary of State for Education and Employment*[35] is   **5–17** how far parents can exercise their rights of religious freedom and expression under Art.9 of the ECHR if these rights appear to contravene the rights of their children or the common consensus of society as expressed in laws. As noted above, since 1998, corporal punishment has been banned in all schools in the United Kingdom, public and private. The appellants sought the right to use corporal punishment in four independent schools as part of their religious beliefs. The House of Lords unanimously rejected their claims. In a pluralist society a balance had to be held between freedom to practice one's own beliefs and the interests of others affected by those practices. The ban on corporal punishment in schools pursued a legitimate aim in protecting the rights and dignity of children. Prohibiting only punishments which might breach Art.3 or Art.9 would be impossible to enforce.

---

[30] 1995 Act s.17(4)(c).

[31] Adoption and Children (Scotland) Act 2007 s14(c). See Adoption (Scotland) Act 1978, s.6(1)(b)(ii), as amended by the 1995 Act s.95.

[32] Under s.12(6), 1978 Act. A similar condition was made in *H and H, Petrs* Unreported, O.H., March 10, 1995.

[33] See paras 4–31 *et seq.*, above. Under s.6(2) of the 1978 Act, a child is presumed old enough at the age of 12 to form a view to which a court or adoption agency should have regard. It is submitted that these bodies should also presumptively have regard to a child's views on his or her own religious upbringing at the same age.

[34] Unless a majority of local voters decide to remove this requirement: Education (Scotland) Act 1980 s.8. See also Provision of Religious Observance in Scottish Schools, Circular 1/2005, available at *http://www.scotland.gov.uk/Publications/2005/03//20778/53820* [Accessed July 2, 2013]. For a general discussion of the rights of children and parentsto freedom of religiouos belief in an educational context, see F. McCarthy, "Prayers in the playground:religion and education in the United Kingdom and beyond", in Mair and E. Orucu (eds), *Religion in Family law: A Comparative Search* (Antwerp: CEFL/Intersentia, 2011), pp.235–262.

[35] *R. (on the application of Williamson) v Secretary of State for Education and Employment* [2005] UKHL 15.

Education[36]

5-18   Parents have both a duty to provide suitable education for their children of school age[37] and a right to determine how their child should be educated.[38] These can be seen as aspects of their general rights and duties as parents under ss. 1 and 2 of the 1995 Act, but are more commonly looked at as statutory rights under the distinct Acts dealing with education.[39] The parental right to have children educated according to their religious or philosophical convictions is also guaranteed by Art.2 of the First Protocol to the ECHR.

5-19   *Children* were, for the first time in Scots legal history, given a statutory right to education under s.1 of the Standards in Scotland's Schools, etc. (Scotland) Act 2000 (the "2000 Act"). Education law is in something of a transitional state from an area largely dominated by parental rights versus the state (particularly in relation to allocation of resources), to an area where children also have a voice, particularly since the incorporation of the ECHR. As Barnes points out, although parents must have regard to the wishes of children when making major decisions about education,[40] children have very few positive rights in domestic education law. While parents have a number of useful statutory rights when seeking to oppose education authority decisions, e.g. to make a placing request for a particular school, or to view the child's school records, the child has almost none. One important exception is that a child now has the right to oppose their own exclusion from school.[41]

5-20   Disputes between parents about how their child should be educated, as we have seen, can be resolved via a s.11 specific issue order.[42] Failure to meet the statutory duty to educate one's children is an offence.[43] Despite the general political emphasis on strengthening parental choice in education, in reality, parental choice, at least for those who do not wish to or cannot

---

[36] This section is not intended to be a comprehensive guide to this specialised area. See further, *Butterworths Family Law Service*, Education, section C 2501 *et seq.*; Barnes, "The right to education in Scotland" (2001) J.L.S.S. July, p.23.

[37] Education (Scotland) Act 1980 s.30(1). This duty can be met "by other means" than by enforcing regular attendance at a school, e.g. by educating the child at home.

[38] Education (Scotland) Act 1980 ss.28(1) and 28A–H (substituted by the Education (Scotland) Act 1981).

[39] A "parent" under s.135 of the Education (Scotland) Act 1980, as amended, is defined as including a guardian, any person who has parental responsibilities in relation to the child, has care of the child or is liable to maintain the child. This latter category brings in the father of a child, even if lacking parental rights and not a carer: see Child Support Act 1991 s.4.

[40] See Children (Scotland) Act 1995 s.6. Note also the 2000 Act s.2(2), which obliges an education authority to take account of the views of the child or young person when fulfilling its duty to educate. This could, e.g. empower a mature child to seek a placement to a different school than that chosen by his or her parents. See further, s.2(1) of the 2000 Act, which, in wording drawn from Art.29 of the UNCRC, also obligates the education authority to secure education which "is directed to the development of the child's personality, talents and mental and physical abilities to their fullest potential". While beyond the scope of this book, this may have considerable implications for the education rights of gifted and special needs children.

[41] 2000 Act, s.41. See, e.g. *S v City of Glasgow Council*, 2004 S.L.T. (Sh. Ct) 128.

[42] See para.4–48, above. See also *Lavelle v Lavelle*, 2001 G.W.D. 4–144, which involved a child bringing an action to enforce payment of her preferred educational option.

[43] Education (Scotland) Act 1980 s.35(1) and see *O'Hagan v Rea*, 2001 S.L.T. (Sh. Ct) 30. Truancy is also a ground for referral to the Children's Hearing.

afford to enter the private sector, is limited by a number of factors including geographical catchment, denominational issues and, most importantly, the financial resources of the authority. In *Harvey v Strathclyde Regional Council*,[44] a mother sought to enforce her wish that her child be sent to a local non-denominational school which the education authority planned to close as part of a general rationalisation scheme. Her claim was that the Regional Council had breached its duty to her under s.28 of the Education (Scotland) Act 1980 by planning to close the school of her choice. Despite evidence that the majority of people in the relevant area opposed the closure plan, the House of Lords eventually held that the region had only to give "regard" to the general principle of parental choice, and that the decision of the authority was an administrative one which could not be faulted unless it was so unreasonable that judicial review would be appropriate. In the wake of *Harvey*, s.28 has been said to place education authorities under "an unenforceable duty".[45]

Names

Parental responsibilities and rights include the legal right and duty to give **5–21** the child a surname. Article 7(1) of the UN Convention on the Rights of the Child that the child shall "have the right from birth to a name". This is also an aspect of private life in terms of Art 8 of ECHR. In *M v C*,[46] a mother, Mrs C, changed her name to her maiden name (McC) following her divorce and at the same time unilaterally changed the name of her son to match. The father opposed the change in court. Distinguishing the pre-1995 Act case of *Flett v Flett*,[47] the sheriff held that providing a name was an aspect of the parental responsibilities implied by s.1(1)(a) of the 1995 Act, and the decision was not therefore simply one for the parent with residence but should be based on the welfare of the child. In that case, it was adjudged to be in the child's interests to preserve the surname he had known all his life until very recently, that of his father—a standard status quo decision. The sheriff was unconvinced by English authority that a child may be stigmatised if he lives in a family where he has a different name than his mother (and/or her new partner). In *D v D*[48] a similar decision was reached. The mother's long-term aim was to exclude the father from the child's life; retaining the child's paternal surname would be a "constant reminder" that the father had a right to play an equal role in the child's life. The choice of name, or a change of name, being a matter of parental responsibility, is something which may be done by either parent without consulting the other. An aggrieved parent has the option of seeking an order under s.11 of the 1995 Act, but if a new name has been used for a lengthy period, it is likely that the court will treat that factor as weighing against a change back.

---

[44] *Harvey v Strathclyde Regional Council*, 1989 S.L.T. 612; and *M v C*, 2002 S.L.T. (Sh. Ct) 82.
[45] Logie, "Parental Choice and the Courts", 1989 S.L.T. (News) 417. See also *Dundee City Council, Petrs*, 1999 Fam. L.R. 130.
[46] *M v C*, 2002 S.L.T. (Sh Ct) 82.
[47] *Flett v Flett*, 1995 S.C.L.R. 189.
[48] *D v D*, 2005 G.W.D. 9–128.

LEGAL REPRESENTATION

5–22 Legal representation embraces the administration of any property belonging to the child, the giving of any legal consent which the child him- or herself is incapable of giving, and acting in any transaction the child is incapable of entering into alone.[49] "Transaction" is widely defined and includes legal contracts, unilateral promises and the bringing and defending of civil proceedings.[50] Litigation was dealt with in Ch.2, paras 2–37 *et seq.*, and we have looked at the issues surrounding the giving of a legal consent in relation to medical treatment in Ch.4, paras 4–32 *et seq.* Here we will principally focus on the administration of a child's property and the making of contracts in relation to that property.

The Child's Property

5–23 Typically, the mother and father (if he has automatic or acquired PRRs) will be the joint legal representatives of the child.[51] Any other person may also apply under s.11 to be granted this responsibility and right. In litigation, the court may appoint a special type of limited legal representative known as a curator *ad litem* to represent the child's interests to the court for the duration of those proceedings only. It is also possible for a parent-substitute known as a "guardian" to be appointed by will[52] who has all the rights and responsibilities of the appointing parent, but whose role is, in practice, often restricted to legal representation. Each parent or other person can act without the consent of the other[53] and disputes over legal representation can be resolved by the court as specific issues under s.11 (para.4.48, above). A third party can thus rely on any one legal representative being entitled to act for the child. There is no need for a majority of representatives to agree, as is the case with trustees administering trust property.

5–24 The right to act as legal representative is restricted in two ways. First, the representative must act, as usual, in the interests of the child.[54] Secondly, the representative only has the right to administer the child's property, or to give a consent or enter any transaction on behalf of the child where the child is incapable of acting for him- or herself.[55] Whether a child has capacity depends on the rules of the Age of Legal Capacity (Scotland) Act 1991.[56]

5–25 *Example*: a boy aged 15 seeks consent from his mother or father to sign a contract for Saturday employment. The parents have the right as legal representatives to refuse to enter the contract on behalf of the child. But if the transaction is seen as one which is commonly entered into by children of that age and in those circumstances, and the terms are not unreasonable, then,

---

[49] 1995 Act s.15(5)(a).
[50] Age of Legal Capacity (Scotland) Act 1991 s.9.
[51] 1995 Act s.3.
[52] See paras 6–10 *et seq.*
[53] 1995 Act ss.2(2) and 7(5).
[54] 1995 Act s.1(1).
[55] 1995 Act s.15(5).
[56] See paras 2–21 *et seq.*

under s.2(1) of the 1991 Act, the child will have capacity to enter into the contract himself. In that case, the parents' rights in connection with the contract terminate, so they cannot veto it.

Administration of the Child's Property

Parents have the right and responsibility as legal representatives to administer a child's property. At common law, parents were restricted in what they could do with the property of their children, with a duty to be conservative in investment and to preserve the child's heritage. Under s.10(1)(b) of the 1995 Act, however, all such restrictions are relaxed and legal representatives are entitled to do anything in relation to that property which the child could do if of he or she was of full age and capacity. Parents can thus pass a good title to assets owned by the child, sell heritage as well as moveable property, donate the child's funds, use the capital as well as the income out of a legacy, and invest in risky as well as safe investments.

5–26

What then is to stop parents maladministering their children's property, e.g. selling the property of a child and putting the proceeds to their own benefit, rather than that of the child? Or putting money bequeathed to a child into their own bank account and refusing to pass it on to the child when he or she is old enough to administer the money himself?

5–27

Before the 1995 Act, the situation was highly unsatisfactory.[57] In theory, parents and guardians were regulated in two ways. First, they were subject to the supervision of the Accountant of Court in their administration of a child's property.[58] Secondly, under the Trusts Acts 1921 and 1961, parents were defined as a type of trustee, and trust law applied to their transactions on behalf of the child. Parents were thus, inter alia, forbidden from acting in their own cause (*auctor in rem suam*) and could be called on to account for their transactions with the child's property. In practice, however, this protection was little-known, obscure in detail and largely illusory.

5–28

The 1995 Act introduces an entirely new scheme in ss.9 and 10 of the 1995 Act.[59] Parents (and guardians) are no longer to be regarded as trustees under the Trusts Acts.[60] Instead the Act attempts to identify and regulate occasions where the child comes into ownership of reasonably large amounts of property.[61] A child most commonly acquires substantial assets via trust, inheritance or an award of damages. In these three cases, the child's property will usually be passed to the parents for future administration, by, respectively, a trustee, an executor or a court. The strategy of the Act then is to focus on these occasions when the property is held at an interim stage by someone other than a parent, and to consider at that time if supervision may be desirable *before*

5–29

---

[57] For a full account, see Wilkinson and Norre, para.15–34.

[58] Judicial Factors Act 1849 ss.10 and 25(2).

[59] See guidance approved by the Professional Practice and Civil Procedure Committees of the Law Society of Scotland, for solicitors taking instructions from a child's legal representative or guardian in relation to a money claim on behalf of the child; reprinted at (2004) J.L.S.S. August, p.38, updated in *Money Claims on Behalf of Children*, JLSS Online, February 14, 2005.

[60] Sch.4, para.2, amending Judicial Factors Act 1849, and para.6, amending Trusts Act 1921 s.2.

[61] See *Report on Family Law*, Scot. Law Com. No.135 (1992), Pt IV.

the money reaches the parents. Section 9 sets out a number of rules *requiring* trustees, executors and other persons holding property worth £20,000 or more for the child, to seek directions from the Accountant of Court as to how the property should be administered, before they pass the property to the parents for administration. Such persons *may* also seek directions voluntarily if they hold property worth between £5,000 and £20,000. When directions are sought, the Accountant of Court may direct that

- a judicial factor be appointed to administer the property. This is usually a solicitor or accountant who is appointed by court to look after the property of a person incapable of doing so, and who is supervised by the Accountant of Court.[62] This might also be a way of placing parents under judicial scrutiny; or
- all or part of the property should be transferred to himself; or
- all or part of the property should be transferred without further ado to the parent or guardian who will administer it on behalf of the child.[63] If there is any dubiety about how the parents will handle the money, conditions may be attached before the property is transferred to the parents, e.g. that there shall be no capital expenditure without the permission of the court.[64]

5–30   Similar provisions apply under s.13 when a court makes an award of damages to a child. When money becomes payable to a child in court proceedings, i.e. damages or settlement, the court may make such order as it thinks fit. *I v Argyll and Clyde Health Board*,[65] provided some useful guidance here. First, s.13 takes precedence over s.9. So even if the sum of damages is over £20,000 it is not mandatory to ask the court or Accountant of Court for directions, though it may be desirable. Secondly, the person who owes the damages—in *I*'s case, the Health Board—is not "the protector of the child" and need not seek directions either from the court or the Accountant of Court. That job should fall to the legal representative—in *I*'s case, his parents. Thirdly, in general it was emphasised that s.13 was more flexible than the pre-1995 Act common law: in particular there was no duty to appoint an expensive judicial factor unless there was some reason to believe the payment to the child's parents could not be secured by some other simpler means, e.g. a reporting condition.

5–31   The Act also protects children by imposing a duty in s.10 on any person administering a child's property as legal representative to act as a reasonable and prudent person would act on his or her own behalf (the standard of care required of a trustee). What remedies does the child have for breach of this duty? A legal representative who fails to meet the s.10 standard can be called on to account for his or her intromissions.[66] No liability is incurred if he or

---

[62] Judicial Factors Act 1849.

[63] Judicial Factors Act 1849 s.9(5).

[64] Judicial Factors Act 1849 s.9(6)(a).

[65] *I v Argyll and Clyde Health Board*, 2003 S.L.T. 231.

[66] 1995 Act s.10(1). This is a remedy derived from the law of trusts. For full details, see Wilson and Duncan, *Trusts, Trustees and Executors*, 2nd edn (1995), pp.451 *et seq.*

she has expended the child's funds in proper discharge of the parental duty to safeguard and promote child's health, development and welfare.[67] However, a child can only require the legal representative to account when he or she has ceased so to act, which will usually not be until the child has reached the age of 16.[68] The child, however, has the right to sue for damages arising out of the parent's failure in fiduciary duty as soon as he or she has capacity to instruct proceedings, which will usually be earlier.[69] Furthermore, an application could be made to the court at any time under s.11, to remove the parent as legal representative, or to replace him with a judicial factor.

Can a child have a contract, which a parent made on his behalf, set aside **5–32** if the parent did not act in the child's interests, as required by s.1(1)? For example, a parent might sell a painting, bequeathed to the child, to a friend for a knockdown price. Although the Act does not say so expressly, by analogy with the law of trusts such transactions should be voidable if the parent has acted in his or her own interests and not those of the child.[70]

On the other hand, a child does not have the right to reduce a contract **5–33** made by a parent just because he or she did not agree with it. Under s.6(1), a child has a right to be consulted in any major decision taken by parents in the exercise of parental responsibility.[71] The sale of important assets belonging to a child, such as a house, may well fall into this category. However, even if the child has not been consulted, or if due regard has not been given to his or her views, this does not give the child, or any other person, a right to reduce a transaction entered into with a third party, as long as that party acted in good faith.[72]

CHILDREN'S RIGHTS

Children share with adults many rights which are generally regarded as being **5–34** part of public law or the law of civil liberties, such as the right to be housed or the right to freedom of speech. In this chapter, however, we shall restrict ourselves to looking at the key private law rights for children: the right not to be discriminated against on grounds of the lack of marital status of one's parents; the right to support during life from one's parents; and the right to claim on death under the rules of succession.

The Right not to be Discriminated Against Because of Parents' Marital Status

Children born to unmarried parents were historically described as "ille- **5–35** gitimate" and suffered serious legal discrimination as a result. As noted in Ch.3, however, discrimination against illegitimate children became steadily

---

[67] 1995 Act s.10(2).
[68] 1995 Act s.2(1)(d) and (7).
[69] An action of accounting is a separate remedy from an action for breach of fiduciary duty. See Walker, *Civil Remedies* (1974), Chs 17 and 58.
[70] See Wilkinson & Norrie, 3rd edn, para.5–06.
[71] A child of 12 or over is presumed old and mature enough to express a view to which parents should have regard.
[72] 1995 Act s.6(2).

less tenable from the late 1970s on, for a number of reasons. In terms of sheer numbers, more and more children are born outside wedlock each year, representing about half of all births. Attitudes towards sexual morality have changed and there is an increasing tendency for children to be born to stable cohabiting couples. In terms of both public ideas of fairness and international human rights standards, legislation providing equal rights for illegitimate children became essential by the early 1980s.[73] This became especially clear after the European Court of Human Rights found, in the case of *Marckx v Belgium*, that rules discriminating against an illegitimate child in relation to succession rights were in breach of the ECHR.[74] Reform was at first accomplished on a piecemeal basis,[75] but in 1986, the Law Reform (Parent and Child) (Scotland) Act s.1(1) laid down the general principle, with some exceptions, that the fact that one's parents were married or not was to have no differential legal effect.

5–36   The Family Law (Scotland) Act 2006 s.21 took this process one step further and amended s.1 of the 1986 Act to abolish completely the status of legitimacy and illegitimacy in Scotland henceforth. No person whose status is governed by Scots law is now to be known as illegitimate, and declarators of legitimacy, legitimation and illegitimacy are abolished. A few connected problems are also tidied up by the 2006 Act. The domicile of a child, once dependent on the marital status of the parents, is now determined by s.22 of the 2006 Act as follows: if the parents of a child are domiciled in the same country as each other, and the child has a home with one or both, the child is domiciled in the same country as the parents: if these conditions do not apply, the child is deemed to be domiciled in the country with which he or she for the time being has the closest connection.

Minor Exceptions

5–37   Deeds executed before, or, indeed, after the commencement of the 2006 Act may still refer expressly to "illegitimate" children, but given the lack of meaning now attached to the term, this is now extremely unlikely to happen. In respect of all deeds executed since the Law Reform (Miscellaneous Provisions) (Scotland) Act 1968,[76] a reference to children will be interpreted as presumptively referring to *all* children whether their parents were married or not. Only for deeds executed before that, does the presumption go the other way.[77] If despite the presumption, there is clearly a reference that needs interpretation according to the old law of legitimacy, then and only then will that law need to be consulted.

5–38   Similarly, statutes which were enacted before the 2006 Act came into force, are also in theory not subject to the abolition of illegitimacy.[78] However, in practice, most statutes affecting children have been amended either by the

---

[73] The UK became a signatory to the European Convention on the Legal Status of Children Born out of Wedlock in 1981.

[74] Under Arts 8 and 14; (1979) 2 E.H.R.R. 330.

[75] Notably by the Law Reform (Miscellaneous Provisions) (Scotland) Act 1968 and the 1985 Act.

[76] 1986 Act s.1(4)(b) and 1968 Act s.5.

[77] *Mitchell's Trs v Cable* (1893) 1 S.L.T. 156 See Wilkinson & Norrie, 3rd edn, para.6.08 et seq.

[78] 1986 Act s.1(4)(a).

1986 Act, or subsequently, to reflect a position of legal equality of all children and to remove offensive terminology.

Finally, nothing in the 1986 or 2006 Act affects the rules relating to the transmission of titles, coats of arms, honours and dignities, and, for these purposes only, declarators of legitimacy, illegitimacy and legitimation are retained.[79] If any question about the effect of a parent's marriage on the status of a person arises as a matter of international private law, then the question shall be determined by the law of the country in which the person is domiciled when the question arises.[80]   **5–39**

The Child's Right to Financial Support

It is a fundamental tenet of the law of both Scotland and England that a child has a right to financial support from both of his or her parents, whether or not they are or have been married and whether or not they live together or apart. The Family Law (Scotland) Act 1985 (hereafter "the 1985 Act") sets out the principles for determining what support is owed by parents to their children ("aliment"). In practice, however, the provisions of the 1985 Act are rarely invoked where the parents share a household with each other and the child, and in cases where the parents live apart, the 1985 Act rules on aliment have largely been eclipsed by the Child Support Act 1991 as amended (hereafter "the 1991 Act") which has introduced wide-ranging changes throughout the United Kingdom in relation to the child's right to support. The 1991 Act does not cover all aspects of aliment, and where it does not, or where the Act is excluded, the 1985 Act is still good law. The 1991 Act does not provide for the educational expenses of children, and so liability for any expense such as school fees must be decided by a court in terms of the principles of sections 1 and 4 of the 1985 Act.   **5–40**

The 1985 Act still applies wherever the 1991 Act does not, in relation to:

(1) claims for top-up aliment under s.8(6)(b) of the 1991 Act in the case of a non-resident parent who has income above the child support cap;
(2) aliment for a child who is disabled in terms of s.8(8) and (9);
(3) aliment for step-children and for children who are not biologically related to the defender and have not been adopted by him but have been accepted by the defender as a member of his family (1985 Act s.1(1)(d));
(4) a claim for aliment, by a child against the parent with whom he lives; (1991 Act s.8(10));
(5) a child between the ages of 20 and 25 who falls within the terms of s.1 of the 1985 Act;
(6) aliment for a child between 16 and 20 in respect of whom no child benefit is payable.

The 1985 Act provides in s.1 that an obligation of aliment is owed by a father and mother to his or her child[81] and by any person to a child who has been   **5–41**

---

[79] 1986 Act s.9(1)(c) as amended by 2006 Act.
[80] 2006 Act s.41.
[81] 1985 Act s.1(1)(c).

"accepted" as part of their family,[82] except where the child has been boarded out as a foster child by the local authority or a voluntary organisation. For the purposes of the 1985 Act, a child is generally defined as a person aged under 18, but may also include a person over the age of 18 but under the age of 25 who is "reasonably and appropriately undergoing instruction at an educational establishment, or training for employment or for a trade, profession or vocation".[83] As we will see later in this chapter, these provisions of the 1985 Act extending alimentary liability beyond genetic or adoptive family do not apply in the context of the rather different provisions of the 1991 Act under which parents have a duty to maintain only those children as defined in the statute[84] Any child within the scope of s.1(1)(d) of the 1985 Act, such as a step-child is similarly excluded from the scope of the 1991 Act and is entitled to aliment under the older statute, with its very different criteria.

5–42   The child's right to support from a parent's estate after death are dealt with in the law of succession, considered below at paras 5–82 *et seq.* Leaving aside questions relating to the death of one or both parents then, there are three main scenarios when discussing a child's rights to support in Scotland:

(1) where the child is living with both parents;
(2) where the child is living apart from both parents;
(3) where the child is living with one parent and the other lives elsewhere.

5–43   Before we go on to consider each of these broad positions in more detail, it should be noted that although the duty of aliment is owed to the child, it is generally the person with care of the child who receives any money that is payable for the aliment of the child. As we have seen in previous chapters, if the child has limited legal capacity this means that financial support owed to a child will usually be administered by a parent or other adult.

Where the Child is Living with Both Parents

5–44   Here, the position is regulated by the 1985 Act. As discussed in para.5–40, both parents are bound to aliment their child and if they fail to do so either the child, or a person acting on behalf of the child, such as a parent, guardian

---

[82] 1985 Act s.1(1)(d). A child whom a father once treated as his own child but subsequently discovers to have been fathered by another man has not been "accepted" by him as a child of the family, i.e. ss.1(1)(c) and 1(1)(d) are mutually exclusive: *Watson v Watson*, 1994 S.C.L.R. 1097.

[83] 1985 Act s.1(5). Since *Macdonald v Macdonald*, 2000 Fam. L.B. 46–4, a number of enterprising students have used or attempted to use this section to support them during their studies, often when they have become estranged from a well-off parent during parental divorce. In quantifying aliment in these cases (see para.5–45 below), a student loan will be regarded as part of the child's own resources: *Park v Park*, 2000 S.L.T. (Sh. Ct) 65. Students will not necessarily be penalised because they do not obtain a part-time job (*Watson v McLay*, 2002 G.W.D. 2–73) or a loan where this might lead to unreasonable debt (*Hay v Hay*, 2000 Fam. L.B. 46–4).

[84] 1991 Act s.1(1) states that each parent of a qualifying child is responsible for maintaining him or her, and s.54 then defines "parent" in relation to any child as meaning any person who is in law the mother or father of the child. For legal definitions of "parent", see Ch.3: broadly this includes genetic and adoptive parents and persons who are to be treated for all purposes as parents under the Human Fertilisation and Embryology Act 1990.

or person with whom the child lives or who is seeking a residence order, can sue to enforce the obligation.[85] An obligation of aliment may also be owed by virtue of s.1(1)(d) of the 1985 Act by a person who has accepted the child as a member of his family. No formal step is required for this liability to arise, though if the defender has married the child's mother it may be all the more difficult for him to maintain that he did not accept the child as a member of his family. In such circumstances, there is no order of liability but any person who is sued for aliment may ask the court to take account of the obligations of aliment owed by other parties.[86]

In determining the amount of aliment to award under the 1985 Act, the court must have regard to the factors in s.4(1),[87] namely the needs and resources of the parties,[88] the earning capacity of the parties, and, generally, all the circumstances of the case. The court can have regard as it wishes to any support given by the defender to any person whom he maintains as a dependant in his household, whether or not there is a legal requirement to maintain that person.[89] Conduct is only relevant if it is manifestly inequitable to leave it out of account.[90] The court when making an order for aliment will usually make an order for periodical payments for a definite or indefinite period[91] but can also exceptionally make orders for lump-sum payments, e.g. for educational expenses.[92]   **5–45**

However, where a child is living as part of a family with both parents, the parental obligation to aliment is usually fulfilled by their provision for the child's everyday needs.[93] It is a defence to an action for aliment that the defender is already fulfilling the obligation of aliment, and intends to continue doing so.[94] Generally speaking, the issue of failure to adequately aliment a child within the household arises more frequently in the context of child protection law and the criminal law of neglect or abuse than in the private law of aliment.[95]   **5–46**

An order for aliment once made can be varied or recalled by the courts on a "material change of circumstances".[96] This is subject, however, to the jurisdiction of the Child Support Agency, discussed below, at paras 5–50 *et seq.*   **5–47**

---

[85] 1985 Act s.2(4).

[86] 1985 Act s.4(2). See, e.g. *Inglis v Inglis*, 1987 S.C.L.R. 608, where a father asked for the alimentary obligation of the aunt and uncle of the child, who were looking after him and had "accepted" him, to be taken into account.

[87] These are also the factors used to assess spousal aliment claims. They are examined in detail in Ch.10, as is the rest of the 1985 Act regime relating to awards of aliment.

[88] This can include the resources of the child him- or herself: see *Wilson v Wilson*, 1987 G.W.D. 4–106.

[89] 1985 Act s.4(3)(a). Support given a *claimant* for aliment by other parties, whether or not legally obligated, can also be taken into account under the head of "resources" in s.4—see, e.g. *Ritchie v Ritchie*, 1989 S.C.L.R. (Notes) 768.

[90] 1985 Act s.4(3)(b).

[91] 1985 Act s.3(1)(a).

[92] 1985 Act s.3(1)(b).

[93] 1985 Act s.2 (6).

[94] 1985 Act s.2(6).

[95] See Chs 7 and 8.

[96] 1985 Act s.5.

Where the Child is living Apart from Both Parents

5–48   It is not uncommon for children to live with neither of their parents either because the parents have chosen to place them elsewhere, e.g. at a boarding school, or because the children have been abandoned or removed from the parents under the rules of child protection law. In these circumstances, the duties of the parents to aliment in principle persist. If the local authority looks after a child under the provisions of Pt II of the 1995 Act, then in general the parents retain their obligation to aliment the child. However, if the local authority removes parental responsibilities and rights from the parents by an order made under s.86 of the 1995 Act or, a permanency order under the Adoption and Children (Scotland) Act 2007, ss 80–84. (see Ch.6), then the parents cease to have a duty of aliment.[97] Where children are living apart from their birth parents because they have been adopted, the duties of the birth parents, including the duty to aliment, are transferred to the adoptive parents.[98] Where the child is living with local authority foster parents, they have no alimentary obligations beyond those agreed in the fostering arrangements.[99] Foster parents are reimbursed by the state for the care of foster children through allowances made under regulations.[100] Finally, where there is no parent or other person who can be identified as having a duty to aliment a child, the child has the right to support from the State. The 1995 Act provides that local authorities have a duty to provide accommodation for a child who has no parent or other person with parental responsibilities or whose parent or guardian cannot provide the child with suitable accommodation or care.[101]

Where Children are Living With One Parent

5–49   The rules on financial support of children living with one parent have been fundamentally altered by the implementation of the Child Support Act 1991, as substantially amended. The Act radically reformed the system of child maintenance in four main ways:

(1) it removed decisions about maintenance from the jurisdiction of the court in most cases and created a Child Support Agency within the social security system to administer the Act;

(2) it provided that decisions about levels of child support were to be made by the application of a rigid formula in nearly all cases, thus altering the position from that which previously existed under the 1985 Act, where the court had a wide discretion in setting the level of aliment;

---

[97] 1995 Act s.86 is silent on this point. However, s.78 of the Social Work (Scotland) Act 1968 provides that "contributions" in respect of a child under 16 who is "looked after" by the local authority (see 1995 Act s.17(6) and para.7–24) are payable *only* by any natural person who has parental responsibilities as defined under s.1(3) of the 1995 Act. This seems to imply that there is no such obligation on parents whose responsibilities have been removed. See Ch.7.

[98] Adoption and Children (Scotland) Act 2007 s.40.

[99] Foster parents with whom the child is boarded out are especially excluded from the duty of aliment under the 1985 Act s.1(1)(d).

[100] See Fostering of Children (Scotland) Regulations 1996 (SI 1996/3263).

[101] 1995 Act s.25. See paras 7–18 *et seq.*

(3) it provided that parents' private agreements as to maintenance could be overridden in the event of either parent applying to the Child Support Agency for a maintenance assessment;

(4) the welfare of the child is not paramount under the 1991 Act, Instead the child's interest is only to be given "regard" when reaching decisions on any matter in respect of which the Secretary of State has a discretion on child support.[102] This is very limited category of decisions.

The Statutory Child Support System

At the time of writing the statutory child support system is in a state of change. The major changes are set out below, but it should be borne in mind that the Child Support Agency (CSA) is the same thing as the Child Maintenance Service (CMS) and the terms may be used interchangeably. In practice the body will call itself 'CSA' when administering CS1 and CS2 cases, and 'CMS' when handling cases under CS3.   **5–50**

Background

The increasing frequency of divorce, as well as the recognition that many non-resident parents were unable or unwilling to contribute to the financial support of their children, led to the need to extend state-provided child (and child-carer) maintenance. Eligibility for supplementary benefits (now income support) was extended first to lone mothers, and in 1975, to lone fathers. All lone parents thus became entitled to receive benefits whether or not they were available for work, a privileged position in the social security system shared only with other special groups, e.g. those over retirement age and those with disabilities. At the same time as extending state benefits for lone parenthood, the Department of Health and Social Security (now the Department for Work and Pensions) began to recover child maintenance from the non-resident parents of children whose resident parent was in receipt of supplementary benefit. These non-residential parents were known as "liable relatives"[103] since the state was taking on the obligation of support which these non-paying parents were legally liable to fulfil. The State thus began to attempt to enforce the private law alimentary obligations of non-resident parents in order to reduce its own expanding social security bill. Until the Social Security Act 1986, non-resident parents were required to pay maintenance at a rate equivalent to the relevant supplementary benefit scales for children. When supplementary benefit was replaced by income support in 1988, the maintenance obligation of non-resident parents was increased to include the amount equivalent to the family and lone parent premiums on top of the allowance for children.   **5–51**

In many cases, however, no attempt was made to recover payment, and in many others only a minimal amount was recovered. In 1988, the DSS's savings from maintenance recovery amounted to £126 million, but this   **5–52**

---

[102] 1991 Act s.2 requires that a child support officer "shall have regard to the welfare of any child likely to be affected by his decision".

[103] Under the Supplementary Benefits Act 1976 s.17 (now repealed).

was a decrease in real terms of 9 per cent since 1981/1982 when the amount recovered in maintenance payments was £103 million. The percentage of income support expenditure recovered almost halved from 13 per cent to 7 per cent during this period. In 1988/1989, the cost of social security to lone parents was reported by the DSS as £3.2 billion, compared with £1.4 billion in 1981/1982.[104]

5–53   As the number of lone parent families rose, the legal arrangements for child maintenance were increasingly criticised. First, the parallel provisions in the private and public law systems were seen as incoherent: while the DSS was concerned to ensure that as many fathers as possible contributed to the financial support of their children after divorce or separation, meanwhile the courts were absolving some fathers from the payment of their alimentary obligations on the grounds that the DSS were supporting their children, and that having to pay aliment for the children of a previous relationship would create financial hardship for the absent parent.

5–54   Secondly, research began to show that even where aliment for children from non-resident parents was ordered by the court, the amounts ordered tended to be small. Moreover, in a large number of cases aliment was never paid, and in a further proportion of cases in which payments *were* made, aliment was paid erratically. For example, in 1980, awards for aliment of children were made in less than half (44 per cent) of the 2,500 Scottish divorce actions involving dependent children. The median amount of aliment per family was £10. In the same year, one-third of all awards for aliment or periodical allowance were never paid at all, while of the remainder over half (54 per cent) were no longer being paid three years later.[105] Later research showed that by 1991, awards for aliment featured in only 40 per cent of Scottish divorces involving children, and that the median amount per week was £23.[106] In any event[107] it became the usual practice in sheriff courts to make no order for aliment in any case in which the payee—almost always the mother—was in receipt of means tested benefits because any such aliment was only going to be clawed back by the DSS, thus making the mother a mere conduit between the father and the State. Aliment, it was felt was properly for the benefit of the child and there was little point in the court making an order from which the child would not gain at all.

5–55   Thirdly, there was increasing evidence that children of lone parents were likely to be living in poverty both because of the failure of the private maintenance system to provide realistic support and because lone parent families

---

[104] Committee of Public Accounts, *DSS: Support for Lone-Parent Families* (1993). See, e.g. *Delaney v Delaney* [1990] 2 F.L.R. 457.

[105] Dobash and Wasoff, "Financial Awards in Divorce and Prospects for Payment", in *Socio-legal Research in the Courts* (Adler and Millar (eds), Central Research Unit Papers), Vol.1. See also, for similar findings in England and Wales, Eekelaar and Maclean, *Maintenance after Divorce* (1986), and Bradshaw and Millar, *Lone Parent Families in the U.K.* (1991), DSS Research Report No.6.

[106] Morris, Gibson and Platts, *Untying the Knot: Characteristics of Divorce in Scotland* (1993).

[107] See the Finer Report, Report of the Committee on One-Parent Families, Cmnd 5629 (1974) for the formula used by the DSS under the supplementary benefit system to calculate the liability of absent fathers.

depend heavily on means tested social security benefits,[108] with consequent low standards of living.

By the end of the 1980s, all these factors had led to social security spending **5–56** on lone parent families being targeted as an area in which savings could be made by reinforcing the principle that parents have an inescapable obligation to support their children.[109] The result was the Child Support Act 1991. However, since implementation of the Act on April 5, 1993, the legislation has attracted an alarming amount of censure and amendment. The Child Support Agency has been criticised for both incompetence and inability to deliver its objectives.[110] Some of the provisions of the 1991 Act have now been substantially modified, particularly those relating to the formulae for determining maintenance due, and to the scope of the Agency's remit. These changes have been detailed in a series of statutory instruments, the Child Support Act 1995, the Child Support, Pensions and Social Security Act 2000, the Child Maintenance and Other Payments Act 2008 and many sets of Regulations. We will now examine the details of the scheme of maintenance provided by the 1991 Act as amended.

THE CHILD SUPPORT ACT 1991 AS AMENDED

The 1991 Act cuts across the existing arrangements for the aliment of **5–57** children in both private law and the social security system,[111] taking priority over the 1985 Act, and effectively removing child support from much of the private law arena.

It may be useful to regard the child maintenance systems having been laid **5–58** over the 1985 Act regime but as having holes in it. Wherever the holes are, the 1985 Act still applies. The most common area of continued relevance for the 1985 Act system of aliment is in educational expenses in respect of which the court retains its role. Child support maintenance takes no account of any educational expenses and CMS will take no account of any parental liability for such expenses when calculating child support liability[112] Other areas where the 1991 Act has no relevance are expenses in respect of a child's

---

[108] Figures from DSS (*Social Security Statistics 1993*, Department of Social Security (1994)) show that nearly 75% of lone mothers receive income support, 15% receive family credit (an in-work benefit for lower paid workers) and less than 1% receive Disability Working Allowance (similar to family credit for those with disabilities).

[109] For commentary on the policy background to the original 1991 Act, see Maclean, "The Making of the Child Support Act of 1991: Policy Making at the Intersection of Law and Social Policy" (1994) 21 Journal of Law and Society 505 and Wilson, "The Bairns of Falkirk: The Child Suppot Act 1991", 1991 S.L.T. (News) 417.

[110] See House of Commons Social Security Committee, *The Operation of the Child Support Act* (1993–1994 HC 69); House of Commons Social Security Committee, *The Operation of the Child Support Act: Proposals for Change* (1994–1995 HC 470); National Audit Office Memorandum on the Child Support Agency, June 1995; Ombudsman report, *Investigation of Complaints against the Child Support Agency* (1994–1995 HC 135). The outstanding sum of arrears in 2009 was £3.7bn. In 2013 it was £3.8bn.

[111] For a concise summary of the 1991 Act as originally enacted from a Scots lawyer's perspective see Wilson, "The Bairns of Falkirk: The Child Suppot Act 1991", 1991 S.L.T. (News) 417.

[112] Child Support Act 1991 s.8(7).

disability—s.8(8) and aliment for a child who, by virtue of his age is no longer subject to the 1991 Act regime.

5–59　　The statutory scheme applies to maintenance for children (i) under 16; (ii) in full-time education which is not advanced education,[113] and under the age of 20; or (iii) under 18 and either available for work or youth training while the PWC is still claiming child support in respect of the child. This contrasts with the wider ambit of the 1985 Act, in which children could qualify for aliment from their parents up until the age of 25 in certain circumstances including "advanced" education, and from non-parents who have "accepted" them as a child of the family. While both parents owe duties of support towards the child, the NRP must meet his obligation of support by making periodical payments of maintenance as determined by the 1991 Act formulae.[114] The extent of the non-resident parent's obligation to provide support as worked out by the Child Support Agency is his or her "maintenance calculation" which can be enforced under the Act.

5–60　　How successful has it been? The 1991 Act and its attendant regulations have had a chequered history. The legislation itself was enacted very speedily: the initial announcement of intention to resort to legislation on this issue was made by The Prime Minister, Mrs Thatcher during a public lecture in 1990. The proposal to legislate on this issue was generally welcomed: the proposition that all parents should support their children financially regardless of whether they live together or not attracted a high level of consensus. Nevertheless, the actual proposals were the subject of much disquiet and parliamentary lobbying and debate. Despite criticisms of the White Paper and Child Support Bill, the Act was passed in June 1991 with implementation to begin in April 1993.

5–61　　Analyses of the outcomes for lone-parent families after implementation of the 1991 legislation showed that very few lone-parent families would ever benefit from the new provisions. It was argued that even where the Act had potential to raise the standards of living for some children living apart from one parent (those who were already in the most advantaged financial positions), the problems of implementation were likely to negate these possible gains.[115] PWCs would also suffer by having their freedom either to make private agreements with the father of their child, or to cut all ties with such fathers, removed. NRPs, too, would suffer inequity in some cases due to the inability of the system to consider their individual financial and personal circumstances.

5–62　　At the time of writing there are three concurrent systems of statutory child support. The first is based on the original Child Support Scheme which came in to effect in 1993. This was a very complicated system in which the calculation of child support liability was based upon information which had to be

---

[113] See ss.3 and 55 of the 1991 Act as amended. Basically what is covered by this is education up to, but not including, the tertiary stage, i.e. university or college. But see para.5–41 for possible claims beyond that point under the Family (Scotland) Act 1985.

[114] 1991 Act s.1(2). The formulae have been very substantially amended over time. See below.

[115] See Millar, "Poor Mothers and Absent Fathers: Support for Lone Parents in Comparative Perspective" and Wasoff and Morris, "The Child Support Act: a victory for women?", both in Jones and Millar (eds), *The Politics of the Family* (1996).

gathered from both parents. The PWC, if she was in receipt of state benefits, had little incentive to cooperate more than passively with the system because any child support maintenance recovered from the NRP (at that time called the Absent Parent) was deducted from the benefit which she received. The calculation became extremely complicated and the Child Support Agency itself was ill-equipped to deal with its own system. The initial rigidity of the 1991 Scheme was to some extent modified by virtue of the Child Support Act 1995 which brought in a system of Departures—special rules whereby the circumstances of some families could be taken in to account either to increase or decrease the level of child support maintenance. Even with these departures the system was complicated, rigid and unpopular.

Eventually the original system, which we now refer to as CS1, was replaced **5-63** by CS2 by virtue of the Child Support, Pensions and Social Security Act 2000 which came in to effect in 2003. CS2 was a simpler system because the income and resources of the PWC were irrelevant. The calculation depended only on the income and resources of the NRP. The calculation itself was much simpler. If there was one qualifying child the NRP paid 15% of his net income for child support maintenance. If there were two qualifying children he paid 20% and if there were three or more he paid 25%. The net income was defined as his gross income less tax, national insurance and pension contributions. Originally only one half of the pension contributions could be deducted but this was changed to include the whole amount of the pension contribution unless the contribution was unreasonably high.[116]

The CS1 departures system was replaced by a system of Variations, which **5-64** allowed either a reduction or increase in the calculation of maintenance. The most frequently litigated of these variations were the Regulations 18 to 20 of the Child Support Variations Regulation 2000. They were known as the "Additional Cases". The NRP, if he had net assets in excess of £65,000 excluding the house in which he lived and some other exclusions was deemed to be earning 8% net per annum on all of those assets. His deemed income was then added to his actual income before the usual formula was applied.

Regulation 20—the "Lifestyle Variation"—permitted the CSA to deem an **5-65** NRP to be earning the level of income which it appeared to them would be necessary for the NRP to fund his lifestyle. This was used if the lifestyle were particular rich and if the declared income of the NRP were particularly low. The usual defences to such an application were that the NRP was either being funded by a third party such as a parent or a new partner or else was spending not income but capital. In the event of the non-resident parent declaring that he was spending capital it was open to the Agency or the PWC to seek to look at that capital in the light of reg.18.

Most recently a system known as CS3 was brought in by a complex series **5-66** of Regulations[117] underpinned by the 2008 Act. At the time of writing CS3 applies to all new cases where there are two or more qualifying children in the same family. Between 2013 and 2017 this will be extended to all new cases and existing CS1 and CS2 cases will be transferred to CS3.

---

[116] See article at 2009 S.L.T. (News) 105.
[117] Most significantly the Child Maintenance Regulations 2012.

5–67   Under each of the three systems of child support the PWC may apply for child support maintenance under s.4 of the 1991 Act. In Scotland a child of 12 or more may make his own application under s.7 of the 1991 Act although this is very rarely done.

5–68   The basis of the calculation under CS3 is the effective date[118] and that is the date when the application is first intimated, no matter how informally, to the NRP. When the calculation is made, which may be weeks or even months later the liability is backdated to that effective date. In the CS1 and CS2 systems information about the income and resources of the NRP was collected principally from the NRP himself. Under CS3 the information will principally be collected from Her Majesty's Revenue & Customs in respect of the last tax year unless under some circumstances that is seen to be impractical.[119] Under some circumstances this information may have to be estimated[120] and then the Child Maintenance Service, as the Child Support Agency has been renamed, will calculate the liability on a differential formula. In respect of the first £800 per week of the NRP's gross income the liability will be 12% for one qualifying child, 16% for two and 19% for three or more. In respect of the NRP's gross income between £800 and £3.000 the liability will change to 9%, 12% or 15% depending on the number of children. This differential is to counter the effect of a higher percentage of the higher rate tax payer being taken from him unfairly.

5–69   CMS will ignore any income which the NRP may have in excess of £3,000 gross per week. If the PWC wishes to receive more payments from the NRP then she must seek aliment from him applying the criteria of s.4 of the Family Law (Scotland) Act 1985 in Scotland.[121] For the NRP with gross income below £200 per weekthe reduced rate, flat rate or nil rate may apply subject to the criteria of regs 43 to 45 of the MCR.

5–70   If there is insufficient information to enable CMS to carry out the calculation they will apply a default rate of £39 per week for one qualifying child, £51 where there are two and £64 per week where there are three or more. It is clear that if this figure is very much lower than the actual maintenance calculation would be on the basis of full correct information then it will be very much in the interests of the NRP to allow the default arrangement to continue. Conversely, if the default rate is higher than the figure which would be properly calculated on full information, the non-resident parent will have an interest to ensure that the information is made available as soon as possible. This, of course, may not be within his control but it will allow the system to operate, even if unfairly. In May 2013, the average weekly maintenance liability across the UK was £23.50 in respect of all cases, regardless of the number of children involved. From this we may say that the default rate seems to have been set at a penal level for most NRPs.

---

[118] Child Support Maintenance Calculation Regulations 2012 (SI 2012/2677) (hereafter "MRC 2012") reg.12.

[119] MRC 2012 regs 35–39.

[120] MRC 2012 reg.42.

[121] Or the Children Act 1989 in England.

Updating Gross Weekly Income

Over the course of any given tax year it is possible that the non-resident 5–71
parent's income will vary considerably. Under CS1 and CS2 the non-resident
parent was able to apply to the CSA to notify them of a decrease in his
income. The PWC was able to notify them of any increase which she felt could
be proven. The CSA would then recalculate the amount of maintenance to be
paid, subject to narrow thresholds. Under CS3 there will be no alteration of
the amount of maintenance liability on a change of circumstances unless that
change of circumstances has been an increase or decrease of at least 25% of
the previously calculated figure. Thus if a non-resident parent with an income
of £1,000 per week were to have an increase of £200 per week the parent with
care and her children would not share in that increase. On the other hand if
his income were to fall to £800 per week he would have no diminution in the
amount of maintenance which he would be obliged to pay at least until the
review date, one year after the original date of calculation.[122]

Shared Care

It is common for a child of separated parents to spend some time with the 5–72
parent with whom the child does not normally live, whether under an informal arrangement between the parties or subject to an order in terms of s.11 of
the Children (Scotland) Act 1995.

If a non-resident parent has the child living with him for at least 52 nights 5–73
per year—1 night per week—then there is a reduction in child support maintenance of one seventh. In the same way the child is with him for 2 or 3 nights
per week on average over the year, the diminution is two sevenths or three
sevenths. If the child is with him or at least 175 nights per year his liability
is reduced by half. These diminutions are repeated from the CS2 system.
However, in an innovation under CS3, by virtue of reg.50(2) of MCR, if
either parent has equal or greater care of the child over the year then that
parent cannot be a non-resident parent at all. Thus a very wealthy non-
resident parent may have a substantial maintenance liability subject to a 50%
deduction and then seek a very slight increase in contact which has the effect
of reducing the money which he pays for his children to nil.

Contact for these purposes depends on the number of nights the child 5–74
spends with the non-resident parent. Regular care during the day, no matter
what money is spent on the child during that time, does not count under the
shared care provisions of the scheme.[123]

Variations

As noted above CS1 was a very rigid system and this rigidity was recog- 5–75
nised as causing injustice. Accordingly in the Child Support Act 1995 the
system of Departures was introduced, modified to a system of Variations
under CS2.[124] Variations under CS3 are further amended and defined under

---

[122] MRC 2012 regs 19–23.
[123] Child Support Act 1991 Sch.1, para.7.
[124] Child Support (Variations) Regulations 2000 (SI 2000/156).

regs 56 to 75 of MCR 2012. The CS2 system included a variation[125] by which a non-resident parent who had assets (subject to some exclusions) in excess of £65,000 could be deemed to be earning 8% net on those assets whether he was actually earning anything on them at all or not. This deemed income was then added to his ordinary income before the application of the usual maintenance formula. Furthermore, under reg.20 of the Variations Regulations a non-resident parent who had a lifestyle which seemed to be substantially more expensive than his declared income could have supported could be deemed to have income which the CSA or the tribunal thought that he would have had to have in order to live that lifestyle. There are two main defences to this lifestyle variation—the first was that the high lifestyle was being funded by a third party such as a parent or new partner, or that the high lifestyle had been funded out of capital rather than income. If the second course was adopted by the NRP, the PWC could ask once again to look at those assets for the purposes of a reg.18 variation. There is no echo of regs 18 nor 20 in CS3.

5–76   There is however a strong echo of reg.19 of the 2000 variation regulations in regs 69 to 71 of MCR 2012, by which an NRP with unearned income in excess of £2500 per year can have that income added to his other income for calculation purposes. Furthermore, if he is thought by the CSA or by the Tribunal to be diverting income then although the CSA is not in a position to prevent that diversion, it can deem him to be receiving the income which has been diverted. A typical example would be a self-employed NRP who, in order to defeat child support maintenance, diverted profits of a business to a close relative or a new partner.

5–77   Variations can also be used by the non-resident parent to decrease the amount of maintenance liability. Regulations 63 to 67 of MRC provide that an NRP who has high costs of exercising contact with a qualifying child, who has costs in relation to the illness or disability of a relevant other child, who is paying prior dates or certain payments in respect of mortgages, etc. of the PWC can have these payments deducted by his income before the application of the maintenance formula.

5–78   Under reg.66 the NRP can seek to deduct payments which he makes in respect of boarding school fees for a qualifying child. This is because during school term time the child has been actually maintenance at the father's expense.

5–79   By virtue of reg.66 a calculation has to be made deducting the cost of tuition from the whole boarding school cost in order to establish the extent of the deduction.

APPEALS

5–80   If a party is dissatisfied with a decision of the CSA or CMS that party and cannot persuade the Agency to change that decision he can apply to the First Tier Tribunal of the Social Entitlement Chamber in an Appeal. The Appeal may proceed on the basis that the Agency has used mistaken facts

---

[125] Child Support Variations Regulations 2000 reg.18.

in its decision, that it has misapplied the Law or that there has been error in the caclulation. A submission is lodged by the CSA Appeals Unit to the First Tier Tribunal and the parties have an opportunity to state their own case in writing although there are no formal written pleadings. The proceedings before the tribunal are informal but once a decision has been reached on fact and law, an appeal will lie to the Upper Tribunal only on a matter of law. From the Upper Tribunal appeal lies to the Court of Session and thereafter to the Supreme Court, although such appeals are extremely rare. Legal Aid is not available in any of these tribunals and it is unusual for parties to be professionally legally represented, although they may bring along another person for moral support. It is not possible formally to cite witnesses to the First Tier Tribunal but evidence can be led from witnesses who appear voluntarily. There are three parties to the Appeal—the NRP, the PWC and the Secretary of State who appears by way of a Presenting Officer, who may or may not take any part in the proceedings.

The decisions of the Upper Tribunal are available on the DWP website **5–81** and these form a corpus of precedent which allows the law in this sphere to develop.

The Child's Right to Support on Death of Parents: Succession[126]

Children have indefeasible common law rights to a portion of the move- **5–82** able estate of both their parents. These rights are known as "legal rights", or sometimes *legitim*, and occur in both testate and intestate succession. In other words, parents in Scotland cannot cut their children out of their will. The *legitim* right is to one third of the moveable estate if there is also a surviving spouse of the deceased, or one half otherwise. (Identical rights go to the surviving spouse of the deceased, if any.) This fund is then divided equally on a *per capita* basis between all the surviving children of the deceased, without any discrimination as to children born outwith marriage[127] or adopted children.[128] However, a blood child of a deceased who has been made the subject of an adoption order or freeing for adoption order, has no claim on the deceased's estate. Any child who has predeceased the parent can be represented by his or her issue.[129] Normally in such circumstances distribution will be on a *per stirpes* basis,[130] unless all claimants are of the same generation in which case distribution is *per capita*.[131]

Example 1: X dies, leaving £90,000 in moveable estate. He leaves a surviv- **5–83** ing spouse and two surviving children, A and B. One child, C, died six months before X, but left two children D and E. The *legitim* fund is £30,000 (one third of moveables), and is divided up £10,000 each to A and B, and £5,000 each to D and E (sharing the £10,000 C would have got if he had survived).

---

[126] See further, Wills and Succession, Vol.25, *Stair Encyclopedia*.
[127] See paras 5–35 *et seq*. above.
[128] 1964 Act s.23.
[129] Succession (Scotland) Act 1964 s.11. "Issue" includes descendants "however remote": s.36.
[130] Succession (Scotland) Act 1964 s.11(2)(b).
[131] Succession (Scotland) Act 1964 s.11(2)(a).

5–84 *Example 2:* same facts as above except that A, B, and C *all* predecease X. A leaves one child, B leaves seven children and C leaves two children, as above. All 10 children share equally in the *legitim* fund as they are all in the same degree of relationship to the deceased, taking £3,000 each.

5–85 Where the deceased parent has made a will and left in it a legacy to a child, that child must choose between taking legal rights or taking the legacy. This election can, it seems, only be made by the child when he or she acquires full legal capacity at the age of 16[132]; if that election is made while the child is between the ages of 16 and 18, it can potentially be set aside as a prejudicial transaction under s.3 of the Age of Legal Capacity (Scotland) Act at any time until the child reaches the age of 21.[133] It is not settled if a parent has the right to make this election for the child as an aspect of legal representation.[134] Lifetime advances by the deceased parent towards the child of a non-alimentary nature can nominally be collated into the *legitim* fund, so as to enhance the share of the other children and diminish the share of the child who had received lifetime monies. However, if a child disclaims legal rights, advances towards that child cannot be collated.[135]

5–86 When a parent dies without making a will, then the child may have rights in intestacy on top of legal rights. Under the Succession (Scotland) Act 1964, on intestacy, "prior rights" which go to any surviving spouse of the deceased are first taken off the estate.[136] These often exhaust the estate, but if assets remain, legal rights are then exigible. Finally, if anything is left after legal rights, and there are surviving children or issue of the deceased, that free estate is divided between them in the same proportions as the *legitim* fund was divided.[137] In effect, this means that if a parent dies intestate, and without leaving a surviving spouse, then the children or remoter issue take the whole estate.

5–87 The succession rights discussed above can be claimed by children under 16 and adult children, without distinction, even if the child has not been in contact with the parent for many years. It can be argued that succession rights, like alimentary rights, should be based on need—especially legal rights which infringe on freedom of testation—and should thus cease at 16 in the same way as aliment and support rights. On the other hand, historically legal rights, and free estate rights, were granted not to meet the needs of dependent children but to keep a certain percentage of family property within the blood-related family.

---

[132] Age of Legal Capacity (Scotland) Act 1991 s.1.

[133] See further, Edwards and Barr, "The Age of Legal Capacity: Further Pitfalls—Part I", 1992 S.L.T. (News) 77.

[134] In current executry practice, executors are advised to retain sufficient funds when distributing an estate to provide for an election for legal rights by the child when he or she reaches 16. But see now Children (Scotland) Act 1995, s.15(5)(b) and 1991 Act s.9.

[135] *Coat's Trs*, 1914 S.C. 744.

[136] 1964 Act ss.8, 9 and 9A. See further, Ch.10.

[137] 1964 Act ss.2(1)(a), 5(1) and 6.

CHAPTER 6

CHILDREN AND NON-PARENTS

When looking at the law relating to children thus far, we have stressed **6–01** the central position granted to the relationship between legal parents and the child. We saw in Ch.3 how the law defines who qualifies as a parent in respect of a child taking account of phenomena such as assisted reproductive techniques. However, many children also enjoy close and significant relationships with persons who are not their parents but who may assist or sometimes even replace parents in the caring role. These persons may include siblings, grandparents, step-parents and new, unmarried partners of one or both parents, as well as temporary carers such as babysitters and child-minders. As will be seen in greater detail in the following chapters on marriage and divorce, it is now not uncommon for families to be established or reconstituted in many permutations other than the classic nuclear family, due to the prevalence of divorce and re-marriage, and the increasing level of cohabitation between both opposite sex and same sex partners. Furthermore, given that many women of working age are now in full- or part-time employment it is likely that children will at some point be cared for at least part-time by persons other than natural parents. In consequence, it is important to look at the rights and duties given by the law to non-parents in relation to children.

Sometimes a child cannot be brought up by either or both natural parents, **6–02** whether through inability, choice, death of the parent, or abandonment of the child. In those cases, the law intervenes to provide alternative care. The law relating to the duties of local authorities to provide care for children is now principally to be found in Pt II of the Children (Scotland) Act 1995 (see Ch.7) and in the Children's Hearings (Scotland) Act 2011 (see Ch.8). However, it is often regarded as the best solution where permanent alternative care is necessary for *a parent-substitute* to be found for the child. The Adoption Policy Review Group (APRG) recognised that in dealing with such children there is a need for permanence and stability in their lives as "delays carry very real risks for children. They suffer more disruption and change and more emotional damage. So permanence must be implemented quickly".[1] There are two main ways in which this can be achieved: first, the appointment of a guardian, an event which is relatively infrequent in modern times; or secondly, much more commonly, the adoption of the child. We will look in detail at the processes whereby substitute parents are provided below.

---

[1] Adoption Policy Review Group (APRG), *Report of Phase II: Adoption: Better Choices for Our children (2005)* (hereafter AGRP2), para.8.

NON-PARENTS

6–03 Persons other than parents do not have automatic PRRs under ss.1 and 2 of the Children (Scotland) Act 1995. However, they may be able to gain PRRs by making an appropriate application under s.11 of that Act. As discussed in Ch.4, anyone claiming "interest" (see para.4–42) has title to make such an application.[2] However, it has not always been easy for a non-parent to win an application for residence in competition with a natural parent, although the paramount criterion will as always be the welfare of the child. In *Kyle v Stewart*,[3] for example, the mother of children took a fatal overdose and left a note asking her sister to take over the care of the children, which she did. In a subsequent custody dispute between the father of the children and the mother's sister, the father won, despite the sister having the benefit of the status quo. Lord Caplan expressed the opinion that the father should not be deprived of his right to care for his children unless some other course would plainly be materially better for the child. Similarly in *Clark v Clark*,[4] a custody dispute between grandparents and the natural parents, it was said that the parents had a "pre-eminent right to custody".

6–04 However, in *Breingan v Jamieson*,[5] the court was quite willing to accept that the child in question was well settled with her maternal aunt and grandparents and the status quo should not be disrupted in order to return her to her natural father (and his new wife), with whom she had not lived for some years.[6]

6–05 Step-parents, who have a purely social, not blood, connection to the child, may have even greater difficulties in convincing a court that their relationship is one which should be supported in law[7] and for many step-parents in a continuing relationship with the natural parent of the child, the simplest and most attractive option is to adopt the child. This solution raises problems of its own, however, which are discussed later in this chapter at para.6–28. Any non-parent who succeeds in obtaining a residence order is given not just the right to regulate residence but also all the parental responsibilities and rights that a mother or married father living with the child would have, for as long as the order remains in force.[8] Thus, a grandparent with a residence

---

[2] Children (Scotland) Act 1995 s.11(3)(a)(i). It is no longer necessary for an applicant for PRRs who is not a parent or guardian of the child either to prove they have special grounds for their application, or to notify the local authority (1995 Act Sch.4, para.26, repealing ss.47–49 of the Children Act 1975). If a court has any dubiety about a non-parental application for, e.g. residence, it can refuse to make an order on general welfare grounds, substitute whatever s.11 order it thinks fit (s.11(2)), or refer the child to the children's hearing under s.62 of the Children's Hearings (Scotland) Act 2011 (replacing s.54 of the 1995 Act).

[3] *Kyle v Stewart*, 1989 G.W.D. 14–580.

[4] *Clark v Clark*, 1987 G.W.D. 35–1240.

[5] *Breingan v Jamieson*, 1993 S.L.T. 186.

[6] See also *Smith v Woodhead*, 1996 G.W.D. 10–533, where a 12-year-old boy's wish to remain with his grandmother in preference to going back to stay with his mother was respected by the court; and *W v B*, 2000 G.W.D. 30–1165, where a deceased mother's wish for her child to go to her sister and brother (who had the status quo) rather than the unmarried father of the child was accepted by the court as in the child's best interests.

[7] See paras 3–19 to 3–22.

[8] 1995 Act s.11(12).

order can also consent to the vaccination of the child or deal with that child's property.

Grandparents are perhaps the class of relatives most discriminated **6–06** against under the current case law on the welfare of the child and s.11 orders. Two particular situations recur again and again. One is where the mother, often unmarried, has been unable to care adequately for her child for whatever reason (age, lack of money, physical or mental problems) and her own mother has stepped into the breach and partly or entirely brought the child up. In such cases, the maternal grandparents often have a great deal to offer the child but have no rights of contact, etc. if circumstances change, e.g. the mother finds a new partner, or moves away. Another common scenario is where the parents separate, the mother has de facto or perhaps *de iure* sole care of the child, and wishes to exclude the father from her life, or, alternately, the father has little interest in pursuing his right and responsibility to maintain contact. In such circumstances, again, it is often the paternal grandparents who are as, or more, keen than the father to maintain contact, which will often be opposed by the mother seeking to make a new life for herself, especially in the all too common domestic abuse scenario.

To deal with these kinds of problems, the possibility of grand-parents **6–07** having automatic limited rights of contact was canvassed during the period prior to the FLSA 2006. However this proposal did not gain popular support and was not implemented. This leaves grandparents with the simple option of persuading a court that it is in the best interests of the child that they should have contact (or residence). In scenario 1, above, this is sometimes possible,[9] especially if an appeal can be made to the status quo principle (discussed in Ch.4 at para.4–66), although difficulties may arise concerning the age and potential infirmity of the grandparents if full residence is sought.[10] But in scenario 2, the odds are stacked against the paternal grand-parents. They are unlikely to have the benefit of the status quo and the mother is likely to be the primary carer, and hostile to contact. Furthermore, allowing contact with the grandparents may also open up the possibility of contact with the father, unfortunate if he has been excluded from the child's life because of a history of violence or criminality. In such cases the courts will rarely make an order in the grandparents' favour, however much they objectively have to give to the child.[11]

Many non-parents caring for children on a temporary basis will not wish **6–08** to seek a residence or any other court order. However, it may still sometimes be important for a person with temporary care, such as a child-minder or baby-sitter, legally to be able to take decisions relating to the child, e.g. to take a child for treatment if he has suffered a minor injury. Section 5 of the 1995 Act makes it plain that any person who has care or control of a child

---

[9] See, e.g. *Wright v Wright*, 1999 G.W.D. 3–115: *A v M*, 1999 Fam. L.R. 42; *C v K*, 2004 G.W.D. 40–813.

[10] But see *Senna-Cheribbo v Wood and Masterton*, 1999 Fam. L.B. 38–4; 1999 G.W.D. 4–162.

[11] See, e.g. *Muirhead v Ness*, 1996 G.W.D. 30–1784; *Rashid v Rashid*, 1999 Fam. L.R. 91; 1998 G.W.D. 25–1241; *Black v McLeod*, 1999 G.W.D. 1219; *N v L and Fife Council*, 2004 G.W.D. 37–750.

under 16[12] can do what is reasonable in all circumstances to safeguard the child's health, development and welfare. In particular, consent can be given to any medical procedure, but only as long as: (i) the child himself does not object, if that child has capacity to give consent on his own behalf; and (ii) the parent of the child has not already indicated that he or she would refuse consent. So, for example, a private foster parent could probably consent to a child being assessed by a local authority doctor for child abuse; but not if the mother or father had previously forbidden the foster parent from allowing the local authority near the child. Furthermore, a parent with responsibilities and rights can expressly or impliedly delegate power to any other person.[13]

6–09   As we saw in the last chapter, the obligation to maintain a child applies primarily between a legal parent and the child. However, it should not be forgotten that under s.1(1)(d) of the 1985 Act, any person owes aliment to a child whom they have "accepted" as a child of their family.

GUARDIANS

6–10   A guardian is someone *other* than a parent who takes on the role of parent-substitute.[14] Guardianship is now primarily regulated by ss.7 and 8 of the 1995 Act. A guardian has all the same responsibilities and rights as a parent has under ss.1 and 2 of the 1995 Act,[15] subject to any court order, including the right to act as legal representative, but has historically been appointed mainly in connection with the administration of the child's property, and possibly civil litigation. A guardian is most commonly appointed by a parent in his will to act after that parents' death, as a so-called "testamentary guardian".[16] A guardian can now also appoint someone to act in turn as guardian after his own death.[17] An appointment as guardian must be in writing and signed by the appointing parent or guardian.[18] A parent or guardian cannot appoint someone as guardian if they were not themselves entitled to act as legal representative at their date of death,[19] e.g. because the local authority had removed parental responsibilities by court order. The guardian appointed must accept the post, either expressly or impliedly by acts which are not consistent with any other intention, e.g. by organising

---

[12] Except teachers (1995 Act s.5(2)) who are given powers to deal with children under the Education (Scotland) Act 1980.

[13] 1995 Act s.3(5). However, such delegation does not reduce the parent's own duties so that parent could still be sued for failure in duty if, for example, a baby-sitter chosen by the parent mistreated the child: 1995 Act s.3(6).

[14] Compare the former law under the Law Reform (Parent and Child) (Scotland) Act 1986, where a "guardian" *included* a parent with parental rights (embracing tutor and curator prior to the Age of Legal Capacity (Scotland) Act 1991). "Guardian" was a confusing term since it was also differently defined in various statutory contexts: see *Report on Family Law*, Scot. Law Com. No. 135 (1992), Pt III.

[15] 1995 Act s.7(5).

[16] 1995 Act s.7(1).

[17] 1995 Act s.7(2).

[18] 1995 Act s.7(1) and 7(2).

[19] Or would have been so entitled if the child is born posthumously.

the sale of an asset belonging to the child.[20] It is also possible for any person claiming interest to apply to be appointed as a child's guardian by the court.[21] If one parent appoints a testamentary guardian, then after that parent dies the other surviving parent will retain parental responsibilities and rights and *act jointly* with the guardian.[22] Disputes between them can be resolved by the courts if necessary.

Example: H and W have a child C, aged 3. H dies, and appoints X as **6–11** testamentary guardian. X wishes to sell investments belonging to C to Y. W disagrees. W and X are joint legal representatives and either can act without the other. We cannot stop X making a valid contract to sell to Y; her remedy is to apply to the court under s.11(2)(f) asking the court to interdict this step on the grounds that it is not in the best interests of the child.[23] Note that if child C had been older, and especially if aged 12 or older, the court would also have to have regard to the child's views on the sale[24] as would W and X.[25]

The appointment of a guardian is specifically defined as a "major deci- **6–12** sion" under s.6(1) of the 1995 Act.[26] Thus mature children (presumptively of age 12 or older) should be consulted about who might become their guardian, as should any other person with parental responsibilities and rights. Guardianship terminates on the death of the guardian, or the child, or when the child reaches 18, unless the deed of appointment otherwise specifies.[27] However, once the child reaches the age of 16, the guardian, like a natural parent, will have only the *responsibility* to provide guidance to the child,[28] and no rights. It is also possible for a guardian, again like a natural parent, to have his rights removed by court order, e.g. for bad behaviour or incompetence.[29]

Guardians are subject, when administering property for children, to the **6–13** same duties of care as natural parents, as laid out in s.10 of the 1995 Act. We considered these duties in detail in Ch.5.[30]

Guardianship, at least in the sense of appointing a person to look after the **6–14** property interests of the child, is a dwindling phenomenon. It is very rare in modern times for children under 16 to be orphaned. Even should this occur, substantial property left to a child without parents is most often tied up in trust and administered by trustees. The physical and emotional care of a child after the death of a parent or parents is by far the more important issue and is much more likely to be resolved by a general application by a relative for parental responsibilities and rights, or a residence order: or, if there are no interested relatives, by the intervention of the state, which is under a duty to provide care in the form of adoptive or fostering parents or residential

---

[20] 1995 Act s.7(3).
[21] 1995 Act s.11(2)(h).
[22] 1995 Act s.7(1)(b).
[23] 1995 Act s.11(7)(a).
[24] 1995 Act s.11(7)(b).
[25] 1995 Act s.6(1).
[26] 1995 Act s.7(6).
[27] 1995 Act s.8(5)(a) and (b).
[28] 1995 Act ss.1(1)(b)(ii), 2(7) and 7(5).
[29] 1995 Act ss.11(2)(h) and 8(5)(c).
[30] paras 5–76 *et seq.*

placement. Guardians are traditionally appointed by will, but many Scottish parents do not make wills at all, let alone put in a guardianship clause. If there genuinely is a specific need to appoint someone to look after the child's property, this may well be best met by the appointment of a judicial factor who will be subject to court supervision.

ADOPTIVE PARENTS

6–15   Adoption[31] is the process by which the legal relationship between a child and his birth parents is severed and a new legal relationship between that child and his adoptive parents is created.[32] When made an adoption order confers both parental status and PRRs on the adoptive parents. PRRs terminate when the child reaches 16 in the usual way, but parental status remains for the rest of the child's life. In 1972, the Houghton Committee Report[33]— which fundamentally shaped adoption law—defined adoption as "the permanent legal transfer of parental rights and responsibilities". The adoption order cuts off the legal relationship between the adopted child and his birth parents, including the right to contact. It also means severing relationships with members of the child's birth family, which may be detrimental to the child's well being as he may have established close ties with siblings, aunts and uncles, as well as with birth parents.[34] For this reason some scholars have promoted "open adoption" as a solution because it allows for a child to be adopted and to maintain some links with his birth family.[35] This is especially important where an older child is adopted, who is more likely to maintain real links with his birth parents and relations. The concept of open adoption covers a whole range of options, including direct and indirect, supervised and unsupervised contact, through face to face meetings or through letters, email etc. Open adoption[36] raises questions about the legal

---

[31]   See further P. McNeill and M. Jack, *Adoption of Children in Scotland*, 4th edn (Edinburgh: W. Green, 2010).

[32]   This chapter does not deal with Intercountry or Transnational adoptions. For legal details see McNeill and Jack, *Adoption of Children in Scotland*, para.1–16; paras 1-43–1-49. For a more socially oriented perspective see S. Howell, *The Kinning of Foreigners: Transnatinal Adoption in a Global Perspective* (Berghahn Books, 2007) and B. Yngvesson *Belonging in an Adopted World: Race, Identity and Transnational Adoption* (University of Chicago Press, 2010).

[33]   Report of the Departmental Committee on the Adoption of Children, Cmnd 5107 (1972).

[34]   See M. Ross for a critical discussion of the Adoption (Scotland) Act 1978 and the need to seriously consider alternative arrangements for adoption in "Adoption in the 21st Century: Still Image Against a Moving Picture", pp.105–128 in J. Scoular (ed.) *Family Dynamics: Contemporary Issues in Family Law* (Butterworths, 2001).

[35]   C.E. Miall and K. March "Open Adoption as a Family Form" Community Assessment and Social Support", 2005 *Journal of Family Issues* 26:380–409; B. Yngvesson, "Negotiating Motherhood: Identity and Difference in 'Open' Adoptions" 1997 *Law & Society Review* 31 (10:31–80; S. Howell, "Adoption of the Unrelated Child: Some Challenges to the Anthropological Study of Kinship", 2009 *Annual Review of Anthropology* 38:149–166; D.H. Siegal, "Open Adoption: Adoptive Parents' Reactions Two Decades Later", 2013 *Social Work* 58(1):43–52; D.H. Siegal and S. Livingston Smith, "Openness in Adoption: From Secrecy and Stigma to Knowledge and Openness", March 2012, Evan B. Donaldson Adoption Institute, downloaded from *www. adoptioninstitute.org/research/2012_03_openess.php* [accessed March 25, 2013].

[36]   See the Minnesota/Texas Adoption Research Project (MTRP), a longitudinal research study

enforceability of agreements as many post adoption arrangements are of a voluntary nature.

While it has been possible for parents in Scotland to seek to make contact a condition of agreement under s.12(6) of the Adoption (Scotland) Act 1978, Scottish courts have generally continued to support the "clean break" model of adoption. While an exception permitting contact was made in the case of *B v C*,[37] the Inner House in that case endorsed the view expressed by Lord Ackner[38] that "in normal circumstances it is desirable that there should be a complete break from the child's natural family".[39] The APRG acknowledged that contact was an important issue where older children may have forged strong ties with their birth parents and relatives and that it should be taken into account.[40] They recommended changes to the law dealing with contact.[41] However, although a number of significant changes were made to the legislation, the basic model for adoption remains the same. The Group recommended retaining the full adoption model, severing legal links between birth parents and the child, and rejected introducing "simple adoption" that represents a type of open adoption.[42] This model, which is in effect in France, allows for a child to retain his birth family name and inheritance rights from the birth family. However, in recognising the importance that contact may have for children, particularly older children, the APRG recommended that contact arrangements to meet these children needs should be taken into account, but only from the perspective of the child's welfare, and only where contact was for a clear purpose.[43] This raises questions about birth parents' rights, such as their rights to respect for private and family life under Art.8, addressed in paras 6–50 *et seq.* below.

6–16

Adoption law has been reviewed in both England and Wales[44] and Scotland.[45] Although a number of significant changes were recommended in both jurisdictions, the basic model for adoption remains the same. Adoption provides a substitute parent or parents for the child where the birth parents are unable, unwilling or unfit to care for the child, and thus the making of an adoption order meets a very much wider set of needs than the appointment of a guardian, which is used almost exclusively to deal with the death of one

6–17

---

that focuses on the consequences of variation in openness in adoption arrangements for all members of the adoptive kinship network; birth mothers, adoptive parents and adopted children, and for the relationships within these family systems. For details see *www.psych.umass. edu/adoption/about_the_project/what_is_mtrp/* [accessed March 25, 2013].

[37] *B v C*, 1996 S.L.T. 1370.
[38] In *Re C (A Minor) (Adoption Order, Conditions)*, 1989 A.C. 1.
[39] *B v C*, 1996 S.L.T. 1370 at 1377.
[40] APRG2 para.4.2.
[41] See *West Lothian Council v M*, 2002 S.L.T. 1155 where the court called for greater flexibility in adoption procedure to better balance the interests of the birth parents, the adoptive parents and the child.
[42] APRG2 paras 3.14 and 3.15.
[43] APRG2 para.4.2.
[44] *Adoption: A New Approach* (2000, Department of Health) leading to the Adoption and Children Act 2002.
[45] *Adoption Policy Review Group—Report on Phase 1* (Scottish Executive, 2002) and *Report on Phase 2* (Scottish Executive, 2005) (APRG2) whose proposals were largely implemented in the Children and Adoption (Scotland) Act 2007.

or both parents. The public perception of adoption is still on the whole a process whereby infants are placed with childless couples who are unrelated to the child. In fact, the demographics of adoption over the years have proved to be very different, with important implications for the development of the law contained in the Adoption and Children (Scotland) Act 2007.[46] Since the 1970s, the number of new adoptions has fallen each year as the supply of young healthy children who can be placed for adoption has declined, for reasons to do with the falling birth rate, changes in sexual morality, universally available contraception and abortion, etc. Over the 20 years leading up to 2003, adoption applications fell by two-thirds—there were almost three times as many adoption applications in 1983 as 2003, when only 373 applications were made.[47] Over a longer period the decline is even more apparent: in 1975, 1,800 adoption orders were made while 30 years later the figure was about 400.[48] In 2011 the number remained relatively stable at 496.[49] Over time, non-relative adoptions of children under the age of four came to account for only around 10 per cent of all adoptions in that age range, and while there were 280 adoptions of children under the age of one year in 1983— one-quarter of all applications in that year—there were only 20 in 2003, representing a steady decrease in infant adoptions. The APRG reporting in 2005 noted that the number of children adopted under the age of one had decreased by some 90 per cent.[50] For a numbers of years the majority of applications for adoption of children have been made by relatives, *not* strangers: some 45 per cent of all applications for adoption were made by a birth parent together with a new step-parent in 1989, which rose to 63 per cent in 2003. In 2005 the APRG found that half of the adoptions tabled involved a relative, typically a step-parent.[51] In 2011, however, this was no longer the case. Of the children adopted in that year, only 27 per cent were adopted by a step-parent compared with 71per cent of children who were adopted by non-relatives.[52] Where adoption by relatives took place this was among the older children placed for adoption.[53] Overall, the total number of applications by relatives especially with regard to younger children is declining. As we will see below, the procedure required for adoption is significantly different in non-relative adoptions, which usually involve an adoption agency, than in step-parent adoptions, where the child is almost invariably not placed by an agency.

6–18   The development which has attracted most attention over the last 20 years has been the increase in numbers in adoption of children originally termed

---

[46] The previous legislation was contained in the Adoption (Scotland) Act 1978 to which important changes were made by the Children (Scotland) Act 1995.

[47] These and other statistics, except where otherwise stated, are taken from *Adoption Statistics 2003* (Scottish Executive National Statistics Publications, 2004).

[48] See *Civil Judicial Statistics* (1975) and above.

[49] *Scotland's Population 2011, The Registrar General's Annual Review of Demographic Trends*, p.61. Note that this number represented 30 more adoptions compared with the number for 2010. Of these children only 14% were under 2; 16% were aged 2; 25% were aged between 3–4; 30% were aged between 5–9; 9% were aged between 10–14 and 5% were aged 15 or over.

[50] APRG2 para.1.2. From around 200 a year to 20.

[51] APRG2 para.6.

[52] *Scotland's Population 2011*, p.61. See also n.49, above.

[53] Of the 74 children aged 10 or over, only 18% were adopted by non-relatives. This may be compared with 69% of children aged under 2 who were adopted by non-relatives.

"hard to place", and now often referred to as "children with special needs" many of whom are "looked after" by a local authority and are on supervision requirements.[54] These children tend to be older than average, or have physical or mental disabilities, or emotional or behavioural difficulties, often related to poor early care or in some cases neglect or abuse. In the case of these children, many of whom have experienced being moved around from placement to placement,[55] it is essential to provide stability and permanence in their lives through timely planning. This may involve parallel planning, that is seeking to do everything that is possible to reunite the child with his family, while at the same time, taking into account long term solutions for permanent care in the event that rehabilitation of the child with her family fails[56]. It is now regarded as preferable, in almost all circumstances, for older children who cannot be cared for by their birth families to live in private homes, with either foster or adoptive parents, rather than to enter long-term residential care.[57] Thus adoption is increasingly being seen by local authorities as another option in the range of approaches it may take towards planning a permanent future for children whose natural families cannot meet the child's needs (discussed further in Ch.7, below). This is a far cry from the original aims of the adoption legislation as introduced in 1930, when adoption was principally seen as a remedy for childless couples, a way to make provision for children whose parents had died, or a means to legitimate children after the re-marriage of one parent. Adoption, however, is not the only option for dealing with such children. It may not suit the needs of all children who cannot live with their birth families but who need a new stable and secure home. An attempt to produce another alternative, in the form of permanence orders, has been introduced under the 2007 Act that aims to produce a much more flexible framework for dealing with those children for whom adoption is unsuitable.[58] We will now consider the law regulating the adoption process that is contained in the Adoption and Children (Scotland) Act 2007 that came into force on the September 28, 2009.[59]

---

[54] See Chs 7 and 8 for details. The APRG noted that while the number of children being adopted has fallen, it drew attention to the fact that the number of children in care in local authorities has risen (APRG2 para.1.2).

[55] The APRG observed that among children who are being looked after away from home there is little stability as they experience an average of 3.07 placement moves in each period in care (APRG2 para.10).

[56] APRG2 para.16.

[57] In 2011/12 there were 13,093 children subject to a supervision requirement (amounting to 1.4% of all children in Scotland. See *SCRA (Scottish Children's Reporter Administration) Annual Report 2011/12*, p.19 downloaded from *www.scra.gov.uk/site/scra/cms_resources/ AnnualReport201112.html on 28/3/2013* [accessed March 28, 2013]. Of these children, around half were living at home and the other half were living away from home with relatives, friends, foster carers, or in a local authority home, residential school or other residential placement (*SCRA Annual Report 2011/12*, Table 5, p.19). The numbers of looked after children in 2011 amounted to 16,171 (representing an increase of 2% since July 31, 2010). Out of these only 5,437 were living at home, while 5,296 were living with a foster carer or prospective adopters, 3,963 were in some other community placement and 1,475 were in a residential school, See *Children's Social Work Statistics Scotland, No 1*, 2012 edn, p.4, downloaded from *www.scotland.gov.uk/Publications/2012/02/7586/1* [accessed March 28, 2013].

[58] For details see paras 6–60 *et seq.* below.

[59] This repealed the Adoption (Scotland) Act 1978, except for Part IV of that Act (that makes

GENERAL DUTIES AND PRINCIPLES: ADOPTION AGENCIES,
COURTS AND CHILDREN

6–19   Every local authority is under the duty to establish and maintain a comprehensive adoption service to meet the needs of all those who are or would be
affected by the adoption process, namely the child, the parents, the rest of
the child's family and the adoptive parents.[60] The 2007 Act[61] maintains the
existing adoption service for placing children with adopters and assessing
adopters. The two key institutions in the adoption process are the courts, to
whom application must be made for an adoption order, and the adoption
agency, who, except in certain cases discussed below, must place the child for
adoption and will vet the suitability of prospective adopters. An adoption
agency is either a local authority or a registered adoption service[62] including
corresponding institutions in England and Wales.[63] Every local authority is
obliged to provide an adoption service in its area[64] and publish a plan for the
provision of adoption services in its area.[65] Where the local authority does
not have its own service it may use a registered adoption service[66] and may
seek assistance from other persons.[67] Under the 2007 Act the term "adoption
agency" covers both a local authority adoption service and a registered adoption service.[68]Adoption agencies and societies[69] are often run by voluntary
or religious bodies. Each local authority is required to seek registration of
its service.[70] Adoption agencies and the adoption process are regulated by Pt
1of the 2007 Act and the Adoption Agencies (Scotland) Regulations 2009.
The 2007 Act seeks to improve access to a broader range of support services,
including information, for people affected by adoptions including members
of adoptive and original families. Both before and after the making of an
adoption order.

6–20   According to s.14(3) of the 2007 Act, both a court and an adoption agency,
when reaching any decision relating to the adoption of a child, must regard the
need to safeguard and promote the welfare of the child concerned throughout
his life as the paramount consideration. This formulation is in keeping with
the ethos of the Children (Scotland) Act 1995. Before 1995, the welfare of

---

provision for children adopted under that Act), and amended the Children (Scotland) Act
1995.
[60] Under s.1(1) and (2) of the 2007 Act.
[61] For a discussion of the 2007 Act see McNeill and Jack *Adoption of Children in Scotland*, 4th edn
(2010); E. Sutherland, *Child and Family Law*, 2nd edn (Edinburgh: W. Green, 2009), Ch.5, paras
5–011 to 5–161; J. Thomson, *Family Law in* Scotland, 6th edn (2011), Ch.13, paras 13.1 to 13.15.
[62] 2007 Act s.119. Where a local authority does not have an adoption service it may use a registered adoption service under s.2(2) of the 2007 Act.
[63] 2007 Act s.119 referring to s.2(1) of the Adoption and Children Act 2002. According to s.2(3)
of the 2007 Act a "registered adoption service" is one registered under the Regulation of Care
(Scotland) Act 2001.
[64] 2007 Act s.1(1).
[65] 2007 Act s.4(1). There must be a review of this plan from time to time, s.4(2).
[66] 2007 Act s.2(2).
[67] 2007 Act s.6.
[68] 2007 Act s.119.
[69] Under s.119 an adoption society is defined as "a body of persons whose functions consist of
or include the making of arrangements for or in connection with the adoption of children".
[70] Under s.33(1) of the Regulation of Care (Scotland) Act 2001.

the child in adoption was only the *first* rather than the paramount consideration. This was intended to preserve a balance between the interests of the child and the right of a natural parent not to have his child removed without very good cause. However, it is inconsistent both with modern child law and the UNCRC not to endorse the paramountcy principle wherever possible. Note also that the court or agency are enjoined to look at the child's welfare *throughout his life*, not just childhood. This should be compared to s.11(7) of the 1995 Act, dealing with court actions for parental rights, which makes no such requirement. Adoption, as we have seen above, is regarded as a status for life and it must therefore enhance the child's welfare not only now but for the foreseeable future. To this end the court must have regard to the likely effect on the child of making an adoption order throughout that child's life.[71]

Courts and agencies are also under a duty to have regard to the views of **6–21** the child when making any decision, taking account of the child's age and maturity,[72] as well as to the religious persuasion, racial origin and cultural and linguistic background of the child.[73] An agency in placing the child must also have regard, so far as practicable, to the views of the child's parent, guardians or other relatives.[74] A child is deemed mature enough to express a view at the age of 12.[75] A child aged 12 or over also has an absolute right to veto his own adoption or to refuse to consent to a permanence order being made on his behalf.[76] Agencies have a duty to consider alternatives to adoption,[77] while courts are required to consider whether it would be better for a child to make an adoption order or not.[78]

Who can Adopt?

A Relevant Couple

The 2007 Act extends the range of persons who can apply to adopt a child. **6–22** Under previous legislation an application to adopt could only be made by a single person, or a married couple.[79] This range of persons was considered unduly restrictive and recommendations were put forward for reform by the APRG who were in favour of allowing unmarried couples, including same sex couples, to adopt jointly.[80] This proposal was accepted and it has been implemented in the 2007 Act by permitting adoption in the case of a relevant couple. Under s.29 a couple qualifies if they are persons who are married to each other,[81] are civil partners,[82] or if they are living together as if

---

[71] 2007 Act s.14(4)(d).
[72] 2007 Act s.14(4)(b).
[73] 2007 Act s.14(4)(c).
[74] 2007 Act s.14(5). For a definition of "relative" see s.119(1) of the Act.
[75] 2007 Act s.14(8).
[76] 2007 Act ss.32(1) and 84(1). The court may, however, dispense with consent under s.32(2) where it is satisfied that the child in incapable of giving consent.
[77] 2007 Act s.14(6) and (7).
[78] 2007 Act s.83(1)(d).
[79] Under ss.14(1) and 15(1) if the 1978 Act.
[80] AGRP2, para.3.42.
[81] 2007 Act s.29(3)(a).
[82] 2007 Act s.29(3)(b)

husband and wife in an enduring family relationship,[83] or if they are persons living together as if civil partners in an enduring family relationship.[84] These reforms take account of the impact of human rights concerns with regard to respect for private and family life (Art.8) and to non-discrimination (Art.14). In particular, the new Act puts to rest questions about the suitability of a non-heterosexual applicant as a prospective adopter.[85] Prior to the 2007 Act, case law had already established that there could be no fundamental objection *in principle* to adoption by a single male adopter living with another man in a stable same sex relationship.[86] Each case had to be decided on its own facts. The 2007 Act now makes it absolutely clear that same sex couples can apply jointly to adopt a child and that there is to be no discrimination on the basis of sexual orientation in the decision-making process.

6–23   What is potentially more problematic is interpreting what gives rise to an "enduring family relationship" where the couple are not married or civil partners. There is no definition of what constitutes such a relationship but the explanatory notes accompanying the legislation[87] indicate that it includes considering the length of the relationship or financial interdependency among the couple, as part of assessing the overall strength of a relationship and the suitability of a couple to adopt. What is clear is that the relationship is viewed as being akin to a marriage or civil partnership involving an intimate element. This means that where a relationship is not of this nature, because, for example, it involves two siblings, or two platonic friends, it will not qualify as an enduring family relationships under the 2007 Act. In the case of a "relevant couple" applicants must be either domiciled or habitually resident for one year preceding the application in any part of the British Islands (United Kingdom, the Channel Islands, or Isle of Man).[88] They must also both be 21 or over,[89] unless one applicant is already the natural parent of the child, in which case that parent need only be 18.[90]

Adoption by One Person

6–24   Where the application is made by a single applicant, he must be over 21 and not be married or in a civil partnership, or in an enduring family

---

[83] 2007 Act s.29(3)(c).

[84] 2007 Act s.29(3)(d). For the position in England and Wales see Adoption and Children Act 2002 Act s.144(4) and (5) as amended by the Civil Partnership Act 2004.

[85] The APRG found that there was no strong evidence to suggest that same sex couples should be excluded from consideration for adoption if a decision was taken to extend the right to apply to adopt to unmarried heterosexual partners (APRG2 *para*.3.34).

[86] See Inner House in *T Petr*, 1997 S.L.T. 724.

[87] See Explanatory Notes to the Adoption and Children (Scotland) Act 2007 that can be downloaded from *www.legislation.gov.uk/asp/2007/4/notes/contents* [accessed on March 28, 2013]. These notes do not form part of the Act but they are useful in providing guidance on it.

[88] 2007 Act s.29(2), set out in s.119.

[89] 2007 Act s.29(1).

[90] 2007 Act s.30(3). This situation applies where one member of a "relevant" couple is applying for an adoption order where the other member of the couple is a parent of the child that is to be adopted. In this context "parent" means a person who has any parental responsibilities or rights in relation to the child (s.30(8)). It applies to step-parents, civil partners and cohabitants and allows them to make an application to adopt the child of their spouse, civil partner or person with whom they are living in an enduring family relationship.

relationship.[91] The applicant must also be domiciled in the British Islands or have been habitually resident there for at least one year before the date of application for an adoption order.[92] In certain circumstances, however, a spouse or civil partner who is aged 21 or over can adopt alone. These circumstances are that the other spouse of civil partner cannot be found, or that the spouse or civil partner have separated and are living apart and the separation is likely to be permanent, or the other spouse or civil partner is by reason of ill health (whether physical or mental) incapable of making an application for an adoption order.[93] The latter also applies in the case where one party to a relevant couple (by virtue of living together as if husband and wife or civil partners) applies alone, and the court is satisfied that the other member of the couple is incapable of making an application because of ill health.[94]

Where a single applicant is the natural parent of the child and wishes to adopt the child (e.g. where he does not have PRRs with regard to the child), before the application can proceed, the court must be satisfied that the other natural parent is dead, or the other natural parent cannot be found, or by virtue of the Human Fertilisation and Embryology Acts 1990 and 2008 there is no other parent,[95] or the exclusion of the natural parent from the application is justified on some other ground.[96]   **6–25**

Step-Parent Adoptions

Either of the child's birth parents can apply to adopt the child alone, but since this would have the effect of severing the legal link between the other birth parent and the child, it must be shown that there is some reason justifying the exclusion of the other parent, e.g. that he or she is dead or cannot be found.[97] In practice, birth parents rarely if ever have reason to adopt their own children, except in conjunction with a new step-parent. Under the 2007 Act there is no provision for a joint application for adoption by a birth parent and a step-parent. This is no longer an option because such applications were considered to be unnecessary. As noted earlier, under the 2007 Act it is possible for a step-parent to apply on his own to adopt the child of their spouse, civil partner or person with whom they are in an enduring family relationship[98] This has the advantage over a joint application by the couple that the natural parent does not have to become an adoptive parent, and thus can continue to appear as a birth parent on the child's birth certificate. The effect of such an adoption is that the child is deemed to be the child of the natural parent and step-parent applicant from his date of birth.   **6–26**

---

[91] 2007 Act s.30(1) and (2).
[92] 2007 Act s.30(6).
[93] 2007 Act s.30(4).
[94] 2007 Act s.30(5).
[95] According to s.28 of the 1990 Act (disregarding s.28(5A) to (51 of that section) or according to ss.34 to 37 of the 2008 Act (disregarding ss.39, 40 and 46 of that Act).
[96] 2007 Act s.30(7).
[97] 2007 Act s.30(7).
[98] 2007 Act s.30(3) of the 2007 Act. This was previously the case with a step-parent who was married to the child's parent under s.15(1)(aa) of the 1978 Act.

6–27   As noted earlier, a number of applications for adoption are made by relatives. Step-parents often wish to adopt the children of their new spouse in order to acquire parental rights and generally take equal responsibility, but such an adoption has the significant disadvantage of severing the legal link not only between the child and the other birth parent, but also with any relatives on that side of the family. This means that if a mother divorces the father of her child, remarries, and her new husband adopts the child, the child loses all succession[99] and alimentary[100] rights in respect of the birth father. This is particularly unfortunate given the high incidence of breakdown of second marriages: the child may lose one family without really gaining another. For these reasons, when the Children (Scotland) Act 1995 was introduced, courts were generally instructed that they should not make an adoption order unless it considered better to do so for the child than not to take any action.[101] This, combined with the general duty on the court to make the welfare of the child its paramount consideration was aimed at getting a court to seriously consider whether it was really necessary to take the extreme step of making an adoption order, or whether some lesser alternative, e.g. a residence order, might suffice. Under the 2007 Act these duties are imposed under s.14(3), which requires a court to regard the child's welfare as the paramount consideration, and s.28(2), which instructs a court not to make an adoption order unless it considers that it would be better for the child to make such an order than not to make one.

6–28   Many step-parent adoptions are undertaken to achieve ends which can be met by procedures less final than adoption, e.g. the child's surname can be changed on his birth certificate to match that of a new step-parent simply by application to the Registrar of Births, Deaths and Marriages.[102] There is also a complementary duty on adoption agencies to consider alternatives to adoption before making arrangements for the adoption of a child.[103] This might extend, for example, to investigating the possibility of a member of the extended family seeking a residence order, rather than placing the child for adoption.

6–29   Birth parents (other than a father who has no PRRs[104]) who wish to oppose the adoption of their child by the new spouse of the other birth parent, have the right to withhold consent to the adoption (discussed further below at paras 6–46 *et seq.*), in which case an adoption order cannot be made unless the court is willing to dispense with their consent.[105] This will not be done lightly. At an early stage the English courts, in *Re B*,[106] considered whether

---

[99] Succession (Scotland) Act 1964, s.23(1).

[100] 2007 Act s.35(2)(b).

[101] This was under the 1978 Act s.24(3) as substituted by 1995 Act, Sch.2, para.16.

[102] Registration of Births, Deaths and Marriages (Scotland) Act 1965 s.20. Note also that a parent can also, later in the child's life, seek a s.11 order to change a child's surname as an aspect of PRRs (see Ch.4) (although this will be dependent on what is in the child's welfare).

[103] 2007 Act s.14(7).

[104] The effect of s.23 of the FLSA 2006 means that that the number of fathers in this situation is diminishing.

[105] 2007 Act s.31(2)(b) of the 2007 Act. This power was previously contained in the1978 Act ss.16 and 16(2).

[106] *Re B* [1975] Fam. 127.

a natural father was unreasonably withholding agreement in refusing to consent to the adoption of his child. Gumming Brace, J. stated that:

> "It is quite wrong to use the adoption law to extinguish the relationship between the protesting father and the child, unless there is some really serious factor which justifies the use of the statutory guillotine. The courts should not encourage the idea that after divorce the children of the family can be reshuffled and dealt out like a pack of cards in a second rubber of bridge".[107]

These comments were affirmed in the Scots case of *A v B*[108] and are all the more true given the emphasis placed by the Children (Scotland) Act 1995 on maintaining contact between the child and both parents after parents split up. In principle, these kinds of issues are more properly dealt with in the original divorce rather than via a later adoption petition.

6–30

Criteria for Adopters

No criteria for adopters other than age, residence or domicile are laid down in the primary legislation. Agencies, like courts, are under a general duty to have regard to the child's welfare throughout his life as the paramount consideration when making any decision to place a child for adoption; and must specifically have regard to the child's own wishes, and to his religious persuasion, racial origin and cultural and linguistic background.[109] This does not mean that, for example, an Asian child cannot be placed with white adoptive parents. In an earlier decision under the 1978 Act, *AH and PH, Petrs*,[110] such an adoption was allowed by the courts, with the caveat that the adopters should use their best endeavours to ensure that the child was brought up to be aware of his black identity and ethnic origins and traditions.[111] In practice, adoption agencies operate detailed criteria for prospective adopters, which they are required under the Adoption Agency Regulations[112] to make available in written form. These criteria are imple-

6–31

---

[107] *Re B* [1975] Fam. 127 at 143.

[108] *A v B*, 1987 S.L.T. (Sh. Ct) 121. Also see the Inner House case of *HQ and LQ v CG* Unreported, October 16, 1992. In both these cases, the court refused to dispense with the consent of natural fathers and thus refused to make an adoption order.

[109] 2007 Act s.14(3) and (4).

[110] *AH and PH, Petrs* Unreported, Outer House, March 10, 1995.

[111] This requirement was added as a condition to the adoption order under s.12(6) of the 1978 Act. Such trans-racial adoptions are not uncommon, partly because it is sometimes difficult to recruit adoptive parents from ethnic groups whose culture does not embrace adoption of children from outside the extended family. They have always, however, been controversial: see, e.g. Hayes, "The Ideological Attack on Trans-Racial Adoption in the USA and Britain" (1995) 9 I.J.L.F. 1.

[112] Adoption Agencies (Scotland) Regulations 2009 (SSI 2009/154) reg. 7. This requires obtaining information set out in Prt 1 of Sch.1 of the 2007 Act for making an assessment. Such information includes age, nationality and ethnicity and where adopters are a couple, the date of marriage or registered civil partnership, details of the prospective adopters' household (including any children and whether or not they are resident in the household), the adopters' educational background and a comprehensive medical report.

mented by the adoption panels which each adoption agency is required to establish and whose function, inter alia, is to consider whether prospective adopters are suitable to be adoptive parents, whether adoption is in the best interests of the particular child in question, and to match the child available for adoption to the proposed adoptive parents. An adoption panel must be composed of six members.[113] It must include a legal adviser[114] and a medical adviser[115] and the qualifications and experience of its members must be sufficient to enable it to discharge its functions effectively.[116] The panel must, under the Regulations, receive information about the child to be adopted and the prospective adopters, including the child's views and a detailed case history of the child.

6–32 The 2009 Regulations prescribe a timescale as well as the process which requires to be undertaken prior to an agency placement or application for a permanence order. In recent years, it has become more common in contested cases for failures to comply with these regulations to be relied upon as a defence against dispensing with parental consent on the grounds of failure to comply with a parent's human rights.[117]

Who can be Adopted?

6–33 An adoption order can only be made in respect of a child who was under 18 at the date the adoption application was made.[118] A child who is or has been married or in a registered civil partnership cannot be adopted.[119] An adopted child can be re-adopted.[120]

6–34 In most cases, the child must be at least 19 weeks old at the date the adoption order is made, and must have had his home with the applicant adoptive parents for the preceding 13 weeks.

THE ADOPTION PROCESS

6–35 There are fundamentally two types of adoption: those in which the child is placed with prospective adopters by an adoption agency, and those where the child is not placed by an agency and is a relative of the adopters.[121] The under-

---

[113] 2009 Regulations reg.3(2).

[114] 2009 Regulations reg.3(4)(a).

[115] 2009 Regulations reg.3(4)(b).

[116] 2009 Regulations reg.3(5).

[117] See *Dundee City Council v M*, 2004 S.L.T. 640. In this case a sheriff raised the issue of whether proceedings involving freeing for adoption prior to proof infringed the parents' rights under Arts 6 and 8. The court held that there have been no infringement as there had been no interference with the parents' civil rights (Art.6) and the parents had had an opportunity to make representation to the children's hearing and would have the opportunity to be heard before the sheriff (Art.8). These proceedings involved a meeting of the adoption panel, to which the parents were not invited, that recommended seeking a freeing for adoption order to the adoption agency dealing with the child.

[118] 2007 Act s.119, previously contained in s.12(1) of the 1978 Act. See *Cameron v Gibson*, 2005 Fam. L.R. 108, which held the age bar to be an absolute bar to validity.

[119] 2007 Act s.28(7).

[120] 2007 Act s.28(6).

[121] 2007 Act s.75. There are a small number of situations which do not fall within this classifica-

lying principle is that children should not be disposed of by their parents, nor acquired by would-be parents on some kind of open market, without the supervision of the state. Thus, private placement is only legal where the child to be adopted is a relative of the adopters (s.75(2)), as for example where a mother places her child for adoption by her sister, the child's aunt. Anyone who privately arranges the adoption of a child in contravention of s.75(1) is guilty of a criminal offence.[122] The prohibitions against private placement do not have extra-territorial effect[123] and thus it is not a crime under Scots law to travel to collect a child in, say, Romania, and then to bring him back to Scotland where an adoption order can be sought in the Scottish courts. Nor is it necessarily the case that if an offence under s.75(1) is committed, then an adoption order cannot be made.[124]

Trafficking in children for money is forbidden in Scots (and United Kingdom) law. It is an offence to pay for the adoption of a child, or for any consent to adoption.[125] Nonetheless despite a contravention of s.72 with regard to payment a court can still go ahead and make an adoption order.[126] Previously it was left to case law to determine what should happen in this situation. For the court's duty in considering whether to make an adoption order was to balance the interest the child has in being adopted against the need to discourage illegal fees and baby-buying. This was addressed in the case *C v S*[127] involving earlier legislation contained in the 1978 Act where an infertile couple commissioned a surrogate mother to bear a child for them and made a payment of some £8,000 to her, supposedly as "expenses". The child was conceived using sperm donated by the prospective father and came to live with the commissioning couple shortly after birth. The couple sought an adoption order. The Inner House held that no illegal payment had been made, since although the money far exceeded the true expenses of the birth, it had been paid to secure a parental order[128] not an adoption order, and was thus not struck at by the Act[129]; but even if it had been, the need to safeguard the child's welfare by allowing an adoption order would have outweighed the public policy objection. This view was endorsed in the case of *H. Petrs*[130] where a placement was made in contravention of a prohibition on private placement. Payment was made to the mother but this was held not to amount to the sale of a child. Although a false declaration as to parenthood had been made, the court held, that as the paramount consideration in granting an

6–36

---

tion, where, for example, a child has been placed on a non-adoptive basis, e.g. with a local authority foster carer, and the carer then lodges an application to adopt the child without the agreement of the agency.

[122] 2007 Act s.75(3).
[123] *Re A (Adoption: Placement)* [1988] 1 W.L.R. 229.
[124] See obiter comments in *D&D v F*, 1994 S.C.L.R. 417 dealing with an earlier prohibition under s.11(1) of the 1978 Act.
[125] 2007 Act s.72. This was also the case under s.51 of the 1978 Act.
[126] 2007 Act s.34.
[127] *C v S*, 1997 S.L.T. 1387. This case also establishes that in Scotland, as in England, an illegal payment can be retrospectively authorised by the court.
[128] Under s.30 of the Human Fertilisation and Embryology Act 1990 that was in force at that time.
[129] Under s.51 of the 1978 Act.
[130] *H. Petrs*, 2010 Fam L.R. 105.

adoption order was the need to safeguard and promote the welfare of the child throughout life it, it would grant the order.

6–37   There is one major exception to the rule on payments in consideration for adoption. Foster parents are often paid allowances in respect of the care they give to the children they foster. If such foster parents seek to adopt the child they foster, which is often desirable to provide "hard to place" children with a permanent and secure home, the termination of foster payments may be a disincentive to adoption. Section 71[131] provides that all adoption agencies are required to establish their own "adoption allowances" schemes so that payments can be made, inter alia, to those such as foster carers in this situation.[132] Such allowances may also be paid, e.g. in recognition of the costs associated with adopting a sibling group. These constitute "excepted" payments[133] and do not fall within the remit of illegal fees.[134]

6–38   Where the child has been placed by an adoption agency, the child must live with the applicants for 13 weeks before application can be made for an adoption order,[135] and the adoption agency must be allowed sufficient opportunity to see the child with the applicant(s) in the home environment, otherwise an order cannot be made.[136] If the child is living with a parent, step-parent or relative, the same rule applies and the local authority must be given adequate access.[137] In a non-agency adoption, notice must be given to the local authority at least three months before the adoption order is made so that they can investigate the suitability of the applicants and whether the adoption was in breach of the rules about private placements.[138] A child is often placed with applicants for some considerable time before an adoption order can be obtained due to court delays. In these circumstances, until an adoption order is made, the natural parents retain their parental rights.[139] In such cases it would be contrary to the welfare of the child if the natural parents could simply change their minds about adoption and remove the child. Section 20 thus provides that if consent[140] has been given by the natural parent(s) to the placement of the child with the prospective adopters, then the parent(s) cannot remove the child without the leave either of the adoption agency or the court.

---

[131] The Adoption Support Services and Allowances (Scotland) Regulations 2009 (SSI 2009/152) generally prescribe the shape of these schemes.

[132] See the Adoption Support Services and Allowances (Scotland) Regulations 2009 (SSI 2009/152).

[133] 2007 Act s.73.

[134] Set out in s.72 of the 2007 Act.

[135] 2007 Act s.15(3)(b).

[136] 2007 Act s.16(1) and (2).

[137] 2007 Act s.16(3) and (4).

[138] 2007 Act ss.18 and 19.

[139] Unless the child is also subject to a supervision order of the children's hearing, or parental responsibilities and rights have already been removed from the natural parents by a court order (see below at para.6–57).

[140] The form in which such consent must be given is prescribed in the Adoption Agency Regulations 2009, regs 14 and 15, and Schs 6 and 7.

Application to the Court for Adoption Order

Application may be made for an adoption order to the Court of Session, or **6–39**
the sheriff court for the sheriffdom where the child resides with the prospective adoptive parents.[141] All adoption proceedings are private.[142] Thus, the
identities of the child and the petitioners are not made public, proceedings
are generally conducted *in camera*, and after the order has been made the
process is sealed and access allowed only to exceptional persons, such as the
child himself on reaching the age of 16.[143] These unusual features of adoption
procedure mean that it is almost impossible to combine an adoption hearing
with another action. This may create difficulties where, for example, a grandparent seeks a residence order in respect of a child whom the adoption agency
have placed with other parties for adoption.[144]

Information about the Application

When an application is made for an adoption order, the court must appoint **6–40**
a curator *ad litem* to safeguard the interests of the child, and provide a report
to this effect to the court.[145] A reporting officer whose role is to obtain and
witness any consents to adoption required from the parent(s) of the child will
also be appointed.[146] These two functions are often performed by the same
person. Furthermore, the adoption agency who placed the child,[147] or in a
non-agency case, the local authority,[148] is required to submit to the court a
report on the suitability of the applicants and the welfare of the child. Great
stress is laid on the reports obtained from the agency or authority and curator
ad litem or reporting officer.[149] The court grants or refuses the order. It may
only grant the order if to do so would be better than making no order at all[150]
and the order may be subject to such terms and as the court thinks fit.[151] It
is no longer competent to make an interim adoption order. [152] Where an
order is refused it will not be competent to make a subsequent application to

---

[141] 2007 Act s.118.
[142] 2007 Act s.109.
[143] See the Adoption (Disclosure of Information and Medical Information About Natural
Parents) (Scotland) Regulations 2009 (SI 2009/268). Part 2 of the regulations deals with the
disclosure of information relating to adoptions. Where an adopted person in Scotland is 16
an adoption agency must disclose any information which it has relating to that person's adoption (reg.3(1)). Where an adopted person is under 16 the agency may disclose information
relating to that person's adoption (reg.3(2)) but prior to disclosure it must take into account
the adopted person's views and welfare and the views of the adoptive parents (reg.3(3)).
However, where the adopted person is under 16 it must not disclose any information which
could identify the adopted person's natural parents.
[144] See *F v F*, 1991 S.L.T. 357; *A v B*, 1955 S.C. 378.
[145] 2007 Act s.108(1)(a).
[146] 2007 Act s.108(b).
[147] 2007 Act s.17.
[148] 2007 Act s.19.
[149] *Central Regional Council v M*, 1991 S.C.L.R. 300; *Petition of AB and CB to Adopt X and Y*,
1990 S.C.L.R. (Notes) 809.
[150] 2007 Act s.28(2).
[151] 2007 Act s.28(3).
[152] Such orders were competent under s.25 of the 1978 Act but the APRG recommended their
abolition (AGRP2, para.3.58).

adopt the child unless a change of circumstances can be demonstrated to a later court.[153] Where an order is granted it must be registered in the Adopted Children's Register and an index thereof and a traceable link to the Register of Births must now be maintained.[154] Access to the link to the Birth Register is restricted to adopted persons, those authorised by a court order, and certain public bodies.[155]

The Requirement of Agreement

6–41   It is a key requirement in Scots adoption law that a court should not make an adoption order unless satisfied that each parent or guardian of the child freely, and with full understanding of what is involved, gives consent to the adoption.[156] For these purposes a parent means a parent who has any PRRs in relation to the child.[157] It also covers a parent who, by virtue of a permanence order which does not include provision granting authority for the child to be adopted, has no PRRs.[158] Thus a parent covers the mother of a child whether married or unmarried[159] and the father if he is married to the mother at the time of the child's conception or subsequently.[160]

6–42   A father who has never been married to the mother does not have automatic parental responsibilities and rights under the 1995 Act.[161] However, an unmarried father who is acknowledged as the father of the child on registration of the birth now has PRRs with regard to that child.[162] This provision is not retrospective. In those cases where registration conferring PRRs does not apply, an unmarried father may still acquire PRRs, either via a s.11 court order, or via s.4 agreement.[163] Where he does not fulfil any of these requirements his consent to the adoption is not needed. It is thought that a father who has acquired one particular parental responsibility or right—who, for example, has applied successfully for an award of contact under s.11 of the 1995 Act—probably also qualifies as a "parent".[164]

6–43   Although not required to consent, a father without PRRs should not however be automatically shut out of the adoption process. He may be able to claim a right to respect for his family life with the child under Art.8 of

---

[153] 2007 Act s.33.
[154] 2007 Act ss.53–55.
[155] 2007 Act s.53(3).
[156] 2007 Act s.31. Subject to the rules on permanence orders, discussed below at para.6–60.
[157] 2007 Act s.31(15)(a)
[158] 2007 Act s.31(15)(b).
[159] Children (Scotland) Act 1995 s.3(1)(a).
[160] 1995 Act s.3(1)(b)(i).
[161] 1995 Act s.3(1)(b).
[162] 1995 Act s.3(1)(b)(ii), added by amendment through s.23 of the Family Law (Scotland) Act 2006.
[163] These are sections of the 1995 Act.
[164] This was not an issue prior to the 1995 Act, as such a father qualified as a "guardian" which was defined in s.65(1) to include a father who had the right of guardianship, custody, access or any other parental right. This part of the definition was repealed by 1995 Act Sch.2, para.29, but it is asserted that these provisions are implicitly subsumed into the new definition of "parent" quoted above.

the ECHR.[165] A father without PRRs may thus still be entitled to appear in the court process dealing with permanence orders or adoption and oppose the application on the question of whether the order is in the best interests of the child. For he is entitled to notification of such proceedings where certain conditions are met. Under s.105 of the 2007 Act, where a local authority proposes to apply for a permanence order or becomes aware that an application for an adoption order for a child in its area is planned, it is under a duty to notify the father of that child where certain circumstances apply. These are that:

(a) the father is not married to the mother of the child at the relevant date[166];
(b) on the relevant date the father of the child does not have, and has never had PRRs in respect of the child[167];
(c) the local authority knows the identity and whereabouts of the father or is able to find out this information using reasonable and practicable steps.[168]

In these circumstance, where s.105(2) applies, a local authority must notify the father either that it proposes to apply for a permanence order or that an adoption application has been made. It must also provide the father with specific information as prescribed in the regulations[169] about the processes of applying for the order in question. The local authority must provide notice at least four weeks before the relevant date on which it intends to apply for the permanence order or as soon as is reasonably practicable when it becomes aware of the application, or intended application, for the adoption order.[170]   **6–44**

A guardian is any person appointed by deed or will or by a court to act as guardian[171] (see para.6–60 above). What happens if a person who is required to consent opposes the adoption? In that case, the court has a discretion to dispense with that person's consent but only under certain conditions.   **6–45**

Dispensing with Consent under the 2007 Act

One of the most significant reforms recommended by the APRG and adopted by the 2007 Act was that the grounds for dispensing with consent should be simplified.[172] As a result, s.31(3) of the 2007 Act has restricted the grounds for dispensing with consent to the following situations: **6–46**

---

[165] See *Keegan v Ireland* [1994] ECHR 18 (May 26, 1994). *Cf* the older Scottish position in *A and B v C*, 1987 S.C.L.R. 514.
[166] 2007 Act s.105(1)(b). The "relevant date" is the date when the local authority decides to apply for a permanence order or becomes aware of the planned application for an adoption order (s.105(5)).
[167] 2007 Act s.105(1)(c).
[168] 2007 Act s.105(1)(d).
[169] The Adoption Agencies Regulations 2009 reg. 25A.
[170] 2007 Act s.105(3) and (4).
[171] 2007 Act s.119.
[172] APRG2 paras 3.20 to 3.25.

(a) the parent or guardian is dead[173];
(b) they cannot be found[174] or are incapable of giving consent[175];
(c) subsection (4) or (5) applies[176];
(d) where neither of those subsections applies, the welfare of the child otherwise requires the consent to be dispensed with.[177]

Unfortunately, the final wording of this section[178] has not achieved its aim as it has raised serious questions about its interpretation, including whether or not it is compatible with human rights provisions, especially Article 8.[179] The key case in this area is *ANS and DCS v ML*[180] where a mother argued that in dispensing with her consent to her child's adoption under s.31(3)(d) her rights under Art.8 had been breached. She argued the ground applied in her case, *that the welfare of the child otherwise requires the consent to be dispensed with*, was insufficiently precise in its meaning. This meant that an order made on that ground was not "in accordance with the law" as required by Art.8(2) to justify any interference with her right to private and family life. In other words, that the Scottish Parliament had acted beyond its competence[181] because the provisions of s.31(3)(d) were not in compliance with the terms of Art.8 of the ECHR. The judgment of the Supreme Court was given by Lord Reed who, in finding that the meaning of the subsection was compatible with the Human Rights Act (HRA) 1998, set out how the issue of compatibility should be addressed.

SUPREME COURT JUDGMENT IN ANX AND DCS v ML

Effect of s.3 of the HRA

6–47   Lord Reed observed that the special interpretative duty imposed by s.3 of the HRA, that empowers courts to give effect to legislation in a manner other than the one which Parliament had intended, only arises where the legislation, if read and given effect to by ordinary principles, would result in a breach of the Convention rights. It is only if the intention of Parliament

---

[173] 2007 Act s.31(3)(a). J. Thomson, *Family Law in Scotland*, 6th edn (2011), para.13.8, p.314 points out that where a parent is dead s/he cannot have PRRs and therefore cannot qualify as a parent under the Act. He concludes that "this provision has been included for the avoidance of any doubt".
[174] In applying this ground it is necessary to establish that all reasonable steps were taken to contact the parent. See *S v M*, 1999 S.C. 388.
[175] 2007 Act s.31(3)(b).
[176] That is that the parent is unable to exercise rights ad discharge responsibilities in relation to the child and is not likely to continue to be able to do so (s.31(4)); or that the parent has had their PRR's removed by a PO and unlikely to get them back (s.31(5)).
[177] 2007 Act s.31(3)(d). These grounds are in line with those applied in England and Wales: Adoption and Children Act 2002 s.52(1).
[178] That replaces s.16(2)(b) of the 1978 Act
[179] For discussion see K. McK Norrie, "Welfare and the new grounds for dispensing with parental consent to adoption", 2008 S.L.T. 32, 213–218 and J. Scott, "Welfare and the new grounds for dispensing with parental consent to adoption: a reply", 2009 S.L.T. 4, pp.17–21.
[180] *ANS and DCS v ML* [2012] UKSC 30.
[181] Under s.29(2)(d) of the Scotland Act 1998.

cannot be given effect, because of an incompatibility with Convention rights, that the courts are authorised in terms of s.3 to read and give effect to the legislation in a manner other than the one which Parliament had intended. What this means is that if an issue of compatibility arises, it is necessary to decide *in the first place* what the legislation means, applying ordinary principles of interpretation. Where the ordinary meaning is not immediately clear the court will apply the presumption, which long antedates the Human Rights Act, that legislation is not intended to place the United Kingdom in breach of its international obligations (including those that arise under the Convention). If, however, the ordinary meaning of the legislation is incompatible with the Convention rights, it is then necessary to consider whether the incompatibility can be cured by interpreting the legislation in the manner required by s.3.[182]

Interpretation of s.31(3) of the 2007 Act

In examining the context in which s.31(3) was drafted, Lord Reed noted **6–48** that the Adoption Policy Review Group sought to dispense with the ground under s.16(2)(b) of the 1978 Act that a parent was withholding consent unreasonably, because it gave rise to considerable litigation. The Group were of the view that the new legislation should be based on the English provisions contained in s.52(1) of the Adoption and Children Act 2002, subject to an amendment designed to reflect more explicitly the requirements of Art.8. He observed that s.31(3)(d) was narrower in scope than the English provision because it would only apply in more limited circumstances.[183] These were that before s.31(3)(d) comes into play neither s.31(4) or (5) must apply. This means that where a parent has PRRs that are more than just rights to contact, then s.31(4) requires the court to consider if the parent is (1) unable to discharge those responsibilities and exercise those rights, and (2) if the parent is likely to continue to be unable to do so. The provisions under s.31(5) apply where a permanence order (that does not include the power to place a child for adoption) has been issued, so that a parent no longer has PRRs and it is unlikely that he will reacquire them. It is only where these conditions are *not* met that s.31(3)(d) becomes relevant. According to Thomson this means that, read literally, s.31(3)(d) applies only to parents whose sole right is to contact.[184] However, it also applies where consent cannot be dispensed with under s.31(4) because the court is of the view that the parent might become able to discharge PRRs and exercise parental rights, or where the court forms the view that it is likely that parental responsibilities and rights will be imposed on or given to the parent. The implications of this are that "a competent and reasonably capable parent could have her consent dispensed with if adoption were a better option for the future of the child"[185] and this would give rise to concerns about infringement of a parent's right to family life under Art.8.

---

[182] *ANS and DCS v ML* [2012] UKSC 30, paras 15–17.
[183] *ANS and DCS v ML* [2012] UKSC 30, paras18–27.
[184] J. Thomson, *Family Law in Scotland*, 6th edn, para.13.12, p.318.
[185] J. Thomson, *Family Law in Scotland*, 6th edn, para.13.12, p.318.

6–49   Lord Reed considered s.31(3)(d) to be of practical importance in two
cases where parents would not fall within the terms of s.31(4) or (5). These
include the situation where a parent was granted PRRs only to the extent
of becoming a relevant person in the children's referral to a children's
hearing,[186] or where a parent continued to have PRRs notwithstanding the
withdrawal of contact.[187] He observed that in these cases it may be possible
that a parent's consent should be dispensed with. He also addressed the situation where a parent may currently be unable to discharge PRRs but where
it may be hard for the court to decide whether s/he will continue to be able
to do so,[188] for example, where dealing with a parent suffering from drug
addiction, where a child may be left in limbo because the future is hard to
predict. In this case Lord Reed points out that, although the terms of dispensing with consent under s.31(4) are not met, the welfare of the child may
require that an adoption order should be made and that in "this situation
s.31(3)(d) provides a basis upon which the court can properly dispense with
parental consent".[189]

Case Law on Convention Rights

6–50   Such considerations pit the welfare of the child throughout his life against
the parent's right to respect for family life under Art.8. How did the Supreme
Court find the provisions of s.31(3)(d) to be compatible with Convention
rights under Art.8? The first point to note is that Art.8(2) allows for discrimination and interference with these rights to take place where "this is
necessary in a democratic society in the interests of national security . . .
or for the protection of other rights and freedoms of others". Looking at
earlier case law dealing with Convention rights, Lord Reed referred to the
judgment in *In re P (Children) (Adoption: Parental Consent)*[190] expressing
the view that "an adoption order made without parental consent . . . must be
proportionate to the legitimate aim of protecting the welfare and interests of
the child."[191]

6–51   Lord Reed then went on to quote the three requirements that must be met
when interfering with Art.8 rights, set out by Hale, L.J., *In re C and B (Care
Order: Future Harm)*[192]

> "first that it be in accordance with the law; secondly, that it be for a
> legitimate aim (in this cases the protection of the welfare and interests of
> the children) and thirdly, that it be 'necessary in a democratic society'."

---

[186] As in the case of *In Principal Reporter v K* [2010] UKSC 56, cited in [2012] UKSC 30, para.29.
[187] As in the case of *NJDB v JEG* [2012] UKSC 21, cited in [2012] UKSC 30, para.29.
[188] For in making a decision in keeping with the child's welfare under s.14(3) this requires a consideration of the situation "throughout the child's life": *ANS and DCS v ML* [2012] UKSC
30, para.30.
[189] *ANS and DCS v ML* [2012] UKSC 30, para.29.
[190] [2008] EWCA Civ 535, para.119–123, cited in [2012] UKSC 20, para.39 at119.
[191] This was referred to by Lord Hope when delivering judgment on this case in the Inner House,
see *ANS, DCS v ML* [2011] CSIH 38, paras 119–123, cited in [2012] UKSC 30, paras 39 at
119.
[192] *In re C and B (Care Order: Future Harm)* [2001] 1FLR 611, para.33 at [2012] UKSC 30,
para.39 at 119.

Lord Reed observed that the word "necessary" takes it meaning from its context but "in Strasbourg jurisprudence [this] has a meaning lying somewhere between 'indispensible', on the one hand and 'useful, 'reasonable' or 'desirable' on the other hand". He notes it "implies a 'pressing social need'".[193] On the third requirement he once again quotes Hale, L.J., that

> "there is a long line of European Court of Human Rights jurisprudence. . .which emphasises that the intervention has to be proportionate to the legitimate aim. Intervention in the family may be appropriate, but the aim should be to reunite the family when circumstances enable that, and the effort should be devoted towards that end. Cutting off all contact and the relationship between the child or children and their family is only justified by the overriding necessity of the interests of the child".[194]

These cases demonstrate that proportionality is key and that a court should adopt the least interventionist approach "unless there are cogent reasons to the contrary".[195] Lord Reed then quoted the conditions that require to be met when dispensing with parental consent for adoption under s.52(1) (b) of the Adoption and Children Act 2002[196]:

> "The Court reiterates that in cases concerning the placing of a child for adoption, which entails the permanent severance of family ties, the best interests of the child are paramount (see *Johansen v Norway* (1996) 23 EHRR 33, para 78; *Kearns v France* (2008) 50 EHRR 33, para 79; and *R and H v United Kingdom* (2011) 54 EHRR28, paras 73 and 81). In identifying the child's best interests in a particular case, two considerations must be borne in mind: first, it is in the child's best interests that his ties with his family be maintained except in cases where the family has proved particularly unfit; and second, it is in the child's best interests to ensure his development in a safe and secure environment (see *Neulinger v Switzerland* (2010) 54 EHRR 1087, para 136; and *R v H*, cited above, paras 73–74). It is clear from the foregoing that family ties may only be severed in very exceptional circumstances and that everything must be done to preserve personal relations and, where appropriate to 'rebuild' the family (see *Neulinger*, cited above, para 136; and *R v H*, cited above, para 73). It is not enough to show that a child could be placed in a more beneficial environment for his upbringing (see *K and T v Finland* (2001) 36 EHRR 18, para 173; and *TS v DS v United Kingdom (Application No. 61540109) (unreported)* given 19 January 2010). However, where the maintenance of family ties would harm the child's health and

---

[193] *ANS and DCS v ML* [2012] UKSC 30, para.39.
[194] *In re C and B, para.*34 cited at [2012] UKAC 30, para.39 at 119.
[195] Hale, L.J., *In re O (Supervision Order)* [2001] 1 FLR 923, para.28, cited at [2012] UKSC 30, para.39 at 123.
[196] See *YC v United Kingdom (Application No. 4547/10)* Unreported, cited by Lord Reed in [2012] UKSC 30, para.40.

development, a parent is not entitled under Article 8 to insist that such ties be maintained (see *Neulinger*, cited above, para 136; and *R v H*, cited above, para 73)".

In reaching its decision that dispensing with consent in this case was compatible with Convention rights the court in *YC v United Kingdom*[197] attached particular significance to a list of factors that should be taken into account in exercising its power under s.52(1)(b). These include "the age, maturity and ascertained wishes of the child, the likely effect on the child of ceasing to be a member of his original family, and the relationship the child has with relatives".[198]

6–52   Applying these considerations to the *ANS* case, what led the Supreme Court to decide that s.31(3)(d) could be construed in a way that did not put it in breach of its international obligations? Referring to the case law outlined above the court held that the test is a test of necessity and proportionality.[199] What this means is that the court must be satisfied "that the interference with the rights of parents is proportionate, that is, that nothing less than adoption will suffice".[200] This test is consistent with the no order principle contained in s.28(2) of the 2007 Act dealing with the making of adoption orders. In treating welfare as the paramount consideration in reaching a decision under s.14(3) this is in keeping with Art.21 of the UNCRC that specifically makes welfare the paramount consideration in adoption proceedings. Under these tests consent will only be dispensed with where the court is satisfied that "there is an overriding requirement that adoption should proceed, for the sake of the child's welfare . . . and that nothing less than adoption will suffice".[201] Thus s.31(3)(d) is compliant with human rights provisions because:

"In considering the child's welfare, and in assessing the overall proportionality of an order. . .the court will have regard in particular to the matters listed in section 14(4). Two of those matters correspond to the factors which are listed in section 1(4) of the 2002 Act and were mentioned by the European Court: the age, maturity and ascertained wishes of the child are covered by section 14(4)(b) and the likely effect on the child of ceasing to be a member of his original family is covered by section 14(4)(d). One would equally expect a court exercising powers under section 31(3)(d) of the 2007 Act to take into account the remaining matter mentioned by the European Court, namely the relationship the child has with relatives, since that is one of the circumstances of the case, and it is plainly relevant to the likely effect on the child on the making of an adoption order. It is therefore a matter which falls within the ambit of sections 14(2) and (4)(d)".[202]

---

[197] *YC v United Kingdom* (Application No4547/10) Unreported given March 13, 2012.
[198] Cited by Lord Reed in [2012] UKSC 30, para.41.
[199] *ANS and DCS v ML* [2012] UKSC 30, para.40.
[200] *ANS and DCS v ML* [2012] UKSC 30, para.34.
[201] *ANS and DCS v ML* [2012] UKSC 30, para.34.
[202] *ANS and DCS v ML* [2012] UKSC 30, para.43.

For these reasons the court rejected the argument that s.31(3)(d) was so imprecisely formulated as to lack legal certainty. While acknowledging that it leaves "a lot to the judgment of a sheriff hearing the case"[203] the court pointed out the impossibility of spelling "out exhaustively the particular circumstances in which dispensing with parental consent is necessary".[204] Given the specific circumstances contained in s.31(3)(a) and (b) and in subss.(4) and (5), the court noted that s.31(3)(d) "is intended to confer a residual power which can be used in such other circumstances as may arise" and that it is "unrealistic to expect that a provision of that nature will spell out the precise circumstances in which it may appropriately be applied".[205]

In its judgment the court drew attention to the fact that in the population **6–53** statistics for the year 2010, there were 911,794 children aged under 16. In that year only 406 adoption orders were made. There were no statistics on how many of these included cases where parental consent was dispensed with; however, most cases where this occurs involve children who are adopted from care, and in 2009/2010, this situation accounted for 218 adoptions. Even if all these cases dealt with dispensation of consent (which is most unlikely) it would account for only 0.02% of the total number of children in that year, that is 1 in 5000.[206] However small the number, however, the authors are of the view that given the long reaching effects of adoption it is important that the process is conducted as fairly as possible with regard to the interests of all parties. The Court also drew attention to the need for quick decisions in adoption cases and expressed concern that adoption proceedings begun, in this case, in 2009 had been subject to a delay that would have profoundly negative effects on the child in question,[207] given that the decision whether to make an order would have to be referred back to the original judge.[208]

The Adoption Order

Once the court is satisfied that any required consent has been given, or that **6–54** a ground for dispensing with consent exists, or that the child is subject to a permanence order which has not been revoked, it can proceed to decide whether, in the welfare of the child, an adoption order should be made.[209] Any condition can be attached to the order under s.28(3), including the right to allow a child to maintain contact with his birth family after the adoption. The order vests parental rights and responsibilities under ss.1(3) and 2(4) of the 1995 Act in the adopters[210] and extinguishes the corresponding rights and duties which

---

[203] *ANS and DCS v ML* [2012] UKSC 30, para.47.
[204] *ANS and DCS v ML* [2012] UKSC 30, para.47.
[205] *ANS and DCS v ML* [2012] UKSC 30, para.47.
[206] *ANS and DCS v ML* [2012] UKSC 30, para.44.
[207] See also *NJDB v JEG* [2012] UKSC 21 where the court was critical of the length of time it had taken to deal with a contact case. See also *Dundee City Council v M*, 2004 S.L.T. 640 where a nine day proof on a freeing for adoption order had to be set aside while a determination was made as to whether parents' human rights had been infringed. In effect this meant that the child's life had been placed in limbo for another year before the matter could be remitted back to a sheriff for a determination as to whether or not to make the order.
[208] *ANS and DCS v ML* [2012] UKSC 30, paras 50 to 52.
[209] 2007 Act s.14(3).
[210] 2007 Act ss.28(1) and 40(1).

any parent or guardian held immediately before the order was made.[211] The obligation of the parent to pay aliment to the child is also ended.[212] Although the adoption order effectively severs the legal link between natural parent and child, some legal connections remain. A child remains related to his natural parents for the purpose of determining prohibited degrees of relationship and incestuous relationship.[213] Marital and sexual relations with the adoptive parents (though not adoptive siblings) are struck at in addition.[214] An adopted child remains the child of his natural parents for any determination of immigration or nationality status.[215] For succession purposes, an adopted child is generally treated as the child of the adopters and not of the natural parents[216] but adoptive status may still affect the rights in succession of a child in executries governed by the law before September 10, 1964.[217]

Reform Under the 2007 Act: Permanence Orders

6–55 As we have seen, establishing a ground for dispensing with consent in contested cases is not always straightforward. In the end, only a very small number of adoption applications made to the court are refused because consent is refused and not dispensed with. But the effect of refusal can be to cause enormous delay in the adoption process. This causes particular difficulty if the child has been placed with, and become settled with, the prospective adopters for some time, on a basis of informal consent from the natural parent or parents. If that consent is subsequently withdrawn when the formal adoption application is made, then lengthy proceedings may need to be initiated for dispensation with parental consent. In the meantime the child is in legal limbo, with the birth parents retaining all rights.

6–56 To prevent this difficulty, the Houghton Committee in 1972 recommended a new procedure known as "freeing for adoption", which was introduced in the Children Act 1975.[218] A freeing for adoption order was sought on the same conditions as an adoption order, but, ideally, could be obtained before the child was placed with prospective adopters. The effect was to transfer PRRs not to adoptive parents, but to the adoption agency.[219] A child who was freed for adoption could thus be placed with prospective adopters without fear that the placement would be disrupted by a change of heart by the natural parent(s).[220] However, in reviewing the adoption process the APRG noted that while freeing for adoption was intended to facilitate adoption where parents

---

[211] 2007 Act ss.35(2)(a) and 40(4).

[212] 2007 Act s.35(2)(b)(i).

[213] 2007 Act s.41(1).

[214] See Ch.9.

[215] 2007 Act s.41(3).

[216] Succession (Scotland) Act 1964 s.23(1).

[217] i.e. when the above section came into force. See further, Wilkinson and Norrie, 2nd edn (1999), pp.522 to 523.

[218] These provisions became part of the 1978 Act, ss.18–21.

[219] 1978 Act s.18(5).

[220] A freeing order could not be made unless the child had been placed for adoption or was likely to be placed for adoption: see s.18(3).

agreed to this, it had become more generally used in contested cases to dispense with parental consent. These contentious cases often concerned children who were "looked after"[221] by the local authority outside the family home, often under supervision requirements imposed by a children's hearing.[222] In these circumstances what was at stake was the long term welfare of the child. While intervention in the lives of children's families is preferably based on co-operation and voluntary engagement[223] with the aim of reuniting children with their families where they are not residing with them and with rehabilitating the family, there are circumstances where this is not possible. In these cases it is desirable that a stable, permanent solution be found for these children as soon as possible, for the uncertainty and instability that being "looked after" can engender has detrimental effects on these children's well being.[224]

Parental Responsibilities Orders

In a small number of cases it is clear that children cannot live with their birth families and that arrangements need to be made to provide them with a new, long term, stable placement. Under the 1978 Act this was achieved through providing for parental responsibilities orders (PROs) that vested PRRs in the local authority and through freeing for adoption orders. In the case of the former, PRRs were removed from the birth parents and vested in the local authority taking care of "looked after" children. In the case of the latter, PRRs were also removed from the birth parents and vested in the local authority pending a placement for adoption. In both cases the children in question remained looked after by the local authority.[225] The APRG were critical of these orders because of their inflexibility and limitations in meeting the needs of individual children.[226] In their view PROs were unsatisfactory because:

6–57

(a) PRRs were transferred to the local authority and not to a substitute family caring for the child;
(b) there was no flexibility to vary the PRRs being transferred to meet the circumstances of the case (for example, by awarding some PRRs to the local authority and others to the carers of the child);
(c) a person who had had PRRs removed by a PRO (such as a birth mother) could not apply for a contact or residence order at a later date.[227]

---

[221] For more detailed discussion on looked after children see Ch.7. While the number of children being adopted over the years has fallen, the numbers of looked after children have increased every year since 2001, and is at its highest in 2011 since 1981 (*Children's Social Work Statistics Scotland, No.1* (2012), p.1).

[222] Above, n.57.

[223] Under Pt II of the Children (Scotland) Act 1995, ss.16–38 dealing with support for children and their families, see Ch.7.

[224] The APRG observed that of the children looked after away from home, an average of 3.07 placement moves were recorded for each period of care (APRG2 para.10).

[225] In the case of freeing orders, however, this status would come to an end on the child's adoption.

[226] APRG 2 paras 5.1 to 5.10.

[227] Such persons could not apply for contact or residence orders under s.11 of the 1995 Act. However, the PRO itself could provide for contact and it was possible to apply for contact when the order was being made or subsequently under ss.89(5) and 88 of the 1995 Act.

For these reasons local authorities made little use of PROs in practice.[228]

Freeing for Adoption Order

6–58   While freeing for adoption orders were intended to avoid conflict between birth parents and prospective adopters by freeing the child from the parents before the adoption took place they also had their limitations.[229] These included:

(a) the fact that pending adoption the child was left in limbo with no-one other than the local authority having PRRs;

(b) the potential danger that if a child was not ultimately adopted there was no "way back" from the situation, allowing for the redistribution of PRRs;

(c) the fact that a child might have some residual contact with a member of his birth family but once a freeing order was made the law provided no protection for that contact to continue pending adoption[230];

(d) that these orders were a precursor to adoption based on the notion of a "clean break" between the child and his birth parents on adoption where contact was not desirable[231];

(e) that freeing orders were introduced as a means of fast tracking adoption but in practice they were subject to delays that were unsatisfactory in securing long term stability for the child.[232]

Long Term Fostering

6–59   There were also concerns about the position of children in long-term fostering arrangements under supervision requirements made by a children's hearing. For while these supervision requirements suspend birth parents' rights (e.g. to residence) they do not confer PRRs on either the local authority looking after the child or on the substitute carer. Given that supervision requirements are subject to an annual review this makes them unstable, as the orders may be varied or revoked, creating uncertainty as to whether a child will remain with particular foster carers. As one child who formed part of a group canvassed for their views on adoption observed:

---

[228] In 2004 there were only 341 such orders in place compared to 4,427 children on supervision requirement away from home (APRG2 para.5.10).

[229] APRG2 para.5.6.

[230] See *D v Grampian Regional Council*, 1995 S.L.T. 519 where the House of Lords held that if parental rights were removed from a natural parent by an adoption order or freeing for adoption order, then that parent should be divested not only of their rights, but also of their title to go to the courts to ask them to make an order for contact or residence in their favour. This ruling took the form of s.11(3) and (4) of the 1995 Act. Thus there was no statutory provision allowing for contact to be made in these circumstances.

[231] While the 1978 Act did allow for contact to be made a condition of the adoption order in exceptional cases under s.12(6), this had to be done at the time the order was made.

[232] This was because of the disruption to the child's life caused by a lack of certainty or stability in their circumstances. The APRG noted four stages at which delays can taken place (1) between a child becoming "looked after" away from home and a review decision to seek permanence; (2) between review and the adoption panel; (3) between the panel and lodging the court application for adoption or freeing for adoption; and (4) during the court process and matching a child with a family (APRG2 para.9).

"I feel more safe when I am with my [adoptive] Mum [than when in foster care] because she is my Mum, she is the only person who has been there for me". (Young woman, aged 14 years.)[233]

Although a carer could apply for PRRs under s.11 of the 1995 Act this is an expensive process which if successful could lead to the child ceasing to be looked after by the local authority and to the foster carers' allowances being terminated.

Permanence Orders

In light of these limitations the Adoption Review Group recommended **6–60** abolishing PROs and freeing for adoption orders and replacing them with a new order, called a permanence order. Such an order would have the advantage of providing "greater legal security and stability for the child and new family, as well as a mechanism for securing clear rights for birth parents where appropriate".[234] For this order would allow children to be brought up by substitute parents leading to greater stability and predictability for children, while also balancing out the interests of children, birth parents and substitute parents in line with human rights requirements. It would deal with long term security for children, both for those for whom return to the family home is not possible but for whom adoption is not the answer, as well as for those children for whom adoption is the preferred option. The great advantage of such orders is that they enable individual solutions to be tailor made for children by taking account of their different needs, including contact with their birth families.

Characteristics of Permanence Orders

Mandatory Provisions

The flexibility referred to above is achieved through the mandatory and **6–61** ancillary provisions attached to the orders and the provision granting authority for the child to be adopted if certain conditions are met.[235] Only a local authority can apply for a PO under s.80 of the 2007 Act. Such an order consists of a mandatory provision that vests the right to regulate the child's residence in the local authority until the child is sixteen years old.[236] It also vests responsibility in the local authority to provide guidance to the child, in a manner appropriate to the child's stage of development until the child reaches eighteen.[237] Where the child in question is subject to a supervision requirement and the court is satisfied that compulsory measures of supervision would no longer be necessary if the PO is granted, it must revoke the supervision requirement when granting the PO.[238]

---

[233] APRG2 para.3.11.
[234] APRG2 para.5.12.
[235] These conditions are set out in s.83 of the 2007 Act.
[236] 2007 Act s.81(1)(b) and (2)(b).
[237] 2007 Act s.81(1)(a) and (2)(a).
[238] 2007 Act s.89.

Ancillary Provisions

6–62　　Ancillary provisions may contain a whole range of orders, including the vesting of PRRs in the local authority or a third party.[239] While parents may retain some PRRs under these provisions, it is also the case that they may have all their PRRs extinguished under s.82(1)(c). The ancillary provisions may:

(a) vest any of the remaining PRRs, except contact, in the local authority[240]; or

(b) vest any of the PRRs, including contact, in another person[241];

(c) extinguish parents' or a legal guardian's PRRs that were vested in them prior to the making of a PO and that now vested in another person after making the order[242];

(d) specify arrangements for contact between the child and any other person the court considers to be appropriate, in the child's best interests[243];

(e) determine any question that has arisen in respect of PRRs or any other aspect involving the welfare or the child.[244]

These provisions allow for flexibility because, apart from residence and guidance, PRRs can be apportioned as the court sees fit so long as each PRR vests in a person.[245] This is important because it means that *all* PRRs, apart from the mandatory provisions, must be allocated to a person or to the local authority.

Order Granting Authority for Adoption

6–63　　When applying for a PO the local authority can request the court to make an order granting authority for the child to be adopted.[246] This has the advantage of fast tracking the adoption process as parental consent to adoption will have been obtained or dispensed with.[247] However, certain conditions must be met before such an order can be granted. These are

(a) that the court is satisfied that the child has been or is likely to be placed for adoption[248];

(b) that the parents or guardian of the child must understand the effect of making an adoption order and consent to such an order being made,[249] or that the parents' or guardian's consent should be dispensed with.[250]

---

[239] 2007 Act s.82. These cover all the remaining PRRs that do not include residence and guidance.

[240] 2007 Act s.82(1)(a).

[241] 2007 Act s.82((1)(b).

[242] 2007 Act s.82(1)(c) and (d).

[243] 2007 Act s.82(1)(e).

[244] 2007 Act s.82(1)(f).

[245] 2007 Act s.80(3).

[246] 2007 Act s.80(2)(c).

[247] 2007 Act s.83(1)(c)(i) and (ii). Thus a PO replaces the old freeing for adoption order.

[248] 2007 Act s.83(1)(b).

[249] 2007 Act s.83(1)(c)(i).

[250] 2007 Act s.83(1)(c)(ii).

In addition, certain other conditions must be adhered to. These are

(a) that an order cannot be made in respect of a child aged 12 or over without the child's consent[251];
(b) that the child should be given the opportunity to express his views and have them taken into account if he is of sufficient age and maturity to form a view.[252] A child aged twelve or over is presumed to be of sufficient age and maturity[253]but this does not preclude a younger child from expressing a view if he can demonstrate sufficient maturity.
(c) that account is taken of the child's religious persuasion, racial origin and cultural and linguistic background,[254]along with the likely effect on the child of the making of the order.[255]

An order cannot be made where a child is or has been married, or is or has been a party to a civil partnership.[256] Where a PO includes authority to adopt and a child is being placed for adoption or has been adopted, the local authority must give notice to persons who consented to the provision or to those whose consent was dispensed with.[257]

Once again, difficulties in granting a PO and a PO with consent to adopt **6–64** arise with respect to dispensing with a parent's or a guardian's consent to the order. Dispensing with consent here is based on the same limited grounds that justify dispensing with consent to adoption.[258] In *Aberdeenshire Council v W*[259] the sheriff principal went through the procedure that should be followed in making a PO. The first step is to consider the conditions and considerations applicable to the making of a PO set out in s.84. In this case, as the child was only two and half years old, the question of the child's consent was not a relevant consideration.[260] Neither was it practicable, given the child's age, to ascertain or take account of her views[261] There were no issues with regard to her religious persuasion, racial origin or cultural and linguistic background that stood in the way of making the order.[262] In considering the likely effect of the order on the child the sheriff principal formed the view that the making of the order would clear the way ahead for her to be adopted by the prospective adoptive parents and "hence to enjoy the benefits of permanence, stability and continuity that ought to be the birthright of every child."[263]

He also considered that the sheriff at first instance had erred by not **6–65**

---

[251] 2007 Act s.84(1). This is in keeping with the general requirements for adoption. However, such consent is unnecessary where the court is satisfied that the child is incapable of consenting to the order under s.84(2).
[252] 2007 Act s.84(5)(a)(i) and (ii) and s.84(5)(b)(i).
[253] 2007 Act s.84(6).
[254] 2007 Act s.84(5)(b)(ii).
[255] 2007 Act s.84(5)(b)(iii).
[256] 2007 Act s.85.
[257] 2007 Act s.101. It must also notify these persons when placement for adoption ceases.
[258] 2007 Act s.31(2)(b) and (3). These grounds are discussed at para. 6–46 above.
[259] *Aberdeenshire Council v W*, 2011 S.L.T. (Sh. Ct) 186.
[260] Thus s.84(1) and (2) could be disregarded.
[261] Under 2007 Act s.84(5)(a) and (b)(i).
[262] Under 2007 Act s.84(5)(b)(ii).
[263] *Aberdeenshire Council v W*, 2011 S.L.T. (Sh. Ct) 186, para.23.

forming the view that child's residence with the parents "is, or is likely to be, seriously detrimental to the welfare of the child".[264] The sheriff principal reached this conclusion on the basis of evidence that this child had been the subject of a child protection order from birth and had been placed with foster carers. She remained in foster care until she was transferred into the care of prospective adoptive parents with whom she was happily living at the time of the case. She had never lived with her parents, who had had two children taken into care and who had been adopted before she was born, but she did have supervised contact with them, that at the time of the case had been reduced to a meeting once a month. In the sheriff principal's view, removing her from the care of her prospective adopters with whom she had been living would be seriously detrimental to her welfare as she was likely to "run the risk—which I consider would be a substantial one—of causing her significant psychological damage."[265]

6–66   The original sheriff appeared to have problems in finding that the parents fell within the remit of s.83(1)(c)(ii) on the basis that the parents were, in the opinion of the court, unable satisfactorily to discharge their responsibilities and exercise their rights and would be likely to continue to be able to do so.[266] The sheriff principal took the view that in interpreting this section the words 'likely to continue' had to be taken into account at "the date of the court's decision and not some indeterminate date in the future".[267] On this basis with the evidence before the court he concluded that this ground had been met.[268]

6–67   The next step was to consider whether the parents' consent should be dispensed with on this ground. This required making a judgment about whether it would better for the child if it were to grant authority for the child to be adopted than if it were not to grant such authority.[269]This had

---

[264] 2007 Act s.84(5)(c)(ii).

[265] *Aberdeenshire Council v W*, 2011 S.L.T. (Sh. Ct) 186, para.19. While the sheriff at first instance considered that the local authority should have carried out a kinship care assessment to see if the child should be transferred to the care of her grandparents, the sheriff principal took the view that as the child had been living for more than thirteen months with her prospective adopters and that there was no realistic prospect of her being returned to her parents, even if her kin were identified as suitable carers "the possible advantage of her being brought up by members of her birth family is clearly outweighed by the potential benefit of her being brought up by the prospective adopters" (para.29). His approach was motivated by the need to "put an end to the ongoing uncertainty of her current situation and clear the way for her to be adopted. . .so that she may be granted the stability and security of a permanent home with committed and capable parents" (para.29).

[266] 2007 Act s.83(3)(a) and (b) and (c).

[267] *Aberdeenshire Council v W*, 2011 S.L.T. (Sh. Ct) 186, para.14.

[268] The sheriff at first instance had had difficulty in reaching this decision because he noted that there was no evidence of dependence on drink or drugs or a propensity for violence from which it could be inferred that the parents had surrendered all capacity to care for a child of any age. In doing so, he was influenced by the provisions of the old s.16(2) of the 1978 Act that placed great emphasis on the parent's behaviour as being inadequate or at fault. However, this is not required under the 2007 Act, where it is the welfare of the child that is the paramount consideration. This case may be compared with that of *Inverclyde Council v T*, 2011 CSOH 27 where the parents were both drug addicts suffering from mental health difficulties. In this case a PO was granted with authority to adopt on the basis that they were unable to discharge their PRRs and to exercise their parental rights and that they were likely to be unable to do so.

[269] 2007 Act s.84(3).

to be read in conjunction with s.14(2) to (4) looking at all circumstances of the case,[270] having regard to the value of a stable family unit in the child's development[271]and other matters,[272] including the likely effect on the child, throughout the child's life[273] of the making of an adoption order.[274] Taking all these factors into account in making an order the court must consider "the need to safeguard and promote the welfare of the child throughout the child's life as the paramount consideration".[275] The sheriff principal acknowledged that reading s.14(2) literally imposes an impossible task upon the court or adoption agency, as it is inevitable that not all circumstances in a particular case will be known to the court or agency. He therefore interpreted "all the circumstances" to mean "all the relevant and material circumstances so far as these have come to its attention".[276]

With all this in mind, returning to a consideration of dispensing with the parents consent under s.83(i)(c)(ii), and whether it would be better for the court to grant authority for the child to be adopted than not to grant it,[277] and taking account of the need to safeguard and promote the welfare of the child throughout childhood as the paramount consideration,[278] the sheriff principal found that the grounds for making an adoption order and for dispensing with parental consent had been met. While observing that in cases of this kind "there will always be a degree of uncertainty about what the future holds, so that one can never be absolutely sure that an order ... will turn out to be the best available option for the particular child"[279] nonetheless "there comes a point in time when the court just has to grasp the nettle and make the best judgment it can on an application ... in the light of all available information and always subject to the provisions of the 2007 Act".[280] In reaching his conclusion the sheriff principal acknowledged that the parents' human rights under Art.8 had been infringed, but held that this could be justified as being in accordance with the law, in pursuing a legitimate aim, namely the protection of the health, rights and freedoms of the child, that can be regarded as "necessary in a democratic society".[281] In making the PO granting authority for the child to be adopted the sheriff principal revoked the supervision requirement that was in place with regard to the child.[282]

6–68

It is important to note that where a supervision is in effect parents still

6–69

---

[270] 2007 Act s.14(2).

[271] 2007 Act s.14(4)(a).

[272] Concerning the child's ascertainable views (s.14(4)(b)) taking account of the child's age an maturity; the child's religious persuasion, racial origin and cultural and linguistic background (s.14(4)(c)).

[273] Note that this is a much longer term consideration than that relating to childhood which ends at 18 under the Act.

[274] 2007 Act s.14(4)(d).

[275] 2007 Act s.14(3).

[276] *Aberdeenshire Council v W*, 2011 S.L.T. (Sh. Ct) 186, para.25.

[277] 2007 Act s.83(1)(d).

[278] 2007 Act s.84(4).

[279] *Aberdeenshire Council v W*, 2011 S.L.T. (Sh. Ct) 186, para.26.

[280] *Aberdeenshire Council v W*, 2011 S.L.T. (Sh. Ct) 186, para.26,

[281] Under Art.8(2).

[282] Under s.89 the court has power to revoke a supervision requirement where it is satisfied that on the making of a PO compulsory measures of supervision would no longer be necessary.

have PRRs even if they are suspended. In *East Lothian Council v S*[283] a sheriff was found to have erred in law when he took the view that, as the child was subject to a supervision requirement, there was no person having the right to have the child with him or otherwise regulate the child's residence in terms of s.84(5)(c)(i). On this basis he proceeded to make a PO with authority to adopt a child without applying the test in s.84(5)(c). This test required the court to make a finding as to whether or not it was satisfied that the child's residence with his parents was, or was likely to be, seriously detrimental to his welfare in terms of s.84(5)(c)(ii). The case was remitted back to the sheriff to consider the test that he had ignored and a curator ad litem was appointed to prepare a report given a change in circumstances that had arisen through the birth mother's subsequent pregnancy.[284]

APPLICATION AND NOTIFICATION OF A PO

6–70 Only a local authority may apply for a PO[285] and where it does so proceedings are conducted in private unless the court otherwise directs.[286] The order may be made in respect of any person under the age of 18, provided he has never been married or registered as a civil partner.[287] Such an order will likely be sought in the sheriff court, but can also be made in the Court of Session.[288] As with many statutory provisions the details of procedure are contained within regulations but the 2007 Act does set out certain minimal requirements.[289] A very important aspect of applications is that notification must be given to a whole range of persons, including the unmarried father who has never had any PRRs, who in the past had difficulty in participating in proceedings but must now be notified of the fact of the application and date and place of the hearing "if he can be found".[290] The Act sets out a list of persons who must be given the opportunity to make representations with regard to the PO if they wish to do so. These include

(a) the local authority making the application;
(b) the child or the child's representative;
(c) any person who has parental responsibilities or parental rights in relation to the child;
(d) any other person who claims an interest.[291]

---

[283] *East Lothian Council v S*, 2011 Fam. L.R. 80.
[284] The parents sought to have the case remitted to a different sheriff for a fresh hearing on the basis that the original sheriff would in fact be reviewing his own decision. The sheriff principal rejected their contention on the basis that the remit was not a form of review but involved applying a distinct legal test that had not previously been considered.
[285] 2007 Act s.80(1).
[286] 2007 Act s.109.
[287] 2007 Act s.85(2). The fact that a child has been adopted is not bar to the making of a PO (s.85(1)).
[288] Under s.118 of the 2007 Act an application can be made to a sheriff court in the sheriffdom "within which the child is" or to the Court of Session.
[289] 2007 Act s.104(2)–(5).
[290] 2007 Act s.104(2)(b).
[291] 2007 Act s.86(2)(a)–(d).

Similar requirements apply to applications for variation and revocation discussed below. Where an application for a PO is pending (including variation of such an order)[292] and a children's hearing is considering making or modifying a supervision requirement, the children's hearing must prepare a report for the court to which the application was made.[293] Where two or more persons have a parental right in respect of a child and at least one of them has the right vested as the result of a PO, each may exercise the right without the consent of the other unless the order vesting the right provides otherwise.[294] Where PRRs are vested in a local authority it may not act in a way that would be inconsistent with any court order of which it is aware relating to the child or the child's property.[295]

EFFECT OF A PO ORDER AND ITS RELATIONSHIP WITH OTHER LEGAL ORDERS

The relationship of a PO to other legal orders depends on its precise terms. **6–71** All orders however have a mandatory element and this extinguishes the parents' or legal guardian's right to determine the child's residence.[296] When made a PO revokes the terms of any previous PO as well as any PRRs vested in a person under s.11 of the Children (Scotland) Act 1995.[297] In the case of the latter, as noted earlier, the court must ensure that *all* PRRs vest in a person or persons by virtue of the PO that it grants.[298] Other than these provisions, the effect of the order very much depends on whether it has ancillary provisions and the form that these provisions take in regulating PRRs in relation to children. A PO remains in effect until varied or revoked or until the child is adopted when the order cease to have effect on the making of the adoption order.[299]

Where POs are granted a question arises as to how they fit in with other **6–72** orders, for example, supervision requirements made by a children's hearing. In dealing with the jurisdiction of courts and children's hearings, the APRG expressed the view that the courts make decisions about the legal status of a child (adoption, etc.) and the conferral or removal of legal PRRs (such as s.11 orders).[300] Hearings, on the other hand, make decisions on measures of supervision necessary for a child's welfare,[301] which can include temporary suspension of PRRs particularly contact and residence of the child. Decisions of hearings take precedence over decisions of the courts in matters within the hearings system's jurisdiction (e.g. requiring an adopted child to be looked after away from home).[302] This means that where a supervision requirement is in place when an application for a PO is pending it remains in force.[303]

---

[292] Variation may include amendment to the order to provide for authority to adopt (s.95(3)).
[293] 2007 Act s.95.
[294] 2007 Act s.91.
[295] 2007 Act s.90(1) and (2)(a).
[296] 2007 Act s.87.
[297] 2007 Act s.88(1) and (2).
[298] 2007 Act s.88(3).
[299] 2007 Act s.102.
[300] APRG2 para.5.37.
[301] For a detailed discussion of the role of children's hearings see Ch.8.
[302] For a detailed discussion of the role of children's hearings see Ch.8.
[303] 2007 Act s.90(2)(b).

Where an application for a PO is pending, if a children's hearing is considering making or modifying a supervision requirement, it must prepare a report to the court dealing with the application for a PO.[304] It may take no action pending the outcome of the application unless the court refers the matter to the Principal Reporter.[305] Where a local authority is not happy with a supervision requirement that is in force it may seek an interim PO.[306] If this is granted the interim order takes precedence over a supervision requirement.[307] When it comes to considering the full PO, the court may revoke the supervision requirement provided the court is satisfied that the granting of the PO would render compulsory measures of supervision unnecessary.[308] If a court does not take this action the supervision requirement will remain in place and the local authority having PRRs may not act in a way that would be inconsistent with its terms.[309]

6–73   In the case of an ordinary s.11 order, a pre-existing supervision requirement takes precedence over a subsequent court order if the order is inconsistent with the terms of the requirement. Once a PO is granted, however, the court may not grant a s.11 order except in so far as it concerns an interdict, prohibiting a person from taking certain steps; appointing a judicial factor; or removing a person as the child's guardian.[310] This means that where a parent, who retains a right by virtue of being a parent (and not under a s.11 order), is in dispute with a person who has the right under a PO, it is not possible to bring an application to the court under s.11 to settle the matter.[311] Instead, the appropriate course of action would be to seek a variation of the PO under s.92 of the 2007 Act.

Variation

6–74   An application is only competent where it involves a variation of any of the ancillary provisions.[312] A local authority is under a duty to apply for variation where it determines that there has been a material change of circumstances directly relating to any of the POs provisions, and, as a result of this change the order ought to be varied.[313] It must do so as soon as is reasonably practicable.[314] Where an application is made by a local authority, the court must allow any person affected by the PO to make representation if they wish to do so.[315] Where the application is not made by a local authority but by another applicant

---

[304] 2007 Act s.95.

[305] 2007 Act s.96(1), (2) and (3).

[306] 2007 Act s.97(1) and (2).

[307] 2007 Act s.97(5). Note that if the interim order is granted it is also open to the court to terminate the supervision requirement under s.97(3) and (4).

[308] 2007 Act s.89(1)(b).

[309] 2007 Act s.90(1) and (2)(b).

[310] 2007 Act s.103.

[311] Unless it had to do with the matters mentioned earlier.

[312] In this context variation to vary includes to "add to, omit, or amend" (s.92(8)).

[313] 2007 Act s.99(1). No guidance is given on what amounts to a "material change of circumstance" but it may be useful to refer to the criteria set out in s.96(4) that guide the court on granting variation.

[314] 2007 Act s.99(2).

[315] 2007 Act s.94(1).

then the court must notify those who were entitled to make representations where the initial PO was applied for.[316] In reaching a decision on variation the court must take the same criteria into account that it used in granting the PO.[317] In doing so it may vary any of the ancillary provisions as it considers appropriate.[318] Variation may include extinguishing a responsibility or right vested in a person immediately before the variation in order to confer and vest that responsibility or right in another person.[319] A local authority may also apply to have a provision granting authority for a child to be adopted added to an existing PO.[320] Where this is done all the same people who are entitled to make representations with regard to the variation of a PO are entitled to make representations regarding adoption.[321] In this process it is important to note that the conditions for granting the application to amend are the same as they would have been if authority to adopt had been sought in the original application.[322]

It is not only a local authority that can apply for a variation. It also includes **6–75** the list of persons listed in s.94(3) who are the same as those who have a right to make representations where an application for a PO is made, including the child.[323] However, in their case, they need to acquire the leave of the court to make an application.[324] The court must grant leave in two circumstances. The first is where it is satisfied that there has been a material change of circumstances directly relating to any of the PO's provisions.[325] Little guidance is given as to what amounts to "a material change of circumstances" but the court is directed in making its decision to have regard to the welfare of the child in respect of whom the PO was made, as well as the circumstances of any parent or guardian of the child and of any persons who had any PRRs immediately before the PO was granted.[326] The second is where the court is satisfied "that for any other reason it is proper to allow the application to be made".[327] This is a very vague provision that affords a great deal of discretion to the court in making a decision, underpinning the flexibility of a PO that is seen to be its greatest strength.

Revocation

It is also competent for a local authority or "any other person affected by **6–76** the order who has obtained the leave of the court" to apply for revocation of

---

[316] 2007 Act s.94(2) and (3). See also s.86 (2) with regard to those entitled to make representations with regard to an initial PO. See para.6–70 above. In the case of variation, such persons expressly include any person on whom a duty was imposed, or power conferred by the order (s.94(2)(d)); and any persons in whom PRRs were vested immediately before a variation under s.92 which vested these PRRs in another person (s.94(2)(f)).
[317] 2007 Act s.92(6). For a discussion of this criteria see para.6–63 above.
[318] 2007 Act s.92(2).
[319] 2007 Act s.92(4) and (5).
[320] 2007 Act s.93(1) and (2).
[321] These are the people set out in s.94(2) and (3), discussed at para.6–70 above.
[322] 2007 Act s.93(2)–(5). These are the same as the conditions set out for adoption in ss.83 and 84, discussed at para.6–63 above.
[323] 2007 Act s.86. See para.6–79 above.
[324] 2007 Act s.94(4).
[325] 2007 Act s.94(5)(a).
[326] 2007 Act s.94(6).
[327] 2007 Act s.94(5)(b).

a PO.[328] A local authority must, apply for revocation "as soon as reasonably practicable"[329] where it has determined that there has been a material change of circumstances directly relating to any of the PO's provisions and, as a result of this change, the order ought to be revoked.[330] Once more, there is almost no guidance as to how to proceed apart from a direction to the court that it should grant the order "if satisfied that it is appropriate to do so in all circumstances of the case."[331] In reaching a decision on revocation the court is also directed to take account of "any wish by the parent or guardian of the child in respect of whom the order was made to have reinstated any PRRs vested in another person by virtue of the order".[332] Where the court takes a decision to revoke a PO it will be necessary to ensure that PRRs are vested in a person or persons. Thus the court must consider whether to make any order under s.11 of the Children (Scotland) Act 1995, imposing any parental responsibility or vesting any parental right in a person.[333]

---

[328] 2007 Act s.98(2).
[329] 2007 Act s.99(2).
[330] 2007 Act s.99(1)(a) and (b).
[331] 2007 Act s.98(1).
[332] 2007 Act s.98(1)(b)
[333] 2007 Act s.100.

CHAPTER 7

THE CHILD IN NEED OF CARE

INTRODUCTION

At 7am on Wednesday, February 27, 1991, social workers and police 7–01 made a planned and synchronised "dawn raid" on six households in South Ronaldsay, Orkney.[1] Nine children aged from 8–15 years from four families were removed by the use of place of safety orders obtained from a sheriff, and flown to undisclosed locations on the Scottish mainland. Neither children nor parents received warning of the planned social work action. The children were removed from their homes because the social work department feared they were at risk, following allegations made by seven children from another family, W, that organised ritual child abuse and satanic practices were taking place on the island. The Orkney children were separated from each other and from their parents and were not allowed to take with them toys and objects from home: one child was housed in a school for young offenders due to an unproven belief he was an abuser as well as a victim. A minimum of contact with parents was allowed, and the children were interviewed intensively by social workers, the police and child experts from the RSPCC. The place of safety orders, which authorised the detention of the children, were upheld at children's hearings which the children themselves were not allowed to attend. In April 1991, some five weeks later, the children were returned home after Sheriff Kelbie declared that the proceedings were "fatally flawed" because of procedural irregularities.[2] As a result, the evidence of abuse was never heard or tested and, subsequently, the police investigation of the parents and others for criminal offences relating to abuse was dropped. In June 1991, Lord Clyde conducted an extensive inquiry into what had gone wrong in Orkney.[3] His remit was explicitly not to explore whether sexual abuse *had* occurred in Orkney, but rather to look at how such allegations should be investigated and how children in such circumstances should be protected and questioned. The terms of reference of the inquiry related to the way in which the children had been removed; how they had been detained and, in particular, how they had been interviewed and cared for; and what proceedings should have followed upon the children's removal. In March 1996, the Orkney Islands Council reached an out of court settlement with

---

[1] Further details of the Orkney case can be found from a number of sources, e.g. Asquith, *Protecting Children—Cleveland to Orkney: More Lessons To Learn* (1993); Reid, *Suffer The Little Children* (1992).
[2] Kirkwall Sheriff Court, April 4, 1991. Further legal points arising out of the removal were decided in *Sloan v B*, 1991 S.L.T. 530.
[3] *Report of the Inquiry into the Removal of Children from Orkney* (1992) ("the Clyde Report").

the four South Ronaldsay families to pay each child £10,000 and each parent £5,000 in damages.[4]

7–02   The facts of the Orkney case, it must be stressed, are idiosyncratic—the allegations of abuse were extremely complex and hard to prove, and the setting for events was isolated and lacking in full professional support—but they illustrate vividly how difficult the work of child protection can be. They also raise many of the fundamental questions which the Scottish legislation governing this area attempts to address. These are questions like

- what level of risk must be suspected, and what facts must be proven, before a child should be removed from the family home?;
- what rights should parents have to maintain contact with a child who has been removed from the home?;
- what rights should the local authority have to investigate suspected abuse?;
- how far should the state be able to make decisions about a child in opposition to the wishes of the parents? To put it another way, what is the correct balance between family autonomy and protection of the welfare of the child?;
- what rights should parents have to oppose the intervention of the state in the *courts*?;
- does removal of a child replace parental with administrative abuse? Would it be better if a suspected abuser was removed from the home, rather than the child?;
- how should the wishes of the *child* concerned be regarded by the state and the courts, as separate from the interests of his parents or family?

7–03   The Orkney facts also make it plain that in child protection cases a number of different legal aims may conflict. The primary aim of the state agencies should be to protect and help the child. But the state also has an interest in prosecuting wrongdoers under the criminal law. The children themselves (and, in Orkney, the parents) may wish to invoke the civil law of delict to seek compensation in damages for harm they have suffered[5]; alternatively they may wish to explore criminal injuries compensation.[6] These are both important remedies; but in this chapter, and the next, our principal focus will be to look at how the state can intervene to help in circumstances in which children appear to be in need of care or protection from outwith their family. Child abuse—both sexual and physical—is one of the most visible phenomena in this area but is by no means all that social workers and courts are concerned with. Children may be in need of support or protection because of poverty or deprivation, because parents may be disabled or mentally ill, or otherwise unable to cope with the demands of parenting, or because parents have died, disappeared or been sent to jail. Children may also, as we shall see, be perceived as in need because they have begun to

---

[4] *The Scotsman*, March 5, 1996. See also Edwards, "Suing Local Authorities for Failure in Statutory Duty: Orkney Reconsidered after *X v Bedfordshire*" (1996) 1 Edin. L. Rev. 115.

[5] See further paras 5–07 *et seq*.

[6] See Criminal Injuries Compensation Act 1995.

commit criminal offences, or play truant from school, or because they are themselves physically or mentally ill or otherwise have special needs, e.g. for educational assistance.

In such circumstances, state agencies have a number of options. In Orkney, **7–04** the immediate remedy chosen in response to suspected abuse at the time was to remove the children from their homes as a form of emergency protection. But in many other, more ordinary, circumstances of need, the first line of state intervention is to provide more resources to the child and the family, which might take the form of financial assistance, support from social workers, day care, added home help *et al.* As we shall see, one of the general tenets of the Children (Scotland) Act 1995 and the Children's Hearings (Scotland) Act 2011is that it is better for the state to intervene as little as possible in the care that is given by families to their children, unless the child's welfare requires such intervention. The emphasis in Pt II of the 1995 Act dealing with support for children and their families places the emphasis on local authorities and families working voluntarily together in a co-operative manner. In some circumstances, parents may decide with the social work department that it is better if the children are accommodated by the local authority for some while. In others, parents will be deeply opposed to their children being removed from home and if this seems necessary in the welfare of the child, the local authority will have to obtain legal authority to accomplish it. They will have to decide if, as in Orkney, emergency protection seems necessary, or whether there is no imminent risk of significant harm. Some children move in and out of local authority care, or remain accommodated by the local authority, for considerable time. In such cases, the social work department must consider if a permanent solution for the child's care and upbringing away from his natural family is necessary. We have already considered such a permanent solution in the last chapter, when looking at adoption and permanence orders.

In this chapter we will be looking in detail at the options for action by the **7–05** state outlined above. The law governing childcare and protection was radically reformed by, and is now principally to be found in ss.16 to 38 of Pt II of the Children (Scotland) Act 1995,[7] the Children's Hearings (Scotland) Act 2011 ("the 2011 Act)[8] and some sections of the Social Work (Scotland) Act 1968 ("the 1968 Act") that are still relevant. It is undoubtedly true that the Orkney crisis described above, and the succeeding Clyde Report, have been catalysts for change; but they have by no means been the only contributors to the major sea-changes taking place in Scots law. Other influences have been the Review of Child Care Law in Scotland which led in 1993 to the White Paper, *Scotland's Children*[9]; the Kearney Report on childcare policy in Fife[10]; the Skinner Report on residential childcare[11]; the Scottish Law Commission

---

[7] Pt II came into force on April 1, 1997.
[8] September 19, 2012 is the date of commencement for most of the Act under the Children's Hearings (Scotland) Act 2011 (Commencement No. 6) Order 2012. But note that at the time of writing this book most of the Regulations governing it have not yet been made public or come into force.
[9] Cmnd 2286 (1993).
[10] *Report of the Inquiries into Child Care Policies in Fife* (1992–1993 HC 191).
[11] A. Skinner, *Another Kind of Home: A Review of Residential Child Care* (Scottish Office, 1992).

Report on Family Law[12] which shaped Pt I of the 1995 Act; and the Children
Act 1989 which, like the 1995 Act after it, brought sweeping reform to the
English law of child protection, and was at least partially a response to an
earlier controversial multiple child abuse case in Cleveland in 1987.[13] Since
then, a much broader approach to support and intervention in the lives of
children has been developed along the lines of principles contained in *A Guide
to Getting it right for every child* (GIRFEC),[14] that built on values promoted
in *The Children's Charter*,[15] *For Scotland's Children*[16] and *The Early Years
Framework*[17], as well as taking account of provisions in the UNCRC and the
ECHR. This approach, outlined in *National Guidance for Child Protection
in Scotland* (2010), marks a shift towards "early, proactive intervention in
order to create a supportive environment and identify any additional support
they [children and families] may need as early as possible".[18] These principles and values are being taken forward by the Children and Young People
Bill the foundation stone on which a legislative programme that embeds a
new approach based on prevention, appropriate early age intervention, and
child-centred service delivery will be built.[19] As part of this programme, the
Bill seeks to promote children's rights through imposing duties on Scottish
Ministers to advance and raise awareness of the rights of children and young
people set out in the UNCRC.[20]

GIRFEC

7–06   At the heart of GIRFEC are 10 components that are set to be applicable in
any setting and in any circumstance. These are:

(1) A focus on improving outcomes for children, young people and their
families based on a shared understanding of wellbeing.
(2) A common approach to gaining consent and to sharing information
where appropriate.

---

[12] Scot. Law Com. No.135 (1992).
[13] The Cleveland Inquiry commenced in August 1987 and culminated in the Butler-Sloss Report
in June 1988 (*Report of the Inquiry into Child Abuse in Cleveland in 1987*).
[14] *A Guide to Getting it right for every child* (GIRFEC), 2005 and 2008, Scottish Executive and
Scottish Government.
[15] *Protecting Children and Young People: The Charter* (2004) Scottish Executive.
[16] *For Scotland's Children* (2000) Scottish Executive.
[17] See *Early Years and Early Intervention: A Joint Scottish Government and COSLA Policy
Statement* (2008) Scottish Government. See also *A Curriculum for Excellence: The Curriculum
Review Group* (2004) Scottish Executive; *Curriculum for Excellence—building to curriculum 1*
(2006); *the contribution to curriculum areas 2: active learning the early years* (2007); *a framework for learning and teaching 3* (2008).
[18] GIRFEC 2008, p.6. For the latest version of GIRFEC see June 2012 downloaded from *www.
scotland.gov.uk/Resource/0041/00417342.pdf* [accessed April 3, 2013].
[19] See The Scottish Government's Response to "A Scotland for Children: A Consultation on a
Children and Young People Bill", March 22, 2013 downloaded from *www.scotland.gov.uk/
Publications/2013/03/9148* [accessed April 3,2013]. Note that 2,400 children and young people
were engaged in responding to the Bill's proposals.
[20] It will be followed by a Children Services Bill that will set out specific powers for
implementation.

(3) An integral role for children, young people and families in assessment, planning and intervention.

(4) A co-ordinated and unified approach to identifying concerns, assessing needs, and agreeing actions and outcomes, based on the *Wellbeing Indicators.*

(5) Streamlined planning, assessment and decision-making processes that lead to the right help at the right time.

(6) Consistent high standards of co-operation, joint working and communication where more than one agency needs to be involved, locally and across Scotland.

(7) A *Named Person* for every child and young person, and a *Lead Professional* (where necessary) to co-ordinate and monitor multi-agency activity.

(8) Maximising the skilled workforce within universal services to address needs and risks as early as possible.

(9) A confident and competent workforce across all services for children, young people and their families.

(10) The capacity to share demographic, assessment, and planning information electronically within and across agency boundaries.[21]

In adopting this approach, the key values and principles, building on the Children's Charter, involve:

* Promoting the wellbeing of individual children and young people.
* Keeping children and young people safe.
* Putting the child at the centre.
* Taking a whole child approach.
* Building on strengths and promoting resilience.
* Promoting opportunities and valuing diversity.
* Providing additional help that is appropriate, proportionate and timely.
* Supporting informed choice.
* Working in partnership with families.
* Respecting confidentiality and sharing information.
* Promoting the same values across all working relationships.
* Making the most of bringing together each worker's expertise.
* Co-ordinating help.
* Building a competent workforce to promote children and young people's wellbeing.[22]

Where children are in need of care and protection there are three main institutions in Scotland that are involved in dealing with them. As will be seen, the local authority has both duties and powers in relation to children, which are usually exercised by its social work department. The courts also have a significant role in preventing the local authority from taking unfettered action and giving children and parents a right to judicial hearing. The third

7–07

---

[21] GIRFEC 2012, p.6.
[22] GIRFEC 2012, p.7.

major institution is the children's hearings system. The hearings system was introduced in 1971 under the Social Work (Scotland) Act 1968 as a system whereby both children who were seen as "delinquent", and those who were seen as in need of care and protection, could be given the measures of care that they needed. The hearing is neither a court nor a department of the local authority but an independent tribunal. It is, however, serviced by the local authority in that they are responsible for implementing its disposals, which most commonly take the form of requirements of compulsory supervision. Its function is to decide in partnership with children and parents what steps should be taken to fulfil the best interests of the children who are referred to it. Children who appear to be in need of help can be referred by any person to an official known as the reporter, whose decision it then is whether there are grounds for convening a hearing to consider the child's case ("grounds of referral"). Disposals of the hearing can be appealed to the courts. The children's panel, as it is sometimes known, has a key role in Scottish childcare law, which will be explored in detail in Ch.8.

GENERAL PRINCIPLES: COURTS AND CHILDREN'S HEARINGS

7–08 Section 16 of the 1995 Act sets out three important principles which apply whenever a court or children's hearing determines any matter relating to a child (subject to exceptions noted below). As can be seen, they parallel the provisions in s.11 in Pt 1 of the 1995 Act laying down the criteria for when an order relating to parental responsibilities and rights should be made[23]:

(1) *The child's welfare is paramount.*[24] However, where the court or hearing consider there is a risk of serious harm to the public (whether physical or not) a decision inconsistent with the welfare principle can be made.[25] This could, for example, allow a children's hearing or sheriff to make a supervision order placing a child in a residential school for young offenders on the basis of public protection rather than on welfare needs[26];

(2) *The child's views, taking account of the age and maturity of the child, are to be given regard as far as practicable.* Children must be given an opportunity to express their views. Children of 12 years or older are presumed mature enough to express a view but such maturity can be shown at a younger age.[27] Children can of course not only now express a view, but instruct their own lawyers to represent them in proceedings.[28] A curator *ad litem* may also be appointed by the court to represent the best interests of the child and at a hearing, or any appeal to the courts from the

---

[23] See paras 4–49 *et seq.*
[24] 1995 Act s.16(1).
[25] 1995 Act s.16(5).
[26] A child may be placed in secure accommodation as a disposal of the hearing but there are further safeguards to this in the form of the criteria in s.83(5) aand (6) of the 2011 Act—see further Ch.8.
[27] 1995 Act s.16(2).
[28] See further paras 2–33 *et seq.*

hearing, an official known as a safeguarder may be appointed to the child for similar purposes[29];

(3) *Neither the court nor the hearing is to make any requirement or order with respect to the child unless it considers that it would be better for the child that the requirement or order be made, than that none should be made at all.*[30] This "no order" or "minimum intervention" principle applies to a very wide range of decisions, including decisions of the children's hearing when making or reviewing supervision requirements, or confirming emergency protection measures; and decisions by the sheriff when hearing appeals from a children's hearing, or when granting emergency protection orders.[31] It does *not*, however, apply to the case where a sheriff considers whether to make a child protection order, nor does it apply to the deliberations of the children's hearing when deciding whether to continue and confirm the child protection order.[32] The duty to consult the child discussed above also does not apply to these decisions.[33]

In practice, this means there is a statutory presumption that neither the hearing nor the sheriff should intervene unless it is clearly the best measure to secure the child's welfare. The appropriateness of this provision in the context of child protection has been questioned. In the private law context, as we saw in Ch.4, the "minimum intervention" principle most often operates to preserve the rights and responsibilities of both parents towards the child even if they have divorced. There is clear evidence this is better for the child than to remove the responsibility of one parent on a routine basis, as was common prior to the 1995 Act.   **7–09**

However, in Pt II cases, as Thomson has argued,[34] it is likely there is already a prima facie case for intervention if the child has come to the attention of the local authority or been referred to the hearing. By definition, these are cases that have already been investigated by the social work department or the reporter as likely to require intervention and so the "minimum intervention" principle may well be inappropriate and not in the interests of the child. Minimum intervention can be justified on the ideological basis that families know best what to do for their children and should be left alone as much as possible by the state.[35] It can be regarded as a principle resetting the balance between families and the state after what was seen as the over-zealous intervention of social workers in cases in the 80s and early 90s. However, a   **7–10**

---

[29] Formerly under 1968 Act, s.34A (introduced by the Children Act 1975, s.66) but now under ss.30 and 31 of the 2011 Act. A safeguarder need not be a lawyer but often is. The expanded rights of independent representation for children under the 1995 Act raise the possibility of clashes between lawyers acting in the "best interests" of the child and those representing the child's own wishes. See further Cleland, in Cleland and Sutherland, *Children's Rights in Scotland*, 3rd edn (Edinburgh: W. Green, 2009), Ch.10.

[30] 1995 Act s.16(3).

[31] See s.16(4)(a)(i) and (ii); s.16(4)(b) and s.16(4)(c) of the 2011 Act.

[32] 1995 Act s.16(3) and (4).

[33] 2011 Act s.27(2).

[34] Thomson, "The Welfare Principle—Under Attack or Strengthened?", 1996 S.L.T. (News) 115.

[35] Thomson himself has argued that "family autonomy may be regarded as a hallmark of a democratic society": J. Thomson, *Family Law in Scotland*, 4th edn, p.289.

minimum intervention principle is also a useful means by which the financial resources devoted to childcare and protection can be rationed and globally restricted, particularly in these uncertain economic times when budgets are being slashed. This gives rise to concern because it is clear that the social work resources that are needed to deal with children in need have risen since 1995. Financial support for these children and their families is essential if local authorities are to be able to channel resources towards the more long-lasting and expensive activity of crisis prevention. Where such support is inadequate or lacking, there is a danger that resources will be allocated towards cases where crisis has already arisen, rather than to promoting more sustained support for children and families in the longer term.[36]

LOCAL AUTHORITY POWERS AND DUTIES

7–11   The 1995 Act, Pt II, in conjunction with what remains of the 1968 Act, attempts to set out a framework to support children and their families in the community, emphasising partnership between parents and local authorities. The local authority is generally under a duty to promote social welfare by making available advice, guidance and assistance to persons in the area for which they are responsible.[37] This assistance can take the form of cash, but only in exceptional circumstances,[38] assistance in kind,[39] the provision of residential nursing accommodation,[40] home helps or laundry facilities.[41] Assistance under s.12 is restricted to persons aged 18 or over.[42] This is because the 1995 Act gives local authorities special duties in relation to children in need.

7–12   In particular, s.22 provides that local authorities have duties to promote and safeguard the welfare of children in their area who are "in need".[43] This phrase is broadly defined[44] to include:

(i) children who are unlikely to achieve or maintain a reasonable standard of health or development without local authority assistance;
(ii) children whose health or development is likely to be significantly impaired without such assistance;

---

[36] For discussion of the possible "laissez faire" approach to intervention see Waterhouse and McGhee, "Justice and welfare—has the Children (Scotland) Act 1995 shifted the balance?" (1998) 20 J.S.W.L. 49.
[37] 1968 Act s.12.
[38] See 1968 Act s.12(3) and (4). The assumption is that a person in need of cash should approach the social security authorities first.
[39] 1968 Act s.12(1).
[40] 1968 Act s.13A.
[41] 1968 Act s.14.
[42] 1968 Act, s.12(2) as amended by 1995 Act, Sch.4, para.15(11).
[43] Note that this duty is a general duty to provide services, the detailed nature and extent of which is left to the local authority's discretion. See *Crossan v South Lanarkshire Council*, 2006 S.L.T. 441. Thus a local authority has a discretion, and not an enforceable obligation, to provide services for a particular child and members of his or her family under s.22(3)(a) of the 1995 Act if it will safeguard or promote the child's welfare to do so.
[44] 1995 Act s.93(4)(a).

(iii) disabled children; and

(iv) children affected by the disability of another member of the family.

Local authorities have powers to assist children who fit this broad definition, and the families of those children, with the aim of improving things for the child *without* removing him from the home environment. Indeed, the authority is expressly charged with promoting the upbringing of such children by their family.[45] Although this *enables* action by the authority, it can thus be seen as working hand in hand with the minimum intervention principle for courts and children's hearings discussed above. **7–13**

One of the major proposals of the White Paper *Scotland's Children* was that local authorities should adopt strategic planning in order to improve the services they could deliver, better utilise resources, facilitate inter-agency co-operation and achieve consistency between different areas. As a result local authorities were placed under a duty to publish plans relating to services for children ("in need" or otherwise).[46] Local authorities also come under specific duties to co-operate in the provision of services to children with other agencies and authorities such as health boards[47]; to provide day care facilities for pre-school children under five[48]; towards disabled children[49]; and to provide after-care assistance for children who are leaving care and who are over 16 but under 19.[50] Local authorities are also given a discretion, though not a duty, similarly to assist children leaving care who are aged 19 to 21.[51] This help can take the form of the provision of cash, or in kind. Provision of accommodation to children and young persons is dealt with below. However, it should be noted that s.38 introduces a framework for the provision of short stay refuges for children under 18 who appear to be at risk of harm and at their own request seek such accommodation. The stay in such refuges will be limited to seven days, or in exceptional circumstances, 14 days.[52] **7–14**

POVERTY AND ITS EFFECTS ON CHILDREN

Poverty[53] remains one of the most serious problems facing children in Scotland and the UK today. Its effects last a lifetime, negatively impacting health, education, social and physical development and seriously harming **7–15**

---

[45] 1995 Act s.22(1)(b).

[46] 1995 Act s.19.

[47] 1995 Act s.21.

[48] 1995 Act s.27.

[49] 1995 Act ss.23, 24.

[50] 1995 Act s.29.

[51] 1995 Act s.29(2).

[52] 1995 Act s.38(5).

[53] According to the Child Poverty Action Group (CPAG) income and material deprivation remain the most fundamental dimensions of poverty (CPAG, *Poverty in Scotland 2011: a more equal Scotland* (ed. J.M. Mckendrick, G. Mooney, J. Dickie and P. Kelly, 2011), p.4). The Demos Report 2012, *A Wider Lens*, by L. Bazalgette, M. Barnes and C. Lord, Demos 2012 underscores the need to understand disadvantage from a multidimensional perspective by identifying households that suffer from a combination of disadvantages (such as poor housing, poor health, wordlessness, as well as low income). It is based on a secondary analysis

future life chances and opportunities.[54] While the numbers living in poverty generally fell in the decade since devolution, nonetheless "poverty [in Scotland] remains widespread and deep".[55] 18 per cent of Scotland's population, and 21 per cent of all children, still live in poverty today.[56] The figure for children in Scotland is line with that for across the UK, where it is 22 per cent,[57] but these figures reflect rates of poverty that are significantly higher than in other European countries.[58] The effects on children growing up in poverty are that they:

- are more than twice as likely as their peers who are not living in poverty to suffer developmental difficulties as they reach school age;
- face challenges with early language and communication, physical health and social skills;
- are less likely to reach their potential in school than other children;
- are more likely to experience lower health outcomes than other children; and
- are less likely to reach their potential in adult life.[59]

Children experience difficulties because they are living in households where lack of money leads to the threat of falling into debt, choosing between necessities of life, going without basics, and often being caught up in a cycle of 'dead end' jobs. Poverty creates a situation where people are unable to save and it leads to lower levels of mental well being, shorter life spans and more years of ill health.[60]

7–16 In recognition of the need to tackle this problem the UK Government passed the Child Poverty Act 2010 that sets out four main targets designed to capture different aspects of child poverty.[61] These are relative poverty,[62] low

---

of a two year data set of the Scottish Household Survey 2009 and 2010 which contains information on 28,000 households in Scotland.

[54] It is acknowledged that children growing up in low-income households are at greater risk of poor outcomes across a variety of domains including health, emotional and behavioural problems, risky behaviours and educational attainment. See *Child Poverty in Scotland: A Brief Overview of the Evidence* (Scottish Government, 2010) downloaded from *http://www.scotland. gov.uk/Resource/Doc/304557/0107230.pdf* [accessed May 22, 2013].

[55] See Joseph Rowntree Foundation, *Devolution's Impact on Low-Income People and Places* (Joseph Rowntree Foundation, 2010).

[56] CPAG et al., *Poverty in Scotland, Summary Briefing*, updated October 2012, downloaded from *http://www.CPAGScot_Poverty_in_Scotland_Summary_Briefing_October_2012.pdf* [accessed April 2, 2013].

[57] *Child Poverty in Scotland: A Brief Overview of the Evidence.*

[58] CPAG, *Summary Briefing*. Note that the figures for children in poverty in Denmark and Norway are less than 10% and are at 15% for Germany.

[59] See Save the Children, *Child poverty in Scotland: The Facts* downloaded from *http://www. savethechildren.org.uk/sites.default/files/images.child_poverty_facts_2013.pdf* [accessed April 2, 2013].

[60] CPAG et al., *Poverty in Scotland, Summary Briefing.*

[61] Note that people are considered to be living in poverty if they live in households whose equivalised income is below 60% of the UK median income in the same year. See *Child Poverty in Scotland: A Brief Overview of the Evidence.*

[62] This is defined as individuals living in households whose equivalised income is below 60% of the UK median income in the same year.

income and material deprivation combined,[63] persistent poverty[64] and absolute poverty.[65] Working with these criteria, the figures for 2008/09[66] reveal that in Scotland the figures are as follows for:

- *Relative poverty*: In 2008/09 21 per cent of the population of children (210,000) were living in relative poverty (before housing costs). The overall reduction in relative poverty rates from 28 per cent to 21 per cent between 1998/99 and 2008/09 was one of the largest seen in any UK region.
- *Low income and material deprivation*: Figures for the percentage of children in low income and material deprivation combined have only been available since 2004/05. Over that period they have not changed much and have remained around 15 or 16 percent.
- *Persistent poverty*: In Scotland 13 per cent of children experienced persistent poverty between 2004 and 2007. This figure fell from 15 per cent during 2001 to 2004.
- *Absolute poverty*: Trends for absolute poverty among children have been similar to those for relative poverty, though more marked. Absolute poverty among children fell from 28 per cent in 1998/99 to 12 per cent in 2005/06. Since then rates have not changed much and the 2008/09 figure was 11 per cent.[67]

The Child Poverty Act 2010 requires Scottish Ministers to publish a child poverty strategy and to lay an annual report in the Scottish Parliament on measures it has taken under the strategy.[68] The strategy has two main aims, to maximise household resources and to improve children's well being and life chances. Research shows that poverty is not evenly distributed throughout the UK but varies considerably.[69] A local poverty map published by End Child Poverty, however, found that almost every Scottish local authority contains wards where more than one in five children live in poverty, along with nearly half of Scottish local authorities where over 30% of children live in poverty.[70] The findings indicate that children are more at risk of poverty than other age groups and that the highest levels of poverty in Scotland can be found in families with young children.[71] The findings show that the family's employment status had the largest impact on the child's risk of persistently

---

[63] Material deprivation involves a measure of children's living standards which, unlike relative and absolute poverty, is not based solely on income.

[64] This is defined as being in relative poverty in at least three out of the last four consecutive years.

[65] This is defined as individuals living in the same household where equivalised income is below 60% of the (inflation adjusted) Great Britain median income in 1998/1999.

[66] Taken from the Family Resources Survey, Households Below Average Income dataset 2008/2009.

[67] These figures are cited in *Child Poverty in Scotland: A Brief Overview of the Evidence*.

[68] The first annual report was published in March 2012.

[69] *The Child Poverty Map of the UK 2013.*

[70] *The Child Poverty Map of the UK 2013* (End Child Poverty, February 2012), lists the top 20 parliamentary constituencies with the highest levels of child poverty across the UK with Glasgow North East ranked number three and Glasgow Central ranked number 15.

[71] See Save the Children, *Child poverty in Scotland: The Facts*. See also the Demos Report 2012

living in poverty, with families that were consistently out of work most at risk of persistent poverty.[72] Other risk factors include lone parent families, large families, families with a young mother (under 25), families with low educational attainment and families living in rented housing (especially social housing).[73] In addition, children living in poverty also include those from minority ethnic backgrounds and those whose mother has a longstanding health problem or disability.[74]

7–17   What is clear is that the risk of poverty is reduced as access to work increases.[75] Education is an important factor here as it is strongly linked with employment opportunities for parents.[76] Those without qualifications are less likely to enter paid employment.[77] Those living in deprived areas have lower rates of participation in education and higher rates of exclusion from school, as well as higher unemployment rates for school leavers.[78] For those families with children, access to child care is seen as a key feature in influencing whether out-of-work parents are able to enter employment. Cost is a major barrier to preventing parents on the lowest incomes from accessing childcare. The costs of childcare in Scotland are amongst the highest in the UK, "which are already among the highest in the world".[79] Research by the Women in Scotland Economic Research Centre suggests that there is a link between the increase in women's employment in Scotland between 1998 and 2008 and the significant decrease in child poverty.[80] They note, however, that the recent economic recession "has impacted negatively on women's employment, most markedly through the 'austerity' measures on public sector employment and severe cuts in welfare spending".[81]

---

that found that 37% of birth cohort children who lived with two or more children were persistently poor compared with 21% of solo children.

[72] *Growing Up in Scotland: Circumstances of persistently poor children.* Scottish Government 2010.

[73] Demos Report 2012, p.19.

[74] *Growing Up in Scotland: Circumstances of persistently poor children.*

[75] *Child Poverty in Scotland: A Brief Overview of the Evidence.*

[76] McQuaid et al., *How Can Parents Escape from Recurrent Poverty?* (Joseph Rowntree Foundation, 2010).

[77] See *Evaluation of the Working for Families Fund* downloaded from *www.scotland.gov.uk/Publications/2009/04/20092521/0* [accessed April 2, 2013].

[78] *Child Poverty in Scotland: A Brief Overview of the Evidence.* Educational attainment related to later life outcomes such as entry to higher education and employment means experiencing poverty can have long-term consequences for individuals and families. See Hill et al., *An Anatomy of Economic Inequality in the UK: Report of the National Equality Panel* [London: Government Equalities Office].

[79] Save the Children, *Child poverty in Scotland: The Facts.*

[80] See WISE and Save the Children, Briefing Sheet, September 2012 on *Child Poverty and Mothers Employment Patterns: Exploring Trends* by Professor Ailsa McKay, Emily Thomson and Susanne Ross downloaded from *www.savethechildren.org.uk/sites.default/files/images/WISESCUKBriefingFinal.110912.pdf* [accessed April 2, 2013].

[81] See WISE and Save the Children, Briefing Sheet, September 2012 on *Child Poverty and Mothers Employment Patterns: Exploring Trends* by Professor Ailsa McKay, Emily Thomson and Susanne Ross downloaded from *www.savethechildren.org.uk/sites.default/files/images/WISESCUKBriefingFinal.110912.pdf* [accessed April 2, 2013]. They express the view that increasing opportunities for mothers to access market work could be of more relevance to child poverty reduction goals than concentrating on increasing employment of both male and female parents.

In reviewing poverty, CPAG note that progress on child poverty has stalled while working age adults' risk of poverty has not significantly altered.[82] There is great concern over the Institute of Fiscal Studies 2012 to 2013 projections for the UK, that as a result of welfare reforms and spending cuts, measures of absolute and relative child poverty are likely to increase between 1.7 and 2.2 per cent as a direct result of changes to tax and benefit policy, as well as a reduction in the entitlement for housing benefit.[83] According to WISE and Save the Children "this analysis does not take account of material employment patterns and could actually underestimate the impacts of recession on poverty".[84]

ACCOMMODATING CHILDREN

It is in this context that local authorities have to exercise their duties in rela- **7–18** tion to children and families in their areas. In certain circumstances, it may be better for a child to be cared for by someone other than the family, usually on a temporary basis, perhaps because one or both parents are ill, hospitalised, pregnant or suffering an episode of depression. Such care is often anecdotally referred to as "respite" or "voluntary" care. Under s.25, local authorities have a *duty* to provide accommodation for children under the age of 18[85] in their area (whether residing there or simply found there) in any of the following circumstances:

(a) no-one has parental responsibility for the child;
(b) the child is lost or abandoned; or
(c) the person caring for him is prevented, whether or not permanently and for whatever reason, from providing him with suitable accommodation or care.[86]

Local authorities may provide accommodation in a family—that is, with foster carers—with a relative of the child,[87] with another suitable person, in a residential setting or make other appropriate arrangements making use of services available to children cared for by their own families. These may be in England and Wales or Northern Ireland.[88]

Local authorities also have the *power* to provide accommodation for **7–19**

---

[82] *Poverty in Scotland: Summary Briefing.*
[83] *Poverty in Scotland: Summary Briefing.* See also WISE and Save the Children, Briefing Sheet.
[84] WISE and Save the Children, Briefing Sheet.
[85] See definition of "child" in 1995 Act s.93(2)(a).
[86] 1995 Act s.25(1).
[87] Increasing attention is being given to kinship care, see Sutherland, *Child and Family Law*, 2nd edn (Edinburgh: W. Green, 2008), para.9.091. It may span a variety of arrangements. There is concern, however, that kinship carers may not receive the same level of support from the local authority, addressed by GIRFEC Fostering and Kinship Care National Strategy 2007 downloaded from *www.scotland.gov.uk/Publications/2007/12/031437041/0* [accessed April 5, 2013].
[88] 1995 Act s.26.

children in their area if this would safeguard and promote their welfare.[89] This power extends to young people who are over 18 years but under 21 years.[90]

7–20   The value of s.25 is that it enables local authorities to offer accommodation to children where this seems appropriate without the need to take more drastic steps such as removing parental rights from the parents or referring the child to the children's hearing. In principle, parents of a child who is being accommodated under s.25 lose none of their parental responsibilities or rights (hereafter "PRRs"). A key requirement of s.25 then is that the authority must obtain parental agreement before receiving the child into their accommodation. The local authority cannot provide a child with accommodation if anyone with *both* parental responsibilities *and* the right to regulate the child's residence and control, direct and guide the child's upbringing,[91] objects, provided that that person is also willing to accommodate or arrange for the provision of accommodation to the child.[92] A child of 16 years or over can give his own consent to be accommodated despite parental objection.[93] While these provisions preserve parental rights to control the residence of the child,[94] they may be, in some cases, problematic.

7–21   *Example*: Husband (H) and wife (W) have separated and their child (C) is living with W; H has taken little interest in C. W is going into hospital and wants the child accommodated by the local authority. H objects and proposes his home as alternative accommodation. As a married father, he has all parental responsibilities and rights unless removed by court order. In terms of s.25(6), the local authority cannot provide s.25 accommodation even if they suspect the husband's care will be inadequate. Nothing within the section provides that the alternative accommodation arranged by H must be suitable or safe. However, if W has obtained, or obtains, a *residence order*,[95] then she can agree to the child being accommodated despite the objection of H.[96] If the non-objecting parent did not or could not obtain a residence order, and respite care still seemed desirable, then the authority would have to consider some other option, such as referral to the children's hearing.

7–22   Before providing a child with accommodation, the local authority, so far as is practicable, must ascertain the child's views, taking account of the age and maturity of the child. A child of 12 years or more is presumed able to form a view.[97] This overcomes, to some extent, the objections made against the corresponding provisions under the 1968 Act that "voluntary care" was voluntary for the parents, but not for the child.

---

[89] 1995 Act s.25(2).
[90] 1995 Act s.25(3).
[91] Under s.2(1)(a) and (b) 1995 Act, as amended by Family Law (Scotland) Act 2006.
[92] 1995 Act s.25(6).
[93] 1995 Act s.25(7)(a). This is consonant with the rule that a child is of full legal capacity at age 16 (Age of Legal Capacity (Scotland) Act 1991 s.1).
[94] 1995 Act s.2(1)(a).
[95] Under s.11(2)(c).
[96] 1995 Act s.25(7)(b).
[97] 1995 Act s.25(5).

Accommodated Children and Parental Rights of Return

As we have seen, parents of a child who is being accommodated under   **7–23** s.25 lose none of their parental responsibilities or rights. As the statute makes crystal clear, a person with parental responsibilities may thus remove the child from the accommodation provided by the local authority *at any time*.[98] However, if the child has been in the accommodation for a continuous period of at least six months,[99] 14 days' notice in writing must be given before the child can be removed.[100] This allows the authority some time in which to consider whether they need to take legal action to retain the child.

Can a local authority *refuse* immediately to return a child accommodated   **7–24** under s.25 of the Act before the six months are up if they fear that to do so is not in the welfare of the child? One thing the authority certainly cannot do is apply to the court for a residence order in respect of the child under s.11 of the 1995 Act, since s.11(5) specifically forbids local authorities from doing this. However, s.11(5) does not prevent an authority from *defending* a s.11 action. In a pre- 1995 Act case, *M v Dumfries and Galloway Regional Council*,[101] a local authority refused to return a child who had been voluntarily placed in its accommodation in its care under the equivalent provision of the Social Work (Scotland) Act 1968. The child had been in care for more than six months but the parents had given the required written notice.[102] The child made allegations of sexual abuse against the father after which the authority refused to return him. The parents raised an action for delivery of the child which the local authority successfully opposed by arguing that the action related to parental rights and was therefore governed by the welfare principle, and that it was not in the child's best interests to return home. It appears possible to similarly defend the child by inaction under the 1995 Act.[103]

This is not, however, the best solution. If the local authority wished to   **7–25** prevent the removal of the child from its care, it could more properly refer the child to the reporter to the children's panel[104] or apply to the court for a Child Protection Order, if there was a risk of immediate significant harm to the child if returned (see paras 7–37 *et seq.* below).

Similar considerations apply to restriction of contact rights. The parents,   **7–26** so long as they have PRRs, retain the right to maintain contact with the child[105] and the authority cannot restrict this without seeking some legal warrant for their action.[106]

---

[98] 1995 Act s.25(6)(b).
[99] This can be accommodation provided by more than one local authority.
[100] 1995 Act s.25(7).
[101] *M v Dumfries and Galloway Regional Council*, 1991 S.C.L.R. 481.
[102] Then, 28 days: see 1968 Act, s.15.
[103] See *M v D and Dumfries and Galloway Council*, 2001 Fam. L.R. 58, and para.4.41, above.
[104] But this would require clear evidence for at least one condition set out in s.52(2): see Ch.8.
[105] 1995 Act s.2(1)(c).
[106] In fact, the authority comes under a duty to *promote* contact between the accommodated child and his parents, subject, however, to the welfare principle—see 1995 Act s.17(1) (c).

"Looked after" Children[107]: s.17

7–27   Children in s.25 accommodation are described in the Act as "looked after" by the local authority, and this means the authority has significant duties towards them.[108] Other groups of children also fall into this category, including

- children subject to a supervision requirement imposed by a children's hearing;
- children under warrants, orders or authorisations, including child protection orders, child assessment orders or permanence orders[109];
- children towards whom the authority has responsibilities who are subject to orders analogous to those described above made in other parts of the United Kingdom.[110]

7–28   In 2012 there were 16,171children in Scotland who were "looked after" children.[111]

Local authority duties towards "looked after" children are set out in s.17[112] and include

(a) the duty to safeguard and promote the welfare of the child as their paramount concern;

(b) the duty to make reasonably available to such children services which are supplied to children cared for by their own parents[113];

(c) the duty to take such steps as are both practicable and appropriate to promote, on a regular basis, personal relations and direct contact between the child and any person with parental responsibilities, having regard to the welfare principle[114];

(d) the duty to provide advice and assistance, with a view to preparing the child for when he or she is no longer looked after by a local authority[115];

---

[107] See J. McRae, *Children looked after by local authorities: the legal framework* (2006) commissioned for the review of looked after children in Scotland and published by the Social Work Inspection Agency.

[108] Guidance on how these children should be dealt with is contained in the Guidance on the Looked After Children (Scotland) Regulations 2009 and the Adoption and Children (Scotland) Act 2007 as updated by the Scottish Government in March 2011. Downloaded from *www.scotland.gov.uk?publications/2011/03?10110037/0* (web only publication) [accessed April 5, 2013].

[109] Discussed below at paras 7–37 *et seq.* For permanence orders see Ch.6, paras 6–60 *et seq.*

[110] 1995 Act s.17(6) as amended by Sch.5, para.2 to the 2011 Act (not yet in force).

[111] *Children's Social Work Statistics Scotland No.1* (2012 edn).

[112] Protecting the public from "serious harm" may allow a local authority to override these duties (s.17(5)).

[113] Notably, schooling, There has been considerable concern about the poor educational experiences and outcomes of children looked after away from home: see Maclean and Gunion "Learning With Care: The Education of Children Looked After Away from Home by Local Authorities in Scotland" (2003) 27(2) Adoption and Fostering 20. See report of the Adoption Policy Review Group that commented on the poor outcomes for looked after children in education and employment, *APRG2*, para 3.7 referring back to their Phase 1 Report, p.12.

[114] 1995 Act s.17(1)(a)–(c).

[115] 1995 Act s.17(2).

(e) the duty, as far as is practicable, to ascertain the views of the child, his or her parent(s) or any other person who has parental rights in relation to the child, or any person whose views are seen as relevant, before making any decision about the child.[116] The authority must then give due regard to these wishes. Account must be taken of the child's age and maturity.[117]

(f) the duty when making decisions relating to the child to take account of the child's religious persuasion, racial origin, cultural and linguistic background.[118]

Parents come under a duty in relation to "looked after" children to advise the local authority of any change of address without unreasonable delay. Breach is a criminal offence.[119]

RESTRUCTURING SERVICES FOR CHILDREN AND FAMILIES IN SCOTLAND

The legal duties of local authorities must be viewed in the context of a restruc- **7–29**
turing of services for children and families in Scotland, particularly with regard to child protection. As the Minister for Children and Early Years has observed the child protection landscape in Scotland has developed considerably since 1998, involving "new legislation, new areas of practice and new approaches" that have "shaped activities at both national and local level".[120] There is a recognition that agencies can improve outcomes for Scotland's most vulnerable "by adopting common frameworks for assessment, planning and action that help them to identify needs and risks and work together to address them appropriately".[121] Building on the principles and values of GIRFEC involves "a shift towards early, proactive intervention"[122] by professionals dealing with children, such as social workers, health workers, doctors, teachers and police, who provide services to children and their families. The aim is to provide for more co-ordinated intervention, extending beyond those cases where children are in need of compulsory measures of supervision.[123] For children and their families come into contact with services at different

---

[116] 1995 Act s.17(3).
[117] 1995 Act s.17(4). Oddly, there is no presumption of maturity at 12 or over as is usual in the 1995 Act.
[118] 1995 Act s.17(4)(c).
[119] Unless the move was to an address where the other parent was resident and the first parent genuinely believed the other had informed the authority (s.18).
[120] Ministerial Forward, p.1 of the *National Guidance for Child Protection in Scotland 2010* downloaded from *www.scotland.gov.uk. Resource/Doc/334290/0109279.pdf* [accessed March 28, 2013]. Thus child protection must be viewed in the context of GIRFEC, the Early Years Framework and the UNCRC.
[121] Ministerial Forward, p.3 of the *National Guidance for Child Protection in Scotland 2010* downloaded from *www.scotland.gov.uk. Resource/Doc/334290/0109279.pdf* [accessed March 28, 2013].
[122] Ministerial Forward, p.6 of the *National Guidance for Child Protection in Scotland 2010* downloaded from *www.scotland.gov.uk. Resource/Doc/334290/0109279.pdf* [accessed March 28, 2013].
[123] Discussed in detail in Ch.8.

points in their lives, for different reasons, and with different needs. In some cases these needs can be met by family members themselves, or a network of support,[124] or by a single agency. However, where complex needs come into play, where children and their families are especially vulnerable "services must come together to take a collective and co-ordinated approach".[125] At the centre of this process is the child.[126]

The Named Person

7–30   Where a child comes into contact with universal services, such as health or education, he will have a Named Person assigned to him until the age of 18. In most cases this person will have little to do other than using the National Practice Model[127] as a starting point for recording routine information about a child or young person. The Named Person becomes more actively involved where a child or young person requires extra help and support beyond that provided by families, teachers and health practitioners in the normal course of their day to day life and work. The Named Person, who is often a health visitor or teacher, becomes a point of contact with whom the child and family can work to sort out any further help, advice or support that may be needed. Where concerns about a child are brought to their attention, they become the first point of contact with the child and family for working out what action needs to be taken, including arranging for help to promote the child's development and well being. Thus the Named Person has an important role to play in supporting early intervention via health or education.

The Lead Professional

7–31   Where two or more agencies need to work together to help a child or young person and family a Lead Professional will be appointed to co-ordinate that help.[128] This means that the child will be subject to a unified plan of action with one agency taking responsibility for its implementation, so that children do not fail to receive services because one agency believes that another is responsible for taking action with regard to the child, when in fact neither are taking any action at all because they each believe that the child is someone else's responsibility. To this end, a single plan of action, the Child's Plan, will be established. It will be managed and reviewed through a single meeting structure, even if a child is involved in several processes, for example, being looked after or having a co-ordinated support plan. In this case it will be the responsibility of the Lead Professional to integrate expertise and to co-ordinate any actions taken to improve outcomes for the child.

---

[124] See GIRFEC 2012, p.11 that defines this network as always including "family and/or carers and the universal services of health and education".
[125] *National Guidance 2010*, p.4
[126] GIRFEC 2012.
[127] GIRFEC 2012, pp.13–14.
[128] For details see GIRFEC 2012, p.13 and *National Guidance 2010*, p.16.

Child Protection and Risk or Likelihood of Significant Harm

In these processes it is vital that children are consulted, get to express **7–32** their views and have an understanding of any decisions that are taken that affect them. It is hoped that this restructuring of services will help to alert professions to child protection issues as soon as they arise. Dealing with child protection involves protecting a child from child abuse or neglect.[129] This requires an assessment of risk, that does not require abuse or neglect to have taken place, but that is based on whether there is a likelihood or risk of significant harm to the child.[130] It is acknowledged that the concept of 'significant harm' is a complex one for which there are "no absolute criteria" that can be applied.[131]

For such harm can result, not only from a specific incident, such as an assault, or a series of incidents, but may also involve "an accumulation of concerns over a period of time".[132] Some factors are outlined for consideration so that:

> "In assessing the severity of ill treatment or future ill treatment, it may be important to take account of – the degree and extent of physical harm; the duration and frequency of abuse and neglect; the extent of premeditation; and the presence or degree of threat, coercion, sadism and bizarre or unusual elements".[133]

In considering events or circumstances that interrupt, change or damage the child's physical and psychological development, those making decisions about children are directed to consider

- the nature of the harm, either through an act of commission or omission;
- the impact on the child's health and development, taking into account their age and stage of development;
- the child's development within the context of their family and wider environment;
- the context in which a harmful incident or behaviour occurred'
- any particular needs, such as a medical condition, communication impairment or disability, that may affect the child's development, make them more vulnerable to harm or influence the level and type of care provided by the family;
- the capacity of parent or carer to meet adequately the child's needs; and
- the wider and environmental family context.[134]

In light of these considerations, where a child or young person is thought to be at risk of significant harm it is necessary to call a Child Protection Conference. At this conference the Lead Professional will be responsible for

---

[129] *National Guidance 2010*, p.14.
[130] *National Guidance 2010*, p.14.
[131] *National Guidance 2010*, p.15.
[132] *National Guidance 2010*, p.15.
[133] *National Guidance 2010*, p.15.
[134] *National Guidance 2010*, pp.15–16.

ensuring the production of an agreed multi-agency Child's Plan, based on an assessment of needs, with a particular focus on the risks to the child and the interventions necessary to reduce these risks. The plan will incorporate and amend, if necessary, any previous plans drawn up by individual agencies. In child protection cases, the role of the Lead Professional will generally be taken by a local authority social worker. The Child's Plan will be known as the "Child Protection Plan" as long as the risk of significant harm is deemed to last.

Child protection register

7-33   To assist professionals and practitioners local authorities are made responsible for creating and maintaining a Child Protection Register in their area for all children who are subject to a Child Protection Plan.[135] Where a Child Protection Case Conference takes place and there is a multi-agency assessment that a child has suffered, or is likely to suffer, significant harm, that child's name will be placed on the Child Protection Register. In this event, there is a need to inform the child or young person, the family and any carer, that the child's name has been placed on the register, giving them information about the register and who has access to it. Where the risk of significant harm is no longer deemed to apply the child's name will be taken off the register and on de-registration the Child Protection Plan may revert to being the Child's Plan (where the child may require to continue receiving support).

Child Protection as Part of Wider Planning Processes

7-34   These measures dealing with planning for child protection are perceived as forming part of wider planning processes in a local area

> "forming part of wider economic and social objectives as expressed through community and integrated children services planning, the national outcomes shared by national and local government and the key national policy frameworks".[136]

Emergency Protection of Children

7-35   It is with this background in mind that we must consider legal measures dealing with the emergency protection of children. While every effort is made to work with a child and family voluntarily, if the local authority feels that the child is imminently at risk in the family home then they must consider what emergency action should be taken. There are basically three options: removing and accommodating the child under s.25 with the agreement of the parents or person with residence order; removing the child against the wishes of the parents using a child protection order;[137] or other emergency measures[138] aimed at safeguarding and promoting the welfare of the child.

---

[135] Note that this register is an administrative one and has no legal status.
[136] *National Guidance 2010*, p.62.
[137] Previously dealt with under ss.57–62 of the 1995 Act and now contained in ss.37–54 of the Children's Hearings (Scotland) Act 2011.
[138] See ss.55 and 56 of the 2011 Act replacing s.61 of the 1995 Act.

Similar orders are to be found in the Children Act 1989 which is in operation in England and Wales.

Prior to the 1995 Act, children could be removed from parents in emergency situations by use of place of safety orders, which could be obtained very speedily from a sheriff or a justice of the peace. These empowered the local authority to remove the child to an undefined "place of safety".[139] Such orders were used to remove the Orkney children and were subjected to detailed criticism by Lord Clyde in his report.[140] The main flaws identified in the old scheme were that

    7–36

  (i) children were not always removed *only* in circumstances when they were actually in imminent danger or risk of harm if not removed. For example, in Orkney, the removal of the children was planned some two weeks in advance. Were they really in danger of harm if their removal could be delayed for so long? Since removal from home is a traumatic event, it should only be "absolutely justified where the alternative is the certain exposure to harm"[141];

  (ii) there were *insufficient alternatives* to the drastic step of removal of the child. For example, in many cases, immediate removal was unnecessary when what would suffice was a power to gain access to the child to examine him or her for evidence of abuse.

 (iii) the *parents* were not given adequate rights in the process. When children were removed by place of safety orders, the parents did not have a chance to oppose the removal for up to a week, and then only at a meeting of the children's hearing. It was felt that parents should be entitled to make an immediate challenge, and to a sheriff rather than the hearing.

 (iv) the *rights of the child* were insufficiently guarded in the process. When a child was taken into care via a place of safety order, the precise rights, duties and powers of those involved with the child were not clear. Nor was the status of the parents, e.g. whether they retained rights to maintain contact with the child.

REMOVAL OF THE CHILD: CHILD PROTECTION ORDERS

The 1995 Act attempted to implement the Clyde recommendations by replacing the place of safety order of the 1968 Act with the child protection order (hereafter "CPO") laid out in ss.57 to 60 of that Act that have now been repealed and replaced by ss.37 to 54 of the Children's Hearings (Scotland) Act 2011. Application for a CPO can be made to the sheriff by "a person",[142]

    7–37

---

[139] Under s.37 of the 1968 Act, now repealed. For a full discussion of the 1968 Act system of emergency protection, see Wilkinson and Norrie, pp.457–462.

[140] See Ch.16 of the Clyde Report; also Lord Clyde, "Lessons from the Orkney Inquiry" in Asquith, *Protecting Children* (NCB, 1993). It should be noted that problems with place of safety orders had been identified as early as the *Review of Child Care Law 1990* (1993), Pt 14.

[141] Lord Clyde, "Lessons from the Orkney Inquiry" in Asquith, *Protecting Children* (NCB, 1993), p.21.

[142] 2011 Act s.37(1).

or specifically, by a local authority.[143] Under s.39(2) the sheriff has a discretion to grant the CPO if:

(a) he is satisfied that there are reasonable grounds to believe that—
    (i) the child has been or is being treated in such a way that the child is suffering or likely to suffer significant harm,
    (ii) the child has been or is being neglected and as a result of the neglect the child is suffering or is likely to suffer significant harm,
    (iii) the child is likely to suffer significant harm if the child is not removed to and kept in a place of safety, or
    (iv) the child is likely to suffer significant harm if the child does not remain at the place at which the child is staying (whether or not the child is resident there), and
(b) the order is *necessary* to protect the child from harm or from further harm.

When the application is made by the local authority under s.38, a CPO can be made if they establish that:

(a) they have reasonable grounds to suspect that—
    (i) the child has been or is being treated in such a way that the child is suffering or likely to suffer significant harm,
    (ii) the child has been or is being neglected and as a result of the neglect the child is suffering or is likely to suffer significant harm,
    (iii) the child will be treated or neglected in such a way that is likely to cause significant harm to the child
(b) the local authority is making enquiries to allow it to decide whether to take action to safeguard the welfare of the child, or is causing those enquiries to be made,
(c) those enquiries are being frustrated by access to the child being unreasonably denied, and
(d) the local authority has reasonable cause to believe that access is required as a matter of urgency.

7–38   The emphasis in both cases is on the current existence or future risk of *"significant harm"*, a key phrase which recurs when we come to look (below) at child assessment orders and exclusion orders. It would seem in line with the provisions of the Clyde Report that harm which has occurred in the *past*, but which is not causing the child to suffer either now or in the foreseeable future, should not form grounds for a child protection order. In such circumstances, the correct action (if any) should be to refer the child to the children's hearing. A different interpretation has however been reached in England and Wales where the same phrase is used in the emergency protection provisions of the Children Act 1989.[144] The term "significant harm" is open to interpre-

---

[143] 2011 Act s.38.
[144] See *Re M (A Minor) (Care Order) (Threshold Conditions)* [1994] 2 F.L.R. 577; also *In Re O (Minors) (Care: Preliminary Hearing)* [2003] UKHL 18. However, the context of English child protection law is so different (and even the wording subtly different) that these cases cannot be regarded as binding or even necessarily persuasive.

tation but Norrie has suggested that it should mean harm of a "not minor, transient or superficial nature".[145]

An issue that has arisen in both Scotland and England is whether a CPO **7–39** can be taken immediately on, or even before, the birth of a child, where the mother or family has a long history of involvement with social work and there are fears of the safety of the newborn infant. In Scotland, a CPO can clearly not be taken in respect of a fetus: a fetus is not a legal person[146] and therefore not "a child" as the Act demands. Furthermore to apply a CPO to a fetus would seriously impinge on the autonomy and human rights of the mother. The Strasbourg court has expressed grave reservations about the practice of taking children into care at birth as an infringement of the rights under Art.8 of the mother and family.[147] They have also been uneasy about the instant removal of children from families who do not at that time have legal representation or advice.[148] In Scotland there is conflicting authority as to whether parents or families in this situation have a right to legal representation before a child can be removed at birth.[149] Lord McCluskey took the view in *K and F Applicants*[150] that "in the case of a child not yet born, the need for urgency is far from obvious" and confirmed to the ECHR-friendly view that the sheriff should receive legal representations in such cases before removal. These cases have now been discounted as authority in *NJ and EH v The Lord Advocate and Others*[151] on the grounds that they both failed to pay adequate attention to discussion of the ECHR and of Convention jurisprudence.[152]

In *NJ and EH* two local authorities obtained CPOs in relation to two new **7–40** born children without giving their mothers a right to be heard. In the case of *NJ*, an eighteen year old mother, she had given birth to a child previously and that child was removed to live with foster carers because of lack of parental care. In *EH's* case, she had two children previously both of whom had been removed from her and placed in the care of her mother. In both cases the petitioners were informed at case conferences that they attended, that the local authority concerned intended to apply to the sheriff for a CPO to authorise the removal of the child into the care of the authority after its birth. Thereafter, each petitioner sought to lodge caveats at their local sheriff courts, which if granted, would have allowed the petitioners to have the opportunity of making representations to the sheriff before the granting of the CPO. Lord Brailsford held that the rejection of the caveats by the sheriff courts in question did not amount to a breach of their Art.6 rights (right to a fair hearing). This was because refusing to allow a caveat to be lodged, was not "a determination of any "civil right" or obligation within the meaning of Art.6.[153] For the decision to refuse the caveat had no substantial influence

---

[145] Norrie, *Children (Scotland) Act 1995*, 2nd edn (Edinburgh: W. Green, 2004).
[146] *Hamilton v Fife Health Board*, 1993 S.L.T. 624.
[147] See, e.g. *K and T v Finland* [2001] 2 F.L.R. 707.
[148] See *P, C and S v UK* (2003) 38 E.H.R.R. 28.
[149] *C Petr* (2001) Fam. L.R. 42; *cf. K and F Applicants*, 2002 S.L.T. (Sh. Ct) 38 and (2001) Fam. L.R. 44.
[150] *K and F Applicants*, 2002 S.L.T. (Sh. Ct) 38 and (2001) Fam. L.R. 44.
[151] *NJ and EH v The Lord Advocate and Others* [2013] CSOH 27.
[152] *NJ and EH v The Lord Advocate and Others* [2013] CSOH 27, para.12.
[153] *NJ and EH v The Lord Advocate and Others* [2013] CSOH 27, para.25. Note that the rules

on the petitioners' civil rights. This was because a "caveat does not check or determine a legal right or obligation, it does no more than alert the caveator of a hearing at which such rights or obligations pertaining to him may be effected in some way."[154] Lord Brailsford rejected the petitioners contention that failure to be informed of a hearing that may affect a person's rights is itself an interference with that right that triggers the provisions of Art.6.[155] For while Lord Brailsford accepted that "the inability of a person to participate in a hearing which affects his rights could engage Article 6" that would be an argument "relevant to a challenge to that hearing, not an argument against any earlier step such as the lodging of a caveat".[156]

7–41   In the case of Art.8, however, there had been a breach of the petitioners' rights to private and family life because the interference with them could not be justified on the basis of there being an immediate risk or threat to the children concerned. In reviewing Convention jurisprudence on this point it was submitted that

> "in emergency cases, taking a child into care without allowing the parent to be heard was a violation of article 8 of the ECHR if it was possible to hear the parent first without depriving that proposed action of its effectiveness".[157]

In the context of emergency orders in the UK under s.44 of the Children Act 1989 it was held that

> "an ex parte application will normally be appropriate only if the case is genuinely one of emergency or other great urgency—and even then it should normally be possible to give some kind of albeit informal notice—or if there are compelling reasons to believe that the child's welfare will be comprised if the parents are alerted in advance of what is going on."[158]

It was acknowledged that article 8 permits interference with its rights under Art.8.2 where this is "in accordance with the law" and "necessary in a democratic society". This requires an assessment as to whether the interference is "proportionate".[159] In assessing proportionality[160] "a court will require to balance all rights and give particular importance to the interests of the child".[161] In this process "it has to be borne in mind that a parent is not enti-

---

of court in relation to caveats did not expressly permit the lodging of them in relation to CPO's.

[154] *NJ and EH v The Lord Advocate and Others* [2013] CSOH 27, para.32.

[155] *NJ and EH v The Lord Advocate and Others* [2013] CSOH 27.

[156] *NJ and EH v The Lord Advocate and Others* [2013] CSOH 27.

[157] *NJ and EH v The Lord Advocate and Others* [2013] CSOH 27, para.14, citing the authority of *K and T v Finland* [2003] 36 EHRR 18 and *Haase v Germany* [2004] 2 FLR 39.

[158] *NJ and EH v The Lord Advocate and Others* [2013] CSOH 27, para.14, citing Munby, J. in *X Council v B* [2004] EWHC 2015 at paras 52 and 53.

[159] *NJ and EH v The Lord Advocate and Others* [2013] CSOH 27, para.22.

[160] On the basis of case law such as *P, C and S v UK* [2002] 35 EHRR 31; *TTP v United Kingdom* [2002] 34 EHRR 2; *Covezzi and Morselli v Italy* [2004] 38 EHRR 28.

[161] *NJ and EH v The Lord Advocate and Others* [2013] CSOH 27, para.23.

tled under article 8 to have measure taken that would harm the child's health and development".[162]

On the basis of information available in this case[163] each petitioner was **7–42** able to seek legal advice as to the local authority's proposed course of action with regard to CPOs and sought to lodge caveats allowing for representations when the applications for CPOs were being made. When the CPOs were sought both petitioners were in hospital with their child. While they could have exercised their legal right to leave hospital taking their new born child with them there were "practical considerations in both cases which significantly reduced that possibility".[164] In the case of *NJ*, the child had been placed in a secure cot and could not be removed from it without the assistance of hospital staff. Any attempt made by the petitioner to remove the child without approval would have resulted in the police being called. In the case of *EH*, "the petitioner was physically incapacitated as a result of surgery".[165] Referring back to Munby J. in *X Council v B*,[166] before the extreme step of depriving the parent of a right to be heard can be taken there must exist "a compelling case for applying without first giving the parents notice" and where there exists ". . .an emergency or other great urgency". What was envisaged was the sort of situation where "intimation to the parents might itself create a risk to the child" or "where any delay in seeking an order may endanger the child's health and well being". [167] The tests were not met in this case because the parents were aware before their children were born of the action that the local authority proposed to take so there was "no question of risk involved in telling them of, or permitting representation at a hearing",[168] In this case, given the children were secure and being looked after in hospital at the time the CPOs were granted, the court could not hold "that the degree of urgency amounted to an emergency".[169]

These tests are highly relevant given that the number of CPOs has **7–43** increased over the years. Earlier research by Francis and McGhee[170] found a downward trend in the use of emergency protection orders overall since the introduction of the 1995 Act, and hypothesised that this was partly due: (i) to the greater judicial scrutiny of CPOs than place of safety order, leading to greater reluctance to seek them, (ii) to the "minimum intervention" principle; and (iii) to the principle of working in partnership with parents. However, the Scottish Children's Reporter Administration (SCRA) observe that the numbers of CPOs have increased from 370 in 1999 to 558 in 2006,[171] to 678

---

[162] *NJ and EH v The Lord Advocate and Others* [2013] CSOH 27; citing *Haase v Germany* [2005] EHRR 19, paras 89–93.
[163] Note Lord Brailsford was critical of the lack of information available to him in the form of affidavits or written evidence, see para.28.
[164] *NJ and EH v The Lord Advocate and Others* [2013] CSOH 27, para.30.
[165] *NJ and EH v The Lord Advocate and Others* [2013] CSOH 27, para.16.
[166] *X Council v B* [2004] EWHC 2015, paras 52–53.
[167] *NJ and EH v The Lord Advocate and Others* [2013] CSOH 27, para.32.
[168] *NJ and EH v The Lord Advocate and Others* [2013] CSOH 27, para.32.
[169] *NJ and EH v The Lord Advocate and Others* [2013] CSOH 27, para.32.
[170] Francis and McGhee, *Child Protection and Social Work Practice: Exploring the Impact of the Children (Scotland) Act 1995* (Edinburgh: Dept of Social Work, University of Edinburgh, 2000).
[171] SCRA, *A Study of Children Subject to Child Protection Orders in Edinburgh 2007/2007*, Executive Summary, p.1.

in 2010 to 2011 and to 781 in 2011 to 2012.[172]In the majority of cases these orders involved new born babies or children under the age of two. In the 2006 to 2007 SCRA study, 30 per cent of the CPOs involved new born babies and over 60 per cent were in relation to children who were under 20 weeks old.[173] In 2011 to 2012, 21.3 per cent of the children concerned were under twenty days old[174] and 49% were aged under 2.[175] The study in 2006 to 2007 also noted that the grounds for 87 per cent of CPOs were lack of parental care and that half the children in respect of whom CPO's were granted were already on the Child Protection Register. In addition, 52.2 per cent of the children already had an existing open referral to the Children's Reporter and/or were subject to a supervision requirement.[176] In 80 per cent of cases a Child Protection Case Conference had been held prior to the application for a CPO.[177] The long term prospects for reuniting these children with their parents are not favourable. Supervision requirements were made or continued at the end of the CPOs in 95 per cent of cases and three months after the CPOs ended only 10 per cent of children were returned to their parents.[178]

MAKING A CPO: TERMS, CONDITIONS AND DIRECTIONS

7–44   The CPO must identify the applicant and as far as is practicable, the child concerned. It should state the grounds on which the application was made and be accompanied by supporting evidence.[179] The sheriff, when making the CPO, should be guided by the welfare principle of the child throughout his or her life as the paramount consideration.[180] He or she is not, however, subject to the duty to consult the child,[181]nor does the minimum intervention principle apply to the making of a CPO or to the deliberations of the children's hearing when deciding whether to continue and confirm the CPO[182] However, if a CPO is granted, the applicant should subsequently implement it only to the extent necessary to safeguard the welfare of the child.[183] The sheriff when making the CPO can make it subject to such terms and conditions as seem appropriate.[184] He or she can, in particular, require any person to produce the child; authorise the removal of the child by the applicant to a place of safety, and the keeping of the child at that place; authorise the

---

[172] SCRA, *Official Statistics 2011/12* as at July 5, 2012.
[173] Executive, Summary, p.1.
[174] That is 166 out of 781 children.
[175] That is 383 out of 781 children.
[176] Executive Summary, p.1.
[177] Executive Summary, p.1.
[178] Executive Summary, p.1.
[179] 2011 Act s.37(5).
[180] 2011 Act s.25(1). and (2). However, s.26 makes provision for this to be ignored where it is necessary to protect members of the public from serious harm whether physical or not (s.26(a)), in which case a consideration of the child's welfare throughout childhood is reduced to a primary rather than a paramount consideration (s.26(2)).
[181] 2011 Act s.27(2).
[182] Children (Scotland) Act 1995 s.16(3) and (4).
[183] 2011 Act s.58(1) and (2)(a).
[184] 2011 Act s.37(2) and (3).

prevention of the removal of the child from any place where the child is staying[185]; and provide that the location of the child once removed to a place of safety should not be disclosed.[186]

It should be stressed that the applicant—who will usually, but not invaria- **7–45** bly be a local authority—is only empowered to do what is specifically author-ised by the sheriff in the CPO. The parental responsibilities and rights (PRRs) of the parent or carer of the child are not removed, nor are they transferred to the applicant. (The local authority does, however, owe duties to the child who has been removed by CPO as a child "looked after" by the authority.[187]) In principle, therefore, the applicant—say, an authority—has no parental rights to, for example, consent to the medical or psychiatric assessment of the child who has been removed for suspected abuse.[188] Nor do they have the power to restrict the parent's contact with the child (unless they have been authorised to keep the child's location a secret) since in principle the parents retain the right and responsibility to maintain contact.[189]

To deal with this, s.37(3) provides a general power and discretion to the **7–46** sheriff when making a CPO to make whatever *directions* seem necessary to safeguard and promote the welfare of the child. The applicant may also apply for a direction in relation to the fulfilment of PRRs in relation to the treatment of the child arising out of any assessment authorised by the order or any other matter the sheriff considers appropriate.[190] Particular provision is made for directions about contact and medical treatment. The sheriff may give directions as to contact[191] (and any conditions that are to be attached to it e.g. that contact be supervised by a social worker[192]) between the child and (a) any parent of the child; (b) any person with parental responsibilities in relation to that child; and (c) any other specified person or class of persons.[193] He may also make a direction *prohibiting* contact between the child and any person.[194] In relation to medical consent, s.37(2)(d) specifically provides that an order may authorise the carrying out of an assessment of the child's health or development[195] or of the way in which a child has been or is being treated or neglected.[196]

The intent of s.37(2)(d) is that the parent's refusal to co-operate with **7–47** medical assessment of the child need not fatally hamper the social work investigation of the abuse. But what if the child *himself is* competent to give a medical consent? s.186 of the 2011 Act expressly recognises that where a child has capacity under s.2(4) of the Age of Legal Capacity (Scotland) Act

---

[185] 2011 Act s.37(2).
[186] 2011 Act s.40. In making a CPO a sheriff must decide whether or not to make a direction that the location of any place of safety at which the child is being kept or any other information specified in the direction relating to the chid must not be disclosed (s.40(3)).
[187] Children (Scotland) Act 1995 s.17, discussed at paras 7–27 *et seq.*
[188] This point was controversial in relation to place of safety orders under the 1968 Act: see Thomson, 1991 S.L.T. (News) 379.
[189] s.1(1)(c) and 2(1)(c) of the 1995 Act.
[190] 2011 Act.42.
[191] 2011 Act s.41.
[192] 2011 Act s.41(3)(b).
[193] 2011 Act s.41(4).
[194] 2011 Act s.41(3)(a).
[195] 2011 Act s.37(2)(d)(i).
[196] 2011 Act s.37(2)(d)(ii).

1991,[197] a medical examination or treatment can only be carried out where the child consents to it. Thus *a parent's* refusal of consent can be overcome but the child's cannot.

When a sheriff makes a CPO the applicant must notify certain persons.[198] These include the person specified in the order[199] (unless the person is the applicant), the child, each relevant person in relation to the child,[200] the relevant local authority for the child (unless the local authority is the applicant),[201] the Principal Reporter and any other person to whom the applicant is required to give notice under rules of court.[202]

Recall, Variation and Duration of CPOs

7–48
As we have seen above, it was one of the major recommendations of the Clyde Report that if children had been removed from the home by emergency action, then parents should have an opportunity as soon as possible to challenge this action before a sheriff. To this end, there are detailed provisions which allow for recall and variation of CPOs. It is important to note that once the CPO is granted, it must be implemented within 24 hours or it will lapse.[203] The intention of the legislation again here is to prevent authorities from applying for CPOs as insurance where there is no actual or imminent threat to the child.

7–49
The reporter to the Children's Panel (the Principal Reporter) must be told forthwith of the implementation of the CPO, and can subsequently decide to liberate the child if circumstances have changed, or further information indicates the conditions for making the CPO are no longer satisfied.[204] If the child is not liberated, the reporter must arrange a children's hearing on the second working day after the implementation of the CPO.[205] This hearing's role is to consider whether the CPO and any directions should be continued, varied, or terminated.[206] It is sometimes known as an "initial" hearing.[207] If the hearing is satisfied that the conditions for a CPO are established it can continue the order and any directions (with or without variation) until a second children's hearing can be arranged to consider whether or not the child is in need of a compulsory supervision order. This second hearing must take place on the eighth working day,[208] after the child was removed to a place of safety,[209]or the order was made.[210]

---

[197] This arises if in the opinion of a qualified medical practitioner, the child is of an age to understand the proposed treatment and its possible consequence. See para. 2–24.
[198] 2011 Act s.43.
[199] Under 2011 Act s.37(2)(a).
[200] See 2011 Act s.200 for the definition of a relevant person,
[201] See 2011 Act s.201 for the definition of a relevant local authority.
[202] 2011 Act s.43(1)(f).
[203] 2011 Act s.52(2).
[204] 2011 Act s.53.
[205] 2011 Act ss.45(3) and 46(3).
[206] 2011 Act s.47.
[207] Norrie, *Children (Scotland) Act 1995*, 2nd edn (Edinburgh: W. Green, 2004).
[208] "Working day" does not include weekends, January 1 and 2, and December 25 and 26: 2011 Act s.202.
[209] 2011 Act s.54(c).
[210] 2011 Act s.54(d).

Thus, if the parents do not successfully challenge the CPO at any earlier stage, the CPO must at latest come to an end on the eighth working day after it was taken,[211] when the hearing meets to decide whether grounds of referral exist. However, parents have an opportunity to challenge the CPO in the courts, at two earlier stages:

7–50

Stage 1 challenge: After a CPO has been made by the sheriff under s.57(1) or (2), application to a sheriff to set aside or vary the CPO (and/or any directions that have been made) is possible before the commencement of the "initial hearing".[212] Such an application must be determined within three working days.[213] The reporter can arrange a hearing to give advice to the sheriff in relation to the CPO.[214] If the sheriff determines that the conditions for making the CPO are *not* satisfied, he or she may terminate the order.[215] If satisfied the conditions for granting the CPO *are* met, the order and any directions granted under it should be confirmed or varied, along with any new directions that are granted.[216] Where this occurs the order continues in force until the full children's hearing on the eighth working day.

7–51

If a "stage 1" challenge is made, there is no "initial" hearing, and if the CPO is confirmed by the sheriff, it will remain in force until the eighth working day hearing when the normal procedure in relation to children's hearings comes into play.[217]

7–52

Stage 2 challenge: If *no* "stage 1" challenge is made prior to the "initial" hearing then there is a second chance to make an application to recall the CPO within two working days of the "initial" hearing.[218] The options available to the sheriff are the same as in the "stage 1" application for recall. If the CPO is continued (with or without variation of the order and/or directions) a full hearing is held on the eighth working day from the implementation of the original CPO as above.

7–53

A stage 1 or 2 challenge may be made by the child, a relevant person in relation to the child, a person who has or recently had a significant involvement in bringing up the child, the person who applied for the CPO, the Principal Reporter, and any other person prescribed by the rules of court.[219] Where an application is made for variation or termination notice must be supplied to the same persons who are entitled to notice on the making of the CPO.[220] There is no further appeal from a sheriff granting, refusing or continuing a CPO, to the sheriff principal or Inner House. This is appropriate given the emergency and time-limited nature of the order.

7–54

---

[211] Note that it may cease to have effect at an earlier date, at the beginning of a children's hearing arranged under s.69 in relation to the child (s.54(a)), or where the person specified in the order or applicant receives notice that the question of whether or not a compulsory supervision order should be made in respect of a child will not be referred to a children's hearing (s.54(b)).

[212] 2011 Act s.48(3)(a).

[213] 2011 Act s.51(3).

[214] 2011 Act s.50.

[215] 2011 Act s.51(5)(a). Where this occurs the order ceases to have effect at the end of the hearing before the sheriff (s.51(6)).

[216] 2011 Act s.51(5)(b) and (c).

[217] See Ch.8.

[218] 2011 Act s.48(3)(b).

[219] 2011 Act s.48(1)(a)–(g).

[220] 2011 Act s.49.

7-55   If it is not "practicable" to make an application to a sheriff for a CPO, emergency authorisation for removal can be made by a Justice of the Peace.[221] This would most likely be used only in rural or remote areas or perhaps on public holidays. However, application would then have to be made for a "proper" CPO within 24 hours.[222] A police constable also retains the power to remove a child to a place of safety, but again, only for 24 hours.[223]

ALTERNATIVES TO REMOVAL OF THE CHILD

Child Assessment Orders

7-56   Removing the child via a CPO is a drastic step both for the child and the family. In line with the general principle of minimum intervention and the recommendations of the Clyde Report, the 1995 Act provided for a child assessment order[224] (hereafter "CAO") that is now dealt with under sections 35 and 36 of the 2011 Act. A CAO is tailored to deal with emergency situations where there are concerns about the child's safety and needs, and the authority is being denied access to the child to find out if their concerns are legitimate and whether further action is necessary. For example, the school may report that a young child had a black eye and bruising, that no explanation had been given by the mother, and that neither the social worker nor the doctor had been allowed to see the child. In such circumstances, it may be possible to clear up the issue by examination of the child without the need to remove the child from the home. It is designed to provide a less invasive procedure for dealing with the child.

7-57   The local authority (and no other person) can apply to a sheriff for a CAO to carry out an assessment of the child's health and development,[225] or of the way in which a child has been or is being treated or neglected.[226] For these purposes a child is a person under 16.[227] In making a decision about whether or not to make the order[228] the sheriff must be satisfied that

(a) the local authority has cause to suspect that
    (i) the child has been or is being treated in such a way that the child is suffering or is likely to suffer significant harm, or
    (ii) that the child has been or is being neglected and as a result of the neglect the child is suffering or is likely to suffer significant harm,
(b) an assessment of the kind mentioned in s.35(2) is necessary in order to establish whether there is reasonable cause to believe that the child has been or is being so treated and neglected, and

---

[221] 2011 Act s.55.
[222] 2011 Act s.55(5).
[223] 2011 Act s.56.
[224] 2011 Act s.55.
[225] 2011 Act s.35(2)(a).
[226] 2011 Act s.35(2)(b). Note this period was up to 7 days under the old legislation.
[227] 2011 Act s.199(1). Also included is a child between 16 and 18 who is subject to a compulsory supervision order: see Ch.8 for details.
[228] 2011 Act s.36(2).

(c) it is unlikely that the assessment could be carried out, or carried out satisfactorily, unless the order was made.

Once again, the welfare of the child throughout his or her childhood is the paramount consideration.[229] In this case however, there is a duty to consult the child in proceedings for an order[230] and the sheriff must also be satisfied that it is better for the child to make an order than not to make an order.[231] If granted, the order must specify the period for which it is to have effect which must begin no later than 24 hours after the order is granted,[232]and not exceed three days.[233] In some circumstances, examination of the child at home will be impractical and so a CAO can also provide authorisation for the child to be taken to "any place", e.g. a hospital, surgery or clinic, for the purpose of assessment and to be kept there for a period of time specified by the sheriff.[234] Once again, if the assessment involves a medical examination, the child must consent to this if under 16 but has the capacity to consent under s.2(4) of the Age of Legal Capacity (Scotland) Act 1991.[235] If the child is to be kept away from home, then the sheriff can make directions about contact between the child, his parents and others.[236] There is no express appeals procedure for such orders when granted, but given the short three- day period for which they are valid this is unlikely to be of any practical importance.

There is little difference between the threshold criteria required for making   **7–58**
a CAO and a CPO and there will be a temptation for the local authority to seek the more all-encompassing remedy on the grounds of expediency—it will be much easier to arrange the assessment of a child removed into their temporary care, as well as easier generally to safeguard his or her welfare. Indeed, s.36(3) expressly states that if the sheriff considers when hearing the application for a CAO that the conditions for making a CPO are met, he may exercise his discretion and make a CPO rather than a CAO. The evidence suggests, however, that a CAO is not much used when a CPO can be applied for.[237]

Another issue raised by the drafting of s.35 is what happens if the parent   **7–59**
refuses to comply with the CAO. Section 35(3) merely provides that the CAO may "require any person . . . to produce the child to the officer for the purpose of carrying out the assessment. "Person" here obviously includes a parent with responsibilities, who would normally have the right to give or withhold consent to medical or other assessment. The section does not transfer parental rights to the authority, it merely places an obligation on the person who does have such rights. What happens if the parent refuses

---

[229] 2011 Act s.25.
[230] 2011 Act s.27.
[231] 2011 Act s.29(1)(a) and (2).
[232] 2011 Act s.35(5)(a).
[233] 2011 Act s.35(5)(b).
[234] 2011 Act s.35(2)(b).
[235] 2011 Act s.186.
[236] 2011 Act s.35(2)(c).
[237] Francis and McGhee, *Child Protection and Social Work Practice: Exploring the Impact of the Children (Scotland) Act 1995* (Edinburgh: Dept of Social Work, University of Edinburgh, 2000).

to produce the child or give consent to assessment? Presumably such a stubborn parent could be held in contempt of court, but this would not immediately assist in the main point of the exercise, namely, assessment of the child. One solution may be for the sheriff to cast his requirement in the form of a s.11 order awarding the appropriate right to the authority on an interim basis.[238]

Exclusion Orders

7–60 Where there is a basis for concern about a child's safety within a household, prior to the 1995 Act the only option was to remove the child from that household unless the suspected abuser would leave voluntarily. The exclusion order (hereafter "EO") allows the suspected abuser to be removed from the household instead. Such an order is in line with the tenet that the child's needs should take precedence over those of the adults involved. However, what the legislation attempts to do rather than provide to the court an unfettered discretion to exclude, is to require the sheriff to balance the interests of the child and the adult involved using multiple tests. In this sense, the provisions of ss.76–80 have many similarities to the provisions of the Matrimonial Homes (Family Protection) (Scotland) Act 1981 which allow the court a discretion to make an order excluding one spouse or cohabitant for the protection of the other.[239]

7–61 Only a local authority can apply for an exclusion order, and application must be made to the sheriff. The grounds on which the sheriff may choose to make an EO are laid out in s.76(2):

(1) the child[240] must have suffered or be likely to suffer "significant harm" as a result of the conduct or threatened or reasonably apprehended conduct of the "named person" who is to be excluded.[241] This is the same test as when a sheriff is asked to make a CPO, appropriately, as the alternative to an EO would be to remove the child via a CPO; *and*

(2) the making of the order must be *necessary* for the protection of the child *and* would better safeguard the child's welfare than removing the child from the family home.[242] Obviously if this test is not met but there *is* a risk of significant harm, the local authority should seek a CPO, or possibly a CAO. Even if it does not do so the sheriff can choose *ex proprio motu* to grant a CPO rather than an EO[243]; *and*

(3) before an EO can be made, there must be a person left in the family

---

[238] It is clear that a sheriff has jurisdiction to make s.11 orders *ex proprio motu*.

[239] See Ch.11.

[240] "Child" means a child under 16 or a child aged 16–18 who is under a supervision requirement of the children's hearing or who has been referred to the hearing: s.93(2)(b).

[241] For an example of the kind of facts involved, see the first reported cases on EOs, *Russell v W*, 1998 Fam. L.R. 25.

[242] "Family home" is defined very widely: see s.76(12). The main thrust of the definition is that it is a family residence where the child ordinarily resides with the parent(s) or other carer(s).

[243] 1995 Act s.76(8).

home who is capable of caring for the child and any other member of the family, and who will go on residing in the family home.

On top of these requirements, the sheriff *shall not* make an exclusion order if it appears to him to be "unjustifiable or unreasonable" to do so.[244] The sheriff is to have regard to all the circumstances of the case, when considering if an EO would be unjustifiable or unreasonable, but in particular[245] to the conduct of members of the child's family, the respective needs and financial resources of members of the family, and the extent to which the family home or any item in it, is used in connection with a trade or profession.[246] It may well be asked how the making of an EO could ever be unreasonable, given the paramountcy of the welfare of the child[247] if tests 1 and 2 above have been met, but what this part of s.76 clearly seems to contemplate is a balancing exercise between the potential trauma to the child of removal and the proprietary/occupancy rights of a resident alleged abuser—rather as the Matrimonial Homes (Family Protection) (Scotland) Act 1981 seeks to strike a balance between protection of the abused spouse or cohabitant, and the occupancy and property rights of the allegedly violent or threatening spouse or partner. It would seem viable, then, for a suspected abusive father to put up as defence to an EO that the mother has enough money to move out with the child(ren) instead—although this does not seem prima facie to be the best option for the child. Such a father has further backing from the principle of minimum intervention, as discussed above, which also applies to a decision to make an EO.[248]

7–62

The sheriff in deciding whether to make, vary or discharge an EO must so far as practicable have regard to the views of the child concerned taking account of its age and maturity.[249]

7–63

Procedure, Effect and Duration

Before a sheriff can make an EO, the "named person" must be given a chance to be heard or represented before the sheriff.[250] However, in emergency circumstances an interim EO can be made forthwith having the same effect as an EO, without hearing the person to be excluded, so long as the sheriff is satisfied the test in s.76(2) is met.[251] A full hearing at which the named person has a right to present his case must then be held within three

7–64

---

[244] 1995 Act s.76(9).

[245] 1995 Act s.76(9) and (10).

[246] In particular, the sheriff must consider if residence in the family home is required as a condition of employment, and the consequences for the family of breaking such a condition, e.g. eviction of the whole family: s.76(9)–(11). An example might be where the named person has lodgings in a pub as a condition of the job, or is a live-in caretaker or janitor.

[247] 1995 Act s.16(1).

[248] 1995 Act s.16(3) and (4)(b)(i).

[249] 1995 Act s.16(2) and (4)(b)(i).

[250] 1995 Act, s.76(3). The sheriff must also consider the views of any person who under Rules of Court must be notified that the EO has been made. This includes the person who will continue to care for the child within the family home.

[251] 1995 Act s.76(4).

working days.[252] At this hearing the sheriff can either make a final order or confirm, vary or recall the interim order.[253] It appears that the obligation to consult the child applies to interim EOs in the same terms as it does to ordinary EOs.[254] But since that obligation is only to consult the child "so far as practicable", in many cases there will probably be deemed insufficient time to notify and consult the child.

7–65 The effect of the EO is to suspend the named person's rights of occupancy (if any), and to prevent him entering the home without the permission of the local authority.[255] Thus permission to re-enter from the excluded person's spouse or partner, even if they own the home, is ineffective, and such entry would be a breach of the order. Without further provision, breach of an EO would have to be enforced by application to a civil court. But as with the Matrimonial Homes Act 1981, an EO can be given extra "teeth" by the addition of an interdict to prevent the named person entering the house, backed up by the attachment to the interdict of a power of arrest for breach.[256] This power of arrest, which must be notified to the excluded person to be effective,[257] enables a police constable to arrest without warrant the excluded person if he has reasonable cause to suspect that person is in breach of the interdict.[258] After such arrest, the excluded person can either be liberated if the police are satisfied there is no further likelihood of breach of the interdict, or they can detain him until he is brought to court for the offence of criminal breach of the interdict.[259] In such circumstances, the court appearance must take place on the first day after the arrest, excluding weekends and court holidays[260]; the procurator-fiscal can also decide not to take any criminal proceedings.[261] If it appears to the sheriff that the interdict was broken and there is a substantial risk of violence by the excluded person against any member of the family, or any other appropriate person, then the excluded person can be detained for up to two days.[262] All this applies to interim EOs in the same terms.[263]

7–66 As well as an interdict prohibiting entry to the home, a sheriff can also attach to an EO a warrant for summary ejection, an interdict prohibiting the removal of named items from the home, e.g. the children's clothes or school books, an interdict prohibiting the excluded person from entering or remain-

---

[252] Act of Sederunt (Child Care and Maintenance Rules) 1997 r.3.36.
[253] 1995 Act s.76(5). An interim EO can also only last a maximum of six months: *Glasgow City Council v H*, 2003 S.L.T. 948.
[254] 1995 Act s.76(12).
[255] 1995 Act s.77(1).
[256] 1995 Act ss.77 and 78. Application to attach the interdict to the EO is made under s.77(2) and (3). Application for the power of arrest can be made *only* by the local authority (not, e.g. the resident spouse) "at any time while an exclusion order has effect": s.78(2).
[257] 1995 Act s.78(3).
[258] 1995 Act s.78(6).
[259] 1995 Act s.78(7), (10)–(14).
[260] 1995 Act s.78(11).
[261] 1995 Act s.78(10)(b).
[262] Not including weekends and court holidays: 1995 Act s.78(13). A father caught trying violently to break into the family home on the Thursday night before a public holiday weekend might therefore be committed to jail until the following Wednesday.
[263] 1995 Act s.76(12).

ing in a specified area in the vicinity of the home, and an interdict prohibiting the excluded person from taking any specified step in relation to the child.[264]

What if the local authority wishes to exclude the abuser not only from the **7–67** family home but from coming into contact with the child at all, perhaps at school or a part-time workplace?[265] In principle, beyond the authority of the exclusion order itself, the authority has no right to restrict a father's contact with the child as the order has no effect on his PRRs including the right (and duty) to maintain contact.[266] One solution might be to ask the sheriff to add an interdict prohibiting the named person from "entering or remaining in a specified area *in the vicinity of the* home".[267] But this would depend on whether the school, for example, fell within that "vicinity".[268] Visiting the child at school might be classified as "taking any step" in relation to the child and an interdict could possibly be sought on that basis.[269] Another alternative might be to ask the sheriff to make an "order regulating the contact between the child and the named person".[270] Such an "order" would override a married father's automatic right to contact with his child while not living with him or her, and if necessary, a power of arrest could be obtained and attached for enforcement purposes.[271]

An EO lasts for a maximum of six months.[272] However a second or sub- **7–68** sequent EO may be sought immediately, and on the same set of facts.[273] A sheriff can direct that it terminates earlier, or it may be varied or recalled.[274] This time limit is only intended to allow the local authority and the family a breathing space to consider how best to secure the child's welfare permanently, e.g. by voluntary exclusion. Application can be made to the sheriff to have the EO varied or recalled by the authority, the excluded person, the non-excluded spouse or partner[275] or any other person left in the family home caring for the child(ren). The statute makes no explicit reference to appeals from an EO but it has been held that appeal lies to the Sheriff Principal.[276]

---

[264] 1995 Act s.77(2).
[265] The child may not be in danger of abuse in a public place but he could be threatened or upset by contact and the authority might also wish to prevent the father intimidating the child not to give evidence in court or to a children's hearing.
[266] Unless, e.g. a children's hearing had made a supervision order with condition relating to contact—see Ch.8.
[267] 1995 Act s.77(3)(d).
[268] Similar problems of interpretation have arisen in the past in relation to Matrimonial Homes Act interdicts and exclusion orders. See Ch.11.
[269] 1995 Act, s.77(3)(e). This subsection does *not* require that the specified step taken be one taken "in the fulfilment of parental responsibilities or exercise of parental rights": *cf.* s.11(2)(f).
[270] 1995 Act s.77(3)(f).
[271] 1995 Act s.78(1).
[272] 1995 Act s.79(1).
[273] *Glasgow City Council v H*, 2003 S.L.T. 948.
[274] 1995 Act s.79(2)(a) and (b).
[275] "Partners" are persons who live together in a family home as if they were husband and wife (1995 Act s.79(4)). Since the Human Rights Act 1998 came into force it is thought that this provision will have to be interpreted to include couples who live together as if they were civil partners.
[276] *Glasgow City Council v H*, 2003 S.L.T. 948.

Exclusion Orders and Sale of the Family Home

7–69   One response by a person who is named in an application for compulsory exclusion under s.76 may be to threaten to sell the family home, if they are sole or co-owner. In the Matrimonial Homes (Family Protection) (Scotland) Act 1981 ("the 1981 Act"), prejudice to the occupancy rights of the non-entitled spouse who has excluded an entitled spouse is avoided by means of conveyancing devices: specifically, a third party who buys the house in question or part of the house cannot enter and prejudice the occupancy of the non-entitled spouse, and the existence of a non-entitled spouse must be declared when missives are entered for sale of the house.[277] Sections 76–80 of the 1995 Act contain no equivalent provisions, probably because it was envisaged that the 1981 Act protection would cover the situation. However, this may still leave some problems, e.g. if the child is left living with someone who does not qualify for protection under the 1981 Act, such as an elder sibling or grandmother, in which case the house is still vulnerable to sale.

Problems with Exclusion Orders

7–70   It would appear that exclusion orders are not widely used in practice. A study by Francis and McGhee reported only 35 being obtained between 1997 and 1999.[278] There may be various reasons for this. In the first place, as we have seen, only a local authority can apply for such an order excluding a suspected abuser from the house. Even where it is sought it does not operate immediately to exclude the abuser from the home but requires a court procedure to be gone through in deciding whether it is "unjustified or unreasonable" which may render it of little value in situations where there is a real emergency. In such situations the child will still have to be removed awaiting the granting of the exclusion order, in which case the value of keeping the child in the home without disruption to his or her life will have been lost. The temporary nature of the order, that only lasts for six months, may not be long enough in practice to make any real changes to the family situation. From the perspective of social work the order may be of little use if the non-excluded spouse or partner does not wish to co-operate or is afraid to enforce the terms of the order against the excluded spouse. This was commented on in *It's Everybody's Job to Make Sure I'm Alright* where there was a general view among social workers that "there was little point in seeking exclusion order as they placed the responsibility on the other adult in the household (usually a woman who had previously been unsuccessful in excluding the man) to keep the abuser out".[279]

---

[277] See further Ch.11.
[278] *Child Protection and Social Work Practice: Exploring the Impact of the Children (Scotland) Act* (2000) discussed in J. McGhee and J. Francis "Protecting Children in Scotland: examining the impact of the Children (Scotland) Act 1995" (2003) 8 *Child and Family Social Work* 133.
[279] *It's Everybody's Job to Make Sure I'm Alright* (Report of the Child Protection Audit and Review, Scottish Government, 2002), para.4.4., downloaded from *www.scotland.gov.uk/publi cations/2002/11/15820/14009* [accessed May 23, 2013].

Assessment of Local Authority Powers and Duties

The powers and duties discussed above and laid down by the 1995 and **7–71** 2011 Acts are more comprehensive, more detailed and more hedged about with safeguards and threshold criteria than was ever the case under the 1968 Act. The 1995 Act for the first time laid out the duties owed towards children looked after by the local authority in one place in primary legislation. The accommodation and emergency protection provisions try hard to meet the injunction of Lord Clyde that "removal of a child in a case of alleged abuse is not a remedy of first resort but rather a remedy to be adopted after all other courses have been considered and found to be inadequate".[280] The exclusion order is an example of an attempt to meet these concerns by removing the abuser rather than the child from the family home. In recent years the exercise of power and duties by local authorities has become subject to far greater scrutiny, as human rights considerations, especially rights contained in article 6 and article 8, have become the subject of challenge as we have noted in the case law discussed earlier. Balancing out the various interests involved, especially those of parents and children is no easy task and must be approached on a case by case basis.

In dealing with statutory duties imposed on local authorities, an area that **7–72** remains uncertain is the extent to which these duties can be enforced in court by members of the public. The leading English House of Lords judgment of *X v Bedfordshire County Council*[281] in 1995 made it seem extremely unlikely that any child, or indeed parent, could ever claim damages for the failure of a local authority to fulfil a public statutory duty. An effective immunity from action was given to public authorities performing statutory duties.[282] The blanket immunity given local authorities performing social welfare functions by *X v Beds*, however, was controversial in discounting any accountability of social services to parents and children at all, even where there had been plain negligence. *X v Bedfordshire County Council* was subsequently challenged by the now grown children in *Z v United Kingdom*[283] that went to the European Court of Human Rights (ECHR). The Court found that the local authority's failure to protect the children from serious, long term abuse and neglect was a violation of Art.3 (prohibition on torture) and of Art.13 (right to an effective remedy). In Scotland, the case of *E v United Kingdom*[284] went to the ECHR where a step father was convicted of indecently assaulting two of his four step-children. He was put on probation, but continued to have contact with the family in breach of his probation order. In 1989 he was convicted of abuse with respect to all four children. The four children sought damages from the local authority, but on the basis of the law at that time, their claim was dismissed. They were awarded criminal injuries compensation but took

---

[280] Clyde Report, para.16.9.
[281] *X v Bedfordshire County Council* [1995] 3 All E.R. 353.
[282] For a full account see Edwards (1996) 1 Edin. L. Rev. 115. For a further discussion of suing local authorities see Norrie (2001) "Suing local authorities for child protection failures" *Scottish Law and Practice Quarterly* 6(4), pp.314–317.
[283] *Z v United Kingdom* (2002) 34 EHRR 3.
[284] *E v United Kingdom* (2003) 36 EHRR 31.

their case to the ECHR where the Court found that their rights under Arts 3 and 13 had been breached. It appears that an action by a child may now be competent where the local authority has failed in the carrying out of its duties to a particular child.[285] More recently, the United Kingdom was required to pay compensation to a child and mother jointly because of a local authority's fundamental failures in respect of Art.8.[286]

---

[285] See *C v Flintshire County Council* (2001) 2 F.L.R. 33 and *S v Gloucestershire County Council and Havering London Borough Council* [2000] 3 All E.R. 346.
[286] See *AD v United Kingdom* (2010) 51 EHRR 8.

CHAPTER 8
NEEDS NOT DEEDS? THE CHILDREN'S HEARINGS SYSTEM

In the last chapter we outlined the legal framework within which Scots law 8–01 attempts to provide for children in need of resources, care or protection. The focus of discussion was on the powers and duties of local authorities, how these interact with the rights of the child and the family concerned, and the role of the courts in ensuring accountability for the acts of local authorities. In this chapter, we will look beyond the local authority to consider the role of the children's hearings system. The hearings system, as discussed below, deals with both children in need of care, and children who have committed offences. It is thus not only a crucial part of the Scottish childcare regime, but also by far the most significant component of the juvenile criminal justice system. In recent years, the hearings system's role in both arenas has been increasingly questioned, perhaps especially in relation to juvenile crime. Initiatives to reduce juvenile crime have been introduced, with a distinctly punitive flavour, as opposed to the hearing's welfarist philosophy, have been introduced: notably the Antisocial Behaviour Orders ("ASBOs") ushered in, in this jurisdiction, by the Antisocial Behaviour etc. (Scotland) Act 2004. Other innovations, such as parenting orders, have for the first time in the juvenile justice system, tried to impose responsibilities, not just on young offenders, but on those who may be deemed to be responsible for their behaviour. It is questionable to what extent these approaches can be harmoniously integrated into the Scottish welfare-based system.

BACKGROUND[1]

The children's hearings system was created by the Social Work (Scotland) 8–02 Act 1968 (hereafter "the 1968 Act"), following the report of the Kilbrandon Committee[2] which was set up in 1961 with the remit:

---

[1] See further for historical background, Martin et al., *Children Out of Court* (Edinburgh: Scottish Academic Press, 1981), Martin and Murray, *The Scottish Juvenile Justice System* (Edinburgh: Scottish Academic Press, 1982) and *Juvenile Justice in Scotland: Twenty Five Years of the Welfare Approach*, Lockyear and Stone (eds) (T & T Clark, 1998). For up-to-date facts and statistics, see the Scottish Executive website, the website of the Scottish Children's Reporter Administration ("SCRA"), *www.scra.gov.uk* and *www.childrenshearingsscotland.gov.uk*. Statistics about the hearings system are now published annually in the *Annual Report of the SCRA*, available at *www.scra.gov.uk/home/index.cfm* [accessed August 18, 2013]. The two standard legal texts are Kearney, *Children's Hearing and the Sheriff Court*, 2nd edn (Butterworths, 2000) and more recently Norrie, *Children's Hearings in Scotland*, 3rd edn (Edinburgh: W.Green, 2013). An overview of the system with proposals for reform in 2006 can be found in A. Griffiths and R.F. Kandel, "The Governance of Children: From Welfare Justice to Proactive Regulation in the Scottish Children's Hearings System" pp.171–189 in F. and K. von Benda-Beckmann and J. Eckert (eds), *Rules of Law and Laws of Ruling: On the Governance of Law* (Ashgate, 2009).
[2] *Report of the Committee on Children and Young Persons*, Cmnd 2306 (1964) (hereafter, the "Kilbrandon Report").

"To consider the provisions of the law of Scotland relating to the treatment of juvenile delinquents and juveniles in need of care and protection
or beyond parental control, and, in particular, the constitution, powers,
and procedure of the courts dealing with such juveniles, and to report".

8–03   From the very outset, then, the Kilbrandon Committee was charged with
considering together two groups of children until then regarded as quite
separate: those who were labelled as juvenile offenders or truants, and those
who were perceived as being in need of care and protection. The conclusions
of the Kilbrandon Report were radical. First, the distinction usually drawn
between juvenile offenders and children in need of care and protection was
seen as being meaningless and unhelpful. Both were "children in trouble".[3]
Juvenile delinquency was perceived as a symptom of underlying social or psychological problems, of the child having needs which were not being met by
the family or the educational system. The aim of the juvenile justice system,
then, should be to meet the needs of such a child, not to punish him or her.

8–04   Secondly, following on from the concept that children who offend, and
children in need, should be treated in a uniform way, came the idea that
such children should be dealt with not in the ordinary courts, but in a special
tribunal where proceedings would be informal and where the welfare of the
child would be the paramount concern in making a decision, or "disposal",
relating to that child.

8–05   Thirdly, the Committee recommended that these new tribunals (to be
known as "children's panels") should be staffed by lay persons rather than
by legally trained judges, and should be fora in which the panel members, the
child, the parents and involved social workers would be able to talk freely,
unrestricted by the rules of legal procedure and evidence which are normally
required in a judicial forum. Ideally, lawyers would be unnecessary. Where
facts were disputed, e.g. whether a child had actually committed an offence,
these should be legally established in the courts, where the safeguards of due
process would be fully retained, rather than in the welfare-centred tribunal.
However, crucially, the court's role would be restricted to proof, and judges
would play no part in assessing the needs of the child and making the final
disposal. The spheres of *justice*, as found in the courts, and *welfare*, predomi-
nant at the children's panel, would therefore be kept separate. The panel,
being interested in meeting the child's needs for care and supervision, not in
retribution or "justice", would have no powers to punish in the conventional
sense, e.g. to fine either child or parents, or to imprison, but only to impose
compulsory measures of supervision.

8–06   The Kilbrandon Report was published in 1964 and following a Government
White Paper in 1966,[4] most of the proposals made were accepted and
implemented in the 1968 Act. The child tribunal became known as the "children's hearing". Minor changes to the system, such as the introduction of
safeguarders,[5] were made by the Children Act 1975. However, the Children
(Scotland) Act 1995 recodified and, in several ways, radically altered the

---

[3] This phrase is taken from Kelly, *Introduction to the Scottish Children's Panel* (1996).
[4] *Social Work and the Community*, Cmnd 3065 (1966).
[5] See para.8–45 below.

scheme of the 1968 Act, following recommendations in, inter alia, the Review of Child Care Law in Scotland, the Clyde Report on Orkney, the White Paper *Scotland's Children*[6] and the Finlayson Report in 1992.[7] Only very minor changes were made by the Family Law (Scotland) Act 2006. Since then, in the light of a major consultation,[8] virtually all of Pt 2 of the 1995 Act[9] dealing with children's hearings has been repealed by the Children's Hearings (Scotland Act) 2011.

This Act, which is about to be brought into force,[10] attempts to address human rights concerns raised in challenges to the previous system as well as bringing about changes to the organisational structure of children's panels. It creates a new national panel for children's panel members and a new national panel for safeguarders, as well as updating and introducing new grounds of referral. It also makes changes to the definition of a "relevant person", along with altering the rules regulating confidentiality and disclosure. In addition, a new permanent scheme of state funded legal representation for children and relevant persons is introduced that will be administered by the Scottish Legal Aid Board. **8–07**

THE CHILDREN'S HEARINGS SYSTEM: PERSONNEL AND PROCEDURE

The Child

The children's hearings system deals principally with children up to the age of 16.[11] However, children age 16 and over, but under 18 in respect of whom a supervision requirement remains in force, may also come before a hearing.[12] Young persons under 18 who have been prosecuted for offences in the criminal courts may also be remitted to the hearing for disposal, rather than being sentenced by the court; the court may also simply seek the advice of the hearing relating to the disposal of such a case.[13] **8–08**

Personnel

The key personnel of the children's hearings system are the members of the children's panel, and an official known as the Principal Reporter who is **8–09**

---

[6] Cmnd 2286 (1993).

[7] Finlayson, *Reporters to Children's Panels: Their Role, Function and Accountability* (Scottish Office, 1992).

[8] See *Strengthening for the Future: A consultation on the reform of the Children's Hearings System*, (2008) Scottish Government, and *The Summary Report on the Consultation Responses Strengthening for the Future: A Consultation on the Reform of the Children's Hearings System* (2009) The Scottish Government.

[9] 1995 Act ss.39–74.

[10] At the time of writing this edition of *Family Law* the Act was not in force, it is due to come into force in June 2013.

[11] 2011 Act s.199. For a detailed discussion of its provisions see K. Mck Norrie, *Children's Hearings in Scotland*, 3rd edn (Edinburgh: W. Green, 2013). For a general guide see also Children's Hearings Scotland *Training Resource Manual*, Vol.1, *Legislation and Procedure; Training Resource Manual*, Vol.2, *Children's Hearings Handbook* (2013), Scottish Government.

[12] 2011 Act s.199(2)–(9). Compulsory supervision orders are discussed below at paras 8–64 *et seq.*

[13] Criminal Procedure (Scotland) Act 1995 s.49(1).

assisted by Reporters throughout Scotland in carrying out his functions.[14] Under the 1995 Act every local government area was under a duty to establish a children's panel whose function is to hear cases referred to the children's hearings system.[15] However, under the 2011 Act this structure has been replaced with a new national body known as Children's Hearings Scotland,[16] headed by a National Convener,[17] who is an independent officer. The first National Convener, appointed by Scottish Ministers, took up post in April 2011 for a fixed term of five years.[18] Subsequent appointments will be made by Children's Hearings Scotland (CHS)[19] The National Convener together with CHS is responsible for appointing and dismissing panel members from local authority areas throughout Scotland, and for establishing area support teams,[20] as well as training panel members and setting standards to ensure consistency across the country.[21] The National Convener and CHS also provide legal advice to hearings and takes over the reporter's role in enforcing decisions against local authorities.

8–10   In this process, a children's hearing consists of a chairing member and two other members,[22] and must include both a man and a woman.[23] They must, so far as practicable, be appointed from the area of the local authority which is the relevant local authority for the child to whom the hearing relates,[24] and their appointment lasts for three years, subject to reappointment.[25] Under the new Act there is a duty to take reasonable steps to involve people under 25, who have previously been to a children's hearing, in the development and delivery of training panel members.[26] It is also expressly required that training must have regard to how panel members can best elicit the views of children.[27] Panel members are supposed to be lay representatives of their

---

[14] The 2011 Act refers to the "Principal Reporter" but this includes other officers of the Scottish Children's Reporter Administration to whom the Principal Reporter's functions are delegated, see Sch.3, para.10.

[15] 2011 Act s.39.

[16] 2011 Act s.2.

[17] 2011 Act s.1.

[18] The first CHS *Corporate Plan 2012–15* (downloaded from *www.chsscotland.gov/uk/doc/ CHSCoporatePlan-colour.pdf* [accessed May 29, 2013]) has been issued setting out priorities for the next three years. These include establishing the national panel and area support teams and setting up the new organisation as laid out in the 2011 Act.

[19] 2011 Act Sch.1 para.8.

[20] 2011 Act Sch.1 para.12.

[21] See s.11 requiring CHS to provide assistance to the National Convener in carrying out his functions. Note that the Children's Hearings (Scotland) Act 2011 (Commencement No.2) Order 2011 (SI 2011/111) has brought into force provisions relating to the establishment, functions and powers of the CHS and the powers of the Scottish Ministers relating to the National Convener and the new body on April 18, 2011.

[22] The National Convener may select one of the members of the children's hearing to chair it, see s.6(4).

[23] 2011 Act ss.5 and 6(3)(a).

[24] 2011 Act s.6(3)(b).

[25] 2011 Act Sch.2, para.1(5).

[26] 2011 Act Sch.2, para.3(2).

[27] 2011 Act Sch.2, para.3(3). Getting children to participate has been a longstanding problem for hearings, see R. Gallagher, *Children and Young People's Voices: The Law, Legal Services, Systems and Processes in Scotland*, (1999) Scottish Child Law Centre, C. Hallet and N. Hazel, *The Evaluation of Children's Hearings in Scotland*, Vol.1, *Deciding in Children's Interests* (1998) The

community with some interest in or experience of children and their problems, and are unpaid, although expenses are met.[28] However, they do receive extensive training in relevant areas of law, social work and child psychology.

The Principal Reporter or reporter is also an independent official[29] whose   **8–11** primary role is to decide which children should come before a children's hearing. Although a reporter acts on behalf of a single local authority area, since the introduction of the Local Government, etc. (Scotland) Act 1994, all reporters have been employed by a national umbrella organisation known as the Scottish Children's Reporter Administration ("SCRA") since April 1, 1996 and not by local authorities.[30] The SCRA was introduced following local government reorganisation, but was also designed to minimise differences in practice between reporters. It is headed by a Principal Reporter for Scotland. The office of Principal Reporter and of the SCRA has been maintained under the 2011 Act.[31] As was previously the case, the reporter need not be legally qualified, but may instead be drawn, for example, from a background in social work or education.[32]

The reporter's role in the hearings system is crucial. His or her function is   **8–12** to receive reports on children who may be in need of compulsory measures of supervision, from sources such as the police, procurators fiscal, social work departments, schools and members of the public. Any one may refer a child to the reporter.[33] This incudes a court involved in relevant proceedings, such as family actions for divorce, separation and adoption,[34] as well as a sheriff dealing with a child under the Antisocial Behaviour, etc. (Scotland) Act 2004.[35] Where a referral is made the reporter must investigate to decide if these children should be referred to a hearing.[36] The reporter also provides legal procedure advice where this is required at the hearing itself, and makes applications to the sheriff to have a ground of referral established if this becomes necessary.[37] The reporter should only refer a child to, and arrange for,[38] a hearing if satisfied that

---

Scottish Office Central Research Unit; Griffiths and Kandel, "Hearing Children in Children's hearings" (2000) *Child and Family Law Quarterly*, Vol.3, pp.283–299; L. Waterhouse and J. McGhee, and R. Stewart (2000) *The Evaluation of Children's Hearings in Scotland*, Vol. 3, *Children in Focus* (The Scottish Office Central Research Unit); L.Waterhouse and J. McGhee, "Children's Hearing in Scotland; Compulsion and Disadvantage" (2002) *Journal of Social Welfare and Family Law*, Vol.24(3), pp.279–296; A. Griffiths and R. Kandel, "Empowering Children? Legal Understanding and Experiences of Rights in the Scottish Children's Hearings System" in S. Halliday and P. Schmidt (eds) *Human Rights Brought Home: Socio-Legal Perspectives on Human Rights in a National Context* (Oxford: Hart Publishing, 2004), pp.231–255.

[28] 2011 Act Sch.2. para. 4.
[29] 2011 Act Sch.3, para.1.
[30] 1995 Act s.40(2).
[31] See Pt 2 of the 2011 Act ss.14–24 and Sch.3.
[32] 2011 Act Sch.3, para.8(4).
[33] 2011 Act s.64.
[34] 2011 Act s.62.
[35] 2011 Act s.70.
[36] 2011 Act s.66.
[37] See para.8–12.
[38] 2011 Act s.201 defines "relevant local authority" in terms of a local authority as one (a) in whose area the child predominantly resides; or (b) where the child does not predominantly

> (i) at least one of the "grounds of referral" under s.67(2) (discussed below) is satisfied in respect of the child; *and*
>
> (ii) the child is in need of compulsory measures of supervision.[39] "Supervision" includes measures for the protection, guidance, treatment, or control of the child.[40]

8–13 If the reporter does *not* choose to refer the child to a hearing, he or she may either decide no action is necessary,[41] in which case the child and parents must be informed of this,[42] or refer the case for advice, guidance and assistance to the local authority,[43] which may then wish to consider if there is a case for action on its part, e.g. an offer to accommodate the child under s.25 of the 1995 Act, or to provide assistance under s.22.[44] In recent years there has been a drop in referrals to the reporter. The year 2011/2012 when 31,593 children were referred represents the fifth consecutive year that the number of children referred to the reporter has decreased, with only 3.1% of all children in Scotland being subject to a referral.[45] It represents a 2.7% drop in numbers from the previous year.[46] Out of those children who were referred, approximately 60% were referred on to a hearing.[47] In 40% of cases the reporter decided no further action was desirable or necessary. Once the reporter has decided no action is necessary, no hearing can subsequently be arranged based solely on the same set of investigated facts.[48]

8–14 The reporter thus has complete discretion to divert a child out of the children's hearings system if he or she feels that that child is not in need of compulsory supervision or would suffer more than gain by becoming involved in the legal process.[49] This discretion is based on the child's welfare rather than the extent of any alleged offence. For example, it might be clear on the facts that a child has committed an offence of joyriding, once, for a prank; but if the subsequent investigation revealed that the child's family were well able to deal with the situation and no need for intervention was disclosed, then the case would not be pursued. Alternatively, a report of a very minor crime, such as the theft of a carton of milk, might on investigation disclose a family in need of help to control the child, or a child who is not being properly cared for. The reporter's discretion cannot be appealed or reviewed, otherwise than by the

---

reside in the area of a particular local authoirty, the local authority with whose area the child has the closest connection.

[39] 2011 Act ss.66(2), and 69(1) and (2).
[40] 2011 Act s.66(1)(b).
[41] 2011 Act s.68(1)(a) and (b).
[42] 2011 Act s.68(3)(a).
[43] 2011 Act s.68(5)(a) and (b). Note that this is where the child and/or family agree to this on a voluntary basis.
[44] 2011 Act s.68(1) and (3). See further, Ch.7 above.
[45] *SCRA Annual Report 2011/12*, p.19.
[46] *SCRA Annual Report 2011/12*, p.22.
[47] *SCRA Annual Report 2011/12*.
[48] 2011 Act s.68(6).
[49] Note that the police must report all children they have arrested and detained, who are *not* to be charged with criminal offences in the ordinary courts, to the Principal Reporter under s.43(5) of the Criminal Procedure (Scotland) Act 1995. The reporter must investigate and decide whether or not to proceed with a hearing under s.66(2) and may exercise his or her discretion to release the child without raising further proceedings.

public law remedy of judicial review of administrative action. Over the years the balance of referrals has shifted from offence grounds to those involving care and protection.[50] In 2011/12 89% of referrals were made on the basis of care and protection.[51] Of these, 13.4% involved children under two years of age.[52] While concerns over the years have focused on a small group of persistent offenders[53] and initiatives such as fast track hearings[54] and youth courts[55] have been initiated to deal with them, the reality is that referrals to the reporter are "at its lowest since 1998/99" and SCRA attribute this to "more effective intervention from other areas within the children's service arena".[56]

It should be noted that although most juvenile offenders will be referred **8–15** to the children's hearings system, in some very serious cases, children aged twelve or over may still be prosecuted in the criminal courts.[57] Such prosecution can be undertaken only on the instructions of the Lord Advocate or at his instance, and may be brought only in the High Court of Justiciary or the Sheriff Court.[58] In practice, such prosecutions are restricted to the more serious crimes, such as murder or rape, and those involving a penalty of disqualification from driving.[59]

The Grounds of Referral

The grounds of referral in s.67(2) represent a set of threshold criteria which **8–16** must be proven to exist, or be agreed to, by both the child and the parents,

---

[50] In 2002/03 a total of 37,727 children were referred, the highest since the children's hearings system began. This increase was, however, almost entirely due to an increase in children being referred on non-offence grounds. For example, there was a 102% increase in children referred on non-offence grounds and 7% increase in children referred on offence grounds between 1992–1993 and 2002–2003, see *SCRA Annual Report 2002–2003*.

[51] *SCRS Annual Report 2011/12*, p.19.

[52] *SCRS Annual Report 2011/12*.

[53] See proposals put forward in GIRFEC (2005) discussed at A. Griffiths and R. Kandel "The Governance of Children: From Welfare Justice to Proactive Regulation in the Scottish Children's Hearings System" pp.171–189 in F. and K. von Benda-Beckmann and J. Eckert (eds), *Rules of Law and Laws of ruling: On the Governance of Law* (2009). For a broader discussion of youth crime and justice see M. Burman, P. Bradshaw, N. Hutton, F. McNeill and M. Munro, "The End of an Era? Youth Justice in Scotland", pp.429–472 in J. Junger-Tas and S. H. Decker (eds) *International Handbook of Juvenile Justice* (2008); and L. McAra and S. McVie, "Youth Crime and Justice: Key Messages from the Edinburgh Study of Youth Transition and Crime" (2010) *Criminology and Criminal Justice*, Vol.10, pp.211–230.

[54] A. Cleland "The Anti-Social Behviour etc.(Scotland) Act 2004: Exposing the Punitive Fault Line below the Children's Hearings System" (2005) 9 Edin. L.R. 439 commenting on M. Hill et al., *Fast Track Hearing Hearings Pilot: Final Report of the Evanluation of the Pilot* (Scottish Executive, 2005).

[55] See L. Piacentini and R. Walters, "The Politicization of Youth Crime in Scotland and the Rise of the 'Burberry Court'" (2006) *Youth Justice*, Vol.6, pp.43–59.

[56] L. Piacentini and R. Walters, "The Politicization of Youth Crime in Scotland and the Rise of the 'Burberry Court'" (2006) *Youth Justice*, Vol.6, pp.43–59.

[57] While the age of criminal responsibility in Scotland is set at eight, no child under twelve can be prosecuted in the criminal courts since the introduction of s.41A, inserted into the Criminal Procedure (Scotland) Act 1995 by s.52 of the Criminal and Justice Licensing (Scotland) Act 2010.

[58] Criminal Procedure (Scotland) Act 1995 s.42.

[59] Successive Lord Advocates have issued directions on prosecution, for the latest see Appendix B, Scottish Law Commission, 2001 Discussion Paper 115 on the Age of Criminal Responsibility.

before a children's hearing can begin to consider if compulsory measures of supervision (CSO) are necessary. New grounds have been inserted into the 2011 Act including, forced marriage, close connections with domestic abuse and with a Sch.1 offender under the Criminal Procedure (Scotland) Act 1995, as well as a general, catch-all provision dealing with conduct likely to have a serious adverse effect on the health, safety or development of the child or another person.

The grounds are that:

(a) The child is likely to suffer unnecessarily, or the health or the development of the child is likely to be seriously impaired, due to a lack of parental care

8–17   Generally this ground refers to poor parenting over a period of time by a parent or carer. The reasons for this may be that the carer may have limited parenting ability, substance misuse problems, mental health issues or relationship difficulties and is unable to prioritise the child's needs before that of their own or of others in the household. Failure to provide parental care involves acts of omission as well as acts of commission. The test is an objective one; that is, whether a reasonable person would infer from the facts that there has been a lack of parental care that is likely to cause a child unnecessary suffering or seriously impair a child's health or development.[60] The lack of parental care may be past or present and the word 'likely' refers to possible and probable future lack of care and the likely impact on the child.[61]

(b) A schedule 1 offence has been committed in respect of the child

8–18   A list of all the Sch.1 offences is contained in the Criminal Procedure (Scotland) Act 1995. Schedule 1 offences include offences involving assault, ill treatment, neglect, exposure, abandonment or any offence involving bodily injury in a manner likely to cause unnecessary suffering.[62] Sexual offences are also contained in Sch.1. The ground is established if, on the balance of probabilities, an offence was committed against the child. Although in some cases the identity of the perpetrator may be known, it is not necessary to prove who has committed the offence, it is sufficient for it to be established that the child has been a victim of such an offence. Note that, even if a perpetrator has had no criminal proceedings brought against him or her, or has been acquitted in criminal proceedings, the ground of referral can still be upheld if there is supporting evidence.[63]

(c) The child has, or is likely to have, a close connection with a person who has committed a Sch.1 offence

---

[60] See *McGregor v L*, 1981 S.L.T. 194; *D v Kelly*, 1995 S.L.T. 1220. These cases involved the old ground of lack of parental care under s.52(2)(c) that is virtually the same as the ground under s.67(2)(a). Note that, where parents have a history of neglecting their children, it is not necessary for a child to have actually suffered parental neglect before the ground can be established.

[61] 2011 Act s.67(2)(a).

[62] The ground may be established if, for example, the physical chastisement of a child is not reasonable, see *B v Harris*, 1990 S.L.T. 208 and *G v Templeton*, 1998 S.C.L.R. 180.

[63] 2011 Act s.67(2)(b).

This ground can be used to protect any child from birth onwards where the **8–19** child has had or is likely to have in the future, a close connection with someone who has committed an offence mentioned in Sch.1 of the Criminal Procedure (Scotland) Act 1995. A child is taken to have a close connection with a person if the child is a member of the same household as the person, or the child is not a member of the same household but has significant contact with the person. The word 'household' has a wide meaning[64] and may involve the person either living in or not living in the same house. If not living in the same house as the child, then that person having a continuing relationship or family tie with the child and/or his family would constitute member of the same household.[65]

(d) A child is, or is likely to become a member of the same household as a child in respect of whom a Sch.1 offence has been committed

For this ground to be upheld, the child has to be a member of the same **8–20** household as a child who has been the victim of a Sch.1 offence. Again, the word 'household' has a wide meaning and may involve the child not actually physically living in the same house as the referred child but having a continuing relationship with the child.[66]

(e) The child is being, or is likely to be, exposed to persons whose conduct is (or has been) such that it is likely that—(i) the child will be abused or harmed, or (ii) the child's health, safety or development will be seriously adversely affected

This ground may be used where more than one person is behaving in such **8–21** a way that the child's safety is or is likely to be compromised. The conduct complained of may be past or present and may arise in a wide range of cases, including, for example, a group of people who are present in a house where substance misuse is taking place or pornography is being shown. In taking account of this ground the word 'likely' also takes account of the impact that such behaviour may have on the child.[67]

(f) The child has, or is likely to have, a close connection with a person who has carried out domestic abuse

---

[64] See *Cunningham v M*, 2005 Fam. L.R. 14.

[65] 2011 Act s.67(2)(c). See *McGregor v H*, 1983 S.L.T. 626 where the court held that a household denoted a family unit that represented a group of person held together by a particular tie, such as a blood relationship. While a family unit normally lived together, it did not cease to be a family unit if individual members were temporarily separated. In this case B, who had been the victim of a schedule 1 offence was temporarily living with foster parents and so was no longer living in the same house as his brother A. Although A and N were living separately at the time of the hearing the court held that A was a member of the same household as B and so the ground of referral was competent.

[66] 2011 Act s.67(2)(d). See *A v Kennedy*, 1993 S.L.T. 118 where the court held that it was the nature of the relationship that determines the existence of a household. In that case the ground was established in relation to a child whose sibling had died of a Sch.1 offence 10 years before. The court held that a household could continue even where the perpetrator had physically left the home, if the person looking after the child still maintained contact regular contact with him.

[67] 2011 Act s.67(2)(e).

8-22　　This ground may be used to protect a child who has a close connection with the perpetrator of domestic abuse regardless of the sex of the perpetrator. A child will be taken to have a close connection with such a person if the child is a member of the same household as the person, or the child is not a member of the same household but has significant contact with the person. The ground not only covers a current connection with a person who has carried out domestic abuse but also encompasses a 'likely' connection. For this ground to apply it is not necessary that the domestic abuse has been carried out in the referred child's family.[68]

(g) The child has, or is likely to have a close connection with a person who has committed an offence under Pt 1, 4 or 5 of the Sexual Offences (Scotland) Act 2009

8-23　　This ground may be used to protect a child who has a close connection with someone who has committed an offence of unlawful sexual intercourse, rape etc of a young child (a child who has not attained 13 years of age) or an older child—a child who has not attained 16 years of age. For these purposes, a child is taken to have a close connection with a person who has committed an offence if the child is a member of the same household as the person, or the child is not a member of the same household but has significant contact with the person.[69]

(h) The child is being provided with accommodation by a local authority under section 25 of the Children (Scotland) Act 1995 and special measures are needed to support the child

8-24　　This ground concerns children who are being voluntarily accommodated by the local authority and whose behaviour is such that they may need special measure of support, This might arise where they are, for example, constantly absconding, or engaging in conduct that is putting themselves and/or others at risk. In such cases the special measures might include a compulsory supervision order, a movement restriction condition, or even, in severe situations, secure accommodation.[70]

(i) A permanence order is in force in respect of the child and special measures are needed to support the child

8-25　　This ground relates to those children in respect of whom a permanence order applies and who are no longer subject to a compulsory supervision order. The idea is that if such a child experiences difficulties, because for example, the placement is not working, the child could be referred to a children's hearing for support and be brought back into the system.[71]

---

[68]　2011 Act s.67(2)(f).
[69]　2011 Act s.67(2)(g).
[70]　2011 Act s.67(2)(h).
[71]　2011 Act s.67(2)(i).

(j) The child has committed an offence

This ground applies only to a child over the age of criminal responsibility, **8–26** that is eight years of age or older, who has committed at least one offence.[72] Where the statement of grounds prepared by the reporter relates to an offence, it must have the same degree of specification as a criminal charge and specify the nature of the offence. The standard of proof in these cases is beyond reasonable doubt. The age of criminal responsibility remains eight, though no child under 12 can be prosecuted in the criminal court.[73]

(k) The child has misused alcohol

This ground brings any child who has misused alcohol into the system **8–27** which is in line with Art.33 of the UN Convention of the Rights of the Child which expects member states to take appropriate action to protect children from illicit drug use.[74]

(l) The child has misused a drug (whether or not a controlled drug)

This ground includes children who have misused a class A, B or C drug, **8–28** prescribed or a non-prescribed drug.[75]

(m) The child's conduct has had, or is likely to have, a serious adverse affect on the health safety or development of the child or another person.

This ground may be used to bring a child before a hearing where s/he is **8–29** engaging in a range of behaviours that is likely to have an adverse effect in terms of the child's health, safety or development or that of others with whom s/he comes into contact. Such behaviour might include running away from home, substance abuse, or sleeping rough. It might also include self-mutilation or harming behaviour.[76]

(n) The child is beyond the control of a relevant person

This ground may be used when a child is behaving in such a way that s/he **8–30** does not respond to the reasonable demands made by a relevant person who has responsibility for him or her. For example, where a child is continually staying out late at night without consent, or continually running away from home.[77]

(o) The child has failed without reasonable excuse to attend school regularly

Children under sixteen are obliged to go to school.[78] They are only excused **8–31** if their non-attendance falls within the range of reasonable excuses defined

---

[72] 2011 Act s.67(2)(j).
[73] Criminal Procedure Act (Scotland) Act 1995 ss.41 and 41A.
[74] 2011 Act s.67(2)(k).
[75] 2011 Act s.67(2)(l).
[76] 2011 Act s.67(2)(m).
[77] 2011 Act s.67(2)(n).
[78] 2011 Act s.199(2).

in section 42 of the Education (Scotland) Act 1980. These refer to difficulties with travel arrangements, health problems or special circumstances acceptable to the education authority or a court. (s 67(2)(o))

(p) The child (i) has been, is being, or is likely to be, subjected to physical, emotional or other pressure to enter into a civil partnership, or (ii) is, or is likely to become, a member of the same household as such a child

8–32   This ground applies to any child who has been or is being or is likely to be put under pressure to enter into a civil partnership. It also protects any child who is a member of the same household as the victim or is likely to become a member of the same household as the victim.[79]

(q) The child (i) has been, is being or is likely to be, forced into a marriage(that expression being construed in accordance with section 1 of the Forced Marriages etc (Protection and Jurisdiction)(Scotland)Act 2011, or (ii) is, or is likely, to become a member of the same household as such a child

8–33   This ground applies to any male or female child who has been, is being or is likely to be forced into a marriage. It covers past, existing and future marriages. The pressure need not be physical but may involve emotional coercion or duress. It may for example, involve the child being held captive somewhere until s/he agrees to the marriage, or it may involve threats to cut the child off from his or her family and community if s/he does not agree to the marriage. It is important to note that arranged marriages do not fall under this category (because although the marriage may be arranged the parties consent to it). However, consenting to an arranged marriage may turn into a forced marriage if either of the parties changes their mind and wishes to withdraw from the marriage and pressure/duress is brought to bear upon him or her to proceed with the marriage. This ground also protects any child who is a member of the same household as the victim or is likely to become a member of the same household as the victim.[80]

PROCEDURE AT THE CHILDREN'S HEARING

Pre-Hearing Panels and Attendance

8–34   If the reporter feels that ground(s) of referral exist in respect of a child and that the child is in need of CSO, then he or she should arrange for a hearing to be convened.[81] In certain cases a pre-hearing panel may be convened to determine certain matters before the hearing.[82] These include whether or not

---

[79] 2011 Act s.67(2)(p). The words "has been" were added by the Children's Hearings (Scotland) Act 2011 (Modification of Primary Legislation) Order (SSI 2013/211). On marriages and civil partnerships entered into under duress see Ch.9.

[80] 2011 Act s.67(2)(q).

[81] 2011 Act s.69 (1) and (2).

[82] 2011 Act s.79.

a person qualifies as a 'deemed relevant person',[83] or whether a child should be excused from attending the hearing.[84] As a child not only has a right but also a duty to attend a hearing[85] in order to be excused one of the following grounds must be met, that:-

- the case involves an offence mentioned in Schedule 1 of the Criminal Procedure (Scotland) Act 1995 or Part 1, 4, or 5 of the Sexual Offences (Scotland) Act 2009, and the attendance of the child at the hearing, or that part of the hearing, is unnecessary for a fair hearing;[86]
- the attendance of the child at the hearing, or that part of the hearing would place the child's physical, mental or moral welfare at risk;[87] or
- taking account of the child's age and maturity, the child would not be capable of understanding what happens at the hearing or that part of the hearing.[88]

In the CHS's Training Resource Manual,[89] the point is stressed that not only do children have an absolute right to attend a hearing, but that their attendance is central to a hearing so that even where they are very young children panel members should recognise that "a great deal of information can be gathered by observing the child's behaviour and the interaction between the child and adults present".[90] It should be noted that even if the panel dispense with a child's duty to attend the hearing it cannot dispense with the child's right to attend if the child wishes to do so.

Another reason for holding a pre-hearing panel is to determine whether a 'relevant person' in relation to the child should be excused.[91] A pre-hearing panel may only excuse a relevant person from attending a hearing if it would be unreasonable to require their attendance for all or part of a hearing, or if their attendance at all or part of the hearing is thought to be unnecessary for the proper consideration of the case.[92] Such a person may also be excused where the rules of procedure allow for this.[93] A pre-hearing panel may also be held to determine whether it is likely that the children's hearing will consider making a compulsory supervision order including a secure accommodation

8–35

---

[83] 2011 Act s.79(2). This may be at the instance of the reporter (s.79(2)(b)), but may also be convened at the request of the individual in question, the child, or relevant person in relation to the child (s.79(2)(a)). The determination is important as in order to have the right to attend a hearing a person has to qualify as a "relevant person".

[84] 2011 Act s.79(3)

[85] 2011 Act s.73(2).The reference to a "fair hearing" reflects taking the human rights considerations of others, as well as the child, into account.

[86] 2011 Act s.73(3)(a).

[87] 2011 Act s.79(3)(b).

[88] 2011 Act s.79(3)(c).

[89] The CHS's *Training Resource Manual*, Vol.1, *Legislation and Procedure* (2013), Scottish Government.

[90] The CHS's *Training Resource Manual*, Vol.1, *Legislation and Procedure* (2013), Scottish Government, p.280.

[91] 2011 Act s.79(3)(b). Who qualifies as a relevant person or deemed relevant person is discussed at paras 8–41 *et seq.* below.

[92] 2011 Act s.79(5)(a).

[93] See 2011 Act s.79(5)(b) referring to s.177.

authorisation in relation to the child.[94] Finally, a pre-hearing panel may be held to deal with any matter specified in the rules.[95]

8–36   Once any of these matters have been dealt with in a pre-hearing panel, the hearing may subsequently take place. The hearing meets in private, and no persons other than those strictly necessary for the proper consideration of the case should be present.[96] The child who is the subject of the hearing now has both the duty and an absolute *right* to attend at all stages of the procedure, even if she or he is too young to understand the full import of the proceedings or may suffer from hearing some of the evidence.[97] However, the child's *duty* to attend can be dispensed with by a pre-hearing panel on the grounds discussed above.

8–37   Where the child fails to attend the grounds hearing and has not been excused from attending, the hearing may require the reporter to arrange another hearing.[98] The hearing may also request the reporter to make an application for a warrant to secure attendance. Where this is granted by a hearing the warrant authorises an officer of the law to

- search for and apprehend the child[99];
- take the child to, and detain the child in, a place of safety[100];
- bring the child before the relevant proceedings[101]; and
- so far as is necessary for the execution of the warrant, to break open shut and lockfast places.[102]

Note that where a place of safety is involved the warrant may prohibit its disclosure (whether directly or indirectly) to any person in the warrant.[103] Under certain conditions a warrant may include secure accommodation authorisation,[104] but only where

- it authorises the keeping of a child in a residential establishment[105]; and
- one or more of the secure criteria are met[106]; and
- having considered all other options the children's hearing consider it necessary to do so.[107]

---

[94] 2011 Act s.79(3)(c). This is important because any such determination will trigger a requirement to notify the Scottish Legal Aid Board so that legal assistance can be made available to the child.

[95] 2011 Act s.79(3)(d).

[96] Only those with a right may attend, 2011 Act s.78(1). No other person may attend unless certain conditions are met, s.78(2).

[97] See 2011 Act s.78(1)(a) confering a right of attendance on the child and s.73(2) conferring a duty on the child to attend.

[98] 2011 Act s.95.

[99] 2011 Act s.88(1)(a)(i).

[100] 2011 Act s.88(1)(a)(ii).

[101] 2011 Act s.88(1)(a)(iii). These are proceedings before a children's hearing or before a sheriff (s.88(4)(d)).

[102] 2011 Act s.88(1)(a)(iv).

[103] 2011 Act s.88(1)(b).

[104] 2011 Act s.88(2) and (3).

[105] 2011 Act s.88(2)(a).

[106] 2011 Act s.88(2)(b).

[107] 2011 Act s.88(2)(c).

The conditions are:

- the child has previously absconded and is likely to do so again and if the child was to abscond, the child's physical, mental or moral welfare would be at risk[108];
- the child is engaging in self-harming conduct[109];
- the child is likely to cause injury to another person.[110]

Where a warrant is issued, a hearing must then be convened to consider the child's case on the next working day where practicable.[111] The warrant has a limited existence and comes to an end either at the beginning of the hearing dealing with the child, or at the latest, on the expiry of seven days beginning with the day on which the child is first detained.[112] In certain situations, a children's hearing may have to make a decision in relation to the child as a matter of urgent necessity, for example, to protect the child. If a child is not subject to a compulsory supervision order (CSO), there is an interim measure, known as an interim compulsory supervision order (ICSO) which can be set in place for the child if it is necessary.[113] Where the child is under a CSO, then an interim measure, known as an interim variation compulsory supervision order (IVCSO) can be put in place in cases of urgent necessity.[114] These are new provisions that have been introduced by the 2011 Act to provide more choices and flexibility in dealing with the child's needs. Where the child is not subject to a CSO, an ICSP may be made where the grounds hearing consider it is necessary as a matter of urgency for the protection, guidance, treatment or control of the child.[115] The order is highly flexible, presenting panel members with a range of options for the child. This means that the child can be removed from the home or remain in the home on an ICSO. The child can be required to reside in a named place or a place of safety. Like a CSO, at least one measure must be attached to the order and the implementation authority must be named. An ICSO lasts for 22 days[116] but can be renewed lasting up to a total of 66 days before the s.67 ground is established in court.[117] The same considerations come into play when dealing with a child who is subject to a CSO.[118] However, in this case the order can only last of 22 days and cannot be renewed although other variations can be made.[119] Any warrant imposed by

8–38

---

[108] 2011 Act s.88(3)(a).

[109] 2011 Act s.88(3)(b).

[110] 2011 Act s.88(3)(c).

[111] Rule 17 of the Children's Hearings (Scotland) Act 2011 (Rules of Procedure in Children's Hearings) Rules 2013 (SSI 2013/194).

[112] 2011 Act s.88(4)(a). Note that where a warrant is granted by a sheriff under s.103(7) this lasts until the beginning of the continued hearing, or the expiry of 14 days beginning with the day on which the child is first detained (s.88(4)(b)), whichever is the earlier.

[113] 2011 Act s.93(5).

[114] 2011 Act s.97(5).

[115] 2011 Act s.93(5).

[116] 2011 Act s.86(3)(d).

[117] 2011 Act s.96(4).

[118] 2011 Act s.97.

[119] 2011 Act s.97(6).

a hearing can be appealed to the sheriff,[120] and then to the Inner House, or to the sheriff principal and thence by his leave to the Inner House.[121]

8–39   In some cases, a hearing will have been convened as a legal requirement because a child has been removed to a place of safety by virtue of a CPO obtained by a local authority or some other person. Once a child has been removed under a CPO, then unless it is subsequently recalled by the sheriff, or the child liberated by the reporter, a hearing must be convened to consider the child's case by the eighth working day after the day on which the CPO was implemented.[122] We considered the complex procedural steps following a CPO in detail in Ch.7, at paras 7–48 *et seq.* A hearing may also be convened where an ASBO or interim ASBO has been made in respect of a child: see para.8–81 below. In such a case, a special ground of referral is regarded as already having been established, and there is no need either for proof or acceptance of a ground of referral,[123] so the hearing can proceed straight to merits and disposal.

8–40   Apart from the child him or herself, the other parties with a right to attend the hearing are members of the press,[124] representatives of the Council on Tribunals[125] and any "relevant persons", who also have a duty to attend unless it would be unreasonable to require their attendance.[126] Others who have a right to be present include the reporter,[127] the three panel members,[128] any appointed safeguarder,[129] a person representing the child and/or relevant person[130] and other required for a proper consideration of the case, e.g. social workers etc. In the interests of keeping the child at the centre of proceedings, with as little distraction as possible, the chairing member is under an obligation to keep the number of people at a hearing to a minimum.[131]

8–41   In recent years who may qualify as a "relevant person" has been the subject of some dispute.[132] Under the 2011 Act a new status is created, that of a "deemed relevant person", who is a person whom a pre-hearing panel determines "has (or has recently had) significant involvement in the upbring-

---

[120] 2011 Act s.154.
[121] 2011 Act s.63.The appeal to the sheriff from the hearing imposing the warrant must be heard within three days or the warrant ceases to have effect: s.157(3).
[122] 2011 Act s.54.
[123] Antisocial Behaviour, etc. (Scotland) Act 2004 s.12(A1). See also s.70 of the 2011 Act.
[124] 2011 Act s.78(1)(i). They can, however, be excluded if this is necessary in the interests of the child or they are causing significant distress to the child (s.78(1)(5)).
[125] 2011 Act s.78(1)(g).
[126] 2011 Act s.78(1)(c).
[127] Children's Hearing Rules 2013 r.13.
[128] 2011 Act s.5.
[129] 2011 Act s.78(1)(f). For discussion of the role of a safeguarder see para.8–45 below.
[130] 2011 Act s.78(1)(c) and of the 2013 Rules r.11(1).
[131] 2011 Act s.78(4).
[132] With regard to the position of the unmarried father under s.93(2)(b)(c) of the 1995 Act the matter went all the way to the Supreme Court in *Principal Reporter v K* [2010] UKSC 56. The section was interpreted by the court to include any person "who appears to have established a family life with the child with which the decision of a children's hearing may interfere". For discussion see "Unmarried fathers as 'relevant persons'—Principal Reporter v K", 2011. S.L.T. (News) 115. See also *Authority Reporter v S* [2010] CSIH 45, also decided under the 1995 Act, and commentary by Evans, "Unmarried fathers, contact and children's hearings; exploring Authority Reporter v S" (2011) Edin. L.R pp.106–111.

ing of the child".[133] Where the pre-panel hearing makes this determination than the deemed relevant person is to be treated as a relevant person.[134] If it is not practicable to hold a pre-hearing panel then a determination of relevant or deemed relevant person status must be made at the beginning of the hearing.[135] Relevant persons include any persons with parental responsibilities or rights (PRRs) in respect of the child under Pt I of the 1995 Act.[136] It also includes anyone who has PRR's under a court order,[137] except where this involves a contact or specific issue order.[138] The draft Children's Hearings (Scotland) Act 2011 (Review of Contact Directions and Definition of Relevant Person) Order 2013 appears to have corrected this position by widening the definition of relevant person to include *all* parents, except those who have had their PRR's removed by a court.[139] When in force, the regulation will rectify the position of unmarried father's whose names were registered on their child's birth certificate before the provisions of the Family Law (Scotland) Act 2006 took effect giving fathers registered on their child's birth certificate automatic PRRs.[140] For these fathers, who did not have PRRs because the 2006 Act was not retrospective in its effect, will now qualify as a relevant person under the Order.

While it is true that any person can now apply to be deemed a relevant **8–42** person this requires the person to establish past or present significant involvement in the upbringing of the child. What this entails is far from clear. Until the draft order is put in place, there is a question as to whether this requirement is in breach of an unmarried father's human rights because is seems to require more than the family ties that are recognised and protected under Strasbourg jurisprudence. In the case of *Keegan v Ireland*[141] the parents separated before the child was born. The mother arranged for the child to be adopted without consulting the father. Although he had no direct "involvement" with the child he did have family ties and the European Court of Human Rights held that his rights under Arts 6 and 8 had been violated. It is not clear how this deeming provision will stand up

---

[133] 2011 Act s.81(3).
[134] See 2011 Act s.83(4), setting out the parts of the Act that apply to that person.
[135] 2011 Act s.80(3).
[136] 2011 Act s.200(1)(a). This is provided that such PRR's have not been removed by a court order. For discussion of who has PRRs see Ch.3.
[137] 2011 Act s.200(1)(b).
[138] See 2011 Act s.200(2).
[139] Art.3. Widening the definition is necessary express denial of relevant person status to a person with a contact order flies in the face of the Inner House's decision in *Authority Reporter v S* [2010] CSIH 45. In this case two unmarried fathers with contact orders were denied relevant status in relation to their children by children's hearings. In one case the father was not notified of the hearing and not invited to attend. In the other, the father was allowed into part of the hearing but not given papers and not allowed to fully participate. The Inner House held that what had happened breached these fathers' right to a fair hearing under Art.6 of the ECHR and so interpreted the definition of relevant person to be read to include a parent who had "a right of contact in terms of a contact order" in order to make the section compliant with human rights. Thus s.200(2) of the 2011 Act, taken on its own, appears to be in breach of fathers' human rights.
[140] Since May 4, 2006, all fathers registered on their child's birth certificate have PRR's under s.3(1)(b)(ii) of the 1995 Act.
[141] *Keegan v Ireland* (1994) 8 E.H.R.R. 342.

to human rights scrutiny as it appears to be setting a higher threshold for recognition. This is particularly problematic because the status of a deemed relevant person may be removed by a hearing. Where it appears to a hearing that and individual no longer has, or had not recently had, significant involvement in the child's upbringing, the hearing must determine whether the individual should continue to be deemed a relevant person in relation to the child. This may give rise to the kind of situation in *Principal Reporter v K*[142] where the father had a contact order but contact did not take place and the child was made the subject of a children's hearing on the basis of allegations of abuse. In this case legal proceedings and hearings dragged out until the Supreme Court upheld the sheriff's interlocutor granting the father PRR's to the extent that he could become a relevant person in terms of the section. In reaching its decision the Supreme Court interpreted the relevant person provision[143] to include a person "who appears to have established family life with the child with which the decision of a children's hearing may interfere". Once again, human rights considerations stressing family ties and family life may be at odds with the requirement of significant involvement which may lead to an unmarried father having his deemed status removed where there is a protracted period of dispute where he is denied contact with the child.

8–43   The status of a deemed relevant person is not confined to unmarried fathers but covers all those who can establish significant involvement in the upbringing of the child. There is no guidance given in the Act as to factors that are to be taken into account. The CHS *Training Resource Manual* does, however, observe that for a person to meet the test's requirement that person must "have been involved in how the child is being brought up in terms of the core decisions in relation to the child's life".[144] According to the Manual these include decisions such as where the child is to live, what school the child is to attend and medical treatment for the child.[145] It would not include a person who looks after the child after school or a professional worker who has no involvement in the child's life beyond his or her professional remit. It might, however, include a member of an extended family who has recently had the care of the child in the "absence of the child's parent for a significant period of time".[146] Where there are problems in the legislation with regard to recognition of a relevant person or deemed relevant person these can be addressed by orders of the Scottish Ministers.[147]

8–44   Once the status has been determined it remains in existence for the purpose of the hearing in question, subsequent hearings, pre-hearing panels, orders, warrants, reviews and court proceedings. It lasts until it is, in effect, reviewed by a hearing. Where a person is unsuccessful in acquiring a deemed relevant

---

[142] *Principal Reporter v K* [2010] UKSC 56.
[143] Under s.93(2)(b)(c) of the 1995 Act.
[144] CHS *Training Resource Manual*, Vol.1, p.245.
[145] CHS *Training Resource Manual*, Vol.1, p.245.
[146] CHS *Training Resource Manual*, Vol.1, p.245.
[147] See 2011 Act s.200(3) and s.81(5)(a). This power was used to draft the Children's Hearings (Scotland) Act 2011 (Review of Contact Directions and Defintion of Relevant Person) Order 2013.

person status an appeal may be made to a sheriff,[148] and from a sheriff to the sheriff principal or to the Court of Session.[149] In any event, any person can be allowed to attend at the discretion of the chairman of the hearing.[150] Normally, social workers associated with the case will be allowed to attend under this discretion.

Representation and Legal Aid

To meet the child's needs, the hearing must consider in every case whether **8–45** it is necessary to appoint a safeguarder,[151] an official who has a function similar to that of a curator *ad litem* in ordinary court proceedings and who is often, though not necessarily, a lawyer. The safeguarder's role is to discover and represent the best interests of the child to the hearing. Thus a safeguarder is not an advocate acting on behalf of the child and promoting the child's wishes, although these are taken into account in a discussion of what is in the best interests of the child presented in the safeguarder's report. A safeguarder is, however, now obliged to take the views of the child and to state how this was done in the report submitted to a hearing.[152] It was originally necessary for there to be a conflict of interest between parent and child before a safeguarder could be appointed, but this is no longer the case. Safeguarders were introduced into the hearings system in 1985,[153] but a much more extended role for them is contained in the 2011 Act, where panel members are required to consider in every case where a substantive decision is being made about the child whether or not a safeguarder should be appointed at any point in the proceedings.[154]

Both parents and the child are allowed to bring along one person to accom-   **8–46** pany them to the hearing.[155] This may be a supportive person such as a friend, but may equally well be a lawyer. Under the 2011 Act a new child advocacy service is introduced under s.122.This will not come into operation until 2014. When it does the chairing member of the panel will be under a duty to inform the child of advocacy services that include the provision of support and representation with a view to assisting a child in engaging with and participating in the hearing. As we saw in Ch.2, a child of sufficient capacity may instruct a lawyer independently of his parents.[156] Apart from this very limited window of opportunity, the Kilbrandon vision, as earlier discussed, was that the hearing would benefit from being a relatively informal tribunal, without the involvement of lawyers for children or parents, or judges, or prosecutors.

---

[148] 2011 Act s.160. Persons who may appeal include the individual who applied, the child, and a relevant person in relation to the child or two or more of these persons acting jointly, s.160(2).

[149] 2011 Act s.164. Persons who may appeal are those set out above, s.164(3).

[150] 2011 Act s.78(2)(b). The chairing member may not, however, grant permission for any person without a right to attend if either the child or a relvant persons objects to their attendance (s.78(3)), unless s/he considers it necessary for the proper consideration of the case (s.78(2)(a)).

[151] 2011 Act s.30.

[152] Children's Hearings (Scotland) Act 2011 (Safeguarder: Further Provision) Regulations 2012 (SSI 2012/336) reg.7.

[153] Under the Children Act 1975 s.66 (now repealed).

[154] 2011 Act s.30(1) and (2).

[155] Children's Hearings Rules 2013 r.11(1) and (2).

[156] Paras 2–33 *et seq.*

Accordingly, in principle (and as is normal with other tribunals, such as employment tribunals) legal aid was not made available for representation at the hearing, but only if the case was appealed to the sheriff court or the Inner House. Limited aid was, however, available for non-representational legal advice and assistance, e.g. advice before the hearing; and some lawyers chose to provide their services free or pro bono to children or families; but, largely, this prohibition ensured that lawyers were absent from the actual hearing.

8–47   The blanket non-availability of legal aid for representation of the child was found to be contrary to Art.6(1) of the European Convention on Human Rights ("ECHR") in the leading case of *S v Miller*.[157] This was the first major human rights challenge to the legality of the hearings system after the coming into force of the Human Rights Act 1998. The Inner House (First Division, comprising of the Lord President (Rodger), Lord Penrose and Lord Macfadyen) first held that the children's hearings were a civil, as opposed to a criminal, tribunal. There was thus no absolute entitlement to legal aid for every child appearing before the hearing, as would have been required if the hearing in question had fallen under Art.6(3). Nor was there such a right even for every child appearing on an *offence* ground of referral. Lord Penrose remarked that "the sole purpose of the hearing is to find a solution to the child's problems which best suits the child's needs on a proper application of the welfare principle". The proceedings as a whole, therefore, were not characterised as criminal proceedings, even where the ground of referral was (as in S's case) based on an offence committed by the child.[158]

8–48   Was legal aid required even if the hearings fell only within the requirements of Art.6(1)? It was already clear from the jurisprudence of the European Court of Human Rights in Strasbourg in *Airey*'s case, that an absolute bar on legal aid could be seen as unfair, and thus a breach of Art.6(1).[159] The Scottish Executive argued strongly that the reason legal aid was not available was to maintain the informality and child-orientated approach of the hearings system. These arguments were, however, rejected. Without access to legal aid, and hence legal representation, it could not be guaranteed that "[no] child would ever be unable to conduct his own case effectively before the hearing". Furthermore, the Lord President pointed out, lawyers were already appearing on a sporadic basis without any apparent destabilising of the system. In such circumstances, it was better to put legal representation on an equal footing rather than leaving it largely available only to those with the means to pay. The Inner House also held that the defect in process was not cured by the availability of legal aid at an appeal stage, since by that time prejudice to the child might have already become embedded. Accordingly, as matters stood, there was a breach of Art.6(1).[160]

---

[157]   *S v Miller*, 2001 S.L.T. 531. See further Edwards, "*S v Miller*: The End of the Childrens' Hearings System As We Know It?", 2001 S.L.T. (News) 187.

[158]   *S v Miller*, 2001 S.L.T. 531 at [50]. On determining whether the hearings were criminal or civil in nature, see also Lord President at [10]–[24] and Lord Macfadyen at [10]–[50].

[159]   *Airey v Ireland*, Series A No.32 (1979). See also *Benhan v UK*, Reports, 1996-III 738.

[160]   However the lack of availability of legal representation in the past does not mean that the disposals made by all hearings before *S v Miller* are retrospectively invalidated, unless there is proof of actual unfairness leading to actual prejudice which had not been corrected by review or appeal remedies available: *M v Caldwell*, 2001 S.L.T. (Sh. Ct) 106. In *S v Miller (No.2)*,

If access to free legal representation was essential in *some* hearings, then   **8–49**
which hearings would those be? Clearly allowing legal aid for every child at
every hearing would not only be expensive to the public purse, but potentially catastrophic for the character of the hearings system which might be
suddenly flooded by lawyers. The Inner House offered some guidance as to
which cases should be afforded free representation[161] including

(1) hearings where there might be a deprivation of liberty, e.g. those poten-
    tially leading to the making of a supervision requirement with a condi-
    tion of secure accommodation;
(2) hearings involving very young children[162] or those of "limited intelli-
    gence or limited social skills";
(3) hearings involving difficult issues of law, e.g. defences such as provo-
    cation or self-defence, or where there are complicated documents and
    reports to consider;
(4) generally, any case of such "complexity" that legal aid is demanded,
    bearing in mind the *Airey* requirement that the child must have *effective*
    access to justice.[163]

The Lord President also made the point that the need for legal aid may arise   **8–50**
at either the "grounds of referral" stage or the "disposal" stage. Since *S v
Miller*, there have been a number of regulations dealing with legal representation[164] that have now been overtaken by the provisions of the 2011 Act.[165] The
2011 Act provides that the term "children's legal aid" means representation
by a solicitor, and where appropriate, by counsel in proceedings.[166] There
are two types of provision for legal aid, one where the child is automatically
entitled to legal aid and assistance,[167] and one where it may be provided at
the discretion of the Scottish Legal Aid Board (SLAB).[168] In addition, there is
provision for legal aid to be made available to a relevant person under certain
conditions.[169] The circumstances where a child is entitled to automatic legal
assistance include the following

2001 S.L.T. 1304, it was held that *S v Miller* itself did not require the court to make a formal
declaration of incompatibility with the ECHR as the legal aid point was to be addressed
by regulations. See also Jamieson, "*S v Miller*: Should A Declaration of Incompatibility be
Made?", 2001 S.L.T. (News) 137.

[161] See Lord Macfadyen at [62] and Lord Penrose at [74].

[162] Although note that this will not include the cases of children too young to accept or deny the
grounds of referral as these will transmit automatically to the sheriff court for proof, where
legal aid is already available. The age group envisaged in *S v Miller* thus seems to be roughly
5 to 12.

[163] The bar on legal aid and possible infringement of Art.6 was not addressed by the Children's
Hearings (Legal Representation) (Scotland) Amendment Rules 2009.

[164] See the Children's Hearings (Legal Representation) (Scotland) Rules 2009.

[165] See s.191 that makes amendments to the Legal Aid (Scotland) Act 1986.

[166] See s.28B(2) of the 1986 Act inserted by s.191.

[167] See s.28C(1)(a)–(d), added to the 1986 Act by s.191.

[168] See s.28B(3) added to the 1986 Act by s.191 where children may be entitled to legal aid if they
pass the means and merits tests set out in s.28D.

[169] See s.28E added to the 1986 Act by s.191. This also depends on the relevant person meeting
means and merits tests under s.28E(3).

- application to vary or terminate a Compulsory Protection Order (CPO)[170];
- proceedings before a sheriff under ss.45/46 (children's hearing following the making of a CP0)[171];
- proceedings before a hearing or pre-hearing panel where a CPO may be made including a secure accommodation authorisation[172];
- proceedings before a CH involving the arrest of a child and detention in a place of safety[173];
- proceeedings under Pt 10 (proceedings before a sheriff) or Pt 15 (Appeals) of the Act.[174]

8–51 In certain other situations, a pre-hearing panel or hearing may consider that in order for a child or young persons to participate effectively in a hearing it is necessary for them to be represented by a solicitor. There are no guidelines as to what amounts to effective participation but the CHS *Training Resource Manual* refers to situation involving complex legal issues where a person may not be able to effectively participate without the assistance of a solicitor.[175] Where this is the case and the pre-hearing panel or hearing are of the view it is unlikely that the child will arrange such representation the hearing must defer making a decision in relation to that child and require the reporter to notify SLAB of the recommendation for legal aid, the reasons for it, and the name and address of the child so the child can be notified.[176] In these circumstances the child requires to have a capacity to instruct a solicitor. As we have seen in chapter 2, children under sixteen have the capacity to instruct a solicitor where they have a general understanding of what it means to do so.[177] While such capacity is presumed from the age of twelve, there is nothing to prevent a younger child from having such capacity. In all cases involving legal aid it is SLAB that make the decision not the panel or hearing who can only make recommendations to the Board. In those cases where legal aid for the child is not automatic three considerations come into play. These are

- that it is in the best interests of the child that legal aid be made available[178];
- that it is reasonable in the particular circumstances of the case that the child should receive legal aid[179];
- that after consideration of the disposable income and disposable capital of the child the expenses cannot be met without undue hardship to the child.[180]

---

[170] Under s.48 of the 2011 Act; 1986 Act s.28B(1)(a).
[171] 1986 Act s.28C(1)(b).
[172] 1986 Act s.28C(1)(c).
[173] 1986 Act s.28C(1)(d). These are proceedings under s.69(3).
[174] 1986 Act s.28C(1)(e).
[175] CHS, *Training Resource Manual, Volume 1, Legislation and Procedure* (2013), p.399.
[176] 2013 Rules r.50.
[177] Age of Legal Capacity (Scotland) Act 1991 s.2(4A).
[178] 1986 Act s.28D(3)(a).
[179] 1986 Act s.28D(3)(b).
[180] 1986 Act s.28D(3)(c). In most cases this will be an easy test for the child to meet.

The Act also recognises that a relevant person may have an interest in receiv-   **8–52**
ing legal assistance given the kind of decisions that a hearing can make that
may involve removing the child from the home. Legal assistance in this case,
however, is not automatic, but is subject to meeting certain conditions. These
include that it is reasonable in the particular circumstance of the case that
the relevant person should receive legal and that they should be granted legal
aid because they cannot meet the expenses of attending the hearing without
undue hardship.[181] There are also provisions in relation to appeals, including appeals dealing with deemed relevant person status.[182] Where legal aid is
granted it may be made subject to conditions.[183] A pre-hearing panel and a
hearing is also under a duty to consider the need for legal aid in relation to
a relevant person where it is of the opinion that the relevant person cannot
participate effectively without legal representation and it is unlikely that s/
he will arrange for such representation.[184] What is new is that, under the
2011 Act, legal representation will be the responsibility of SLAB who has
a duty to establish and maintain a register of solicitors who will be eligible
to provide assistance to children and/or relevant persons as outlined above.
In compliance with these requirements, the Board has established a code of
practice in relation to solicitors carrying out children's legal assistance that
solicitors must comply with.[185] Only a solicitor who is on the register may
provide children's legal aid and assistance and the Board is under a duty to
monitor the service to ensure compliance with its Code of Practice. As with
other provisions in the Act there is provision for Scottish Ministers to modify
the circumstances in which children's legal aid is available.[186]

Exclusion and Confidentiality

In some circumstances, it may be very difficult for a child to speak freely to   **8–53**
the panel members if one or both parents are present. Parents will usually be
entitled to be present as "relevant persons", but under s.76 the hearing has the
right to exclude any relevant person (and any representative of theirs)[187] for
so long as is necessary either to obtain the child's views, or to avoid causing
the child significant distress. However, the child cannot be guaranteed confidentiality even after exclusion, because the excluded person must be informed
by the chairing member what has taken place in his or her absence.[188]

Confidentiality has always created a problem for hearings.[189] On the one   **8–54**
hand, parents who face the possible imposition of measures of compulsory

---

[181] 1986 Act s.28E(3).
[182] See 1986 Act s.28 E and F.
[183] 1986 Act s.28G, these may include requiring the assisted person to make a contribution, see
s.28K.
[184] 2013 Rules r.50.
[185] See SLAB, *Code of Practice in relation to Children's Legal Assistance Cases*, Feburary 2013,
prepared in terms of s.28N of the Legal Aid (Scotland) Act 1986.
[186] 1986 Act s.28L.
[187] Under 2011 Act s.77.
[188] 2011 Act s.76(3).
[189] For the problems of the exclusionary provision under the 1995 Act and the way in which
panel members sought to get round it see Griffiths and Kandel, "Half-told Truths and
Partial Silence: Managing Communication in Scottish Children's Hearings" in F. and B. von

supervision have basic rights as a matter of procedural justice (under Art.6 of the ECHR, and also at common law) to know what the case is against them or their children. On that basis, all information that is given to panel members should be shared with the parents. On the other hand, cases will sometimes involve sensitive information which neither the hearing nor, sometimes, one or more of the parties may wish disclosed to all other parties. For example, one parent might discover that the other is adulterous, or has a history of violence. Most importantly, given full disclosure, the hearing cannot guarantee that views expressed by a child about his or her parent(s) will remain private. Despite these difficulties, following the European Court of Human Rights case of *McMichael v UK*,[190] the Principal Reporter became obliged[191] to make available to each parent[192] a copy of any report made available to the children's hearing. This still left the children themselves without a statutory right to access to reports concerning their own case, a position conceded in *S v Miller* (above) to be contrary to Art.6 of the ECHR.

8-55   There is now power under s.178 of the 2011 Act allowing for non-disclosure in certain circumstances where a person has been excluded from a hearing. This provisions provides express statutory authority for non disclosure of information "if disclosure of that information. . .would be likely to cause significant harm to the child".[193] While this new provision is to be welcomed it raises questions about what constitutes "significant harm to the child". Again, there is no guidance given in the Act as to what this might entail. Given the human rights considerations that arise, it is submitted that the test used for confidentiality regarding children's views in court as set out in the case of *McGrath v McGrath*[194] may be applied. This involved following a decision of the House of Lords in *Re D*[195] that established a three-part test. This required a determination of (a) whether disclosure of the material would involve a real possibility of significant harm to the child; (b) if it would involve such a risk, a consideration of whether the overall interests of the child would benefit from non-disclosure; and c) if satisfied that interest of the child pointed to non-discloure, then weighing that consideration against the interest of the parent or other party in disclosure.

PROCESS

8-56   Any decision or determination made by a children's hearing must be informed by the basic three principles applied under the 2011 Act:

Benda-Beckmann and A. Griffiths (eds), *The Power of Law in a Transnational World: Anthropological Enquiries* (2009), pp.176–195.

[190] *McMichael v UK* [1995] Fam. Law 478; ECHR, February 24, 1995.

[191] Children's Hearings (Scotland) Rules 1996 r.5(3). Reports prepared before this date in the expectation of non-disclosure to parents will be replaced by composite reports.

[192] See Children's Hearings (Scotland) Rules 1996 r.5(3)(b).

[193] 2011 Act s.178(1). This applies despite any requirement under the Act to give a person an explanation of what has taken place at proceedings or to provide him or her with information about the child or the child's case or reasons for a decision made by a hearing, s.178(2).

[194] *McGrath v McGrath*, 1999 S.L.T. (Sh. Ct) 90.

[195] *Re D* [1995] 4 All E.R. 385.

(1) the need to safeguard and promote the welfare of the child throughout the child's childhood as the paramount consideration[196]
(2) that the child must be given an opportunity to express a view and regard must then be given to those views as far as is practicable having regard to the age of maturity of the child.[197] Competence to express a view is presumed at 12 or over[198];
(3) the hearing should not make any requirement unless it feels it is better to do so than to do nothing (the "minimum intervention" principle).[199]

These principles are similar but not identical to those contained in s.11(7) of the Children (Scotland) Act 1995 discussed in depth at Ch.4, paras 4–49 *et seq*.[200] It is important to note, however, that a hearing can make a disposal or decision which is inconsistent with the child's welfare where they consider there is a risk of serious harm to the public.[201] So, for example, a child might be subject to an order for secure accommodation authoristion[202] for the protection of the public even if this did not best meet the needs of that child. As noted earlier, however, this step should only be taken as a last resort and under certain conditions.   **8–57**

The procedure of the hearing is primarily laid down in the Children's Hearings (Scotland) Act (Rules of Procedure in Children's Hearings) Rules 2013.[203] and is intended to foster informal discussion between the child, parents, and hearing members. The first task of the chairman of the grounds hearing is to explain the ground or grounds under which the child was referred to the hearing as being in need of a CSO and then to establish if these ground(s) are accepted by both the child and any "relevant person".[204] If any of these persons refuses to accept any of the grounds, then the reporter must make an application to the sheriff court under s.93 for the sheriff to establish as proven the ground(s) that are disputed, unless the hearing is willing to discharge the referral on the grounds that the child no longer seems to be in need of a CSO[205] The sheriff must hear the s.93 application within 28 days of it being lodged.[206]   **8–58**

If the *child* fails to attend the hearing without being excused then the grounds hearing may ask the reporter to arrange another hearing.[207] The child's acceptance cannot be dispensed with and either the referral must be discharged, or an application made to the sheriff for proof.[208] If the child or relevant person in relation to the child is incapable of understanding the   **8–59**

[196] 2011 Act s.30.
[197] 2011 Act s.27(3).
[198] 2011 Act s.27(4).
[199] 2011 Act s.28(2).
[200] Under 2011 Act s.11(7)(a) the reference is simply to welfare being the paramount consideration.
[201] 2011 Act s.26(1)(a), in which case welfare is downgraded to a primary consideration.
[202] See below, para.8–69.
[203] Note that at the time of writing this chapter the rules have not been formally approved and remain in draft form.
[204] 2011 Act s.90.
[205] 2011 Act s.93(2)(b).
[206] 2011 Act s.101(2).
[207] 2011 Act s.95(2).
[208] 2011 Act s.93(2).

grounds of referral, because of age or otherwise, or has not understood the explanation given in relation to the ground, then an application must be made to the sheriff for proof, or else the referral must be discharged.[209] If one or more, but not all, of the grounds are accepted, then the hearing may either move on to dispose of the case under s.91 with respect to those grounds which *are* accepted,[210] or if they feel this is inappropriate, they can await the determination of the sheriff who is charged with establishing the disputed grounds before moving on to the disposal stage.[211]

Establishing the Grounds of Referral—s.101 Proofs

8–60   Proceedings before a sheriff under s.101 are not to be held in open court although they are held in court.[212] The application to have the ground(s) of referral established is presented by the reporter, and legal aid is available for representation of both parents and child.[213] The need for the appointment of a safeguarder must be considered by the court.[214] All grounds of referral must be established on the balance of probabilities, i.e. the civil standard of proof, except grounds relating to s.67(2)(j) dealing with the committal of an offence in which case the ground must be established beyond reasonable doubt.[215] Other grounds which may require proof of an offence being committed by someone *other* than the child, can be established on the usual civil standard. Thus, it is not at all anomalous that an alleged abuser of a child might be found not guilty of the crime in the criminal courts, but then be proven to be the abuser in a s.101 proof. As Lord Justice-Clerk Ross said in *Harris v F*:

> "The purpose of a ground of referral such as [this] is to advance the welfare of the child and to protect the child . . . Protection of a child is in my opinion a justification for applying a lower standard of proof in applications under s 42 [now s.101] and it is still a justification even if the person concerned is ultimately acquitted of the offence in the criminal courts".[216]

A proof that a child has been the victim of an offence can proceed even if a criminal prosecution is pending, although this is undesirable because of the potential prejudice to the accused in criminal proceedings.[217] The basic rules of evidence and procedure are observed at a s.68 proof but there are various judicial dicta that proceedings are neither civil nor criminal but

---

[209] 2011 Act s.94(1) and (2).
[210] 2011 Act s.91(1)(b).
[211] 2011 Act s.108(2).
[212] 2011 Act s.101(3).
[213] Both the child and any "relevant person" may also be represented by a non-legally qualified person: 2011 Act s.104.
[214] 2011 Act s.31.
[215] 2011 Act s.102(3).
[216] *Harris v F*, 1991 S.L.T. 242 at 246 dealing with abuse under earlier legislation. See also *Kennedy v B*, 1992 S.C.L.R. 55.
[217] *P v Kennedy*, 1995 S.L.T. 476.

uniquely *sui generis*,[218] and in *W v Kennedy*,[219] Lord Sutherland went so far as to say that,

> "it would be quite wrong for [the interests of the child] to be thwarted by the application of rigid rules of evidence or procedure just because such rigidity may be appropriate in other types of proceedings".

As at the hearing stage, the child has a right and a duty to attend but can be released from this obligation by the sheriff[220] and parents have a right to attend but can be excluded in the interests of the child by the sheriff.[221]

If the ground(s) for referral are established or accepted, the sheriff remits the case back to the children's hearing to consider and dispose of the case.[222] If none of the grounds are found to be proven, then the sheriff must dismiss the application and discharge the referral and any warrant by means of which the child has been detained.[223]

A child, or relevant person can apply for a review of a sheriff's grounds **8–61** determination.[224] However, a review will only be carried out if

- there is evidence in relation to the ground that was not considered by the sheriff when making the grounds determination[225];
- the evidence would have been admissible[226];
- there is a reasonable explanation for the failure to lead that evidence before the grounds determination was made[227]; and
- the evidence is significant and relevant to the question of whether the grounds determination should have been made.[228]

If these conditions are not met, the sheriff must dismiss the appeal.[229]

New Evidence

However, the 2011 Act allows for a review of a ground of referral that has **8–62** been established under s.110. It may be brought by either the child or a relevant person.[230] The review may only take place where

- there is evidence in relation to the ground that was not considered by the sheriff when making the grounds determination[231];

---

[218] *McGregor v D*, 1977 S.L.T. 182; *A v Kennedy*, 1992 S.C.L.R. 387.
[219] *W v Kennedy*, 1988 S.C.L.R. 236.
[220] 2011 Act s.103(2) and (3).
[221] Act of Sederunt (Child Care and Maintenance Rules) 1997 r.3.47(6).
[222] 2011 Act s.108(2).
[223] 2011 Act s.108(3).
[224] 2011 Act s.110 (except in relation to s. 67(2)(j) where the case has been remitted to the reporter under s.49 of the Criminal Procedure (Scotland) Act 1995).
[225] 2011 Act s.111(3)(a).
[226] 2011 Act s.111(3)(b).
[227] 2011 Act s.111(3)(c).
[228] 2011 Act s.111(3)(d).
[229] 2011 Act s.111(4).
[230] 2011 Act s.110(2).
[231] 2011 Act s.111(3)(a).

- the evidence would have been admissible[232];
- there is a reasonable explanation for the failure to lead that evidence before the grounds determination was made[233]; and
- the evidence is significant and relevant to the question of whether the grounds determination should have been made.[234]

If the sheriff is satisfied that notwithstanding the above, the s.67 ground is established the application for review must be dismissed.[235] If, however, the sheriff finds that the ground is not established, s/he must recall the grounds determination and make an order discharging (wholly or to the extent that it relates to the ground) the referral of the child to the children's hearing.[236]

8–63   More generally, the child, a relevant person or the reporter can appeal the sheriff's decision on the grounds determination to the Inner House or to the sheriff principal and thence, with his leave, to the Inner House.[237] A safeguarder can also appeal a sheriff's decision.[238] The appeal is by way of stated case either on point of law or in respect of any irregularity in the conduct of the case. If the appeal is upheld by either the sheriff principal or the Inner House then the case is remitted back to the sheriff for disposal in accordance with such instruction as the appeal court gives.[239]

DISPOSAL OF THE CASE: COMPULSORY SUPERVISION ORDERS

8–64   Once the grounds of referral have been either accepted or established in court, the case is remitted back to the children's hearing who can either continue the case to gather further relevant information, discharge the referral or make a CSO under s.83 if they feel this is necessary in respect of the child.[240] If a CSO is imposed by the hearing, then the local authority has the responsibility of implementing it, e.g. placing the child with foster parents to meet a residential order.[241] One of the key problems in the hearings system which emerged in the responses[242] to the *Getting It Right* consultation was the lack of any ability by the reporter or the panel to compel the local authority to implement a supervision requirement. Given a global lack of resources in social services, this was a serious issue in the panel achieving effective results, particularly in relation to persistent offender cases. An amendment to the 1995 Act was made to deal with this,[243] and the issue has been addressed in s.146 of the 2011 Act. Under this provision a children's hearing may require the National Convener

---

[232] 2011 Act s.111(3)(b).
[233] 2011 Act s.111(3)(c).
[234] 2011 Act s.111(3)(d).
[235] 2011 Act s.114(2).
[236] 2011 Act s.114(3).
[237] 2011 Act s.163.
[238] 2011 Act s.163(3)(c).
[239] 2011 Act s.163(10).
[240] 2011 Act s.119(3).
[241] 2011 Act s.144.
[242] The Scottish Executive, Stevenson and Brooks, *A Report on Responses* (2004).
[243] 2011 Act s.71A.

to give the local authority notice specifying where it considers the authority to be in breach of its duties, stating that if the authority does not remedy this within twenty one days from the date of the notice the National Convener will make an application to the court for an order of enforcement. [244] If, on further review, it appears that the authority continues to be in breach of its duty, the children's hearing may direct the National Convener to apply to the sheriff court for an order.[245] Where the National Convener is so directed an application for enforcement must be made to the relevant sheriff court to enforce implementation of the authority's duty in relation to the child.[246]

In making a disposal, the hearing is not restricted to consideration merely **8–65** of the facts that have been proven as part of the grounds of referral. Rather, proof of any ground is the key that unlocks the door to consideration of *all* the circumstances of the case, proven or unproven.[247] Thus, even evidence which was inadmissible at a s.101 proof, e.g. hearsay statements made by a child who was not a competent witness, might be used by the hearing to formulate their disposal. However, any fact which was specifically *disproven* at proof cannot be relied upon by the hearing at the disposal stage.[248] While this approach can be criticised as contrary to natural justice, it is in line with the conception of the hearing as a child-centred forum whose paramount concern is welfare not justice. The hearing is of course bound by the minimum intervention principle and the welfare principle to make no disposal and discharge the case if it seems to them this meets the needs of the child as well as making a CSO would.

Review of Compulsory Supervision Orders

As a fundamental principle, a child should be subject to a CSO no longer **8–66** than is necessary to secure his or her welfare. An order can last no longer than a year[249] unless continued by a review hearing,[250] which can also choose to terminate or vary the order.[251] This ensures that a child's case is regularly reconsidered. As well as the mandatory annual review, a review *must* be requested by the local authority if:

- they are satisfied the CSO ought to be terminated or varied[252]; or
- a condition in the requirement is not being complied with[253];
- the best interests of the child would be served by the authority making an application for a permanence order or by placing the child for adoption.[254]

---

[244] 2011 Act s.146(3)
[245] 2011 Act s.146(6). Note that in making this decision the children's hearing is expressly required not to take account of the adequacy of the authority's means; s. 146(7).
[246] 2011 Act s.147(1).
[247] *O v Rae*, 1993 S.L.T. 570.
[248] *M v Kennedy*, 1993 S.L.T. 431.
[249] 2011 Act s.83(7)(a)(i). This is the case, unless there is a review and the reporter must initiate a review of the CSO within three months of the expiry of the order (s.133).
[250] 2011 Act s.138(3)(c).
[251] 2011 Act s.138 (3)(a) and (b).
[252] 2011 Act s.138(2)(a)
[253] 2011 Act s.138(2)(b).
[254] 2011 Act s.131 (2)(c) and (d).

In this case, the hearing's role at review is to provide advice to any future court who may deal with application for the order in question.

8-67   Furthermore, the child or any relevant person may require a review at any time at least three months after the original hearing or last review hearing.[255] Finally, the hearing making the CSO may itself set a date for the next review.[256]

8-68   It is also now possible under the Antisocial Behaviour (Scotland) Act 2004 s.12(1A) that if a child comes before a court which makes an ASBO or interim ASBO in respect of a child, and that child is already subject to a supervision requirement, then the court may require the reporter to convene a hearing to review the supervision requirement.[257]

Conditions and Effect of Compulsory Supervision Orders

8-69   The hearing may attach such conditions to a compulsory supervision order as they see fit,[258] including a requirement that the child must reside at any place.[259] Effectively, there are two main types of supervision orders: those where the child is required to live outside the family home (hereafter "residential supervision orders") and those where the child is supervised by social workers within the family setting ("home supervision orders").[260] Children under residential supervision orders may live in local authority residential homes, or with foster parents. The panel can order that the address of a child under a supervision order should not be disclosed, for example an abusing father or mother.[261] In exceptional circumstances, the hearing may require that a child should be made subject to a CSO with a secure accommodation authorisation.[262] The hearing must be satisfied that having considered other options such a requirement is necessary[263] *and* that one of the following conditions applies[264]:

- the child has previously absconded or is likely to abscond again and in that event the physical, mental or moral welfare of the child would be at risk[265]; or
- that the child is likley to engage in self-harming conduct[266];or
- that the child is likely to cause injury to another person.[267]

8-70   Children under a secure accommodation condition are effectively subject to an unlimited sentence of detention which can potentially last until the age of

---

[255] 2011 Act s.132.
[256] 2011 Act s.125(3).
[257] 2011 Act s.129.
[258] 2011 Act s.83(2).
[259] 2011 Act s.83(2)(a).
[260] Most supervision orders made are home supervision orders.
[261] 2011 Act s.83(2)(c).
[262] 2011 Act s.83(5).
[263] 2011 Act s.83(5)(c).
[264] 2011 Act s.83(5)(b).
[265] 2011 Act s.83(6)(a).
[266] 2011 Act s.83(6)(b).
[267] 2011 Act s.83(6)(c).

18, albeit subject to review within three months of the condition first being made.[268] It is hard to reconcile this either with the welfare aims of the hearings system or the requirements of natural justice.[269] However it was held in *S v Miller*[270] that a secure accommodation condition was not a breach of Art.5 of the ECHR, because although it *was* a "deprivation of liberty", it was excusable as made "for the . . . educational supervision" of a minor child. Drawing on the Strasbourg case of *Koniarska v UK*,[271] the court held that

> "the words 'educational supervision' must not be equated rigidly with the notion of classroom teaching. In particular in the present context of a young person in local authority care, educational supervision must embrace many aspects of the exercise, by the local authority, of parental rights for the benefit and protection of the person concerned".

A more recent human rights challenge to the system was lodged in *J v Children's Reporter for Stirling*.[272] It was not successful as the Inner House unanimously held that the provisions relating to the placing and keeping of a child in secure accommodation are Convention compliant.[273] As noted above, a child now has a right to free legal representation and assistance at any hearing where an order authorising secure accommodation is made or likely to be made.

An option of last resort, a possible alternative to secure accommodation authorisation is for the hearing to make a condition restricting movement, or an "electronic tagging" order.[274] This involves intensive support and monitoring services (monitoring is facilitated by an electronic "tag") where the young person is restricted to, or away from, a particular place. The electronic tag must be supported by a full package of intensive measures to help the young person change their behaviour. The conditions for the making of an electronic tagging order are the same as for secure accommodation,[275] and the implication is clearly that this may be an effective way to deal with persistent young offenders without actually locking them up. In this sense it can be seen as a welfarist initiative. There have been debates on how effective and desirable such a measure is since its inception.[276] Studies suggest

8–71

---

[268] See r.13 of the Secure Accommodation (Scotland) Regulations 2013 (SSI 2013/212).

[269] Harris and Timms describe the equivalent English regime as "punishment disguised as care". (Harris and Timms, *Secure Accommodation in Child Care: Between Hospital and Prison or Thereabouts?* (1993), p.50).

[270] See above, para.8–32.

[271] *Koniarska v UK* ECHR, 12 October 2000.

[272] *J v Children's Reporter for Stirling* [2010] CSIH 85.

[273] While the case was decided on the basis of the 1995 Act, the court's ruling is relevant as the provisions of the 2011 are in line with the requirements set out by the court.

[274] Antisocial Behaviour etc. (Scotland) Act 2004 s.135, amending s.70 of the 1995 Act. Under s.83(2)(d) of the 2011 Act a CSO may contain a movement restriction order if certain conditions are met. The Intensive Support and Monitoring (Scotland) Regulations (SSI 2008/75) may be replaced by regulations made by the Sottish Ministers under s.150 of the 2011 Act.

[275] See 2011 Act s.83(6). Note that the hearing must also be satisfied that it is necessary to include a movement restriction condition in the order (s.83(4)).

[276] See Cleland, "The Antisocial Behaviour etc. (Scotland) Act 2004: Exposing the Punitive

that while it may have had some effect, there is no evidence to suggest that it is any more effective than other measures of supervision in reducing offending behaviour,[277] and that there is a substantial variability in outcomes, making it clear that success depends "on a range of factors, involving the person, the intervention, the quality of implementation and the research design".[278]

Contact

8-72   The hearing, in particular, *must* consider whether to attach a condition regulating contact with the child.[279] This is because contact is viewed as central to a child's relationship with his or her family. Article 9 of the UNCRC upholds the child's right to personal relations and direct contact with both parents on a regular basis. We have seen how Part I of the Children (Scotland) Act 1995 expressly stipulates that the maintenance of contact is both a parental responsibility and right, and Article 8 of the ECHR requires respect for private and family life, of which contact forms a part. Where contact becomes problematic is where dispute arises over contact where a child is subjected to a residential supervision requirement. What rights do parents have if the hearing adds as a condition to such a requirement that contact with their child is to be limited or terminated? The effect of the supervision requirement, and any condition, is not to *remove* the statutory rights and duties a parent would normally be able to exercise under ss.1 and 2, but to "suspend" them for the duration of the requirement. Thus, the parent cannot exercise his or her parental rights in any way incompatible with the terms of the supervision requirement.[280] A condition restricting contact therefore takes precedence over the parent's ordinary right to maintain contact. Even if the panel do not place particular restrictions on contact, they can legitimately provide that it be at the discretion of the local authority, in which case the authority has the right to restrict contact as it sees fit.[281] However, since a child under a supervision requirement is a "looked after" child [282] the local authority are required

---

Fault Line Below the Children's Hearings System" (2005) 9 Edin L.R. 439. See also M.Nellis, "'The Tracking' controversy: The Roots of Mentoring and Electronic Monitoring" (2004) *Youth* Justice, Vol.4, pp.77–99; L. Mcara and S. McVie, "Youth Justice? The Impact of system Contact on Patterns of Desistance From Offending" (2009) *European Journal of Criminology*, Vol.4(3), pp.25–345.

[277] M. Sapouna, C. Bisset and A. Conlong, *What Works to Reduce Reoffending; A Summary of the Evidence* (2011) Justice Analytical Services, Scottish Government.

[278] M. Sapouna, C. Bisset and A. Conlong, *What Works to Reduce Reoffending; A Summary of the Evidence* (2011) Justice Analytical Services, Scottish Government, p.38. See the call for more rigorous research in this area in IRISS (The Institute for Research and Innovation in Social Services), "Intensive supervision, surveillance and monitoring of young people", *Insight No. 9*, at *www.iriss.org.uk/resources/intensive-supervision-surveillance-and-monitoring-young-people* [accessed June 1, 2013].

[279] 2011 Act s.83(3). This is the case when a hearing is making, continuing or varying a CSO or any interim order.

[280] 1995 Act s.3(4).

[281] *Kennedy v M*, 1995 S.C.L.R. 88. Note that the hearing cannot restrict contact merely to facilitate the adoption of the child as they are not an adoption agency and would be acting ultra vires: *M v Children's Hearing for Strathclyde*, 1988 S.C.L.R. 592.

[282] Children (Scotland) Act 2006 s.17(6)(b).

to promote, on a regular basis, direct contact between parent and child in so far as this is compatible with the child's welfare.[283]

If parents are denied contact, either by the specific terms of the CSO made by the hearing, or by the decision of the local authority, can they mount a challenge? In *D v Strathclyde*,[284] the Inner House found that the effect of a condition of contact in a supervision requirement[285] was not only to suppress the parental rights of contact, but to remove from the parent title to sue for contact in the courts. This was because any award by the court would interfere with the obligations of the local authority to implement the supervision requirement. As the court asserted in *D v Strathclyde*, "a collision would always be on the cards".[286] This had the unfortunate effect, however, that for parties who were not "relevant persons", they had neither the right to attend the hearing and argue their view on contact there (the "public law" remedy), nor the right to raise the matter in the ordinary civil courts (the "private law" remedy). This was particularly unfortunate for unmarried fathers without PRRs who nonetheless wished to stay in touch with their child, sometimes against the wishes of the mother and/or the reporter.

8–73

Contact Direction Review Hearing

This situation will no longer arise under the 2011 Act because s.126 makes provision for a review of a contact direction where certain conditions are met. It allows persons, who are not relevant persons but who have a right of contact with the child, for example, through a contact or permanence order, certain rights of participation in relation to a children's hearing, including calling for a review. This occurs where the hearing makes a contact direction within a CSO, an interim CSO, an interim variation of a CSO or a medical examination order which lasts more than five days.[287] It also allows for participation where a hearing continues or varies a CSO under s.138. The conditions that must be met are, that the orders are "a contact order regulation contact between an individual (other than a relevant person in relation to the child) and the child",[288] or "a permanence order which specifies arrangement for contact between such an individual and the child".[289] Where these conditions apply, the contact direction review hearing, which must take place no later than five working days after the original hearing,[290] may confirm or vary the order in question. Unlike other hearings, this is one that neither the child or relevant person are required to attend.[291]

8–74

In other situations, however, it may be possible to apply to the court for an order where a child is subject to a supervision order. In *P v P*[292] a

8–75

---

[283] Children (Scotland) Act 2006 s.17(1)(c).
[284] *D v Strathclyde*, 1985 S.L.T. 114. Affirmed in *A v G*, 1996 S.C.L.R. 186 (Updates).
[285] This was the terminology that was used before the 2011 Act.
[286] *D v Strathclyde*, 1985 S.L.T. 114 at 116.
[287] Note that the category of persons who may apply may be extended by an order made by the Scottish Ministers (2011 Act s.126(2)(b)).
[288] 2011 Act s.126(3)(a).
[289] 2011 Act s.126(3)(b).
[290] 2011 Act s.126(4).
[291] 2011 Act s.126(7).
[292] *P v P*, 2000 S.L.T. 781.

two-year-old girl was subject to a supervision requirement, which included a condition that she reside with her grandmother. There was no condition as to contact, which meant it was left to be regulated by the local authority in accordance with their duties under s.17 in respect of a "looked after" child. The natural mother had dropped out of the picture but the natural father wanted to apply for contact. The grandmother raised an action under s.11of the Children (Scotland) Act 1995 for a residence order. Her intention was to make sure she had power to do all things necessary for the child's welfare in relation to third parties, e.g. deal with her education, which was not a power the hearing could give her. The Inner House held, in these circumstances, that they had power to grant the residence order sought.

Medical Consent

8–76   The hearing also has the right to attach a condition requiring the child to submit to medical examination or treatment.[293] Again, a parent cannot exercise any parental right in a way which is incompatible with the terms of the supervision requirement. So a mother cannot veto a medical examination ordered by the hearing by virtue of her rights as legal representative. However, the rights of some children *themselves* to give or receive consent must be taken into account. The Age of Legal Capacity (Scotland) Act 1991 s.2(4) provides that a child can give a valid consent to treatment if he or she is capable, in the opinion of a medical practitioner, of understanding the nature and possible consequences of the procedure or treatment. Such a competent child also has the right to *refuse* treatment.[294] Under s.186 of the 2011 Act, a child of sufficient maturity retains these rights even if required to submit by a supervision requirement.

Duration

8–77   A CSO terminates:

(i) when the child reaches 18[295]; or
(ii) after a year if not renewed by a review hearing[296] (see above).

APPEALS AGAINST DISPOSAL

8–78   Either the child or any "relevant person", or a safeguarder[297] may appeal the disposal of the hearing to the sheriff within three weeks.[298] The sheriff receives the same reports that were available to the hearing but may also hear oral evidence from the reporter, the appellant(s) and any other party. The sheriff may confirm the decision and may take certain steps if satisfied that

---

[293] 2011 Act s.83(2)(f).
[294] For the full argument supporting this point, see paras 4–37 to 4–38.
[295] 2011 Act ss.83(7)(a)(ii) and 83(7)(b)(ii).
[296] 2011 Act s.83(7) (a)(i).
[297] Safeguarders are now given power to appeal a hearing's decision under s.154 of the 2011 Act.
[298] 2011 Act s.154(1) and (5).

the circumstances of the child have changed since the decision was made.[299] If, however, the sheriff is not satisfied that the hearing's disposal was justified, then she or he must allow recall the warrant where the decision is a decision to grant a warrant to secure attendance,[300] or terminate the order where the decision is a decision to make an interim CSP or a medical examination order.[301] Otherwise under s.156(3) she or he may

(a) require the Principal Reporter to arrange a children's hearing for any purpose provided for under the Act[302];
(b) continue, vary to terminate the order[303];
(c) discharge the child from any further hearing or proceedings[304]; or
(d) make an interim CSO or an interim variation CSO; or
(e) grant a warrant to secure attendance.

A further appeal against the disposal lies from the sheriff to the sheriff principal[305] and thence to the Inner House (with the leave of the sheriff principal)[306] or directly to the Inner House.[307] There is no appeal to the Supreme Court.[308] As with appeals against a finding that grounds are proven, the basis of appeal is either point of law or procedural irregularity.[309] On deciding an appeal, the sheriff principal or the Court of Session must remit the case to the sheriff for disposal in accordance with such directions as the court may give.[310]

ANTISOCIAL BEHAVIOUR ORDERS AND PARENTING ORDERS

As we noted at the start of this chapter, since around 1995 there has been an increased emphasis in both Scotland and England on what can be done to control the perceived increase in youth crime and offensive behaviour, and, in particular, persistent offending. The Antisocial Behaviour etc. (Scotland) Act 2004 (the "2004 Act") introduced into Scotland, for children, the antisocial behaviour orders ("ASBOs"), which had already arrived in England and Wales somewhat earlier via the Crime and Disorder Act 1998. The 2004   **8–79**

---

[299] 2011 Act s.156(1).
[300] 2011 Act s.156(2)(a)(i).
[301] 2011 Act s.156(2)(a)(ii).
[302] 2011 Act s.156(3)(a). Note that this reflects that fact that the case may be at different stages in the process.
[303] The fact that the sheriff takes these steps does not prevent a children's hearing from continuing, varying, or terminating the order or warrant (2011 Act s.156(5)).
[304] Where this occurs the sheriff must also terminate any order or warrant which is in effect in relation to the child (2011 Act s.156(4)).
[305] 2011 Act s.163(1).
[306] 2011 Act s.163(2).
[307] 2011 Act s.163(1).
[308] 2011 Act s.163(11). Note, however, that where a human rights issue is raised under the ECHR this may fall within the scope of a devolution issue, and a party may appeal against a determination of a devolution issue by the Court of Session, see the Scotland Act 1998 Sch. 6, paras 12 and 13(b). Such an appeal requires the permission of the Court of Session, or if that is not forthcoming, the permission of the Supreme Court.
[309] 2011 Act s.163(9).
[310] 2011 Act s.163(10).

Act applies to children in Scotland age 12 and over but under 16 (ASBOs for adults in Scotland were also introduced by the 1998 Act.) It was argued during the passing of the 2004 Act that ASBOs were unnecessary for under 16s, since there was already in place a wide range of diversionary measures to keep offending young people out of the criminal courts, including the children's hearings, early intervention projects and restorative justice projects. However the government insisted that a small number of persistently anti-social young people existed for whom no current measures were effective.[311] In Scotland, this has meant that, in addition to the welfare-centred hearings system, we now have, sitting rather oddly in conjunction with the Kilbrandon model, an alternate means of controlling the behaviour of delinquent children via the courts.

8–80 ASBOs, rather like interdicts, are court orders, made in the civil sheriff court, which constrain persons not to commit certain types of antisocial behaviour, usually in specified locations. Examples might be hanging round in front of a specified cashpoint, or building exit, or inside a supermarket, or shopping mall; making undue noise in domestic areas; littering; fly-posting; or spray-painting. The court will make an ASBO if satisfied that a person age 12 and over has engaged in antisocial behaviour, and that the ASBO is necessary to protect other persons from further antisocial behaviour.[312] Anti-social behaviour is defined as acting in a manner that causes, or is likely to cause alarm or distress; or a course of conduct[313] that causes, or is likely to cause, alarm or distress to at least one person who is not part of the household of the person served with the ASBO. Local authorities and registered social landlords may apply for ASBOs; they cannot be sought by the police, procurator fiscals or the Crown. An ASBO is an order sought in the civil courts under civil procedure.[314] It is not proof of a criminal conviction, and does not form part of a criminal record. However *breach* of an ASBO is a criminal offence,[315] punishable by fine, or by imprisonment (although detention is not allowed for children under 16[316]).

8–81 The relationship between the hearings system and the "ASBO system" is complex. Before deciding to apply for an ASBO for a child, the guidance suggests that a multi-agency approach should be taken, with the local authority consulting with other agencies who have already been involved with the child, including the SCRA.[317] Where an ASBO is sought in relation to a 12–15 year old, the court *must* ask the reporter to arrange an advice hearing before determining the application.[318] However although "regard" must be given to the advice of the hearing, it need not be followed. Notably, the court, unlike the hearing in Pt II of the 1995 Act, is under no obligation to regard the child's welfare as paramount. In determining an *interim*

---

[311] See *Guidance on Antisocial Behaviour Orders: Antisocial Behaviour etc. (Scotland) Act 2004* (Scottish Executive, 2004), para.20.
[312] 2004 Act s.4(1) and (2).
[313] i.e. at least 2 occasions of conduct. Conduct includes speech (2004 Act s.143(2)).
[314] 2004 Act s.4(1) and Scottish *Guidance on ASBOs*, above n.94, para.33.
[315] 2004 Act s.9.
[316] 2004 Act s.10.
[317] Scottish *Guidance on ASBOs*, para.20.
[318] 2004 Act s.4(4).

ASBO, or an application for variation or revocation of an ASBO, the sheriff must similarly take account of the reporter's views[319]. If either a full or interim ASBO is made, the court *may* require the reporter to bring the child before a hearing,[320] which will then decide whether to impose a supervision requirement (or, more likely, if an existing one should be varied). If there is no existing supervision requirement in place, there is no need to prove, or have a ground of referral accepted: a ground of referral is deemed to have already been established, and the hearing can proceed straight to disposal.[321] Similarly, the court may refer the child to the hearing to have his or her supervision requirement reviewed, without any need for the reporter to exercise their usual discretion whether to seek review.[322] Effectively in both these cases, the will of the court trumps the discretion of the reporter. Thus the provisions create a tension between the hearings system, where the welfare of the child is paramount, and the antisocial behaviour legislation where the focus lies in supportive local communities and controlling antisocial children. How best to achieve these goals is a matter that remains open to debate.

Parenting Orders

The 2004 Act also introduced radical new orders to alter the conduct of **8–82** the *parents* of children and young persons.[323] If a child[324] has engaged in antisocial behaviour, or offended, then the local authority in whose area the child lives, or the Principal Reporter, can apply to the sheriff (under summary procedure) to make a parenting order for up to a year[325]. The Principal Reporter can also seek a parenting order solely on the ground that the order is desirable in the interests of the child.[326] The reporter and the local authority are required to consult before making an application for a parenting order.[327] The court can also be asked to consider if a parenting order should be made in certain proceedings,[328] e.g. if an ASBO is made in respect of a child.[329]

The parenting order will require the parent to comply "during a specified **8–83** period . . . not exceeding twelve months . . . with such requirements as are

---

[319] 2004 Act ss.7(3) and 5(2).
[320] 2004 Act s.12.
[321] 2004 Act s.12(4). See also s.70 of the 2011 Act where the grounds are to be treated as if having been established by the sheriff under s.108 of the Act. This means there is no need for a grounds hearing.
[322] 2004 Act s.12(5).
[323] See generally Pt 9 of the 2004 Act and *Guidance on Parenting Orders: Antisocial Behaviour (Scotland) Act 2004* (Scottish Executive, April 2005). These orders were in a "pilot" phase until April 2008.
[324] Defined for these purposes as a person under 16: see 2004 Act s.117.
[325] 2004 Act s.102.
[326] 2004 Act s.102(3).
[327] 2004 Act s.102(9).
[328] 2004 Act s.114. In any relevant proceedings, e.g. a divorce, the court may require the Principal Reporter to consider whether to apply for a parenting order. It is not clear if these are restricted to civil proceedings.
[329] 2004 Act s.13. The sheriff must be satisfied that making the order is desirable in the interests of preventing antisocial behaviour by the child *or* protecting their welfare.

specified".[330] As Sutherland says, this is a "breathtakingly broad" phrase.[331] In practice this is likely to mean that parents are required to attend counselling, or guidance sessions for a particular period. A "parent" is defined to be the same as a "relevant person" under s.93(2)(b) of the 1995 Act.[332] Unlike with ASBOs, the paramount consideration in making a parenting order is the welfare of the child.[333] As with ASBOs, although a parenting order is a civil order obtained in the civil sheriff court, breach of a parenting order (without reasonably excuse) is a criminal offence[334] punishable by a fine, and eventually jail if the fine is not paid.

8–84   A hearing may now require the Principal Reporter to consider making an application to the sheriff for a parenting order.[335] If obtained, this means a hearing has been able to (albeit indirectly) exert compulsory powers over the behaviour of the parents it sees, rather than just the child.[336] Some commentators see this as a major step forward for the effectiveness of the hearing. Sutherland on the other hand argues that (unlike in the United States, from which legal system parenting orders have been borrowed) we have no tradition of compulsion of parents in the interests of the child in Scotland, and that parenting orders are a culturally alien transplant which are unlikely to work. Other scholars point to the punitive element of these orders, that focus on holding children and their parents responsible for their behaviour, while ignoring their relationship with poverty and disadvantage.[337] In subsequent chapters we will move on to look at how the law regulates the status and relationships of children when they have emerged as adults, and left both the safeguards and the restrictions of child status behind.

---

[330] 2004 Act s.103.

[331] Sutherland, "Parenting Orders: A Culturally Alien Response of Qustionable Efficacy?", 2004 Jur Rev 105 at p.117.

[332] See para.8–28 above.

[333] 2004 Act s.109(1). The court also has to have regard to the views of the child, with, as usual, a child of 12 presumed mature enough to express a view (ss.109(2) and 108(6)).

[334] 2004 Act s.107.

[335] 2011 Act s.128.

[336] Supervision requirements made by the hearing prior to the 2004 Act (and any conditions attached) affected only the behaviour of the *child*.

[337] See R. Walters and R, Woodward, "Punishing 'Poor Parents': 'Respect', 'Responsibility' and Parenting Orders in Scotland" (2007) *Youth Justice*, Vol.7(1), pp.2–20; G. Scott and G. Mooney, "Poverty and social justice in the devolved Scotland: Neoliberalism meets social democracy" (2009) *Social Policy and Society*, Vol.3(4), pp.379–389; C. Burgess, M. Malloch, "Evaluation of the National Parenting Development Project", Research conducted for the Aberlour Child Care Trust, *Report No 02/2008*, the Scottish Centre for Crime and Justice Research.

CHAPTER 9

FAMILIES AND FORMALISED ADULT RELATIONSHIPS

Families take many forms in Scotland today. They include lone-parent **9–01** households, cohabiting opposite sex and same sex couples with or without children, as well as marital relationships and civil partnerships. Individuals may enter into a number of these forms of family in their lifetime as they move *from* marriage to lone-parenthood on to a cohabiting relationship, perhaps, or from cohabitation to marriage.

Here are some data on contemporary families and households: **9–02**

- In 2011, there were 17.9 million families in the UK. Of these, 12 million consisted of a married couple with or without children, and 2.9 million of an opposite-sex cohabiting couple with or without children.[1] The 2001 census data showed that only 43 per cent of Scottish families consisted of a married couple with or without children.[2] The UK figures suggest this percentage is likely to be higher in the 2011 census data.

- At the time of the 2001 Census, there were 163,434 "cohabiting couple" family households in Scotland. Of these, 62,443 had one or more dependent children.[3] At the time of writing, 2011 census data has yet to be published. However, the figures seem likely to be significantly higher: the number of cohabiting couple households in the UK as a whole has doubled from around 1.5 million in 1996 to almost 3 million in 2012, of which around 1.1 million had dependent children.[4]

- In 2011, 51 per cent of births were to unmarried parents, compared with 43 per cent in 2001 and 29 per cent in 1991. However, the number of births registered solely in the mother's name fell from six to seven per cent during the 1990s to five per cent in 2011, suggesting the increase

---

[1] Office for National Statistics ("ONS"), *Statistical Bulletin: Families and Households, 2001–2011*, p1. Available at: *http://www.ons.gov.uk/ons/rel/family-demography/families-and-households/2011/stb-families-households.html* [accessed August 5, 2013].

[2] Taken from Scottish Census Data in 2001 discussed in A. Morrison, D. Headrick, F. Wasoff, and S. Morton, *Family formation and dissolution: Trends and attitudes among the Scottish Population* (Research Finding 43/2002), p.3. In contrast, the proportion of cohabiting couples, ungrouped individuals and lone-parent families in Scotland rose between 1991 and 2001.

[3] Registrar General for Scotland ("RGS"), *Mid 2003 Population Estimates for Localities in Scotland*. Available at *http://www.gro-scotland.gov.uk/statistics/theme/population/estimates/special-area/settlements-localities/archive/mid-2003-localities.html* [accessed August 5, 2013].

[4] ONS, *Statistical Bulletin: Families and Households, 2012*, p1. Available at: *http://www.ons.gov.uk/ons/rel/family-demography/families-and-households/2012/index.html* [accessed August 5, 2013].

in births to unmarried parents has been in babies born to unmarried partners in a stable relationship.[5]

- There were 29,135 marriages in Scotland in 2011. Of these, around 24 per cent represented people who had previously been married. There were also 554 civil partnerships registered.[6]
- There were 9,862 divorces and 44 civil partnership dissolutions in Scotland in 2011.[7]
- 71 per cent of children adopted in Scotland in 2011 were adopted by non-relatives of the child.[8]
- Around 3 million children were living in lone parent families in the UK in 2011. 92 per cent of lone parents are mothers. Around 40 per cent of children in lone parent families live in poverty, as opposed to around 20 per cent of children in families with two parents.
- In 2011, 29 per cent of households in the UK consisted of one person.[9]
- Caring responsibilities continue to impact on the economic activity of women in the UK. In 2011, 35 per cent of women reported that looking after home/family was the primary reason for economic inactivity, as opposed to only 5.7 per cent of men.[10]

DEFINING FAMILIES

9–03 Historically, the concept of family in Scots law was focused on the ancestral line, with marriages brokered to secure alliances between different houses, maintaining property and power within the hands of an elite group. Our modern ideal of marriage for love, sometimes referred to as "companionate marriage", did not take hold until Victorian times. Since then, the ancestral family model has been replaced by the nuclear family model as the most significant family unit in our lives. At the heart of the nuclear family is an intimate relationship between two adults. At one time, the only intimate relationship recognised in law was marriage between a man and a woman. However, increasing acceptance of same-sex couples

---

[5] RGS, *Scotland's Population 2011: The Registrar General's Annual Review of Demographic Trends*, 157th edn, Ch.2. Available at *http://www.gro-scotland.gov.uk/statistics/at-a-glance/annrev/2011/index.html* [accessed August 5, 2013].

[6] RGS, *Scotland's Population 2011: The Registrar General's Annual Review of Demographic Trends*, Ch.6. RGS marriage records show that the number of marriages has been on a general downwards trend.

[7] RGS, *Scotland's Population 2011: The Registrar General's Annual Review of Demographic Trends*, Ch.7. While there was a marked increase in the number of divorces in Scotland up to the early 1980s, since then the numbers have fluctuated. Increasing levels of cohabitation may be related to the recent decline in divorces as the breakdown of cohabiting relationships is not subject to divorce proceedings.

[8] RGS, *Scotland's Population 2011: The Registrar General's Annual Review of Demographic Trends*, Ch.8.

[9] ONS, *Statistical Bulletin: Families and Households, 2001–2011*, p1. Available at: *http://www.ons.gov.uk/ons/rel/family-demography/families-and-households/2011/stb-families-households.html* [accessed August 5, 2013].

[10] ONS, *Social Trends 41: Labour Market*, p19, available at *http://www.ons.gov.uk/ons/rel/social-trends-rd/social-trends/social-trends-41/social-trends-41---labour-market.pdf* [accessed August 5, 2013].

and non-marital relationships has given rise to significant changes in the law over the past two decades. Judicial recognition of same-sex relationships as "family relationships" began in relation to the benefits system,[11] with civil partnership,[12] adoption rights[13] and provision for assisted reproductive treatment for same-sex couples[14] following soon afterwards. Legislation enabling same-sex couples to marry was introduced into the Scottish Parliament in 2013.[15] Cohabiting couples are also eligible to adopt[16] and to receive assisted reproductive treatment.[17] Since 2006, on the breakdown of the relationship, a former cohabitant is entitled to make a financial claim against her former partner,[18] or if the relationship ends by death of one of the cohabiting parties, the survivor can make a claim on the intestate estate.[19]

Human Rights Influence

One important driver behind the increase in formal legal recognition of same-sex and non-marital relationships has been the jurisprudence of the European Court of Human Rights at Strasbourg. The Human Rights Act 1998 sets out that a domestic court or tribunal faced with a Convention question must take into account the jurisprudence of the Strasbourg court wherever relevant.[20] Notwithstanding the discretion implied by the obligation merely to "take account of" the Strasbourg position, the House of Lords has indicated that a European precedent should be followed unless there is a strong reason to deviate from it.[21]   **9–04**

Over the years the European Court of Human Rights has expounded the concept of what constitutes a "family" together with the range of persons that fall within its ambit and the rights accorded to them. Its approach is generally functionalist in nature, in the sense that it focuses on the reality of how parties have lived rather than on the formal legal ties between them. Accordingly, two adults living in a committed relationship which is not legally formalised through a mechanism such as marriage will nevertheless be regarded as a family unit[22] and children of such a family should not be   **9–05**

---

[11] *Fitzpatrick v Sterling Housing Association* [1999] 4 All E.R. 705 (HL).
[12] See generally Civil Partnership Act 2004, Prt 3 of which is applicable in Scotland.
[13] Adoption and Children (Scotland) Act 2007, s.29(3)(b) and (d).
[14] Human Fertilisation and Embryology Act 2008, ss.42–44.
[15] Marriage and Civil Partnership Bill, discussed at paras 9–18 *et seq.*
[16] Adoption and Children (Scotland) Act 2007 s.29(3)(c) and (d).
[17] Human Fertilisation and Embryology Act 2008 ss.36–37 and 43–44.
[18] Family Law (Scotland) Act 2006 s.28.
[19] Family Law (Scotland) Act 2006 s.29.
[20] Human Rights Act 1998 s.2(1)
[21] *R (Anderson) v Secretary of State for the Home Department* [2003] 1 A.C. 837. For more detail on the effect of the Human Rights Act 1998 and the Scotland Act 1998, see R. Reed and J. Murdoch *Human Rights Law in Scotland*, 3rd edn (Haywards Heath: Bloomsbury Professional, 2011), Chs 1 and 3.
[22] *Johnston and Others v Ireland* (1986) 9 E.H.R.R. 203; *EB v France* (43546/02) [2008] 1 F.L.R 150. Being "unmarried" was recognised domestically as a status within the meaning of Art.14 (which prohibits discrimination on the basis of certain statuses) in the House of Lords decision in *P (A Child) (Adoption: Unmarried Couples)* [2009] 1 A. C. 173.

discriminated against simply by dint of the fact their parents are unmarried.[23] (It seems that some distinction in treatment between married and unmarried fathers may still be justified,[24] although such justifications are increasingly hard to find.[25]) Similarly, a person who acts as a parent to a child is likely to be regarded as having a family relationship with that child regardless of whether that relationship is recognised in law.[26]

9–06   Strasbourg case law has had a particular influence on the development of our law on formation of families through its decisions on two connected topics: gender identity and same-sex marriage.

Gender Identity

9–07   As a broad definition, a transperson[27] is someone who has the physical characteristics of one sex, but psychologically and emotionally identifies as the other sex.[28] In Scotland, sex is assigned at birth on the basis of the child's physical characteristics. As medical and societal understanding of transgenderism increased in the late twentieth century, so too did calls for a legal mechanism by which birth certificates could be amended in cases where the birth-assigned sex turned out to be incorrect. Domestic challenges to the status quo were initially unsuccessful.[29] *Corbett v Corbett*[30] in England and *X Petr*[31] in Scotland found that gender was determined at birth based on immutable biological features.[32] Human rights challenges founded on the argument that transpersons were entitled to have their gender correctly identified in law as part of the Art.8 right to private life were similarly unsuccessful. The Strasbourg court cited a lack of clarity in the medical evidence

---

[23] *Marckx v Belgium* (1979–1980) 2 E.H.R.R. 330.

[24] *McMichael v UK* (1995) 20 E.H.R.R. 205.

[25] *Principal Reporter v K* [2011] Fam L.R. 2.

[26] *Marckx v Belgium* (1979–1980) 2 E.H.R.R. 330; *Boyle v United Kingdom* (1995) 19 E.H.R.R. 179

[27] The term "transsexual" is found often within the legislation and case law. The term "transgender" is preferred here as more inclusive of the range of trans identities and experiences without an express or implied focus on gender reassignment surgery. It is acknowledged however that the terminology in this area is complex and evolving. See *http://www.scottishtrans.org/ Transgender_Umbrella.aspx* [accessed August 5, 2013].

[28] This very simplistic definition is used as a basis for illustration of the legal arguments in the Scottish system, which operates on the Judeo-Christian basis that sex is a binary, meaning a person can only be either male or female. Some transgender accounts of sex and gender incorporate arguments that more than two sexes and/or genders exist, and that gender is a spectrum rather than a binary. These accounts have yet to obtain any real attention in Scots law. For a general discussion of the position of transpersons within Scots law, see L. Barnes, "Gender identity and Scottish law: the legal response to transsexuality", 2007 Edin. L.R. 162.

[29] But note the decision of a trial court in the US state of Hawaii: *Baehr v Miike*, Civil Case No. 91 1394 (First Circuit Court Hawaii, December 3, 1996), that the state had no reason to deny a marriage licence to a male same sex couple. In expectation of this judgment, the US Congress passed the Defence of Marriage Act 1996 which provides that any other US state need not recognise such a marriage.

[30] *Corbett v Corbett* [1971] P.83.

[31] *X Petr*, 1957 S.L.T. (Sh. Ct) 61.

[32] For a different approach see the Australian case of *Att-Gen (Cth) v Kevin and Jennifer* [2003] Fam CA 94 (February 21, 2003) where the full bench of the Family Court declined to follow *Corbett*, finding that post-operative transsexuals will normally be members of their reassigned sex.

on transgenderism and a lack of consensus amongst Convention signatory states as to how it should be dealt with legally as justifications for the position in UK law, which was said to fall within the state's margin of appreciation.[33]

This all changed in 2002 with the landmark Strasbourg decision in **9–08** *Goodwin v UK*.[34] The court held that, by that time, medical and societal views on transgenderism had evolved to the point where the lack of recognition for the correct genders of transpersons within UK law was no longer acceptable. It found that the right of transpersons under Art.8, to personal development and to physical and moral security in the full sense enjoyed by others in society, could no longer be regarded as a matter of controversy requiring the lapse of time to cast clearer light on the issues involved.

In order to bring the law into line with the Convention, the Gender **9–09** Recognition Act 2004 was enacted. Under the Act, a gender recognition certificate can be issued which gives full legal recognition to the applicant's correct gender, referred to in the legislation as the "acquired gender." A certificate can be issued by a Gender Recognition Panel if satisfied that the applicant (who must be at least 18)[35]:

- has or has had gender dysphoria. This is defined by s.25 as meaning "the disorder variously referred to as gender dysphoria, gender identity disorder and transsexualism"; and
- has lived in the acquired gender throughout the preceding two years; and
- intends to continue to live in the acquired gender until death.[36]

The application must contain a statutory declaration as to whether or not the applicant is married or in civil partnership.[37] Where the application is successful, the panel must grant a full gender recognition certificate so long as the applicant is not in a formalised adult relationship.[38] Where the successful applicant *is* in a formalised relationship, an interim gender recognition certificate is issued.[39] If the relationship is brought to an end on the basis of the interim certificate, the court must grant a full certificate at the same time as granting the decree of divorce or dissolution.[40] If the relationship is brought to an end in some other way within six months of the grant of the interim certificate, the person with the interim certificate may apply again to the panel within six months of the end

---

[33] See *Rees v UK* (1986) 9 E.H.R.R. 56; *Cossey v UK* [1991] 13 E.H.R.R. 622; *Sheffield v UK* [1998] 2 F.L.R. 928.
[34] *Goodwin v UK* (2002) 35 E.H.R.R. 18.
[35] 2004 Act s.1.
[36] 2004 Act s.2. This is to be established through the medical evidence of the type laid down in s.3. This includes a report from a registered medical practitioner, or a chartered psychologist, either of whom must be practicing in the field of gender dysphoria. This report must include details of diagnosis. The second report need not be from a medical professional practicing in the field of gender dysphoria, but could be from any registered medical practitioner. At least one of the reports must include details of any treatment that the applicant has undergone, is undergoing or that is prescribed or planned, for the purposes of modifying sexual characteristics.
[37] 2004 Act s.3(6).
[38] 2004 Act s.4(2).
[39] 2004 Act s.4(3).
[40] 2004 Act s.5(1).

of the relationship in order to obtain a full certificate. Where an application is rejected, applicants may appeal on a point of law to the Court of Session.[41] The Marriage and Civil Partnership (Scotland) Bill contains provisions that remove the requirement for a couple to divorce before a full certificate can be issued.[42]

9–10 On issuing a full gender recognition certificate, the Secretary of State must send a copy to the Registrar General for Scotland, where the applicant is entered in the United Kingdom birth register, so that a new entry may be created.[43] As a result the applicant will be entitled to a new birth certificate reflecting the correct gender.[44]

9–11 From that point onwards, the general principle is that the gender identified on the certificate is the legally relevant gender. Specific provision is made in the statute for some potentially complicated situations which result from this rule. In relation to succession, s.15 establishes that if a will refers to the "eldest daughter" and a person who was previously identified as a son comes to be identified as the "eldest daughter" following the grant of a certificate, that person (subject to s.18)[45] will inherit as the "eldest daughter". Likewise, s.13 establishes that persons are to be treated in their acquired gender for the purposes of obtaining state benefits,[46] although gender distinctions in benefits are being phased out and should have disappeared entirely by 2021.[47]

9–12 The Act also includes some exceptions to the general principle. Section 12 provides that where a transperson was the legal father or mother of a child prior to issue of the gender recognition certificate, that parental status will remain unchanged in order to ensure the continuity of parental responsibilities and rights. In other words a transwoman will remain the father of her

---

[41] 2004 Act s.8(1).

[42] Marriage and Civil Partnership (Scotland) Bill s.28 and Sch.2.

[43] 2004 Act s.10(4) brings Sch.3 dealing with registration into effect. Under Pt 2 of Sch.3 that deals with Scotland, the Registrar General is to maintain, in the General Register Office of Births, Deaths and Marriages in Scotland, a Gender Recognition Register ("GRR"). This register will not be open to public inspection or search. Where a full gender recognition certificate is issued the Registrar General must make an entry in the GRR and mark the original entry referring to the birth (or adoption) of the transsexual person to show that the original entry has been superceded. This will ensure that caution is exercised when an application is received for a certificate from the original birth (or adoption) record. If applicants for a birth certificate provide details of the name recorded on the birth certificate, they will be issued with a certificate from the birth record. If they supply details recorded on the GRR, they will receive a certificate complied from the entry in the GRR. The mark linking the two entries will be chosen carefully to ensure that the fact that an entry is contained in the GRR is not apparent. The mark will not be included in any certificate compiled from the entries on the register.

[44] 2004 Act s.9(1).

[45] This provides for an application to be made to the court in situations where the devolution of property may be adversely affected by the changes brought about by this Act.

[46] See Sch.5.

[47] Widowed Mother's Allowance, available for a maximum of 18 years under s.37 of the Social Security Contributions and Benefits Act 1992, and Widow's Pension, available for a maximum of 20 years under s.38 of the same Act, are available only to women widowed prior to April 2001, meaning the first will become obsolete by April 2019, and the second by April 2021. Category A retirement pensions—paid from a person's NI contributions—had for many years been available earlier to women (at age 60) than to men (age 65), but women's pensionable age is in the process of being raised gradually so that by 2020 both men and women will reach pensionable age at 66. For current information, see: *https://www.gov.uk/state-pension* [accessed August 5, 2013].

child after issue of the certificate; a transman will remain the mother of his child. Similarly, when it comes to dealing with criminal law, some definitions of sexual offences remain gender-specific and hence refer specifically to acts committed by a man upon a woman. Section 20 ensures that where criminal liability would exist, but for the fact that a person—either the victim or the perpetrator—has subsequent to the offence obtained a certificate, then criminal liability will exist regardless of the certificate.

Potentially the most complicated consequence of a gender recognition **9–13** certificate arises where the applicant is already party to a marriage or civil partnership. The right to marry had been at the heart of the human rights discussion of gender identity from the beginning; one of Christine Goodwin's arguments in support of legal recognition of her correct gender was that her birth-assigned sex prevented her from marrying her male partner. The 2004 Act resolved this problem, by enabling Goodwin and transpersons in her situation to marry in their correct gender following the issue of a certificate. But what of a case where a transperson was *already* married to someone of the opposite birth-assigned sex? Marriage is competent only between a man and a woman; civil partnership only between same-sex couples.[48] The 2004 Act does not presently permit a full gender recognition certificate to be issued in circumstances where the gender correction would result in a man being married to a man, a woman being married to a woman, or an opposite-sex couple being in civil partnership with each other. In such cases, an interim certificate is issued, on the basis of which the applicant may seek to dissolve the existing relationship. If decree of divorce or dissolution is granted, the applicant can then apply for a full certificate. This approach gave rise to further human rights challenges from married transpersons, who contended that their Art.8 rights were violated by being forced to make a choice between their gender and their marriage.[49] Although the court acknowledged this to be an accurate description of the situation in which transpersons found themselves, it was considered a necessary consequence of the institution of marriage as understood in the United Kingdom.

Same-sex Marriage

The position of married transpersons under the 2004 Act contributed to **9–14** a broader human rights debate on whether marriage should be available to same-sex couples. The Strasbourg court had historically adopted the position that regulation of the rights of same sex couples fell within the margin of appreciation of individual states, enabling same sex couples to be treated differently in law than opposite sex couples.[50] However, during the first decade of the twenty first century, the legal treatment of same sex relationships underwent a process of rapid change throughout Europe. At the start of the decade, same sex marriage was not possible anywhere in Europe. By the end,

---

[48] See the discussion at para.9–22.
[49] *R v United Kingdom* (35748/05) and *Parry v United Kingdom* (42971/05) Unreported November 28, 2006.
[50] *X and Y v United Kingdom* (1983) 32 D.R. 220; *Mata Estevez v Spain* (56501/00) Unreported May 10, 2001.

same sex couples could marry in seven European states[51] and register a form of civil union in a further 11.[52]

9–15 The Chamber of the Strasbourg Court considering the application in *Schalk and Kopf v Austria*[53] in 2010 therefore did so against a very different factual background than in previous cases on this topic. The applicants, a same sex couple, contended that their rights under Arts 8, 12 (right to marry) and 14 (freedom from discrimination) were not respected in Austrian law since it was not possible for them to marry or otherwise obtain formal recognition of their relationship.[54] The court adopted a middling position. It accepted that same sex couples can establish family life for the purposes of Art.8 and indicated that Art.12 was applicable to same sex couples in some circumstances. The language of the court broadly suggested that an absence of legal recognition in any form for same sex relationships will soon be found in violation of the Convention: it referred to the state margin of appreciation as encompassing the *timing* of legislative changes in this area, apparently presupposing that such changes will occur.[55] However, beyond that it considered regulation of same sex marriage to be an issue falling within the margin of appreciation of individual member states, particularly given that there is as yet no European consensus on the issue and therefore no obligation on states to extend marriage to same sex couples.

9–16 The decision can be criticised for a lack of internal consistency. The court accepted that Art.12 is relevant for same sex couples. Excluding them from marriage is therefore discrimination that requires to be justified under art.14. However, the decision offers no guidance on whether or why the distinction between marriage and civil unions is so justified. It may be hard to see what justification *could* be offered, although references to the "deep-rooted social and cultural connotations" of marriage "that may differ largely from one society to another"[56] and to the protection of "traditional" family as a "weighty and legitimate reason which might justify a difference in treatment"[57] may offer some clues to the court's thinking.

9–17 It seems likely that the matter will come before the Strasbourg court again in the near future. One pending application from the United Kingdom, *Ferguson v UK*,[58] has been made jointly by four same sex couples refused the right to marry and four opposite sex couples refused the right to register a civil partnership. The case does not argue that marriage should be available to same sex couples as of right, but that in a state where legal recognition is given to same sex partnerships by other means, it is discriminatory to only

---

[51] The Netherlands, Belgium, Spain, Norway, Sweden, Portugal and Iceland.

[52] France, Germany, Finland, Luxembourg, United Kingdom, Andorra, Czech Republic, Slovenia, Switzerland, Hungary and Austria.

[53] *Schalk and Kopf v Austria* (2011) 53 E.H.R.R. 20.

[54] The application was made in 2004. By 2010, Austria had introduced a form of civil union for same sex couples, although marriage continued to be reserved for opposite sex couples.

[55] *Schalk and Kopf v Austria* (2011) 53 E.H.R.R. 20 at para.105.

[56] *Schalk and Kopf v Austria* (2011) 53 E.H.R.R. 20 at para.62.

[57] *Schalk and Kopf v Austria* (2011) 53 E.H.R.R. 20 at para.77.

[58] A copy of the application is available at *http://equallove.org.uk/the-legal-case/* [accessed August 5, 2013].

allow opposite sex couples access to one and same sex couples access to the other. A hearing date is awaited.

In the meantime, the position within the United Kingdom has contin- **9–18**
ued to change. Following a consultation on religious civil partnership and same sex marriage in late 2011,[59] the Scottish Government announced an intention to legislate for same sex marriage.[60] Following a further period of consultation,[61] the Marriage and Civil Partnership (Scotland) Bill was introduced into Parliament in June 2013.[62] At Westminster, similar legislation for England and Wales in the form of the Marriage (Same Sex Couples) Act received Royal Assent in July 2013. Notwithstanding the continued strong opposition from certain quarters, it seems almost certain that same sex marriage will be possible throughout the United Kingdom in the near future. Account will be taken of this likely development in the following sections, as we consider in detail the process by which adult relationships are formed in law.

FORMATION OF ADULT RELATIONSHIPS

Three forms of adult relationship are recognised in Scotland – marriage, civil **9–19**
partnership and cohabitation. To marry, or to register a civil partnership, involves following a detailed process laid out in statute, the result of which is that a new legal status is acquired. Cohabitation, on the other hand, is a matter of fact rather than law. To be a cohabitant is something a person *does* rather than something a person *is*, strictly speaking. A cohabiting relationship is therefore "formed" simply by the parties living together and meeting the relevant statutory test. It is possible to find more than one statutory definition of cohabitation,[63] since different pieces of legislation seek to protect different aspects of non-marital cohabiting relationships. The most important in practice will be the definition in s.25 of the Family Law (Scotland) Act 2006, which determines whether a couple were cohabiting for the purposes of allowing financial claims at the end of the relationship. This will be discussed in detail in Ch.13.

The marriage process is governed by the Marriage (Scotland) Act 1977. **9–20**

---

[59] Scottish Government, *Consultation on registration of civil partnership, same sex marriage and related issues* (2011), available at: *http://www.scotland.gov.uk/Publications/2011/09/05153328/0* [accessed August 5, 2013]. The consultation received around 77,500 responses—the highest number for any Holyrood consultation to date.

[60] See the news release at *http://www.scotland.gov.uk/News/Releases/2012/07/same-sex25072012* [accessed August 5, 2013]. Criticisms have been levelled that the responses to the consultation did not support the Government's decision, for which see *Registration of Civil Partnerships, Same Sex Marriage: Consultation Analysis* (2012), available at: *http://www.scotland.gov.uk/Publications/2012/07/5671* [accessed August 5, 2013].

[61] Scottish Government, *The Marriage and Civil Partnership (Scotland) Bill: A Consultation* (2013). Available at *www.scotland.gov.uk/publications/2012/12/9433/0* [accessed August 5, 2013].

[62] Available at *www.scottish.parliament.uk/parliamentarybusiness/bills/64983.aspx* [accessed August 5, 2013].

[63] See for example Family Law (Scotland) Act 2006 s.25; Family Law (Matrimonial Homes) (Family Protection) (Scotland) Act 1981 s.18.

Registration of a civil partnership is governed by the Civil Partnership Act 2004. Since these two processes mirror each other, they will be treated together here, with differences pointed out where they arise. The impact of the proposed equal marriage legislation is also taken into account wherever relevant, although it should be kept in mind that the legislation as enacted may differ in the particulars from the Bill under consideration at the time of writing. In order to marry or register a civil partnership, parties must have capacity to do so, give their free consent, and comply with the requisite legal formalities. Each of these requirements will be considered in turn.

Capacity

9–21   The rules on capacity are set out in s.5 of the 1977 Act and s.86 of the 2004 Act. Where these rules have not been complied with, any purported marriage or civil partnership which results will be void. A declarator of nullity of marriage may be sought as evidence of this fact where, for example, a person wishes to have an erroneous entry deleted from the Marriage Register.

9–22   In the first place, parties seeking to marry must be of opposite sexes[64]; parties seeking to register a civil partnership must be of the same sex.[65] The proposed equal marriage legislation will open marriage to same-sex couples.[66] There is no intention at present to open civil partnership to opposite sex couples.[67] For these purposes, a party's sex will be as indicated on their birth certificate or gender recognition certificate, should one have been obtained.[68]

9–23   A person may not marry or register a civil partnership in Scotland until he is 16 years old.[69] It is also incompetent for an under-16 domiciled in Scotland to enter a formalised adult relationship in another jurisdiction, regardless of the age limit in place there.[70] Unlike in England, where parental consent is required for parties aged 16 or 17 to formalise their relationship,[71] consent or opposition by a parent is irrelevant in Scotland. The age of 16 is also the age at which the law recognises the right of individuals to enter into sexual relations with one another without incurring criminal sanctions.[72] These age limits reflect a concern to protect children from exploitation while at the same

---

[64] Marriage (Scotland) Act 1977 s.5(4)(e).
[65] Civil Partnership Act 2004 s.86(1)(a).
[66] Marriage and Civil Partnership (Scotland) Bill s.2.
[67] Scottish Government, *The Marriage and Civil Partnership (Scotland) Bill: A Consultation* (2013), para.4.20–4.21. Available at *http://www.scotland.gov.uk/Publications/2012/12/9433/0* [accessed August 5, 2013].
[68] The Gender Recognition Act 2004 enables transpersons to obtain a certificate giving recognition in law to the fact that the gender assigned to them at birth was incorrect.
[69] 1977 Act s.1(2); 2004 Act s.86(1)(c).
[70] 1977 Act s.1(1); 2004 Act s.217(3) and (4)
[71] Marriage Act 1949 s.3(1A); 2004 Act s.4.
[72] Sexual Offences Act 2003 s.9. Sexual activity between men of any age was a criminal offence in Scotland until the Criminal Justice (Scotland) Act 1980 s.80 introduced an age of consent at 21. This was reduced to 18 by the Criminal Law (Consolidation) (Scotland) Act 1995 s.13 and then to 16 by the Sexual Offences (Amendment) Act 2000 s.1. Section 1 of the 2000 Act also applied to sexual activity between women, which previously been neither illegal nor subject to an age of consent. The Sexual Offences Act 2003 replaced all earlier legislation.

time recognising an age at which young persons become sufficiently mature to make their own decisions. The age limit for adult relationships is in line with the broader provision that children obtain full legal capacity at 16,[73] discussed in Ch.2 above.

A person is not permitted to enter a formalised adult relationship if he is **9–24** already married or in civil partnership.[74] Any prior relationship must have been brought to an end by divorce, dissolution or death. A person who purports to enter a marriage or civil partnership whilst in a prior subsisting relationship commits a criminal offence.[75] Although it is not competent to enter a formalised polygamous relationship in Scotland, recognition will be given for certain purposes to polygamous relationships validly contracted in other jurisdictions.[76] The Scottish Government has made clear that it has no intention to introduce polygamous marriage here.[77] The proposed equal marriage legislation contains provisions enabling couples who are in civil partnership when the legislation is enacted to convert their relationship to marriage if they wish to do so. It will be necessary for such couples to participate in a marriage ceremony in the usual way. The marriage will bring the civil partnership to an end. However, rights and responsibilities accrued during the civil partnership will continue on into the marriage, making the two in effect one longer relationship recognised in law.[78]

A couple may not marry or register a civil partnership where they fall **9–25** within the forbidden degrees of relationship.[79] An individual may not enter a formalised adult relationship with any person who is related to him within a prohibited degree. The list of prohibited degrees is as follows:

(1) Relationships by consanguinity

Parent
Child
Parent's parent (grandparent)
Child's child (grandchild)

---

[73] Age of Legal Capacity (Scotland) Act 1991 s.1(1). In the past, Scots law recognised that girls could marry at 12 and boys at 14. These were the respective ages at which the sexes acquired the status of minor. However, the age limit for marriage was raised to 16 for both sexes by the Age of Marriage Act 1929.

[74] 1977 Act s.5(4)(b); 2004 Act s.86(1)(d).

[75] A person who attempts to marry whilst already married commits the common law offence of bigamy. A person who attempts to register a civil partnership whilst already married or in civil partnership commits an offence under the 2004 Act s.100. A person who attempts to marry whilst already in civil partnership is not covered by either of these offences, but would be guilty of making a false declaration under the 1977 Act s.24. The Government proposes to replace this legal patchwork with a new statutory offence of bigamy which applies to all the situations outlined above: Marriage and Civil Partnership (Scotland) Bill s.26.

[76] Matrimonial Proceedings (Polygamous Marriages) Act 1972; Private International Law (Miscellaneous Provisions) Act 1995 s.7(2).

[77] Scottish Government, *The Marriage and Civil Partnership (Scotland) Bill: A Consultation* (2013), paras 3.37–3.40. Available at *http://www.scotland.gov.uk/Publications/2012/12/9433/0* [accessed March 2013].

[78] Marriage and Civil Partnership (Scotland) Bill ss.7–9.

[79] 1977 Act s.2 and Sch.1; 2004 Act s.86 and Sch.10.

Sibling
Parent's sibling (aunt or uncle)
Sibling's child (niece or nephew)
Parent's parent's parent (great-grandparent)
Child's child's child (great-grandchild)

Relationships of the half blood are treated as being of the same order as relationships of the full blood.[80] So, for example, a half brother and sister (who share only one parent in common), are prohibited from marriage in just the same way as a brother and sister who share both parents in common. First cousins are permitted to enter a relationship.

(2) Relationships by affinity

Child of former spouse or civil partner (step-child)
Former spouse or civil partner of parent (step-parent)
Former spouse or civil partner of grandparent
Grandchild of former spouse or civil partner

An individual may enter a relationship with a person related to him by affinity as listed here provided that: (i) both parties have attained the age of 21 at the time of the marriage or civil partnership; and (ii) the younger party has not at any time before reaching the age of 18 lived in the same household as the other party and been treated as a child of the family.[81] So, for example, a woman may register a civil partnership with her ex-husband's daughter provided both are over the age of 21 *and* her former step-daughter never lived as a child within her former matrimonial household. The aim here is to allow parties who fall within the technical restriction of affinity to marry or enter a civil partnership, so long as they have never assumed a parent and child type of relationship with each other.

(3) Relationships by adoption

Adoptive parent or former adoptive parent
Adopted child or former adopted child

A person may enter a relationship with an adoptive sibling, provided no other prohibition applies. Although adoption severs all legal ties between biological parent and offspring, marriage or civil partnership between a child and a biological parent is nevertheless caught by the rules relating to consanguinity.[82] These rules also prohibit an adopted child from entering a relationship with a genetic sibling.

9–26   Relationships which fall within the prohibited degrees are definitively listed, so that where a relationship is not expressly struck at by the Act, the parties know they are free to marry or enter a civil partnership (barring some other type of impediment).

---

[80] 1977 Act s.2(2)(a); 2004 Act s.86(9).
[81] 1977 Act s.2(1A); 2004 Act s.86(3)–(5).
[82] Adoption and Children (Scotland) Act 2007 s.41(1)(a).

What are the policy reasons underlying these prohibitions? The division **9–27** between the categories derives from Christian morals and values embedded in canon law. So, for example, marriage with affinal relations was struck down on the basis of the Augustinian doctrine that when a man and a woman married they become of one flesh rendering the blood relations of one the blood relations of the other and thus ineligible for marriage.[83] The prohibitions have been maintained despite the waning influence of canon law since other policy considerations continue to underpin their existence. The risk of birth defects in children born to parents who are closely genetically related is one obvious reason for consanguinity-related prohibitions on marriage. The risk of abuse where one person is in a position of trust in relation to the other, as with a step- or adoptive parent and child, may help to explain the other rules.

Consent

Formalised adult relationships in Scotland must be entered voluntarily. **9–28** Consent is therefore a vital component of entering such a relationship. The emphasis that Scots law places on consent may be traced back as far as the Institutional writers and Stair's observation that marriage "is, and ought to be, of the most free consent".[84] Parties are ineligible to enter a relationship where they are incapable of giving consent.[85] Where both parties have the requisite capacity, a purported relationship will be void where consent is given only by reason of duress or error.[86]

A person may be incapable of giving consent as a result of a mental illness **9–29** or impairment of some kind. The mere existence of mental illness is not an issue in itself: what matters is whether the individual is "capable of understanding the [relationship] and giving consent thereto"[87] at the time that the marriage or partnership ceremony takes place. Marriage and civil partnership are easy contracts to understand. Proving that a person did not hold the requisite capacity is therefore a difficult task. In *Long v Long*,[88] it was held that although a young woman had been subject to supervision in an institution for long periods of time as a result of learning or developmental difficulties, she was nonetheless capable of understanding the nature of marriage and of giving her consent at the time when she participated in a wedding ceremony. Where a person does not have the required capacity at the time of the ceremony, any purported relationship will be void.[89]

---

[83] It has been observed that at one stage in Scottish history this doctrine, taken to its extreme, gave rise to a situation where it "was surprising that any valid marriage could have taken place in Scotland at all": Clive and Wilson, *The Law of Husband and Wife in Scotland* (Edinburgh: W. Green, 1974), p.88.

[84] Stair, i.4.1.

[85] 1977 Act s.5(4)(d); 2004 Act s.86(1)(e).

[86] 1977 Act s.20A; 2004 Act s.123.

[87] *Long v Long*, 1950 S.L.T. (Notes) 32.

[88] *Long v Long*, 1950 S.L.T. (Notes) 32.

[89] 1977 Act s20A(3); 2004 Act s.86(1)(e).

Duress

9–30   Where a person does have the necessary capacity, his consent may never-theless be vitiated by duress or error. Duress refers to a situation in which a party has uttered words of consent only because he has been threatened or subjected to some kind of external pressure. In the general law of contract in Scotland, this is referred to as "force and fear."[90] A bride who goes through a wedding ceremony only because she has a gun to her head, for example, could not be said to have freely consented to the marriage. In practice, duress is more likely to come in the form of emotional or financial threats. For duress to be established, it must be shown that the free will of the party raising the plea was genuinely overcome by external pressure. If consent was given only by reason of duress, any purported relationship will be void.[91]

9–31   Arranged marriages have subjected this difficult area of law to scrutiny. In *Mahmood v Mahmood*[92] and *Mahmud v Mahmud*[93] the petitioners, a woman and a man respectively, sought to have their marriages annulled on the basis of force and fear in the form of familial pressure. In *Mahmood*, the marriage was arranged between the two families in 1983 without the woman's knowl-edge. She was informed of the arrangement in March 1988 and pressure was put on her to consent to the marriage. It was alleged that her parents had threatened to disown her, to stop supporting her financially and to send her to live in Pakistan if she refused to go through with the marriage. In addition, she was informed that her failure to consent to the marriage would bring disgrace not only on herself, but on the Pakistani community in Edinburgh. Aged 21, aware that her elder brother and sister had been disowned by her family for this reason, and totally dependent on her family financially, she went through with the marriage ceremony in April 1988, although she had informed her prospective husband that she did not want to marry him. The parties lived together for only three months (until the end of July) during which time they rarely spoke to each other and had sexual intercourse only twice. At the end of that time the woman raised an action to have the mar-riage annulled on the basis of her lack of consent.

9–32   The husband argued that the threats were not of such gravity as to sway or overcome the will of an ordinary person. Previous case law had established that threats must be sufficient to cause fear of immediate danger to life, limb or liberty.[94] Lord Sutherland, however, held that the specific threats averred would support a plea of force and fear if they exceeded the limits of proper parental influence. It was not sufficient for the pursuer simply to claim that her will had been overcome by fear of her parents' or community's disap-proval. Nonetheless, the whole circumstances leading up to the marriage cer-emony, combined with evidence of what happened after the ceremony, might demonstrate that her consent was not genuine and was made under duress.[95]

---

[90] McBryde, *The Law of Contract in Scotland*, 2nd edn (Edinburgh: W. Green, 2001), para.17.02. Duress, the equivalent term in English law, is the term used in the 1977 and 2004 Acts.

[91] 1977 Act s.20A(1) and (2); 2004 Act s.123(1)(c).

[92] *Mahmood v Mahmood*, 1993 S.L.T. 589.

[93] *Mahmud v Mahmud*, 1994 S.L.T. 599.

[94] See *Szechter v Szechter* [1971] P.286.

[95] This was the term used by Lord Sutherland, 1993 S.L.T. 589 at 592.

This approach was followed in *Mahmud*, in which the male petitioner **9–33** was 31 years old. As in the previous case, a marriage had been arranged on his behalf many years earlier with a woman in Pakistan. In 1992, he found himself under pressure to marry this woman on the basis that, as the youngest son in a Muslim culture, it was his duty to provide a wife to look after his ailing mother, and that failure to follow through on the marriage would bring dishonour to his family and the Pakistani community in Scotland and Pakistan. At this time he was living with another woman in Scotland and they were expecting their first child. Bowing to family pressure, he went through a ceremony of marriage with the woman from Pakistan. However, he did not see this woman before the marriage ceremony, which took place in a registry office on his way to work, or after the event. The woman was subsequently deported back to her home in Pakistan. In this case, Lord Prosser held that the sustained pressure from the man's family had destroyed the reality of his consent to the marriage and overborne his will.

A more recent example can be found in *Sohrab v Khan*.[96] The pursuer, who **9–34** was 19 years old at the time of the action, had been 16 when she went through a marriage ceremony arranged by her parents without her consent. She had been told of the wedding a week before it was due to take place, and when she protested, in addition to the threat of ostracism from her family and the community, her mother said she would commit suicide if the pursuer did not comply. The ceremony had taken place in December 1998. The parties ceased living together the following April, and their cohabitation during that four-month period was described as "short, unhappy and interrupted".[97] Lord McEwan accepted that the pursuer had been put under more pressure than a 16 year old could bear, and that her will had been broken. The marriage was declared void.

It is important to stress that these cases do not establish a general ruling **9–35** that arranged marriages are invalid. The fact that a marriage has been arranged does not, in itself, represent an inherently forceful imposition of the parents' will. The question in every case is whether the will of the party has been overcome by the pressure imposed.

A clear distinction should also be drawn between the broad category of **9–36** arranged marriage and its abusive subset of forced marriage. This refers to cases in which an individual, usually a woman, is intimidated and threatened with or subjected to physical violence in order to compel her to go through with a marriage. Under the Forced Marriage etc (Protection and Jurisdiction) (Scotland) Act 2011, the court is empowered to grant a "forced marriage protection order" effectively interdicting threatening conduct designed to coerce a person into entering a marriage.[98] Breach of this order is a criminal offence.[99] The Act also makes provision for persons subject to threatening behaviour to be taken to a place of safety.[100] Orders under the Act can be

---

[96] *Sohrab v Khan*, 2002 S.C. 382.
[97] *Sohrab v Khan*, 2002 S.C. 382 at 392.
[98] 2011 Act ss.1 and 2.
[99] 2011 Act s.9.
[100] 2011 Act s.2.

sought by the person seeking protection or a relevant third party,[101] which might include a social worker or a representative of a relevant organisation such as Scottish Women's Aid.

Error

9–37   Consent to marriage or civil partnership may also be vitiated by error on limited grounds. Where a person is in error as to the nature of the ceremony, any purported relationship which follows will be void.[102] Although there is no reported case law, it is possible to imagine that this type of error could arise, for example, where the practice amongst adherents of a particular religion was for the legal marriage ceremony to take place at a separate date and time from the religious marriage ceremony. In such a situation, it might be reasonable that a party to the marriage did not comprehend the significance of the legal ceremony, considering rather that the religious ceremony would be the one which "counted".

9–38   The other potential ground of error sufficient to vitiate consent is described in the 1977 Act as

> "a mistaken belief held by a person ('A') that the other party at the ceremony with whom A purported to enter into a marriage was the person whom A had agreed to marry."[103]

Equivalent wording is found in the 2004 Act.[104] The essence of this ground is that the person who appeared at the ceremony must have impersonated the party A intended to enter a relationship with. If Anna went through a wedding ceremony with her long-term partner Bob, only to discover after the ceremony that it was actually Bob's identical twin brother Colin who had been standing in his place, the marriage would be void. What will not be sufficient to vitiate consent is a mistaken belief as to the character, wealth or any other quality of the other party to the relationship. If Anna went through a wedding ceremony with Bob believing him to be a millionaire, only to discover after the ceremony that he was penniless, the marriage would remain valid.

9–39   Examples can be found in the case law. In the leading authority of *Lang v Lang*,[105] a man was induced to marry a pregnant woman in the belief that he was the father of her child. When it became clear that he could not be the father, due to the very short gestational period that would have been involved, he sought to have the marriage annulled on the basis of essential error and fraudulent misrepresentation. He was not successful. In *McLeod v Adams*,[106] the pursuer married a man who told her he was a sergeant in the Black Watch with a substantial sum in the bank. After the wedding, he disap-

---

[101] 2011 Act s.3.
[102] 1977 Act s20A(5)(a); 2004 Act s.123(2)(a).
[103] 1977 Act s.20(5)(b).
[104] 2004 Act s.123(2)(b).
[105] *Lang v Lang*, 1921 S.C. 44.
[106] *McLeod v Adams*, 1920 1 S.L.T. 229.

peared, taking her life savings with him. It transpired he was a deserter from the army who had no money. The marriage was nevertheless valid.

Formalities of Constitution

Parties who fulfil the capacity requirements and give free consent must   **9–40** also go through the necessary procedural formalities in order to validly constitute their marriage or civil partnership. In the first place, parties must submit a notice of intention to marry or a notice of proposed civil partnership to the registrar of the district in which the ceremony is to take place.[107] Each party must submit a notice, accompanied by a birth certificate,[108] and where either party has previously been in a formalised relationship, evidence of the dissolution of that relationship.[109] After receipt of the notice, the registrar—if satisfied that there is no legal impediment or if so informed by the Registrar General—issues a marriage or civil partnership schedule which is the authority for the formalisation of the relationship.[110] The schedule may not, however, be issued before the expiry of 14 days from receipt of the notice unless on the written request of a party to the relationship and with the authority of the Registrar General.[111] The Marriage and Civil Partnership (Scotland) Bill contains provisions increasing this time period to 28 days.[112]

Once the marriage or partnership schedule is issued, parties participate   **9–41** in a ceremony to formalise the relationship. The terminology varies: marriages are said to be solemnised at such ceremonies; civil partnerships are said to be registered. For the sake of simplicity, the word "formalise" will be used here to refer to all instances of this process. Marriages in Scotland can be formalised in a civil ceremony or a religious ceremony. Civil partnerships can only be formalised in a civil ceremony at present,[113] but when the new equal marriage legislation is enacted, religious ceremonies will also be possible.[114] The Government additionally intends to introduce a third form of ceremony—known as a "belief ceremony"—to be celebrated by representatives of non-religious organisations such as the Scottish Humanist Society.[115]

A civil ceremony must be conducted by an authorised registrar[116] and is   **9–42** normally conducted at the registrar's office.[117] At present, parties who wish

---

[107] 1977 Act s.3; 2004 Act s.88(1).
[108] 1977 Act s.3(1); 2004 Act s.88(2)(a).
[109] 1977 Act s.3(1); 2004 Act s.88(2)(b).
[110] 1977 Act s.6; 2004 Act s.94.
[111] 1977 Act s.6(4); 2004 Act s.91.
[112] Marriage and Civil Partnership (Scotland) Bill s.16(2).
[113] 2004 Act s.93.
[114] Marriage and Civil Partnership (Scotland) Bill s.22.
[115] Marriage and Civil Partnership (Scotland) Bill ss.10–12. Humanist celebrants have been authorised to conduct religious ceremonies since 2005, but since the beliefs of such organisations are not religious, it was considered appropriate to introduce a third category of ceremony.
[116] This is a district or assistant district registrar appointed in term of s.17 of the 1977 Act.
[117] In exceptional cases, e.g. where a person is seriously ill or suffering from serious bodily injury and is unable to attend and there is good reason why the marriage cannot be delayed, a

to conduct a civil marriage ceremony somewhere other than the registry office must seek approval for the venue from the local authority.[118] This restriction is to be removed by the new marriage legislation, so that parties may hold their ceremony at any place agreed by the registrar and the couple,[119] as is already the case for partnership ceremonies.[120] The marriage or partnership schedule must be available to the authorised registrar. Both parties must be present together along with two witnesses aged 16 or over.[121] There is no prescribed form of ceremony laid down by the Act but it generally follows a certain procedure which involves the registrar explaining the nature of the relationship in Scots law and asking the parties to declare if they know of any legal impediment to their relationship. The parties are then asked to take each other as spouses or civil partners and to exchange consent to the relationship. After they have done so, the registrar declares them to be married or civil partners. The schedule is signed by both parties, the witnesses and the registrar.[122] The relationship is then entered into the Marriage or Civil Partnership Register.

9–43   A religious ceremony may be conducted by a minister of the Church of Scotland, a minister, clergyman, pastor or priest of a religious body prescribed by the regulations, or other approved celebrant.[123] Celebrants of prescribed religious bodies are automatically authorised to conduct opposite sex marriages, but will have to opt-in to conduct same sex marriage or civil partnership ceremonies.[124] Again, the schedule must be produced to the celebrant and both parties to the relationship must be present along with two witnesses aged 16 or over. Where the celebrant belongs to the Church of Scotland or a prescribed religious body, the ceremony must be in accordance with a form recognised as sufficient by the church or body to which the celebrant belongs.[125] In any other case, the statutory requirement is that the ceremony must include a declaration by the parties, in the presence of each other, the celebrant and the witnesses, that they accept each other as spouses and a declaration by the celebrant thereafter that they are spouses.[126] After the ceremony, the schedule is signed by both parties, the witnesses and

---

registrar may give special dispensation for it to be solemnised elsewhere, e.g. in a hospital. See s.18(4)(a) and (b).

[118] 1977 Act ss.18 and 18A.
[119] Marriage and Civil Partnership (Scotland) Bill s.19.
[120] 2004 Act s.93.
[121] 1977 Act s.19(2); 2004 Act s.85. The requirement in the 1977 Act is for two witnesses "professing to be 16 years of age or older", whereas the 2004 Act requires the witnesses to have "attained the age of 16". It is not thought that this difference in wording would lead to different results in practice.
[122] 1977 Act s.19(3); 2004 Act s.85(4).
[123] 1977 Act ss.8(1), 9 and 12. See also Marriage (Prescription of Religious Bodies) (Scotland) Regulations 1977 (SI 1977/1670). Amendments are proposed to the 2004 Act to mirror the 1977 Act scheme here; Marriage and Civil Partnership (Scotland) Bill s.19.
[124] This approach was found necessary to protect the right to freedom of thought, conscience and religion of celebrants who consider formalised same sex relationships to be contrary to their religious beliefs. See the discussion at Scottish Government, *The Marriage and Civil Partnership (Scotland) Bill: A Consultation* (2013), paras 3.03–3.07 and Annex A. Available at *http://www.scotland.gov.uk/Publications/2012/12/9433/0* [accessed March 2013].
[125] 1977 Act s.14(a).
[126] 1977 Act s.14(b) and s.9(3).

the celebrant. It must then be returned to the district registrar for registration within three days of the ceremony, to be entered into the appropriate Register.[127]

Belief ceremonies will operate in the same way as religious ceremonies. **9–44** Belief bodies will be prescribed by regulations made by Scottish Ministers. Celebrants ascribed to those bodies will automatically be authorised to conduct opposite sex marriage ceremonies, and will be able to opt-in to conduct same sex marriage or civil partnership ceremonies.[128]

It is an offence for anyone who is not within the classes of person author- **9–45** ised to formalise a relationship to conduct a ceremony in such a way as to lead the parties to believe that he is formalising a valid relationship. It is also an offence for the celebrant to conduct a religious ceremony without at the time having the schedule, or for either a religious celebrant or an authorised registrar to conduct a ceremony without both parties being present.[129] Provided both parties had capacity, gave consent, were present at the ceremony *and* the relationship has been registered, its validity is not to be questioned in any legal proceedings on the ground of failure to comply with a requirement or restriction imposed by the legislation.[130] This provision does not save a relationship that has never been registered and where no schedule was ever issued.[131] In such a case the relationship is void.

Impediments to Formalising a Relationship

At any time before the formalisation of a relationship, any person may **9–46** submit an objection in writing to the registrar.[132] Where the objection relates to a matter of misdescription or inaccuracy, the registrar may, with the approval of the Registrar General, make any necessary correction. In any other case he must, pending consideration of the objection by the Registrar General, suspend the completion or issue of the schedule or, if a schedule has already been issued for a religious ceremony, notify the celebrant of the objection and advise him not to formalise the relationship.[133] If the Registrar General is satisfied on consideration of an objection that parties do not have capacity to enter the relationship for any of the reasons discussed at paras 9–21 to 9–27 above, he must direct the registrar to take all reasonable steps to ensure that the ceremony does not take place. If on the other hand he is satisfied that there is no legal impediment, he must inform the registrar and the schedule may then be completed and issued at that stage so that the ceremony may proceed.[134]

---

[127] 1977 Act s.15(2).
[128] Marriage and Civil Partnership (Scotland) Bill s.10.
[129] 1977 Act, s.24; 2004 Act, s.100(2).
[130] 1997 Act, s.23A; 2004 Act s.95A.
[131] *Saleh v Saleh*, 1987 S.L.T. 633.
[132] 1977 Act s.5(1); 2004 Act s.92(1).
[133] 1977 Act s.5(2); 2004 Act s.92(4).
[134] 1977 Act s.5(3) and s.6(1); 2004 Act s.92(5).

Defects and Invalidity: Effect on Relationship

9-47   Where a relationship is void as a result of lack of capacity, absent or defective consent, or failure to comply with the procedural formalities in a way that cannot be resolved by s.23A of the 1977 Act or s.95A of the 2004 Act, either party can apply to the sheriff court or petition the Court of Session for declarator of nullity. A court, on granting declarator of nullity, has the same powers to award financial provision in respect of a void relationship as it has on granting a decree of divorce or dissolution.[135]

Irregular Marriage

9-48   It used to be possible to constitute a marriage in Scotland without complying with the formal requirements set out above. Such marriages, referred to as irregular marriages, came into being by operation of law where parties fulfilled certain requirements.[136] Only one form of irregular marriage has any continuing relevance today; marriage by cohabitation with habit and repute.[137] (Despite the overlapping terminology, it should be noted that this is quite separate from the legal relationship of (non-marital) cohabitation which is dealt with elsewhere.) This form of marriage arises where a couple have set up home together without going through *any* form of ceremony, or where the ceremony was invalid. It operates on the presumption that *tacit* consent to marriage is constituted by the cohabitation, as man and wife,[138] in Scotland,[139] of a couple free to marry, who are generally reputed to *be* husband and wife. The presumption is rebuttable. There are two major hurdles to be overcome in establishing a marriage of this kind, first, by satisfying the requirement that the cohabitation must be for a considerable period,[140] and secondly, fulfilling the requirements of habit and repute.[141] It has been established that there is no minimum period required for cohabitation.[142] To meet the second requirement however, not only must the parties behave towards one another as husband and wife but they must also be believed to be such by third parties. According to *Low v Gorman*,[143] "although repute need not be universal it must be general, substantially unvarying and consistent and not divided". The opinion of others comes into play and the weight attached to their opinions varies.[144] It is clear that if parties openly admit that they are

---

[135] Family Law (Scotland) Act 1985 s.17(1).

[136] For discussion, see Sutherland, paras 12-095–12-102.

[137] The other two were declaration *de praesenti* and promise *subsequent copula* both of which were abolished by s.5 of the Marriage (Scotland) Act 1939.

[138] Note that it is not cohabitation *per se* that gives rise to the presumption but cohabitation as husband and wife.

[139] See Lord Watson's dicta to this effect in the *Dysart Peerage Case* (1881) L.R. 6 App. Cas. 489 at 537–538.

[140] *Campbell v Campbell* (1866) 4 M. 867.

[141] See *Ackerman v Blackburn*, 2002 S.L.T. 37 where the court held that the evidence fell far short of establishing the pursuer's averments of general repute.

[142] See *Kamperman v MacIver*, 1994 S.L.T. 763 where the court held that a period of cohabitation lasting 6 and a half months after an impediment to marriage was removed was not insufficient.

[143] *Low v Gorman*, 1970 S.L.T. 356 at 395.

[144] See *Petrie v Petrie*, 1911 S.C. 360 where the court placed greater weight on the evidence of the man's professional colleagues and relatives, who considered him unmarried, compared with

not married then marriage on the basis of cohabitation with habit and repute can never be established. The issue of admissions to certain third parties is, however, less clear cut. In *Mackenzie v Scott*,[145] the court refused to grant a declarator of marriage on the basis that, as several friends knew that the couple were not in fact married, and that they had discussed getting married on several occasions, all they had was a *future* intention to marry and that they did not regard themselves as married. This case may be contrasted with that of *Shaw v Henderson*[146] where the court granted a declarator in circumstances very similar to those of *MacKenzie v Scott*, adopting the view that while relatives knew that the couple had never gone through *any* form of ceremony this did not mean that they did not regard themselves as being husband and wife. This approach was criticised in *Kamperman v McIver*[147] but followed in *Dewar v Dewar*.[148]

The fact that there was a legal impediment to marriage when the cohabita-   **9–49**
tion began does not preclude the constitution of marriage by continuance of the cohabitation with repute after the parties become free to marry,[149] although circumstances after the removal of the impediment must be sufficient in themselves to establish the inference of tacit consent.[150] Consent to marriage may be proved by cohabitation with habit and repute where spouses have previously been married to one another and divorced.[151] A declarator of marriage must be sought from the court before the legal rights and obligations that attach to marriage will apply to a marriage constituted by consent following relevant cohabitation with habit and repute.[152] The SLC recommended that, given the uncertain status of habit and repute marriage, such marriages should be abolished.[153] After consultation, the Scottish Executive initially declined to implement this recommendation on the basis that they did not "wish to penalise those who wish to benefit from this form of marriage, however irregular it may be".[154] The Scottish Parliament, however, took the view that this type of marriage was obsolete and abolished it prospectively, except in the case of invalid marriages entered into abroad, where

---

the views of persons such as the cleaner and the postman. See also *Ackerman v Blackburn*, 2002 S.L.T. 37, above, where the parties were considered married by neighbours, customers of the pursuer's shop and members of the various organisations with which the deceased was involved, but not by close family members of the deceased. In weighing the evidence the views of the latter prevailed. Also *Skeikh v Skeikh*, 2005 Fam. L.R. 7 in which the woman's parents knew she was not married but those encountering the couple in daily life assumed they were. The woman had not wanted to enter marriage via a muslim ceremony as offered by the male. Declarator was granted.

[145] *Mackenzie v Scott*, 1980 S.L.T. (Notes) 9.
[146] *Shaw v Henderson*, 1982 S.L.T. 211.
[147] *Kamperman v McIver*, 1993 S.L.T. 732.
[148] *Dewar v Dewar*, 1995 S.L.T. 467.
[149] *Campbell v Campbell* (1867) 5 M. (HL) 115.
[150] *Low v Gorman*, 1970 S.L.T. 356; *S v S*, 2006 S.L.T. 471.
[151] *Mullen v Mullen*, 1991 S.L.T. 205.
[152] Where such a declarator is granted the court must, under s.21 of the 1977 Act, state the date on which the marriage was constituted and forward it to the Registrar General for registration.
[153] See *Report on Family Law* (1992), para.7.9.
[154] See *Parents and Children* (2000), para.10.5.

one of parties to that marriage has died.[155] In this situation, where the parties were married "outwith the United Kingdom" and the marriage proves to be invalid under the law of the place where the purported marriage was entered into, a marriage by cohabitation with habit and repute may be established. This is dependent upon *all* the following factors being met, namely:

- both parties' belief that they are married to one another up until the death of one of them[156];
- both the deceased and surviving party are domiciled in Scotland at the date of death[157]; and
- that the surviving party only became aware of the invalidity of the purported marriage after the other party's death.[158]

9–50 In all other cases, it will no longer be competent to establish marriage by cohabitation with habit and repute for cohabitation entered into *on and after* May 4, 2006 when the Family Law (Scotland) Act 2006 came into effect. This will not, however, have any effect on the validity of marriages of this type entered into before the Act took effect or where the cohabitation with habit and repute:

- ended before the commencement of s.3(1)[159]; or
- began before, but ended after commencement[160]; or
- began before, and continues after, commencement.[161]

Parties in either of the latter two categories will have the alternative of exercising rights under ss.25 to 29 of the 2006 Act, discussed at paras 13–91 to 13–102. Parties who did not commence cohabiting until after May 4, 2006 will have no option but to use the provisions of the 2006 Act.

9–51 In the next chapter we consider the effect of marriage, civil partnership and cohabitation upon the legal rights of individuals entering such a relationship and upon their property.

---

[155] FLSA 2006 s.3(3) and (4).
[156] FLSA 2006 s.3(4)(d).
[157] FLSA 2006 s.3(4)(a) and (b).
[158] FLSA 2006 s.3(2)(a).
[159] FLSA 2006 s.3(2)(a).
[160] FLSA 2006 s.3(2)(b).
[161] FLSA 2006 s.3(2)(c).

CHAPTER 10

DOMESTIC RELATIONS, PERSONS AND PROPERTY

In Ch.9, we discussed the rules for establishing a valid marriage and a valid **10–01** civil partnership. Logically, the next question that arises is, what legal effect does marriage and civil partnership have on the person and property of spouses and civil partners? Further, are such persons treated in a different manner from unmarried heterosexual and same-sex couples?

At one time, a husband acquired, on marriage, complete rights to his wife's **10–02** moveable property, a right known as *the jus mariti*. He also acquired the more limited right to administer her heritable property by virtue of *the jus administrationis*. Even after *the jus mariti* was abolished in 1881,[1] the husband retained the right of administration in respect of the whole of a wife's property, heritable and moveable, until 1920. At that date, however, the Married Women's Property (Scotland) Act 1920 established the basic principle of modern Scots law (now to be found in s.24 of the Family Law (Scotland) Act 1985) that marriage "shall not of itself" affect the respective rights of the parties to the marriage in relation to

(a) their property, or
(b) their legal capacity.

Thus, spouses are free to acquire, own and dispose of property as though unmarried; enter into contracts as independent persons; sue each other in delict; and may be prosecuted for crimes committed one against the other (such as theft or assault). However, these general propositions are subject to certain qualifications which will be examined in this and succeeding chapters.

MARRIAGE, CIVIL PARTNERSHIP, AND PERSONAL STATUS

Domicile and Residence

At one time, the domicile of both the wife and any children of a marriage **10–03** was dependent on, and followed, that of the husband. The husband also had the right to determine where the matrimonial home should be located and a wife who refused to reside there could be divorced for desertion, unless she could establish that the husband's choice was not genuine or reasonable.[2] Section 1 of the Domicile and Matrimonial Proceedings Act 1973 abolished the wife's domicile of dependence, and established that a married woman

---

[1] Under the Married Women's Property (Scotland) Act 1881 s.1.
[2] *Stewart v Stewart*, 1959 S.L.T. (Notes) 70.

could acquire a domicile of choice in the same way as any other person over the age of 16.[3] Further, in 1984, the husband's right to determine the location of the matrimonial home was abolished along with certain other outdated rules affecting spouses.[4] In Scots law, a woman has always been entitled to retain her own surname on marriage. The custom of women adopting their husband's surnames on marriage is said to have crept into Scotland in the first half of the nineteenth century.[5] Prior to that, it was the custom for a married woman to retain her own name.[6] Current practice in formal legal documents is for a married woman to be cited by reference to both her maiden name and her husband's surname.

10–04   The domicile of a child is determined by the domicile of his/her parents under the age of 16[7] or, if the parents do not live in the same country as each other, then the domicile "for which the child has for the time being the closest connection".[8] Once a child attains the age of 16 s/he becomes capable of having independent domicile.[9]

Sexual Relations, Fidelity, and Marital Rape

10–05   It is clear that spouses have a duty to adhere, i.e. to live together and be sexually faithful with respect to one another. The duty of adherence can no longer be enforced by court action,[10] but where a spouse is unfaithful, grounds exist for divorce.[11] What has been controversial in recent years is the extent to which spouses are obliged to have marital sexual relations. Scots law certainly recognises that sex is an important component of marriage, and that incurable and permanent impotency at the date of marriage (as opposed to wilful non-consummation) gives either party the right to have the marriage declared voidable.[12]

10–06   Does this mean that a husband may use force to compel his wife to accede to sexual relations? Where this occurs between parties who are not spouses, this constitutes the crime of rape. It is only over the last 26 years or so that

---

[3] Transitional problems persisted for women who had already acquired a domicile of dependence before the 1973 Act came into force: see *IRC v Duchess of Portland* [1982] 1 All E.R. 784.

[4] Law Reform (Husband and Wife) (Scotland) Act 1984 s.4.

[5] See E. Clive, *The Law of Husband and Wife in Scotland*, 4th edn (Edinburgh: W.Green, 1997), para.11.019 for further details.

[6] See *Grieve v Pringle* (1797) Mor. 5951.

[7] Family Law (Scotland) Act 2006 s.22(1) and (2). Prior to the 2006 Act, a legitimate child took domicile of dependence from the father (unless s/he did not reside with him as there was a statutory exception to the general rule under the Domicile and Matrimonial Proceedings Act 1973). Under the common law, however, a child whose parents were unmarried took the domicile of his or her mother.

[8] Family Law (Scotland) Act 2006 s.22(3).

[9] Age of Legal Capacity (Scotland) Act 1991 s.7.

[10] Law Reform (Husband and Wife) (Scotland) Act 1984 s.2.

[11] On the basis of adultery under s.1(2)(a) of the Divorce (Scotland) Act 1976.

[12] Impotency is the only ground on which a marriage can be declared voidable in Scots law. The Scottish Law Commission recommended its abolition in *Improving Scottish Family Law* (Scottish Office, 1999). However, as this would effectively remove the only civil law remedy available to those whose religious beliefs forbid divorce, the recommendation was not followed. For a fuller discussion of voidable marriage see Edwards and Griffiths, *Family Law*, 1st edn, paras 9.31 *et seq.*

marital rape has been recognised as a crime by the courts, first in Scotland[13] and then in England.[14] The courts were reluctant to accord recognition to marital rape, not only because of difficulties of proof in a situation where the parties already have an intimate relationship, but also because of antique Institutional authority. According to Hume, a husband could not rape his wife.[15] This rested on the belief that when a woman consented to marriage, she thereby irrevocably consented to sexual intercourse with her husband. Over the last 25 years, however, the Scottish courts have unpicked the husband's immunity from prosecution for marital rape, at first only in cases where the parties were actually living apart when the alleged rape took place,[16] and latterly even where spouses continued to cohabit.[17] As the Lord Justice-General put it in *S v HM Advocate*:

> "Nowadays it cannot seriously be maintained that by marriage a wife submits herself irrevocably to sexual intercourse in all circumstances . . . the fiction of implied consent has no useful purpose to serve today in the law of rape in Scotland . . . logically the only question is whether or not as matter of fact the wife consented to the acts complained of".[18]

Contract and Delict

As noted earlier, married women and men can sue and be sued, in contract and delict, even though the other party to the action is their spouse.[19] Marriage does not make one spouse automatically liable for the debts, obligations or delicts of the other spouse.

10–07

At one time, a husband was responsible for his wife's antenuptial debts, and was also personally liable for household debts contracted by his wife, since by law she had ostensible authority to contract on behalf of her husband in the domestic sphere (*praepositura rebus domesticis*). These rules have now been repealed.[20] But it is still, anomalously, possible for a woman to pledge her husband's credit for necessaries at common law,[21] and he would then be liable for any debt. However, this rule of law has now become obsolete as very few shopkeepers would today hand over goods on a mere private pledge of credit, nor are most members of the public aware the rule exists. The rule extends

10–08

---

[13] *S v HM Advocate*, 1989 S.L.T. 469.

[14] *R v R* [1992] A.C. 599, HL. An attempt to challenge the concept of marital rape by taking the matter to the European Court failed in *SW v UK; CR v UK* [1996] Fam law 275, ECtHR.

[15] Hume, I, 302.

[16] *HM Advocate v Duffy*, 1983 S.L.T. 7; *HM Advocate v Paxton*, 1985 S.L.T. 96.

[17] *S v HM Advocate*, 1989 S.L.T. 469.

[18] *S v HM Advocate*, 1989 S.L.T. 469 at 473.

[19] While the Married Women's Property Act 1920 s.1 gave married women the same legal capacity to *enter into* contracts as unmarried women, it was not until *Horsburgh v Horsburgh*, 1949 S.C. 227 that it was established that it was competent for spouses to sue each other in contract. The right to sue one another in delict was established by s.2 of the Law Reform (Husband and Wife) Act 1962.

[20] The ante-nuptial debts rule (by s.6) and the *praepositura* (by s.7) of the Law Reform (Husband and Wife) (Scotland) Act 1984.

[21] As the common law has developed, it has never been, and is not, the case that a *husband* can pledge his *wife's* credit for necessaries.

from a husband's obligation to aliment his wife, however such a duty is also now owed by a wife to a husband.[22] The same obligation applies to those in civil partnerships also.[23] A modern gender-free equivalent therefore is probably for spouse A to allow spouse B to use a credit card which is paid off by spouse A, or alternatively for both spouses to draw cheques on a joint current account. There is, of course, no reason why one spouse cannot expressly or impliedly appoint the other spouse their agent under ordinary principles of contract, and thus allow that spouse to bind them to contracts.

10–09   In the field of delict, statutory rules allow the surviving spouse or cohabiting partner of a deceased person to claim damages where that person has died due to the negligence of a third party.[24] These rules have been extended to cover civil partners."[25] Such damages include amounts for both financial loss of support and non-financial consequences such as loss of society and grief, distress and anxiety caused.[26] A claim can now be made by a homosexual cohabitant of the deceased, as the definition of relative under s.14(1)(a) of the Damages (Scotland) Act 2011 covers

> "a person who immediately before the death is the deceased's spouse or civil partner or is living with the deceased as if married to, or in a civil partnerhsip with the deceased".[27]

10–10   In the past the courts were generally reluctant to ascribe status to same-sex relationships,[28] but this approach has been challenged by the implementation of the Human Rights Act 1998 and the Court of Appeal's ruling in *Ghaidan v Mendoza*.[29] Subsequent legislation in Scotland takes account of this to provide parity in the treatment of heterosexual and same-sex couples (except with regard to marriage).[30] However, the development of the law in this area

---

[22] Married Woman's Property Act s.4 introduced a limited obligation of aliment on a wife of sufficient means. The current mutual obligation of spouses to each other is governed by the Family Law (Scotland) Act 1985. See s.1(1).

[23] Family Law Scotland Act 1985 s.1(1)(bb) as amended by the Civil Partnership Act 2004 Sch.28, Pt 2, s.11.

[24] Claims may also be made by a parent or child of the deceased: ss.1 and 10 of and Sch.1 to the Damages (Scotland) Act 1976; Administration of Justice Act 1982 ss.9(2) and 14.

[25] CPA 2004 Sch. 28, Pt 4, para.42, that made the necessary amendments to the definition of "relative" in Sch.1 of 1976 Act (interestingly, these amendments were repeated in Sch.2 of the 2006 Act); also Sch.28, Pt 4, para.47 of the 2004 Act makes the necessary changes to the Administration of Justice Act 1982.

[26] See ss.1 and 10 of and Sch.1 to the Damages (Scotland) Act 1976, as amended by the Damages (Scotland) Act 1993 and ss.9(2) and 14 of the Administration of Justice Act 1982 and the Family Law (Scotland) Act 2006 s.35 extending the definition of "immediate family" set out in Sch.6.

[27] These persons were previously covered by the Damages (Scotland) Act 1976 s.10(2), as amended, before that Act was repealed and the 2011 Act came into force.

[28] See paras 9–13 to 9–18, in particular the UK courts' insistence on interpreting "man" and "woman" in biological terms for the purposes of entry to marriage.

[29] *Ghaidan v Mendoza* [2002] 4 All E.R. 1162. In this case the court held the statutory meaning of the words "as his or her wife" must be interpreted in the light of Art.8 to mean "as if they were his or her wife" in order to avoid discrimination under Art.14 and thus to enable a same-sex partner to be treated as if he or she were a spouse.

[30] e.g. Adults with Incapacity (Scotland) Act 2000 s.87 and s.24C Home Owner and Debtor Protection (Scotland) Act 2010. For a general overview overview of the way in which same-

has not always been consistent. In *Telfer v Kellock*[31] a woman's claim that she was "family" for the purposes of the 1976 act, after her female partner (with whom she had exchanged vows and rings) had been killed in a road traffic accident, was dismissed. This case was decided five months after the House of Lords ruling in *Ghaidan* that the difference in treatment between same-sex and heterosexual couples was eliminated by the duty under s.3 of the Human Rights Act 1988 to interpret legislation of the United Kingdom parliament in a manner consistent with the provisions of that act.

Where a person is injured so that he or she finds it necessary to call on **10–11** a relative for "personal services" such as nursing care or domestic help, a claim may be made against the negligent party to repay these services at a reasonable rate.[32] The definition of relative has been extended to cover civil partners[33] and has been further amended by the 2006 Act to cover same-sex cohabiting partners.[34] Where such a claim is successful, the claimant is under a duty to account to the relative who provided the services. If the injured person is unable to perform certain personal services *for* a relative, as a result of the negligence of a third party, then that party can also be asked to pay in respect of this loss of services.[35] The "personal services" in question are the kind of domestic duties which would normally be supplied free to a family member, but would be paid for if provided to a stranger, e.g. house cleaning or gardening.

Duty to Act as a Witness

In civil proceedings, spouses of parties to the action are competent and **10–12** compellable witnesses: that is, they can both be called and compelled to give evidence.[36] In criminal cases, the situation was somewhat different but the law in this area has been amended by the Criminal Justice and Licensing (Scotland) Act 2010. Under s.86 of the 2010 Act, a spouse or civil partner of an accused is now a competent and compellable witness for the prosecution, accused or co-accused in *any* proceedings against the accused. In effect they will be treated no differently to any other witness in criminal proceedings.[37]

Taxation

Only a brief outline can be given here of the key ways in which the taxation **10–13** system is affected by marriage. Spouses were taxed as one unit for income

---

sex couples were treated in Scots law up to prior to the 2004 and 2006 Acts see B. Dempsey, "Same-Sex Couples in Scots Law—Part 1" (2002) SCOLAG No. 300, 181 and "Same-Sex Couples in Scots Law—Part 2" (2002) SCOLAG No. 301, 201.

[31] *Telfer v Kellock*, 2004 S.L.T. 1290.
[32] Administration of Justice Act 1982 ss.7 and 8, as amended.
[33] Now contained in s.14(1)(a) of the Damages (Scotland) Act 2011.
[34] FLSA 2006 s.30.
[35] Administration of Justice Act 1982 s.9 as amended.
[36] Evidence (Scotland) Act 1853 s.3. At common law the spouse of a party was not, in general, a competent witness.
[37] The section will also take away the common law right of an accused's spouse to refuse to give evidence of matrimonial communings. These changes in the law were brought about because of concerns about not being able to compel a spouse or civil partner to give evidence in child abuse cases.

tax purposes, with a married woman's income being deemed to be that of her husband.[38] The husband was given the married man's allowance[39] to set off against their joint income, in addition to income relief against any earned income of his spouse.[40] However, since the tax year 1990/1991,[41] the married couple has been no longer treated as a tax unit for most tax purposes. Each spouse is responsible for making a return of income and paying the relevant tax.[42] The married couple's allowance was no longer available from the tax year 2000/2001, except for couples in which one of the spouses was aged 65 or more on or before April 5, 2000.[43]

10–14   However, the tax system has not adopted a consistent policy of neutrality as between married couples and those living together outside marriage. For example, transfers between spouses (where on death or by way of lifetime gift) are exempt from inheritance tax[44] as are such transfers between civil partners.[45] However, transfers between a cohabiting couple are not. Similarly, a transfer between spouses or civil partners does not give rise to a chargeable gain for the purposes of capital gains tax[46]; but there is no comparable provision in transfers for cohabiting couples. On the other hand, there are certain situations in which a married couple and, more recently, civil partners may be treated less favourably than an unmarried couple. For example, there is an exemption from capital gains tax on the disposal of a dwelling house which has been the only or main residence[47]; but while a husband and wife or civil partners are only allowed one residence for this purpose,[48] *both* partners in a relationship outside marriage are entitled to relief on a residence. Many of these rules have evolved over time to meet specific problems rather than reflecting any coherent policy towards the taxation of the family unit.

SEPARATION OF PROPERTY: ACCESS TO RESOURCES

10–15   The rule that marriage shall not of itself affect the property rights of spouses is sometimes known as the "separate property" rule.[49] Neither spouse acquires a right to own or administer the property of the other on marriage (except by express agreement). This is in line with the emphasis placed in modern

---

[38] See Income and Corporation Taxes Act 1988 ("ICTA 1988") s.279.

[39] ICTA 1988 s.257(1).

[40] ICTA 1988 s.257(6).

[41] When the repeal of s.257 of the Finance Act 1988 came into effect.

[42] Finance Act 1988 s.32.

[43] ICTA 1988 s.257A.

[44] Under s.18 of the Inheritance Tax Act 1984. There are also limited exemptions from Inheritance Tax in respect of gifts in consideration of marriage under s.22 of the 1984 Act.

[45] Tax and Civil Partnership Regulations 2005 (SI 2005/3229) reg.7(4) which amended s.18 of the Inheritance Tax Act 1984.

[46] Under s.282 of the Income and Corporation Taxes Act 1988, as amended by SI 2005/3229 reg.62 to include civil partners.

[47] Under s.58 of the Taxation of Chargeable Gains Act 1992, as amended by SI 2005/3229 reg.107(2) to cover civil partners.

[48] Under s.222 of the 1992 Act.

[49] Family Law (Scotland) Act 1985 s.24.

family law on marriage as an equal partnership rather than a dependent relationship.[50] However, there are arguments against a strict application of the separate property rule, and in favour of a certain degree of flexibility and pooling of assets. Spouses (and unmarried couples), because of their family obligations, often do not have the same freedom of action as single people. Furthermore, women and men in both marital and cohabiting relationships tend to have different and unequal opportunities to earn and amass property because they take on different roles within the family.

This is particularly so when we consider not just traditional forms of **10–16** wealth such as heritage and capital, but also assets such as wages from employment, and benefits associated with such labour, or purchased by it, such as pensions, insurance rights and contribution-based social security benefits. These assets are of crucial importance in most Scottish households. Recent research estimates that the number of owner-occupied households in Scotland has remained relatively stable over the last seven years, rising from 63 per cent[51] to 64%,[52] with around a third of all households still being rented. In 1981 only 8 per cent of Scots in 1981 had savings of £10,000 or over and only 15 per cent had savings £5,000 or over.[53] Since then the proportion of households without any type of bank or building society account has fallen, especially since 2000.[54] In 2012 only 4% of households surveyed did not have any banking facitilies.[55] However, those in the lowest income category were more likely to have no facilities compared with less than 1% of those with household incomes above £30,000.[56] By 2011, 27% of households[57] did not have any savings in investments, with almost 12% of households having less that £1,000 in savings.[58] When it comes to income, most households acquire this through wages, salaries and self-employed

---

[50] See, e.g. the Family Law (Scotland) Act 1985 ss.9 and 10(1), which deal with the principles to be applied to financial provision on divorce. These provide for a fair sharing of the net value of the property acquired during the marriage, which by s.10(1) means equal shares for spouses except where special circumstances justify a departure from this norm.

[51] Scottish Executive, *Scottish Household Survey Bulletin* (No.8), November 7, 2005, p.1. Research online downloaded from *www.scotland.govuk/Resource/Doc/46746/ 0030438.pdf* put the figures at 63% owner-occupied with 29% social renters and 6% renting from a private landlord. Of these 18% of households are in receipt of housing benefit. *Scotland's People: results from the 2003 Scottish Household Survey* (published February 23, 2005), Figure 4–1, p.19 put the figures as 65%, 20% and 6% respectively. Overall, the number of owner-occupied dwellings in Great Britain increased by 44% between 1981 and 2003 while the number of rented dwellings fell by 17% according to *Social Trends—35 years of social change*, News Release (March 22, 2005), p.3. National Statistics downloaded from *www.statistics.gov.uk/ socialtrends35* [accessed August 2013].

[52] *Scotland's People Annual Report; Results from the 2011 Scottish Household Survey* (2012, Office for National Statistics) p.3 (hereafter referred to as "SHS 2011").

[53] See Manners and Rauta, *Family Property in Scotland: An enquiry carried out on behalf of the Scottish Law Commission* (OPCS, HMSO, 1981), Table 2.16, p.9.

[54] *Monitoring poverty and social exclusion in Scotland 2005: findings informing change* (Joseph Rowntree Foundation, December 2005).

[55] SHS 2011, p.57.

[56] SHS 2011, p.74.

[57] That is 3 in 10.

[58] SHS 2011, p.46. Note that this figure rises to 56% of households in the social rented sector that have no savings at all.

earnings.[59] Access to employment and income generating activities for women and men still reflect a gender bias that has an impact on their ability to acquire life insurance policies and pension schemes that form the major assets of many Scottish households. Statistics demonstrate that women are less likely to acquire these resources than men, for a number of reasons to do with their domestic role within the family, and, in particular, their responsibilities for childcare that are discussed below.

10–17   While it is clear that over the last forty years there has been a transformation in the gender component of the UK workforce, with women increasingly likely to be in paid employment for most of their adult lives, nonethless gender imbalances remain with regard to the scale and form of employment and in remuneration.[60] In Scotland, the demographic composition of the labour market has changed dramatically over the last few decades, with around two thirds of women featuring in paid employment.[61] This marks a significant increase since the 1970s when only around 45% of women worked outside the domestic realm.[62] According to the 2011 Scottish Household Survey, 59% of men and 49% of women are in paid work.[63] Of these, 46% of men and 29% of women are in full-time employment.[64] Women, however, are more likely to be engaged in part-time work than men,[65] while more men than women are self-employed.[66] Even though the figure for women's employment has increased, the figures for male employment have been declining.[67] This is attributed to changes in the labour market facilitated mainly by economic restructuring and deindustrialisation "which have seen huge increases in the use of non-standard forms of employment such as part-time, temporary and casual employment contracts, as well as changing attitudes to women's socio-economic role".[68]

10–18   However, despite increased employment, women are more likley than men to have primary caring responsibilities, which means they are more likely to work part-time or have some flexible working arranements.[69] It is estimated

---

[59] In 2006/2007 to 2008/2009 an average of 73% of household income was derived from these sources, while 13% was derived from state retirement and other pensions, 9% from benefits and tax credits and 3% from investments, see *Social Trends: Income and Wealth?* p.5. See also P. Bradshaw et al., *Growing Up in Scotland: Birth Cohort 2, results from the first year* (2013), where it is noted that for families in Scotland income is most likely to come from wages and salaries and Child Tax Credit (p.32).

[60] D. Perrons, *Women and Gender Equity in Employment: Patterns, progress and challenges,* Institute for European Studies (IES), Working Paper WP23 (February 2009), p.1.

[61] Office for National Statistics (ONS), Regional Labour Market Statistics (April 2012), Newport, National Statistics, *www.ons.gov.uk/ons/rel/subnational-labour/regional-labour-market-statistics/index.html* [accessed April 18, 2013] ONS (2012).

[62] T. Hogarth, D. Owen, L. Gambin, C. Hastuck, C. Lyonette and B. Casey, "The Equality Impacts of the Current Recession", *Equality and Human Rights Commission Research Report No.47* (Manchester: Equality and Human Rights Commisssion, 2009).

[63] SHS 2011, p.5.

[64] SHS 2011, p.5.

[65] This amounts to 17% of women compared with 4% of men, SHS 2011, p.5.

[66] 9% of men compared with 3% of women, SHS 2011, p.39.

[67] From 94.9% in the 1970's to 76.1%, see ONS 2012.

[68] Mckay, Thomson and Ross, *Child Poverty and Mothers Employment Patterns—Exploring Trends, WiSE and Save the Children Briefing Sheet,* September 2012.

[69] Mckay, Thomson and Ross, *Child Poverty and Mothers Employment Patterns—Exploring Trends, WiSE and Save the Children Briefing Sheet,* September 2012. See also P.Bradshaw et

that there are 657,000 in Scotland[70] and many of them are women.[71] The overall prevalence of women to male carers is around 60% of women to 40% of men, with women featuring predominantly among the age group 30 to 69.[72] Those inovlved in caring responsibilities appear to be involved for a period of more than five years.[73] Motherhood is also seen to be a key variable in employment, with full-time work falling from 90% to 40% on the birth of the first child in the 2000s.[74] Figures show that a higher proportion of women with no dependent children in the household are employed full-time compared with women who have dependent children present.[75] They also reveal that a higher proportion of women with dependent children take on domestic responsibilites for the home or family than those without such children.[76] As a result, although more women are experiencing some form of paid employment it varies from that of men, the majority of whom still work in traditional full-time positions in the labour market.[77] For women's employment varies from that of men in its nature and form. It tends to cluster around work that involves caring, teaching and clearning that is not as well paid as employment in other sectors.[78]

This means that women often earn less than men given occupational seg- **10–19** regation that is "a key feature of modern labout market".[79] There is also the problem of women's under-representation in managerial positions[80] so that while more women are experiencing employment they are confined "to a narrower range of sectors and occupations, where many experience downward occupational mobility and a much wider pay gap".[81] While the gender pay gap appears to be falling this may be accounted for by the fact that many men have had to move into lower paid service work as manufacturing employment has declined.[82] In any event, the UK has an above average gender pay gap compared with other member states of the European Union.[83]

Such conditions have had an impact on women's abilities to make savings **10–20**

---

al., *Growing Up in Scotland: Birth Cohort 2, results fromm the first year* (2013) where it was reported that mothers were more likely to be workig part-time, that is leass than 35 hours per week, than full-time. Thus 40% of women taking part in the survey who were mothers worked part-time compared with only 17% of mothers who worked full-time (p.36).

[70] SHS 2007/2008 referred to the *Caring Together: The Carer Strategy for Scotland 2010–2015*, Scottish Government at para.3.1.

[71] 11% of women compared with 8% of men, *Caring Together*, para.3.9

[72] *Caring Together*, para.3.9.

[73] This involves 70% of carers, see *Caring Together*, para.3.7.

[74] D. Perrons, n.60 above, p.3.

[75] That is 43% of women without dependent children compared with 28% of women with dependent children, SHS 2011, p.44.

[76] That is 22% of women with dependent children compared with 5% of women without dependent children, SHS 2011, p.44.

[77] McKay, Thomson and Ross (2012).

[78] McKay, Thomson and Ross (2012). Note that more women are employed in the public sector in Scotland than men, with 4 out of 10 women being employed in this sector compared with 2 out of 10 men, see ONS 2012b.

[79] McKay, Thomson and Ross (2012).

[80] McKay, Thomson and Ross (2012).

[81] D. Perrons, n.60 above, p.5. See also M. Jyrikinen and L. McKie, *Women in Management: gender, age and working lives*, Briefing No.56 (2011), Centre for the Study of Families and Relationships, Edinburgh University.

[82] D. Perrons, n.60 above, p.4.

[83] It ranks 23rd of 27 EU states. See D. Perrons (2009), p. 3.

or to contribute to pension schemes. The Scottish Widows Report on Women and Pensions in 2012 noted the growing gap betwen the amount women and men are saving for retirement. They acknowledge that this is due to the fact that "men still tend to be the main breadwinners with women more likely to take career breaks to look after children or become carers for elderly relatives" with the result that "they usually also take a break from pension contributions".[84] They also recognise that "divergent career paths for the genders clearly plays out in the relative pension levels we see for men and women.[85] This leads to a position where they report that over a quarter of women are not saving anything for retirement. Their findings are in line with those of the Commons Work and Penisions Committee Report 2013 that found that one third of women retiring in 2010 had not accumulated enough insurance credits to entitle them to more than 60% of the full, basic state pension. While contributions to pension schemes have been falling, with the Prudential Survey of 2011 revealing that one out of five people who retire today have no pension savings and have to rely on the state to provide for them in their retirement, these figures reveal a gender imbalance, with 28% of women having to rely on the state compared with 10% of men.[86] In referring to government statistics, the Prudential note that income for women is so low that 65% are reliant on the Pension Credit.

10–21   The Prudential attribute women's failure to contribute to a pension scheme to their lack of disposable income.[87] The Scottish Widows Report noted that one of the reasons women are not contributing to a pension scheme is because they are opting to repay short-term debt. Where women do save, they tend to be putting money into instant access accounts or regular savings schemes that do no generate sufficient income for retirement.[88] Where women and men are contributing to penison schemes they tend to be schemes that are provided by employers. According to the Office of National Statistics, 30% of men and 61% of women who are employed full-time are contributing to a pension scheme.[89] It also recorded participation among women working part-time, amounting to 41% of part-time female employes.[90] What is clear is that membership rates vary according to socio-economic status so that the highest rates of membership are to be found amongst those who are managers or who have professional status.[91]

---

[84] Scottish Widows Report (2012), p.6.
[85] Scottish Widows Report (2012).
[86] See *Women and Pensions Guide* 2011.
[87] In their survey 78% of the women claimed to have little or no disposable income to enable them to save for retirement.
[88] See the Prudential Class of 2011 Survey and the Scottish Widows Report (2012).
[89] ONS, *Occupational and Personal Pensions Schemes (General Lifestyle Survey Overview—a Report on the 2011 Lifestyle Survey)*, published March 2013, downloaded from *www.ons.gov. uk/ons/dcp171776_302345.pdf* [accessed April 25, 2013].
[90] *Occupational and Personal Pension Schemes (General Lifestyle Survey Overview — a report on the 2011 General Lifestyle Survey)*, p.2. It notes that the increase in numbers of women working part-time contributing to a pension scheme may be "partly explained by changes following a European Court of Justice ruling in 1995 that made it illegal for pension schemes to exclude part time workers", p.5.
[91] *Occupational and Personal Pension Schemes (General Lifestyle Survey Overview — a report on the 2011 General Lifestyle Survey)*, p.3.

The lowest rates are found among women in the routine and manual workers group, covering full and part-time employment.[92] The figures give cause for concern because the overall numbers contributing to pension schemes are falling. While membership of a pension scheme is higher among public sector workers[93] the numbers are still alarming because "even including he public sector where participation rates are much higher less than half of all employees were saving in workplace pensions.[94] The figures are not much better for the self-employed, where only 31% of men and 20% of women were contributing to a pension scheme in 2011.[95] It remains to be seen what effect automatic enrollment into a pension scheme that took effect in 2012 will have over the longer term.

Thus while more women are experiencing employment this has, according to one commentator, involved women in "being partially assimilated into the largely unmodified masculinised model of working to a greater extent than men have been assimilated into the feminised world of domestic reproduction and care".[96] As a result there is an aysmmetric convergence in women and men's lives that means women experience continuing gender segregation in the labour market, together with a gender pay gap, especially in part-time work that "contributes to enduring disadvantages to women in the labour fource, in their life time earnings and in retirement incomes".[97]

10–22

Among those women who are particularly disadvantaged are those who head lone-parent families. It is acknowledged that a quarter of all families in the UK fall within this category[98] and that one in five children is now cared for in a lone-parent family.[99] A great majority of these families are headed by a lone mother.[100] While the proportion of families headed by a lone-parent appears to have stabilised over the years, what has not changed is the fact they they remain among the poorest type of family in the UK.[101] Thus 57% of lone-parent households in the UK lacked the income required for an adequate standard of living in 2011.[102] This may be compared with only 23% of couple households with children who found that they lacked the income required for an adequate standard of living.[103] Compared with couple families, lone-parent

10–23

---

[92] While 44% of men among this group, working full-time are enrolled only 31% of women feature. This figure for women falls to 25% among women working part-time. ONS 2013 (see n.89), p.3.

[93] 83% of public sector employees are enrlled compared with 32% of employees in the private sector. See ONS 2013, p.6.

[94] That is less than 46%, see ONS 2013, p.6.

[95] ONS 2012.

[96] D. Perrons, n.60 above, p.11.

[97] D. Perrons, n.60 above, p.11.

[98] National Statistics, *Social Trends 41*, Families and Households, p.7.

[99] *One Parent Families—A Profile*, August 2009 downloaded from *www.opfs.org.uk/files/one-parent_families_aprofile_2009/pdf*.

[100] National Statistic, *Social Trends 41*, p.7. Note that, according to *One Parent Families—A Profile* (2009), over half of these women were previously married.

[101] *Social Trends 41*.

[102] See M. Padley and D. Hirsch, *Households Below a Minimum Income Standard: 2008/9 to 2010/11*, April 25, 2010, p.4. Downloaded from *www.jrf.org.uk/publications/people-below-mis* [accessed May 22, 2013].

[103] M. Padley and D. Hirsch, *Households Below a Minimum Income Standard: 2008/9 to 2010/11*, April 25, 2013.

families are more likely to be in lower income groups, have lower educational qualifications and live in areas of higher deprivation.[104] According to the Scottish Household Survey in 2011, where a household is headed by a woman she is less likely to report having any savings compared with a man.[105] Indeed, young mothers and lone mothers are less likely to be in employment than older mothers and those in couple families.[106] For almost twice as many lone mothers as mothers in couple familes are not in employment.[107]

10–24   While the numbers of these families at a very high risk of falling below adequate living standards appears to have fallen, this may be associated with the rise in tax credits in this period and before the reduction in child-care tax credit in 2011.[108] It has since been observed that "cuts in the tax credit entitlement since then are likely to have made the trends for families with children less favourable".[109] The Scottish Widows 2012 *Report on Women and Pensions* observed that "having dependent children is much more likely to result in reductions to long-term savings, including pensions, for women than for men".[110] They attribute this to women prioritising the family before themselves and noted that, where women get divorced, they lose out because the law on pensions and divocre "is largely ignored".[111] Where lone-parent families exist, almost half live in social housing[112] and it is amonst this group that the highest group of households with no savings are to be found.[113]

10–25   Over the years attempts have been made to tackle childcare issues. The National Childcare Strategy launched in 1998 aimed to increase the quantity, quality and affordability of childcare, primarily to enable more women to enter paid employment. In addition, the Employment Act 2002 extends parents' rights in work and may encourage fathers to become more involved in child rearing as paternity leave became a statutory requirement and new fathers receive two weeks paid leave. The most significant change has been the introduction of flexible working "rights". This allows parents and guardians with children under six or a disabled child under 18 to request changes in working hours, working times and the place of work. Since then, as part of the commitment of successive governments "to give every child in Scotland the best start in life",[114] two of the central featues of policy have been a major expansion of early years childcare provision and tax credits subsidising the

---

[104] P. Bradshaw et al., *Growing Up in Scotland: Birth Cohort 2, Results from the first year* (2013), p.27. For example, 59% of lone-parent families had incomes in the lowest 20% compared with 14% of parents in couple families (p.27).

[105] Only 56% of households headed by a woman reported having any savings compared with 68% of households headed by men. SHS 2011, p.53.

[106] *Growing Up in Scotland* (2013) p.37.

[107] *Growing Up in Scotland* (2013) p.37.

[108] See *Households Below A Minimum Income Standard* (2013), p.3.

[109] *Households Below A Minimum Income Standard* (2013).

[110] Scottish Widows 2012 Report, p.6. Downloaded from *www.scottishwidows.co.uk/about_us/ media_centre/reports.html* [accessed May 21, 2013].

[111] Scottish Widows 2012 Report, p.10.

[112] That is 47%.

[113] That is 56% of households in Scotland; see SHS 2011, p.46.

[114] See Scottish Government and COSLA, 2008; Scottish Executive, 2003; Scottish Executive, 2006.

costs of childcare. The early years childcare model that has been developed over the last decade

> "is that of maternal care for the first year, supported by up to one year of maternity leave and, since April 2007, nine months of maternity pay, and a mixed economy of childcare, including informal, voluntary, private and statutory providers, and culminating in universal funded part time pre-school education for children aged 3 and 4".[115]

Scotland appears to have been well ahead of England and Wales in this respect, with statistics[116] estimating that "96% of 3 and 4 year olds eligible for free pre-school education were registered with local authority or partnership pre-school education centres, a greater level of take-up of nursery places for the under 5s than in England and Wales".[117] The changes to maternity leave and pay introduced by the Work and Families Act 2006 have had a clear impact on the use of childcare for children aged ten months in Scotland.[118] Since then a second cohort of children have featured in the research and what is emerging is that the rise in childrcare costs have made it more difficult for parents to meet these costs.[119] Thus employment and household income are key drivers of the duration of childcare being used for the child.[120] This has implcations for those on low incomes, especially lone-parent families.

The question that arises is the extent to which Scots family law should take **10–26** take account of these economic and social factors. In the next section, we will look at the property rights that apply to domestic relationships *while the relationship subsists*, comparing the position of spouses and civil partners with that of heterosexual cohabiting couples. We shall examine the rules relating to the division of property on termination of a domestic relationship (including "financial provision on divorce") in Chs 11 to 13.

Exceptions to "Separate Property" Rule

There are however certain exceptions to the general rule that marriage does **10–27** not affect the spouses' property rights. These include:

- a spouse's right to aliment[121];
- provisions under the Matrimonial Homes (Family Protection) (Scotland) Act 1981[122];
- spousal presumption of equal shares in household goods[123];

---

[115] P. Bradshaw and F. Wasoff, *Growing Up in Scotland: Multiple Childcare Provision and its Effect on Child Outcomes* (2009), Ch.1, Introduction.
[116] Scottish Government 2008.
[117] *Growing Up in Scotland* (2009), Ch.1, Introduction.
[118] *Growing Up in Scotland* (2013), p.174.
[119] *Growing Up in Scotland* (2013), p.170. The proportion of parents reporting that childcare costs were "very easy" to pay has reduced slightly from 14% to 10%, whereas the proportion saying costs were difficult to pay increased a little from 21% to 24% (p.170).
[120] *Growing Up in Scotland* (2013), p.166.
[121] 1985 Act s.1(1)(a). Extended to civil partners by Sch.28, Pt 2, paras 11–13 of the CPA 2004.
[122] Discussed in paras 11–10 *et seq.*
[123] 1985 Act s.25. This provision has now been extended to cover civil partners and cohabitees both heterosexual and same-sex couples by s.26 of the FLSA 2006.

- spousal presumption of equal shares in money and property derived from any housekeeping allowance[124];
- exception to requirement of delivery where insurance policy in favour of spouse and/or children[125];
- right to retain possession of tenancy where spouse who is tenant leaves matrimonial home[126];
- right to succeed to private tenancy on spouse's death as statutory tenant[127];
- right to succeed to public sector secure tenancy on death of spouse[128];
- right to financial provision on divorce where matrimonial property is subject to fair sharing between the spouses regardless of who holds title to it.[129]

ADULTS AND RIGHTS OF SUPPORT

10–28   Each spouse owes a duty of support or "aliment" to the other for the duration of the marriage. This duty terminates on the dissolution of the marriage. Unmarried partners, apart from civil partners, do not owe each other private law duties of aliment either during or after the termination of the relationship. When a marriage is terminated by divorce or a civil partnership is dissolved, a periodical allowance may be awarded by the court to be paid by one spouse or civil partner to the other for a limited or unlimited time: this should not be confused with an award of aliment which can be made only while the marriage or civil partnership subsists.

10–29   During marriage, spouses usually support each other informally and do not often seek legal awards. Separated spouses seeking support often prefer to rely on state social security benefitsor minutes of agreement, rather than seek an award from a court which may involve contact with a hostile ex-partner and be difficult to enforce.[130] Aliment, unlike social security benefits,

---

[124] 1985 Act s.26. This provision has now been extended to cover civil partners and cohabitees by s.27 of the 2006 Act.

[125] Married Women's Policies of Assurance (Scotland) Act 1880 s.2. In this case the policy vests in the spouse and his or her representatives as soon as the policy is effected, without delivery. This has now been extended to cover civil partners by s.132 of the Civil Partnership Act 2004.

[126] 1981 Act s.2(8). This has now been extended to civil partners by s.102(8) of the CPA 2004.

[127] Sch.1, para.2 of the Rent (Scotland) Act 1984. Also protected under para.3 is "a person who was a member of the original tenant's family residing with him". After the House of Lords decision in *Fitzpatrick v Sterling Housing Association* [1999] 4 All E.R. 705, a member of the tenant's family may now be interpreted to include a tenant's same-sex cohabitee. Civil partners now come within the ambit of the 1984 Act through amendment by Sch.28, Pt 4, paras 48–49 of the CPA 2004.

[128] Under the Housing (Scotland) Act 2001 ss.108(3), 22,and Sch 3. Note that the definition of "spouse" under s.108(3) now extends to "another person living together with that person as husband and wife or in a relationship which has the characteristics of the relationship between husband and wife except that the persons are of the same sex". Where the parties are cohabitees (heterosexual or same-sex) and a secure tenancy is involved, the property must have been the person's only or principal home throughout the period of six months ending with the tenant's death, a condition which does not apply to spouses.

[129] 1985 Act s.10. Extended to civil partners by Sch.28, Pt 2, para.16 of the CPA 2004.

[130] *Report of the Committee on One-Parent Families*, Cmnd.5629 (1974), p.115; Dobash and Wasoff, *Financial Aspects of Divorce* (1986), p.31.

has the advantage that it is awarded at the discretion of the court rather than being set at a fixed amount. However, research evidence indicates that where aliment is replaced by periodical awards made by the courts on divorce, such discretionary awards made by courts tend to be on the low side where they are awarded at all.[131] Individuals seeking support for children of the marriage may come to their own voluntary arrangements or will come within the jurisdiction of the Child Support Act 1991.[132] There are very few actions raised for spousal aliment, with those raised most often seeking aliment as an interim award only for the duration of divorce proceedings. Private law rules on spousal aliment therefore are of dwindling importance in comparison to the private law regime governing financial provision on divorce and the public law rules regulating social security, welfare and child support.

Nonetheless, current government policies continue to endorse and, indeed, **10–30** aggressively pursue the policy that it is the family, rather than the state, which should be the primary source of maintenance and provision for family members.[133] Spouses and civil partners, can also claim property rights out of each other's estate on *death* under the rules of both testate and intestate succession. While the FLSA 2006 has for the first time given the courts discretionary powers to make some provision for heterosexual/same-sex cohabiting couples, these are not on a par with the provisions that apply to spouses and civil partners.[134]

Aliment

The legal obligation on family members to maintain or aliment each other **10–31** pre-dates the state system of maintenance and support. In the past, the obligation to provide aliment was broadly construed at common law to include the extended, and not just the nuclear, family.[135] So, e.g. grandparents could become liable to aliment grandchildren where the parents were unable to do so,[136] and grandchildren could reciprocally find themselves liable to aliment their grandparents. Within this framework, husbands were liable to aliment their wives, but there was no reciprocal requirement for wives to aliment their husbands until 1920.[137]

Who Owes an Obligation of Aliment?

The law on aliment is now contained in the Family Law (Scotland) Act **10–32** 1985.[138] Under this Act, the number of persons liable to pay aliment has been

---

[131] See Wasoff et al., *Impact of the Family Law (Scotland) Act 1985 on Solicitors' Practice* (Scottish Central Research Unit, 1990), pp.73–75.
[132] As amended by the Child Support Act 1995 and by the Child Support Pensions and Social Security Act 2000.
[133] See the Family Law (Scotland) Act 1985 s.1(1) requiring individuals to maintain their spouse/civil partner and children as well as the Child Support Act 1991 (discussed in full in Ch.5).
[134] FLSA 2006 s.28.
[135] See Bankton's *Institute of the Laws of Scotland*, i,6,15; Bell's *Principles of the Law of Scotland*,10th edn (1633).
[136] See, e.g. *Mackenzie's Tutrix v Mackenzie*, 1928 S.L.T. 649.
[137] See Married Women's Property Act 1920 s.4.
[138] References in this section are to the 1985 Act unless otherwise stated.

strictly limited. Section 1(1) states that an obligation of aliment is now owed only by

(a) a husband to his wife[139] *or vice versa* and a partner in a civil partnership to the other partner[140];
(b) a father or mother to his or her child; and
(c) a person to a child who has been accepted as a child of his or her family.[141]

Aliment (and child support) for children is dealt with in Ch.5.

How Much is Owed?

10–33   Where aliment is due, it is an obligation to provide a party with "such support as is reasonable in the circumstances",[142] having regard to the factors specified in s.4(1), namely

(a) the needs and resources of the parties;
(b) the earning capacities of the parties; and
(c) generally all the circumstances of the case.

The s.4 factors are also relevant when determining an award of *interim* aliment.[143]

10–34   The court is thus given extensive discretion. Unlike social security law, where need is defined in terms of set rates of benefit, the "rates" for aliment are flexible, with the needs and resources of the parties being considered in the light of the parties' standard of living during the marriage, their earning capacity, their age and their health. However, it would appear that, in practice, a number of solicitors estimate claims for aliment not on the particular circumstances of the case but rather on the basis of certain "rule of thumb" rates developed over the years.[144]

10–35   "Resources" are not just confined to income. They may also include capital,[145] (particularly where such capital has regularly been encroached upon for maintenance or where it is reasonable for them to be used towards living expenses),[146] support from relatives, third parties or cohabitants or parental contributions,[147] as well as child tax credit.[148] So, e.g. in *Munro v Munro*[149] a wife sued her husband for aliment. The court took into account

---

[139] The terms "husband" and "wife" include parties to a valid polygamous marriage: s.1(5).
[140] Amendment made to the 1985 Act by Sch.28, Pt 2, para.11 of the Civil Partnership Act 2004. References hereafter to spouses should be taken to include civil partners.
[141] 1985 Act s.1(1)(d). This does not include a child who has been boarded out for fostering by a local or other public authority or voluntary organisation.
[142] 1985 Act s.1(1) and (2).
[143] *McGeachie v McGeachie*, 1989 S.C.L.R. 99.
[144] See Wasoff et al., *Impact of the Family Law (Scotland) Act 1985 on Solicitors' Practice* (Scottish Central Research Unit, 1990).
[145] *Alexander v Alexander*, 1957 S.L.T. 298.
[146] *Dowswell v Dowswell*, 1943 S.C. 43.
[147] *Alexander v Alexander*, 1957 S.L.T. 298 at 303. See also *Syme v Syme* (1833) 11 S.305.
[148] *Dupuy v Dupuy*, 2010 Fam L.R. 19.
[149] *Munro v Munro*, 1986 S.L.T. 72.

the fact that the husband's cohabitant was contributing to the joint outlays of that household as these formed part of the resources which were available to the husband. It refused, however, to take account of the cohabitant's *income* and aggregate it with that of the husband, as that would amount to placing the cohabitant under an obligation to aliment the wife, when she was under no such legal obligation.[150]

"Resources" also include state benefits to which a party is entitled, **10–36** except those based exclusively on need—such as Income Support and the non-contributory part of the jobseeker's allowance—which will be left out of account. In addition, resources are not limited to present resources but may also include *foreseeable* resources,[151] such as payoffs from insurance or pension plans, rights of inheritance or imminent statutory redundancy payments. Income is normally assessed on the basis of the parties' net income after tax,[152] because aliment is now normally payable out of post-tax income, and is not taxable in the hands of the recipient.[153]

The court has discretion, when considering "all the circumstances of the **10–37** case", to take account of any support, financial or otherwise, given by the defender to *any person* whom he or she maintains as a dependant in his or her household, *whether or not* the defender owes an obligation of aliment to that person.[154] Prior to the 1985 Act if a person choose to voluntarily maintain another—not by virtue of a legal obligation of aliment—then such support could not be taken account of by the courts as a drain on the resources of the payer.[155] This often led to the making of an unrealistic assessment.

Example: Husband (H) leaves his wife (W) and sets up a new household **10–38** with his girlfriend (X) and her children A and B. H has no legal obligation to support X but if he does in fact support her (by paying a portion of his salary towards the household budget for example), his payments can be taken into account when quantifying his resources so as to determine how much aliment he owes W.[156]

The court is specifically enjoined *not* to take account of the conduct of the **10–39** parties when quantifying aliment, unless it would be "manifestly inequitable to leave it out of account".[157] This should be the case only in circumstances

---

[150] See also *Frith v Frith*, 1990 G.W.D. 5–266.
[151] 1985 Act s.27(1). Note that it is within the discretion of the court whether or not to take foreseeable resources into account in the initial action, or whether to leave them to be taken into account at a later date on an application for variation under s.5.
[152] See *Wiseman v Wiseman*, 1989 S.C.L.R. 757; *Harper v Harper*, 1990 G.W.D. 40–2322; *Pryde v Pryde*, 1991 S.L.T. (Sh. Ct) 26, but *cf. MacInnes v MacInnes*, 1993 S.L.T. 1108 and Lord Marnoch's observation (at p.1109) that the calculation should be on the basis of gross income, where a husband continues to get tax relief in the form of the married person's allowance under s.36 of the Finance Act 1988, despite changes in the tax treatment of his payments.
[153] See further, Barr, *A Vintage Year for Aliment*, 1989 S.L.T. (News) 57.
[154] 1995 Act s.4(3)(a).
[155] See *Henry v Henry*, 1972 S.L.T. (Notes) 26.
[156] Note: Whilst initially H would have no obligation to support the children A and B, if he acts in a manner which indicates he "accepts them as a child of his family" then such a duty will exist: s.1(1(d) of the 1985 Act. It is interesting to note that in this respect the 1985 Act is far more realistic in its acceptance of the fact that separated spouses tend to acquire new dependants and new responsibilities, than is the Child Support Act 1991, even after considerable amending of its formulae to enable reduced payments in the event of acquired dependants.
[157] 1995 Act s.4(3)(b).

where conduct has actually affected the parties' finances, e.g. where a party blatantly disposes of assets or income in order to exhaust their estate, thereby depriving the other party of their right to aliment. Either spouse can claim aliment even if they have given the other grounds for divorce.[158] If one spouse feels aggrieved by the other's matrimonial conduct, then the remedy lies in seeking a divorce which, when granted, terminates the obligation to aliment a spouse (but not children).[159] The statutory attempt to downplay the significance of conduct goes hand in hand with the general move away from a fault-based approach in matrimonial matters.[160]

Court Actions for Aliment

10–40   An action for aliment may be raised in the sheriff court or the Court of Session.[161] It may be raised as an independent action or as an action ancillary to other proceedings such as divorce, dissolution of civil partnership, separation, nullity of marriage or civil partnership, financial provision, or declarator of paternity.[162] It may also be claimed in any other action where the court considers it appropriate.[163] Whether an independent action, or ancillary to other proceedings, a court may make an award of interim aliment, pending the final disposal of the action.[164] Those who may apply to the court for aliment are those to whom an obligation of aliment is owed,[165] as well as representatives of children and incapax claimants.[166]

10–41   At common law, spouses had to separate before an action of aliment could be raised. Section 2(6) of the 1985 Act expressly provides that it is competent to bring an action for aliment, notwithstanding that the pursuer is living in the same household as the defender. Where such an action is brought, however, it may be met with the defence that the defender is fulfilling the obligation of aliment in the household (whether in money or in kind), and intends to continue doing so.[167]

10–42   Other defences are also competent. The defender may argue that he or she has made an offer to receive the pursuer into his or her household and to fulfil the obligation of aliment there, so long as the offer is one which it is reasonable to expect the other spouse to accept.[168] In considering what is "reasonable",

---

[158] *Donnelly v Donnelly*, 1959 S.C. 97.

[159] However, note that even where a decree of divorce has been granted, but a claim for financial provision is still pending, an award of interim aliment remains competent, as in *Neill v Neill*, 1987 S.L.T. (Sh. Ct) 143.

[160] Compare the similar provision in s.11(7) of the 1985 Act dealing with conduct in respect of financial provision on divorce, discussed in Ch.13; and see also the non-fault grounds for divorce in s.1(2)(d) and (e) of the Divorce (Scotland) Act 1976.

[161] 1985 Act ss.2 and 27(1).

[162] 1985 Act s.2(2)(e).

[163] 1985 Act s.2(2)(e).

[164] 1985 Act s.6(1)(a) and (b).

[165] 1985 Act s.2(4)(a). But note that by ss.27(1) and 17(2), a person may claim *interim* aliment even if they are not owed an obligation of aliment, e.g. a pursuer in an action of nullity of marriage. If she succeeds in her action, the result will be that the defender does not owe her a duty of aliment, but she will nonetheless be entitled to seek and retain interim aliment.

[166] 1985 Act ss.2(4)(b) and (c), and 2(5).

[167] 1985 Act s.2(7).

[168] 1985 Act s.2(8).

the court is expressly allowed to have regard to conduct.[169] For example, where there is a history of domestic violence, adultery or alcoholism, the pursuer may be justified in refusing the offer. However, the mere fact that a husband and wife have agreed to live apart shall not of itself make the offer "unreasonable".[170]

The court has a number of powers in relation to an action for aliment. It can order either party to provide details of his or her resources.[171] Furthermore, by common law powers, it can grant a commission and diligence to recover documents detailing the parties' resources, such as employment slips. When granting decree, the court usually makes an order for a periodical payment for a definite or indefinite period or until the happening of a specified event, e.g. "two years", or, "until the pursuer re-enters full-time employment".[172] Exceptionally, the court can order the making of alimentary payments of an occasional or special nature, including payments in respect of inlying,[173] funeral and educational expenses.[174] The court can also back-date an award of aliment,[175] either to the date of the bringing of the action or to such later date as the court thinks fit; or, exceptionally, to a date prior to the bringing of the action.[176] It does not, however, have the power to backdate an award of interim aliment. The Act expressly states that the court has *no* power to substitute a lump sum for a periodical payment.[177]

10–43

Variation and Recall of Court Orders

Under the 1985 Act the court has power to vary or recall a decree for aliment[178] or interim aliment.[179] In an application for variation or recall the court has all the powers that it has in an action for aliment. Variation normally requires that since the date of the decree there has been a material change of circumstances[180] but this is not necessary in the case of variation of an award of interim aliment.[181] Divorce is not a change of circumstances, but rather an event which causes the obligation of aliment to terminate. A "change of circumstances" must be one which affects the resources of either party, e.g. an increase or decrease in the earnings or means of either party, such as

10–44

- where one spouse inherits property[182];
- takes up employment[183]; or

---

[169] 1985 Act s.2(9), which also refers the court to all other relevant circumstances.
[170] 1985 Act s.2(9).
[171] 1985 Act s.20.
[172] 1985 Act s.3(1)(a).
[173] These are expenses connected with the period of confinement associated with childbirth.
[174] 1985 Act s.3(1)(b).
[175] But not an award of interim aliment.
[176] 1985 Act s.3(1)(c). The court also has the power to award less than the amount claimed even if the claim is undisputed: s.3(1)(d).
[177] 1985 Act s.3(2).
[178] 1985 Act s.5.
[179] 1985 Act s.6(4).
[180] 1985 Act s.5(1).
[181] *Bisset v Bisset*, 1993 S.C.L.R. 284.
[182] *Donald v Donald* (1862) 24 D. 499.
[183] *Dowswell v Dowswell*, 1943 S.C. 23.

• loses his or her job.[184]

The making of a maintenance assessment under the Child Support Act 1991 is specifically designated as a "material change of circumstances" justifying variation of aliment paid to a spouse as well as to a child,[185] although an order for the payment of aliment in respect of matters falling ouwith the sphere of the statutory child support system will not be taken into account by the CSA when making their calculation for child support maintnenance.

10–45   Cases involving applications to the court to vary a decree of aliment often occur in respect of children. In *Ahmed v Ahmed*[186] the mother applied to the Court of Session to increase the amount of aliment payable for the younger child of the marriage. In 1994 the Court of Session awarded aliment of £50 per week for each of the two children. In October 2000 the mother applied for an increase in respect of the younger child. After proof the judge awarded £220 per week and back-dated the increase to the date of the application. The father reclaimed, attacking both the scale of the increase and its backdating. The actual expenditure on the child's recurring needs was found to have been £160 per week. Apportioning four fifths of that to the father meant an award of about £130 per week. The Inner House held, however, that awarding aliment was not a purely arithmetical exercise, but that the child's needs ought to be related to the standard of living she was entitled to in terms of her parents' earnings and that there should be no disparity between her and the defender's other children in America. Thus the award should not be constrained by what her relatively poorer mother had been able to afford over the past few years without a sufficient contribution from the father.

10–46   In this case, costs also involved medical expenses of £10,000. The Lord Ordinary had added this sum to the other expenditure and averaged it out over the period from the date of the application to the date of decree to arrive at the appropriate amount of aliment. The Inner House held that aliment of £130 per week plus £8,000 (which was the father's share of medical expenses) came to very near the same total as the £220 per week that had been awarded for the period until the child reached 18. It would not, therefore, interfere with the Lord Ordinary's award. It also held that backdating was justified because the father had not been frank about his income and financial circumstances when the application was made, and but for the delay caused by the lengthy proof, an increase would have been awarded soon after the date of application.

10–47   In *Sutherland v Sutherland*,[187] the father of two children sought to vary an agreement reached in 2001 that provided aliment for his two children and their mother on the grounds that his income had decreased to a material extent since late 2001 while the mother's income had increased as she was now in full-time employment. The sheriff decided that there had been a material change in the father's financial position and that it was appropriate to look at his current

---

[184] *Brotherston v Brotherston* (1938) 54 Sh. Ct. Rep. 218.
[185] 1985 Act s.5(1A).
[186] *Ahmed v Ahmed*, 2004 S.C.L.R. 247.
[187] *Sutherland v Sutherland*, 2004 Fam. L.B. 70–4.

income and expenditure. The parties' agents agreed that on the father's current income new statutory rules applied by the Child Support Agency would produce a figure of £475 per month per child. The sheriff regarded this sum as being fair and reasonable and varied the amount of aliment accordingly. We should remember, however, that the criteria provided in s.4 of the 1985 Act are completely different from the formula for child support maintenance and the Sheriff's decision may be thought unsound for that reason alone. The criteria under s.4 of the 1985 Act include the needs and resources of the payee as well as those of the payer. The CSA system entirely ignores the payee's means.

In this case, as the minute of agreement had been registered in the Books of **10–48** Council and Session in October 2001, the Child Support Agency would have had to decline jurisdiction to assess child support should the mother have made such an application.[188] Nonetheless, in reaching his decision the sheriff was influenced by the amount that would have been payable by the non-resident parents according to the Child Support Agency's calculations.

In *Higgins v Higgins*,[189] a couple had two daughters aged 11 and 7. **10–49** The parents separated in 1998, entered into a minute of agreement in mid 2000 and divorced a few months later. The wife then sought an order for payment of school fees in respect of the younger daughter plus a variation in both children's aliment because childcare costs had risen faster than the retail price indexation allowed for in the agreement. In the agreement, both parents had discharged their rights to financial provision and/or to an order for interim aliment or aliment under the terms of the Family Law (Scotland) Act 1985. They acknowledged that they had been independently legally advised and that the terms of the agreement were fair and reasonable. The father argued that the agreement precluded the mother from claiming an alimentary payment in respect of school fees under s.3(1)(b) of the 1985 Act.

However, the court held that there had been no express discharge of the **10–50** right to claim aliment on behalf of a child and, looking at the other terms of the agreement, such a discharge could not be reasonably inferred from them. All that had been discharged were the financial claims of the couple vis-à-vis one another. It also noted that there had been several material changes in circumstances since the date of the agreement, namely that

* the father's pay had increased from £160,000 to well over £1 million;
* school fees and associated expenses had risen faster than the inflationary increases granted by the agreement;
* the cessation of the wife's allowance at the end of 2003 would mean that her resources and those of the children would fall below their reasonable needs.

---

[188] This is because commissioner's decision CSCS/5/97 reported in 1999 that an extract registered agreement on aliment for a child was equivalent to a maintenance order which removes jurisdiction for the Child Support Agency in *non-benefit* cases. A Minute of Agreement made after March 2003 will exclude the jurisdiction of the CSA/CMS but only for one year. Thereafter an application for maintenance is competent and a calculation following application will nullify any part of any alimentary obligation under the agreement which is for any purpose other than those mentioned in s.8(7) to (10) of the 1991 Act.

[189] *Sutherland v Sutherland*, 2004 Fam. L.B. 67–7.

It was agreed that the father's ability to pay was not an issue. He considered that he had made a generous agreement and was not prepared to pay all the younger daughter's school fees or "reinstate" his wife's allowance by means of an increase in the children's aliment.

10–51 The court held that need was a relative concept but that generally speaking it should be assessed against the standard of living which the couple envisaged for the children when the agreement was made. In this case, the agreement had provided in principle for the private schooling of the younger daughter when she became old enough. Thus, the court held that the father should pay school fees to enable the younger daughter to continue at the private school where she had already been for some time. In reaching this decision it took account of the fact that her elder sister and the father's daughter by his remarriage were both being privately educated as well as the fact that the mother's attempts to obtain a better job were constrained by her need to care for the children, especially during school holidays.

10–52 The father's argument that the increase in child aliment sought by the mother was an attempt to replace her allowance (which was due to come to an end) was met by s.4(4) of the 1985 Act. This section empowers the court in awarding aliment to a child under 16 to include reasonable provision for the expenses of the carer in caring for the child and in this case the evidence showed that the mother's expenditure on herself was modest.

10–53 Overall, these cases set out three stages for dealing with aliment:

- the first, is to ask whether there has been any material changes in circumstances since the agreement was made[190];
- the second is, if there have been material changes, do they justify any variation in the amount due; and
- if so, by how much should the award be varied?

In assessing need it is also relevant to take account of how a father treats his other children. This is recognised in s.4(3)(a) of the 1985 Act and underpinned by the decision in *Ahmed* that equal treatment of children by parents in old and new families is an important consideration that should be upheld.

10–54 Unfortunately the 1985 Act did not extend these powers of variation to a court dealing with a variation of aliment payable in terms of an agreement. The FLSA 2006 has corrected this oversight and inserted new powers into s.7[191] of the 1985 Act that are identical to those for variation of aliment due in terms of a decree discussed above. The FLSA 2006 has also made it clear that when dealing with an action of aliment against a non-Scottish defender the Scottish courts should apply the Scots law on aliment.[192]

Awards of interim aliment may also be varied or recalled.[193] In this case no change of circumstances is required,[194] although such a change will ground a claim for variation.

---

[190] 1985 Act s.7(2).
[191] 1985 Act s.7, subss.(2ZA), (2ZB) and (2ZC) inserted by s.20 of the FLSA 2006.
[192] 1985 Act s.40.
[193] *Johnsen v Johnsen*, 1995 Fam. L.B. 14–10.
[194] *Higgins v Higgins*, 2004 Fam. L.B. 67–7.

Backdating of Court Orders

At common law, there was no provision for an award of aliment to be   **10–55**
backdated to cover time periods before the application was made to the
court, because aliment was intended to relieve the present needs of an applicant. Thus a spouse could not, in general, recover arrears of aliment on the
basis that the other spouse had failed to provide support in the past[195] unless
the aliment was at that time already due under a court decree,[196] separation
agreement, or other voluntary obligation.[197]

However, under the 1985 Act, the court has limited powers to backdate   **10–56**
aliment.[198] Aliment can be backdated from the date of the decree to the
date of the bringing of the action,[199] or, on special cause shown, to a date
prior to the bringing of the action.[200] In addition, the court also has the
power to backdate when varying or recalling an award.[201] Where the court
exercises this power, it may order any sum paid under the decree to be
repaid.[202] But note that where *interim* aliment is concerned, the courts do
not have these powers to backdate although, as we have seen, it may vary
future payments.[203] Thus, the defender cannot be compelled to pay *interim*
aliment in respect of any time period before the award of interim aliment
was granted.

Voluntary Agreements

It is not necessary to go to court to obtain aliment. Parties may reach their   **10–57**
own agreements with respect to aliment[204] which the courts will enforce.[205]
Parties are also free to make "clean break" agreements excluding future liability for aliment, or barring either party from bringing an action for aliment
in the future. However, such agreements can be attacked subsequently in
court on the statutory ground that they were not fair and reasonable in all
the circumstances at the time they were made.[206] The courts also have power
to vary or recall the amount of aliment specified within such agreements
where there has been a material change of circumstances since the date of the

---

[195] *McMillan v McMillan* (1871) 9 M. 1067.
[196] *Fletcher v Young*, 1936 S.L.T. 572.
[197] *Hood v Hood* (1871) 9 M. 449.
[198] 1985 Act s.3(1)(c).
[199] 1985 Act s.3(1)(c)(i).
[200] 1985 Act s.3(1)(c)(ii).
[201] *Abrahams v Abrahams*, 1989 S.L.T. (Sh.Ct) 11.
[202] 1985 Act s.5(4).
[203] *McColl v McColl*, 1993 S.L.T. 617.
[204] 1985 Act s.7.
[205] An "agreement" under s.7(5) is one that is entered into before or after the commencement
of the 1985 Act, and includes a unilateral voluntary obligation. In practice, agreements for
aliment are usually in probative writing and registered in the Books of Council and Session
for execution to ease any future enforcement. They often combine provisions relating to
aliment with other clauses relating to financial provision on divorce, succession and matters
relating to children of the marriage. See further, Ch.15.
[206] 1985 Act s.7(1). This, of course, refers only to agreements in respect of aliment between
spouses. As seen in Ch.5, it is never possible under the Child Support Act 1991 to agree to
exclude future liability to support a *child*.

agreement.[207] The defences which apply when applying for aliment also apply when a party seeks to enforce an *agreement* for aliment.[208]

Termination

10-58   An award of aliment terminates at the date indicated by the court when making the order. This may be at a definite date, or on the happening of a specified event.[209] The obligation on spouses to aliment each other terminates when the marriage ends, whether by death[210] or divorce. However, an ex-spouse may still be allowed to claim support in the form of a periodical allowance as part of an award of financial provision on divorce.[211]

Enforcement of Aliment

10-59   A court order for aliment, or an agreement for aliment executed in probative form and registered in the Books of Council and Session, can be enforced under the Debtors (Scotland) Act 1987 by means of a current maintenance arrestment,[212] which requires the employer of the debtor to deduct a sum, determined according to a statutory formula, from the debtor's earnings each pay day, and to pay the sum deducted to the creditor. The deductions continue for as long as the arrestment is in effect, which means that aliment can be recovered at weekly or monthly intervals, as it falls due. But these provisions have certain limitations, namely that: (i) a current maintenance arrestment cannot be used to enforce *arrears* of aliment; and (ii) it can only come into operation four weeks after decree has come into effect, and after the debtor has defaulted on at least one instalment of aliment.[213]

Where parties have reached agreements on aliment which have *not* been registered in the Books of Council and Session, a current maintenance arrestment cannot be used. In such cases, where the debtor defaults, a court action must be raised to obtain a decree for aliment, which can then be enforced only by the ordinary means of diligence.[214]

---

[207] 1985 Act s.7(2). Again note that under s.7(2A), the making of a child maintenance assessment under the Child Support Act 1991 constitutes a "major change of circumstances".

[208] 1985 Act s.7(3).

[209] 1985 Act s.3(1)(a).

[210] But a widow has an independent claim against her husband's estate for temporary aliment after his death. See *Stair Encyclopaedia*, 1.4.22. The Scottish Law Commission in their *Report on Succession*, Scot. Law Com. No.124 (1990), recommended the abolition of this right (para.9.10.).

[211] See paras 13–64 to 13–67.

[212] Debtors (Scotland) Act 1987 ss.51–56 as amended by the Bankruptcy and Diliengence, etc. (Scotland) Act 2007, The Diligence Against Earnings (Variation) (Scotland) Regulations 2009, the Civil Jurisdiction and Judgments (Maintenance) Regulations 2011 and the Internationa Recovery of Maintenance (Hague Convention 2007) (Scotland) Regulations 2012.

[213] Sch.5 to the Child Support Act 1991 has reduced the number of instalments on which the debtor has defaulted from three to one.

[214] Note again that the right to raise an action for aliment in the courts may be barred if aliment for children is also sought under the provisions of the Child Support Act 1991. See further Ch.5.

Recovery from Liable Relatives

What if a woman living alone, but still married to her husband, applies   **10–60**
for an income-related benefit? Although she may qualify for the benefit—
and be awarded it, under the private law rules examined above—it is legally
the duty of her husband to aliment her. The same is true for civil partners.
However, it will often be more convenient for a person in this position to
claim state benefit rather than to seek and enforce a court award for aliment.
Accordingly, the state reserves the right to recover the cost of such an award
from those who fall within the category of "liable relatives" under the Social
Security Administration Act ("SSAA") 1992,[215] for spouses and civil partners are liable to maintain each other.[216] Liability under the 1992 Act previously covered spouses who are liable to maintain each other[217] and parents
who were, until the Child Maintnenance and Other Payments Act 2008,
liable to maintain their children under public law.[218] Thus the Secretary of
State can recover benefit paid to a spouse or civil partner by raising civil
proceedings against a liable relative.[219] Note that since the obligation to
aliment terminate on divorce or dissolution of a partnership, an ex-spouse
or ex civil partner cannot be a "liable relative" under the 1992 Act. A major
change that has taken place is that parents are no longer "liable relatives"
for the purposes of child support.[220] Under s.6 of the Child Suport Act
1991 a claim for either income support or income-based jobseeker's allowance automatically triggered an application to the Child Support Agency
for child support. Section 15 of the 2008 Act has now repealed ss.6 and 46
of the 1991 Act. According to Wikeley the repeal of s.6 "is one important
consequence of the emphasis under the new post-Henshaw arrangements
is private ordering. Parents with care on benefit therefore have the same
choice as private clients in terms of the child support options",[221] although
as he points out "it remains unclear how many parents with care on benefit
will actually 'go private'".[222] Under the CS3 system of child support parties
will be encouraged not to use the statutory system at all, but will be guided
by CM Options towards extra-judicial informal settlements expressed in
Family Based Arrangements. At the time of writing it is uncertain how this
scheme will work.

---

[215] SSAA s.106 as amended by the Child Amintenance and Other Payments Act 2008.
[216] Welfare Reform Act 2012 Sch.14, Pt 8 (from August 1, 2013); CPA 2004, Sch.24, para 61 as
read with para.46 as amended by the 2008 Act.
[217] Under the Civil Partnership Act 2004 the definition under the 1992 Act has been extended to
cover civil partners: s.254, Sch.24, Pt 4, para.61(4).
[218] Paraphrased from s.78(6) of the 1992 Act prior to amendment under the 2008 Act. This is
repealed with effect from August 1, 2013 by virtue of the Welfare Reform Act 2012: see above.
[219] Social Security Administration Act 1992 s.105 as amended by Child Maintenance and Other
Payments Act 2008.
[220] For discussion of reforms see N. Wikeley, "The Strange Death of the Liable Relative Rule"
(2008) *Journal of Social Welfare and Family Law*, Vol.30(4), pp.339–351.
[221] N. Wikeley, "The Strange Death of the Liable Relative Rule" (2008) *Journal of Social Welfare
and Family Law*, Vol.30(4), p.344.
[222] N. Wikeley, "The Strange Death of the Liable Relative Rule" (2008) *Journal of Social Welfare
and Family Law*, Vol.30(4), p.344.

SUCCESSION[223]

10–61 Marriage and civil partnership have important consequences for adults in relation to both testate and intestate succession. The provisions of the 1964 Succession (Scotland) Act 1964 dealing with succession have now been extended to cover civil partners.[224]

Intestate Succession[225]

Prior Rights

10–62 Where a person dies without leaving a will, any surviving spouse or civil partner will be entitled to prior and legal rights out of the deceased's estate, according to the law of intestate succession under the Succession (Scotland) Act 1964.[226] This provides important protection to such parties given that a survey found that only 37% of Scots make a will.[227] Prior rights include rights to the deceased's interest in the dwelling-house which the deceased and surviving spouse/civil partner formerly shared, and the furniture and plenishings,[228] and to monetary provision.[229] As the name implies, these are distributed first out of the deceased's estate before legal rights (although after debts, funeral expenses and taxes). Where the surviving spouse/civil partner was ordinarily resident in a dwelling-house in which the deceased had a "relevant interest" at the date of death,[230] the surviving spouse/civil partner is entitled to the deceased's interest in the house where its value is not in excess of £473,000, or to the sum £473,000 where its value exceeds this limit.[231] The surviving spouse/civil partner is also entitled to furniture and plenishings[232] from the deceased's estate up to a value of £29,000.[233] In addition, the surviving spouse/civil partner is also entitled to monetary provision out of the deceased's estate.[234] The value of the monetary right depends on

---

[223] For fuller details see J. Kerrigan, *Drafting for Succession* (Edinburgh: W.Green, 2004) and D.R. Macdonald, *Succession*, 3rd edn (Edinburgh: W.Green, 2001).

[224] Civil Partnership Act 2004 s.261(2), Sch.28, Pt 1.

[225] For details see Meston, *The Succession (Scotland) Act 1964*, 5th edn (2002). Note that figures for dwelling-house, furniture, plenishing and monetary rights are updated from time to time by statutory instrument. The current figures took effect from the February 1, 2012 under the Prior Rights of Surviving Spouse and Civil Partner (Scotland) Order 2011 (SSI 2011/436).

[226] These rights are extended to civil partners by Sch.28, Pt I, para.1 of the 2004 Act.

[227] See S. O'Neill, *Wills and Awareness of Inheritance Rights*, Scottish Consumer Council (2006), p.5, n.40.

[228] Succession (Scotland) Act 1964 s.8. For application to civil partners see para.4, Pt 1, Sch.28 of the 2004 Act.

[229] Succession (Scotland) Act 1964 s.9 as amended by Prior Rights of Surviving Spouse (Scotland) Order 2011 (SSI 2011/436).

[230] A "relevant interest" can be that of an owner or a tenant, other than a tenancy under the Rent and Mortgages Acts, s.8(6). Where there is more than one qualifying house, the surviving spouse has six months to elect which is to qualify for prior rights.

[231] 1964 Act s.8(1).

[232] These are defined in s.8(6)(b) of the 1964 Act.

[233] These can come from a different house from that which the dwelling-house rights were taken.

[234] 1964 Act s.9; para.1, Pt 1, Sch.28 of the 2004 Act.

whether or not the deceased is survived by issue.[235] Where there are issue, the surviving spouse/civil partner is entitled to a sum of £50,000, and where there are none, to £89,000. The monetary right is borne by the heritable and moveable parts of the estate in proportion to their respective amounts after the dwelling-house and plenishings rights have been taken off.[236] This ensures that the moveable estate, out of which legal rights are claimed, is not unfairly depleted since the children have indefeasible rights in the moveable estate which are exigible only after prior rights have been taken off. In practice, prior rights are fixed at rates such that they may exhaust the majority of intestate estates.[237]

LEGAL RIGHTS

The surviving spouse or civil partner is also entitled to legal rights,[238] which are taken from what is left of the deceased's moveable estate, after prior rights have been deducted. Once again, the sum the surviving spouse receives depends on whether or not there are children or remoter issue of the deceased, since the children are also entitled to legal rights.[239] Where there are no issue, the surviving spouse/civil partner is entitled to half the moveable estate, but otherwise only to one-third. **10–63**

The remaining half or third of the moveable estate (known as the dead's part), plus any remaining heritage, is left for the deceased's heirs to inherit. Under s.2 of the 1964 Act, the heirs of the deceased are listed in order of preferential right. A surviving spouse or civil partner inherits under this head only if there are no children or remoter issue, parents, siblings or sibling's descendants left alive. **10–64**

Testate Succession

Where the deceased leaves a will but fails to provide for the surviving spouse/civil partner or issue, then again legal rights can be claimed by them out of the moveable estate. This right cannot be excluded by the deceased in his or her will. Thus, the surviving spouse/civil partner and issue can only truly be cut out of the will of the deceased if the deceased is willing to convert all the moveable property into heritage. For the surviving spouse/civil partner is entitled to a one-half or one-third share of the moveable estate, depending on whether or not there are surviving children or issue. **10–65**

Where the deceased leaves a will in which provision *is* made for the **10–66**

---

[235] "Issue" includes descendants however remote, and makes no distinction between children whose parents were married and those who were born out of wedlock: s.36(1) of the 1964 Act.

[236] 1964 Act s.9(3).

[237] SSI 2011/436 amending the 1964 Act.

[238] These used to be referred to under the 1964 Act as the *jus relicti* (where the husband is the surviving spouse) and the *jus relictae* (where the surviving spouse is the wife). These terms have been abolished and replaced with the general term "legal rights" by Sch.28, Pt I, para.6 of the 2004 Act.

[239] In the past these legal rights under the 1964 Act were known as *legitim* but this term, along with *jus relicti* and *jus relictae* has been abolished and replaced with the general term "legal rights" by Sch.28, Pt I, para.6 of the 2004 Act.

surviving spouse and children, these parties can elect whether to take such provision or whether to renounce it and claim legal rights instead. It is not possible to do both, i.e. to both "approbate" and "reprobate" the will. In some cases, it may be in the interests of the surviving spouse/civil partner to renounce the legacy, even if it is of the whole estate, thereby forcing the whole estate into "artificial intestacy".[240] If the spouse merely took the testamentary gift, and there were also children or remoter issue of the deceased, then those children could claim legal rights which would be taken from the estate leaving only the residue for the surviving spouse. But if the spouse/civil partner *renounces* the testate gift, then the whole estate falls into intestacy, in which case prior rights take precedence over legal rights. In many cases, these prior rights will exhaust the estate, and so the surviving spouse will obtain the whole estate without having to meet the children's claim for legal rights.

10–67   It should be noted that the divorce of a testator does not automatically revoke a will in Scotland, so that the words "my wife" are usually interpreted as being descriptive, especially if the person is also named.

10–68   Where parties are separated complications may arise as in the case of *Price v Baxter*.[241] In this case the parties who were married, separated before the deceased's death without getting divorced. However, the parties had executed a minute of agreement in 2007 (a year before the deceased died) that was registered in the Books of Council and Session. The minute contained a reunciation and discharge of any rights to financial provision and other matters on divorce. The deceased's relations argued the the terms of the minute operated to revoke the will that he had made in the defender's favour in 1999 making her the sole beneficiary and appointing her as executor. The parties did not have any children. The court held that the terms of the minute did not operate to revoke the will, discharging the rights under it as the minute's sole purpose was to regulate financial and other matters with a view of the divorce. As a result the minute did not have any effect on the will so that the defender was entitled to her rights under it and to act as executor.

Succession and Cohabitants

10–69   In the past, cohabitants could not claim rights in the estates of their deceased partners unless they had explicitly been left a legacy by that partner. Over the years, however, as the number of cohabiting couples has increased, there has been a recognition that some kind of provision needs to be made for them on death and dissolution of their partnership.[242] As noted earlier, 51% of children are now born out of wedlock to parents who are both registered on the birth certficate, many of whom are living at the same addresss.[243] These figures have remained relatively constant over the last few years

---

[240] See *Kerr, Petr*, 1968 S.L.T. (Sh. Ct) 61.

[241] *Price v Baxter*, Case No. A1186/08, Sheriffdom of South Strathclyde, Dumfries and Galloway at Hamilton, March 2009; and 2009 Fam. L.R. 138.

[242] 80% of Scots took this view, *Scottish Omnibus Survey* (2005). See Chapter 13 for a discussion of legal reform in relation to dissolution of a cohabiting relationship. See also *Report on Family Law*, Scot. Law Com. No.135 (1992), which includes discussion of the range of "permeations" of cohabitation and the inevitable difficulties it poses for legislation: p.16.24

[243] Registrar General for Scotland, *Scotland's Population 2011 (Annual Report)*, p.23.

demonstrating the proportion of the population for whom cohabitation features as a way of life. While cohabitants are still not entitled to claim prior or legal rights, reforms implemented by s.29 of the Family Law (Scotland) Act 2006 mean that they can now apply to the court for discretionary provision on intestacy. In order to qualify under s.25(1) of that Act, a cohabitant must first estabish that they fall within the definition set out in the Act which is defined as either member of a couple consisting of:

(a) a man and a woman who are (or were) living together as if they were husband and wife;
(b) two persons of the same sex who are (or were) living together as if the were civil partners.

In determining whether or not a person is a cohabitant the court is to "have regard to—

(a) the length of the period during which A and B have been living together (or lived together);
(b) the nature of their relationship during that period; and
(c) the nature and extent of any financial arrangements subsisting, or which subsisted during that period."[244]

In applying to the Court of Session or the sheriff court[245] for discretionary provision, a cohabitant must establish that immediately before the deceased's death the deceased was domiciled in Scotland, was *intestate* and cohabiting with the cohabitant "survivor".[246] Application to the court must be made within six months of the deceased's death.[247] Where the applicant establishes that s/he was a cohabitant the court may make an order or interim order as it thinks fit

(a) for payment to the survivor out of the deceased's net intestate estate of a capital sum of such amount as may be specified in the order;
(b) for transfer to the survivor of such property (whether heritable or moveable) from that estate as may be so specified.[248]

In reaching its decision the court is directed to consider

(a) the size and nature of the deceased's net intestate estate;
(b) any benefit received, or to be received by the survivor—
    (i) on, or in consequence of, the deceased's death; and
    (ii) from somewhere other than the deceased's net intestate estate; and

---

[244] FLSA 2006 s.25(2).
[245] FLSA 2006 s.25(3). Where the court concerned is the sheriff court it must be in the sheriffdom in which the deceased "was habitually resident at the date of death" or, if this is uncertain, Edinburgh Sheriff Court: s.29(5)(b) and (c).
[246] FLSA 2006 s.29(1).
[247] FLSA 2006 s.29(6).
[248] FLSA 2006 s.29(2)(a).

(c) the nature and extent of any other rights against, or claims on, the deceased's net intestate estate; and

(d) any other matter the court considers appropriate.[249]

In the 2006 Act the "net intestate estate" that a surviving cohabitant may make a claim for a capital sum out of is defined to mean so much of the intestate estate as remains after provision for the satisfaction of

(a) inheritance tax;

(b) other liabilities of the estate having priority over legal rights and the prior rights of a surviving spouse or surviving civil partner; and

(c) the legal rights, and the prior rights, or any surviving spouse or surviving civil partner.[250]

Therefore if the deceased died leaving a surviving spouse/civil partner, a surviving cohabitant partner may not receive anything out of the deceased's estate.

10–70 Further, when a court does make an order or interim order it must not exceed "the amount to which the survivor would have been entitled had the survivor been a spouse or civil partner of the deceased".[251] If a capital sum is involved this may be payable by instalments.[252] There is provision for the court, on an application "by any party having an interest", to vary the date or method of payment where a capital sum is concerned.[253]

10–71 If a cohabiting partner dies testate and made testamentary provision for his/her partner then the partner may of course inherit, however this will not defeat the rights of any subsisting spouse or civil partner of the deceased.

10–72 The reforms are to be welcomed although they exist on a discretionary footing rather than representing the kind of entitlement that is embodied in the Succession (Scotland) Act 1964. They do go further than the reforms proposed by the Scottish Law Commission in 1990 who, while noting there was some public sentiment in favour of extending succession rights to cohabitants,[254] expressly discounted proposals for extending rights to *same-sex* couples.[255] No doubt the legislative response to including same-sex couples is the result of case law and jurisprudence on human rights emanating from Strasbourg and United Kingdom courts that rejects discriminatory treatment on the basis of sex or gender.

10–73 Since the legislation was passed there have been very few reported cases in this area. In a study conducted in 2010 researchers found that the number of cases family lawyers have dealt with, roughly 1,000, is "well below the likely number of cohabiting relationships that end in separation or an intestate

---

[249] FLSA 2006 s.29(3).

[250] FLSA 2006 s.29(10).

[251] FLSA 2006 s.29(4).

[252] FLSA 2006 s.29(7)(b).

[253] FLSA 2006 s.29(9).

[254] *Report on Succession*, Scot. Law Com. No.124 (1990); also, *The Effects of Cohabitation in Private Law*, Scot. Law Com. Discussion Paper No.86 (1990).

[255] *The Effects of Cohabitation in Private Law*, Scot. Law Com. Discussion Paper No.86 (1990), p.6.12.

death".[256] What is clear is that the discretion given to the court is so broad that it is hard to assess what the outcome of an application will be, a factor which may account for the small number of reported cases.

Case Law on s.29

Given the breadth of discretion that courts have, it is hard to predict whether or not an application will meet the terms of section 29 and what type of award might be made if the applicant is successful. Each case will be judged on its own merits but there are a few general interpretive points that have emerged from the case law to date. Firstly, that s.29 of the 2006 Act does not not confer a right to succession on cohabitants. The Scottish Law Commission rejected the idea that cohabitants should have an automatic right to succession.[257] This view was upheld in *Savage v Purches*[258] and in *Kerr v Mangan and Others*.[259] In the latter case the Sheriff Principal noted that while a spouse's claim on an intestate estate is fixed and formulaic, a cohabitant's claim is variable and determined by a discretionary decision of the court (para.14). It was argued that, like s.28, s.29 is "a free-standing, self-contained statutory innovation".[260] The second consideration involves what contstitutes the 'net intestate estate'. In *Kerr* the Sheriff Principal interpreted this phrase as meaning the net estate that is to devolve *according to Scots law*. For the estate of the deceased in the *Kerr* case included heritable property in Ireland. The sheriff at first instance included this property as part of the deceased's estate out of which an award under s.29 could be made. On appeal, the Sheriff Principal held that the section should be read in a way that is consistent with the rules of intestate succession set out in the 1964 Act and in a way that is consistent with the rules of international private law. The latter provide that it is the location of the heritable property that determines jursidiction over it.[261] The Sheriff Principal reached the view that to include the heritable property in Ireland as part of the estate would be to interpret s.29 in such a say as to give the section "an extraterritorial effect which is contrary to the principles of private international law".[262] As a result the propety in Ireland was not treated as forming part of the deceased's estate for the purposes of making an award under s. 29.

The third consideration involves the interpretation of s.29(4) when it comes to assessing the amount which may be awarded to a cohabitant. In interpreting its terms the Sheriff Principal took into account the mischief that

10–74

10–75

---

[256] See "No longer living together: how does Scots cohabitation law work in practice?", *Briefing 51* (October 2010, *Centre for Research on Families and Relationships*).

[257] *Report on Succession*, Scot. Law Com, No.215 (2009), p.80.

[258] *Savage v Purches*, 2009 S.L.T. (Sh. Ct.) 36.

[259] *Kerr v Mangan and Others*, Case No, A56/08, Sheriffdom of Tayside Central and Fife, at Perth, February 15, 2013.

[260] *Kerr v Mangan and Others*, Case No, A56/08 at para.6, where reference was also made to the view being consistent with the reports of the Scottish Law Commission, firstly, on succession (No.124 of 1990) and, secondly, on family law (No.135 of 1992) which clearly distinguished between the cohabitant's right to claim on the estate of the deceased and a right of succession. The Sheriff Prinicpal accepted this submission (para.18).

[261] This is according to the *lex situs* that applies to immoveable property.

[262] *Kerr v Mangan and Others*, Case No, A56/08 at para.21.

the section was intended to address. This was the fact that without legislation a cohabitant would receive no benefit from the estate of the deceased under the law of intestate succession, when fairness might dictate that s/he should receive an award. Section 29 allows for such an award "the only proviso qualifying that objective being that the rights of a surviving spouse or civil partner are to remain intact and that the cohabitant should be no better off than if they had been a spouse or civil partner".[263] Thus, in applying s.29(4) the Sheriff Principal held the sum to be awarded could not exceed the amount to which a spouse or civil partner would have been entitled to under Scots law.

10–76 Cases involving cohabitants become even more complex where they also involve family members who are entitled to the deceased's estate under the law of intestate succession. In the first reported case, *Savage v Purches*,[264] the deceased had been cohabiting with his male partner, Mr Savage, for two and a half years before he died. Had the couple been in a civil partnership, Mr Savage would have received the whole of the net intestate estate of £186,113 under a prior rights claim under ss.8 and 9 of the 1964 Act. In this case, however, the deceased was survived by a half sister Sandra Purches and she was entitled to his estate under the 1964 Act. On the deceased's death, the tustess of a pension scheme of which he was a member split the proceeds equally between Sandra Purches and Mr Savage. As an adult dependent Mr Savage was also awarded an annual pension of £9.543, subject to inflationary increases. While recognising that Mr Savage qualified as a cohabitant under s.25, the court went on to consider the terms of s.29(3) dealing with any benefits received as a result of the deceased's death that the court is directed to take into account when considering whether or not to make an award. In this case, the court assesed that benefits that Mr Savage had received as an aggregate of £420,000 before turning to deal with any payment of an award under s.29.[265]

10–77 In assessing Mr Savage's claim under s.29 the court held that he had already received a substantial sum, especially when the net value of the intestate estate as a whole was taken into account. Under s.2 of the 1964 Act a sibling was to inherit the net inetstate estate in preference to a spouse or civil partners (after deduction of prior rights). Considering all the circumstances of the case the court established the value of Mr Savage's claim at nil. For it observed that, while a cohabitant cannot receive more than a spouse or civil partner, the court is not bound by any lower limit that it may set on an award. It is clear that in reaching its decision it was influenced by the fact that the deceased had been in a cohabiting relationship with a different partner for fifteen years and that he had made a will in that partner's favour. When the relationship ended and the will was destroyed no subsequent will was made in favour of Mr Savage and the couple did not share a bank account. The court also considered that that Mr Savage had benefitted from the cohabitation as

---

[263] *Kerr v Mangan and Others*, Case No, A56/08, para.16.

[264] *Savage v Purches*, 2009 S.L.T. (Sh. Ct) 36, For discussion of the case see F. McCarthy, "Rights in Succession for Cohabitant", 2009 *Edin. L.R.*, Vol.13, pp.325–329.

[265] In calculating this sum the court took into account the cost of purchasing an annuity from the insurance company that would provide the same amount of income that Mr Savage was receiving as an annual pension. This was calculated at £298,900.

the deceased had provided him with free accommodation and several foreign holidays a year. In reaching this decision the sheriff acknowledged that the court cannot claim to ignore the duration and nature of the cohabitation which are "part of the contextual hinterland in which the claim . . . presents itself".[266] Taking all the circumstances of the case into account the sheriff held that the benefits Mr Savage had already received as a result of the deceased's death were sufficient to militate against payment of anything more.

That case invovled a short and childless cohabitation. It may be con- **10–78** trasted with the case of *Windram v Windram and Marshal* (Third Party).[267] In this case the couple lived together for 24 years and had two children at the date of the deceased's death. It was viewed as having a different character from the case of *Savage v Purches*[268] on the basis that if no order was made under s.29 the children would be entitled to the whole of the deceased's estate,[269] leaving thier mother, the pursuer, Mandy Windram with nothing. In reviewing the circumstances of the case, the sheriff found that the couple had divided responsibilites between them, with Mandy Windram providing most of the physical care for the family while her partner, Mr Giacopazzi provided financial support. The pursuer had given up work when the first child was born and did not return until the second child went to school, making her a full time housewife "for about 11 years"[270] with the result that she "places herself in a position of dependency on the deceased".[271] In addition, the pursuer worked in the deceased's business without pay and nursed the deceased while he was dying.[272]

In this case a curator ad litem was appointed for the children, who argued that the status quo under the 1964 Act should not be distrubed and that the entire estate should pass to the children. At the time of the case the deceased's net estate was valued at £304,918 and the pursuer, aged forty five, had no pension or resources of her own, apart from a lump sum payment of £25,451 that came from the deceased's pension fund. She was constrained in the work she could take on as she still had to care for the younger child who had around eight more years of education to complete. The sheriff observed that the pursuer was under a duty to aliment the older child while he was under the age of twenty five and undergoing further education or training. The sheriff acknowledged the need to "strike a fair balance between the children's interests and those of the pursuer in the particular circumstances of the case".[273] However, if the house were to be held in trust for the children althoughthe puruser would be likely to remain there in the short-term the sheriff did not consider this to be satisfactory "given that the pursuer had

---

[266] *Savage v Purches*, 2009 S.L.T. (Sh. Ct) at para.15.
[267] *Windram v Windram and Marshal*, Case Ref A86/08, Sheriffdom of Lothian and Borders at Jedburgh, October 21, 2009; 2009 Fam. L.R. 157.
[268] *Savage v Purches*, 2009 S.L.T. (Sh. Ct) 36.
[269] Under s.2(1)(a) of the 1964 Act.
[270] *Windram v Windram and Marshal*, Case Ref A86/08, at para.14.
[271] *Windram v Windram and Marshal*, Case Ref A86/08.
[272] The sheriff surmised that it was likely the couple would have married had Mr Giacopazzi not died so precipitously.
[273] *Windram v Windram and Marshal*, Case Ref A86/08, at para.13.

foregone the opportunity to establish herself financially during her twenties and thirties"[274] with the result that "she would have no certainty of a home during her later middle years and beyond".[275] Under these circumstances the sheriff considered it would be unfair to leave here with no property, and especially "unfair to leave her with no security in the home she shared with the deceased".[276]

10–79   The sheriff therefore held that the home was to be transferred to the pursuer together with a capital sum that would enable her to repay the mortgage and leave her sufficient funds to maintain the home. The pursuer was also awarded the deceased's share of the furniture and plenishings valued at £2,000. Such an award would, in the sheriff's view benefit both her and the children "by allowing them to live in a mortgage free home, releasing such income as the pursuer has to meet their daily needs".[277] This award would leave £148,500 (before expenses were deducted) that would mean that the children would still remain "entitled to about £70,000 each from the father's estate".[278]

10–80   In this case, the award made in favour of the pursuer was only around £11,000 less than she would have received from prior and legal rights had she been a surviving spouse.[279] However, as the cases demonstrate they very much turn on their own facts and it still remains hard to judge what the likely outcome of a section 29 claim to a court will be.

SCOTTISH LAW COMMISSION PROPOSALS FOR REFORM

10–81   As the laws of succession currently stand they are somewhat inflexible. In 2007 the Scottish Law Commission published a discussion paper on sucession[280] and issued a report in 2009.[281] In examining both intestate and testate succession the report highlighted two main areas for reform. With regard to the former, it highligted the position of the surviving spouse or civil partner after prior rights, noting that s/he ranks below the deceased's children, parents or siblings as regards the remainder of the deceased's estate. This raises concerns about the spouse or civil partner's position vis a vis other family members, especially in cases where s/he cannot claim the prior right to housing with the result that s/he may receive only a small fraction of the intestate estate. With regard to testate succession the Commission examined claims which immediate relatives, such as a spouse or civil partner or children should have to the deceased's estate where they find themselves in a position where they are left little or nothing under the deceased's will. While some protection is afforded against complete disinheritance, under legal rights

---

[274] *Windram v Windram and Marshal*, Case Ref A86/08, at para.15.
[275] *Windram v Windram and Marshal*, Case Ref A86/08. The sheriff also noted that her children were under no legal duty to aliment her.
[276] *Windram v Windram and Marshal*, Case Ref A86/08.
[277] *Windram v Windram and Marshal*, Case Ref A86/08, para.17.
[278] *Windram v Windram and Marshal*, Case Ref A86/08, para.18.
[279] *Windram v Windram and Marshal*, Case Ref A86/08, para.18.
[280] Discussion Papers on Succesion, (DP 136) issued in August 2007.
[281] See Scottish Law Commission, *Report on Succession*, No.215 (2009).

and legitim, this takes the form of a fixed shared of the deceased's moveable estate. Where the deceased's estate contains little or no moveable property (with most of the deceased's estate being of a heritable nature) this can lead to negligible awards being made under these provisions.

In order to create greater flexibility and fairness among family members **10–82** the Commission made several recommentdations for reform in its Report in 2009. These cannot be discussed in detail here, but they included making the rights of the surviving spouse or civil partner non-property specific.[282] Under the current law of intestate succession, if s/he is not ordinarily resident in the house s/he has no entitlement to the house of the furniture and plenishings under prior rights. Instead of these rights, the Commission proposed that the surviving spouse or civil partner should get the entire net estate if there is no issue.[283] In the case of issue, then s/he should have a right in the estate up to a threshold sum[284] and to the whole estate if it amounts to less than the threshold sum.[285] There were also proposals for dealing with the situation where the value of the house is over the limit provided for in prior rights, that would entitle him or her to a recalculated capital sum that would be in excess of the currently stipulated threshold sum. This would amount to the spouse or civil partner taking half of any balance in excess of the threshold sum, with the issue taking the other half of the balance.[286]

In respect of testate succession where the surviving spouse or civil partner **10–83** is disinherited, the report proposed replacing legal rights for a surviving spouse or civil partner with a legal share of 25% of the whole of the deceased's net estate to which s/he would have been entitled had the deceased died intestate,[287] When dealing with children, however, there was disagreement as to how they should be dealt with. This lead to two sets of recommendations being tabled. The first, involved replacing legitim with a fixed legal share of the deceased's estate amounting to 25% of what they would have been entitled to had the deceased died intestate.[288] The second was a more controversial proposal, providing that that legal rights for children should be replaced with a provision that on death children under twenty five should be given a capital sum payment which would be calcalcutated to provide reasonable financial support for the child until s/he reaches the age of 25.[289] As a result, adult children would have no claim on either the deceased's testate or intestae estate. This recommendation was not supported by the public, 70% of whom still thought that adult children should have a claim on their parent's estate if not provided for in a will.[290]

The 2009 report also dealt with the position of cohabitants. It was critical **10–84**

---

[282] Para.2.3 of the 2009 *Report on Succession*, No. 215, p.2.
[283] Para.1.6 of the 2009 *Report on Succession*, No. 215, p.2.
[284] This was set at £300,000 subject to approval by the Scottish Parliament. See para.1.8 of the 2009 Report, p.3.
[285] Para.1.8 of the 2009 *Report on Succession*, No. 215, p.2.
[286] Para.1.8 of the 2009 *Report on Succession*, No. 215, p.2.
[287] Paras 1.15 and 1.17 of the 2009 *Report on Succession*, No. 215, p.4.
[288] Para.1.19 of the 2009 *Report on Succession*, No. 215, p.5.
[289] Para.1.19 of the 2009 *Report on Succession*, No. 215, p.5.
[290] See *Attitudes Towards Succession Law: Findings of a Scottish Omnibus Survey*, July 21 2005, published by Scottish Executive Social Research.

of the lack of guidance given to courts in exercising their discretion under s.29 of the 2006 Act which was far too broad. It obseved that the court was being asked to do the imposisble in balancing conflicting family interests without any guidance as to the relative weight to be given to the needs and interests of each party.[291] Indeed there was no indication of the principle underlying the award, whether it was to provide for the applicant's future needs, or whether it was to be in recognition of the financial and non-financial contribution that the applicant has made for the benefit of the deceased and their family during their relationship.[292] For this reason the report recommended replacing s.29 with a new statutory regime providing succession rights to cohabitants.[293] This would require cohabitants, unlike spouses or civil partners, to "earn" the right to succession that would cover two stages. The first would involve taking account of the following factors in deciding whether or not the applicant qualified as a cohabitant. These were

- whether or not the parties were members of the same household;
- that stability of the relationship;
- whether or not there was a sexual relationship;
- whether the parties had children together or have accepted children as children of the family; and
- whether the parties appear to family, friends and members of the public to be a married couple, civil partners or cohabitants.[294]

If the test of qualifying as a cohabitant is passed then the court must decide the extent to which the applicant is to be treated as a spouse or civil partner, which is to be expressed in terms of a percentage. This seems odd, as cohabitants are neither spouses nor civil partners so that making an award based on the percentage to which they conform to these roles appears to be forcing them to conform to particular stereotypes with regard to relationships. In reaching this decision as to the percentage attributed to the applicant, the court is to have regard to only three matters:

- the length of the period of cohabitation;
- the interdependence financially or otherwise between the cohabitant and deceased during the cohabitation; and
- what the cohabitant contributed to the life togeher of the cohabitant and the deceased (whether such contributions were financial or otherwise, as for example, running the household, caring for the deceased and their children or any children accepted by them as children of the family).[295]

---

[291] Para.4.7, 2009 *Report on Succession*, No. 215, p.68.

[292] Para.4.3, 2009 *Report on Succession*, No. 215, p.67.

[293] Para.4.9, 2009 *Report on Succession*, No. 215, p.69.

[294] Para.4.11, 2009 Report, pp.69–70. The last factor covers two situations, one where the parties hold themselves out as a married couple or civil partners when they are not and one where the parties openly state they are not a married couple or civil partners but nevertheless live together. While appearing to look to the quality of the relationship this last factor appears to do no more than rest on actually living together.

[295] Para.4.14, 2009 *Report on Succession*, No. 215, p.71.

The importance of curtailing the court's consideration to these three matters would mean that factors such as the size of the estate, or the interests of the decased's children or other relatives would be irrelevant.[296] Under the report's recommendations a cohabitant would have a claim under both intestate and testate succession. Where the deceased died intestate, the cohabitant would be entitled to the appropriate precentage of the estate to which a spouse or civil partner would have been entitled.[297] Where the deceased left a will, the cohabitant would be entitled to the appropriate precenatge of the legal share to which a spouse or civil partner would have been entitled.[298]

The report also recommended extending the limit placed on applications **10–85** from six months to a year, with power to extend this period on cause shown.[299] This is important because under the current law the six month period starts to run from the date of death and not from the date of the appointment of an executor dative and there is no discretion within the existing legislation to allow for any extension of this time period. The may cause problems where, for example, a cohabitant seeks to succeed to the deceased's estate under a will which is later found to have been revoked, by which time it may well be too late to initiate a claim under s.29.[300] The problems of adhering to time limits was also highlighted by family lawyers in the 2010 survey.

It is clear that succession law in its current form is unsatisfactory and is in **10–86** need of further reform. However, none of the recommendations discussed above have yet been implemented.

---

[296] Para.4.19, 2009 *Report on Succession*, No. 215, p.72.
[297] Para.1.24 of the 2009 *Report on Succession*, No. 215, pp.6–7.
[298] Para.1.24 of the 2009 *Report on Succession*, No. 215, pp.6–7.
[299] Para.4.32, 2009 *Report on Succession*, No. 215, p.77.
[300] See para.4.31, 2009 *Report on Succession*, No. 215, pp.76–77.

CHAPTER 11

THE FAMILY HOME AND DOMESTIC ABUSE

11–01 For most families, the most important asset they possess is the house in which they live. The family home may be owned privately, or occupied under a public or private sector tenancy.[1] In the case of private ownership, title to heritable property is conferred by a document known as the disposition which must be recorded in the Register of Sasines, or registered in the Land Register of Scotland. It is only on recording or registration of the disposition that ownership of the property passes to the purchaser, who then acquires full rights as proprietor, including the right to occupy and dispose of the property. A mere agreement to purchase property, although (if properly executed) an enforceable contract, does not, of itself, transfer the real right in the property, merely giving the purchaser a personal right against the seller.

11–02 Most house purchases need to be financed by a loan from a building society or bank. Such a loan, colloquially known as a mortgage, is invariably made on condition that the building society or bank becomes a heritable creditor. As such, the lender acquires a real right in security over the property to the value of its interest in the property. This is accomplished by the house purchaser granting a standard security over the house to the lender.[2] This standard security becomes a burden on the property as soon as it is registered or recorded, which gives the lender the right to sell the house if the purchaser fails to make the necessary repayments (including interest). The proceeds of such a sale are held in trust by the lender, and any surplus over from the sale after expenses and the loan have been paid off must be returned to the former debtor.[3]

11–03 Where the house is rented, title to occupy is conferred on the tenant by way of a lease, which lays down the terms and conditions under which the tenancy is held, including the duration of the lease,[4] as well as the period of notice which must be given on either side to terminate the tenancy. Statutory provisions have, over the years, provided the tenant with greater security of tenure than existed at common law.[5]

11–04 In Ch.10, we discussed the general proposition that marriage has no effect

---

[1] Public sector tenancies are regulated principally by the Housing (Scotland) Act 1987 as amended by the Housing (Scotland) Acts of 2001, 2006 and 2010. Private sector tenancies are regulated by the Rent (Scotland) Act 1984, Housing (Scotland) Act 1988 as amended and by the Private Rented Housing (Scotland) Act 2011.

[2] Conveyancing and Feudal Reform (Scotland) Act 1970.

[3] Conveyancing and Feudal Reform (Scotland) Act 1970 s.27. This procedure has been amended by the Home Owner and Debtor Protection (Scotland) Act 2010. For more general discussion see G.L. Gretton and KGC Reid, *Conveyancing*, 4th edn (Edinburgh: W. Green, 2011), Ch.22 at 22–40.

[4] Which may not exceed 20 years under Land Tenure Reform (Scotland) Act 1974 s.8.

[5] See, further, *Stair Encyclopaedia*, Landlord and Tenant (Reissue) published February 25, 2011.

on the property rights of the spouses. We noted that the Matrimonial Homes (Family Protection) (Scotland) Act 1981 ("1981 Act") provided an important exception to this rule. In this chapter, we will discuss in detail the key aspects of the 1981 Act[6] that was implemented to provide protection in the home for spouses and children (and, to a limited extent, heterosexual cohabitants) subject to domestic abuse. This protection has subsequently been extended to cover civil partners as well as same sex cohabitants.[7] It was a controversial piece of legislation as it was seen to curtail the property rights of those with legal title to the family home.

THE MATRIMONIAL HOMES (FAMILY PROTECTION) (SCOTLAND) ACT 1981

Background to the 1981 Act

Under the ordinary rules relating to property, only the person who owns property is entitled to possess it, occupy it and alienate it by sale or gift. In respect of heritable property, i.e. land and buildings, the person whose name is on the disposition, i.e. the disponee, is the legal owner (upon registration in the Register of Sasines or the Land Register of Scotland), regardless of who actually financed the sale, e.g. a bank, the other spouse or a relative. Thus, in principle, the person who owns the family home has the power to evict any other occupants, and to interdict them from returning to the premises,[8] provided obligations of aliment are met. A husband or wife may do this if they have sole title.[9]   **11–05**

Clearly, this can cause hardship in the domestic sphere.[10] Particular concern arose in the 1970s after empirical research showed that domestic abuse[11] was   **11–06**

---

[6] A full analysis of the conveyancing implications of the 1981 Act is outside the scope of this book. See, further, Gretton and Reid, *Conveyancing*, 4th edn (Edinburgh: W. Green, 2011), Ch.10 pp.176–189.

[7] See Civil Partnership Act 2004 ss.101–116 and the Family Law (Scotland) Act 2006 ss.31 and 32.

[8] In *Maclure v Maclure*, 1911 S.C. 200, a husband who was the sole tenant of the family home was granted an interdict to exclude his drunken wife from the premises, on the condition that he continued to aliment her.

[9] In *Millar v Millar*, 1940 S.C. 56, a wife who let property to her husband gave him notice to quit, just like an ordinary tenant. The court upheld her action regardless of the fact that the property in question was used as the family home and that she had deserted her husband.

[10] See the *Report from the Select Committee on Violence in Marriage* (1974–1975, HC 533) and the *Observations* on that report, Cmnd.6690 (1976).

[11] There are different ways of defining what this entails. The nationally agreed definition as stated in the ACPOS/COPFS Protocol is "Any form of physical, sexual or mental and emotional abuse which might amount to criminal conduct and which takes place within the context of a close relationship. The relationship will be between partners (married, cohabiting or otherwise) or ex-partners. The abuse can be committed in the home or elsewhere." See *http://www.crownoffice.gov.uk/publications/prosecution-policy-and-guidance* [accessed August 2013] and *http://www.scotland.police.uk/keep-safe/advice-for-victims-of-crime/domestic-abuse/what-is-domestic-abuse/* [accessed August 2013]. This definition was adopted by the police through the Domestic Violence Working Group of the Scottish Criminal Statistics Committee, involving the Association of Chief Police Offers in Scotland (ACPOS) and the Crown Office and Procurator Fiscal Service (COPFS). It may be contrasted with the more specific and detailed definition contained in the Scottish Government's National Strategy to Address Domestic Abuse (now referred to as the National Strategy) that states "Domestic abuse (as gender-based abuse), can be perpetrated by

a prevalent and apparently increasing problem,[12] primarily for women living with violent male partners. It is now widely recognised that "the pattern of abuse is asymmetrical. Overwhelmingly it is men who use violence against women partners, not the obverse."[13] While the numbers of women abusing men in recorded[14] incidents has risen this still represents a minority of perpetrators overall.[15] As early as 1976, studies documenting violence and abuse

---

partners or ex-partners and can include physical abuse (assault and physical attach involving a range of behaviour), sexual abuse (acts which degrade and humiliate women and are perpetrated against their will, including rape) and mental and emotional abuse (such as threats, verbal abuse, withholding money and other types of controlling behaviour such as isolation from family or friends)". See Domestic Abuse: A National Training Strategy, section 1 downloaded from *http:// www.scotland.gov.uk/Resources/Doc/47171/0025041.pdf* [accessed May 20, 2013].

[12] In 2011–2012, 59,841 incidents of domestic abuse were recorded compared with 55,698 incidents recorded in 2010–2011, an increase of 7%, continuing the generally upward trend. See Domestic Abuse Recorded by the Police in Scotland 2010–2011 and 2011–2012, *Statistical Bulletin, Crime and Justice Series*, October 30, 2012, p.1. According to the 2010/2011 *Scottish Crime and Justice Survey: Partner Abuse*, while the risk of experiencing partner abuse was similar for women and men "the nature and impact of the abuse differed" (p.8). For over the course of their adult lives "women experienced a greater number of forms of partner abuse on average than men and were more likely to have experienced particular forms of physical abuse than men" (p.12). They were also more likely to experience psychological abuse and a greater range of forms of this type of abuse than men" (p.18). Note that the definition of abuse used in 2010–2011 was wider than that used in 2006 and includes physical, emotional/psychological, sexual and financial abuse by partners (p.59). For discussion of the psychological impact of domestic abuse see M. Tagg, "Psychological Impact On Those Who Experience Domestic Abuse", in H. Hughes (ed), *Domestic Abuse and Scots Law* (2011), pp.158–180. According to the *Women's Aid Annual Survey 2012: Executive Summary*, for England and Wates only, 139,100 women and 19,145 children were directly supported by outreach and other non-refuge services, while 19,510 women and 19,440 children were accommodated in refuges (pp.1–2). It was also estimated that specialist domestic and sexual violence services were provided for a total of 158,610 women and 38,585 children. Scottish Women's Aid no longer compile annual statistics but on one day, in Scotland, September 18, 2012, 827 women and 522 children and young people were supported by Women's Aid groups, while 349 women and 323 children were living in a Women's Aid refuge. See *Scottish Women's Aid Census Day 2012*. Women's Aid in England estimated that their capacity to provide refuge is just at 65% of the number of places needed, based on an estimate of one family per place per 10.000 population as recommended by the Council of Europe.

[13] In 2011–2012, 81% of the incidents recorded involved a female victim and a male perpetrator, see 2012 *Statistical Bulletin, Crime and Justice Series*, p.5. Scottish Women's Aid observe that one in five women experience domestic violence in their lifetimes. See *Changing Lives: Women's Aid in Scotland* (2012), p.3. According to the 2010/2011 *Scottish Crime and Justice Survey: Partner Abuse*, in 61% of recorded cases the perpetrator was male compared with 37% of cases where the perpetrator was female (p.21). When considering the gender of the most recent or only abusive partner in the last 12 months, 54% were male and 39% were females (p.21), so that 93% were subject to abuse by an opposite-sex partner. In the majority of cases those who had experienced partner abuse since the age of 16 were of the opposite gender to their abusive partners. Only 5% of the men and 2% of women were of the same gender as their abusive partners (p.21).

[14] It is important to note that all these statistics are based on recorded incidents which tend to be under representative of the actual numbers involved. See Home Office, Policy document on *Ending violence against women and girls in the UK*, downloaded from *https//www.gov.uk/ government/policies/ending-violence-against-women-and-girls-in-the-uk* [accessed May 20, 2012] where it is estimated that fewer than one in four people who suffer abuse at the hand of their partner, and only one in ten women who experience serious sexual assault report it to the police. It is, of course, possible that for various reasons men are less likely to report abuse than women are.

[15] The percentage of domestic abuse with a male victim and female perpetrator has risen from 9% in 2001–2003 to 17% in 2011–2012. See *Statistical Bulletin, Crime and Justice Series*, p.5.

identified a number of key areas for concern,[16] including the family home as a site of abuse.[17]

In recent years there has been concern over children and the effects that abuse **11–07** against a parent that they have witnessed or heard has had on their lives.[18] The *2010/2011 Scottish Crime and Justice Survey: Partner Abuse* found that over one third of those who had experienced partner abuse in the last twelve months had children living with them at the time of the more recent incident.[19] In this situation children were more likely to be living with women who had experienced partner abuse in the last twelve month than with men.[20] Of those who had experienced partner abuse in the last twelve months who had children living with them, 69% said the children were present when the abuse occurred.[21] This is extremely disturbing, though hardly surprising, given that the vast majority of incidents that are recorded take place in a house or family home.[22]

In these circumstance a major concern was the fact that if a violent partner **11–08** was the sole owner of the home (and most perpetrators of such violence are male) than he had the sole right to occupy and thus to eject all other inhabitants of the house as he pleased, e.g. as a reprisal for calling out police because of assault. If the victim left the house she would have no right to re-enter the family home against his will.

This had implications for women, namely that **11–09**

- they might be rendered homeless, or forced to accept substandard accommodation for themselves and their children; and
- for this reason many women put up with abuse or violence because they did not have anywhere suitable to go.

These findings made a great impression on both English and Scottish Law Commissions and led to legislation being drafted to deal with the situation. In

---

The *Women's Aid Annual Survey 2012* for England and Wates only estimated that a total of 3,050 males approached the service for support and that this number represented less than 2% of the total number of female victims and survivors using specialist domestic violence support services. For information on how men are affected by domestic abuse see *Scottish Women's Aid Position Statement: Men Affected by Abuse, Summary Statement*, October 2012.

[16] See n.10, above.

[17] In 2011–2012, 87% of recorded incidents took place in a house or home. In cases where the victim and perpetrator cohabited (as spouse or partner) this number rose to 93%, leading to the conclusion that the "overwhelming majority of domestic abuse incidents still take place 'behind closed doors'". See *Statistical Bulletin, Crime and Justice Series* (2012), p.9.

[18] See *Safer Lives: Changed Lives: A Shared Approach To Tackling Violence Against Women in Scotland* (2009) Scottish Government, downloaded from *www.scotland.gov.uk/ Publications/2009/06/02153519/0* [accessed May 20, 2013]. See also M. Tagg, "Psychological Impact on Children in Domestic Abuse Situations" in H. Hughes (ed.), *Domestic Abuse and Scots Law* (2011), pp.181–204.

[19] M. Tagg, "Psychological Impact on Children in Domestic Abuse Situations" in H. Hughes (ed.), *Domestic Abuse and Scots Law* (2011), p.22.

[20] That is 43% of these children were living with women compared with 25% who were living with men (p.22).

[21] *2010/2011 Scottish Crime and Justice Survey: Partner Abuse*. Note that in 28% of these incidents the children not only saw or heard the abuse but became involved in some way, and in 7% of these incidents they were hurt or injured during the incident.

[22] See n.17, above.

Scotland this took the form of the Matrimonial Homes (Family Protection) (Scotland) Act 1981. The Act has two main aims:

- to provide a spouse (and now a civil partner)[23] who has no legal right to live in the home with that right (and to extend this to a limited extent to cohabitants); and
- to provide increased protection for a spouse (and now a civil partner)[24] and children (and to a limited extent a cohabitant)[25] who are at risk from domestic abuse.

Law reform in this area has focused[26] on providing the spouse, and now civil partner, who had no legal title to the house where she[27] resided with the rights

- to occupy and re-enter the matrimonial home, and
- to exclude the violent spouse or partner, even where he was the sole legal proprietor or tenant.

A principal area for concern which has been subjected to modifications since the passage of the 1981 Act has been how to provide workable *enforcement* mechanisms to protect these rights.

THE STRUCTURE OF THE 1981 ACT

Entitled and Non-Entitled Spouses

11–10   The 1981 Act is primarily concerned with providing rights to spouses in respect of the matrimonial/family home. The Act refers throughout to "entitled" and "non-entitled" spouses.[28] These terms are also used to cover civil partners, namely an "entitled partner" and "non-entitled partner", and their rights in the "family home" under the 2004 Act.[29] The entitled spouse ("ES")

---

[23] See s.101, Pt 3, Ch.3 of the Civil Partnership Act 2004.

[24] Under ss.102–112 and ss.113–116, Pt 4 of the 2004 Act.

[25] 1981 Act s.18, dealing with cohabitants, is now amended by s.31 of the Family Law (Scotland) Act 2006. Section 31 created "domestic interdicts" and added these into the 1981 Act. The intention was to allow unmarried cohabitants, either opposite-sex or same-sex, the same protection as married couples have under matrimonial interdicts. Domestic interdicts will have much the same effect in relation to cohabitants as matrimonial interdicts have for married couples with similar scope. See *http://www.legislation.gov.uk/asp/2006/2/notes/division/2/13/1* [accessed August 2013].

[26] The 1974–1975 Select Committee Report (*op. cit.*, above, n.10) led to the enactment of the Domestic Violence and Matrimonial Proceedings Act 1976 in England, which has now been replaced by Pt IV of the Family Law Act 1996. In Scotland, it took longer for such legislation to be passed in the form of the 1981 Act, which emerged out of the Scot. Law Com. Consultative Memorandum No.41 (1978) on *Occupancy Rights in the Matrimonial Home and Domestic Violence* and the subsequent report on this subject (Scot. Law Com. No.60 (1980)).

[27] In this chapter, the pronoun "he" will be used for the entitled spouse and "she" for the non-entitled spouse as reflecting the commonest situation. The provisions of the 1981 Act are, however, gender neutral.

[28] As defined in ss.1 and 22.

[29] Under ss.101–112 of Pt 3, Ch.3 of the 2004 Act.

or entitled civil partner ("EP") is the one who has legal title to the matrimonial/ family home, as owner or tenant, or who is granted permission to occupy the matrimonial/family home from a third party, e.g. a trustee.[30] The non-entitled spouse ("NES") or non-entitled civil partner ("NEP") is the spouse or partner who has no legal title to the property, but is given certain rights of occupation under the 1981 or the 2004 Act. The rights of the NES arise automatically under the 1981 Act by virtue of marriage to the ES as is the case also with registration of a civil partnership under the 2004 Act and such rights do not require any additional form of registration or notification to come into effect. As will be discussed below, without adequate safeguards this could raise problems for third parties who could not tell from examining the title documents of a property that it is a matrimonial or family home and that a NES/P has rights in respect of it.[31]

Matrimonial/Family Home

The NES/P's rights under the 1981 or 2004 Act apply only in respect of a **11–11** matrimonial[32] or family[33] home. What counts as a matrimonial home is very broadly defined to include "any house, caravan, houseboat or other structure which has been provided or has been made available by one or both spouses as, or has become, a family residence".[34] This definition may cover more than one residence. So, for example, where a couple buy a house in the town and a cottage in the country, and use them both as family residences, they may both qualify as a "matrimonial" or "family" home within the definition of the Acts. As a house may "become" a matrimonial or family home, the fact that it was purchased before the parties married is irrelevant. It is important to bear in mind the distinction between 'matrimonial home' for these purposes, and 'matrimonial property' for the purposes of the division of assets in divorce. A house can be a matrimonial/family home even if neither of the spouses/civil partners has ever lived in it, for the definition is satisfied by a house which is merely "provided" or "made available" as a family residence. On the other hand, not all properties which are purchased during marriage/ civil partnership necessarily qualify as a matrimonial/family home. Where, for example, one party buys a property for his or her exclusive use, or for investment purposes, and can argue that it was not acquired as a family residence, the Acts will not apply.[35] Where a house is provided or made available by one spouse/civil partner for the other to reside in *separately* it is not to be

---

[30] 1981 Act, s.1(2). A spouse who is entitled to occupy the matrimonial home along with a third party is also an entitled spouse, but only where the third party has waived his or her right of occupation in favour of the entitled spouse. See *Murphy v Murphy*, 1992 S.C.L.R. 62

[31] See paras 11–39 to 11–48.

[32] 1981 Act, s.22.

[33] See s.31 of the FLSA 2006 inserting s.18A(3) into the 1981 Act defining "family home" in the same terms as a matrimonial home.

[34] 1981 Act, s.22; see also s.135 of the 2004 Act defining a "family home" for civil partners and at s.18A(3) of the 1981 Act for cohabitees as inserted by s.31 of the FLSA 2006. The definition also includes "any garden or other ground or building attached to, and usually occupied with, or otherwise required for the amenity or convenience of, the house, caravan, houseboat or other structure".

[35] See the attempt to argue against a house being a matrimonial home in *Mazur v Mazur*, 1990 G.W.D. 35–2011.

regarded as a "matrimonial" or "family" "home".[36] Where the matrimonial/family home is a tenancy that has been transferred from one spouse/civil partner to the other by agreement or under any enactment it ceases to qualify as a matrimonial/family home.[37]

11–12   Application for an order under the 1981/2004 Act may be made to either the sheriff court or the Outer House of the Court of Session.[38]

Occupancy and Related Rights

Occupancy Rights—Spouses

11–13   Under s.1(1) of the 1981 Act, the NES has the right

(a) if in occupation, to continue to occupy the matrimonial home; and
(b) if not in occupation, to enter into and occupy the matrimonial home.

These rights include the right to occupy and re-enter together with any child of the family.[39] The Act was amended to this effect in 1985 to ensure that a NES's occupancy rights could not be defeated by threats to eject any children of the marriage from the matrimonial home. In its initial form, the Act did not confer any occupancy rights on children, who also had no right to occupy the home at common law except by permission of the person with title. It is still the case that children do not have independent rights under the Act, but only indirect rights of occupancy attached to an adult's occupancy rights. Nor is the protection of any child of the marriage a matter of compelling concern in the scheme of the 1981 Act, although the needs of the child are a factor the courts will consider under s.3(3)(c) (discussed in para.11–22).[40] In *Hampsey v Hampsey*[41] the court held that a sheriff had no power to grant an exclusion order simply because the best interests of the child required it. Compare the more recent provisions of the Children (Scotland) Act 1995, ss.76–80, which give the court the right to grant an exclusion order excluding a suspected abuser from the home of a child where this is necessary for the child's protection.[42] Under these provisions, the court *is* enjoined to treat the welfare of the child as paramount,[43] and

---

[36] 1981 Act s.22 for spouses; 2004 Act s.135 for civil partners
[37] 1981 Act, s.22(2) as inserted by s.7 of the FLSA 2006. The equivalent tenancy provisions for civil partners is at s.135(2) of the 2004 Act (as inserted by Sch.1, para.12 of the FLSA 2006). For cohabitants, similar provision is at s.18A(4) of the 1981 Act as inserted by s.31 of the FLSA 2006. Note that when an order is made during a divorce action requiring one spouse to sell his interest to the other it has been held that the vendor is entitled to continue to occupy the matrimonial home until the point of divorce in the absence of grounds for an interim exclusion order under s.4 of the 1981 Act. See *Adams v Adams*, 2010 S.L.T. (Sh. Ct) 2.
[38] 1981 Act s.22 for spouses; 2004 Act s.135 for civil partners.
[39] Under s.22 this includes "any child or grandchild of either spouse, and any person who has been brought up or treated by either spouse as if he or she were a child of that spouse, whatever the age of such a child, grandchild or person may be". Note that in this context, somewhat unusually, no age limit is placed on the child.
[40] See, e.g. *Assar v Assar*, 1993 G.W.D. 2–102.
[41] *Hampsey v Hampsey*, 1988 G.W.D. 24–1035.
[42] Discussed in detail in paras 7–60. and 7–70. Note that s.76 exclusion orders last for a maximum of only six months.
[43] 1995 Act s.16.

the underlying policy is that it is better, where there is compelling evidence, to prejudice the occupancy rights of an alleged abuser, rather than traumatically remove the child. The 1995 Act does not, however, give children express rights of occupancy in the family home any more than the 1981 Act does.

Occupancy Rights—Civil Partners

Corresponding rights under s.101 of the 2004 Act apply to civil partners. In this context, a child of the family is defined as **11–14**

> "any child or grandchild of either civil partner, and any person who has been brought up or treated by either civil partner as if the person were a child of that partner whatever the age of such a child, grandchild or person".[44] For these purposes "family" is defined as "the civil partners in the civil partnership, together with any child, grandchild or person so treated".[45]

Occupancy Rights—Cohabitants

In the past the definition of a cohabiting couple was restricted to "a man **11–15** and a woman who are living with each other as if they were man and wife".[46] However, the section has been extended[47] to include persons living with one another "as if they were civil partners". In determining the issue of whether or not the parties are a cohabiting couple, the court is expressly directed to consider all the circumstances of the case, including the length of the cohabitation and whether there are any children of the relationship.[48] In assessing the question of occupancy the First Division took the view that the appropriate test to be applied is whether the parties were living together as husband and wife at the time of the conduct that gave rise to the application.[49]

Unlike spouses and civil partners, cohabitants *do not* have automatic occu- **11–16** pancy rights (unless they are the owner of the property) but must apply to the court to have them declared. Further, occupancy rights may only be granted for a period not exceeding six months requiring further application to obtain another declarator, again for no longer than six months.[50]

In respect of the definition of "family" home discussed above,[51] similar **11–17** provision exists and similarly, where a property has been made available by one partner for the other to reside in separately, it falls outwith the definition of family home.[52]

Where occupancy rights are granted to cohabitants, ss.2 of the 1981 Act (which deals with subsidiary and consequential rights) and s.3 (which

---

[44] Under s.101(7) of the 2004 Act, as amended by Sch.1, para.3(b) of the FLSA 2006.
[45] 2004 Act s.101(7).
[46] 1981 Act s.18(1). Given this wording a same-sex couple could not come within the definition of a cohabiting couple. The section has now been amended to read "as if they were husband and wife" by s.31 of the FLSA 2006.
[47] By s.31 of the FLSA 2006.
[48] 1981 Act s.18(2).
[49] *Armour v Anderson*, 1991 S.C.L.R. 628.
[50] 1981 Act s.18(1).
[51] See para.11–11.
[52] 1981 Act s.18A(3) for cohabiting couples, inserted by s.31 of the FLSA 2006.

concerns the regulation of rights of occupancy of a matrimonial home by court) also apply to cohabitants by virtue of s.18(3) of that Act. Since 2006 cohabitants have included same-sex couples.[53]

Consequential and Subsidiary Rights

11–18   Granting occupancy rights to the non-entitled spouse/civil partner is not, on its own, enough to guarantee that person's ability to remain in the home. Certain ancillary rights are also necessary. For example, if the right to occupy was not accompanied by a right to the use of furniture and plenishings in the home, then the ES/P might remove such items as belonged solely to him from the matrimonial or family home, thus making occupation very difficult.[54] To prevent this, either spouse or civil partner may apply to the court for an order regulating possession or use of any furniture and plenishings in the matrimonial home.[55] Section 2(1) of the 1981 Act for spouses (at s.102 of the 2004 Act for civil partners), further empowers the NES without the consent of the ES to:

(a) make payments, such as rent, that are due by the entitled spouse[56];
(b) perform any other obligation incumbent on the entitled spouse;
(c) enforce performance of an obligation owed to the entitled spouse by a third party, e.g. a contract to re-paint the house[57];
(d) carry out essential repairs;
(e) carry out non-essential repairs or improvements which the court considers appropriate for the reasonable enjoyment of the occupancy rights[58]; and
(f) take such other steps as an entitled spouse would have been entitled to take to protect his occupancy rights.

It is of little use however, for the NES/P to be given the *right* to pay the mortgage or rent if she has not enough funds with which to pay it because the ES/P

---

[53] Under s.34 of the FLSA 2006.
[54] This problem, however, is alleviated by s.25 of the Family Law (Scotland) Act 1985, which sets up a presumption that "household goods" are owned in equal shares by spouses. See paras 12–04 to 12–08. This presumption is now extended to civil partners by Sch.28, Pt 1, para.28 of the 2004 Act and to heterosexual cohabiting as well as same-sex couples who are not civil partners by s.22(6) of the FLSA 2006.
[55] 1981 Act s.3(2) for spouses; 2004 Act s.103(2) for civil partners. 1981 Act s.22 for spouses; 2004 Act s.135 for civil partners: "furniture and plenishings" is defined to include items which are owned, hired or acquired under a hire-purchase or conditional sale agreement by one of the spouses. The court has a discretion as to what order to make having regard to all the circumstances of the case, including the factors set out in the 1981 Act s.3(3) for spouses; 2004 Act s.103(3) for civil partners.
[56] Payment includes "rents, rates, secured loan instalments, interest or other outgoings (not being outgoings on repairs or improvements)": 1981 Act s.2(1)(a) for spouses; 2004 Act s.102(1)(a) for civil partners.
[57] But only to the extent that the entitled spouse could enforce such performance: 1981 Act s.2(1)(c) for spouses; 2004 Act s.102(1)(c) for civil partners.
[58] These must be repairs which the entitled spouse could have legally undertaken and which have been authorised by court order: 1981 Act s.2(1)(e) for spouses; 2004 Act s.102(1)(e) for civil partners.

is refusing to pay his share. Accordingly, the court has power to apportion expenditure on rent, mortgage, or essential repairs made by one spouse, between *both* spouses/civil partners,[59] provided application is made within five years from the date on which the payment was made.[60]

Cohabitants

Section 2 of the 1981 Act which deals with subsidiary and consequential rights and s.3 which concerns the regulation of rights of occupancy of a matrimonial home by court also apply to cohabiting couples by virtue of s.18(3) of that Act.[61] Further, this also now applies to cohabiting same-sex couples by virtue of s.34 of the FLSA 2006.

Orders Regulating Occupancy Rights

Although occupancy rights of the NES/P arise from their status, when it **11–19** comes to taking any action to enforce or restrict such rights, it may be necessary to ask the court to declare the existence of these rights.[62] The ES/P may also wish to have his common law rights of occupancy declared. The court can also be asked to regulate the exercise of, protect, declare, enforce, or restrict, the occupancy rights of the spouses/civil partners.[63] In each case, it has discretion to make such order as it considers just and reasonable, having regard to all the circumstances of the case including[64]:

(a) the conduct of the spouses/civil partners in relation to each other and otherwise;
(b) the respective needs and financial resources of the spouses/civil partners;
(c) the needs of any child of the family;
(d) the extent (if any) to which—
  (i) the matrimonial (or family) home; and
  (ii) [any relevant] item of furniture and plenishings . . . is used in connection with a trade, profession or vocation of either spouse/civil partner; and
(e) whether the entitled spouse/civil partner offers or has offered to make available to the NES/P any suitable alternative accommodation.

These factors are important considerations as they apply not only to regulatory orders but also to exclusion orders, discussed below.

The court has power to grant an interim regulatory order.[65] The main **11–20** restriction on s.3 (1981 Act) and s.103 (2004 Act) is that the court cannot issue an order which would, in effect, amount to excluding an ES/P from the matrimonial/family home.[66] This is because this would be a derogation from

---

[59] 1981 Act s.2(3) for spouses; 2004 Act s.102(3) for civil partners.
[60] 1981 Act s.2(7) for spouses; 2004 Act s.102(7) for civil partners.
[61] With the exception of s.3(1)(a).
[62] 1981 Act s.3(1)(a) for spouses; 2004 Act s.103(1) for civil partners.
[63] 1981 Act s.3(1) for spouses; 2004 Act, s.103(1) for civil partners.
[64] 1981 Act s.3(3) for spouses; 2004 Act, s.103(3) for civil partners.
[65] 1981 Act s.3(4) for spouses; 2004 Act, s.103(4) for civil partners.
[66] 1981 Act s.3(5) for spouses; 2004 Act, s.103(5) for civil partners.

the common law rights of the proprietor to occupy his or her own property; rather, this requires a special statutory exclusion order as provided for under s.4 of the 1981 Act and s.104 of the 2004 Act.

Exclusion Orders

11–21   Notwithstanding s.3, the court does, however, have the power, in certain cirumstances, to exclude a spouse/civil partner whether entitled or non-entitled, from the matrimonial home, under s.4(2) of the 1981 Act and s.104(2) of the 2004 Act. Section 4(2) states:

> "Subject to subsection (3) below, the court *shall* make an exclusion order if it appears to the court that the making of the order is *necessary* for the protection of the applicant or of any child of the family from any conduct *or threatened or reasonably apprehended conduct* of the non-applicant spouse which is *or would be* injurious to the physical *or* mental health of the applicant or child." [Emphasis added.][67]

On first reading, the sections may appear extremely broad in application as

(i) the court *shall*, not may, grant an order where it feels the test is met;
(ii) the test is met not just by actual conduct, but also by conduct which is threatened or merely apprehended;
(iii) mental, not just physical, injury[68] may be caused by the conduct;
(iv) the injury *itself may* be potential rather than actual.

As Clive[69] has observed, this test could be wide enough to justify excluding a spouse who did nothing worse than smoke tobacco in the family home, were it not for the provisos[70] stating that the court shall *not* make an exclusion order if it would be unjustified or unreasonable having regard to all the circumstances including the factors discussed above (under regulatory orders). In the particular case of a matrimonial home which is, or forms part of, an agricultural holding,[71] or is a tied house, there are further reasons given why a court should not make an exclusion order. Effectively, the court is asked to have regard to the fact that where the family home is a farmhouse and the defender spouse/civil partner is a farm worker, or where that spouse/civil partner is in some other form of employment where residence in the family home is a condition of employment, then his exclusion may not only jeopardise that employment, but possibly also lead to the eviction of the whole family.[72]

---

[67] In s.104(2) of the 2004 Act, the words "is to make" are substituted for "shall".
[68] See, e.g. *Anderson v Anderson*, 1993 G.W.D. 35–2258 where the injury complained of was stress-related illness.
[69] E. Clive, *The Law of Husband and Wife in Scotland*, 4th edn (Edinburgh: W.Green, 1997), para.15.043.
[70] 1981 Act s.4(3) for spouses; 2004 Act s.104(3) for civil partners.
[71] Defined in Agricultural Holdings (Scotland) Act 1991 s.1.
[72] 1981 Act s.4(3)(b) for spouses; 2004 Act s.104(3)(b) for civil partners.

Case Law on s.4[73]

Early judicial interpretation of s.4 was so restrictive that it rendered the   **11–22**
section virtually inoperable.[74] The two leading cases of *Bell v Bell*[75] and *Smith
v Smith*[76] placed interpretative glosses on the words used in s.4 which made
it extremely difficult to obtain an exclusion order. The test of "necessity"
was held to be a "high and severe" test[77] which involved an element of "real
immediate danger of serious injury or irreparable damage"[78] (although these
terms were not to be found in s.4 itself). This emphasis on *physical* violence
was reinforced by the finding that unless the applicant was living in the home
at the time of the application, an exclusion order was not necessary for protection of the applicant or child, for no immediate danger could be present.[79]
In addition, in order to prove the application was necessary, the applicant
was required to have already obtained a non-molestation interdict against the
other spouse. However, where such an interdict *had been* obtained, but had
not been breached, an exclusion order was *also* deemed unnecessary, because
there was no indication that the applicant was in imminent danger, or likely
to suffer irreparable harm.[80]

However, subsequent judicial decisions and legislative amendments have   **11–23**
reduced the effect of these early decisions almost to nil. It is now clear that
an applicant can apply for an exclusion order regardless of whether or not
she is living in the matrimonial home.[81] Nor is it any longer a pre-requisite
for an exclusion order that the applicant spouse has previously obtained a
non-molestation interdict against the other spouse, although it is still a factor
to be considered.[82] What amounts to necessity is no longer predicated upon
immediate danger, risk of serious injury or irreparable harm. Instead, the
court has been directed to consider four questions:

(1) what is the nature and quality of the alleged conduct?;
(2) is the court satisfied that the conduct is likely to be repeated if cohabitation continues?;
(3) has the conduct been or, if repeated, would it be injurious to the physical
or mental health of the applicant or to any child of the family?;

---

[73] Note: the case law pre-dates the coming into force of the 2004 Act, therefore, references
throughout this section are to the 1981 Act and use the term "spouse".

[74] See Robertson and Robson, "Exclusion Orders: The Emerging Criteria", 1983 J.L.S.S. 397.

[75] *Bell v Bell*, 1983 S.L.T. 224.

[76] *Smit v Smith*, 1983 S.L.T. 275.

[77] *Bell v Bell*, 1983 S.L.T. 224, *per* Lord Robertson at 230.

[78] *Bell v Bell*, 1983 S.L.T. 224, *per* the Lord Justice-Clerk at 228.

[79] This was the situation in *Bell*, where no order was made since Mrs Bell was, in fact, living
temporarily with her son when she applied for the order.

[80] *Smith v Smith*, 1983 S.L.T. 275, *per* Lord Grieve at 279.

[81] See *Colagiacomo v Colagiacomo*, 1983 S.L.T. 559 and s.13(5) of the Law Reform (Miscellaneous
Provisions) (Scotland) Act 1985, which expressly amended s.4 to provide that a spouse may
apply for an exclusion order "whether or not that spouse is in occupation at the time of the
application". Although this is still a factor to be taken into consideration, according to Lord
Wheatley in *Colagiacomo*, exclusion orders *have* since been granted (in *Ward v Ward*, 1983
S.L.T. 472; and Brown v Brown, 1985 S.L.T. 376), where the applicant spouse has been living
outside the home.

[82] See *Brown v Brown*, 1985 S.L.T. 376.

(4) if so, is the order sought *necessary* for the future protection of the physical or mental health of the applicant or child?[83]

Since *Bell*,[84] and *Smith*,[85] applications for exclusion orders have clearly become more viable, though much still depends on the view the individual first instance judge takes of the facts at hand. Indeed, in a number of cases where application has been made for *interim* exclusion orders,[86] they have been granted on the basis of limited affidavit evidence[87] although it should be noted that interim exclusion orders can be granted only where the non-applicant spouse has been afforded an opportunity of being heard or represented before the court.[88] At one time in danger of interpreting the 1981 Act too restrictively, the courts may now have to guard against too liberal an application of the Act's provisions, and there may be a danger that judges grant orders on the basis of a balance of convenience test (judging one spouse's interests against the other) rather than on the criteria set out in s.4.[89] The role of the court under the 1981 Act is not to act as arbiter over the spouses' arrangements for sharing the matrimonial home, nor to provide relief to one spouse who no longer wishes to live with the other; but rather to provide protection where one spouse is genuinely causing, or in danger of causing, injury of some kind to the other spouse or any child of the family. The injury complained of should therefore derive directly from the acts of the defender spouse, and not just be stress or unhappiness generally induced by the breakdown of the marriage.[90] However, in a few cases, courts have held that stress taken together with the interests of the children can provide sufficient grounds for the granting of an order under s.4.[91]

---

[83] These questions were set out in *McCafferty v McCafferty*, 1986 S.L.T. 650 at 656. They have been approved in subsequent cases. See *Millar v Millar*, 1991 S.C.L.R. 649 where the court held that an exclusion order was still *necessary* to protect the applicant spouse although she had been living apart from her abusive husband for 10 months.

[84] *Bell v Bell*, 1983 S.L.T. 224.

[85] *Smith v Smith*, 1983 S.L.T. 275.

[86] Under s.4(6). The Act does not specify the test for an interim order but it has been held to be the same as for an ordinary exclusion order: *Bell* (n.68), *Smith* (n.71), *Ward* (n.72) and *Brown* (n.73).

[87] See *Mather v Mather*, 1987 S.L.T. 565 where an interim exclusion order was granted on this basis, although it was then suspended for three months to enable the defender to find other accommodation.

[88] See *Armitage v Armitage*, 1993 S.C.L.R. 173 where the court held that, unless there were circumstances in which the need for protection of the applicant was sufficiently urgent to justify a decision being taken immediately, the defender should have been afforded an opportunity to present his case by lodging his own affidavits.

[89] See *Ward v Ward*, 1983 S.L.T. 472; also *Pryde v Pryde*, 1996 G.W.D. 39–2245. *Cf.*, however, *Barbour v Barbour*, 1990 G.W.D. 3–135 where the court declined to grant an exclusion order because it did not appear that it was necessary to protect anyone.

[90] See *Matheson v Matheson*, 1986 S.L.T. (Sh. Ct.) 2. But see also *Anderson v Anderson*, 1993 W.L. 966116; *Assar v Assar*, 1994 W.L. 1716350; and *Roberton v Roberton*, 1999 S.L.T. 38 (1st Div.) where the court upheld the sheriff's granting of an interim exclusion order on the basis that the defender's conduct was part of a continuing process with which the pursuer's deteriorating health was consistent and that on the material before him the sheriff was entitled to conclude that the pursuer's health problems were not attributable simply to the distress of the breakup but to the defender's conduct which might be expected to damage her health.

[91] See *Anderson v Anderson*, 1993 W.L. 966116 and *Assar v Assar*, 1994 W.L. 1716350.

Cohabitants

A cohabitant with no occupancy rights who wishes to use s.4 of the Act to **11–24** exclude a violent partner who has occupancy rights must first raise an action for full occupancy rights, which, due to the procedure involved, may take several months. However, it appears that in practice, sheriffs grant interim exclusion orders pending the determination of a cohabitant's application for occupancy rights. Where the application is granted the court can only make an order for a limited period of up to six months, initially, and that may be extended on application for further six month periods.[92]

Additional Orders

Where the court grants an exclusion order it *must* also make certain other **11–25** specific orders where these are requested by the applicant, and *may* grant certain others. The court *must* grant[93]

(a) a warrant for the summary ejection of the non-applicant spouse/civil partner from the home;
(b) an interdict prohibiting the excluded spouse/civil partner from entering the matrimonial home without the express permission of the applicant; and
(c) an interdict prohibiting the non-applicant spouse/civil partner from recovering any furniture or plenishings from the house except with the consent of the other spouse/civil partner or by further order of court.

In the case of (a) and (c), however, the defender spouse/civil partner can plead that the order is unnecessary.[94]

The court *may*, in addition, grant certain other orders, including, impor- **11–26** tantly, an interdict prohibiting the other spouse/civil partner "from entering or remaining in a specified area in the vicinity of the matrimonial home",[95] ("family home" in the 2004 Act). Such an interdict may be particularly useful, as the protection that can be afforded by s.4(4) of the 1981 Act/s.104(4) of the 2004 Act alone is limited. Orders made under these sections cannot prevent a spouse/civil partner entering a house bought or rented after separation which is *not* a matrimonial/family home, nor a refuge where a spouse/civil partner is staying temporarily, nor the place of work of a spouse/civil partner, nor the school which the parties' children attend. These are all areas, as experience demonstrates, where couples are likely to come into contact and where one party may be vulnerable and put at risk. Where the NES/P wishes to keep the ES/P away, not only within the home but also, for example, when picking up the children from school or when

---

[92] 1981 Act s.18(1) which as amended by s.31 of the FLSA 2006 applies to same-sex as well as opposite-sex partners.
[93] 1981 Act s.4(4) for spouses; 2004 Act s.104(4) for civil partners.
[94] These additional orders are extended to cohabitees under section 18(3) of the 1981 Act: *http://www.legislation.gov.uk/ukpga/1981/59/section/18* [accessed August 2013].
[95] 1981 Act s.4(5)(a) for spouses; 2004 Act s.104(5)(a) for civil partners.

getting the car out of a nearby car park, then the protection an interdict under s.4(5) of the 1981 Act/s.104(4) of the 2004 Act offers some help but may still be inadequate.

11–27   To address these deficiencies, the Scottish Law Commission recommended that the definition of matrimonial interdicts be extended to cover areas outwith the matrimonial home, such as schools and work places,[96] and this has been implemented by the FLSA 2006. This amends s.14(2)(b) of the 1981 Act and s.113(2)(b) of the 2004 Act[97] so that a spouse/civil partner is prohibited from entering or remaining in:

   (i)   the matrimonial (or family) home;
  (ii)   any other residence occupied by the applicant spouse (or civil partner);
 (iii)   any place of work of the applicant spouse (or civil partner);
 (iv)   any school attended by a child in the permanent or temporary care of the applicant spouse (or civil partner).

These additional orders are important because they help to secure the position of the applicant spouse/civil partner. In particular, as we will see below, an interdict can be enforced by the police if a power of arrest is attached by the court.[98]

Cohabitants

11–28   To ensure that the protection afforded spouses above was also extended to cohabitees, the FLSA 2006 introduced "domestic interdicts" into the 1981 Act by the insertion of ss.18A and 18B.[99] These domestic interdicts offer protection both to same-sex and opposite-sex cohabitants to a similar extent, as provided by the FLSA amendments above in relation to the coverage of matrimonial interdicts.

Enforcement of Interdicts

Matrimonial Interdicts

11–29   An interdict is an order granted by a court preventing an individual from carrying out a specified action and can be specifically used to prohibit certain conduct of one person towards the other. For the purposes of the 1981 Act, a *matrimonial* interdict is defined under s.14(2) as any interdict or interim interdict which:

   (a)   restrains or prohibits any conduct of one spouse towards the other spouse or child of the family, or
   (b)   prohibits a spouse's movements as outlined above.[100]

---

[96]   Recommendation 57(c), *Report on Family Law*, Scot. Law Com. No.135 (1992).
[97]   FLSA 2006 s.10 amends s.14(2)(b) of the 1981 Act; Sch.1, s.8 of the FLSA 2006 amends s.113 of the 2004 Act.
[98]   See paras 11–35 to 11–37.
[99]   Inserted by s.31 of the FLSA 2006.
[100]   See paras 11–26 to 11–27.

Section 14(1) makes it clear that a matrimonial interdict may be granted **11–30** where the spouses are still cohabiting. A s.14(2)(a) interdict must specify in detail the conduct which is prohibited, and this should be no wider than is necessary to prevent the act which the pursuer seeks to have prohibited, i.e. the molestation of the other spouse or child of the family.[101] A s.14(2)(b) interdict, like a regulatory order under s.3, *cannot* serve to exclude the entitled spouse from his own home, since the function of an interdict is merely to enforce existing legal rights, not to declare new rights or restrict existing ones.[102] The 1981 Act has been amended by s.10 of the FLSA 2006 to allow that a matrimonial interdict may be granted which excludes an ES from his property when the matrimonial interdict is *ancillary* to an exclusion order *or*, by virtue of s.1(3), the court refuses leave to exercise occupancy rights. This amendment was included to ensure that a matrimonial interdict not be used as an easy alternative to an exclusion order.

A s.14(2)(b) interdict is, in practice, usually ancillary to an exclusion **11–31** order as—due to the nature of domestic relationships—it is a difficult remedy in practical terms if the parties are still residing in the same house.[103] Furthermore, a NES/P who wishes to exclude the other spouse *has* to seek the statutory remedy under s.4. The difference between seeking an interdict and an exclusion order is that, as we have seen, an exclusion order can be granted only where the court is satisfied that it is *necessary*; whereas an interdict may be granted, like any ordinary civil order, on the balance of probabilities.

INTERDICTS FOR CIVIL PARTNERS

Section 113 of the 2004 Act governs interdicts obtainable by Civil Partners. **11–32** This mirrors s.14 of the 1981 Act as amended by the FLSA 2006 Act.[104]

The Importance of Powers of Arrest Under the 1981 Act

At common law, a interdict (including a matrimonial interdict), like other **11–33** civil orders, could be enforced only by going back to the civil court and seeking to have the party who had failed to obey the interdict penalised for breach of interdict.[105] Such a return to the courts would inevitably involve expense and, even worse in the context of domestic abuse, delay. Without further provision, an exclusion order under s.4 of the 1981 Act and s.104 of the 2004 Act would also be enforceable by civil means only.

---

[101] See *Murdoch v Murdoch*, 1973 S.L.T. (Notes) 13, where an interim interdict preventing a husband from telephoning his wife or calling at her house was rejected on the basis that its scope was too wide.

[102] *Tattersall v Tattersall*, 1983 S.L.T. 506. This is now expressly embodied in the new s.14(2)(b)–(5) of the 1981 Act inserted by s.10 of the FLSA 2006.

[103] K. Norrie, E. Sutherland, A. Cleland, *The Laws of Scotland, Stair Memorial Encyclopaedia*, Reissue (Edinburgh: Law Society of Scotland, 2004), pp.495–496.

[104] FLSA 2006 s.33 and Sch.1, para.8.

[105] For practice and procedure in the Sheriff Court see further, Macphail, *Sheriff Court* Practice, 3rd edn, Sheriff T. Welsh Q.C. (ed.) (Edinburgh: W. Green, 2006). For the Court of Session rules, see Court of Session Act 1988 s.47(1).

11–34 For most NES/Ps faced with an abusive spouse attempting to re-enter the family home in breach of an interdict or exclusion order, clearly the most useful remedy would be if the police could be asked to enforce the interdict. But as a general rule the function of the police is to enforce the *criminal* law, and although conduct in breach of a matrimonial interdict might also be criminal, e.g. an assault, the police have tended in the past to be reluctant to become involved in abusive issues of this kind.[106]

11–35 The 1981 Act, heeding these problems, provides a novel enforcement mechanism now mirrored in the 2004 Act, whereby a breach of the matrimonial interdict can nonetheless be responded to by the police under certain circumstances. As we saw at para.11–30 above, where an exclusion order is granted by the court under s.4,[107] an ancillary matrimonial interdict *must be* made as well by virtue of s.4(4).[108] Other interdicts may also be granted under s.4(5).[109] These interdicts qualify as "matrimonial interdicts" under s.14(2) of the Act. By s.15(1)(a), the court is *required* to attach a power of arrest to any matrimonial interdict which is made ancillary to an exclusion order.[110] This provision is mandatory in order to avoid the prior English experience, which was that the courts were reluctant to attach a power of arrest when given unfettered discretion.[111] The courts also have discretion to attach a power of arrest to a matrimonial interdict which is *not* ancillary to an exclusion order. In that kind of case, the non-applicant spouse must have had the opportunity of being heard or represented before the court, before the power of arrest can be granted.[112]

11–36 The power of arrest gives the interdict "teeth". It enables the police to arrest the non-applicant spouse without warrant, where they have "reasonable cause for suspecting that spouse of being in breach of the interdict".[113] It is not necessary for a breach of the ordinary criminal law to have occurred, or be suspected, before the power of arrest can be exercised by a constable, merely actual or suspected breach of the interdict.[114] This represented a major step forward in providing protection for those at risk of domestic abuse. This has now changed under s.4 of the Protection from Abuse (Scotland) Act 2001, discussed below. Under s.4(1) of the 2001 Act the police can now only arrest the interdicted person without warrant if the constable (a) has reason-

---

[106] See Morley and Mullender, *Preventing Domestic Violence to Women* (Police Group Crime Prevention Series, Paper No.48, HMSO, 1994). See also Grace, *Policing Domestic Violence in the 1990s* (Home Office Research Study, No.139, London, HMSO, 1995). Theoretically, another remedy for potential victims of domestic violence lies in the common law remedy of lawburrows, under which a potential lawbreaker is asked to give security in respect of future behaviour. In practice it is of little use in preventing domestic violence from materialising: see *Liddle v Morton*, 1996 G.W.D. 22–1292.

[107] 2004 Act s.104.

[108] 2004 Act s.104(4).

[109] 2004 Act s.104(5).

[110] 2004 Act s.114. Power of arrest may be attached to an interdict which is ancillary to an *interim* exclusion order.

[111] See *Report on Occupancy Rights in the Matrimonial Home and Domestic Violence*, Scot. Law Com. No.60 (1980), para.4.35 and *Lewis v Lewis* [1978] 1 All E.R. 729.

[112] 1981 Act s.15(1)(b) for spouses; 2004 Act s.114(1)(b) for civil partners.

[113] 1981 Act s.15(3) for spouses; 2004 Act s.114(4) for civil partners.

[114] See s.15(3) and Lord Advocate's guidelines to chief constables on the Matrimonial Homes (Family Protection) (Scotland) Act 1981 (outlined in 1986 SCOLAG 170).

able cause for suspecting that person of being in breach of the interdict *and* (b) considers that there would, if that person were not arrested, be a risk of abuse or further abuse by that person in breach of the interdict. However, the efficacy of exclusion orders with powers of arrest was limited by the fact that under the 1981 Act they orginally terminated when the marriage comes to an end.[115] Although powers to regulate the occupation of the matrimonial home on divorce do exist, they are very rarely used.[116] This is a serious defect for the applicant spouse who may suddenly be left unprotected on divorce. The difficulty lies in the fact that, while the law may regard the parties' relationship as at an end, this does not necessarily reflect reality, particularly where an abusive partner is concerned. Experience and research show that an abusive partner often continues to harass a former spouse or cohabitant, regardless of the fact that a divorce has taken place or that the parties are no longer cohabiting.[117] Recognising the problems that this caused, the Scottish Law Commission recommended that the law be reformed to provide that a power of arrest would last for a fixed term of three years and remain effective even where the parties' marriage had come to an end.[118]

This recommendation has been enacted in the Protection from Abuse **11–37** (Scotland) Act 2001[119] that also provides for powers of arrest to be attached to interdicts granted to protect against abuse as defined in the Act.[120] For reasons outlined below,[121] there were discrepancies in the procedures dealing with powers of arrest under the 1981 and 2001 Acts. To maintain consistency in dealing with such powers, an amendment has been made to the 2001 Act instructing the court to attach a power of arrest to a matrimonial interdict which is ancillary to an exclusion or interim order made under the 1981 Act,[122] or to any relevant interdict as defined by s.113(2) of the 2004 Act, which is ancillary to an exclusion or interim order made under the 2004 Act.[123] As a result the 2001 Act now has *exclusive* control over powers of arrest attached to interdicts dealing with domestic abuse.[124] Its terms have

---

[115] 1981 Act s.5(1)(a) for spouses; 2004 Act s.105(2)(a) for civil partners.

[116] Family Law (Scotland) Act 1985 s.14(2)(d). Incidental orders (of all kinds) were made in only 2% of all ordinary divorce actions for 1989 and 1% in 1991. See Morris, Gibson and Platts, *Untying the Knot: Characteristics of Divorce in Scotland* (Edinburgh: Scottish Central Research Unit, 1993), p.34.

[117] In *An Evaluation of the Protection from Abuse (Scotland) Act 2001* (Scottish Executive Social Research, 2003), the authors K. Cavanagh, C. Connelly and J. Scoular reported that: "Much literature indicates that separating from an intimate partner is a dangerous and potentially lethal time for women. This was significantly reinforced in our finds. Men's threats to maim, disfigure and kill an intimate partner who had left them were widely and vividly reported in the court records, as was the actual execution of many of these threats. The need for effective legal protection for women at this time is absolutely critical": p.85.

[118] Recommendation 60 of the *Report on Family Law*, Scot. Law Com. No.135 (1992).

[119] Protection from Abuse (Scotland) Act 2001 s.1(3).

[120] See paras 11–61 to 11–64 below.

[121] See para.11–60 below.

[122] Protection from Abuse (Scotland) Act 2001 s.1A(a), inserted by s.32 of the FLSA 2006.

[123] Protection from Abuse (Scotland) Act 2001 s.1A(b). Domestic interdicts dealing with cohabitees under s.18A of the 1981 Act are covered by the amendment made to s.2(1) of the 2001 Act that inserts the words "in the case of any other interdict" into that section that deals with the duration, extension and recall of powers of arrest.

[124] See further, discussion at paras 11–61 and 11–64 below.

created more stringent requirements for the granting and enforcement of powers of arrest than existed under the 1981 Act.[125]

Cohabitants

11–38   Protection in the form of "domestic interdicts" has been extended to cohabitants by s.31 of the FLSA 2006 which introduces ss.18A and 18B into the 1981 Act. Further, as s.32 of the FLSA 2006 amends the Protection from Abuse (Scotland) Act 2001 so that the power of arrest is attached "in the case of any other interdict", it may be attached to these domestic interdicts subject to conditions.[126]

THIRD PARTY DEALINGS AND THE MATRIMONIAL/FAMILY HOME

11–39   Sections 1 and 4 of the 1981 Act and ss.101 and 104 of the 2004 Act, as we have seen, combine to give the NES/P the right to occupy and re-enter the matrimonial home and, if necessary, even to exclude the ES/P. But, crucially, the NES/P does *not* acquire any rights of ownership in the home under the 1981 or 2004 Acts. The ES/P is still entitled to sell the whole of the property. Since, under s.1(1) of the 1981 Act,[127] the NES's occupancy rights depend on there being an *entitled* spouse in respect of the particular home in question, without further provision, these occupancy rights would fall at the moment of sale. Thus the NES/Ps rights could be easily defeated by selling the property, either to a bona fide third party or perhaps just to a "straw man", such as a relative or friend, who could then re-convey the house to the originally entitled spouse.

11–40   A similar problem arises where the spouses/partners are co-owners. At common law, each is entitled to sell his or her *pro indiviso* share to another party. Spouse A therefore could sell his half of the house to stranger X who as co-proprietor would then be entitled to occupy the former matrimonial home along with spouse B. Effectively this would be likely to render spouse B's common law occupancy rights unworkable.

11–41   In order to prevent the first problem, the 1981 Act provides at s.6(1)(a) that the NES/P is not to be prejudiced by reason only of any dealing of the ES relating to the matrimonial home.[128] "Dealing" is very broadly defined to include the sale or lease of the matrimonial home, or grant of a heritable security over it or the creation of a trust over it.[129] Although the ES/P retains his legal right to sell the home, under s.6(1A)[130] the NES/P's occupancy rights are protected from the entitled spouse's dealing except in the circumstances outlined in paras 11–53 and 11–54 below. Not only that, but the purchaser is not entitled to claim rent from the non-entitled spouse in respect of her continued occupancy. These provisions protect the NES/P from eviction by a

---

[125] For further discussion see paras 11–60 *et seq.* below.
[126] Protection from Abuse (Scotland) Act 2001 s.1(2).
[127] 2004 Act s.101(1) for civil partners.
[128] 2004 Act s.106 for civil partners.
[129] 1981 Act s.6(2); 2004 Act s.106(2).
[130] Substituted by s.6(2) of the FLSA 2006 in place of s.6(1)(b) of the 1981 Act. Sch.1, para.5 of the FLSA 2006 substitutes s.106(1A) in place of s.106(1)(b) of the 2004 Act.

third party. The protection against dealings given to NES/P in s.6 is extended in similar terms to protect *co-owning* spouses under s.9(1) of the 1981 Act and to *co-owning* civil partners under s.109 of the 2004 Act.

Example: A and B are married to each other and own the matrimonial **11–42** home in common. A sells his *pro indiviso* half share to a third party, X. X now co-owns with B but cannot occupy because B has the protection of s.9(1)(a) and (b). Obviously this will usually discourage X from purchasing.[131]

Consents, Renunciations and Affidavits

Although the function of the provisions of the 1981 Act (which have been **11–43** mirrored in the 2004 Act) is to protect the interests of NES/Ps, it also has to balance them against the interests of third parties, and provide for the ordinary situation where a married couple both wish to sell the family home to a third party. No third party will purchase a matrimonial home which is burdened with the occupancy rights of a NES/P. The Act's solution is to provide that where the NES/P consents to the "dealing" in writing, and in prescribed form, the protection afforded against adverse dealings will not apply.[132] The court can dispense with the consent of the NES/P in certain circumstances,[133] especially where consent is unreasonably withheld[134]; where the spouse/civil partner cannot consent because of physical or mental disability; or the spouse/ civil partner cannot be found.[135] However, an order dispensing with consent can only be made if the heritable security is granted for a loan of no more than such amount as the court specifies in the order, and the security is executed before the date prescribed in the order.[136] Where the court refuses an application for an order, it has power to require a NES/P "to make such payments to the owner of the home in respect of that spouse's occupation of it as may be specified in the order" and "to comply with such other conditions relating to that spouse's occupation of the matrimonial home as may be so specified".[137]

It is also competent for the NES/NEP to renounce his or her rights in the **11–44**

---

[131] But if he does, X still has the indefeasible common law right as co-owner with B to raise an action of division and sale of the house. Note that that the protection given in respect of such actions under s.19 applies only where the co-owners are spouses.

[132] 1981 Act s.6(3)(a) for spouses; 2004 Act s.106(3)(a) for civil partners. The prescribed form is set down by the Matrimonial Homes (Form of Consent) (Scotland) Regulations 1982 (SI 1982/971) Schs 1 and 2. The equivlaent came into force for civil partners on March 30, 2006 under the Civil Parntership Family Homes (Form of Consent) (Scotland) Regulations 2006 (SI 2006/115), The writing requires to be carried out in the presence of a notary public.

[133] These now include a proposed sale where negotiations with a third party have not begun, or where they have begun but a price has not been agreed under s.7 of the FLSA 2006 which amends s.7 of the 1981 Act. Under these circumstances an order dispensing with consent may only be made if the price agreed for the sale is no less than such amount as the court specifies in the order and the contract for the sale is concluded before the expiry of such period as may be so specified under s.7(1B) inserted by s.7 of FLSA 2006. In the case of civil partners see s.107 of the 2004 Act as amended by s.33, Sch.1, para.6 of the FLSA 2006.

[134] e.g. *O'Neill v O'Neill*, 1987 S.L.T. (Sh. Ct) 26.

[135] 1981 Act s.6(3)(b). Similar provisions apply to the dispensation with a civil partner's consent to dealing under s.107 of the 2004 Act.

[136] 1981 Act s.7(1D) inserted by s.7 of the FLSA 2006. For civil partners see s.107(1D) of the 2004 Act inserted by Sch. 1, para.6 of the FLSA 2006.

[137] 1981 Act s.7(3A) inserted by s.7 of the FLSA 2006. For civil partners see s.107(3A) inserted by Sch. 1, para.6 of the FLSA 2006.

matrimonial/family home.[138] To guard against undue pressure on the non-entitled spouse, such renunciation must be done in writing before a notary public.

11–45   From a conveyancing perspective, the important question is how the prospective purchaser of a house is to know if he or she is buying a matrimonial home in respect of which a NES/P has occupancy rights? Given that occupancy rights under the 1981 Act are not registered, there is no way in which a potential purchaser can check to find out if a NES/P exists.[139] This places the purchaser in a difficult position. The solution, as provided by s.6(3)(e), is that where there has been "a transfer for value",[140] a third party who acquires an interest in heritable property will not be prejudiced by the occupancy rights of any spouse of the seller, if

> "(a) the third party acted in good faith, and
> (b) the transferor[141] produces to the third party *either*
>   (i) a written declaration signed by the transferor, or a person acting on behalf of the transferor under a power of attorney or as a guardian (within the meaning of the Adults with Incapacity (Scotland) Act 2000 (asp 4), that the subject of the transfer are not, or were not at the time of the dealing, a matrimonial home in relation to which a spouse of the transferor has or had occupancy rights; or
>   (ii) a renunciation of occupancy rights or consent to the dealing which bears to have been properly made or given by the non-entitled spouse or person acting on behalf of the non-entitled spouse under a power of attorney or as a guardian (within the meaning of the Adults with Incapacity (Scotland) Act 2000 (asp 4)".[142]

In practice, therefore, during exchange of missives for sale of a house, the seller is routinely required as a condition of the sale to produce either a consent to the dealing or renunciation of occupancy rights which appears to have been given by the NES/P, or an affidavit declaring *either* that the subjects of the transfer for value are not a matrimonial/family home *or* that there is no spouse/partner with occupancy rights in respect of that home. It should

---

[138] 1981 Act s.6(3)(a)(ii) for spouses. The Act allows rights to be renounced in respect of: (a) a particular matrimonial home; or (b) a particular property which it is intended by the spouses will become a matrimonial home. For civil partners see s.106(3) of the 2004 Act.

[139] The NEP's rights are treated as an overriding interest over the property, and as such are not noted in the title sheet. See s.6(4) which amends the Land Registration (Scotland) Act 1979. Checking the Register of Marriages is not conclusive either, as the parties may have married abroad or be married by cohabitation with habit and repute.

[140] These word replace the word "sale" that existed under the original s.6(3)(e) by s.6(3) of the FLSA 2006. For civil partners the same substitution has been made by the insertion of subs. (1A)(b)(i) after s.106(1) of the 2004 Act by s.33, Sch.1, para.5 of the FLSA 2006.

[141] This has been substituted for the word "seller" that existed under the original s.6(3)(e) by s.6(3) of FLSA 2006. For civil partners see insertion of subs.(1A)(b)(ii) after s.106(1) of the 2004 Act by s.33, Sch.1, para.5 of the FLSA 2006.

[142] 1981 Act, s.6(3)(e) as amended by s.6(3) of the FLSA 2006. For civil partners see subs.(1A)(b) (ii)(i) and (ii), after s.106(1) of the 2004 Act by s.33, Sch.1, para.5 of the FLSA 2006.

also be noted that where the NES/P has not occupied the home for years their protection under the 1981 Act comes to an end.[143]

Where the correct documentation, detailed above, is supplied and the **11–46** third party has acted in good faith, then s/he can enter the contract free of any occupancy rights of a NES/P. The Act does not specify what amounts to good faith. It is clear that where the purchaser has actual knowledge of the existence of a NES/P, e.g. because they are a relative of the family, then he or she will not be in good faith. What is not clear is whether the third party is under any duty to make inquiries about the marital/civil partnership position of the seller. As Clive points out, the result of a requirement to make reasonable inquiries could be an unacceptable and embarrassing invasion of privacy.[144]

What if a seller fraudulently declares in the matrimonial affidavit that there **11–47** is no NES/P, or forges a consent or renunciation? It is clearly the intent of the section that the purchaser can still enter and occupy the subjects and that the non-entitled spouse's occupancy rights fall. The only remedy open to the NES/P will then be to apply to the court for "just and reasonable" compensation from the entitled spouse.[145]

Double Dealing

Consider the scenario where A and B are married and A, the sole owner of **11–48** the family home, sells it to C who then in his turn sells it to D. It is clear that the sale to C could not have prejudiced B's right of occupancy as NES (unless a matrimonial affidavit, consent or renunciation was fraudulently given by A). But in this scenario, does D have the right to occupy? Do B's occupancy rights still operate to prevent him? In Clive's view, the NES's occupancy rights were no longer enforceable in this situation, but the wording of s.6(1) was ambiguous enough to make this contestable.[146] To clarify the position s.6 has now been amended to provide that the NES's occupancy rights will not be exercisable, following a dealing by the entitled spouse where

(a) a person acquires the home, or an interest in it, in good faith and for value from a person other than the person who is or, as the case may be, was the entitled spouse; or
(b) a person derives title to the home from a person who acquired title as mentioned in paragraph (a).[147]

---

[143] 1981Act, s.6(3)(f).
[144] E. Clive, *The Law of Husband and Wife in Scotland*, 4th edn (Edinburgh: W.Green, 1997), para.15.076.
[145] 1981 Act s.3(7) for spouses; 2004 Act s.103(8) for civil partners.
[146] E. Clive, *The Law of Husband and Wife in Scotland*, 4th edn (Edinburgh: W.Green, 1997), paras 15.081, 15.083. This is also the argument put forward by the Scottish Law Commission in its *Report on Family Law*, Scot. Law Com. No.135 (1992), para.11.10. But see a contrary view in Nichols and Meston, *The Matrimonial Homes (Family Protection) (Scotland) Act 1981*, 2nd edn (1986), para.6.05.
[147] 1981 Act s.6(1A) as inserted by s.6(2) of the FLSA 2006. For civil partners, see s.106(1A) inserted to the 2004 Act by s.33. Sch.1, para.5 of the FLAS 2006.

Pre-Marital and Pre-Act Dealings or Obligations

11–49   Where a dealing or obligation entered into by the entitled spouse with respect to property takes place before his or her marriage to the non-entitled spouse, it remains unaffected by s.6 of the 1981 Act.[148] The same is true of those dealings or obligations entered into by such a spouse before the 1981 Act came into effect.[149]

Co-owners/Co-tenants of the Matrimonial Home

11–50   Until now, we have been dealing mainly with the remedies granted by the 1981 Act (and mirrored by those of the 2004 Act) where one spouse (the ES) is sole owner and the other (the NES/P) is not. However, it is increasingly common for both spouses to share legal title to the matrimonial home, whether as co-owners or co-tenants. Neither party in this situation may eject the other from the matrimonial home.[150] But the Act makes it clear that a regulatory order under s.3, and an exclusion order under s.4, can be obtained where both spouses are entitled to occupy the matrimonial home.[151]

11–51   As noted above, at common law, where parties own property in common, each party is free to sell his or her *pro indiviso* share of the property without the other's agreement. The protection given by s.9(1) in this situation was discussed in paras 11–45 and 11–47 above. Another right given to co-owners, however, is the right to raise an action of division and sale. Until the 1981 Act, the court had no discretion to refuse an application of this kind, even if it left the non-applicant spouse without a home. Effectively, therefore, raising an action of division and sale was a foolproof way to defeat the occupancy rights of the co-owning spouse.

11–52   To deal with this, s.19 of the Act provides that when an action is brought for division and sale, the court has a discretion to refuse or postpone the granting of decree, or to grant decree subject to conditions, having regard to all the circumstances of the case including the factors listed in s.3(3).[152] Similar provisions apply to civil partners under s.110 of the 2004 Act. Whether the applicant spouse/civil partner has made an offer of suitable alternative accommodation to the other spouse/civil partner is also relevant.[153] Children are regarded as a very important consideration under s.19, although as is always the case with the 1981 Act, their needs are not paramount. In *Crow v Crow*[154] the court held it competent to postpone granting decree for division and sale beyond a date when the marriage would

---

[148] 1981 Act s.6(3)(c) for spouses; 2004 Act s.106(3)(c) for civil partners.

[149] 1981 Act s.6(3)(d) for spouses; 2004 Act s.106(3)(d) for civil partners, in which the wording is "before commencement of this section".

[150] 1981 Act s.4(7) and the 2004 Act s.104(8) make it clear that common-law powers to eject, if they were ever competent between co-owning spouses/partners, no longer apply.

[151] 1981 Act s.4(1) for spouses and the 2004 Act s.104(1) for civil partners.

[152] 1981 Act s.19(a).

[153] 1981 Act s.19(b). The offer must be of specific alternative accommodation. So, e.g. a general offer to help a co-owning spouse find somewhere to live, as in *Hall v Hall*, 1987 S.L.T. (Sh. Ct.) 15, is not sufficient. For civil partners see s.110(b) of the 2004 Act.

[154] *Crow v Crow*, 1986 S.L.T. 270.

be terminated by divorce where the needs of the children required this.[155] The question of onus of proof established in *Milne v Milne*[156] has been questioned in the case of *B v B*[157] where the court did not agree that the onus should be on the husband to prove decree for division and sale should be granted, but took the view that the onus was placed on the wife, as the party relying on the statutory limitation to the common law right of a co-owner to apply for division and sale.

While there was some doubt as to where the onus of proof lies in s.19 applications,[158] the case of *B v B*[159] held that, in accordance with the general rule applicable to persuasive and evidential burdens of proof, the party who raises the statutory defence must prove it. The court is, in practice, unlikely to allow a sale to go ahead where this would adversely affect the children's interests and those of the parent with whom they live. It is important to note that s.19 of the 1981 Act and s.110 of the 2004 Act apply only to co-owners who are spouses or civil partners. In all other cases where a house is jointly owned, e.g. by cohabitants, or *ex*-spouses or *ex*-civil partners, the court *must* grant decree where it is applied for, as a matter of common law.[160]   **11–53**

Tenancies

In many cases, the matrimonial/family home is held under a sole or shared tenancy agreement rather than owned by the spouses or partners. Particular problems may arise for NES/P living in homes of this kind. In some tenancies, security of tenure can be guaranteed only where the legal tenant is in continuous occupation. This requirement will be met under the 1981 Act even if the sole legal tenant has abandoned the tenancy if the tenant's spouse is in occupation.[161] Where the ES/P fails to meet his or her obligations, or has left or been excluded from the matrimonial/family home, the NES/P may wish to have the tenancy transferred into her name.   **11–54**

Transfer

This may be accomplished in one of two ways. Under the Housing (Scotland) Act 2001, social landlords (such as local authorities) may apply to the court for recovery of possession on the basis that he or she wishes to transfer the tenancy to the tenant's spouse, former spouse, civil partner,   **11–55**

---

[155] See also *Milne v Milne*, 1994 S.L.T. (Sh. Ct) 57.

[156] *Milne v Milne*, 1994 S.L.T. (Sh. Ct) 57.

[157] *B v B*, 2010 G.W.D. 24–454.

[158] Compare *Hall v Hall*, 1987 S.L.T. (Sh. Ct) 15 and *Milne v Milne*, 1994 S.L.T. (Sh. Ct) 57, with *Berry v Berry*, 1988 S.C.L.R. 296 where it was held that the onus lay on the defender to show why it was unreasonable for the sale to go ahead.

[159] *B v B*, 2010 G.W.D. 24–454.

[160] Note that if divorce or dissolution of partnership takes place and does not deal with a co-owned matrimonial home then neither s.19 of the 1981 Act nor s.110 of the 2004 Act would be available to postpone an action of division and sale. The court, however, has power under s.14 (2)(d) of the Family Law (Scotland) Act 1985 to regulate the occupancy of the former matrimonial or family home and this power may be used to avert division and sale.

[161] Sch.2, para.15. Spouse includes same-sex and opposite sex cohabiting partner. Civil partners are also included by virtue of CPA 2004, Sch.28, para.65.

former civil partner or cohabitant.[162] This is competent where one of these parties has applied for the transfer, and one of the parties to the relationship no longer wishes to live with the other in the house. Alternatively, the NES may apply to the court for a transfer under s.13 of the 1981 Act, provided that he or she is prepared to pay the other spouse such compensation as the court deems just and reasonable in the circumstances.[163] Where an application is made under s.13, the court is directed to have regard to all the circumstances of the case[164] including the suitability of the applicant to become a tenant and the applicant's capacity to perform the obligations under the lease.[165] In assessing the situation, the court may take account of the parties' conduct[166] as well as the children's interests.[167] Where both spouses are common tenants, the court may vest the tenancy solely in the applicant's name, provided that the applicant pays just and reasonable compensation to the other spouse.[168]

11–56   In such cases, a copy of the application for transfer must be served on the landlord, who must be given an opportunity of being heard or represented before the court makes a transfer order.[169] The court may not transfer a tenancy in certain cases where it represents an incident of employment, or is an agricultural holding or croft, or let on a long lease.[170] Where, however, the transfer is competent and the court makes an order, the tenancy vests immediately in the transferee and the transferee becomes subject to all the liabilities under the lease, except for arrears of rent, which remain the liability of the transferor.[171]

11–57   The court's power to transfer a tenancy under s.13 can also be exercised on decree of divorce[172] or nullity of marriage.[173] In either case, the court may

---

[162] See s.48 of, and Sch.3, para.16 to, the 1987 Act. Sch.28, para.54 amends s.83 of the Housing (Scotland) Act 1987.

[163] 1981 Act s.13(1) for spouses; 2004 Act s.112(1) for civil partners.

[164] Including the factors set out in s.3(3) of the 1981 Act. See s.103(3) of the 2004 Act for civil partners.

[165] 1981 Act s.13(3) for spouses; 2004 Act s.112(3) for civil partners.

[166] See *McGowan v McGowan*, 1986 S.L.T. 112 where the court granted a transfer partly because the husband's extremely unreasonable conduct had been solely responsible for the breakdown of the marriage and partly because the wife had been having to stay with her daughter and her family in a house which was too small for them. See also the case of *McMillan v McMillan*, 2004 Fam. L.B. 70–5 where the court also took the view that given that the incomes of husband and wife were roughly similar, it was reasonable for the tenancy to be transferred as the husband's behaviour had been the principal reason for the breakdown of the marriage.

[167] In *Guyan v Guyan* (Note), 2001 Fam. L.R. 99, the wife sought a transfer of her husband's share of a joint tenancy into her name. He did likewise. In reaching its decision the court held that in balancing the interests of adults and children, the children had to come first and made an order transferring the tenancy to the wife on the grounds that the children would have more security, live in better accommodation and surroundings (than their current temporary accommodation) and be able to continue at their existing school.

[168] 1981 Act s.13(9) for spouses; 2004 Act s.112(10) for civil partners.

[169] 1981 Act s.13(4) for spouses; 2004 Act s.112(4) for civil partners.

[170] 1981 Act s.13(7) for spouses; 2004 Act s.112(8) for civil partners.

[171] 1981 Act s.13(5) for spouses; 2004 Act s.112(5) for civil partners.

[172] 1981 Act s.13(2)(a) 1981 Act. Also dissolution of civil partnership at s.112(2)(a) of the 2004 Act.

[173] 1981 Act s.13(2)(b) 1981 Act. Also nullity of civil partnership at s.112(2)(b) of the 2004 Act.

make an order transferring the tenancy when it grants decree, or within a specified period thereafter.[174]

Cohabitants

When it comes to a transfer of tenancy the court can only make such an order in favour of the NEP if that party has been granted occupancy rights by the court, or to either partner, if both are entitled to jointly occupy the home, e.g. as joint tenants.[175] **11–58**

Termination of Rights Under the 1981 and 2004 Acts

Rights for spouses and civil partners will cease to exist where: **11–59**

- the marriage/partnership comes to an end by death or divorce/dissolution of partnership (except where a transfer of tenancy is concerned[176] or where powers of arrest have been attached to a matrimonial or domestic interdict in which case such powers of arrest expire three years after they have been granted (regardless of whether or not a marriage is still in existence)[177];
- where the ES/P ceases to be entitled[178];
- where the court recalls an order regulating occupancy rights[179];
- where the NES/P consents to the dealing or renounces his or her occupancy rights[180];
- the NES/P's rights under s.6 of the 1981 Act or s.106 of the 2004 Act do not operate where the ES/P has permanently ceased to be entitled to occupy the home in question and for a continuous period of two[181] years thereafter, during which time the NES/P has not occupied the home[182];
- the six-month period of occupancy rights granted to a cohabitant by a court has elapsed (and a re-application to the court has not been made).[183]

LIMITATIONS OF THE 1981 ACT

Our discussion of the 1981 Act highlights the difficulties that arise in framing legislation aimed at combating domestic abuse on the paradigm of marriage. **11–60**

---

[174] 1981 Act s.13(2) for spouses; 2004 Act s.112(2) for civil partners.
[175] 1981 Act ss.13 and 18(4).
[176] 1981 Act ss.1(1) and 5(1)(b); 2004 Act, s.105(2)(a). Also see *Clarke v Hatten*, 1987 S.C.L.R. 527.
[177] Protection from Abuse (Scotland) Act 2001 s.1(3).
[178] As the NES/P's rights under the 1981 Act are derived from the ES's rights, it follows that where the ES ceases to have such rights those of the NES/P must fall (except in relation to dealings under s.6). The same applies to civil partners (except in relation to s.106 of the 2004 Act).
[179] 1981 Act s.5(1)(a); CPA 2004 s.105(1)(a).
[180] 1981 Act s.6(3)(a)(i) and (ii) and s.6(3)(e); 2004 Act s.106(3)(a)(i) and (ii).
[181] Originally this was five years but it has been changed to two by s.5 of the FLSA 2006. For civil partners see insertion of subs.(6A) after s.101(6) by s.33, Sch.1, para.3 of FLSA 2006.
[182] 1981 Act s.6(3)(f). *Stevenson v Roy*, 2002 S.L.T. 445.
[183] 1981 Act s.18(1).

While the 1981 Act has been amended to allow interdicts with powers of arrest to continue after divorce and for domestic interdicts with powers of arrest to apply to cohabiting couples, and while provisions similar to those contained in the 1981 Act have been enacted to apply to same-sex couples who are registered as civil partners under the 2004 Act, there are still situations in which family members find themselves without adequate protection from domestic abuse.

MOVING BEYOND THE FAMILY HOME

Protection from Abuse (Scotland) Act 2001

11–61   This Act[184] extends the range of interdicts to which powers of arrest may be attached. These include any interdicts (or interim interdicts) obtained before or after the passing of the Act for the purposes of protecting against "abuse". Under its provisions, applicants no longer need to demonstrate any particular personal relationship to an alleged abuser. Nor are occupancy or property rights of any relevance. There is therefore no need for any person applying for a power of arrest to share, or to have shared, a home with the abuser. Instead the court simply has to find that granting the power of arrest is necessary to protect the applicant from the risk of abuse through a breach of interdict. Those currently excluded from using the 1981 Act, noted above, may use the 2001 Act to have powers of arrest attached to an interdict that has been obtained, or is being sought, to provide protection from abuse. Such an order may be obtained from either the Court of Session or the sheriff court.[185] Abuse under the Act is widely defined to cover psychological as well as physical abuse as well as "violence, harassment, threatening conduct, and any other conduct giving rise or likely to give rise, to physical or mental injury, fear, alarm or distress".[186] It includes conduct, which need not be active, and which covers a relatively wide category of behaviour including presence in a specified place or area.[187]

11–62   The FLSA 2006 has repealed s.15(3) of the 1981 Act and s.114(4) of the 2004 Act, the sections dealing with power of arrest without warrant. There was a risk under the previous regime of two powers of arrest being attached to interdicts prohibiting the same person from doing the same thing, although provision was made in both Acts to try to ensure that two powers of arrest could not be attached to interdicts prohibiting the same person doing the same thing.[188]

11–63   Before granting powers of arrest the court must be satisfied that

"(a) the interdicted person has been given an opportunity to be heard by, or represented before, the court;

---

[184] Which came into force on February 6, 2002.
[185] 2001 Act s.7.
[186] 2001 Act s.7.
[187] 2001 Act s.7.
[188] Protection from Abuse (Scotland) Act 2001 s.1(2)(b) and s.15(1A) of the 1981 Act inserted by s.6 of the 2001 Act.

(b) attaching the power of arrest is necessary to protect the applicant from a risk of abuse in breach of the interdict".[189]

The court must be satisfied that the attachment of the power of arrest is necessary to protect the applicant from a risk of abuse in the interdict. The fact that a woman has an interdict and that the interdicted person is abusive or potentially abusive is not sufficient proof to the court of risk of abuse. The court must be satisfied that attaching the power of arrest is necessary to protect the applicant from a risk of abuse in breach of the interdict.[190] So, for example, fear of another's presence in a specified place will not in itself justify the granting of powers of arrest unless there is an interdict prohibiting that person's presence. If a power of arrest is attached to an interdict under the terms of the legislation, police have discretionary powers to arrest and detain the person in breach of the interdict.[191] There is a two-step test before the police can use this power. They must:

(a) have reasonable cause to suspect that a breach of the interdict has occurred[192]; and
(b) also be satisfied that if not arrested, the person in breach will continue to cause abuse, or further abuse, which will be in breach of the interdict.[193]

In other words the police have to carry out a risk assessment on the spot. It is not enough for the police to suspect that the interdict has been breached. They must also be satisfied that there is a potentially abusive situation that the victim needs to be protected from and that this abuse would be in breach of the interdict. It is also not enough to satisfy this test for the police to suspect that the interdicted person would be likely to be abusive if not arrested where the likely abusive behaviour is not prohibited by the interdict. This is now the test that applies to *all* interdicts.[194]

Where a power of arrest is attached to an interdict under the 2001 Act, **11–64** the court must specify the length of its duration up to a maximum period of three years from the date of attachment.[195] After this date it will cease to have effect, although an application may be made to the court for an extension of up to three years.[196] There is no limit to the number of times an extension

---

[189] 2001 Act s.1(2).
[190] 2001 Act s.1(2).
[191] Protection from Abuse (Scotland) Act 2001, s.4(1). However, this discretionary power may be compared with the discretionary power that was (prior to the FLSA 2006) exercised under the 1981 Act where the Lord Advocate's guidelines issued in 1986 provided that "the offending spouse will be arrested in all but the most trivial cases".
[192] Protection from Abuse (Scotland) Act 2001 s.4(1)(a).
[193] Protection from Abuse (Scotland) Act 2001 s.4(1)(b).
[194] In research commissioned by Scottish Women's Aid, the researchers listed one of the reasons for women's lack of use of protective provisions as being due to the increased burden of proof that applicants faced in applying for powers of arrest in having them enforced by the police. See *The use and effectiveness of exclusion orders under the Matrimonial Homes (Family Protection) (Scotland) Act 1981 in preventing homelessness*, Research Report 2010 by Avizandum Consultations and AAJ Associates, p.18.
[195] 2001 Act s.1(3).
[196] 2001 Act s.2(4).

may be granted. On arrest, a person must be detained in police custody until
s/he is either charged with an offence or brought before a court.[197] In a study
evaluating the 2001 Act, the authors noted that it appeared "to be successful
in increasing access to powers of arrest".[198] However, the study also noted
that these gains were limited

> "due to the continued reliance on police discretion and the requirement
> that the breach of the interdict must amount to a crime before prosecu-
> tion can be considered".[199]

It also observed that

> "Civil law interdicts place an unfair burden on victims of abuse to
> pursue actions due to strict criteria for legal aid and the cost of privately
> funding civil court actions".[200]

PROTECTION FROM HARASSMENT ACT 1997

11–65   Another way of regulating abusive conduct is to utilise the provisions of the
Protection from Harassment Act 1997. The Act imposes an obligation on
persons not to

> "pursue a course of conduct which amounts to harassment of another
> which is either intended to amount to harassment of that other or which
> he knows or ought to know amount to harassment of another. For these
> purposes such conduct occurs in circumstances where it would appear to
> a reasonable person that it would amount to harassment of that other".[201]

Where such conduct occurs, a civil delict is created in Scotland against which
an order restraining harassment may be sought. In this context, "conduct" is
broadly defined to include speech[202] and that harassment includes "causing
the person alarm or distress".[203] Where an application is made to the court it

---

[197] 2001 Act s.4(2).
[198] K. Cavangh, C. Connelly and J. Scoular, *An Evaluation of the Protection From Abuse
(Scotland) Act 2001* (Scottish Executive Social Research, 2003), p.86.
[199] K. Cavangh, C. Connelly and J. Scoular, *An Evaluation of the Protection From Abuse
(Scotland) Act 2001* (Scottish Executive Social Research, 2003), p.87.
[200] *An Evaluation of the Protection from Abuse (Scotland) Act 2001* (Scottish Executive Social
Research, 2003). This continues to be the case and is reflected by the fact that the number of
firms providing civil legal aid has fallen by 12% in the period 2003/04 to 2008/09, see *SLAB,
Research Briefing*, July 2009 "Patterns of Civil Supply: National Findings". Such a contrac-
tion in this sector has an impact on women's accessibiity to legal services in seeking court
orders for protection. Eligilbility for civil legal aid is regulated by the Legal Aid (Scotland)
Act 1986, the Civil Legal Aid (Scotland) Regulations 2002, the Civil Legal Aid (Scotland)
(Fees) AmenmentREgulations 2009 and the Advice and Assistance Civil Legal Aid (Special
Urgency and Property Recovered or Preserved) (Scotland) Regulations 2011.
[201] 1997 Act ss.1(1) and (2).
[202] 1997 Act s.8(3).
[203] 1997 Act s.8(3).

may award damages[204] as well as granting an interdict or interim interdict.[205] As such an interdict is designed to protect the applicant from abuse, it may have a power of arrest attached to it in terms of the Protection from Abuse (Scotland) Act 2001. Damages may include damages for any anxiety caused by the harassment or any financial loss arising from it.[206] The court may also, if appropriate, issue a non-harassment order ("NHO").[207] An NHO is more difficult to obtain than an interdict, as the applicant has to prove a "course" of harassing conduct on at least two separate occasions before the court will make an order.[208] However, this requirement is reduced to one occasion where the NHO is being sought because of domestic abuse under s.1 of the Domestic Abuse (Scotland) Act 2011, which amended the 1997 Act by introducing a new s.8A. A defence to an action exists where the conduct was

- authorised by, under or by virtue of any enactment or rule of law;
- was pursued for the purpose of preventing or detecting crime; or
- was, in the particular circumstances, reasonable.[209]

However, in *Marinello v City of Edinburgh Council*[210] the Inner House held that where there was a gap of eighteen months between the alleged incidents of harassment the later incident might be considered part of the course of conduct.

Case law has demonstrated that the courts have encountered difficulties, **11–66** and have adopted differing interpretations of the Act when it comes to the granting of NHOs. In *Heenan v Dillon*[211] the sheriff questioned the proposition set out in *Furber v Furber*[212] that a court could grant an NHO at any time during the proceedings without the defender having an opportunity of being heard.[213] In *Alexandra v Murphy*,[214] the Sheriff Principal upheld this view on the grounds that, given the order could render the defender liable to imprisonment, such an action would amount to a fundamental breach of natural justice. He also formed the view (which was obiter) that:

---

[204] 1997 Act s.8(5)(a).
[205] 1997 Act s.8(5)(b)(i).
[206] 1997 Act s.8(6).
[207] 1997 Act s.8(5)(b)(ii).
[208] This understanding was established following the case of *Glennan v McKinnon*, 1998 S.C.C.R. 285. In this case the court held that it was not permissible to take previous convictions into account so that for an NHO to be available there had to have been averments of conduct *on at least two occasions* in relation to the current offence. However see *Riley v HM Advocate*, 1999 S.C.C.R. 644 which somewhat mitigates the effects of the previous case although it still upholds the position that "a course of conduct" must be demonstrated before an NHO can be contemplated. In the Scottish Executive Consultation Paper, *Stalking and Harassment* (2000), reform was canvassed on whether such conduct should "cover not only the present charge but also a previous incident where that had formed part of a previous conviction" at p.3.
[209] 1997 Act s.8(4).
[210] *Marinello v City of Edinburgh Council*, 2002 S.L.T. 66.
[211] *Heenan v Dillon*, 1999 S.L.T. (Sh. Ct) 32.
[212] *Furber v Furber*, 1999 S.L.T. (Sh. Ct) 26.
[213] The sheriff in *Heenan* did observe that it was not clear from the judgment whether the "interim" NHO made by the sheriff in that case was made without the defender having had an opportunity of being heard. The sheriff observed that while the order was made ex parte, "that does not mean that the defender did not have notice of the motion" (at 32L).
[214] *Alexandra v Murphy*, 2000 S.L.T. (Sh. Ct) 44.

- it is incompetent to make an interim NHO[215];
- a determinative NHO can be pronounced once only and that having been pronounced, it cannot be continued, varied or reviewed by application under s.8 of the 1997 Act or by appeal;
- in a defended cause a determinative order should not generally be granted without proof.[216]

11–67 While the court is empowered to grant an interdict or a NHO, this is subject to the proviso that,

> "a person may not be subjected to the same prohibition in an interdict or interim interdict and a non-harassment order at the same time".[217]

In *McCann v McGurran*,[218] the court held that the clear implication is that in exercising its power it cannot "grant both remedies but must, if circumstances require it, choose between the two".[219] It goes on to note:

> "This is perfectly consistent with the situation where in the same action, in applying remedies, the different remedies may be thought appropriate at different times (or perhaps even in respect of different conduct). Thus, since the non-harassment order is not an interim provision, there can be occasions where the court thinks it appropriate to grant an interdict at the early stage of the action but then, if the harassment is proved at a later stage of the case, wants to confer on the pursuer the more powerful protection of a non-harassment order".[220]

In stating this the court held that the restriction on the power to pronounce a NHO was "aimed alone at interdict orders pronounced within the framework of the action of harassment" and went on to observe that

> "while the fact that the pursuer had the protection of a permanent interdict [granted in an earlier divorce action] was a significant factor to be considered in determining whether or not to grant a non-harassment order, the application was technically competent".[221]

However, in this case, the court held that there were no circumstances which justified the granting of a NHO *at this stage* as the defender had given notice of intention to defend and the issues relevant to the merits could not be identified until they had been focused by the defences and the defender had had the opportunity to be heard.

---

[215] Note: for the avoidance of confusion, it is the non-harassment order that in the Sheriff Principal's opinion could not be interim. This is not to be confused with an interim interdict which may be granted under the Act at s.8(5)(b)(ii).

[216] *Alexandra v Murphy*, 2000 S.L.T. (Sh. Ct) 44 at 48G.

[217] 1997 Act s.8(5)(b)(ii).

[218] *McCann v McGurran*, 2002 Fam. L.R. 74.

[219] *McCann v McGurran*, 2002 Fam. L.R. 74 at 13–11, p.76.

[220] *McCann v McGurran*, 2002 Fam. L.R. 74.

[221] *McCann v McGurran*, 2002 Fam. L.R. 74 at 13–02, p.74.

Where an NHO is made and breached, the party breaching it is guilty of **11–68** an offence and may be liable to imprisonment,[222] or to a fine,[223] or both (see above). Note that breach of the order is still a criminal offence even if the order is granted in a civil court which means that it automatically attracts greater sanction than the civil protection orders outlined above. However, in the past, breach of an NHO did not in itself constitute an offence for which the police could arrest without a warrant. Amendments to the 1997 Act and the Criminal Procedure (Scotland) Act 1995[224] now give the police statutory powers to arrest those in breach of the order without such a warrant.[225]

THE CRIMINAL JUSTICE LICENSING (SCOTLAND) ACT 2010 AND THE DOMESTIC ABUSE (SCOTLAND) ACT 2011

Amendments to the 1997 Act have been made to deal with the problems **11–69** faced by applicants in applying for NHO's, especially for women dealing with domestic abuse. The first set of amendments was made by s.15 of the Criminal Justice and Licensing (Scotland) Act 2010. These made it easier for Fiscals generally to obtain criminal NHO's against offenders for incidents occurring after March 28, 2011.[226] Amendments to the 1997 Act have also been made by the Domestic Abuse (Scotland) Act 2011.[227] Firstly, the 2011 Act amends the 1997 Act by removing the requirement that there be a course of conduct before an NHO may be obtained where the conduct referred to amounts to domestic abuse, through the addition of s.8A. As a result of this reform, the protections available under the Act are significantly extended as the victim no longer needs to wait to be harassed a series of times before seeking protection as the course of conduct requirements no longer apply under s.8A of the 1997 Act. Section 8A, however, only applies wherever the conduct which has led to the pursuer bringing the action of harassment to court amounts to domestic abuse. Thus a person under this section must not "engage in conduct which will amount to harassment". Harassment of a person is defined as including or causing the person alarm of distress.[228]

---

[222] This may be up to five years where conviction is on indictment or up to six months on summary conviction under s.9(1)(a) and (b).

[223] Protection from Harassment Act 1997 s.9(1)(a) and (b).

[224] Made by s.49 of the Criminal Justice (Scotland) Act 2003.

[225] Protection From Harassment Act 1997 s.9 and s.234A of the Criminal Procedure (Scotland) Act 1995.

[226] Due to the amendments made by s.15 of the 2010 Act an NHO can now be applied for where a person is convicted of an offence involving misconduct that "causes alarm or distress". Misconduct requires a lower threshold of than that existing for harassment; an order can now be made to prevent "harassment" rather than merely to prevent any "further harassment", meaning that a woman can go to court at a much earlier stage; the court can now have regard to information or other offences which involved misconduct towards the victim which the offender has been convicted of, or has accepted a fixed penalty, compensation offer or work order; and the court can now see the relevant details of previous convictions, rather than simply referring to a list, which allows the court to have a more detail and a greater understanding of the abuser's past offending.

[227] This Act came into effect on July 20, 2011, three months after it received Royal Assent, under s.5(2) of the Act.

[228] 1997 Act s.8A(3)(b)(ii).

There is also an altered definition of conduct that comes into play where this section is engaged that may involve conduct one or more occasions and includes speech and presence in any place or areas.[229] Secondly, the 2011 Act makes it a criminal offence to breach a "domestic abuse interdict" which has a valid power of arrest attached.[230] This applies to interdicts made on or after the July 20, 2011. The penalites imposed for breach inlcude imprisonment and/or a fine.[231]

11–70   It is important to note that these criminal penalties on breach only apply to those cases that involve "domestic abuse interdicts." To allow the provisions of the Act on criminal penalties for breach to apply to a particular interdict, the court must first make a determination under s.3 of the Act that the interdict is a "domestic abuse interdict". According to s.3(2) of the Act a "domestic abuse interdict " is one granted for the protection of the applicant applicant against his or her spouse or civil partner, cohabitant or person with whom he or she is in an "intimate personal relationship". Further, under s.2, the criminal penalties on breach only apply if the domestic abuse interdict also has a valid power of arrest attached.

11–71   It is also important to note that breach of a domestic abuse interdict only gives rise to criminal penalties after the 2011 Act came into force. It is not possible for those holding interdicts with powers of arrest prior to the Act coming into force, to apply to the court for a recognition that the existing interdict with attached powers of arrest qualifies as a domestic abuse interdict.[232] Before making such a determination under the 2011 Act, however, the court must give the abuser an opportunity of being heard.[233] It is also the case that the determination will have no effect with regard to criminal penalties until a copy of the court interlocutor containing the determination has been served on the abuser.[234] It should be recognised that the new offence of breach of interdict does not replace the option of pursuing a civil hearing for contempt of court. This means that where conduct gives rise to a conviction under the 2011 the same conduct cannot be used in civil proceeding for a contempt of court action and vice versa.[235]

New Offence of Stalking

11–72   Additional protection that may now be utilised by victims of abuse is the new statutory offence of stalking introduced under section 39 of the Criminal Justice and Licensing (Scotland) Act 2010. While victims of abuse and violence are at risk in their home they are also at risk of being pursued by their partners or ex-partners outwith the home. Section 39 of the 2010 Act creates a new statutory offence of stalking. The offence occurs where a person (A) stalks another person (B) where A engages in a course of conduct

---

[229] 1997 Act s.8A(3)(a) and (b)(i) and (ii).
[230] 2011 Act s.2(2).
[231] Under s.2(3) where the offender has a summary conviction imprisonment may be up to 12 months, and where the offender is convicted on indictment it may be up to 5 years.
[232] 2011 Act s.2(1)(a).
[233] 2011 Act s.3(3).
[234] 2011 Act s.3(4).
[235] 2011 Act s.2(5) and (6).

(involving conduct on at least two separate occasions) which causes B to feel alarm or distress, where A either acts with the intention of causing B to feel fear or alarm or where A knew or ought to have known that engaging in the s.34 of the FLSA 2006 course of conduct would be likely to cause B to feel fear or alarm. The definition of conduct in section 39(6) is extremely broad and includes following, contacting or attempting to contact the other person, publishing any statement in relation to the other person, monitoring electronic communication, interfering with property and watching or spying or loitering in any place (whether public or private). Where a person is convicted of an offence under this section that person is liable to imprisonment and/or a fine.[236] As with the Protection from Harassment Act 1997, and the Domestic Abuse (Scotland) Acts 2001 and 2011 the provisions are not status dependent requiring any form of prescribed relationship (such as spouse or civil partner) between the offender and the recipient of the defender's behaviour before they can take effect.

TACKING HOMELESSNESS: INTERSECTIONS BETWEEN PRIVATE AND PUBLIC LAW

It is clear that over the years the Scottish Government have made great efforts to tackle domestic abuse with regard to both adults and children. It is beyond the scope of this chapter to deal with all the measures that have been put in place,[237] including the Gender Equality and Violence Against Women Team, the Rape Crisis Specific Fund and the Children Services Fund set up to provide direct therapeutic support to children in refuges, leaving refuges and in outreach settings.[238] What remains evident, however, is the link between domestic abuse and homelessness.[239] While the Matrimonial Homes (Family Protection) (Scotland) Act 1981 attempted to deal with this situation by offering protection to spouses, civil partners and cohabitants and their children, by excluding an abuse partner, there is evidence to suggest that in practice little use is made of exclusion orders. Research[240] commissioned

11–73

---

[236] Under s. 39(7), where the offender has a summary conviction imprisonment may be up to 12 months, and where the offender has a conviction on indictment imprisonment may be up to a period of 5 years,

[237] For discussion of the criminal justice system see P. Leach "The Criminal Justice System" in H. Hughes (ed.), *Domestic Abuse and Scots Law* (2011), pp.89–108; for discussion of specialist responses see C. Connelly, "Specialist Responses to Domestic Abuse" in H. Hughes (ed.), *Domestic Abuse and Scots Law* (2011), 109–129.

[238] For details see *www.scotland.gov.uk/Topics/People/Equality/Violence-women/VAWFund2012-15* [accessed May 24, 2013].

[239] The Scottish Government recognises that domestic abuse is a major contributory factor to homelessness. It notes that a violent or abusive dispute within the household was the fourth most common reason for all homelessness applications in 2008–2009 in Scotland. See "Domestic Abuse, Housing and Homelessness in Scotland: An Evidence Review", Scottish Government, November 2010, downloaded from *wwww.scotland.gov.uk/Publications/2010/10/27085309/0* [accessed May 22, 2013].

[240] This research was based on a sample of 34 women, 16 of whom were interviewed individually and 18 of whom were interviewed in groups; participation of 36 local Women's Aid groups, data from six sheriff courts and in-depth work in four local authority areas to explore the reasons why women were not using exclusion orders and the factors that influenced their choices. See "The use and effectiveness of exclusion orders under the Matrimonial Homes

by Scottish Women's Aid revealed that women appear to be using exclusion orders as a remedy less frequently than in the past.[241] The researchers attribute this to a number of factors including developments in the area of homelessness policy and practice through implementation of the Housing (Scotland) Act 2001 and the Homelessness etc (Scotland) Act 2003 that deal with local authorities' duties towards housing the homeless.

11–74   Building on the Housing (Scotland) Act 1987 these Acts give women a strong legal entitlement to housing as a homeless person where they are fleeing from domestic abuse. The 1987 Act provided that a person can be homeless even if s/he has legal rights to accommodation, e.g. as co-owning spouse. The definition of a homeless person in terms of the 1987 Act[242] is normally a person who has no accommodation in Scotland or England or Wales, but it also includes a person who has accommodation, but

(a) cannot secure entry to it, or
(b) it is probable that occupation of it will lead to violence from some other person residing in it or to threats of abuse (within the meaning of the Protection from Abuse (Scotland) Act 2001 (asp 14) from some other person residing in it and likely to carry out the threats, or
(bb) it is probable that occupation of it will lead to
　　　(i) abuse; or (ii) threats of violence which are likely to be carried out, from some other person who previously resided with that person, whether in that accommodation or elsewhere.[243]

11–75   Local authorities do not have a duty to house those who are intentionally homeless. However, the 1987 Act expressly provides that a person is not intentionally homeless simply because he or she leaves accommodation which it was unreasonable to expect him or her to occupy, e.g. because of the fear of domestic abuse.[244] The Housing (Scotland) Act 2001 strengthened the rights of homeless households more generally and introduced a requirement for local authorities to produce homeless strategies which could be integrated with their domestic abuse strategies. The Homelessness etc (Scotland) Act 2003 increased the safety net for homeless households, including phased expansion of priority need categories leading to eventual abolition of priority need. This expansion included "persons at risk of domestic abuse" as a priority category, making this priority explicit. The concept of priority need has now been abolished giving all unintentionally homeless people a legal

(Family Protection) (Scotland) Act 1981 in preventing homelessness", 2010 Report, by Avizandum Consultants and AAJ Associates, commissioned by Scottish Women's Aid.
[241] "The use and effectiveness of exclusion orders under the Matrimonial Homes (Family Protection) (Scotland) Act 1981 in preventing homelessness", 2010 Report, p.5.
[242] As amended by the Law Reform (Miscellaneous Provisions) (Scotland) Act 1990 and by the Homelessness, etc. (Scotland) Act 2003.
[243] Housing (Scotland) Act 1987 s.24(3) as amended by the Law Reform (Miscellaneous Provisions) (Scotland) Act 1990 and by the Homelessness, etc. (Scotland) Act 2003. Para.(bb) was added by the Law Reform (Miscellaneous Provisions) (Scotland) Act 1990.
[244] 1987 Act s.26(1).

entitlement to housing.[245] The Act also defined domestic abuse in terms set out in s.7 of the Protection from Abuse (Scotland) Act 2001. This is important because it extends the concept of abuse beyond that of physical violence to include threatening behaviour or psychological, financial or emotional abuse.

These provisions attempt to provide individuals fleeing domestic abuse and seeking a home, with at least the choice of asserting occupancy rights under the 1981 Act, or seeking accommodation from the local authority. However, although those experiencing domestic abuse are entitled to be rehoused, public housing is still difficult to obtain[246] and, even where provided, may not come up to the same standard as previous accommodation.   **11–76**

The Scottish Government have produced guidance on homelessness prevention which identifies domestic abuse and sexual abuse of a child in the household as an indication of risk of homelessness, and an area for homeless prevention activity by local authorities.[247] They have also provided guidance on the needs of children in homeless households that emphasises the need for a multi-agency approach to support, geared to helping applicants to stay in their home safely, while also providing an option for rehousing in alternative accommodation.[248] What emerged from the research commissioned by Scottish Women's Aid, was the need to promote increased security in the home (whether in family home or reallocated housing). This could be brought about by providing more advice and information about the remedies available for tackling domestic abuse, including exclusion orders.[249] There is also a need for a simplified legal process (both civil and criminal), as well as better access to legal aid to pursue civil legal remedies, along with the need for wider changes in the legal system to counteract the perception among women that it favours the rights of the abuser.[250] While real attempts have been made to tackle domestic abuse in recent years there is still a long way to go. Many of the initiatives that are being promoted require sustained financial investment and it remains to been seen how viable they will be given the constraints on public expenditure in a current climate of economic austerity.   **11–77**

---

[245] See the Homelessness (Abolition of Priority need Test) (Scotland) Order 2012 (SI 2012/330), that amends Pt 2 of the 1987 Act, abolishing the priority needs test under ss.31 and 32, and s.25 that set out which persons were accorded priority need for accommodation.

[246] This may be due to a shortage of housing stock. In its 2010 Report on *Domestic Abuse, Housing and Homelessness in Scotland* the Scottish Government acknowledged that "the problem lies in the gap in housing provision" to meet the legal entitlement (p.7). There is a lack of concrete data on how local authorities are dealing with the situation. In one case, *Mcmillan v Kyle and Carrick District Council*, 1995 S.C.L.R. 365 a local authority alleged it had no jurisdiction over the homeless applicant, and therefore no duty to provide housing, because the applicant did not have sufficient family or local connections with the area.

[247] See "the use and effectiveness of exclusion orders under the Matrimonial Homes (Family Protection) (Scotland) Act 1981 in preventing homelessness" 2010 Report, by Avizandum Consultants and AAJ Associates, commissioned by Scottish Women's Aid, p.21.

[248] See *Meeting the Best Interests of Children Facing Homelessness*, Scottish Government, June 2010.

[249] The study found that a number of women and service providers lacked knowledge about the existence of exclusion orders and how to acquire them.

[250] See n.239 above

11–78   There is another option for those women who have left husbands who own or co-own the family home, that is to initiate divorce proceedings, and to attempt to stake a claim to all or part of the family home as part of a claim for financial provision on divorce. We examine this further in Ch.13 along with the rights that apply to civil partners. In Ch.12, however, we will look at other strategies for disputing *ownership*, as opposed to *occupation*, of the family home, while the marriage or civil partnership subsists, as well as looking at ownership of other types of matrimonial or family property.

CHAPTER 12

FAMILY PROPERTY

As a general principle, the rules of property law in Scotland are not affected **12–01** by marriage, civil partnership or cohabitation. Every legal person in Scotland has a patrimony, which contains anything with a financial value that the person owns. A person normally becomes the owner of a piece of property by buying it. The fact that a buyer is in a formalised adult relationship has no affect on this process. Each party to the relationship has his own patrimony; anything he acquires during the relationship becomes part of his sole patrimony. In the last chapter, we explained that this is sometimes referred to as a "separate property regime".

However, as touched upon in the last chapter, this general principle **12–02** is subject to various exceptions to account for the realities of family life. Although parties to a relationship retain their individual patrimonies, the decisions they make about property are likely to be taken jointly to a significant extent. Imagine that Donald and Edith are a married couple who have just had their first child. As parents, they have a shared responsibility to care for their child physically, emotionally and financially. They decide that Edith will shoulder the bulk of the day-to-day physical and emotional care by working at home, and Donald will shoulder the bulk of the financial care by continuing in paid employment. The separate property regime does not comprehend this type of shared endeavour that is common in relationships. Donald will use his wages to buy property, and that property therefore becomes part of his patrimony. The fact that he could not earn those wages without Edith caring for their child is not reflected in his patrimony. Donald can invest some of his wages to generate further income, all of which goes into his patrimony. Edith cannot invest her care. After ten years, Donald may have considerable assets in his patrimony; Edith may have very few. Alternatively, Donald may have run up considerable debts during this period. Debt collectors may be knocking on the door. Although the debts fall solely within Donald's patrimony, they may have been run up in the interest of the family, and both Edith and the child will be affected if Donald's creditors were to repossess the family home. The exceptions to the separate property regime are designed to give recognition to the operation of family life.

Exceptions to the separate property regime fall into three main categories. **12–03** In the first place, the law tends to disapply the rules of separate property in relation to day-to-day household items and expenses. In the second place, the law will allow a party to the relationship to assert a claim in respect of the other party's property in some limited contexts. Finally, the law puts in place certain protections both for creditors and for other members of the family where one party to a relationship has run up debts he is unable to pay.

HOUSEHOLD PROPERTY

Household Goods

12–04   Section 25(1) of the Family Law (Scotland) Act 1985 sets out a presumption that household goods obtained in prospect of or during a formalised adult relationship are owned in common between the parties to the relationship. It goes on to provide in s.25(2) that this presumption cannot be rebutted merely by the fact that the goods were solely paid for by one of the parties.[1] Although expressed as a presumption, these two provisions taken together seem in effect to create a rule[2] that household goods acquired for or during a marriage or civil partnership will be owned in equal shares by the parties, irrespective of who actually paid for them. Accordingly if Donald purchased a toaster for the family home from his wages, ownership of that toaster will be held in equal shares by himself and Edith.

12–05   This provision solves both a practical and an ideological problem. The practical problem is that over the course of a long relationship it is unlikely that parties will even remember who paid for each household item, far less be able to prove as much by, for example, producing a receipt. A presumption of shared ownership saves time and effort that would otherwise have to be spent trying to establish who owns which items. The ideological problem relates back to the idea of joint endeavour discussed in para.12–02 above. Donald may buy a microwave because he has received a bonus at work; Edith may buy a vacuum cleaner six months later with money won on a scratch card. In both cases, the decisions on how to spend the money were likely taken jointly, and the items purchased intended for the use and benefit of the whole household. It is sensible for the law to recognise that context by disapplying the usual rule that the buyer becomes the owner.

12–06   Household goods are broadly defined to cover

> "any goods (including decorative or ornamental goods) kept or used at any time during the marriage or civil partnership in any family home[3] for the joint domestic purposes of the parties to the marriage or the partners, other than—
>
> (a) money or securities;
> (b) any motor car, caravan or other road vehicle;
> (c) any domestic animal".[4]

Where goods are not kept or used "for joint domestic purposes" they will not qualify as household goods and s.25(1) will not apply. This means that where one party has specifically purchased goods for his own purposes, for example

---

[1] Section 25(2) does not apply where parties are married but not living together. In that situation, it may be possible to rebut the presumption with proof of payment.

[2] It is not clear how the presumption of shared ownership can ever be rebutted if it is not sufficient to *prove* one party is the sole owner by virtue of having paid for the goods.

[3] This has the same meaning as "matrimonial home" in s.22 of the Matrimonial Homes (Family Protection) (Scotland) Act 1981. See Ch.11.

[4] 1985 Act s.25(3).

in connection with a hobby which his spouse or civil partner does not share, he will retain sole ownership of the goods in question. A husband who buys jigsaw puzzles, or a wife who collects graphic novels, can attempt to prove that these were not acquired for "joint domestic purposes" and the presumption of ownership in equal shares will not arise.

Section 25 does not apply to goods gifted by or inherited from third **12–07** parties. Ownership of such goods is therefore regulated by the usual property law rules. If Edith receives a coffee machine as a birthday present from her mother, that coffee machine remains in Edith's sole ownership despite the fact it is a household good. Where a gift is given to the couple together, as with wedding presents for example, ownership depends on the intention of the donor. Was the gift meant to be owned in common by the couple, or by one party only? As Thomson has pointed out,[5] although a gift may be intended for the parties' joint *use*, it does not necessarily follow that the donor intended that the gift should be *owned* jointly by them. On their wedding day, Donald's parents may have made the couple a gift of antique jewellery, handed down in the family for generations. The intention may have been for Edith to have sole *use* of the jewellery, but for Donald to have sole *ownership*, so that the items can be retained on that side of the family.[6] If the donor's intention has not been expressly communicated, it may be possible to infer the correct intention from the circumstances surrounding the gift, so that for example a gift from the wife's family might be inferred as intended for her sole ownership.[7] Clive has suggested that a presumption of shared ownership of wedding presents would be appropriate.[8]

Household goods[9] are also presumed to be held in shared ownership by **12–08** cohabitants, subject to the same exception in respect of goods acquired by gift or inheritance from a third party.[10] However, in the case of cohabitants, it *is* possible to rebut the presumption by providing proof of ownership.[11] It may be inferred that the policy argument underlying the presumption for spouses and civil partners is not considered as strong in the case of cohabitants.

Money and Bank Accounts

Money is expressly excluded from the definition of "household goods,"[12] **12–09** meaning the presumption of shared ownership does not operate and the ordinary rules of property law apply. Wages paid to Donald are owned by

---

[5] J. Thomson, *Family Law in Scotland*, 6th edn (Edinburgh: Bloomsbury Professional, 2011), pp.82–83.

[6] Note that such items may be regarded as "heirlooms" and therefore be unaffected by the wife's prior right to furniture and plenishings if the husband dies first and does not leave a will: Succession (Scotland) Act 1964 s.8(6)(c).

[7] See *McDonald v McDonald*, 1953 S.L.T. (Sh. Ct) 36.

[8] Clive, *The Law of Husband and Wife in Scotland*, 4th edn (Edinburgh: W.Green, 1997), para.14.041.

[9] The definition of "household goods" used in s.25(3) of the 1985 Act is also used in s.26(4) of the 2006 Act.

[10] FLSA 2006 s.26.

[11] FLSA 2006 s.26(3).

[12] 1985 Act s.25 for spouses and civil partners; FLSA 2006 s.26 for cohabitants.

Donald. Confusion can arise here where money is paid into a bank account held in joint names. In such cases, the names on the account are not conclusive of ownership of the funds held in the account; instead, they merely indicate to the bank or building society concerned that each of the named account-holders may draw freely on the account. There is no presumption of shared ownership of the funds raised by the fact that they are in joint names. Instead, ownership must be proved by reference to the actual contributions made by the account-holders, and whether or not there is any evidence of donation. If Donald's wages are paid into an account he holds jointly with Edith, in the absence of contrary evidence, it will be assumed that the money belongs solely to Donald, and that the account was opened merely to allow Edith to draw conveniently on his funds.[13]

12–10   Where there is evidence that *both* parties have contributed to the funds in a joint account, but the precise amounts remain vague, it is submitted that donation of whatever amount is necessary to give each a half share should be inferred, unless there is specific evidence to the contrary.[14]

12–11   Joint accounts set up by spouses frequently incorporate a survivorship clause which allows the surviving spouse to withdraw all the funds on the death of the other. Such a clause does not of itself imply that the deceased spouse intended to leave such proportion of the funds as belonged to him or her to the surviving spouse on death. It merely allows the surviving spouse to ingather the funds, which will then be due to the deceased's heirs. However, it is sometimes possible in these circumstances to prove *donatio mortis causa*.[15]

Savings from Housekeeping Allowance

12–12   At common law, where a wife managed to save money from a housekeeping allowance paid to her by her husband, the savings were considered to belong to her husband since it was his money in the first place.[16] Injustice arose, however, where the wife saved money out of the allowance by for example spending her own earnings on household provisions. The money saved was still her husband's. The only way in which a wife could claim a share of the money saved was if she could establish, as in *Pyatt v Pyatt*,[17] that the savings had increased due to her management skills. In *Pyatt*, the wife saved money out of her allowance and used it to put a winning stake on the football pools. The question was whether the pay-out from the win on the pools should go wholly to the husband since the stake had been bought using his money. The court held that the winnings had derived not only from the stake money which had come out of the housekeeping allowance provided by the husband, but also from the wife's luck and skill. Accordingly, both were entitled to an equal share of the winnings.

---

[13] See *Cuthill v Burns* (1864) 24 D. 849.
[14] Proposals for the introduction of a presumption of equal ownership of money held in joint accounts by spouses were dropped, reportedly because of the opposition of the Committee of Scottish Clearing Banks. See *Report on Matrimonial Property*, Scot. Law Com. No.86 (1984), para.4.9.
[15] *Forrest-Hamilton's Trs*, 1970 S.L.T. 338.
[16] *Preston v Preston*, 1950 S.C. 253.
[17] *Pyatt v Pyatt*, 1966 S.L.T. (Notes) 73.

The common law position was altered by s.26 of the Family Law **12–13** (Scotland) Act 1985[18] which provides that money derived from an allowance for joint household expenses or similar purposes is presumed to be owned in equal shares by the spouses or civil partners.[19] The same presumption applies to any property obtained with money derived from that allowance. Accordingly, if Mrs Pyatt were to win the pools today, the money would be presumed to be owned in equal shares by herself and her husband irrespective of any luck or skill involved.

Almost identical provision is made for cohabitants in s.27 of the Family **12–14** Law (Scotland) Act 2006.[20] It is important to note, however, that the home in which the couple reside is expressly excluded from the definition of "property" in which equal shares will be presumed.[21]

Enforcement of Life Assurance Policies

A life assurance policy is a contract between the insurance company and **12–15** the insured person. The insured is contracted to pay a regular contribution to the company, who in turn are contracted to pay out a sum of money in the event of the insured's death. Normally, a contract cannot be enforced by a person who is not a party to it. In the case of life assurance, however, the third party who is to receive the pay out in the event of the insured's death can obtain a right to enforce, known as a *jus quaesitum tertio*.[22] Normally, a JQT can only be obtained where the policy is delivered to the third party, or where intimation of the policy is made to him. Without delivery or intimation, the third party cannot enforce the insurance company's contractual obligation to pay out. However, where the insurance policy has been taken out by a spouse or civil partner for the benefit of his spouse or civil partner, it is artificial to demand delivery or intimation because of the nature of the relationship. Section 2 of the Married Women's Policies of Assurance (Scotland) Act 1880[23] therefore makes an exception to the ordinary rule in the case of a husband or wife taking out a life policy in favour of the other spouse or children of the relationship. The effect of the statute is that the policy proceeds are deemed to be held in trust by the insured for the third party beneficiaries whose rights are therefore enforceable against the insured (or his estate) even if there was no delivery or intimation. This provision was extended to civil partners by s.132 of the Civil Partnership Act 2004. The Scottish Law Commission recommended that the rule should also be extended to cohabitants,[24] but this recommendation has yet to be given effect.

---

[18] As amended by Sch.28, Pt 2, para.29 of the 2004 Act.

[19] This section (prior to its redrafting by the 2004 Act to include civil partners) replaced the similar provision in s.1 of the Married Women's Property Act 1920, which only covered savings made by a *wife* from a housekeeping allowance made to her by her *husband*. The provisions of s.26 of the 1985 Act clearly apply equally to husband and wife.

[20] Implementing *Report on Family Law*, Scot. Law Com. No.135 (1992), para.16.12.

[21] FLSA 2006 s.27(3).

[22] *Carmichael v Carmichael's Exrx*, 1920 S.C. (H.L.) 195.

[23] As amended by the Married Women's Policies of Assurance Act (Scotland) (Amendment) 1980.

[24] *Report on Family Law*, Scot. Law Com. No.135 (1992), para.16.45.

Gifts

12–16   As a general rule, where A hands over property or money to B, there is a presumption *against* donation by A to B. (A may, for example, merely be depositing the item with B for safekeeping.) As with all presumptions, it may be rebutted. While the nature of the relationship between husband and wife is such that one might expect them to exchange gifts, case law suggests that the courts are wary of holding that the presumption is rebuttable simply because the donor and donee are married to each other.[25] The courts are, however, aware that intention to donate is more likely between spouses than between strangers.[26] Gifts made between spouses are as irrevocable as gifts to other people.[27] However, gifts between parties to a relationship to defraud creditors in the bankruptcy of the donor spouse may be struck down as gratuitous alienations under the Bankruptcy (Scotland) Act 1985, discussed further below.[28]

CLAIMS ON THE OTHER PARTY'S PROPERTY

12–17   The exceptions to the separate property regime outlined above go some way towards recognising that families tend to operate as an economic unit, with decisions taken jointly by couples for the benefit of the family. However, these presumptions of shared ownership are limited in their scope, dealing principally with day-to-day household assets. They do not apply to more significant family assets, in particular the family home, which for most families will be by far the most valuable asset in question. Yet the public policy arguments that underlie the presumptions of shared ownership discussed above are just as likely to apply to ownership of larger assets.

12–18   Consider the following example. Donald and Edith have bought a house. Ownership of the house is taken in Donald's name only, since Donald as the wage-earner is able to obtain a better mortgage in his sole name than the couple can obtain jointly. Donald covers the mortgage repayments each month from his wages: as discussed above, he would not be able to earn these wages without Edith taking on his share of the day-to-day care of their child. Edith also adds to the value of the house by regularly redecorating and

---

[25] See, e.g. *Jamieson v McLeod* (1880) 7 R. 1131; *Newton v Newton*, 1923 S.C. 15; *A v B* (1925) 41 Sh. Ct Rep. 23.

[26] Thomson, *Family Law in Scotland*, 6th edn (Edinburgh: Bloomsbury Professional, 2011), p.79, asserts the presumption is "not difficult" to rebut between spouses. Clive, *The Law of Husband and Wife in Scotland*, 4th edn (Edinburgh: W.Green, 1997), para.14.029 comments that while "the natural affection and obligation to provide support which subsists between parent and child can cancel out a presumption against donation . . . these considerations have, for some reason, not been given much weight in husband and wife cases" although he acknowledges that "there is no reason to doubt that they at least reduce the strength of the presumption".

[27] The old common law rule that gifts between spouses were revocable during the donor's lifetime was abolished by s.5 of the Married Women's Property (Scotland) Act 1920. But death-bed gifts by a spouse may still be revocable where the donor unexpectedly recovers, under the general rules of *donatio mortis causa*.

[28] Gifts made by a spouse/civil partner to third parties up to five years before a divorce/dissolution of partnership that are intended to reduce a person's resources in order to avoid an order for financial provision are also struck down by s.18 of the Family Law (Scotland) Act 1985, as amended by s.261(2), Sch.28, Pt 2, para.24 of the 2004 Act (to apply to civil partners).

undertaking various DIY projects. After 10 years, the house has increased substantially in value as a result of the party's efforts together with a rising property market. However, the property is entirely within Donald's patrimony. Edith has no right of ownership in the house.

While the relationship subsists, and the parties continue to operate as an economic unit, this imbalance in property rights is unlikely to cause problems. However, if the relationship breaks down, and Donald and Edith wish to go their separate ways, obvious difficulties arise. **12–19**

Where a formalised adult relationship is brought to an end by divorce or dissolution, a detailed legislative framework exists to untangle and hopefully neutralise the economic consequences by allowing one party to make a claim for financial provision against the other.[29] To put it very simply, in a case such as Donald and Edith's, it might be expected that the court would order Donald to transfer half the value of the house to Edith as her fair share. This is discussed in detail in the next chapter. Cohabitants are also entitled to make more limited financial claims against each other on the breakdown of the relationship,[30] also discussed in Ch.13. **12–20**

In some cases, neither of these options will apply. For example, Edith may not wish to divorce Donald for religious reasons, so cannot make a claim for financial provision on divorce. Where a party wishes to make a claim against the property of the other during the course of the relationship, it may be possible to do so under the law of unjustified enrichment. An alternative may be to do so using the law of trusts. It should be stressed that these remedies are unusual, but the discussion is included for completeness. **12–21**

Unjustified Enrichment

Where a party to a relationship has made contributions towards property he does not own, then in theory one option is to seek a remedy in unjustified enrichment. The principles of enrichment law are complex, but in this context the key idea is that the party who did not own the property (Edith, in the example above) made contributions that enriched the other party on the basis of the underlying assumption that the relationship would continue. If the relationship ends, the rationale for those contributions no longer exists. This mode of enrichment was categorised in Roman law as the *condictio ob causam finitam*. An alternative argument under enrichment law, of relevance in non-marital cohabitation cases, could be that the contributions were made on the basis of an anticipated future contract of marriage which did not ultimately result. This was known as the *condictio causa data causa non secuta*. In either case, the advantage obtained by the party who owns the home becomes unjustified in the legal sense by the breakdown of the relationship. The contributing party is entitled to recompense for his contributions, so long as this is equitable in the circumstances. **12–22**

In the reported jurisprudence, the small number of cases on unjustified enrichment in a domestic context have invariably concerned non-marital **12–23**

---

[29] Family Law (Scotland) Act 1985 ss.8–10.
[30] Family Law (Scotland) Act 2006 s.28.

cohabitants. The leading case is *Shilliday v Smith*[31] where the pursuer successfully recovered the money she had spent on repairs and improvements to the defender's home during the course of their cohabiting relationship. In *Satchwell v McIntosh*,[32] the pursuer had contributed a sum of money towards the purchase price of the family home, although title was taken in the name of the defender only. He had also contributed financially towards refurbishment work. Again, he was successful in recovering the amount he contributed. In *McKenzie v Nutter*,[33] the parties had been in a longstanding relationship whilst living in separate homes. They agreed to sell their separate properties and buy a new house in which they would live together. The pursuer sold his house, and the couple used the proceeds to purchase a new property with title taken in both their names. The defender then refused to go through with the sale of her house, declining also to move into the new property with the pursuer. On the sale of the new house, the court found the pursuer entitled to the defender's half-share of the proceeds on the basis of unjustified enrichment.

12-24   Although these cases show the types of situation in which enrichment principles offer some remedy, it should be stressed that the extent to which enrichment can be relied on in a relationship context is limited. One particular difficulty which arises is in attributing a value to non-financial contributions made to the household. In Donald and Edith's situation, Edith may be able to recover the cost of DIY materials or money she has paid to tradesmen. She may even be able to seek payment in respect of any increase in the value of the house resulting from her redecorating efforts. However, the broader non-financial contributions she has made in taking care of the child of the family, cooking and cleaning cannot be tied directly to the value of the house, which in practice is likely to be the bulk of its value. Enrichment law is not designed to take account of the breadwinner/homemaker division of labour common in family relationships. A further difficulty is that enrichment can only take account of what has happened in the past. In the event of the relationship ending, the financial impact on Edith, who has been out of the employment market for many years and is likely to have difficulty finding a job as a result, will continue long after the break up. The rules of financial provision on divorce and, to a lesser extent, the statutory regime on breakdown of cohabitation are better suited to provide remedies in this situation, as discussed in Ch.13.

Constructive Trust?

12-25   In a trust, property is owned by one party (the trustee) for the benefit of a different party (the beneficiary.) As a general rule, trusts must be explicitly created in a written document. However, in English law it is accepted that a trust can come into existence through implication: in other words, that the law can deem one person to be holding property as a trustee for another party, despite the fact this was never explicitly agreed. Attempts have been

---

[31] *Shilliday v Smith*, 1998 S.C. 725.
[32] *Satchwell v McIntosh*, 2006 S.L.T. (Sh. Ct) 117.
[33] *McKenzie v Nutter*, 2007 SLT (Sh. Ct) 17.

made to use this doctrine in a family law context to argue that one party to a relationship owns property at least in part as a trustee for the other party to the relationship. In the typical case, although one spouse owns a home in his sole name, it will be contended that the house was purchased with assets generated by both himself and the other spouse. The other spouse therefore asserts that a trust favouring her as a beneficiary has been constructed in law, despite the fact no trust was ever expressly constituted. What substitutes for express constitution of trust, and therefore founds the claim, is a finding of an express or implied agreement or "imputed common intention" between the parties that ownership of the house was to be shared.[34]

In Scotland, the law of trusts is very different from the equivalent English **12–26** law, and it is unclear whether equivalent claims can be made. In fact, it is not clear that the doctrine of constructive trust has any application in Scotland at all, and attempts to use trust law in a family context have not been successful.[35] Extension of the doctrine of constructive trust would tend to undermine the security of the Scots system of land tenure, and use of the doctrine in England within family situations has caused problems which it would be undesireable to replicate here.[36]

DEBTS AND BANKRUPTCY

Family assets may be put at risk where a debt owed by one party to an **12–27** adult relationship cannot be paid. In these circumstances the law seeks to balance the interests of creditors with those of families to ensure that both are fairly treated. In the past, marriage could result in one spouse sharing liability for debts incurred by the other,[37] but with the exception of certain statutory debts,[38] this is no longer the case. Debts incurred by one party to an adult relationship impose no liability on the other party. Similarly, debts owed by one party in a relationship to another are not privileged – a spouse, civil partner or cohabitant has no greater claim to repayment of a loan than any ordinary creditor. These are logical outcomes of the separate property regime.

The law does, however, recognise that the existence of an adult relationship **12–28** between parties may give rise to certain risks in relation to debt. In the first

---

[34] For recent authority, and a summary of the development of the law in this area, see *Kernott v Jones* [2011] UKSC 53.

[35] *Newton v Newton*, 1923 S.C. 15.

[36] e.g. in their failure to recognise uniformly the value of non-financial contributions towards the shared household. Gretton has commented that "few English lawyers would regard their system in this regard as being a suitable article for export" and, later, "The idea that into this labyrinth [the Scottish legal system] should walk and lose ourselves fills me with horror", *Constructive Trusts* (1997) 1(3) E.L. Rev 281.

[37] Thus a husband was liable for his wife's ante-nuptial debts until this was abolished by the Law Reform (Husband and Wife) (Scotland) Act 1984 s.6(1) and (2) and he was bound by his wife's capacity to act as his agent in domestic affairs (under the *praepositura domesticiis rebus*) until this was abolished under s.7 of the 1984 Act.

[38] See the Local Government Finance Act 1992 s.77 which imposes joint and several liability on spouse and cohabitants for council tax, and the Social Security Administration Act 1992 s.78 that does the same for repayment of social fund loans.

place, parties to a relationship may collude to defeat creditors by transfer-ring assets from the debtor-party's patrimony into his partner's patrimony. Creditors are given certain legal protections to prevent this from being suc-cessful. In the second place, assets owned by the debtor-party may be used by other members of the family, who would suffer through no fault of their own if those assets were seized by creditors. Certain protections for the family are provided in this situation. Finally, the debtor-party to a relationship may unfairly manipulate or coerce the other party into taking on responsibility for that debt by lying or concealing information. The law also sets out certain protections for the non-debtor party in that situation.

Protection of Creditors

12–29   In the case of a debtor's sequestration (colloquially referred to as "bank-ruptcy"), a creditor may make claims over property that the debtor has transferred to his spouse or civil partner. Under the provisions of the Bankruptcy (Scotland) Act 1985, any transfer made by a debtor to an "asso-ciate" within five years of his sequestration can be challenged by the trustee in sequestration,[39] who is the person with responsibility for administering the sequestration process. A spouse or civil partner would fall within the definition of associate.[40] If a challenge is made, the debtor must show either that he was solvent at the time of the transfer,[41] or that the transfer was made for adequate consideration,[42] or that the transfer was a gift that was reasonable in all the circumstances.[43] If he is successful, the transaction will stand. Otherwise, the court may reduce the transaction or grant such other redress as is appropriate. So, imagine that Edith has taken a loan from the bank which she has become unable to repay. Edith also owns an expensive antique painting. It is likely that the bank would be able to make use of debt enforcement procedures to seize the painting and sell it, recovering the loan they made to Edith from the proceeds of sale. Edith does not want this to occur, and so donates the painting to Donald. The painting is now in his patrimony, but still part of their wealth as a couple. Provided this donation had been made within five years of the bank's enforcement action, the court could set aside the transaction, returning the painting to Edith's patrimony and making it available to the bank.

12–30   A similar common law remedy predating the 1985 Act also continues to exist. A creditor may challenge a transfer made by the debtor (regardless of the debtor's relationship with the person to whom it is transferred) if

- it was made at a time when the debtor was insolvent; or
- making the transfer rendered the debtor insolvent and the debtor remains insolvent at the date of the challenge,

---

[39] Bankruptcy (Scotland) Act 1985 s.34.
[40] Bankruptcy (Scotland) Act 1985 s.74.
[41] Bankruptcy (Scotland) Act 1985 s.34(4)(a).
[42] Bankruptcy (Scotland) Act 1985 s.34(4)(b).
[43] Bankruptcy (Scotland) Act 1985 s.34(4)(c), e.g. for a birthday, Christmas or other conven-tional gift.

and in *both* cases there was no onerous consideration for the transfer.[44] However, as it is difficult for creditors to establish that the debtor was insolvent at the time of the transfer, the statutory remedy under the 1985 Act is more usually relied upon.

Where premiums are paid by spouses or civil partners in respect of a policy **12–31** under the Married Women's Policies of Assurance (Scotland) Act 1880, a creditor may seek to recover their repayment but only if it can be established that they were paid with intent to defraud the creditor, or if the person effecting the policy is made bankrupt within two years from effecting the policy.[45]

Creditors also receive a particular protection in respect of the operation **12–32** of the Matrimonial Homes (Family Protection) (Scotland) Act 1981. As discussed in Ch.11, the occupancy rights of a non-entitled spouse or partner under the 1981 Act prevail in principle over the rights of third parties, such as a person who buys the family home from the entitled spouse. Another third party who will often have an interest in a family home is a creditor such as a bank who has loaned the entitled spouse funds to purchase the property in exchange for a standard security (colloquially referred to as a "mortgage") over the house. The essence of a security over property is that, should the debtor cease making repayments on the loan, the creditor is entitled to sell the property in order to recoup his funds. If the house is subject to the occupancy rights of a NES, however, the bank would find it impossible in practice to make a sale, since who would buy a house they are not permitted to occupy? Section 8 of the 1981 Act protects heritable creditors here by providing that, so long as the creditor was in good faith when the security was granted, occupancy rights will not prevail over the rights of the creditor. The creditor will be in good faith if, at the time the security was granted, the non-entitled spouse gave written consent to the security or (more unusually) renounced occupancy rights entirely.[46] The court also has the power to make an order enabling the non-entitled spouse to make the mortgage payments on behalf of the entitled spouse,[47] which may be a more practical solution for both the heritable creditor and the NES in cases where the NES can afford the repayments.

Protection of Family Members Against Creditors

A family home is likely to have been purchased using a loan from the bank, **12–33** granted in exchange for a standard security. As mentioned in para.12–33, the essence of a security over property is that, should the debtor cease making repayments on the loan, the creditor is entitled to sell the property in order to recoup his funds. The law recognises that where a heritable creditor exercises this power of sale in respect of a family home, the whole family will be

---

[44] *Boyle's Trustee v Boyle*, 1988 S.L.T. 581.

[45] Married Women's Policies of Assurance (Scotland) Act 1880 s.2.

[46] 1981 Act s.8(2) and (2A). The drafting of this section is hard to follow: if the NES has granted a consent or a renunciation, there is no question of occupancy rights prevailing over the rights of the heritable creditor, and so the protection offered in s.8(1) is redundant. Yet if no consent or renunciation is granted, s.8(1) does not apply. The purpose of s.8(1) is therefore hard to discern.

[47] 1981 Act s.8(1).

affected, even if the home is in the sole ownership of only one member of the family. Various pieces of legislation provide protection to debtors who are at risk of homelessness as a result of a heritable creditor enforcing a security.[48] In particular, a creditor cannot exercise power of sale under a security without a warrant from the court, which will be granted only if reasonable to do so taking into account the reasons for the debtor's default on repayments, whether the debtor is likely to make good the arrears within a reasonable time and the availability of anywhere else to live.[49] An entitled resident of the home, which would include a spouse, civil partner, cohabitant or any other person who occupied the house as their sole or main residence, may also apply to the court for a suspension of the action or to make any other order the court thinks fit.[50]

12–34   Where a person with sole ownership of the family home is sequestrated, his spouse or civil partner is entitled to receive intimation of the sequestration from the trustee and be advised of the right to apply under the Bankruptcy (Scotland) Act 1985[51] for recall of the sequestration, or for such order as the court thinks fit to protect the occupancy rights of the family. This is only possible where the court is satisfied that the purpose of the petition for sequestration was wholly or mainly to defeat the occupancy rights of the non-owning spouse or partner. A trustee in sequestration who wishes to sell the family home cannot do so without the consent of the court, who will grant it only if reasonable taking into account the needs and resources of other family members who occupy the house as their sole or main residence.[52] Household goods are generally protected from sale by a creditor for repayment of debt, whether in relation to action for repayment of debt by an individual creditor,[53] or as part of sequestration proceedings.[54]

Protection of Parties to a Relationship Against Each Other

12–35   Imagine that Donald and Edith own a house between them. Donald runs a business, which falls entirely within his patrimony. He wishes to borrow money from the bank in order to fund the business, but the bank will only allow him to do so if he offers the family home as security for the debt. As a co-owner of the house, Edith would be offering her share of the house as security for a debt belonging entirely to her husband. Edith is of course free to take on this obligation if she wishes to do so. Difficulties arise, however, if Donald takes advantage of his close relationship with Edith, and the trust she places in him, to convince her to sign the security without a full and accurate understanding of the risk she is taking on. A number of cases have arisen in the last decade where this situation has arisen: a problem which Gretton

---

[48] Mortgage Rights (Scotland) Act 2001; Homelessness (Scotland) Act 2003; Home Owner and Debtor Protection (Scotland) Act 2010.
[49] Home Owner and Debtor Protection (Scotland) Act 2010 s.24 and 24A.
[50] Home Owner and Debtor Protection (Scotland) Act 2010 s.24B and 24C.
[51] 1985 Act s.41.
[52] 1985 Act s.40.
[53] Debt Arrangement and Attachment (Scotland) Act 2002 ss.46–48.
[54] 1985 Act s.33.

refers to as "sexually transmitted debt".[55] The courts have developed a line of authority aimed at protecting spouses, typically wives, who may find themselves homeless as a result of their husband's business debts.[56]

The key authority in Scotland is *Smith v Bank of Scotland*.[57] The wife in **12–36** this case said that she had been induced to grant security over her husband's debts (known in Scotland as "giving caution") by his misrepresentation or undue influence. The court found that the creditor in a situation of this kind should be aware of the risk of deception between parties to a relationship, and therefore owed a duty of good faith to the cautioner to make sure she was aware of the risks of the transaction. For the duty to arise, the first requirement is that the caution must be gratuitous: in other words, that the spouse or partner does not benefit from the loan she is guaranteeing. This requirement will usually be satisfied if the loan is made solely to the other party, or to his business. The second requirement is that there is a relationship of trust and confidence between the cautioner and the principal debtor. Spouses (and presumably therefore civil partners)[58] and cohabitants[59] meet this requirement. If the requirements are fulfilled and the duty of care arises, it seems the creditor can discharge it by advising the cautioner to take independent legal advice before entering into the transaction. The more stringent duties placed on the creditor in England, to the effect that the creditor must have signed confirmation from the cautioner that she has been advised of the risks ad warned not to proceed without independent legal advice,[60] do not appear to be replicated in Scotland.[61] If the duty of good faith is not discharged, the cautioner may avoid the grant of caution.

This chapter has focused on the property law consequences of an adult **12–37** relationship whilst it continues to exist. For the most part, these consequences are quite limited, arising only in a closely constrained set of contexts. Far more wide-reaching are the property consequences where an adult relationship is brought to an end. In the following chapter we consider in detail the division of property upon divorce or dissolution of a civil partnership, or breakdown of cohabitation.

---

[55] G. Gretton, "Sexually Transmitted Debt", 1997 S.L.T. (News) 195.
[56] *Barclay's Bank v O'Brien* [1994] 1 A.C. 180; *Smith v Bank of Scotland*, 1997 S.C. (HL) 111; *Royal Bank of Scotland v Etridge (No.2)* [2001] 4 All E.R. 449.
[57] *Smith v Bank of Scotland*, 1997 S.C. (HL) 111.
[58] *Smith v Bank of Scotland*, 1997 S.C. (HL) 111.
[59] *Barclay's Bank v O'Brien* [1994] 1 A.C. 180.
[60] *Royal Bank of Scotland v Etridge (No.2)* [2001] 4 All E.R. 449.
[61] *Clydesdale Bank v Black*, 2002 S.C.L.R. 857.

CHAPTER 13

FINANCIAL CONSEQUENCES OF TERMINATION OF ADULT RELATIONSHIPS

13–01 When spouses, civil partners or cohabitants decide to terminate their relationship, financial consequences inevitably follow. The resources which previously financed one home now have to sustain two separate households and assets shared during the course of the relationship must be divided between the couple. The law makes provision for the redistribution of assets at the end of a marriage or civil partnership in the Family Law (Scotland) Act 1985,[1] in particular ss.8 to 16.[2] Under the 1985 Act, parties to a relationship must establish grounds for divorce or dissolution before they can apply for an award of financial provision.[3] That the relationship should be terminated is rarely a matter of disagreement in court. However, the financial implications may well lead to dispute. For this reason, we will look first at the principles governing financial provision, before examining the grounds for divorce and dissolution in the next chapter. This chapter will also consider the legislative regime which applies on the breakdown of cohabitation. Court orders relating to arrangements for children after the end of a relationship were considered in Ch.4. Issues of childcare and finance are, of course, not always separable. In many relationships where there are children, residence and contact will be key bargaining issues when negotiating a division of property, as is the subsequent question of whether the parent with care of the children may retain the family home while they are growing up.

13–02 The rules regulating distribution of resources after termination of a relationship can be tailored to implement one or more not always compatible objectives. Different jurisdictions favour some objectives over others. For example, the rules could be intended to penalise the party responsible for the breakdown of the relationship, to ensure continued support of the economically weaker party by the other or to provide *transitional* support while former parties to a relationship re-establish financial independence. They may seek to equitably adjust any economic disadvan-

---

[1] References in this chapter are to the 1985 Act, unless otherwise indicated.

[2] These provisions were extended to civil partnerships, where the partnership is being dissolved, through amendments made to the 1985 Act by Sch.28, Pt 2 of the Civil Partnership Act 2004 ss.11–30.

[3] Divorce (Scotland) Act 1976 s.1 for spouses; Civil Partnership Act 2004 s.117 for civil partners. The grounds for dissolution, set out in Pt 3, Ch.5 of the 2004 Act, s.117 (as amended by Sch.1 of the FLSA 2006) are the same as they are for marriage with the exception of "adultery" which is omitted from the 2004 Act. See discussion in Ch.14. Financial provision under the 1985 Act may also be available where divorce or an equivalent has been granted in a different jurisdiction. The 1985 Act also applied were a decree of nullity is granted in relation to a formalised relationship.

tage one party has suffered in the interests of the family.[4] In Scotland, the law of financial provision on divorce prior to the 1985 Act, found in s.5 of the Divorce (Scotland) Act 1976,[5] suffered from the lack of any clear statement of its objectives. The court was given almost no guidelines to aid it in the exercise of its discretion to make an award. By contrast, under the 1985 Act, the court is assisted by a set of principles laid out "in considerable and almost clinical detail"[6] in s.9, which to some extent incorporates all the objectives mentioned above bar the first. The regime governing financial claims on the breakdown of cohabitation, set out in the Family Law (Scotland) Act 2006, ss.25 to 28, is arguably less clear in its aims as discussed below.[7]

FINANCIAL PROVISION ON DIVORCE AND DISSOLUTION

The two grounds for divorce/dissolution are irretrievable breakdown of marriage/civil partnership or the granting of an interim gender recognition certificate to either spouse or civil partner.[8] The principal philosophy underlying the 1985 Act is that divorce or dissolution should be as far as possible a "clean break" between the parties, that is, the former spouses or civil partners should be free to lead separate lives afterwards, unrestricted by continuing financial obligations to each other. The relationship is seen as akin to a business partnership "wound up" by divorce or dissolution and, ideally, the assets of that business should be distributed to the former partners once and for all on its termination in the form of capital, or by transfer of property. Accordingly, the 1985 Act restricts the making of a periodical allowance award, requiring one party to continue to maintain the other after the termination of the relationship, to occasions where a capital or property transfer award is insufficient to meet the objectives of the Act.[9] Furthermore, the court is given a wider range of powers than was provided under the 1976 Act to make it easier for it to award an equitable clean break settlement. In particular, the court can make an award of capital by instalments,[10] and make a property transfer order.[11]

It is important to note that parties cannot expect a clean break from any **13–04** children of the relationship. While divorce or dissolution may end legal ties between the parties, the relationship between parent and child persists, and the court, where it has jurisdiction still to do so since the advent of the Child

13–03

---

4 See *Report on Aliment and Financial Provision*, Scot. Law Com. No.67 (1981).
5 See further, *Aliment and Financial Provision*, Scot. Law Com. Memo No.22 (1976), Vols 1 and 2, and *Report on Aliment and Financial Provision*, Scot. Law Com. No.67 (1981), paras 3.41–3.46.
6 *Per* Lord President Hope in *Little v Little*, 1990 S.L.T. 785 at 786L–787A.
7 See paras 13–96 *et seq*.
8 Divorce (Scotland) Act 1976 s.1(1)(a)–(b) for spouses; 2004 Act Pt 3, Ch.5, s.117(2)(a)–(b) for civil partners. Note that prior to the passage of the Gender Recognition Act 2004, irretrievable breakdown was the sole basis for divorce.
9 1985 Act s.13(2)(a) and (b).
10 1985 Act s.12(3).
11 1985 Act s.12(1).

Support Act 1991,[12] will make such award of aliment for children of the relationship as is justified in the circumstances, before turning to any question of financial provision.[13]

13–05   Under the 1985 Act, the same regime applies to spouses on divorce and to civil partners on dissolution. For the sake of brevity, references throughout this chapter will be to marriage and divorce, which should be taken to include civil partnership and dissolution. References to husband and wife or spouses should be taken to include civil partners. Occasional terminological differences exist in the legislation—for example, married couples have matrimonial property whereas civil partners have partnership property—and these will be explained where relevant.

THE LEGAL FRAMEWORK

13–06   Where an application is made for financial provision on divorce, under s.8(2) the court[14] is directed to make such orders as are

(a) justified by the principles set out in s.9; and
(b) reasonable, having regard to the resources of the parties.

Both considerations must be taken into account before an order can be made. Thus, lack of resources on the part of one party at the date of divorce may sometimes lead the court to award a lower sum than would be suggested by the norm of equal sharing of matrimonial property set out in s.10(1) (see paras 13–07 *et seq.*). For example, in *Crockett v Crockett*,[15] a slump in the value of the husband's business between the relevant date[16] and the date of divorce led the court to make a much lower award to the wife than it would have made purely on the basis of the s.9 principles. However, *resources* are not limited to those assets which qualify as "matrimonial" property[17] but comprise all assets available to the parties,[18] including "foreseeable" resources.[19] These might include assets such as insurance policies which are due to mature after the divorce, lump sum payments and "golden handshakes" due on retirement or termination of employment.

---

[12] See the discussion at paras 5–40 to 5–81.

[13] See Ch.5 for discussion of child support and child aliment.

[14] Under s.27, this may be the Court of Session or the sheriff court.

[15] *Crockett v Crockett*, 1992 S.C.L.R. 591. But *cf. Shand v Shand*, 1994 S.L.T. 387, where the husband's lack of assets at the date of divorce was due to his having caused his own bankruptcy. The wife was awarded the maximum possible sum out of the assets remaining at the date of divorce.

[16] FLSA 2006 s.16 now requires matrimonial/partnership property be valued at either a date the parties agree upon or the date of the order or a date as close to the date of making the order as the court may determine. See discussion at paras 13–12 and 13–22 to 13–24 below.

[17] See para.13–09 below.

[18] See, e.g. *Buczynska v Buczynski*, 1989 S.L.T. 558 where a flat purchased for one spouse by a third party as a gift was taken into account as a "resource" when determining financial provision.

[19] 1985 Act s.27(1).

THE S.9 PRINCIPLES

Section 9 of the 1985 Act sets out the five principles which govern financial **13–07** provision. The basic premise in s.9(1)(a) is that all matrimonial or partnership property should be shared fairly between the parties. Fair sharing, as we shall see, is defined to mean equal sharing unless there are special circumstances to depart from this norm. In addition, account is also to be taken under ss.9(1)(b)–(e) of economic advantages or disadvantages which have been sustained by either person; the economic burden of childcare; the need for readjustment following substantial dependence; and severe financial hardship. Where one party would not be adequately compensated in any of these circumstances by an equal share of the property under s.9(1)(a), then the court may award more than a half share to that person. The s.9 principles are intended to be flexible enough to produce a fair result in a variety of different types of marriage, including those of long and short duration, as well as those where the couple have children and those where they do not. Even after a division of property has been worked out in principle, under s.8(2) the court has substantial discretion as to what orders to make to implement that division. That is, depending on the available resources at the date of divorce, it may make an order for immediate payment of a capital sum or for payment deferred to a certain date or for payment of the capital sum by instalments, possibly out of the salary of the payer.

FIRST PRINCIPLE: S.9(1)(A)—FAIR SHARING OF VALUE OF MATRIMONIAL/ PARTNERSHIP PROPERTY

The first principle contained in s.9(1)(a) is that **13–08**

> "the net value of the matrimonial property should be shared fairly between the parties to the marriage or as the case may be the net value of the partnership property should be so shared between the partners in the civil partnership".

Under s.10(1), fair sharing is defined as equal sharing except where "special circumstances" justify an alternative division.

Matrimonial/Partnership Property

The first question, then, is what qualifies as "matrimonial" or "partner- **13–09** ship" property? Section 10(4) of the 1985 Act defines "matrimonial" property as

> "all the property belonging to the parties or either of them at the relevant date which was acquired by them or him (otherwise than by gift or succession from a third party)—
>
> (a) before the marriage for use by them as a family home or as furniture or plenishings for such a home; or
> (b) during the marriage but before the relevant date".

Section 10(4A) of the Act defines "partnership" property in conformity with this definition. For the sake of brevity, the term matrimonial property will be used in the remainder of this chapter, which should be understood to include partnership property.

13–10   Property acquired for the purposes of the relationship, or obtained during the relationship, is matrimonial property regardless of which spouse's patrimony the property happens to be in. The idea here is that, during the relationship, parties are acting as a unit. Any property they have acquired is the result of both their efforts, regardless of whose money was actually spent. Accordingly, on leaving the relationship, it is fair that they should each have an equal share of those relationship assets.

13–11   When an asset falls into the definition of matrimonial property set out above, it is important to understand that this does not *in itself* change the legal ownership of that item. The owner remains the owner. Defining the item as matrimonial property means only that parties are *entitled* to share it on divorce. This does not happen automatically. Rather, the court has to make an order transferring a share of ownership from the owning spouse to the non-owning spouse. Imagine that Graeme and Fiona are a divorcing couple. Graeme owns a house at the relevant date: his is the only name on the title deeds. If that house was bought during the marriage, or before the marriage for use as a family home, the house will be matrimonial property in the meaning of s.10(4). This does not alter the fact that Graeme owns the house, or that his name alone is on the title. What it means is that the value of the house should be included in the pot of property which the parties are entitled to share on divorce. In a very simple case where only s.9(1)(a) applied, and the house was the only piece of matrimonial property, Fiona and Graeme would each be entitled to half the value of the house on divorce. The court would therefore make an order transferring a share of half the ownership of the house to Fiona, so that Graeme would retain half and Fiona would now own half. Alternatively, the court might order Graeme to pay a capital sum of half the value of the house to Fiona. In this simple situation, if the house was already owned in common between the two of them, the court would not have to make any orders, since the current legal position matches up with the parties' entitlement on divorce.

13–12   Only property acquired before "the relevant date" falls into the matrimonial property pot. The relevant date is the either the date on which parties ceased to cohabit,[20] or the date of service of the summons raising divorce proceedings,[21] whichever is earlier.[22] Usually, the date on which parties cease to cohabit will be the appropriate date, since most divorces are now founded on one or two years' non-cohabitation.[23] The fact that parties live together in the same house does not necessarily indicate that they are still "cohabiting" in the meaning of this section.[24] Financially, continuing to live

---

[20] 1985 Act s.10(3)(a).
[21] 1985 Act s.10(3)(b).
[22] 1985 Act s.10(3). For effect of resumption of cohabitation with regard to fixing the relevant date see *Brown v Brown*, 2003 Fam. L.B. 64–2.
[23] Divorce (Scotland) Act 1976 s.1(2)(c) and (d), discussed at paras 14–21 to 14–32 below.
[24] See *Buczynska v Buczynski*, 1989 S.L.T. 558 where the court held that cohabitation ceased

in the same house but sleeping in separate rooms may be the only option for some couples until the divorce is settled, particularly if there are children to care for. Similarly, whether or not parties are in a sexual relationship will not be determinative of cohabitation, although it may be relevant.[25] The Act makes special provision for calculating the relevant date in situations where parties have resumed cohabitation for a period in an attempt at reconciliation.[26]

Once the relevant date has been identified, determining whether property   **13–13** was acquired prior to it is usually a simple question of fact. A difficulty can arise, however, in situations where the right to the property was acquired before the relevant date, but the property itself was not acquired until afterwards. Where an event giving rise to an award of damages takes place before the relevant date, the damages payment will be considered matrimonial property even where it is not handed over until after the relevant date. This has been established in the case law with reference to delictual damages for wrongful dismissal[27] and patrimonial loss following an injury.[28] However, the time and nature of such a payment may constitute "special circumstances" to depart from the norm of equal sharing, discussed further below.[29] If the event giving rise to the claim for damages occurs before the marriage, a payment made during the marriage will not be considered matrimonial property.[30] Redundancy payments may qualify as matrimonial property if they have been paid to one spouse before the relevant date, even though they are payments made in compensation for loss of future earnings.[31] A refund of income tax may also qualify as matrimonial property, even where it is paid after the relevant date, if the right to repayment refers to a financial period before the relevant date.[32]

Property Acquired Before Marriage/Partnership

Property acquired before formalisation of the relationship will not form   **13–14** part of the matrimonial property. If Graeme has bought a car prior to the marriage, he will remain the owner of that car throughout the relationship and on divorce. If Graeme and Fiona have bought a car which is owned in common between them prior to the marriage, it will remain in common

---

while the parties were still living in the same premises, but had ceased to share the same bedroom, the wife had ceased to cook for her husband and the husband's solicitor had notified the wife of the husband's intention to raise a divorce action.

[25] 1985 Act s.27(2).

[26] 1985 Act s.10(7).

[27] *Louden v Louden*, 1994 S.L.T. (OH) 381.

[28] *Skarpaas v Skarpaas*, 1993 S.L.T. 343. The portion of damages referable to solatium was not matrimonial property since the defender's suffering was endured by him solely. Any damages referable to loss of future earnings will also be excluded, as in *Carroll v Carroll*, 2000 Fam. L.B. 58–6.

[29] See *Skarpaas v Skarpaas*, 1991 S.L.T. (Sh. Ct) 15 at 19.

[30] See *Petrie v Petrie*, 1988 S.C.L.R. 390 where damages awarded after the relevant date for injuries sustained before the marriage were held not to constitute matrimonial property because the property right in that case, the right to damages, had accrued before the date of the marriage.

[31] See *Smith v Smith*, 1989 S.L.T. 668; *Tyrrell v Tyrell*, 1990 S.C.L.R. 244.

[32] *MacRitchie v MacRitchie*, 1994 S.L.T. (Sh. Ct) 72.

ownership throughout the marriage and on divorce. The s9 principles cannot apply to the car in this situation because it is not matrimonial property.

13–15   The exception to this rule is where property has been acquired prior to formalisation of the relationship for use by the couple as a family home, or furniture for that home. Case law has established it is not a requirement of this provision that either party need have contemplated marriage when purchasing such a home.[33] For example, imagine Graeme purchased a house for himself and Fiona to live in together as a "family", with no intent of marriage at that date. A few years later, perhaps following the birth of a child, the couple decide to marry after all. In this situation, should the couple later divorce, the house will be regarded as matrimonial property under s.10(4). In *Buczynska v Buczynski*,[34] the husband bought a house at a time when he was still married to his first wife but having a sexual relationship with the pursuer. He and the pursuer cohabited there from the date of purchase of the home, and continued to do so after their marriage in 1969, and until the relevant date in 1987. The court held that the house was matrimonial property since it had been bought "for use as a family home", apparently having no difficulty in finding that a cohabiting couple could be a "family" even where one party was still married to another person. However, in these circumstances, it must still be proved that there was an intention to purchase the house for use as a family home: not, for example, as a single person's residence, as a buy-to-let investment, or as a home for another person such as an ex-spouse. Had Graeme lived in the house for several years alone, following which Fiona moved in with him and the parties married, the house would not be matrimonial property.[35] Alternatively, imagine Graeme bought the house to live in with his former partner Harry. When that relationship deteriorated, Harry moved out, and some time later Fiona moved in, following which she and Graeme married. Again, the house would not be matrimonial property in this situation, since it had not been bought as a home for Graeme and Fiona. In *Maclellan v Maclellan*,[36] the husband bought a croft before marriage for his sole use. Later the wife moved into the croft and it became the family home. The court held that although the couple had lived together there for 26 years, it was not matrimonial property, as it was not bought "for use . . . as a family home".

13–16   *Maclellan* illustrates a real source of hardship in the way the legislation is phrased. The wife had no claim on the family home, which was the sole substantial asset of the marriage, despite having lived in it and helped maintain it for 26 years. If the husband had chosen to sell that croft and purchase another home, either during or in contemplation of the marriage, then the new home would have comprised matrimonial property.[37] A similar problem arises where a husband purchases a house to live in with wife 1, divorces her but

---

[33] See *Mitchell v Mitchell*, 1995 S.L.T. 426 at 428.

[34] *Buczynska v Buczynski*, 1989 S.L.T. 558.

[35] In *Willson v Willson*, 2009 Fam. L. R. 18, the wife owned a home prior to meeting her husband, and disponed a half share in that home to him after the wedding. His half-share was considered matrimonial property whereas the share she retained was not.

[36] *Maclellan v Maclellan*, 1988 S.C.L.R. 399.

[37] See, e.g. *Jacques v Jacques*, 1995 S.L.T. 963, affirmed by House of Lords at 1997 S.L.T. 459.

goes on living in that home, and then marries wife 2 who moves in. However long he and wife 2 live in that home, it will not be regarded as matrimonial property in respect of the second marriage. In *Buczynska*, Lord Morton suggested[38] that by analogy with the Matrimonial Homes (Family Protection) (Scotland) Act 1981 s.22, a home which "becomes" a family home should be regarded as falling into matrimonial property, whatever the intention at the time of purchase. Helpful as this approach might be, it cannot be said to be justified by the wording of the 1985 Act.[39]

It is not necessary for a house acquired in contemplation of marriage to be used continuously by the parties as a family home from the date of acquisition. In *Mitchell v Mitchell*[40] the parties married, bought a family home, divorced, remarried and then divorced again. The husband retained the house used as a family home after the first divorce, and the question arose whether it was "matrimonial property" in respect of the second marriage. The husband argued that the house was purchased in contemplation of the first marriage, not the second, and therefore should not be regarded as "matrimonial property". The court held that the parties had, as a matter of intention, acquired the house "for use by them as a family home", and nothing in the section stipulated that the property should have been acquired for use in relation to a particular marriage. **13–17**

Property Acquired by Gift or Succession from a Third Party

Property acquired by either party before or during the relationship by way of gift or succession from a third party is excluded from matrimonial property, under s.10(4) of the 1985 Act. If Graeme is given a watch by his brother for Christmas, or Fiona inherits a necklace from her aunt during the marriage, these items will not be matrimonial property. This remains the case if the gift or inheritance is shared by the parties.[41] If a mutual friend gives Fiona and Graeme a painting for their wedding anniversary, the painting will be owned in common between them during the marriage and on divorce, but will not fall into the definition of matrimonial property, meaning the s9 principles cannot apply. Difficulties can arise here in determining the intention of the donor, as we discussed relative to the presumption of shared ownership of household goods in the previous chapter.[42] In *Mukhtar v Mukhtar*[43] title to the family home was taken in both names, but the wife's father had provided a £50,000 deposit toward the house, guaranteed a secured loan for the balance of £146,000 and made all but two of the monthly payments on the property. The sheriff rejected the husband's claim that the house was a joint gift by the wife's father, finding it clear in the circumstances that all the **13–18**

---

[38] *Buczynska v Buczynski*, 1989 S.L.T. 558 at 560. Section 22 of the 1981 Act defines a "matrimonial home" as including a house which "has become" a family residence.

[39] For criticism of this approach, see Clive, *The Law of Husband and Wife in Scotland*, 4th edn (Edinburgh: W.Green, 1997), para.24.025, n.74; Meston, "Matrimonial Property and the Family Home", 1993 S.L.T. (News) 62.

[40] *Mitchell v Mitchell*, 1995 S.L.T. 426.

[41] *Smith v Smith*, 1992 G.W.D. 23–1324.

[42] para.12-07.

[43] *Mukhtar v Mukhtar*, 2002 Fam. L.B. 60–7.

father's expenditure had been undertaken to benefit his daughter. The title had only been put in joint names because both the husband and the wife's income had to be taken into account to support the loan that was taken out. The exception for property acquired by gift or succession applies only where that property has come from a third party. If the parties give gifts to each other during the course of the relationship, they *will* fall within the definition of matrimonial property.

13–19   Property acquired by gift or succession by a third party can, however, become matrimonial property if it changes form or substance during the course of the relationship. In *Latter v Latter*,[44] questions arose as to whether: (i) the family home; and (ii) shares belonging to the husband fell into matrimonial property. The family home had been purchased with a sum of money donated by the wife's family and handed over to her solicitors to buy the property, title to which was then taken in the wife's name alone. On divorce, the court held that the home was not matrimonial property as it had been acquired as a gift, choosing to disregard the fact that the gift had been of the sum of money used to purchase the home, and not the home itself. In Lord Marnoch's view

> "to draw a distinction as between a gift of the purchase price and a gift of the heritable property itself, simply because of the conveyancing techniques employed, would be over precise".[45]

On the other hand, the court held that the husband's shares *did* amount to matrimonial property. These shares had been acquired by the husband prior to marriage, and so were prima facie excluded. However, during the course of the marriage, these shares, which were originally held in a number of family companies, were reconstructed into a single holding of shares in one parent company and this change of form was sufficient to transmute them into matrimonial property. The court noted that even if the shares had been excluded from matrimonial property, the increase in value of the shares over the period of the marriage could have been included.

13–20   Contrast *Whittome v Whittome (No.1)*[46] where Mr Whittome acquired shares, by gift and as a beneficiary under trusts, which formed part of a private family company. Although the nature of the shareholding changed considerably over time, e.g. the private company in which shares were held was publicly floated, it was held that none of these developments led to the creation of new property which would fall within the definition in s.10(4). The facts were distinguished from *Latter* in that Mr Whittome's shares were held in one company which existed throughout the whole period of the marriage.[47] Furthermore, the court rejected the *Latter* approach in holding that the whole value of the gift at the relevant date, not just the original value at the date of donation, should be excluded from matrimonial property. The general rule seems to be that if the reorganisation of a company results in new

---

[44] *Latter v Latter*, 1990 S.L.T. 805.
[45] *Latter v Latter*, 1990 S.L.T. 805 at 808.
[46] *Whittome v Whittome (No.1)*, 1994 S.L.T. 115.
[47] *Whittome v Whittome (No.1)*, 1994 S.L.T. 115 at 125.

shares being acquired in place of the old, the new shares will be matrimonial property; but, if the shareholding remains as it was before, albeit in a different structural form, the property will not qualify as matrimonial property.

These cases must not be confused with the common scenario where   **13–21** property acquired by gift or succession is sold during the course of the marriage, and the proceeds used to purchase some other form of property. For example, a gift of shares may be sold to purchase a house, furniture or other shares. In these cases, what is purchased with the money so derived will fall into matrimonial property.[48] However, the fact that the funds used to acquire this property came from a gift to one spouse/civil partner, may be taken into account as "special circumstances" under s.10(6)(b).[49]

Valuation

Valuation is important because it is the *net value* of the matrimonial prop-   **13–22** erty that is to be divided fairly between the spouses for the purposes of s.9(1)(a). Prior to s.16 of the FLSA 2006, matrimonial property was also *valued* as at the "relevant date".[50] However, in the common situation where the relevant date is the date on which parties ceased to cohabit, several years may subsequently pass before divorce is granted and the assets divided. The value of property at the relevant date may be quite different from its value on the date of divorce. This caused difficulties in practice, particularly in respect of the family home.

In *Wallis v Wallis*,[51] the spouses owned the family home in common.   **13–23** The property was worth a gross amount of £44,000 at the relevant date but £68,000 at the date of divorce, an increase in value of £24,000. The husband sought an order transferring the wife's half of the house to himself. At first instance, the sheriff agreed to make such an order and, by compensation, awarded a half share in the value of the house as at the date of divorce to the wife. The husband appealed. Both the Inner House and the House of Lords subsequently held that the value of an item of matrimonial property had clearly to be established as at the *relevant date*, and that accordingly the wife could only be compensated by an award of half the value of the house at that date, unless there were special circumstances to do otherwise. An increase in value in a house after the relevant date could not be treated as matrimonial property.[52] Effectively this meant that the husband received the wife's half of the house, worth £34,000 gross, for an outlay of £22,000, a result clearly unreasonable to the wife and recognised as such by the House of Lords.[53]

---

[48] See *Jacques v Jacques*, 1995 S.L.T. 963. See also *Fulton v Fulton*, 1998 S.L.T. (OH) 1262 where the court held that shares purchased with money that was a gift were matrimonial property.
[49] See also para.13–38.
[50] 1985 Act s.10(2).
[51] *Wallis v Wallis*, 1992 S.L.T. 676 (1st Div.); affirmed by the House of Lords at 1993 S.L.T. 1348.
[52] See also *Lewis v Lewis*, 1993 S.C.L.R. 32.
[53] For a more detailed discussion of the Inner House decision see E.M. Clive, "Financial Provision on Divorce: 'A Question of Technique'", 1992 S.L.T. (News) 241; see also J.M. Thomson, "Financial Provision on Divorce: Not Technique but Statutory Interpretation", 1992 S.L.T. (News) 245; E.M. Clive, "Dr Clive Replies", 1992 S.L.T. (News) 247; A. Bissett-Johnson and J. M. Thomson, "Sharing Property in a Fluctuating Market", 1994 S.L.T. (News) 248.

13–24   Following governmental consultation with the public in the wake of the decision in *Wallis*,[54] s.10 of the 1985 Act was amended to the effect that matrimonial property should be valued not on the "relevant date", but rather on the "appropriate valuation date."[55] This term is defined to mean

(a) where the parties to the marriage or, as the case may be, the partners agree on a date, that date;
(b) where there is no such agreement, the date of the making of [a property transfer order].[56]

In exceptional cases, where the court decides that the date of making the order should not apply, "the appropriate valuation date shall be such other date as the court may determine",[57] however that date should be as near as possible to the making of the order.[58]

13–25   Prior to the amendment of the 1985 Act, in order to avoid the inequity arising from *Wallis*, parties owning the house in common were free either to agree that one should sell his or her half interest to the other or, in the absence of agreement, to seek an order for division and sale.[59] In both cases, the value of the house at the date of sale is divided and so both parties receive their due. The disadvantage in the latter case, however, is that the party wishing to realise the value of his or her share in the house must raise a separate action to do so after concluding divorce proceedings. Another alternative, therefore, is to seek an incidental order for sale and equal division of the proceeds on divorce, rather than a property transfer order.[60] In *Jacques*,[61] in order to avoid the problems presented by *Wallis*, at first instance the sheriff expressly refrained from making any order at all with respect to the matrimonial property. On appeal, the Inner House found that the sheriff should have granted an order for sale and equal division of the property under the 1985 Act, rather than forcing the parties to resort to separate proceedings for division and sale of the property which would involve them in further expense and delay.[62] This was what had been done in *Quinn v Quinn*[63] where the sheriff declined to make a property transfer order and opted, instead, for

---

[54] In its Consultation Paper, *Family Matters: Improving Scottish Family Law* (Scottish Office, Edinburgh, March 1999) the Scottish Office raised the issue of whether the effect of *Wallis* should be reversed, while the White Paper on *Parents and Children: A White Paper on Scottish Family Law* (2000) postponed any changes in this area until a comprehensive review of matrimonial property had been undertaken.
[55] Family Law (Scotland) Act 2006 s.16.
[56] See s.16 of the FLSA 2006 inserting subss.(2A), (3A) and (2B) after s.10(2) of the 1985 Act.
[57] 1985 Act s.10(2B). In this case, where the court selects a date, it should be as near as possible to the date of making the order.
[58] For a discussion of s.16 see David Nichols' "Comment" in 2006 Fam. L.B. 80–2.
[59] See *MacKenzie v MacKenzie*, 1991 S.L.T. 461 and *Crockett v Crockett*, 1992 S.C.L.R. 591.
[60] Under s.14(2)(a) and (k). See *Jacques v Jacques*, 1995 S.L.T. 963; *MacKenzie v MacKenzie*, 1991 S.L.T. 461; *Reynolds v Reynolds*, 1991 S.C.L.R. 175; *Symon v Symon*, 1991 S.C.L.R. 414; *Crockett v Crockett*, 1992 S.C.L.R. 591; *Lewis v Lewis*, 1993 S.C.L.R. 32. The case of *Lewis* established that this did not run counter to *Wallis* since that only governs where a property transfer order is made.
[61] *Jacques v Jacques*, 1995 S.L.T. 963.
[62] *Jacques v Jacques*, 1995 S.L.T. 963 at 966.
[63] *Quinn v Quinn*, 2003 S.L.T. (Sh. Ct) 5.

granting an order for the sale of the parties' matrimonial home.[64] Although a transfer is justified by the fair sharing of matrimonial property principle, it is often not reasonable in the light of the spouse's resources. However, it may be a preferable option where it is considered necessary for maintaining a family home for children of the marriage, especially if they are young[65] and may be offset, for example, by a transferee spouse not making a claim on the pension of the transferor spouse.

Some types of matrimonial property are particularly difficult to value. Notable amongst these are family or small businesses, and rights in occupational pension schemes. The value of a public limited company can be determined by Stock Exchange prices. But the value of other types of businesses may be dependent on a number of factors, such as whether there is a prospective purchaser,[66] whether the business is sold on a voluntary or forced basis, whether the business is geared for short or long term profits, or for maximum income or maximum capital growth, and how far the value of the business lies in the persons currently running it, and the goodwill they personally command.[67]

13–26

Pensions: Valuation[68]

The 1985 Act expressly provides in s.10(5)[69] that rights to, or interests in, pension schemes[70] or life policies, and similar arrangements[71] fall within the definition of matrimonial property. In a modern marriage, an occupational pension will often be the largest item of matrimonial property, and that item will often be held entirely within the husband's patrimony. Women tend to acquire less in the way of pension rights as a result of reducing or leaving paid

13–27

---

[64] See *Webster v Webster*, 2003 Fam. L.B. 62–6 and 62–7 where the sheriff endorsed the sheriff's observations in *Quinn* that the court should consider whether special circumstances exist (see para.13–37 below) to justify the transfer of one party's share to the other—with the consequent inequality of division—as opposed to allowing the parties to sell the property and divide the proceeds. In this case there were no special circumstances justifying an unequal division of the matrimonial property which had increased substantially in value since the relevant date. So, the sheriff opted for an sale of the property, with the husband paying the wife a lump sum out of his share of the proceeds. He viewed this as representing an easier and fairer way of equalizing matrimonial property. See also *McCaskill v McCaskill*, 2004 Fam. L.B. 72–3. See also *Weir v Weir*, 2005 Fam. L.B. 76–5 where because post-*Wallis* the transfer of the wife's half share of the family home to the husband would have produced a result not fair to her the court felt obliged to order division and sale rather than property transfer.

[65] See paras 13–42 and 13–43 below discussing deviation from equal sharing under "special circumstances" relating to the nature and use of the property under s.10(6)(d) of the 1985 Act.

[66] See, e.g. *Savage v Savage*, 1993 G.W.D. 28–1779, where the value of the business was reduced to reflect the difficulty of selling it for full value.

[67] See *McConnell v McConnell*, 1993 Fam. L.B. 6–7, where evidence was led to the effect that the company was a "people" company.

[68] See also paras 13–32 to 13–35 for a more detailed discussion.

[69] As amended by the Pensions Act 1995 s.167(2).

[70] The definition of "pension scheme" under s.10(10) is not limited to tax-approved schemes, to funded schemes, or to schemes which provide pension benefits as opposed to lump sum benefits. It includes Hancock annuities, provision for parties' pensions payable by the continuing partners in terms of a partnership agreement, and the state pension including the State Earnings Related Pension Scheme (SERPS).

[71] Similar arrangements have been held to include private pension plans for employed or self-employed people, but not gratuities paid by employers after separation (*Gibson v Gibson*, 1990 G.W.D. 4–213) or redundancy payments (*Smith v Smith*, 1989 S.C.L.R. 308).

employment for periods of time in order to care for children or other family members. Wives are accordingly often dependent on the pension rights of their husbands, including any associated benefits to wives and widows, to protect them from old-age poverty. Once a couple are divorced, any rights accruing in terms of the pension scheme to the husband's "spouse or widow" will generally go to the second wife (if any) and not to an ex-wife. By including pension rights in the definition of matrimonial property, therefore, the Act recognises that women have a right to (prima facie) an equal share in the pensions earned by their husbands for the period during which they were married, and that this right cannot be extinguished by the simple expedient of divorce.

13–28   At the most basic level, an occupational pension operates by an employee paying contributions each month into a pension fund, which is looked after by a financial investment company. The company will use the employee's contributions, along with those of all the other members of the fund, to make various investments on the stock market and elsewhere. The company's expertise should ensure that these combined investments generate considerably more profit than if each employee simply saved his pension contribution in a bank account every month of his working life. The pension fund rules will set out what share of the profits generated by the investment is available to the employee. Usually, the longer the employee pays into the fund, the greater his entitlement to the benefits will be, so the value of his pension rights gradually increases over the course of his employment. It will not normally be possible for the employee to start taking money back out of the fund until after a set period of time (normally 25 years) has passed, or a specific event such as his retirement occurs.

13–29   Where pension rights form part of the matrimonial property, it is necessary to determine the Cash Equivalent Transfer Value (CETV) of the pension at the relevant date.[72] This is the figure that the pension fund member would be entitled to transfer into another pension scheme if he left his current employment at the relevant date.[73] This figure will be provided by the pension fund administrator. In the event that the husband did not start contributing to his pension fund until after the parties were married, the entirety of the CETV will be matrimonial property. However, if contributions began prior to the marriage, and continued during it, only the portion of the CETV related to contributions made during the marriage will be matrimonial property. This is determined using the formula "A × B/C" where:

A is the CETV at the relevant date;

---

[72] The law is set out in the Divorce etc. (Pensions) (Scotland) Regulations 1996 (SI 1996/1901) and the Divorce etc. (Pensions) (Scotland) Regulations 2000 (SSI 2000/112). For commentary, see Bissett-Johnson, "Recent Changes in Valuation and Division of Pensions on Divorce", 1996 S.L.T. (News) 295; S. Eden, "Pensions and Divorce (Pt II)", 1996 Fam L.B. 23–3; S. Smith, "Valuation of Pension Rights on Divorce", 1999 Fam L.B. 38–3; I. Talman, "Pensions on Divorce", 1999 Fam. L.B. 41–3 and H. Smith, "Valuation of Pension Rights Revisited", 1999 Fam. L.B. 42–3.

[73] If the fund member is due to receive his pension benefits within 12 months of the relevant date, the actual value of his benefits at that date will be used.

B is the period during the marriage when the party is a member of the pension scheme; and

C is the total period of membership of the scheme before the relevant date.

So, imagine Graeme started contributing to a pension plan in June 1993. He married Fiona in June 2008 and ceased cohabiting with her in June 2013, which is therefore the relevant date. His pension was valued at the relevant date at £40,000. In this scenario, A is £40,000, B is five years (from 2008 to 2013) and C is 20 years (1993 to 2013.) The proportion of the pension which represents matrimonial property is therefore £40,000 x 5/20 = £10,000. This valuation mechanism has been subject to various criticisms.[74]

A final valuation problem is what associated benefits should be   **13–30** included when calculating the total value of the pension. Typically, occupational pensions give rise to a bundle of benefits on top of the basic member's pension, including a spouse's pension and lump sum if the pensioner survives to retirement, or death in service benefit and widow/ widower's pension if he or she does not. There was considerable doubt as to which of these extra benefits should be included when valuing an occupational pension for divorce purposes,[75] until amendments made to s.10(5) by the Pensions Act 1995[76] made it clear that any benefit given by a pension to the surviving spouse or civil partner, including any death in service benefit, is to be included in the value of that pension for divorce purposes.

Pensions: Options

Once the value of the pension rights forming part of the matrimonial prop-   **13–31** erty has been ascertained, there are three options for dividing it on divorce. The first option is that the non-member spouse receives money or property equivalent to her share of the CETV at the date of divorce. So, imagine that Graeme has a pension with a CETV of £10,000, and also a bank account containing savings of £20,000, both of which are matrimonial property. Applying s.9(1)(a), Fiona is entitled to a half share of each of those assets, meaning £5,000 in respect of the pension and £10,000 of savings. It may be agreed that Graeme will transfer £15,000 of savings to Fiona and keep his pension rights in full. In other words, Fiona's share in the pension rights is offset against an equivalent value from the savings account. Research

---

[74] Since CETV is based on what a member would receive if he left the scheme, it may understate the value of rights in a final salary scheme, where a member would effectively be penalised for leaving: see *Logan v Logan*, 2002 Fam. L.B. 55–4. There is also no mechanism for taking into account the fact that the value of pension rights may change significantly from what is predicted in the CETV, either as a result of economic factors or because of changes in to the rules of the pension scheme itself. This will be of relevance in pension sharing cases. For discussion and suggested solutions, see: J. Buchanan, "Pension Rights: Valuation and Sharing Issues", 2005 Fam. L.B. 75–4.

[75] See previously, *Brooks v Brooks*, 1993 S.L.T. 184; *Crosbie v Crosbie*, 1996 S.L.T. (Sh. Ct) 86 and *Gribb v Gribb*, 1996 S.L.T. 719.

[76] Pensions Act 1995 s.167(2).

suggests that such trade-offs are commonly agreed in preference to splitting the value of pension rights.[77]

13–32 Alternatively, parties may split the pension fund.[78] The appropriate share of the CETV (as agreed by parties or determined by the court) is transferred to the pursuer, who would normally pay it into an existing pension scheme, or start a pension scheme with the funds. Occasionally, it may be necessary for the transferee to become a member of the same pension scheme as the transferor, but the pension is held in the tranferee's sole name. The pension then becomes available in the usual way when the transferee retires

13–33 A third option is that the court may make a pension lump sum order earmarking a portion of the lump sum to which the pension fund member is entitled on death or retirement to be paid to the other spouse.[79] Many pension schemes have provision for a lump sum to be paid out to the member's family if the member dies before the pension matures, or alternatively have the option for the member to take a lump sum on retirement with the effect that periodical payments he receives subsequently will be less than if he had not taken the lump sum. Since it is not possible to obtain both a lump sum order and a pension sharing order,[80] and since there is no guarantee that the pension fund member will choose to take the lump sum on retirement, this option is almost never used in practice.

13–34 The advantage of these latter two options is that they do not require any immediate payment out of available resources. Both parties will receive payment only when the pension rights become due, normally on retirement.

Pension Protection Fund

13–35 Following problems with employers going bankrupt and the effect this has on employees' pension rights, the government introduced the Pension Protection Fund under the Pensions Act 2004. This is a government fund to which pension schemes contribute by way of a levy. Its purpose is to pay out compensation to members whose pension schemes have collapsed. Where such a payout is made, s.17 of the FLSA 2006 governs how such compensation is to be dealt with in relation to financial provision as it may well form part of the matrimonial or civil partnership property. The 1985 Act is amended by adding a new subs.(5A) to s.10 of that Act[81] which makes it clear that the compensation may form part of the matrimonial (or civil partnership) property. As with ordinary pensions, compensation received also has to be apportioned so that only that part attributable to the marriage or civil partnership is available for distribution between the

---

[77] Wasoff, McGuckin and Edwards, *Mutual Consent: Written Agreements in Family Law* (Scottish Office Central Research Unit 1997), Ch.4.

[78] This does not apply to state pensions. For discussion of changes in non-state pension rules see A. Bissett-Johnson, "Changes in Pension Division on Divorce", 2000 S.L.T. (News) 297.

[79] 1985 Act s.12A.

[80] 1985 Act s.8(4), (5) and (6).

[81] By s.17 of the FLSA 2006.

parties.[82] Compensation can be subject to a pension sharing order[83] or be made subject to an order earmarking a lump sum.[84]

Net Value of Matrimonial Property

It is the "net" value of the matrimonial property which is to be shared   **13–36**
between the parties under s.9(1)(a). This is calculated by taking the gross value of the matrimonial property at the relevant date, and deducting any outstanding debts. The debts must have been incurred by either party before or during the marriage, in connection with matrimonial property, and be outstanding at the relevant date.[85] For example, a mortgage taken out on the security of the family home will be deducted to produce the net value of the home; while loans incurred to purchase moveables should similarly be deducted.[86] However, capital gains tax which is notionally payable on such property is not deductible.[87]

Special Circumstances

Where an item or asset has been identified as falling within the definition   **13–37**
of matrimonial property, s.10(1) provides that it should be shared equally between the parties unless there are "special circumstances" to justify a different division. Without prejudice to the generality of s.10(1),[88] s.10(6) lists certain circumstances which particularly justify such a departure, and which are examined below. It should be noted that although these circumstances may justify departure from equal sharing, they cannot *require* it: where the circumstances cited are of negligible significance, or opposing special circumstances counter-balance each other, then equal division may be allowed

---

[82] This is to be done in accordance with regulations made by the Scottish Ministers under s.10(8B).
[83] 1985 Act s.8(1)(bab).
[84] 1985 Act s.8(1)(ba) and (bb).
[85] 1985 Act s.10(2). In *Mackin v Mackin*, 1991 S.L.T. (Sh. Ct.) 22, a house was purchased from the husband's employers with a penalty attached to resale within five years. When this penalty was imposed because the spouses separated within 5 years, the value of the property was treated as being the market value less the imposed penalty. In *Buchan v Buchan*, 1992 S.C.L.R. 766, arrears of tax and penalties relating to the period before separation were held to be deductible debts although not calculated until after separation. But *cf. McCormick v McCormick*, 1994 G.W.D. 35–2078 where estimated tax on H's business profits was not deductible; and *Latter v Latter*, 1990 S.L.T. 805, where notional capital gains tax was not deductible from the value of shares held by one spouse.
[86] See *Jesner v Jesner*, 1992 S.L.T. 999.
[87] The Lord Ordinary in *Sweeney v Sweeney*, 2003 S.L.T. 892 held that in determining the net value of the matrimonial property it was permissible to deduct the capital gains tax notionally payable by the husband. However, the Inner House in *Sweeney v Sweeney*, 2004 S.C.L.R. 256 found that the Lord Ordinary had erred in upholding such a deduction for: "it is, rightly, conceded on behalf of the husband that any hypothetical liability of his to capital gains tax arising on the assumption that he had disposed of matrimonial property on that date does not fall to be deducted as being an outstanding debt. No 'netting' provision in respect of matrimonial property other than for outstanding debts is expressly made in the statute [1985 Act]", at 264D.
[88] One "special circumstance" not listed in s.10(6) is where one party has had the sole use of the family home since the date of separation. The usual practice in these circumstances is, however, to seek an incidental order for interest: see para.13–82 below.

to stand.[89] In each case, what matters is what constitutes *fair* sharing in the circumstances.

Source of Funds

13–38   The court is directed to consider the source of the funds or assets used to acquire any of the matrimonial property where those funds or assets were not derived from the income or efforts of the persons during the marriage.[90] As we have seen above, where property owned by one of the parties is acquired by gift or succession from a third party, then it is not matrimonial property. However, if the property is sold and the proceeds used to buy new property, those assets will be matrimonial property. In this situation, unequal sharing of the assets may be justified.[91] Similarly, where property owned solely by one party before the marriage is sold during the relationship and the proceeds used to buy new assets, the same argument can be made. If Graeme uses £50,000 of his pre-relationship savings to buy a house in contemplation of his marriage to Fiona, that house will be matrimonial property, but an unequal split may be justified to reflect Graeme's original contribution.[92] (Bear in mind that had Graeme saved £50,000 from his wages during the marriage and used that money to buy a house, no special circumstances argument could be made, because the £50,000 in this situation has derived from his income and efforts during the marriage.)

13–39   Where the source of funds is a relevant circumstance, there is no defined rule about how that should be taken into account by the court. Much will depend on the broader facts and circumstances of the case. The reported decisions demonstrate a range of potential outcomes. In *Cordiner v Cordiner*,[93] the court held that where the husband's assets had amounted to £107,000 prior to marriage and the wife had had no capital assets, this justified a departure from equal sharing of matrimonial property under ss.10(1) and 10(6)(b) and deducted the value of the husband's pre-marital assets from the net value

---

[89] *Jacques v Jacques*, 1997 S.L.T. 459, *per* Lord Clyde.
[90] 1985 Act s.10(6)(b).
[91] See *Davidson v Davidson*, 1994 S.L.T. (OH) 506 where the court awarded the wife more than a half share of the value of the matrimonial home, which represented the parties' only matrimonial property, on the grounds that it had been purchased entirely by the wife with money derived from her inherited shareholdings. See also *R v R*, 2000 Fam. L.R. 43 where the court held that the fact that to a large extent the net value of the matrimonial property derived from assets donated to or inherited by the defender did constitute a special circumstance which justified departure from the presumption of an equal division of these assets. However, in this case the court also acknowledged that, although special circumstances existed, due weight had to be given to the other s.9 principles, especially s.9(1)(b), as the wife had suffered a financial disadvantage in being unable to pursue her career because of her commitment to caring for their children and the family home (although it did not quantify this). This case has been criticised on the grounds that whatever special circumstances exist they *cannot* be circumstances which constitute successful claims under other s.9 principles because the other principles are not factors to be used in determining a fair division of assets under s.9(1)(a). They represent claims that exist *in addition to* those associated with a fair division.
[92] In *Watt v Watt*, 2009 S.L.T. 931, the husband had owned various interests in a fishing business which had generated further assets during the course of the marriage. This amounted to special circumstances which justified dividing the matrimonial property on a 52/48 basis in favour of the husband.
[93] *Cordiner v Cordiner*, 2003 Fam. L.R. 39.

of the matrimonial property at the relevant date, distributing what remained in equal shares. In *Scott v Scott*,[94] the husband had paid a significant deposit on the family home using money from a pre-relationship damages payment. The sheriff found that this money should be returned to the husband first, before the remaining value of the house was split equally between the parties. In *Phillip v Phillip*,[95] the court went further, not simply returning the figure paid as a deposit by the husband from pre-marriage property, but finding him entitled to a quarter of the value of the family home at the time of divorce to reflect the fact he had paid a quarter of the original purchase price, with the remainder to be split equally between the couple.[96] In *Kerrigan v Kerrigan*,[97] the husband's mother provided the whole of the deposit put down on the matrimonial home, and the husband paid the whole mortgage during the marriage, which lasted only two months. Although title to the house was taken in joint names, the court awarded the whole of the house to the husband. A similar decision was reached in *Mukhtar v Mukhtar*[98] where Sheriff Horsburgh ordered the husband to transfer his half share of the family home over to his wife, effectively giving her the whole of the matrimonial property, since her father had paid the deposit on the house and all but two of the monthly mortgage repayments

With the exception of *Phillip*, each of the marriages in the cases above had been of relatively short duration (from 12 years down to two months) and no children had been involved. In a longer relationship, or one with children, the dictum of Lord MaFadyen in *Cunningham v Cunningham*[99] to the effect that the source of funds used to purchase the matrimonial home is less important than would be the case with other kinds of matrimonial property may be applicable. The intention of the parties will also be relevant: in *Le Riche v Le Riche*,[100] where the couple were married for two years, Sheriff Lothian declined to depart from the norm of equal sharing where the funds for the family home had come almost entirely from the wife's family. He took the view that if the couple had intended to reflect the substantial contribution by the wife's family, the title to the property should have been taken in unequal shares. **13–40**

As a contrast from the decisions above, in *Jacques v Jacques*,[101] the Inner House and subsequently the House of Lords held that although the matrimonial home had been purchased during the marriage with the proceeds of a house owned solely by the husband prior to the marriage, this was, in the circumstances, of little importance and did not justify unequal division. The particular facts of the case leading to this decision were that the spouses had **13–41**

---

[94] *Cordiner v Cordiner*, 2011 G.W.D 37–762.
[95] *Phillip v Phillip*, 1988 S.C.L.R. 427.
[96] See also *Budge v Budge*, 1990 S.C.L.R. 144, where the matrimonial home was purchased with £7,000 derived by the husband from the sale of a home inherited solely by him: the court held that only the increase in value of the house since the marriage should be equally shared with the wife.
[97] *Kerrigan v Kerrigan*, 1988 S.C.L.R. 603.
[98] *Mukhtar v Mukhtar*, 2002 Fam. L.B. 60–7.
[99] *Cunningham v Cunningham*, 2001 Fam. L.R. 12.
[100] *Le Riche v Le Riche*, 2001 Fam. L.B. 51–8.
[101] *Jacques v Jacques*, 1995 S.L.T. 963; affirmed by the House of Lords, 1997 S.L.T. 459.

occupied the house owned by the husband together before their marriage, and had agreed to take title to the new home in both names.[102] As the Lord President observed in *Little v Little*[103]:

> "The concept of sharing the net value of the matrimonial property fairly, the flexibility which is given by the expression 'special circumstances' in section 10(6) and the repeated references in section 11 to all the other circumstances of the case serve to emphasise that, despite the detail, the matter is essentially one of discretion, aimed at achieving a fair and practicable result in accordance with common sense. It remains as important as it always has been that the details should be left in the hands of the court of first instance and not opened up for reconsideration on appeal".

Nature and Use of Property

13–42   A further circumstance the court is directed to consider is the nature of the matrimonial property, the use made of it (including use for business purposes or as a family home) and the extent to which it is reasonable to expect it to be realised or divided or used as security.[104]

13–43   This may be the special circumstances mostly likely to result in unequal division, since the realities of family life mean the equal division that is desirable on paper cannot necessarily be brought about in practice. One obvious example of this is where property is used as a family home for the children of the relationship, especially if they are still quite young.[105] In *Peacock v Peacock*,[106] it was argued that if the value of the matrimonial home was to be divided equally between the spouses, then neither spouse would have sufficient funds to purchase a new home which could house the two children of the marriage. In these special circumstances, the sheriff ordered the husband to transfer his half share in the matrimonial home to the wife, who had legal custody of the children, although all she could transfer to him in return was an insurance policy worth £643. The decision was upheld by both the sheriff principal and the Inner House.[107] But in *Adams v Adams (No.1)*[108] the Lord

---

[102]   The agreement to take the house in joint names was arguably another "special circumstance" under s.10(6)(a) which counter-balanced the issue of the source of the purchase price of the house.

[103]   *Little v Little*, 1990 S.L.T. 785 at 787B–C.

[104]   1985 Act s.10(6)(d).

[105]   See *Cooper v Cooper*, 1989 S.C.L.R. (Sh. Ct) 347 where the sheriff held that the fact the house was required as a home for the pursuer and the three children of the marriage (one of whom was under 16 and another who was still in full-time education and had special needs) that if sold would render them homeless was a circumstance that made it unreasonable to expect the house to be realised and that s.19(6)(d) applied. See also *Murphy v Murphy*, 1996 S.L.T. (Sh. Ct) 91 where the court held that given the wife would have care of the parties' child after divorce, that the house was necessary for the child's welfare, that the husband had alternative accommodation and that the wife would receive no payment from the pension rights or otherwise, special circumstances existed justifying an unequal division of matrimonial property in the wife's favour to the extent of transferring the husband's interest in the matrimonial home.

[106]   *Peacock v Peacock*, 1994 S.L.T. 40.

[107]   See also *Murphy v Murphy*, 1996 S.L.T. (Sh. Ct) 90.

[108]   *Adams v Adams (No.1)*, 1997 S.L.T. 144.

Ordinary refused to accept an argument that the two children of the marriage, aged 14 and 12, would experience an unacceptable disruption to their lives if they were forced to leave the family home.[109]

An alternative approach may be to accept that the matrimonial home **13-44** should be divided in equal shares, but to ask the court to make an incidental order that sale be delayed and that the spouse with care of the children should continue to reside there as a sole occupier until the last child reaches, say, the age of 16.[110] Orders of this kind were once frequently used in the English courts. They have, however, fallen from favour because, on the one hand, they create short-term hardship for the non-resident spouse, whose capital is locked up without compensation and, on the other hand, may produce sudden homelessness for the spouse with care of the children at a future date, when there is no guarantee that he or she will have more in the way of assets to acquire a new home.

Another case where matrimonial property may be unevenly divided because **13-45** of its use is where the family home is used by one spouse to run a business, such as a farm, a bed and breakfast or a dental practice. In *Geddes v Geddes*[111] the husband purchased a farm with his own money for use as a family home. This was the couple's only significant asset. The sheriff awarded the wife not one-half of the net value, which would have required the sale of the farm, but only one-fifth, to be paid by six instalments from the date of divorce. This was because, as the court remarked in *Mayor v Mayor*,[112] "one should hesitate long and hard before ordaining the disposal of an income producing asset such as the family business". As in *Geddes*, the power of the court to order the payment of a capital sum by instalments out of the income of the payer may be usefully applied to resolve the conflict between giving one spouse a reasonable award, and not destroying the livelihood of the other spouse, where the marriage is poor in capital assets.

Another issue arising under this subsection is the realisability of matrimo- **13-46** nial property, which can be problematic particularly in respect of pensions. Although the law has devised rules for valuing pension rights as discussed above,[113] in reality it may be years or even decades after the divorce before the pension matures. The pension fund member who is asked to pay a share of the fund to his former spouse on divorce may not, in reality, be able to make that payment until the pension pays out. Unlike most other assets, pensions cannot be sold and the proceeds used to make the necessary payment on divorce: for tax reasons, pension schemes invariably forbid their members from doing so. The law has developed three mechanisms for circumventing this problem as outlined above: offsetting the value of the pension rights against other matrimonial property; a pension sharing order; or a pension lump sum order.[114] As an alternative, it is possible to argue that "special circumstances" exist to depart from equal sharing of the value of the pension

---

[109] *Adams v Adams (No.1)*, 1997 S.L.T. 144 at 148.
[110] Under s.14(2)(d)(i) and (ii).
[111] *Geddes v Geddes*, 1993 S.L.T. 494.
[112] *Mayor v Mayor*, 1995 S.L.T. 1097 at 1101.
[113] See paras 13–27 to 13–30 above.
[114] See paras 13–31 to 13–34 above.

rights because of the unrealisable nature of the asset.[115] In a number of cases, judges have on this basis awarded less than 50 per cent of the value of the pension rights to the non-member spouse, and sometimes as little as a third.[116] These cases were decided before pension sharing orders and pension lump sum orders were added to the 1985 Act, however, and it is difficult to see how such discounting could be considered either equitable or necessary under the current legislative framework.

Destruction, Dissipation or Alienation of Assets

13–47   The rationale of this head is that a party who has wilfully reduced the total value of the matrimonial property which would otherwise have been available for distribution by destroying, dissipating or alienating the assets should not be entitled to a full half-share of the property.[117] In *Short v Short*,[118] a wife dissipated assets by fraudulently borrowing £20,000 on the security of the matrimonial home without the knowledge of her husband. Her half-share of the matrimonial property was reduced by subtracting nominally the debt she had run up from the total value of the matrimonial assets, before equal division of what remained.[119] Dissipation requires some positive action by a spouse. Thus, in *Park v Park*[120] the husband's failure to meet mortgage payments led to the forced sale of the matrimonial home at a loss. The court did not reduce his share of the matrimonial property, holding that "a passive failure to take definite steps to prevent destruction, dissipation or alienation is not sufficient".[121] The spouses were joint owners in *Park* and the wife could have made the payments herself or at least taken steps to deal with the situation.

13–48   Where dissipation occurs its effects cannot always be rectified, especially where there are few matrimonial assets. In *Fraser v Fraser*[122] the only matrimonial property was the husband's interest in a pension scheme valued at £105,000 at the relevant date. On equal division of the matrimonial property the wife should have been entitled to £52,500. However, the husband retired early, received a lump sum and dissipated it on a failed business. At the date of divorce no resources existed sufficient to justify the making of a capital award in favour of the wife.[123]

---

[115] This approach was expressly approved by the Inner House in *Little v Little*, 1990 S.L.T. 785.

[116] See *Fleming v Fleming*, 1993 G.W.D. 9–621; *Stephen v Stephen*, 1995 S.C.L.R. 175 where only a third of the transfer value of the pension was awarded to the pensioner's wife (amounting to £38,240) and, of that sum, payment of £15,000 was deferred until the death or retirement of the husband (who was aged 52 and expected to retire at 65).

[117] 1985 Act s.10(6)(c).

[118] *Short v Short*, 1994 G.W.D. 21–1300.

[119] See also *Goldie v Goldie*, 1992 G.W.D. 21–1225.

[120] *Park v Park*, 1988 S.C.L.R. 584.

[121] *Park v Park*, 1988 S.C.L.R. 584 at 587. This approach was followed in *Russell v Russell*, 1996 G.W.D. 15–895 where the court held that s.10(6)(c) required something more than the course of bad luck which had affected the wife's business decisions including losing her job and investing capital in unsuccessful business ventures.

[122] *Fraser v Fraser*, 1994 Fam. L.B. 10–3.

[123] The court *could* have awarded a capital sum payable by instalments out of the annual periodical element of the pension, which still existed. It did not do so, however, because the husband needed this income to support his 13-year-old son who lived with him.

Agreement Between Parties

The court will also take account of any agreement between the parties as   **13–49**
to how matrimonial property is to be owned or divided.[124] This will include
agreements made before the relationship (ante-nuptial contracts, sometimes
known colloquially by the Anglo-American term "pre-nup") and during the
relationship, whether or not in contemplation of divorce. Where parties have
entered into an agreement, the court will enforce it unless any term in it is successfully challenged on the ground that it was not fair and reasonable at the
time that it was entered into.[125] The way in which couples have agreed to take
title to property, such as buying the family home in both names, is not generally regarded as an "agreement" since it does not relate explicitly to division
of matrimonial property.[126]

Expense of Valuation/Transfer

A final circumstance for the court to consider is the actual or prospective[127]   **13–50**
liability for any expenses of valuation or transfer of property in connection
with the divorce.[128] This provision ensures that any one party who is ordered
to transfer all or part of an item of property to the other is not unfairly burdened with the expenses of the transfer, such as the solicitor's fees that must
be incurred when transferring ownership of a share of a house from one party
to the other. The expenses of one party can be taken into account to reduce
the other spouse's share of the matrimonial property. However in *Sweeney v
Sweeney*,[129] the court took the view that capital gains tax payable on a transfer of property is not an expense for this purpose.

Conduct

In reaching a decision as to whether or not special circumstances apply   **13–51**
to divert from equal sharing in any particular case, the court is expressly
directed to ignore the issue of conduct on the part of either party unless it
has adversely affected relevant financial resources or it would be manifestly
inequitable to leave the conduct out of account.[130] This is most likely to
arise under the head of dissipation of assets, for example where a spouse
has gambled away the assets of the marriage. The amoral behaviour is not
relevant as "special circumstances" *per se*, but the financial consequences
of that behaviour are. This provision on conduct is not just limited to a
consideration of special circumstances but pertains generally to the application of s.9 principles.

---

[124] 1985 Act s.10(6)(a).
[125] See s.16(1)(b). This is discussed further at paras 15–08 *et seq.* and 15–20.
[126] But see obiter comments of Lord Clyde in *Jacques v Jacques*, 1997 S.L.T. 459, who felt s.10(6)
(a) might not be so limited.
[127] See *Farrell v Farrell*, 1990 S.C.L.R. 717, where the court took account of the future costs of
division and sale of the matrimonial home at a date after divorce; but *cf. Adams v Adams
(No.1)*, 1997 S.L.T. 144
[128] 1985 Act s.10(6)(e).
[129] *Sweeney v Sweeney*, 2003 S.L.T. 892 (OH) at 901C–D.
[130] 1985 Act s.11(7)(a)–(b).

Conclusion on Special Circumstances

13–52   The foregoing give rise to situations in which special circumstances may come into play, but the mere fact that they are found to exist does not render it mandatory for the court to depart from the norm of equal sharing, for the court must not only be satisfied that such circumstances justify a departure but also that such a departure is fair and reasonable having regard to the parties' resources. In considering the facts of a case there may well be an overlap between circumstances that support the application of other s.9 principles (apart from s.9(1)(a)) and that may also fall within the remit of the special circumstances referred to in s.10(1) of the 1985 Act. Where this is the case, as a commentator on the case of *Dehvasati v Dehvasati*[131] has observed, courts must be careful not to focus unduly on such circumstances, as "the tendency to treat everything as special circumstances devalues these other principles".[132]

SECOND PRINCIPLE: S.9(1)(B)—BALANCING ECONOMIC ADVANTAGE AND DISADVANTAGE

13–53   In some cases, the norm of equal sharing of matrimonial property is inappropriate for reasons which do not fall within the special circumstances set out in s.10(6). Decisions made during the course of a relationship can have an ongoing economic impact after the relationship has ended. Imagine that Fiona and Graeme have two children. Prior to the birth of their first child, both were employed as nurses, earning similar wages. As parents, they have a shared responsibility to care for their children physically, emotionally and financially. When the first baby arrived, they decided that Fiona would shoulder the bulk of the day-to-day physical and emotional care by working at home, and Graeme would shoulder the bulk of the financial care by continuing in paid employment. In this situation, both parties might be said to have received some advantages and suffered some disadvantages, but so long as they continue to function as a unit, these could be argued to balance out. Ten years pass and the couple are seeking a divorce. Graeme has been promoted several times during that decade, and is now earning a much higher wage, with the prospect of further promotion on the horizon. Fiona has no wage at all. She foresees difficulty returning to work as a nurse now that her knowledge is ten years out of date. If she is able to find a job, it will be at the same salary level as the position she left 10 years ago, if not lower. As an older woman without an established employment history, promotion is much less likely. Had the couple stayed together, this would not have mattered: both would have enjoyed the financial security offered by Graeme's job. Since they are divorcing, the law must find some other way to compensate Fiona for the

---

[131] *Dehvasati v Dehvasati*, 2003 Fam. L.B. 63–3.
[132] *Dehvasati v Dehvasati*, 2003 Fam. L.B. 63–3 at 63–4. In this case what amounted to "special circumstances" could just as easily have been dealt with under principles 9(1)(b) and (c).

ongoing economic disadvantage she will suffer as a result of being out of the job market for 10 years.[133]

Section 9(1)(b) is designed to deal with this type of situation. It provides **13–54** that, in addition to the principle of fair sharing under s.9(1)(a),

> "fair account should be taken of any economic advantage derived by either person from contributions by the other, and of any economic disadvantage suffered by either person in the interests of the other person or of the family".[134]

"Economic advantage" extends to include any advantage gained before or during the relationship and includes gains in capital, income and earning capacity, while "economic disadvantage" is defined as the converse.[135] "Contributions" are defined to include any contributions made before or during the relationship[136] and expressly cover indirect and non-financial contributions, in particular, any such contributions made by looking after the family home or caring for the family.[137] Where the court is satisfied that

---

[133] For a particularly clear and comprehensive analysis of the disadvantages experienced by the "homemaker" post divorce and the comparative advantages of the "wage earner" post divorce, see the opinions of the House of Lords in the joint English cases of *Miller v Miller* and *McFarlane v McFarlane*, 2006 UKHL 24, in particular the opinion of Lord Nicholls of Birkenhead, especially paras 90–99.

[134] 1985 Act s.9(1)(b). See *Buchan v Buchan*, 2001 Fam. L.R. 48 where the court held that it was pertinent to take into account the pursuer's various roles throughout the marriage as joint breadwinner, housekeeper, mother and teacher which justified an award under this heading. The court also took other factors into account, such as the contribution of a capital sum made by the pursuer's parents towards the family home (which was repossessed through the defender's failure to maintain mortgage payments) as well as the defender's conduct which had an adverse affect on the parties' financial resources. As a result of all these considerations the court elected to depart from the norm of equal sharing and to make property transfer orders that would have the effect of giving the pursuer sole title to the matrimonial home and to an endowment policy. See also *Symanski v Symanski (No.2)*, 2005 Fam. L.R. 2 where the Sheriff Principal upheld a finding by the sheriff that no share of the matrimonial property should be paid to the defender/husband because, inter alia, he had gained economic advantage from the pursuer before the marriage from the injections of capital into his businesses (which subsequently failed). The defender had attempted to argue that when he was discharged from bankruptcy this had the effect of discharging him of all debts and obligations from the date of discharge, including any economic advantage derived from the pursuer. He argued that the pursuer, in seeking an unequal share of the matrimonial property as a spouse, was seeking to derive a financial benefit which would not be available to the defender's creditors. His argument was unsuccessful because the court held that the matrimonial property was entirely derived from property owned by the pursuer and so, far from seeking to obtain any advantage over other creditors, the pursuer was simply seeking to prevent the defender from obtaining a share of that property on account of the imbalance between contributions made by the pursuer and the total absence of any contributions by the defender.

[135] 1985 Act s.9(2). See *Wilson v Wilson*, 1999 S.L.T. 249 (OH) where the court held that where a wife did not receive the expected gains in lifestyle during marriage because her husband ploughed his earning back into his farming business this amounted to a "contribution" by the wife. See also *Quinn v Quinn*, 2003 S.L.T. (Sh. Ct) 5 where the court observed that maintaining the family home after separation, which on divorce will be shared equally, might qualify as a disadvantage if it can be quantified appropriately.

[136] 1985 Act s.9(2).

[137] 1985 Act s.9(2). See *Cahill v Cahill*, 1998 S.L.T. (Sh. Ct) 96 where the court took into account renovations that that the pursuer husband had made during the marriage to a cottage owned

one party has suffered economic disadvantage, a common way of taking this into account is to order that the matrimonial property should be divided unequally, with the disadvantaged party receiving a greater share than the other party. So, Fiona might be entitled to 60% of the matrimonial property and Graeme to 40% to account for Fiona's ongoing economic disadvantage. This principle can also be used to make an award even if there is no matrimonial property.[138] Imagine Graeme owned substantial pre-relationship assets. If the couple had no matrimonial property to be shared, s.9(1)(b) could allow the court to order Graeme to make a payment from his other assets to account for Fiona's economic disadvantage.

13–55   In practice, the courts have tended to be reluctant to make awards under s.9(1)(b). This is because they are instructed when applying s.9(1)(b) to take into account the extent to which

> "(a) the economic advantages or disadvantages sustained by either person have been balanced by the economic advantages or disadvantages sustained by the other person, and
>
>   (b) any resulting imbalance has been or will be corrected by a sharing of the value of the matrimonial property or the partnership property or otherwise".[139]

It is often successfully argued that either the advantages and disadvantages suffered or gained by the spouses have balanced themselves out,[140] or that any imbalance has been sufficiently accommodated through the equal sharing of matrimonial property under s.9(1)(a). So, for example, in *Welsh v Welsh*,[141] the husband was employed throughout the whole 18 years of the marriage and had acquired a full pension and other benefits. The wife argued that their standard of living had only been achieved because she had given up a good job to look after the family and home, and as a result she had been economically disadvantaged. The court found, however, that as the husband had supported her throughout the marriage and as she was now sharing in the value of the home purchased solely with his earnings, their contributions balanced each other out, and so no s.9(1)(b) award was appropriate.[142]

13–56   The prevailing judicial view seems to be that in most cases, domestic

---

by the defender that was not matrimonial property. The court held that the economic advantage that the defender derived from the improved cottage was one that came about through the pursuer's efforts during the marriage, the advantage being gained when the improvements were carried out although the benefit might not be realised until a subsequent date.

[138] In *Dougan v Dougan*, 1998 S.L.T. (Sh. Ct) 27 there was no matrimonial property to be shared out but the court did make an award to the pursuer under s.9(1)(b) because "it is quite clear that the pursuer suffered an economic disadvantage in giving up a well paid position in the interests of the family and, even though the marriage was a short one, the disadvantage to the pursuer was substantial" (at 30). See also *Johnston v Johnston*, 2004 Fam. L.B. 70–6 where a wife tried unsuccessfully to get an award under this heading in order to get at the much more valuable non-matrimonial property that represented her husband's interest in a farming partnership.

[139] 1985 Act s.11(2).

[140] *Adams v Adams (No.1)*, 1997 S.L.T. 144.

[141] *Welsh v Welsh*, 1994 S.L.T. 828.

[142] See also *Petrie v Petrie*, 1988 S.C.L.R. 104.

family arrangements work to the mutual benefit of both spouses, and that the spouse who earns the most does not necessarily gain an unfair advantage over the spouse who opts not to work, or to work part-time. Where awards have been made under s.9(1)(b), they have tended to provide compensation for actual financial contributions made during the marriage by one spouse to the other,[143] or where the labour of one spouse has enhanced the value of an asset which does not form part of the matrimonial property, e.g. a house acquired before marriage by one spouse and subsequently used as the family home or business.[144] However, giving up professional employment to look to the family's needs over a number of years *has* been taken account of by some courts, especially where this has resulted in reduced employment prospects for that spouse.[145]

The court's restrictive approach to s.9(1)(b) is well illustrated in **13–57** *De Winton v De Winton*.[146] In this case, although the marriage was a wealthy one, there was no matrimonial property at all to divide under s.9(1)(a), as all the property had been acquired by the spouses prior to the marriage. The husband owned property amounting to some £1 million, while the wife had a shareholding in a family company worth £160,000. During the marriage, the wife used her money to pay for the children's education at private schools and to raise the standard of living in the household. On divorce, the wife's only possible claim was under s.9(1)(b) as there was no matrimonial property and the children were over the age of 16. The court accepted that she had suffered economic disadvantage, but found that no economic *advantage* had been conferred on the husband, as he would not have chosen by himself to pay for the children to attend private schools, and her other expenditures were on unnecessary luxuries. An award of £30,000 was, however, made, to compensate the wife for financial contributions she had put into the husband's business.

The kind of problem that arises in establishing a claim under the section **13–58** is demonstrated in *Coyle v Coyle*.[147] In this case the wife pursuer had given up a successful career at her husband's request to undertake domestic tasks and childcare after they married. Had she continued working she would have earned substantial sums during the marriage and have built up a substantial pension. She argued that these losses should be compensated. However, the court held that the section did not provide for automatic compensation and that

---

[143] See *Buchan v Buchan*, 1993 G.W.D. 23–1515, where the court took into account the fact that the wife continued to make the same financial contribution to the parties' joint bank account despite the fact that she had taken a substantial cut in salary on marriage. See also *Macdonald v Macdonald*, 1994 G.W.D. 7–104 and *Farrell v Farrell*, 1990 S.C.L.R. 717.

[144] See *Ranaldi v Ranaldi*, 1994 S.L.T. (Sh. Ct) 25 where the court awarded the wife half the increase in value of the family home (which was not matrimonial property) over the period of the marriage, to reflect the labour she had put into running it as a boarding house.

[145] See *Louden v Louden*, 1994 S.L.T. 381, where 55% of the property was awarded to the wife because she had given up a job as a secretary and looked after a child, while the husband pursued a successful business career during their 17-year marriage. In *Clokie v Clokie*, 1994 G.W.D. 3–149, the property was unequally divided in favour of the wife because she had prejudiced her academic career to further that of her husband. See also *McCormick v McCormick*, 1994 G.W.D. 35–2078.

[146] *De Winton v De Winton*, 1996 Fam. L.B. 23–6.

[147] *Coyle v Coyle*, 2004 Fam. L.B. 67–6 and 67–7.

the pursuer had not established an identifiable economic advantage her spouse had enjoyed which derived from an identifiable contribution of hers and which was fair to take account of. While it was true that the husband would have had to pay for domestic and childcare services if she had continued to work it was also the case that she would have been earning a good salary and thus increasing the family's wealth. There was not any obvious connection between the increase in the value of his business and her non-financial domestic contributions.

13–59   In dealing with this ground the court had to balance the economic disadvantages suffered by each party and then see whether any resulting imbalance had been corrected by a fair sharing of the matrimonial property or otherwise. It had to take account of the interplay between the two principles and reach an overall view of the fairness and reasonableness of the financial provision to be awarded. In this case, a move away from the usual 50/50 split was not justified as there was sufficient matrimonial property to compensate her adequately by a share of it. Indeed the wife benefited from a property transfer order in relation to the former family home which had increased substantially in value from the relevant date to the date of proof. This was held to correct any economic disadvantage which she suffered in the interests of her husband and family. While this appears to be fair in the circumstances of this case, the failure to make an award on the basis of the wife's non-financial contributions to the home and family because of the failure to establish a nexus between her domestic activities and the increase in the value of her husband's business may cause hardship in other cases where there is insufficient matrimonial property to be divided among the parties.

THIRD PRINCIPLE: S.9(1)(C)—FAIR SHARING OF ECONOMIC BURDEN OF CHILDCARE

13–60   Section 9(1)(c) requires that

> "any economic burden of caring,
>
> (i)   after divorce, for a child of the marriage under the age of 16 years should be shared fairly between the persons
> (ii) after dissolution of the civil partnership, for a child under that age who has been accepted by both partners as a child of the family."

Section 9(1)(c) is not designed directly to provide for the maintenance of the child, as this is the function of the rules relating to aliment and child support.[148] Instead, this principle allows the court to make allowance for the fact that even where aliment or child support is paid, there may be further economic consequences involved in child care: for example, the parent with primary care of the children may be unable to work full time for some years after the divorce. When assessing the level of award under s.9(1)(c), the court is directed to consider a range of factors under s.11(3) which include the age

---

[148] See Ch.5.

and health of the child,[149] the educational, financial and other circumstances of the child,[150] and the needs and resources of the persons.[151] The court may also take into account any support provided by the defender to dependants, whether or not he is legally obliged to provide such support.[152]

An award under s.9(1)(c), unlike s.9(1)(a) and (b), may be made in the **13–61** form of a periodical allowance order (in other words, weekly or monthly payments) as well as an order for a capital sum or transfer of property.[153] As with s.9(1)(b), the most appropriate mechanism for making an award under this head may be to order an unequal division of the matrimonial property, with the parent with care receiving a greater share.

The courts have often appeared more willing to make substantial capital **13–62** awards under s.9(1)(c) than s.9(1)(b). In *Morrison v Morrison*,[154] for example, the wife was awarded two-thirds of the value of the home and contents so that she could look after the children aged 13 and 10. In *Macdonald v Macdonald*,[155] a wife who assumed the financial burden of bringing up five children, paying for the mortgage and hiring domestic help, was awarded more than half of the capital of the marriage. In some cases the burden of childcare may constitute "special circumstances" to divert from equal sharing under s.9(1)(a), as well as justify an award under s.9(1)(c).[156] In *Russell v Russell*,[157] the husband received substantially more than a half share of the pension rights which were the entirety of the matrimonial property, on the basis that in order to bring up the three children of the marriage, he had had to take early retirement, which meant reduction of these rights. Under these circumstances a s.9(1)(c) award was justified. Courts are, however, reluctant to give the parent who is caring for children an increased share of the value of the matrimonial home, through ordering the other parent to make a property transfer order, where there are insufficient funds or resources to maintain the property. In *Shipton v Shipton*,[158] for example, the court declined to order the husband to transfer his half share in the family home over to the wife who wanted to continue living there with the children because the wife could not afford to keep up the mortgage payments. For this reason the sheriff ordered the home to be sold.[159]

Since the introduction of the Child Support Act 1991, s.9(1)(c) has become **13–63** less important. However, in *Maclachlan v Maclachlan*[160] Lord Macfayden expressed the view that although the enactment of the Child Support Act 1991 had greatly reduced the scope for reliance on s.9(1)(c), it had not wholly superseded it:

---

[149] 1985 Act s.11(3)(d).
[150] 1985 Act s.11(3)(e).
[151] 1985 Act s.11(3)(g).
[152] 1985 Act s.11(6).
[153] 1985 Act s.13(2).
[154] *Morrison v Morrison*, 1989 S.C.L.R. 574.
[155] *Macdonald v Macdonald*, 1994 G.W.D. 7–104.
[156] See, e.g. *Peacock v Peacock*, 1994 S.L.T. 40.
[157] *Russell v Russell*, 1996 Fam. L.B. 21–5.
[158] *Shipton v Shipton*, 1992 S.C.L.R. (Sh Ct) 23.
[159] The same result occurred in *Symon v Symon*, 1991 S.C.L.R. (Sh Ct) 414 and in *Adams v Adams (No.1)*, 1997 S.L.T. 144 (OH) for the same reason.
[160] *Maclachlan v Maclachlan*, 1998 S.L.T. 693 (OH).

"The fact that one parent has to purchase a house large enough, not only to accommodate herself, but also to provide suitable accommodation for the children, seems to me to be an aspect of the economic burden of caring for the children after divorce. If an award of a capital sum would enable that burden to be more fairly shared, I see no reason why reliance cannot be placed on section 9(1)(c) as justifying such a capital sum".[161]

FOURTH PRINCIPLE: S.9(1)(D)—ADJUSTMENT FROM FINANCIAL DEPENDENCE

13–64   Section 9(1)(d) can be relied on only where the principles in s.9(1)(a)–(c) are insufficient to provide adequately for one party after the divorce. The preference of the legislation is for parties to have a "clean break" from one another at the end of the marriage, with no continuing financial relationship. However it was recognised that in a very narrow range of circumstances—namely where one spouse had removed herself for some time from the labour market in order to look after the family, had become financially dependent on the other spouse, and could not now be expected to re-enter employment—it might not be possible for an adequate clean break settlement to be constructed under s.9(1)(a)–(c). This is particularly likely in the case where there is little or nothing in the way of capital assets to share under s.9(1)(a), or where the wife has taken her half share of the matrimonial property in the form of the family home, leaving her with no resources for day-to-day expenses, In such cases, an award under s.9(1)(d) may be justified.

13–65   Section 9(1)(d) provides that a person who has been financially dependent to a substantial degree on the financial support of the other person should be awarded such financial provision as is reasonable to allow her to adjust to the loss of that support on divorce, over a period of not more than three years from the date of divorce.[162] What the Act clearly envisages is that for

---

[161] *Maclachlan v Maclachlan*, 1998 S.L.T. 693 at 698K. However, such an award was not justified in this case as the wife would have more than sufficient resources to purchase a suitable house for the children and herself out of the proceeds of sale from the matrimonial home. Nor was he prepared to award a capital sum to the wife to enable her to make provision for future school fees. He took the view that: "While I do not go so far as to exclude the possibility of its ever being appropriate to make a capital award to enable such future expenditure to be provided for, I am of opinion that the court should be slow to make capital provision for a revenue expense" (at 698F).

[162] But see *Sullivan v Sullivan*, 2003 Fam. L.R. 53 (OH) where the court held that an award of a periodical allowance until remarriage or death was competent (although it might extend beyond a three-year period) given that the capital sum awarded to the defender was modest and that she also had the burden of looking after the two children of the marriage. Lord Emslie held: "In such circumstances, it was in my view open to the sheriff to conclude that there was a continuing dependency here which could not adequately be satisfied by means of a capital award alone, and that in order to avoid hardship a continuing periodical allowance at the specified date would be justified" (at 59). The time limit of three years for a periodical allowance payable under s.9(1)(d) was criticised in the House of Lords as part of the opinions in the joint case of *Miller v Miller* and *McFarlane v McFarlane*, 2006 UKHL 24. Lord Hope of Craighead opined *obiter* that: "The length of the period for which a periodical allowance should be awarded should no longer be confined to an absolute maximum of three years. The court should have a discretion to provide for a longer period . . . in exceptional circumstances" (at para.121).

many homemakers the three-year period will provide a transitional stage during which they can retrain or re-enter the labour market with a view to reacquiring financial independence.[163] Section 11(4) lists various factors the court should consider when making an award under s.9(1)(d), including notably "the duration and extent of the dependence of [the claimant] prior to divorce". In *Sweeney v Sweeney*,[164] the sheriff made an order for periodical allowance to be payable monthly for one year from the date of decree of divorce. This was justified by the fact that the pursuer had not worked independently since the birth of her first child in 1982 (twenty years earlier), during which time she had been wholly dependent upon the defender, who had been making monthly payments to her backdated to the date of separation. The sheriff accepted her contention that she would try to retrain, but that while she would like to do office work again, it might be hard for her to get a job given the length of time since she had last worked and her age. As a result she would need time to adjust to the loss of support and while acknowledging that she would in due course

> "be able to have the benefit of income produced by any capital paid, it will, on the face of it, take some time for her to obtain the full benefit of that, and I see no reason why she should be expected to use part of the capital to meet her income needs".[165]

Where a spouse has managed to survive in the period between separation and divorce without any financial support from her partner, even if only by reducing her standard of living, this is often viewed by the courts as showing lack of dependence and hence may prejudice any award under this head, especially if the period between separation and divorce has been lengthy.[166]

In dealing with claims under s.9(1)(d), the court must consider a number of factors including the age, health, and earning capacity of the claimant, as well as the needs and resources of both parties[167] together with all other circumstances of the case.[168] In addition, the court has a discretion to take account of any support given by the defender spouse to dependants within the household.[169] Conduct is relevant not only where it has affected the financial resources of the marriage, but also where it would be manifestly inequitable to leave it out of account.[170]   **13–66**

Where a s.9(1)(d) award is made, it usually takes the form of a periodical   **13–67**

---

[163] 1985 Act s.11(4) specifically requires the court when making a s.9(1)(d) award to have regard to the claimant spouse's earning capacity, and any intention they have to undertake a course of education or training.

[164] *Sweeney v Sweeney*, 2003 S.L.T. (Sh. Ct) 892.

[165] *Sweeney v Sweeney*, 2003 S.L.T. (Sh. Ct) 892 at 902.

[166] See *Dever v Dever*, 1988 S.C.L.R. 352; also *Millar v Millar*, 1990 S.C.L.R. 666, where the Sheriff Principal commented that one must consider the level of support prior to the date of divorce and ask whether an award of financial provision is desirable to enable the claimant to adjust to that loss.

[167] 1985 Act s.11(4)(a) and (d). "Needs and resources" are defined to include foreseeable needs and resources under s.27(1).

[168] 1985 Act s.11(4)(e)

[169] 1985 Act s.11(6).

[170] 1985 Act s.11(7)(b).

allowance order,[171] although a capital sum or property transfer order is also competent.

FIFTH PRINCIPLE: S.9(1)(E)—SERIOUS FINANCIAL HARDSHIP

13–68   As with s.9(1)(d), the principle in s.9(1)(e) can be relied on only where application of s.9(1)(a)–(c) are insufficient to provide adequately for one party after the divorce. Section 9(1)(e) provides that a person who, at the time of the divorce/dissolution seems likely to suffer serious financial hardship as a result of the divorce/dissolution should be awarded such financial provision as is reasonable to relieve this hardship over a reasonable period.[172] There are two crucial points to note here. First, whereas an award under s.9(1)(d) is limited in duration to three years, a s.9(1)(e) award can be of unlimited duration.[173] Secondly, the "serious financial hardship" that is to be relieved is restricted to that occurring at the time of, and *as a result of*, the divorce. A direct causal link between the divorce and the hardship is thus required. Hardship occurring as a result of a post-divorce event, such as a job loss, is not relevant. In *Barclay v Barclay*,[174] the wife was permanently disabled by multiple sclerosis. The court, however, declined to make an award under s.9(1)(e) because although the wife was indeed suffering serious financial hardship, this was caused not by the separation and pending divorce, but by a deterioration in her medical condition. However, a periodical allowance for three years was awarded under s.9(1)(d) to allow for adjustment from dependence.

13–69   Interestingly, although s.9(1)(e) requires that the hardship stem from the divorce itself and not any other factor such as illness, it does *not* apparently require, as s.9(1)(d) does, that the claimant spouse be financially dependent on the other spouse. In *Haugan v Haugan*[175] a 51-year-old woman was left by her high-earning husband after 27 years of marriage. There was no matrimonial property nor capital assets and she applied for a periodical allowance for an indefinite period under s.9(1)(e) on the basis that she had negligible employment prospects due to physical and mental illness as well as the lack of any qualifications. Her husband argued that any hardship suffered by her was not "as a result of the divorce" as, since their separation a year or so earlier, he had not paid her any aliment. During this time she had lived off income support and was thus strictly financially dependent at the date of divorce on the state, rather than her husband, which would normally exclude a s.9(1)(d) claim. The court found that the loss of the right to aliment on divorce

---

[171] 1985 Act s.13(2)(a).

[172] See *Galloway v Galloway*, 2003 Fam. L.R. where court awarded a periodical allowance of £1,000 a month on this ground to be payable until the pursuer, aged 55, reaches the age of 60 (when she could access deferred pension rights) or her death or remarriage, whichever of the foregoing dates comes first.

[173] See *Mackenzie v Mackenzie*, 1991 S.L.T. 46 and *Johnstone v Johnstone*, 1990 S.L.T. (Sh. Ct) 79, where in each case periodical allowance awards were made to wives until their remarriage or death; *Bell v Bell*, 1988 S.C.L.R. 457 where an award was made payable until the wife reached 60 or remarriage or death, whichever was earlier.

[174] *Barclay v Barclay*, 1991 S.C.L.R. 205.

[175] *Haugan v Haugan*, 1996 S.L.T. 321.

would itself be a hardship brought about by the divorce, and that accordingly a s.9(1)(e) award, of unlimited duration, was appropriate. This view was upheld by an extra division of the Inner House,[176] who made it clear that:

> "While the pattern of actual support afforded prior to the divorce, including any period of separation, is among the factors to be taken into account when assessing whether the loss of the right to aliment is likely to give rise to that hardship, the presence or absence of such actual support cannot be determinative of that matter. The fact that prior to divorce a spouse has failed to fulfil his or her obligation of support to the other cannot, even when active steps have not been taken to enforce it, exclude the making of financial provision in accordance with the principle set out in section 9(1)(e); nor can the fact that at the date of the divorce the claiming party is already suffering such hardship".[177]

However, the court accepted that since the first case there had been a material change in the defender's financial circumstances and that a reduction to £500 a month was reasonable having regard to the parties' resources.

At the end of the day *Haugan* has the rather odd result that it may in some   **13–70**
cases be easier to establish a right to unlimited support under s.9(1)(e) than three-year support under s.9(1)(d), a result surely not intended by the drafters of the Act. But, as Thomson has suggested,[178] a better approach might have been to order a capital award under s.9(1)(b), payable if necessary by instalments out of the husband's income.[179]

In assessing what amounts to "serious" financial hardship, the applicant's   **13–71**
access to sources of support other than the spouse, which includes state benefits, must be considered.[180] As *Haugan* demonstrates, the fact that a spouse may be entitled to state benefits does not automatically mean he or she is not suffering serious financial hardship (indeed it is often the fact of serious financial hardship which makes a person eligible for state benefits). The courts have tended to consider the degree to which the standard of living of a particular spouse will drop on divorce,[181] and the extent to which this has already been cushioned by an award for financial provision based on s.9(1)(a)–(d) of the Act.[182] Where the drop in standard of living as a result of divorce is minimal, because the spouses were already living at a low income level prior to separation, an award has usually not been granted.[183] It must be remembered that s.9(1)(e) is concerned not with alleviating serious financial

---

[176] 2002 S.L.T. (Ex Div) 1349.
[177] 2002 S.L.T. (Ex Div) 1349 at 1352H–I.
[178] Thomson, *Family Law in Scotland*, 6th edn (2011), p.146.
[179] But see A. Bissett-Johnson's concerns about the limitations of a capital sum in "Financial Provision on Divorce in Scots law—Does it Need Reform?", 2000 J.R. 265 discussed at para.13–90 below.
[180] See s.11(5)(a) and (d).
[181] 1985 Act s.11(5)(c).
[182] But see *MacKenzie v MacKenzie*, 1991 S.L.T. 461 where an award under s.9(1)(e) was made to a wife although she was also receiving a substantial capital sum under the other principles.
[183] See *Barclay v Barclay*, 1991 S.C.L.R. 205 where s.9(1)(e) was not applied because the reduction in the wife's weekly income post divorce amounted to only around 5%.

hardship in general, but only that arising as a result of the divorce. Hence it is has been sometimes said anecdotally that s.9(1)(e) is mainly of use to middle-class wives, who are accustomed to a standard of living which may plummet as a direct result of divorce.

13–72 In dealing with claims under s.9(1)(e), again the court must consider a number of factors including the age, health, and earning capacity of the claimant, as well as the needs and resources of both parties[184] together with all other circumstances of the case.[185] In addition, the court has a discretion to take account of any support given by the defender spouse to dependants within the household.[186] Conduct is again relevant not only where it has affected the financial resources of the marriage, but also where it would be manifestly inequitable to leave it out of account.[187]

COURT ORDERS

13–73 In order to implement the objectives of the 1985 Act, the courts are given power to make a wide range of orders. These can be divided into:

(a) orders making financial provision for the parties, including an order for payment of a capital sum,[188] for transfer of property,[189] and for payment of a periodical allowance[190];
(b) incidental orders under s.14(2);
(c) anti-avoidance orders under s.18; and
(d) enforcement orders under ss.19 and 20.

Financial Orders

13–74 The courts are directed as far as possible to deal with financial provision by means of orders for payment of a capital sum or transfer of property. Periodical allowances, where one party makes a regular financial payment to the other, are possible only in limited circumstances where justified by s.9(1)(c)–(e). This is in line with the legislative aim of allowing parties to make a "clean break" at the end of the relationship.

13–75 In some cases it is difficult to order a capital settlement sufficient to allow for a clean break because there are few or no liquid capital assets available at the date of divorce. However, a party who has no current access to capital may nonetheless have an expectation of acquiring some at a future date, perhaps under an insurance policy, pension scheme, or other investment. Alternatively, the paying spouse may have a high enough salary to be able

---

[184] 1985 Act s.11(5)(a) and (d). "Needs and resources" are defined to include foreseeable needs and resources under s.27(1).
[185] 1985 Act s.11(5)(e).
[186] 1985 Act s.11(6).
[187] 1985 Act s.11(7)(b).
[188] 1985 Act s.8(1)(a).
[189] 1985 Act s.8(1)(aa), as inserted by the Law Reform (Miscellaneous Provisions) (Scotland) Act 1990 Sch.8, para.34.
[190] 1985 Act s.8(1)(b).

to pay off a capital sum by instalments out of income. The courts are there-fore given the power to defer the date of payment of the capital sum,[191] and to order payment of capital by instalments.[192] The kind of flexibility that the courts have can be illustrated by *Crosbie v Crosbie*,[193] where the sheriff made an order for payment of a capital sum to be made in three stages. The first payment was to be made on decree of divorce; the second within seven days of sale of the matrimonial home; and the third was to be made out of monthly instalments payable for a fixed period of time after the divorce. An order for payment of capital by instalments is quite different from an order for payment of a periodical allowance. Although both may be paid out of recurrent income, the amount payable under a capital sum order cannot be varied once made. The courts are, however, empowered to vary the date or method of payment on a material change of circumstances,[194] for example if an expected pay-out from an investment fails to materialise or if a job is lost or pay-cut imposed.

The flexibility of capital sum orders is further enhanced by s.12A of the 1985 Act, which empowers the court to make an order for payment of a lump sum out of a pension fund at the date of maturity of the pension (a "pension lump sum order")[195] against the trustees or managers of a pension scheme. The effect of such an order was discussed above at para.13–33.   **13–76**

Despite the importance of clean break settlements in the scheme of the 1985 Act, the number of capital sum orders made by the courts has histori-cally been surprisingly low. In 1991, such orders were only made in five per cent of ordinary divorce actions with an average amount payable of £4,000–£6,000.[196] One of the reasons for the relatively low incidence of court orders for capital sums is because in many marriages with substantial amounts of capital, such payments are agreed under the terms of a separation agreement rather than sought by means of a court order.[197] More recent figures are not available, although anecdotal evidence suggests capital sum orders continue to be made infrequently.   **13–77**

Another option open to the courts, and in keeping with the philosophy of a clean break, is to make a property transfer order. The transfer may be stipulated to take place at the date of divorce or at a future specified date.[198]   **13–78**

As noted above, in theory, periodical allowance orders should only excep-tionally be made under the s.9 principles.[199] A periodical award under s.9(1)   **13–79**

---

[191] 1985 Act s.12(2).
[192] 1985 Act s.12(3).
[193] *Crosbie v Crosbie*, 1995 Fam. L.B. 14–6.
[194] 1985 Act s.12(4).
[195] Under s.8(1)(ba) as inserted by s.167(1) of the Pensions Act 1995.
[196] See Morris Gibson and Platts, *Unfying the knot: Characteristics of Divorce in Scotland* (Edinburgh: Scottish Central Research Unit, 1993), p. 33.
[197] Capital sum payments from one spouse to the other are agreed in some 30% of minutes and joint minutes of agreement: see Wasoff, McGuckin and Edwards, *Mutual Consent: Written Agreements in Family Law* (Scottish Office Central Research Unit 1997), p.20.
[198] 1985 Act s.12(2). For discussion of the difficulties that this may create see Cusine, "Property Transfer Orders: Some Conveyancing Imponderables" (1990) 35 J.L.S.S. 52 and E. Clive, "Reply" (1990) 35 J.L.S.S. at p.118.
[199] For an argument in favour of extending their use see A. Bissett-Johnson, "Lifestyle Support or Provisions for the Middle Aged Wife", 1999 S.L.T. 37.

(d) is limited to a maximum duration of three years.[200] Periodical allowances granted under s.9(1)(c) or (e) can be granted for a definite or indefinite period, or until the happening of a specified event such as. the youngest child reaching the age of 16.[201] If the party receiving the allowance dies or enters into a marriage or civil partnership with someone else, the periodical allowance is brought to an end.[202] Like an order for transfer of property or payment of a capital sum, a periodical allowance can be postponed until the defender is in a position to pay it.[203]

13–80   Either party or his executor may apply to the court for variation or recall of a periodical award if they can show that a material change of circumstances has occurred.[204] The court has power to backdate, vary or recall any award to the date of the application, or on cause shown, to an earlier date.[205] In addition, it has the power to convert a periodical allowance order into a capital sum or property transfer order.[206]

Incidental Orders

13–81   The court has the power to make one or more incidental orders to assist it in implementing its decision under the s.9 principles.[207] Section 14(2) gives the court power, inter alia, to order the sale or valuation of property,[208] to regulate the occupation of the matrimonial home after divorce, to declare the property rights of the parties, to allocate liability for household outgoings after the divorce, and to order that security be given in respect of any financial provision ordered.[209] In general, the court can make any ancillary order which it feels necessary in order to give effect to the s.9 principles.[210]

---

[200] An award under s.9(1)(d) need *not* of course be made for the full possible period of three years. See *Muir v Muir*, 1989 S.L.T. (Sh. Ct) 20 where a wife was awarded a periodical allowance for one year under s.9(1)(d); *Sheret v Sheret*, 1990 S.C.L.R. 799 (periodical allowance awarded for 13 weeks). But see *Sullivan v Sullivan*, above, para.13–65, n.162, where a sheriff's award until remarriage or death was upheld even although it might extend beyond the three year period.

[201] 1985 Act s.13(3).

[202] 1985 Act s.13(7)(b). Where the *payer* rather than *payee* dies, the order continues to operate against the Deceased's estate: s.13(7)(a).

[203] *Shipton v Shipton*, 1992 S.C.L.R. (Sh Ct) 23.

[204] 1985 Act s.13(4).

[205] 1985 Act s.13(4)(a) and (b).

[206] 1985 Act s.13(4)(c). This is useful where the payer dies since the liability for payment on his estate can be converted into a lump sum.

[207] A spouse cannot apply for an incidental order under s.14(2) in isolation but only in connection with an order for financial provision: *MacClue v MacClue*, 1994 S.C.L.R. 933. See also *Reynolds v Reynolds*, 1991 S.C.L.R. (Sh. Ct) 175.

[208] See *Thomson v Thomson*, 2003 Fam. L.R. (Sh. Ct) 22 where the sale was ordered but postponed.

[209] In *Murley v Murley*, 1995 S.C.L.R. 1138, the court used this power to guarantee payment to the husband of a certain percentage of the value of the family home at a date after the divorce. The husband was ordered to transfer his share in the house to his wife, on condition that she took out a standard security over the property to the value of a certain sum which would be payable to the husband on either the wife's sale of the home, or the youngest child's 18th birthday, whichever was earlier.

[210] 1985 Act s.14(2)(k).

Any incidental order made must be justified under the s.9 principles and be reasonable having regard to the resources of the parties.[211]

An incidental order for interest[212] is frequently sought where there is a   **13–82** lapse in time between the date at which payment of a capital sum or transfer of property is ordered—usually the date of divorce—and the date at which the capital is actually paid or the property transferred. There was for a time some disagreement as to whether interest on a capital sum could be awarded in respect of a period prior to the date of divorce. The Inner House made it clear in *Geddes v Geddes*[213] that such an award is competent[214] and would be justified, inter alia, where one spouse had had sole occupation of a family home owned in common since the date of separation, and the other party had therefore suffered loss of use for that period.[215]

Sheriffs now have power to dispense with the grantor's execution of a   **13–83** deed dealing with moveable property in favour of execution by the sheriff clerk.[216]

Anti-avoidance Orders

It is possible a party may seek to reduce his potential liability to make   **13–84** financial payments to the other party on divorce, by giving away property or selling assets at a below market value, with the intention of reducing the total value of the matrimonial property or reducing his apparent resources at the date of divorce. In order to prevent such fraudulent behaviour, the court may, under s.18, set aside or vary the terms of any transaction or transfer of property which had the effect of defeating a claim for financial provision.[217] Lady Clark has pointed out that, on a strict reading of the statue, a transaction which has the *effect* of defeating a claim can be set aside even if it was not *intended* to do so, although it would be a "rare case" in which the court would intervene if that intention was not present.[218] The court may in addition make such an order in relation to the property as it thinks fit.[219] Application under s.18 may be made up to a year after the date of the divorce.[220] However, transactions or transfers can only be reduced or varied if they have occurred

---

[211] See *Geddes v Geddes*, 1993 S.L.T. 494 at 499.

[212] 1985 Act s.14(2)(j).

[213] *Geddes v Geddes*, 1993 S.L.T. 494.

[214] Overruling *Carpenter v Carpenter*, 1990 S.L.T. (Sh. Ct) 68 and *Skarpaas v Skarpaas*, 1991 S.L.T. (Sh. Ct) 15.

[215] See also *Welsh v Welsh*, 1994 S.L.T. 828.

[216] See sub.(ja) inserted into s.14(2) by s.18 of the FLSA 2006. Sheriffs previously could do so in relation to heritable property where the grantor of deeds could not be found, refused or was unable, or failed to execute the deed. However, in an increasing number of matrimonial cases, courts are being asked to make orders for the transfer of moveable property such as insurance policies.

[217] 1985 Act s.18(1).

[218] *M v M*, 2011 Fam LR 24. In this case, the court did partially set aside the transaction by which the husband had set up a trust in favour of his children despite the fact it was not an avodiance transaction. This was said to be justified by the "unique circumstances" of the family concerned.

[219] 1985 Act s.18(2). In *Tahir v Tahir (No.2)*, 1995 S.L.T. 451 the court set aside decree pronounced against the former husband for payment of a loan which was found to be fictitious.

[220] 1985 Act s.18(1).

within the previous five years.[221] The court also has power to act proactively to prevent such fraudulent transactions, by issuing interdict against either party.[222] The rights of third parties who acquire property in good faith and for value from a spouse or a party further down the chain are protected.[223]

13–85   As an example, imagine that Graeme owns a flat in his sole name worth £100,000 which he acquires whilst married to Fiona. Graeme begins having an affair with Harry, and gives him the flat as a gift. Two years later, Graeme divorces Fiona. If he had still owned the flat at the date of divorce, it would have been matrimonial property. In this situation, the court has the power to set aside the gift of the flat to Harry if it thinks fit.[224] What if, by the time of the divorce, Harry had sold the flat on to a third party who paid market value for it and had no knowledge of Fiona, Graeme or the divorce? The court has no power to reduce the third party's title to the flat. However, it could be argued that the sale proceeds received by Harry should be restored to Graeme if Harry was not in good faith.[225]

Enforcement Orders

13–86   The court has the power, on cause shown, to grant warrant for inhibition or arrestment on the dependence of the action in which a claim is made.[226] Any party pursing or defending a claim for financial provision must provide a statement of his assets and liabilities at the relevant date.[227] The court may also order that either party reveals details of their financial resources.[228]

13–87   Finally, it should be noted that until decree of divorce is granted, the court has power to award interim aliment to either party.[229]

Assessment

13–88   The five principles contained in s.9 of the 1985 Act attempt to strike a balance between providing a framework which limits and regulates the discretion of the court when awarding financial provision on divorce or dissolution of civil partnership, and allowing the court room for manoeuvre to produce an equitable solution on the very different facts of each case. The principles can only ever be guidelines in a process whose aim is to reach an outcome that is both justified by the law and fair to the parties. Each

---

[221] 1985 Act s.18(1)(i).
[222] 1985 Act, s.18(1)(ii). See *Hernandez-Cimorra v Hernandez-Cimorra*, 1992 S.C.L.R. 611.
[223] See 1985 Act s.18(3).
[224] 1985 Act s.18(3)(a).
[225] *Hay v Jamieson* (1672) Mor. 1009; Erskine IV, I, 36; Bell, *Comm.*, iii, 183. Where this argument fails, however, the gift can be regarded as dissipation, and thus as special circumstances to justify W being given more than 50% of the matrimonial property under s.10(6)(c). But this will be of little consolation if there is no matrimonial property by the date of divorce to divide.
[226] 1985 Act s.19.
[227] Declaration must be made in a statutory form, Form 13A; Ordinary Cause Rules 33.9, 33A.9, 33.34 and 33A.34.
[228] 1985 Act s.20.
[229] 1985 Act s.6.

case can give rise to a number of different disposals, each of which can be justified under the law. In certain cases, such as *Little v Little*,[230] the courts have quite clearly not restricted themselves to a textbook application of the s.9 principles but have taken a more flexible approach in the interests of efficiency and equity. On the other hand, as we saw in the discussion of *Wallis*, the courts cannot ignore the clear words of the statute simply to produce what seems a fairer result. In *Little* itself, the Lord Ordinary declined to aggregate the total net value of the spouses' assets and share it equally between them, or in some other division justified by special circumstances, as is the normal procedure under s.9(1)(a). Instead, he held that certain items of matrimonial property already de facto divided up by the spouses, such as their cars, were to be left out of calculation, and then went on to split the remaining assets, including the matrimonial home, in equal shares according to their valuation at the date of divorce. In effect, this did not produce an equal split of the total value of the matrimonial property as at the relevant date. The Inner House found this approach a practical one which, in the circumstances of the case, gave rise to fair sharing of the property as required in s.10(1). Thomson has criticised the decision in *Little* as erroneous in terms of the s.9 scheme[231]; but it can also be endorsed as reflecting an underlying current of equity and pragmatism often found in first instance decisions on financial provision.

The fact that the decision in *Little* was upheld by the Inner House highlights the extent to which appeal courts are reluctant to reverse the decisions of the court of first instance, which has the benefit of hearing all the evidence first-hand. This is particularly true in relation to decisions on financial provision, where despite the detail of the legislation, the decision taken is fundamentally an exercise of discretion. An appeal court will thus only reverse the decision reached by a lower court if the court misdirected itself in law, failed to take into account a relevant or material factor or reached a result which was manifestly inequitable or plainly wrong.[232] To reiterate Lord Hope's comment in *Little*   **13–89**

> "the matter is essentially one of discretion, aimed at achieving a fair and practicable result in accordance with common sense. It remains as important as it always has been that the details should be left in the hands of the court of first instance and not opened up for reconsideration on appeal".[233]

---

[230] *Little v Little*, 1990 S.L.T. 785. A similar broad practical approach was applied in the case of *McVinnie v McVinnie (No.2)*, 1996 G.W.D. 24–1383 and upheld by the Sheriff Principal.

[231] J. Thomson, "Financial Provision on Divorce—Undermining the 1985 Act", 1990 S.L.T. (News) 313.

[232] *Little v Little*, 1990 S.L.T. 785, per Lord President Hope at 786K–L, citing Lord Guthrie's dictum in *Gray v Gray*, 1968 S.L.T. 254 at 258. But see J. Thomson, "Essentially Discretionary? Financial Provision on Divorce", 2000 Scottish Law Gazette 169 critiquing this approach on the grounds that it ignores the clear and rational structure of the Act by over privileging judicial discretion.

[233] *Little v Little*, 1990 S.L.T. 785 at 787D; affirmed by the House of Lords in *Jacques v Jacques*, 1997 S.L.T. 459.

13–90 It is important to realise that the s.9 principles, and the powers of the court, however skilfully manipulated, are not in themselves capable of preventing poverty on the breakdown of every relationship. In many marriages, there simply is no property to divide on divorce, although the 1985 Act does help by providing the possibility of the payment of a capital sum by instalments out of income or future resources, and by contemplating the splitting of pension rights. Bissett-Johnson has drawn attention to what he perceives to be weaknesses under the Act,[234] questioning whether a "clean break" on divorce, established through a capital award, is always desirable. He makes the case for extending the courts' discretion to award a periodical allowance on the grounds that capital sums may in some cases be disadvantageous. The House of Lords have also discussed the undesirability of limiting the time period over which any periodical allowance can be made.[235] Lump sum payments are not inflation proof and low return on interest rates may force the recipient to encroach on capital in order to meet living costs. Furthermore, in such circumstances it is questionable whether the lump sum will adequately provide a wife with a sum equal to the loss of salary and career prospects that she may have suffered during marriage. In addition the payment of a capital lump sum, unlike transfer of the family home, will usually result in the recipient being excluded from eligibility for state benefits. Those most at risk here are older women who may find it hard to increase their income through employment given the "age prejudice" they may encounter. Despite legislation[236] prohibiting such discrimination, this is hard to police in practice. The difficulties such women experience may be compounded by the fact that there is some evidence from English solicitors that the lump sum payments sought may not have been adequately calculated where they are intended to cover both lost income and relocation and housing expenses or where they are used to "top up" a pension or provide a retirement income.[237] In addition, if such capital is payable by instalments, there is a risk that the balance of the sum may be lost if the husband becomes bankrupt.[238] The advantage of awarding a periodical allowance is that, unlike a capital sum, it can be varied up or down to take account of a material change in the parties' circumstances, and where bankruptcy occurs, periodic payments from income to meet the needs of a bankrupt's former spouse and family are protected as income does not vest in the trustee in sequestration.[239]

---

[234] A. Bissett-Johnson, "Lifestyle Support or Provision for the Middle Aged Wife", 1999 S.L.T. 37; A. Bissett-Johnson, and C. Barton, "Financial Provision on Divorce in Scots Law—Does it Need Reform?", 2000 J.R. 265.

[235] *Miller v Miller* and *McFarlane v McFarlane* [2006] UKHL 24.

[236] Age is a protected characteristic under the Equality Act 2010.

[237] S. Arthur, and J. Lewis, *Pensions and Divorce: Exploring Financial Settlements* (HMSO Research Report 118, Social Security, 2000), p.31.

[238] W. McBryde, "Financial Provision on Divorce and Sequestration", 1996 S.L.T. (News) 389.

[239] Bankruptcy (Scotland) Act 1985 s.32 as amended by s.261(2), Sch.28, Pt 3, para.34 of the 2004 Act extending cover to civil partners.

BREAKDOWN OF COHABITATION

Since the introduction of the Family Law (Scotland) Act 2006, couples who   **13–91**
live together without entering a formalised adult relationship have been
subject to a legislative regime governing financial claims on the breakdown of
the cohabitation.[240] The regime is intentionally quite distinct from the rules of
financial provision on divorce, with the government citing both the "special
place" of marriage in society[241] and the right of persons who have chosen not
to marry to be free from marriage-like obligations[242] as justifications for maintaining a distinction between the financial consequences of different types of
relationship. Nevertheless, it was recognised that the breakdown of cohabitation could sometimes have uneven economic outcomes in the same way as
formalised relationships, a problem compounded by confusion amongst the
Scottish public as to what the exact rights of cohabitants were in such a situation.[243] It was considered appropriate to introduce legislation which would
create legal certainty and protect those who might find themselves in a situation of economic vulnerability at the conclusion of a cohabiting relationship,
including former cohabitants themselves as well as children of the family.[244]

Cohabitants are defined in the 2006 Act as a man and woman living   **13–92**
together as if husband and wife,[245] or two persons of the same sex living
together as if civil partners.[246] In determining whether two persons are or
were cohabiting, the court is given a non-exhaustive list of factors to take
into account, namely the length of the cohabitation,[247] the nature of the relationship[248] and the nature and extent of any financial arrangements between
the parties.[249] Claims for financial provision where a relationship ends other
than by death are dealt with under s.28.[250] The court is empowered to award
a capital sum, a payment in respect of childcare or such interim order as it
thinks fit after "having regard to the matters mentioned in subsection (3)".[251]
Those matters are:

> "(a) whether (and, if so, to what extent) the defender has derived eco-
> nomic advantage from contributions made by the applicant; and

---

[240] Family Law (Scotland) Act 2006 ss.25–29.
[241] Policy Memorandum on the Family Law (Scotland) Bill (SP Bill 36-PM) at [71], available
at: *http://www.scottish.parliament.uk/S2_Bills/Family%20Law%20(Scotland)%20Bill/b36s2-
introd-pm.pdf* [accessed August 7, 2013].
[242] Policy Memorandum, above n.241, at [70].
[243] Former cohabitants may have had some remedy in unjust enrichment, although such cases
were difficult to prove and fell far short of the "common law marriage myth" which seemed
to retain a hold in the public consciousness. For further discussion, see H. MacQueen
"Unjustified Enrichment and Family Law" (University of Edinburgh School of Law Working
Paper 2010/01, 2010).
[244] Policy Memorandum, above n.241, at [64] and [65].
[245] 2006 Act s.25(1)(a).
[246] 2006 Act s.25(1)(b).
[247] 2006 Act s.25(2)(a).
[248] 2006 Act s.25(2)(b).
[249] 2006 Act s.25(1)(c).
[250] Where one cohabitant dies, his former partner can make a claim under s.29 as dicussed at
paras 10–69 to 10–80 above.
[251] 2006 Act s.28(2).

> (b) whether (and, if so, to what extent) the applicant has suffered eco-
> nomic disadvantage in the interests of—
>> (i) the defender; or
>> (ii) any relevant child"

If awarding a capital sum, the court is also directed to consider the extent to which economic advantage obtained by the defender is offset by economic disadvantage sustained by him in the interests of the applicant or any relevant child.[252] The applicant's disadvantage is similarly to be offset against any economic benefit she has derived.[253] Definitions of key terms are provided in s.28(9), with "contributions" defined to include indirect and non-financial contributions. Economic advantage is construed to encompass gains in capital, income and earning capacity, with economic disadvantage defined as the opposite.

13–93   Empirical research into practitioners' experiences with the legislation in the three years following its introduction[254] makes clear that it is being used by cohabitants and former cohabitants, with claims generally being settled in the shadow of the legislation. One particular difficulty in practice is the time limit set out in s.28(8), which requires that any claim must be made not later than one year after the day on which the parties cease to cohabit.[255] The number of reported cases to date remains fairly modest, and the courts have not found the construction of s.28 to be a straightforward process. The essence of the difficulty appears to be a lack of clarity in the legislation as to the redistributive rationale upon which any award should be based.[256] It is clear that contributions of some kind must have been made, and that an advantage must have been received or a disadvantage suffered, but what is intended to be the connection between these elements? A number of different models have been proposed.

13–94   One initial approach, posited by Lord Matthews in *CM v STS*,[257] was that s.28 of the 2006 Act should be viewed as analogous to s.9(1)(b) of the 1985 Act, with the cohabitation legislation therefore operating in a similar way to the rules of financial provision on divorce. Lord Matthews considered that the similarity in wording between the two sections was so marked that Parliament must have intended both to be understood in the same way.[258] Accordingly, he considered the cohabiting relationship in question in the case to be a joint endeavour, and essentially split both the benefits and the burdens which had arisen over the course of the cohabitation between the parties. Use was made of the divorce jurisprudence to inform his conclusions. Such an approach is in clear conflict with the expressed intention of the legislature to retain a distinction between marriage and non-marital relationships, and

---

[252] 2006 Act s.28(4) and (5).
[253] 2006 Act s.28(4) and (6).
[254] F. Wasoff, J. Miles and E. Mordaunt "Legal practitioners' perspectives on the provisions of the Family Law (Scotland) Act 2006" (October 2010), available at *http://www.crfr.ac.uk/ assets/Cohabitation-final-report.pdf* [accessed August 7, 2013].
[255] Wasoff et al., see n.254 above, p.74–76.
[256] F. McCarthy "Cohabitation: lessons from north of the border?" (2011) 23(3) CFLQ 277.
[257] *CM v STS*, 2008 S.L.T. 871 (OH), also reported as *C v S* and *M v S*.
[258] *CM v STS*, 2008 S.L.T. 871 at 890.

in the academic commentary, it was pointed out that there was no reference to "fair sharing" in the 2006 provisions.[259] Through the subsequent jurisprudence it seems that the *CM v STS* model has now been discredited, with the Supreme Court in *Gow v Grant*[260] noting that

> "[s.28] does not seek to replicate the arrangements that are available for financial provision on divorce or the termination of a civil partnership. For this reason, it would not be right to adopt the same approach to the application of that section as would be appropriate of the exercise was being conducted under s.9 of the 1985 Act."[261]

As the only Supreme Court decision on the 2006 Act to date, the approach   **13–95** to the legislation adopted in *Gow v Grant* carries the most authority. The decision is not without its problems, however. The case concerned a couple who had embarked on a relationship later in life. Both had adult children from previous relationships who had since left home. Both were owner-occupiers of their own houses. At the defender's insistence, the claimant sold her property in order to move in with the defender in his house. She used the majority of the proceeds of the sale for her own purposes, paying off debts and loaning money to her son. At the end of the relationship, the defender's home had increased greatly in value. The claimant, having no legal title to the defender's home and having dissipated the proceeds from the sale of her house, was in no position to buy a property. As an older woman without much prospect of employment, this left her economically vulnerable and likely to be reliant on the state. In the first instance decision,[262] the sheriff had adopted a compensation-type approach to interpretation of the provisions. The claim was valued on the basis that the claimant should be returned to the position she would have been in had the cohabitation never happened.[263] Accordingly, she was awarded a figure made up primarily of the amount by which the property she had owned at the start of the relationship would have increased in value by the end of the relationship, minus the debt which would have remained outstanding at that time.[264] This decision was overturned on appeal,[265] the Inner House preferring the restitutionary interpretation of s.28, discussed further below. The Supreme Court, however, reinstated the decision at first instance.[266] The compensation approach, it was said, built upon a principle of fairness that could be read into the legislation despite the fact it was not explicitly stated.[267] The reference in s.28(3) to disadvantage suffered by the applicant in the interests of the defender should be interpreted broadly, so as not to exclude disadvantage that was suffered *also* in the interests of the

---

[259] J.M. Thomson, "Palimony – Scottish style" [2008] Scottish Law Gazette 95.
[260] *Gow v Grant*, 2013 S.C. (UKSC) 1.
[261] *Gow v Grant*, 2013 S.C. 1 at [35].
[262] *Gow v Grant*, 2010 Fam L.R. 21 (SC).
[263] *Gow v Grant*, 2010 Fam L.R. 21 at [39]–[47].
[264] *Gow v Grant*, 2010 Fam L.R. 21 at [59].
[265] *Gow v Grant*, 2011 Fam L.R. 50 (IH (2 Div.)).
[266] *Gow v Grant*, 2013 S.C. (UKSC) 1.
[267] *Gow v Grant*, 2013 S.C. 1 at [35].

applicant herself.[268] Although the court accepted that the defender did not benefit financially from the sale of the applicant's house, it was found that he did benefit in a broader sense by having the relationship develop on the footing that he desired.[269] Accordingly, a reinstatement of the decision at first instance was considered in keeping with the overriding principle of fairness, rather than economic calculation.[270]

13–96   The Supreme Court's approach is quite surprising, in that the award to the applicant places her ultimately in a much stronger financial position than the defender: he will essentially have to pay the majority of the increased equity in his own home over to the applicant to recompense her for the increased equity on which she had "lost out." This is so notwithstanding the fact the applicant had used the proceeds of the sale, the "nest egg" which might have enabled her to make a future house purchase, for her own purposes rather than applying them in the course of the relationship. In fact, the applicant seems likely to have ended up with a greater award here than if the parties had been married, where the increased equity in the defender's house, as the only real asset of the marriage, would at least have been shared between them. It is not clear that this is the distinction between marriage and non-marital relationships that the legislature intended to maintain when introducing the 2006 Act!

13–97   *Gow* has been followed in one subsequent decision at the time of writing, *Whigham v Owen*.[271] In this case, the pursuer had no assets at the start of the relationship and was living with her mother. The defender had assets of around £2,000. By the end of the 26-year cohabitation, during which the pursuer had worked in the home and periodically in the defender's business whilst raising the three children of the family, the pursuer had assets of around £10,000 while the defender's assets including the family home totalled almost £748,000. The pursuer and one of the children now lived in social housing, supported by state benefits, whilst the defender continued running his business whilst living in the family home. The court awarded the pursuer £250,000, based on somewhat "rough and ready" reasoning. Focus was placed on the dicta in *Gow* that regard must be had to the financial position of the parties at the beginning of the relationship and again at the end. It was noted that, in a divorce situation, the pursuer would be entitled to 50% of the defender's assets as of right. The court asserted that it was clear, generally speaking, that cohabitants should receive lower awards that former spouses. The court also found that the pursuer had made substantial contributions to the relationship, without specifying the nature or extent of these contributions. With an overall focus on the principle of fairness, the court found that a figure of £250,000 was appropriate, without detailing how the figure had been reached. It remains to be seen whether the decision will be appealed.

13–98   The decisions in *Gow* and *Whigham* may be hard to parse on a strict reading of the legislation. On the other hand, their broadly compensa-

---

[268] *Gow v Grant*, 2013 S.C. 1 at [37-38].
[269] *Gow v Grant*, 2013 S.C. 1 at [37-38].
[270] *Gow v Grant*, 2013 S.C. 1 at [40].
[271] *Whigham v Owen* 2013 Fam L.R. 30

tory approach does have the benefit of protecting the claimant, now an economically vulnerable former cohabitant, as the legislature had intended. From this perspective, the compensation approach adopted by the Supreme Court is certainly preferable to the restitutionary interpretation of the legislation adopted elsewhere.

The restitutionary approach starts from the proposition that legal title to   **13–99** assets at the conclusion of the relationship should not be disturbed, unless there is proof that the applicant has made contributions that would justify some alteration in that title. In other words, the applicant must have "earned a share".[272] *Selkirk v Chisholm*[273] offers a clear illustration of this model in action. The parties to the case had cohabited for around nine years in a house held in the defender's sole name. They had no children. Both parties worked for the majority of the relationship, the defender becoming self-employed running a "bodyshop" for motor repairs after a few years. Broadly speaking, the applicant undertook the majority of the homemaking work but contributed little financially to the household, spending her wages on her own interests. The defender paid the household bills, including the mortgage repayments. The applicant was ultimately unsuccessful in her pursuit of an award. The sheriff noted that she had made no financial contribution towards the household, but went further to say that even if she *had* made regular payments towards the bills, this would not represent an economic advantage to the defender: bills would have to have been paid by both parties regardless of their relationship. Even had the claimant contributed every month towards the mortgage repayments, the only advantage that would have accrued would be the diminution in the mortgage debt resulting from the payments. Specifically, such payments would *not* entitle the claimant to any share in the increased equity in the home over the course of the relationship, since this was down entirely to market forces, rather than any contribution by the parties.[274] The same logic was applied in respect of her non-financial contributions.[275]

The popularity of the restitutionary approach to interpretation of s.28 in   **13–100** the reported jurisprudence[276] suggests it may be the most obvious reading of the provisions. However, if it is the correct reading of s.28, then the legislation must necessarily fall some way short of the objectives claimed for it by the legislature at the time of its enactment.[277] For one thing, it is not clear that this interpretation of s.28 is distinct from the unjust enrichment principles which might previously have allowed a cohabitant who had contributed

---

[272] Further discussion of this approach can be found in P. Parkinson "Property rights of cohabitees—is statutory reform the answer?" in A. Bainham, D. Pearl and R. Pickford (eds) *Frontiers of Family Law: Part II* (Chichester: John Wiley & Sons, 1995) at 309 and G. Douglas, J. Pearce and H. Woodward "Cohabitants, property and the law: a study of injustice" (2009) 72 MLR 24 at 29–30.

[273] *Selkirk v Chisholm*, 2011 Fam L.R. 56 (SC).

[274] *Selkirk v Chisholm*, 2011 Fam L.R. 56 (SC) at [116]–[118].

[275] *Selkirk v Chisholm*, 2011 Fam L.R. 56 (SC) at [120].

[276] A preponderance of the reported cases have been decided on roughly restitutonary principles: *Jamieson v Rodhouse* 2009 Fam L.R. 34 (SC), *Falconer v Dods* 2009 Fam L.R. 111 (SC), *Lindsay v Murphy* 2010 Fam L.R. 156 (SC) and *G v F* 2011 G.W.D. 21-483 (SC) in addition to *Selkirk v Chisholm* 2011 Fam L.R. 56 (SC), discussed below, and the appeal decision in *Gow v Grant* 2011 Fam L.R. 50 (IH (2 Div)).

[277] Policy Memorandum, above n.241.

financially to property held in the name of their former partner to make a claim for restitution.[278] Given that the uncertainty engendered by these somewhat arcane common law rules was one motivation for the introduction of the statute, it is difficult to understand how a similarly arcane statutory restatement of the same principles could alleviate that difficulty. More significantly, the legislation sought specifically to protect economically vulnerable former cohabitants and their children on the breakdown of a relationship.[279] The restitutionary approach adopted simply does not achieve this goal. If homemaker contributions, and even direct financial contributions, cannot entitle a party to any share in a family home to which they do not hold title, vulnerability will frequently result. Imagine the couple had children and Ms Selkirk had not contributed financially to the household as a result of taking on the homemaker/carer role full time.[280] Following the reasoning in *Selkirk v Chisholm*, her application would have been just as unsuccessful in these circumstances. Ms Selkirk would leave the relationship with no claim on the family home, an uncertain level of employability and quite possibly primary responsibility for the couple's child. In fact, the earlier decision of *Jamieson v Rodhouse*[281] illustrates precisely this type of outcome to a s.28 claim. Ms Jamieson emerged from 30 years of cohabitation, the majority of which she had spent as homemaker and primary carer of the child of the family, without an award. At her stage in life and after so many years out of the labour market, her employment prospects seemed bleak. Her former partner was entitled to retain ownership of the family home including the equity therein, the only real asset of the couple, as a beneficiary of "the good fortune of property price appreciation."[282]

13–101   The Scottish cohabitation regime may at this stage be said to be in something of a state of confusion. The legislation is ambiguously drafted, and no one reading of the provisions can be proved correct, leaving the courts, practitioners and cohabitants themselves in an unenviable situation. The expertise developed over the past 25 years in respect of the regime for financial provision on divorce is of limited assistance with construction or application of the 2006 legislation. Perhaps of most concern, the restitutionary understanding of the provisions that seems to be emerging from the jurisprudence fails to meet the objectives of the cohabitation scheme, neither improving on the pre-existing common law provision nor protecting the people it was designed to protect.

13–102   Where the 2006 Act fails to provide a remedy in a particular case, for example because a claim has not been made within the one year statutory time limit,[283] it is open to a party to consider an alternative claim on the basis

---

[278] The leading Scottish authority in this area is *Shilliday v Smith* 1998 S.C.725 (IH (1 Div)). See also *Grieve v Morison* 1993 S.L.T. 852 (OH), *Moggach v Milne* 2005 G.W.D. 8-107 (SC) and *Satchwell v McIntosh* 2006 S.L.T. 117 (SC).

[279] Policy Memorandum, above n.241, at [64] and [65].

[280] F. McCarthy "Progress towards principles on the breakdown of cohabitation: *Selkirk v Chisholm*" (2011) 15 Edin L.R. 270.

[281] *Jamieson v Rodhouse*, 2009 Fam L.R. 34 (SC).

[282] *Jamieson v Rodhouse*, 2009 Fam L.R. 34 at [48].

[283] 2006 Act s.28(8).

of unjustified enrichment, as discussed in Ch.12.[284] An alternative approach for cohabiting couples is to regulate the division of their assets on breakdown of the relationship by entering a separation or cohabitation contract. Married couples and civil partners may also sometimes have good reason to wish to exclude the jurisdiction of the courts and make their own enforceable agreements about division of property should their relationship end in divorce/dissolution.[285] The benefits for them are the avoidance of uncertainty as to how a court will exercise its discretion under the Act, the fact that the couple are empowered to regulate their own affairs rather than submitting to the approach taken by the court, and the possibility of conducting often acrimonious disputes in privacy rather than in open court.[286] Agreements have become of increasing importance since the introduction of the 1985 Act, and will be discussed in detail in Ch.15.

---

[284] Paras 12–22 to 12–24. See also H. MacQueen, "Unjustified Enrichment and Family Law" (2010) *University of Edinburgh School of Law Working Paper No. 2010/01*, available at *http://papers.ssrn.com/sol3/papers.cfm?abstract_id=1536600* [accessed at August 7, 2013].

[285] See s.16. Grounds for setting aside such agreements under common law and by virtue of s.16(1) are discussed in Ch.15.

[286] Solicitors are conscious of, and promote these benefits: see Wasoff, Dobash and Harcus, *The Impact of the Family Law (Scotland) Act 1985 on Solicitor's Divorce Practice* (Edinburgh: Scottish Central Research Unit, 1990), pp.77–79.

CHAPTER 14
DIVORCE AND DISSOLUTION: GROUNDS AND PROCESS

DIVORCE

14–01 The Divorce (Scotland) Act 1976 ("1976 Act"), s.1(1), provides that the only two grounds for divorce are that the marriage has broken down irretrievably or that an interim gender recognition certificate has been issued to either party after the date of marriage.[1] Irretrievable breakdown can be established only on the basis of one of the fact situations set out in s.1(2). As Lord Prosser observed in *Findlay v Findlay*:

> "The question for the court is thus not a general one, as to whether the marriage has broken down irretrievably in any ordinary sense of those words, but is a particular question as to whether the subsequent provisions of the Act have been satisfied".[2]

OVERVIEW

14–02 Prior to reforms instituted by the Family Law (Scotland) Act 2006, irretrievable breakdown of the marriage could be established on the following grounds:

- adultery (s.1(2)(a));
- behaviour (s.1(2)(b));
- desertion (s.1(2)(c));
- two years non-cohabitation with consent (s.1(2)(d));
- five years non-cohabitation without the need for consent (s.1(2)(e)).

Since May 4, 2006,[3] the grounds for establishing irretrievable breakdown are:

- adultery;
- behaviour;

---

[1] Under the Gender Recognition Act 2004 Sch.2, Pt 2, para.6 which amended s.1(1) of the 1976 Act.

[2] *Findlay v Findlay*, 1991 S.L.T. 457 at 458.

[3] The Family Law (Scotland) Act 2006 (Commencement, Transitional Provisions and Savings) Order 2006 (SSI 2006/212).

- non-cohabitation for one year with the other party's consent to divorce; or
- non-cohabitation for two years without the need for consent.

Civil Partnership[4]

The provisions governing the dissolution of a civil partnership are to be found at Pt 3, Ch.5, ss.117–122 of the Civil Partnership Act 2004.[5] As is the case for divorce, there are two grounds on which an action for dissolution may be founded, being irretrievable breakdown of the civil partnership or the granting of an interim gender recognition certificate to either party after the registration of the civil partnership.[6] The grounds for establishing irretrievable breakdown are the same of those for married couples with the omission of adultery as a ground.[7] Consistent with the changes to the 1976 Act, desertion was removed as a grounds for dissolution by the FLSA 2006.[8]

14–03

The Grounds for Divorce—Discussion

Divorce can only be obtained on the basis of "irretrievable breakdown" if it is established on one of the grounds set out in s.1(2) of the 1976 Act as amended. These may be summarised as adultery, behaviour, one year's non-cohabitation by the spouses where both consent to the divorce, and two years' non-cohabitation by the spouses without any requirement for mutual consent. When the Gender Recognition Act 2004 came into force on the April 4, 2005, the second basis on which divorce may be granted was added to Scots law, namely, that an interim gender recognition certificate has been issued to either spouse.[9] Divorce for adultery was recognised at common law from the Reformation onwards[10] while desertion was introduced as a ground by statute in 1573. These were the only grounds of divorce until 1938, when the Divorce (Scotland) Act 1938 introduced the grounds of cruelty, incurable insanity, sodomy and bestiality. It was not until 1976 that it became possible to obtain a divorce without proof of matrimonial fault on the part of one of the spouses. The current mixture of fault-and non-fault-based criteria is thus the product of continuing reform over the years. As a result, Scots law has moved from a position where marriage could be ended only

14–04

---

[4] For a discussion on the formation of a civil partnership see Ch.9, paras 9–60 *et seq.*

[5] As amended by s.33, Sch.1 of the FLSA 2006.

[6] 2004 Act s.117(2)(a)–(b).

[7] This is because, due to the heterosexual definition of adultery, there was broad consensus at the time of consultation that sexual infidelity need not be a separate ground, for it could be incorporated within unreasonable behaviour. See Scottish Executive, *The Consultation on Civil Partnership Registration: Analysis of the Responses* (February 5, 2004), para.7.27.

[8] FLSA 2006 s.45(2), Sch.3.

[9] Divorce (Scotland) Act 1976, s.1 as amended by the Gender Recognition Act 2004, Sch.2, Pt. 2, para.6. This at the time of writing, may be subject to amendment by virtue of marriage and Civil Partnership (Scotland) Bill 2013.

[10] See Fraser, *Husband and Wife*, 2nd edn (1878), Vol.II, pp.1139–1140.

by proof of matrimonial offence on the part of one spouse, to the current regime where more divorces are obtained by mutual consent after a period of non-cohabitation than on any other basis.[11] How successful this process of reform has been in establishing a satisfactory level of access to divorce is still controversial. On the one hand, there has been much support for further liberalisation of the divorce laws,[12] but, on the other, concern for the high and increasing rate of breakdown of marriage and its effect on the family.[13] Before turning to the issue of reform, we shall consider the grounds prior to the FLSA 2006.

14–05   First, though, we should note the changing incidence of the use of the various grounds in Scottish divorces. In 2008 there were 11,474 divorces of which 94 were on the ground of adultery and 796 on the ground of behaviour. Non-cohabitation for one year with consent accounted for 2,976 cases and two years' non-cohabitation 6,342. Desertion was the ground in only 17 cases.

14–06   In financial year 2011 to 2012 the number of divorces had fallen to 9,863 of which 64 were for adultery and 497 for behaviour. The one and two year non-cohabitation grounds accounted for 2,485 and 6,695 cases respectively. There was only one case on the ground of gender recognition certificate.

14–07   It is important to note that these were the grounds on which the divorces were granted. It is not at all uncommon for an action to be raised on one of the fault-based grounds and later amended to a non-cohabitation ground as part of a general settlement when other matters have been successfully negotiated.[14]

Adultery

14–08   Under s.1(2)(a), it is a ground of divorce that "since the date of the marriage the defender has committed adultery".

14–09   Adultery has been defined as "voluntary sexual intercourse between a married person and a person of the opposite sex, not being the marriage partner".[15] Accordingly, pre-marital sex with someone other than the future spouse cannot be adultery. A single act of adultery will suffice to give rise

---

[11] See "The Future for Scottish Divorce Law, A 'No Fault' or Mixed system for Scotland" in S. Harvie-Clark, *Family Law (Scotland) Bill: Grounds for Divorce (Updated)* (SPICe briefing, April 21, 2005, The Scottish Parliament) pp.12–

[12] See *The Ground for Divorce: Should the law be changed?*, Scot. Law Comm. Discussion Paper No.76 (1988); *Report on Reform of the Ground for Divorce*, Scot. Law Com. No.116 (1989), paras 2.1–2.11.

[13] Recent years have seen a decline from the number of divorces taking place in the 1980s and 1990.In 1995 almost 40% of marriages in Scotland ended in divorce (RGS, *Annual Report 1995*). In 2003 there were 10,928 divorces in Scotland representing just over one-third of the 30,757 marriages taking place in the same year (RGS, *Annual Report 2003*). In 2004 there were 11,277 divorces representing just under one-third of the 32,154 marriages that took place, (RGS, *Annual Report 2004*) downloaded from *www.gro-scotland.gov.uk/statistics/* [accessed August 2013], Ch.1, p.9. In the year 2011 to 2012 the figure had dropped still further to 9,503.

[14] *http://gro-scotland.gov.uk/statistics/theme/vital-events/general/ref-tables/archive/2008/ section-8-divorces.html and http:www.scotland.gov.uk/Topics/Statistics/Browse/CrimeJustice/ DatasetsCJS/civlawscot1112?refresh=0.09949338570896027* [accessed August 2013].

[15] Clive, *The Law of Husband and Wife in Scotland*, 4th edn (1997), para.21.004.

to grounds for divorce. If the sex is not voluntary, e.g. if rape is involved, then there is no adultery on the part of the victim.[16] If consent cannot be given due to mental incapacity, e.g. dementia, then again there is no adultery even if the sexual act physically took place.[17] So long as sexual intercourse is voluntary, then the state of mind in which it was undertaken (such as a mistaken belief that one's spouse is dead) is irrelevant.[18] For the purposes of establishing adultery, sexual intercourse must involve some degree of physical penetration of the vagina by the penis. Penetration elsewhere, or by other means, does not amount to adultery. Nor do acts that fall short of such penetration, such as oral sex. Accordingly, if a wife is artificially inseminated with the sperm of someone other than her husband, this does not found adultery, even if the insemination was done without the husband's knowledge or consent.[19] These types of activity, less than full intercourse, can found an action for divorce on the basis of behaviour under s.1(2)(b) (see para.14–11 below).

Adultery is not commonly used as a ground of divorce today. In 1995 only eight per cent of divorces were obtained on that ground[20] and in 2002 this number had dropped to six per cent of divorce in the Court of Session and four per cent in the sheriff court.[21] For this reason, we will not discuss in full two somewhat archaic and now very rarely pled, defences to adultery. These are *condonation*,[22] that is, the claim that the pursuer forgave the defender for his or her adultery in the full knowledge it had occurred, and *lenocinium* (or "whoremongering"),[23] the claim that the pursuer actively encouraged or induced the defender to commit adultery.[24] Collusion—where parties to a marriage agree to permit a false case most usually in order to achieve a quicker divorce (discussed below at para.14–33), was also a defence to adultery and indeed to other grounds until s.14 of the FL(S)A 2006 removed this as a bar to divorce.[25]

14–10

---

[16] *Stewart v Stewart* (1914) 2 S.L.T. 310.

[17] Difficulty may arise where incapacity to consent is due to the voluntary consumption of drink or drugs ingested: see Clive, *The Law of Husband and Wife in Scotland*, 4th edn (1997), para.21.005.

[18] *Hunter v Hunter* (1900) 2 F. 771.

[19] The physical requirements for adulterous sexual intercourse were discussed in *MacLennan v MacLennan*, 1958 S.C. 105 where the issue was indeed that of non-consensual artificial insemination by donor (AID).

[20] See RGS, *Annual Report 1995*, Table 8.1.

[21] Scottish Executive, *Civil Judicial Statistics for 2002* (HMSO, Scotland, 2004). Divorces for adultery dropped to less than 1 per cent of the total in 2011–2012.

[22] 1976 Act s.1(3). Condonation requires something more than *verbal* forgiveness, e.g. resumption of cohabitation after the adultery (subject to a three-month grace period for attempted reconciliation (see s.2(2))). See further, Clive, *The Law of Husband and Wife in Scotland*, 4th edn (1997), paras 22.011–22.021.

[23] See *Thomson v Thomson*, 1908 S.C.179.

[24] 1976 Act, s.1(3). See, further, Clive, *The Law of Husband and Wife in Scotland*, 4th edn (1997), paras 22.002–22.010.

[25] However, it remains the case at common law that the court should not grant a decree of divorce if satisfied that the pursuer has put forward a false case or the defender has withheld a good defence.

Behaviour

14–11   Under s.1(2)(b) a marriage has irretrievably broken down if

> "since the date of the marriage the defender has at any time behaved (whether or not as a result of mental abnormality and whether such behaviour has been active or passive) in such a way that the pursuer cannot reasonably be expected to cohabit with the defender".

Identical provision for registered civil partners is to be found at s.117(3)(a) of the 2004 Act with the substitution of the word "registration" for "marriage".

14–12   While behaviour was the commonest ground for divorce at the beginning of the 1980s,[26] in recent years it has been overtaken in popularity by the two years' non-cohabitation and consent ground. In 2002, one-half of the divorces in both the Court of Session and the Sheriff Court were based on this ground, that is, 56 per cent[27] compared with 15 per cent on behaviour. More recent figures shown at para.14–06 above show that the trend is continuing.

14–13   It is only behaviour which has occurred "since the date of the marriage" which is relevant. Thus, if a woman fraudulently induces a man to marry her on the grounds that he is the father of her expected child then this behaviour will not found a divorce, as it occurred prior to the marriage.[28] However, where behaviour commenced prior to marriage continues after marriage, then provided it meets all the other requirements of the section, it may justify a divorce. While the word "behaviour" suggests a course of conduct which takes place over time, the wording "at any time" makes it clear that one single act or occurrence will qualify.[29]

14–14   The behaviour must be "such that the pursuer cannot reasonably be expected to cohabit with the defender". Under s.13(2), parties to a marriage cohabit only where they are "in fact living together as man and wife". While at one time the only behaviour that could be taken into account was that which amounted to cruelty,[30] the current Act makes it clear that conduct need not be culpable, unjustifiable, or even directed towards the pursuer, to found a divorce. The statute expressly states that the behaviour may be "active" or "passive" and may arise as the result of a "mental abnormality". Thus, insanity is not a defence to divorce under this head[31] and behaviour related to illness may justify a divorce. It is no defence that the defender spouse is not to blame for his or her behaviour, and does not intend in any way to

---

[26] Behaviour was the commonest ground of divorce in 1981. By 1984 the combined total of divorces obtained on two or five years' non-cohabitation had overtaken the number obtained on behaviour grounds. By 1986 the total number of divorces obtained on the basis of two years' non-cohabitation alone had overtaken those on the behaviour ground.

[27] *Op. cit.* above n.20.

[28] But *cf. Hastings v Hastings*, 1941 S.L.T. 323 where a wife's fraudulent inducement of marriage by pretending that her husband was the father of her expected child, was held to give husband reasonable cause for desertion (under the Divorce (Scotland) Act 1938).

[29] See dicta in *Gray v Gray*, 1991 G.W.D. 8–477.

[30] Under the Divorce (Scotland) Act 1938.

[31] This was also the case under the Divorce (Scotland Act) 1964 s.5(2)(b), and see the English case of *Williams v Williams* [1964] A.C. 698.

harm or upset the other spouse.[32] For example, in *Fullarton v Fullarton*,[33] a husband was divorced on the basis that as a result of a schizophrenic condition, he had lost all interest in his wife and children and slept abnormally long hours. There must, however, be something more than a mere state of affairs that exists, i.e. there must be some degree of action or conduct by one party which affects the other.[34] It is arguable that some minimal mental element is required in order to distinguish behaviour from a mere state of being,[35] but the fact that the statute refers to "passive behaviour" seems to suggest that that is not the case.

When considering whether it is reasonable to expect the pursuer to cohabit with the defender, the court will consider the personality and experiences of the actual pursuer in question, not some hypothetical reasonable, objective pursuer.[36] In other words, a subjective, not objective, approach is taken in this regard. It is important to stress that the court is not asked to discuss whether the defender's behaviour *itself is* unreasonable, but only whether or not the pursuer can reasonably be expected to cohabit with the defender. What is crucial is that there is a causal link between the defender's behaviour and the pursuer's desire to no longer cohabit with the defender. In *Knox v Knox*,[37] a husband raised an action of divorce on the basis that his wife nagged and shouted at him and had written abusive letters to him while he was living with another woman. The court found that the letters had no effect upon the pursuer, and that the real reason for his leaving home was not his wife's alleged nagging, but his desire to pursue a relationship with another woman. The action for divorce was therefore dismissed since the husband had failed to show that his unwillingness to continue cohabiting with his wife was actually caused by her behaviour.[38]

14–15

When parties separate prior to divorce, the pursuer's acts *after* separation are relevant when assessing whether or not it is reasonable to expect him or her to cohabit with the defender. This is because facts sufficient to form a ground of divorce must be established as at the date of proof, not the date of separation. In *Findlay v Findlay*[39] the wife formed an association with another

14–16

---

[32] See *O'Neill v O'Neill* [1975] 3 All E.R. 289 (where husband was an excessive do-it-yourself enthusiast and made his family's life a misery although his behaviour was not intended to upset them in any way); *Gollins v Gollins* [1964] A.C. 644 (where an idle, lazy husband got into debt while the wife struggled to maintain the family); *Thurlow v Thurlow* [1975] 2 All E.R. 979 (where a wife, because of a neurological disorder, took to bed and ceased to do any housework); and *Friday v Friday* [1970] 3 All E.R. 554 (where a wife existed in a state of blank passivity as a result of a schizophrenic condition).

[33] *Fullarton v Fullarton*, 1976 S.L.T. 8.

[34] See *Katz v Katz* [1972] 1 W.L.R. 955, per Sir George Baker at 960.

[35] There seems to be no such requirement in England: see *Thurlow v Thurlow* [1975] 2 All E.R. 979. *Cf.* Clive, *The Law of Husband and Wife in Scotland*, 4th edn (1997), para.21.013.

[36] *Meikle v Meikle*, 1987 G.W.D. 26–1005.

[37] *Knox v Knox*, 1993 S.C.L.R. 381.

[38] See also *Smith v Smith*, 1976 S.L.T. (Notes) 26, where a wife raised an action for divorce for cruelty on the basis that her husband had been convicted of murder and she was undergoing treatment for her nerves. The court found she had failed to establish any causal connection between her husband's crime and her unwillingness to cohabit with him.

[39] *Findlay v Findlay*, 1991 S.L.T. 457 at 461.

man after she and her husband had separated. She raised an action divorce based on her husband's behaviour. The issue was whether she was unwilling to cohabit with her husband because of her husband's behaviour, or because she had entered a relationship with another man. Lord Prosser held that:

> "On its own, I should doubt whether a party could contend that an association formed since separation by that party could make it unreasonable to expect that party to cohabit with the other party to the marriage".

But he went on to state that he had, however,

> "come to the view that where, as here, a pursuer originally separated from a defender for reasons which flowed from the conduct of the defender, and where after such a separation the parties' lives change over a period of time, and a new association is formed, then it is only realistic to see that association as arising in a sense from the earlier conduct and separation, and as being a relevant factor in considering whether, at the date of proof, the pursuer can reasonably be expected to cohabit with the defender".[40]

Thus, Lord Prosser was satisfied that, taking account of the whole history of events leading up to and since separation, the pursuer could not reasonably be expected to cohabit with the defender, and that this flowed directly from the original conduct of the defender.

14–17   The range of behaviour which may found a divorce under s.1(2)(b) is very broad. It includes non-physical assaults on the pursuer's person or feelings as well as physical violence.[41] It also covers various types of sexual conduct, including sodomy and bestiality (which were formerly grounds of divorce in their own right),[42] along with habitual drunkenness or drug use, and neglect, indifference, taciturnity, and passive or obsessive behaviour. It can include behaviour towards third parties within or outwith the family,[43] the latter even where there is no sexual relationship involved.[44]

14–18   In *AB v CB*[45] a husband, while temporarily insane, murdered his child. His wife, the child's mother, refused to live with him after he was released from hospital. He raised a divorce action on the grounds of her desertion, but the court held that she had reasonable grounds for non-adherence and dismissed the action. A single act of this type would certainly give rise to grounds for divorce under s.1(2)(b) of the 1976 Act. In *Hastie v Hastie*,[46] the wife made

---

[40] *Findlay v Findlay*, 1991 S.L.T. 457.
[41] See *Macleod v Macleod*, 1990 G.W.D. 14–767 (where a jealous husband constantly accused his wife of being unfaithful, although such claims were unfounded).
[42] Under the Divorce (Scotland) Act 1938.
[43] See *White v White*, 1966 S.L.T. 288 (where a husband's criminal conviction for an act of gross indecency with another man in a public toilet held grounds for divorce for behaviour).
[44] See *Stewart v Stewart*, 1987 S.L.T. (Sh. Ct) 48 (where a husband's non-sexual association with another woman after work and late at night was considered sufficient to give his wife grounds for divorce).
[45] *AB v CB*, 1959 S.C. 27.
[46] *Hastie v Hastie*, 1985 S.L.T. 146.

false allegations that her husband was unfaithful and had committed incest with his niece. The court held that, although the wife's conduct was unlikely to recur, nonetheless her allegations had been destructive of the mutual confidence essential to the continuance of a marriage, and so the husband was granted a divorce.

The ground of behaviour is steadily following adultery into decline, especially since the reduction in the non-cohabitation grounds from 2 years and five, to one year and two, by virtue of the FLSA 2006. **14–19**

Desertion

Desertion as a ground of divorce disappeared under the Family Law (Scotland) Act 2006 because the period of non-cohabitation under s 1(2)(e) was reduced from five years to two. Desertion used to require, inter alia, that the parties should have been apart for at least two years and thus the ground of desertion became redundant. Anyone who could show non-cohabitation for two years could divorce on that ground without having to satisfy the other criteria for deserion such as an initial willingness to adhere. **14–20**

One Year's Non-Cohabitation Plus Consent

Under s.1(2)(d), a marriage has irretrievably broken down if **14–21**

> "there has been no cohabitation between the parties at any time during a continuous period of one year after the date of the marriage and immediately preceding the bringing of the action and the defender consents to the granting of decree of divorce".[47]

Identical provision exists for civil partners at s.117(3)(c) of CPA 2004 with the obvious substitution of the words "registration" for "marriage" and "dissolution" for "divorce".[48]

Before amendment by the FLSA 2006, the predecessor of this provision— two years' non-cohabitation plus consent—was the most common ground for divorce, with 48 per cent of divorces obtained in this way in 1995[49] and 56 per cent of divorces in 2002.[50] There must be a continuous period of non-cohabitation, together with the consent to divorce of the spouse who has not raised the action. Non-cohabitation is a question of fact, regardless of the actual intentions of the parties and therefore cohabitation depends simply on whether the parties are "in fact living together as man and wife".[51] The period of non-cohabitation must be "continuous", and rules exist on exemption of periods of cohabitation to encourage reconciliation.[52] That is, if parties separate but then resume cohabitation for a period before separating once again, when considering whether the period of non-cohabitation has been "continu- **14–22**

---

[47] As amended by s.1 of the FLSA 2006.
[48] As amended by s.33, Sch.1, para.9 of the FLSA 2006.
[49] Scottish Executive, *Civil Judicial Statistics for 2002* above, n.21.
[50] Scottish Executive, *Civil Judicial Statistics for 2002*. See para.14–06 above for more recent figures
[51] Divorce (Scotland) Act 1976 s.13(2).
[52] Divorce (Scotland) Act 1976 s.2(4).

ous", no account is taken of periods of resumed cohabitation as long as such periods do not exceed six months in *total*.

14–23   *Example 1*: Sue leaves Joe on March 31, 2011. Joe implores her to come back and the couple attempt a reconciliation when Sue resumes cohabitation with Joe on August 1, 2011. Their attempt is unsuccessful and they agree Sue should leave for good on December 1, 2011. The four-month period of cohabitation from August 1 until the beginning of December will not interrupt the running of the one-year period but it will not count towards it either. This means that either party can raise an action for divorce on the basis of one year's non-cohabitation but not until July 31, 2012. If they had not had a period of attempted reconciliation such an action could have been raised on March 31, 2012.

14–24   *Example 2*: Sue leaves Joe on March 1, 2011. They resume cohabitation on August 1, 2011 until March 15, 2012. As the resumption of cohabitation has extended beyond the six-month period provided for in s.2(4), it has interrupted the running of the one-year period. This means that if either party wishes to raise an action for divorce the one-year period can only start to run from March 15, 2012. Similarly, for civil partners, identical provision is made for calculating a period of non-cohabitation at s.119(3) of the 2004 Act.

14–25   A defender must positively consent to the divorce/dissolution, and has the power to withdraw consent at any time during the one-year period right up until the granting of the decree.[53] Withdrawal of consent is competent even where it represents a tactical manoeuvre on the part of the defender to improve his or her bargaining position.[54]

14–26   For civil partners, it was included in the 2004 Act that provision was to be made for an Act of Sederunt to be passed to ensure that in an action for dissolution raised on the basis of one year's non-cohabitation with consent that:

- the defender be given such information as enables that civil partner to understand—
    - (i) the consequences of consenting to the granting of decree; and
    - (ii) the steps which must be taken to indicate such consent; and
    - (iii) as to the manner in which the defender in such an action is to indicate such consent and withdrawal of such consent;
- and where the defender has indicated and not withdrawn such consent in the prescribed manner, that indication will be sufficient evidence of consent.[55]

Two Years' Non-Cohabitation Without the Need for Consent

14–27   Finally, under s.1(2)(e), a marriage has irretrievably broken down if

---

[53] *Taylor v Taylor*, 1988 S.C.L.R. 60 (Sh. Ct). This has been enabled by statute for civil partners at s.117(3)(4).

[54] *Boyle v Boyle*, 1977 S.L.T. (Notes) 69.

[55] Such notices of consent to dissolution of civil partnership or separation of civil partnership may be found at Ch.33A.18 of the Act of Sedurunt (Sheriff Court Ordinary Cause Rules) 1993 (SI 1993/1956), Sch.1, Ch.33A (Civil Partnership Cases).

"there has been no cohabitation between the parties at any time during a continuous period of two years after the date of the marriage and immediately preceding the bringing of the action".[56]

Identical provision exists for civil partners at s.117(3)(d) of CPA 2004with reference to the "date of registration" rather than to a "marriage".[57]

The same rules discussed under "one year's non-cohabitation with **14–28** consent" apply in relation to what is non-cohabitation[58] and what amounts to a continuous period.[59] Prior to the amendment by the FLSA 2006, its predecessor—five years' non-cohabitation without the need for consent—was the third most popular ground with 18 per cent of divorces obtained in this way in 1995.[60]

This is the only ground which allows a disgruntled spouse/civil partner uni- **14–29** laterally to terminate his or her marriage/partnership without the other party having committed any fault. Prior to amendment by the FLSA 2006, the court had discretion under s.1(5) of the 1976 Act and s.117(6) of the 2004 Act to refuse an action for divorce/dissolution on this ground "if in the opinion of the court the grant of decree would result in grave financial hardship to the defender".[61]

"Hardship" included the loss of the chance of acquiring any benefit, e.g. **14–30** a wife's or widow's benefit under the occupational pension scheme of a husband, or a life policy. This discretionary power might be used or not by the court even if grave financial hardship was established.[62] Courts determined only *financial* hardship as a consequence of a divorce was relevant.[63] Emotional hardship arising from, e.g. loss of companionship or belief that divorce is not proper, was held to be of no significance.

This hardship defence was successful mainly where future benefits would **14–31** be lost as a result of a decree of divorce. Spouses, particularly older wives in long marriages who had never worked, or who had failed to work long enough to build up independent pensions, could claim with reason that divorce would defeat their rights in their husbands' pensions and that this will directly cause them grave financial hardship in the future. In *Nolan v Nolan*[64] the court agreed to refuse decree of divorce because the defender, if divorced, would have lost: (i) a chance of receiving two-fifths of the income element of her husband's index-linked pension; (ii) her indefeasible legal rights in succession in respect of the lump sum element of the pension if it still formed

---

[56] As amended by s.11 of the FLSA 2006.

[57] As amended by s.33, Sch.1, para.9 of the FLSA 2006.

[58] 1976 Act s.13(2).

[59] 1976 Act s.2(4).

[60] See RGS, *Annual Report 1995*, Table 8.1. See also para.14-06 above for more recent figures.

[61] FLSA 2006 s.13 repeals s.1(5) of the 1976 Act.

[62] See *Norris v Norris*, 1992 S.L.T. (Sh. Ct) 51.

[63] If the defender is already living at an impoverished level before the divorce, the defence will not be competent. In *Boyd v Boyd*, 1978 S.L.T. (Notes) 55, the wife had already suffered grave financial hardship during the subsistence of the marriage because her husband was able to pay her only £4.50 per week in aliment. Hence the court found that she would not be significantly worse off as a result of the divorce, and so the defence failed.

[64] *Nolan v Nolan*, 1979 S.L.T. 293.

part of his estate on his death and she survived him; and (iii) dependent again on survivorship, her entitlement to the State widow's pension. Although the husband offered to take out an insurance policy for her benefit, the judge was not satisfied that this would adequately compensate her for the potential loss.

14–32   However, as discussed in Ch.13, since the enactment of the Family Law (Scotland) Act 1985 s.10(5), this is no longer a compelling issue as the matrimonial property divisible on divorce is expressly defined to *include* the value of any pension rights of either spouse referable to the period of the marriage.[65] Furthermore, since the Pension Regulations 1996 have been enacted they have eliminated the previous doubt as to whether any widow's or widower's benefit portion of the pension forms part of the value. Even if there are no liquid assets with which to pay off pension rights at the date of divorce, a pension lump sum order can now be made under s.12A, earmarking a portion of the benefits to be paid at the date the pension matures. Thus we arrived at a point where there seemed no case to justify—purely for financial reasons—keeping alive a marriage which had irretrievably broken down. To do so goes against the general spirit of the 1976 Act.[66] Hence, this discretionary power had been abolished by the FLSA 2006.[67] Nevertheless a spouse will oftern defend the action on the financial ground and this defence will proceed and be dealt with before the granting of any decree of divorce.

Collusion

14–33   This defence was abolished by s.14 of the FLSA 2006 as there was broad agreement that the legislative provision no longer served a useful purpose. Previously, where the spouses agreed to put forward a false case to obtain a divorce, or to hold back a good defence, if discovered, divorce was refused on the ground of collusion.[68] If collusion emerged *after* decree had been granted, then it could be reduced. Nevertheless, it is still the case at common law that a court should not grant a decree of divorce if satisfied that the pursuer has put forward a false case or the defender has withheld a good defence. Co-operation by spouses in seeking a divorce or reaching agreement on its terms, e.g. relating to finance, did not amount collusion unless there was also deceit.[69]

REFORMING THE GROUNDS FOR DIVORCE

14–34   Given that divorce is supposed to be based on the concept of irretrievable breakdown of marriage, current law remains an uneasy partnership between fault and non-fault-based grounds. It is evident that despite the introduction of no-fault divorce, some divorce actions are still obtained on the basis

---

[65] See paras 13–26 *et seq*.

[66] This is the view of the Scottish Law Commission; see *Report on Family Law*, Scot. Law Com. No.135 (1992), para.13.12.

[67] FLSA 2006 s.13 repealing s.1(5) of the 1976 Act, and FLSA 2006 Sch.3 repealing s.117(6) of the 2004 Act.

[68] *Walker v Walker*, 1911 S.C. 163 at 169.

[69] *McKenzie v MacKenzie*, 1935 S.L.T. 198.

of behaviour or adultery, primarily because the parties do not wish to wait for one year for a divorce.[70] This subverted one of the main aims of the 1976 Act, which was to avoid "an unnecessary emphasis on blame and recrimination and an unnecessary increase in bitterness and hostility".[71] In 1988, the Scottish Law Commission consulted on the idea of making divorce available after a period of notice, or after a short period of non-cohabitation lasting from three months to a year.[72] This proposal proved too radical however and in its subsequent report, it merely recommended the dropping of the ground of desertion and shortening the periods of non-cohabitation to one year with consent, and two years without.

REFORMS MADE BY THE FAMILY LAW (SCOTLAND) ACT 2006—OVERVIEW

While other countries, such as Australia, New Zealand, Sweden and Finland have opted for "no fault" systems of divorce,[73] the reforms implemented by the FLSA 2006 continue to promote a mixed system of divorce, that is, a combination of fault and non-fault grounds along the lines of the Scottish Law Commission's recommendations.[74] A further amendment made by the FLSA 2006 is the insertion of a new s.3A into the 1976 Act providing the court with the discretion to postpone decree of divorce where a religious impediment to remarry exists. In such a case the court has to be satisfied that the party seeking divorce has removed or has contributed to the removal of the impediment preventing the other party from remarrying once divorced. A power is given to Scottish Ministers to make regulations to prescribe the religious faiths which can rely on this provision.[75]

14–35

NULLITY

A person who is a party to an apparent marriage which is nevertheless void for lack of capacity or true consent may seek a decree of nullity in the Court of Session or Sheriff Court.[76] The grounds on which marriage is void for lack of consent are set out in s.20A of the Marriage (Scotland) Act 1977 as amended by s.2 of the 2006 Act. Subsection (2) allows a marriage to be void if either partyconsented to the marriage by reason only of duress[77] or error,

14–36

---

[70] See *Report on Reform of the Ground for Divorce*, Scot. Law Com. No. 116 (1989), para.2.2.

[71] *Report on Reform of the Ground for Divorce*, Scot. Law Com. No. 116 (1989), para.2.3.

[72] See *The Ground for Divorce: Should the Law be Changed?*, Scot. Law Com. Discussion Paper No.76 (1988).

[73] England also attempted to institute no-fault divorce by providing that irretrievable breakdown would only be inferred after the expiry of a one-year period for consideration of the practical consequences of divorce, and reflection on whether the marital relationship was irreparable under Pt II of the Family Law Act 1996. However, in 2001 the UK Government repealed this part of the Act with the result that England and Wales continues to retain its mixed system of divorce on irretrievable breakdown of marriage.

[74] See *Report on Reform of the Ground for Divorce*, Scot. Law Com. No.116 (1989).

[75] 1976 Act s.13(3A)(9) inserted by s.15 of the FLSA 2006.

[76] FLSA 2006 s.3.

[77] *Mahmood v Mahmood*, 1993 S.L.T. 589; *Mahmud v Mahmud*, 1994 S.L.T. 599.

or was incapable of understanding the nature of marriage and of consenting to the marriage.

14-37   Error in this context can mean either error as to the nature of the ceremony or as to the identity of the other party. By virtue of subsection (4) a party who consents to the marriage and does not do so because of duress or error cannot claim that the marriage is void by reason only that he had tacitly withheld genuine consent at the time of solemnisation.

14-38   A valid marriage must have the consent of both parties who both must have the mental capacity to consent. No very great intellectual capacity is required for a person to have the mental capacity to consent to a marriage.[78]

14-39   The pursuer in *Sorab v Khan*[79] was only 16 years old when her motherinformed her, only a week in advance, thaqt a wedding had been Arranged. When she protested her mother said that she would disown her and send her to live in Pakistan. The mother also threatened to commit suicide if the marriage did not go ahead. The court granted decree of nullity because the pursuer had been put under more pressure than a 16 year old could reasonably be expected to bear.

14-40   *Singh v Singh*[80] is even more clear cut. There the pursuer was a UK citizen who had been taken to India to visit relations. Contrary to the woman's wishes her mother had arranged for a marriage to take place. The mother theatened to destroy the pursuer's passport and other docvuments and to leave her in India if she did not proceed with the marriage. The marriage did proceed but the pursuer refused to have sexual relations with her new husband, left his house a week later and returned to Scotland. The court had no difficulty in finding that the mother's threats had been serious and amounted to an immediate danger to the pursuer's liberty, causing her will to be overborne and nullifying her consent to marriage.

14-41   Duress is not a common ground of successful actions for nullity, but the coming into force of the Forced Marriage (Protection and Jurisdiction) (Scotland) Act 2001 may encourage parties who have applied, either directly or indirectly for a Forced Marriage Protection Order to seek nullity. The duress need not include any threat of physical violence but it must be sufficient to overcome the free will of the party. It is clear that the test is a stronger one than the test for an order under the 2011 Act.

JUDICIAL SEPARATION—SPOUSES AND CIVIL PARTNERS

14-42   For couples who wish to separate but are opposed to divorce or dissolution, the option of judicial separation remains.[81] Judicial separation is rarely

---

[78]   *Long v Long*, 1950 S.L.T. (Notes) 32.
[79]   *Sorab v Khan*, 2002 S.L.T. 1255.
[80]   *Singh v Singh*, 2005 S.L.T. 749.
[81]   1976 Act s.4 for spouses; 2004 Act s.120 for civil partners.

resorted to today,[82] given the decline in the social stigma of divorce and the possibility of obtaining a divorce without proof of matrimonial fault. The grounds for obtaining a decree of judicial separation are now identical to those for obtaining divorce or dissolution and subject to the same defences and bars. A spouse who has obtained a judicial separation thus always has grounds subsequently to raise an action of divorce if he or she wishes[83] as will a civil partner to obtain dissolution having previously obtained judicial separation.[84]

If in an action for judicial separation between *spouses* it appears to the court there is a reasonable prospect of a reconciliation between the parties, it shall continue the action for such a period as it thinks proper to enable attempts to be made to effect such a reconciliation.[85] No similar provision has been included in the 2004 Act for civil partners in an action for separation in Scotland, however, such provision does exist in an action for *dissolution*[86] and a court cannot grant dissolution without hearing evidence from the pursuer even where a decree for separation has previously been granted.[87]

14-43

In an action for judicial separation between spouses where the defender is suffering from mental illness, the court is directed to appoint a curator *ad litem* to the defender.[88] Similar provision exists for the appointment of a curator *ad litem* for defenders to an action for judicial separation for civil partners.[89]

14-44

A decree of judicial separation provides judicial sanction for spouses or civil partners to separate and live apart without terminating the marriage/civil partnership. Apart from this, the ordinary obligations and restrictions of marriage/civil partnership continue to apply. Thus, neither can remarry and the obligation of aliment subsists. The 1976 Act makes reference to actions for "separation and aliment",[90] whilst the 2004 Act refers to actions for "separation" only.[91] However, the 2004 Act amends the Family Law (Scotland) Act 1985 to make actions for aliment competent in an action for separation.[92]

14-45

JURISDICTION AND PROCEDURAL ASPECTS OF DIVORCE/DISSOLUTION

Jurisdiction—Spouses

Until 1983, all actions dealing with personal status, including divorce, could be raised only in the Court of Session. However, the Sheriff Court now

14-46

---

[82] For a discussion of the importance of judicial separation in the past, see Clive, *The Law of Husband and Wife in Scotland*, 4th edn (1997), para.19.043.

[83] 1976 Act s.3(1); Law Reform (Miscellaneous Provisions) (Scotland) Act 1968 s.11.

[84] 2004 Act s.121.

[85] 1976 Act s.2.

[86] 2004 Act s.118.

[87] 2004 Act s.121(2).

[88] 1976 Act s.11 as enacted by OCR 33.16 (SI 1993/1956) (S.223).

[89] OCR 33A.16 (SSI 2005/638).

[90] 1976 Act s.4(1).

[91] 2004 Act s.120.

[92] 2004 Act s.261(2), Sch.28, Pt 2, para.11 inserting s.2(2)(aa) into the 1985 Act.

has concurrent jurisdiction[93] and most divorces are raised in that forum. The Sheriff's jurisdiction now includes nullity by virtue of s.4 of FLSA 2006. The Court of Session has jurisdiction to hear a divorce where either party to the marriage

(a) is domiciled in Scotland on the date of commencement of the action; or
(b) was habitually resident in Scotland through the period of one year ending with that date.[94]

Jurisdiction exists in the Sheriff Court where either (a) or (b) above is satisfied *and* either party to the marriage:

(i) was resident in the sheriffdom for a period of 40 days ending with that date; or
(ii) was resident in the sheriffdom for a period of not less than 40 days ending not more than 40 days before the said date, and has no known residence in Scotland that date.[95]

Unlike the position in England, where spouses must be married for one year before either one of them can raise an action for divorce,[96] there is no minimum time bar in Scots law.

Jurisdiction—Civil Partners[97]

14-47   The courts[98] in Scotland have jurisdiction in relation to proceedings for the dissolution or annulment of a civil partnership or for the separation of civil partners where

(a) both civil partners are habitually resident in Scotland;
(b) both civil partners were last habitually resident in Scotland and one of the civil partners continues to reside there;
(c) the defender is habitually resident in Scotland;
(d) the pursuer is habitually resident in Scotland and has resided there for at least one year immediately preceding the date on which the action is begun; or
(e) the pursuer is domiciled and habitually resident in Scotland and has resided there for at least six months immediately preceding the date on which the action is begun.

Brussells II

14-48   Since March 1, 2001, the Convention on Jurisdiction and the Recognition

---

[93] Divorce Jurisdiction, Court Fees and Legal Aid (Scotland) Act 1983 s.1.
[94] Domicile and Matrimonial Proceedings Act 1973 s.7.
[95] Domicile and Matrimonial Proceedings Act 1973 s.8(3) as amended by the Divorce Jurisdiction, Court Fees and Legal Aid (Scotland) Act 1983 Sch.1, para.18.
[96] Family Law Act 1996 s.4.
[97] The Civil Partnership (Jurisdiction and Recognition of Judgments) (Scotland) Regulations 2005 (SSI 2005/629).
[98] Both the Court of Session and the Sheriff Court under s.135 of the 2004 Act.

and Enforcement of Judgments in matrimonial matters dealing with Member States has been effective.[99] The Convention's aim is the reciprocal recognition and enforcement of decrees relating to divorce, separation and nullity throughout the EU.[100] As a result appropriate amendments have been made to Scottish legislation to bring it into line with the Convention[101] although jurisdiction still remains primarily dependent on the parties' habitual residence or domicile and if either or both party is habitually resident in Scotland then the Scottish courts will have jurisdiction. However, this may encourage forum shopping, with parties rushing to raise an action in the court that they perceive of as being most favourable to them, as a court first seised of the issue, as defined in Art.16, has jurisdiction over courts later seised in the matter.

The current Convention applies to "the attribution, exercise, delegation, **14–49** restriction or termination of parental responsibility".[102] In particular, it will apply to the following:

- rights of custody and access (residence and contact);
- guardianship;
- the designation and functions of a person having charge of the child's person or property;
- the placement of a child in a foster family or institutional care; and
- protective measures relating to the child's property.[103]

It does not, however, apply to:

- establishing a parent/child relationship;
- adoption;
- the child's name;
- emancipation;
- maintenance obligations;
- trusts or succession;
- measures taken in respect of a criminal offence committed by a child.

---

[99] See Council Regulation (EC) No.1347/2000 known as "Brussels II" now repealed and replaced by Council Regulation (EC) No.2201/2003 known as "Brussels II *bis*" that came into effect on March 1, 2005. Note that much of the earlier regulation has been retained and incorporated into its replacement, although the scope of Brussels II *bis* in addressing issues relating to children is broader than that of the original and is independent of the previous link to parental matrimonial proceedings. For further details see Morris, *The Conflict of Laws*, 6th edn.

[100] According to *Singh v Singh*, 2005 S.L.T. 749 the Council Regulation was not restricted to cases where both parties could found jurisdiction under Art.2(1) and applied in a case, such as the present, where the respondent was not habitually resident or domiciled in, or a national of, a Member State.

[101] See EC (Matrimonial Jurisdiction and Judgments) (Scotland) Regulations 2001 (SSI 2001/36) repealed and replaced by EC (Matrimonial and Parental Responsibility Jurisdiction and Judgments) (Scotland) Regulations 2005 (SSI 2005/42). Also, The Civil Partnership (Jurisdiction and Recognition of Judgments) (Scotland) Regulations 2005 (SSI 2005/629).

[102] Brussels II *bis* Art.1(1)(b).

[103] Brussels II *bis* Art.1(2).

Under the Convention, the child is given the right to be heard on matters relating to his or her custody "unless this appears inappropriate having regard to his or her age or degree of maturity".[104]

CROSS-BORDER DIVORCE AND DISSOLUTION

14–50 In respect of cross-border divorces within the United Kingdom, jurisdiction in these cases is dependent upon one of the spouses or civil partners having been domiciled within a particular United Kingdom legal jurisdiction or having been resident there for at least a year immediately preceding the raising of the action. Where spouses/civil partners are domiciled or resident in different United Kingdom legal jurisdictions then each has a choice as to where to raise the divorce action.

14–51 In actions for divorce where there is competition between actions raised in different United Kingdom legal jurisdictions it is governed by the Domicile and Matrimonial Proceedings Act 1973, Sch.3 which provides for the mandatory sisting by Scottish courts of actions raised here where the criteria set out in para.8 are met. These are

- the competing proceedings relate to the same marriage;
- the couple resided together after the marriage;
- the couple were resident together in the other jurisdiction when the Scottish action was raised or they last resided together there; and
- either spouse was habitually resident in that other jurisdiction for at least a year immediately preceding their last residence together.

There are also provisions set down in para.9 for a discretionary sist where this would serve the balance of fairness and convenience, including the convenience of witnesses and time-scales and expenses in the competing jurisdictions.[105]

CROSS-BORDER RECOGNITION OF DECREE

Divorce

14–52 Provision is made for recognition throughout the United Kingdom of a decree of divorce, annulment or legal separation granted by any court of civil jurisdiction in the British Islands[106] by the Family Law Act 1986.[107] There are only two grounds for refusal of recognition. These are

- that it was granted or obtained at a time when it was irreconcilable with a decision determining the question of the subsistence or validity of the marriage previously given by a court of civil jurisdiction in Scotland

---

[104] Brussels II *bis* Art.11(2).
[105] For further discussion see L. Mair, "Cross-Border Divorces within the UK", 2004 Fam L.B. 70–3.
[106] These cover England and Wales, Scotland, Northern Ireland, the Channel Islands and the Isle of Man.
[107] Family Law Act 1986 s.44(2).

or by a court elsewhere and recognised or entitled to recognition in Scotland[108];

- that the divorce or legal separation was granted or obtained at a time when, according to Scots law, there was no subsisting marriage between the parties.[109]

However, even where these circumstances arise, the court is not obliged to refuse recognition but may go ahead and uphold the divorce, annulment or legal separation.

Dissolution

In respect of civil partnerships, s.233 of the 2004 Act provides that the validity of a dissolution or annulment of a civil partnership or a legal separation of civil partners which has been obtained from a court of civil jurisdiction in one part of the United Kingdom is to be recognised throughout the United Kingdom unless irreconcilable with a decision determining the question of the subsistence or validity of the civil partnership.   **14–53**

Recognition of Overseas Decrees

Provision is also made for the recognition of overseas divorces, annulments and legal separation from countries outside the British Islands.[110] Jurisdiction in the Court of Session and the Sheriff Court has been devised for those actions where a pursuer is seeking recognition in Scotland of a decree of divorce, nullity or separation granted in a country outwith the EU.[111]   **14–54**

Proof

Before a decree of divorce/dissolution can be granted, the ground of the action must be proven on the balance of probabilities.[112] The burden of proof rests with the pursuer who must prove the ground in all cases, regardless of whether the action is defended or undefended.[113] While corroboration is no longer necessary,[114] there must be evidence from someone other than the spouses/civil partners to support the conclusion for divorce.[115] Such evidence need not, however, take the form of parole evidence, i.e. evidence given by witnesses in court, but may be tendered by way of affidavit, i.e. a statement in writing sworn and affirmed in the presence of a notary public or other competent authority). In undefended actions—which are overwhelmingly the majority of divorces in Scotland—the rules of court   **14–55**

---

[108] Family Law Act 1986 s.51(1).
[109] This includes the rules of Scottish private international law, see s.51(2).
[110] For further discussion see *Scottish Family Law Service*.
[111] Domicile and Matrimonial Proceedings Act 1973 as amended by s.37 of the FLSA 2006.
[112] 1976 Act s.1(6) for spouses; 2004 Act s.117(8) for civil partners.
[113] Civil Evidence (Scotland) Act 1988 s.8(1) as amended.
[114] Civil Evidence (Scotland) Act 1988 s.1(1) abolished the need for corroboration in all civil proceedings.
[115] Civil Evidence (Scotland) Act 1988 s.8(3) as amended by s.261(2), Sch.28, Pt 4, para.55 of the 2004 Act to include civil Partners.

provide that evidence is to take the form of affidavit evidence unless the court directs otherwise.[116]

Simplified Divorce/Civil Partnership

14–56 In addition, a simplified, speedy and cheap form of do-it-yourself divorce was introduced in 1982. This is available only where certain conditions are met.[117] These are that

> "(i) the action is undefended;
> (ii) the action is brought on the basis of—
>   a) one or two years' non-cohabitation;
>   b) or a interim gender recognition certificate has been issued to one of the parties;
> (iii) the pursuer is able to state that there are no other proceedings pending in any court which could have the effect of bringing the marriage to an end;
> (iv) there are no children of the marriage under the age of 16 years;
> (v) neither partner is applying for an order for financial provision on divorce;
> (vi) neither party suffers from mental disorder; and
> (vi) there is no religious impediment to the remarriage of either party in terms of section 3A of the Act of 1976."[118]

Similar procedure is available for civil partners as contained within the Act of Sederunt (Ordinary Cause Rules) Amendment (Civil Partnership Act 2004) 2005.[119]

14–57 Legal representation is not required in this form of action although it is always adviseable, since there may be financial claims which a lay party may not know about. The action can be initiated using a standard application obtainable from the Sheriff Clerk, the Court of Session or the local Citizens Advice Bureau. To simplify matters further, the general requirement for evidence from someone other than the spouses/civil partners is dispensed with.[120] On introduction, the aim of rendering the divorce process more accessible to ordinary people was laudable. However, given that many divorces in Scotland involve spouses who have children under 16,[121] or who

---

116 See RCS 49.28(2), as amended by the Act of Sederunt (Rules of the Court of Session Amendment No.5) (Family Actions and Miscellaneous) 1996 (SI 1996/2587), para.2(20), and the Act of Sederunt (Rules of the Court of Session Amendment No.9) (Civil Partnership Act 2004 etc.) 2005 (SSI 2005/632), para.14; and OCR 33.28(2) for spouses and OCR 33A.28 for civil partners.

117 RCS 49.72 (derived from SI 1982/1679) and OCR 33.73. In 2011–12 there were 9453 divorces in Scotland. 62% used the simplified procedure. In the same period there were 50 civil partnership dissolutions of which 94% used the simplified procedure (*http://www.scotland.gov.uk/Publications/2012/* [accessed August, 2013]).

118 RCS 49.72 as amended by the Act of Sederunt (Rules of the Court of Session Amendment No.3) (Family Law (Scotland) Act 2006) 2006 (SSI 2006/206), para.15.

119 SSI 2005/638.

120 Civil Evidence (Scotland) Act 1988 s.8(4) and (5) empower the Lord Advocate to dispense with the requirements of s.8(3) in specified classes of action by statutory instrument.

121 In 1995, over one-third of divorces ended by final judgment involved children under 16,

wish to apply to the court for financial provision,[122] or both, the value of this procedure is limited. Nonetheless, in 1994–1995 the procedure was used in one-third of divorces.[123] The disadvantage of the procedure is that an economically weaker party may sign the form of consent without appreciating that any financial claim must be made in the context of the action and that she will exclude her own claim by signing and returning the document.

Ordinary Divorces

Divorces/dissolutions which do not qualify for the simplified procedure (being the majority of divorces) are known as "ordinary" and proceed through the formal court system. Some particular points relating to procedure should be noted.[124] **14–58**

Options Hearings in the Sheriff Court

Where a divorce is defended in the Sheriff Court, rules of court[125] now provide for an additional step in the legal process, known as an options hearing, to take place. This hearing is intended to give the parties a chance to meet together before the sheriff in order to ascertain if agreement can be reached without proceeding to a full proof, or if this is not possible, to focus the precise disagreement between the parties. The aim is to save judicial time as well as legal aid,[126] and also to reduce delays in concluding the action. To this end, both parties are required to attend the hearing in person[127] and the sheriff is directed to adopt an interventionist role.[128] On the basis of information gathered, the sheriff may order a proof[129] or proof before answer,[130] or remit the action to additional procedure.[131] S/he may also appoint the cause to debate if satisfied that there is a preliminary matter of law which if established following debate would lead to decree in favour of either party, or to limitation of proof to any subsequent degree.[132] In addition, a sheriff has **14–59**

---

see Scottish Courts Administration, *Civil Judicial Statistics 1995*, pp.26–28. Current Civil Judicial Statistics no longer record this information. However, in England and Wales in 2003, 153,500 children under 16 were affected by their parents divorcing in England and Wales, just over one in five were under five years old. Downloaded from *www.statistics.gov.uk/CCI/nugget.asp?ID=1163*.

[122] A party in receipt of an application under the simplified procedure will lose the opportunity to make a capital claim if he or she allows decree to pass.

[123] See *Civil Judicial Statistics 1994*, p.30 and *Civil Judicial Statistics 1995*, p.28. Current Civil Judicial Statistics no longer record this information.

[124] For general discussion of procedure see S.A. Bennett, *Divorce in the Sheriff Court*, 10th edn (Edinburgh: Barnstoneworth, 2005).

[125] OCR 9.12; OCR 33.36 for spouses and OCR 33A.36 for civil partners.

[126] But see A. Gibb, "Time Heals-But not on Legal Aid", 2005 Fam. L.B. 75–1.

[127] OCR 33.36 for spouses; OCR 33A.36 for civil partners.

[128] OCR 9.12.

[129] OCR 9.12(3)(a).

[130] OCR 9.12(3)(b).

[131] OCR 9.12(4).

[132] OCR 9.12(3)(c) added by the Act of Sederunt (Ordinary Cause, Summary Application and Small Claim Rules) Amendment (Miscellaneous) 2004 (SSI 2004/197) (effective May 21, 2004), para.2(6).

power, on cause shown, to continue the options hearing for up to 28 days.[133] However, this power may be used only once.[134] While the aims of the options hearing are to be applauded, questions have been raised as to how effective this new procedure is in practice.[135] As the rules currently stand it is not actually necessary for a defender in a family action to appear at an options hearing in person as representation by a solicitor will suffice to avoid being held in default by the court,[136] except possibly where a sheriff has expressly ordered the defender to appear in person and he or she has failed to obey that order.[137]

Children—Child Welfare Hearing

14-60   Many divorces involve children under 16 and it is not uncommon for parents to seek a s.11 residence, contact or parental responsibilities order at the same time as the principal decree of divorce. The court may exceptionally refuse to grant a decree of divorce/dissolution if it is not satisfied that appropriate arrangements have been made for the children dependant on the spouses/civil partners.[138] In such cases, the best option for the court may be to refer the child to SCRA who will then convene a children's hearing. In such a case, a proof will have to be held to decide if a ground of referral to the hearing exists.[139] Alternatively the sheriff may order a report from a local solicitor who will interview the children (if appropriate) and other relevant witnesses before reporting to the sheriff in writing, with or without a recommendation as to the decision. Any such recommendation is not, of course, binding on the Sheriff. Where divorce/dissolution proceedings involve a child under 16, the court has a duty to give that child an opportunity to express his or her views, which must then be given due regard, depending on the age and maturity of the child.[140] The action must be intimated to that child so that he or she knows that the action is underway and has a chance to participate. Where the child is considered too young to be able to give a view, or distress might be caused to the child, the court can dispense with intimation.[141]

14-61   It is strongly desirable for the welfare of the child that disputes involving children should be resolved as speedily as possible. This is particularly true in disputes over residence for, where the longer the child remains settled with one parent on an interim basis pending resolution of the dispute, the harder it is for the court to contemplate making a change.[142] For this

---

[133] OCR 9.12(5).

[134] OCR 9.12(5).

[135] See Gibb, 1994 Fam. L.B. 7–2 and McTaggart, 1995 Fam. L.B. 13–10.

[136] OCR 33.37 and 9.12(7).

[137] *Grimes v Grimes*, 1995 S.C.L.R. 268.

[138] Children (Scotland) Act 1995 s.12(2)(c) as amended by s.261(2), Sch.28, Pt 4, para.60 of the 2004 Act.

[139] 1995 Act s.54 as amended by s.261(2), Sch.28, Pt 4, para.61 of the 2004 Act. See further, paras 8–15 *et seq*.

[140] 1995 Act s.11(7). A child is presumed competent to express a reasonable view at the age of 12 (s.11(10)).

[141] OCR 33.7(7), as amended, for spouses; OCR 33A.7(7) for civil partners.

[142] See para.4–66.

reason, a new "fast-track" procedure, known as the child welfare hearing, was created to deal with any defended actions in the Sheriff Court[143] which involve a s.11 order under the Children (Scotland) Act 1995, or any other actions where a sheriff considers that such a hearing should be fixed.[144] The aim of the child welfare hearing is to identify and process any disputes concerning children as expeditiously as possible. All parties (including a child who has indicated his or her wish to attend) are required to attend the hearing personally, except on cause shown.[145] Parties are also under a duty to provide the sheriff with as much information as possible so that the court can take whatever steps are necessary to deal with the matter.[146] In conducting the hearing, the sheriff is expected to adopt the same kind of interventionist role that is promoted in the options hearing, in the hope that disputes involving children can be processed as efficiently as possible.[147]

Power to Refer Parties to Mediation

The court also has power to suspend the divorce/dissolution proceed-   **14–62** ings and to refer the parties to mediation.[148] The purpose here is not to encourage parties to reconcile,[149] but to bring them together with the help of a third party mediator so that they can try to reach agreement about the terms of their divorce, especially with regard to children and, more recently, property. Mediation helps the parties to reach agreement by operating outwith the formal adversarial process of the courts and legal advisers.[150] Both the Court of Session[151] and the sheriff court[152] have power to refer parties in any dispute involving parental responsibilities or rights to a family mediation service though attendance cannot be made compulsory. Unreasonable refusal to attend can be taken into account by the sheriff in due course.

Registration

When decree of divorce or dissolution is granted, the clerk of court is   **14–63** required to notify the content of the decree to the Registrar General who

---

[143] OCR 33.22A, as amended, for spouses; OCR 33A.23 for civil partners.

[144] OCR 33.22A(1)(c) for spouses (these might include for, e.g. paternity proceedings); OCR 33A.23(1)(c) for civil partners.

[145] OCR 33.22A(5), as amended, for spouses; OCR 33A.23(5) for civil partners.

[146] OCR 33.22A(6), as amended, for spouses; OCR 33A.23(6) for civil partners.

[147] See A. Gibb, above, n.30 where he talks about the difficulties that practitioners face regarding the payment of legal aid fees in respect of a child welfare hearing and where he observes that where family litigation is concerned, "The situation is at crisis point" (at 75–2).

[148] Note: s.261(2), Sch.28, para.58 of the 2004 Act amends s.1(2) of Civil Evidence (Family Mediation) (Scotland) Act 1995 pertaining to the inadmissibility in civil procedure of information as to what occurred during family mediation.

[149] Mediation was originally referred to as conciliation, but this term was changed to avoid confusion with reconciliation.

[150] See further, Ch.15.

[151] RCS 49.23 as amended.

[152] OCR 33.22, as amended, for spouses; OCR 33A.22 for civil partners.

must make an entry in the relevant register, being the Register of Divorces[153] or the Register of Dissolution of Civil Partnership.[154]

In the final chapter, we consider how parties in Scotland can themselves regulate the terms of dissolution of their marriage/civil partnership or other relationship by agreement—with or without the help of a mediator—and to what extent the courts can, or should, act to protect the weaker party in the relationship, as well as the public interest in the stability of family life.

---

[153] Registration of Births, Deaths and Marriages (Scotland) Act 1965 s.48.
[154] 2004 Act s.122.

CHAPTER 15
PRIVATE ORDERING: MINUTES OF AGREEMENT

Despite the emphasis which has been placed on conflict in divorce in earlier **15–01** chapters, by no means all divorces are defended in court and resolved by full adversarial proceedings. While couples do get into dispute with one another which may require adjudication in court, this is by no means always the case. In fact the cases that make it to court tend to be in the minority of cases rather than the majority. Despite the image of the legal profession as an adversarial profession rather than an enabling one, many couples opt to use legal advice to help them to reach their own agreements on matters such as childcare, aliment and the distribution of their property at the end of their relationships. Although all divorces and dissolutions of civil partnerships must go to court, very few in practice are defended or involve litigation.[1] Research on what people do and think about going to law in both Scotland[2] and England and Wales[3] also reveals that very limited use is made of formal legal proceedings to resolve justicable problems. Reaching consensus has been the goal of much contemporary family law in Scotland (see the Children (Scotland) Act 1995) and England and Wales (see the Family Law Act 1996). It is not therefore surprising to find that many couples reach their own agreements on matters like childcare, aliment and the distribution of their property.[4] One Scottish study estimates that these agreements, referred to as minutes of agreement ("MoA") and joint minutes ("JM") account for around one-third of the total number of divorces in any year.[5] Among the claimed benefits of reaching agreements are that they

- save time and money; and
- may reduce the kind of hostility that full open court proceedings generate.[6]

---

[1] See Morris, Gibson and Platts, *Untying the Knot: Characteristics of Divorce in Scotland* (Edinburgh: Scottish Central Research Unit, 1993), p.15.

[2] H. Genn and A. Paterson, *Paths to Justice Scotland* (Oxford: Hart Publishing, 2001).

[3] H. Genn, *Paths to Justice* (Oxford: Hart Publishing, 1999).

[4] See A.M. Cubie, "Comment: Agreements and Divorcing Clients", 2003 Fam. L.B. 62–2.

[5] Wasoff, McGuckin and Edwards, *Mutual Consent: Written Agreements in Family Law* (Edinburgh: Scottish Central Research Unit, 1997). It is surprising to note that in reaching these agreements, mediation as an alternative form of dispute processing is so little in evidence. This was especially true for Scotland, H. Genn and A. Paterson, *Paths to Justice Scotland*, pp.211–213 where, out of all 472 respondents to the main questionnaire, only seven stated that they had had any involvement with a mediation or conciliation organisation.

[6] See Wasoff, Dobash and Marcus, *The Impact of the Family Law (Scotland) Act 1985 on Solicitors' Practice* (Edinburgh: Scottish Central Research Unit, 1990), Ch.8.

It is worth noting, however, that parties who make agreements,

> "reported that high emotion, conflict, antagonism and compromise were the norm in reaching such agreements. The term 'agreement' is, in itself, misleading, since almost all of those interviewed said that they had not willingly agreed but had felt pressured into signing because they thought that the alternatives were worse. They did not feel in control of the process or the outcome. No one felt empowered".[7]

In fact, Wasoff suggests that the term "settlement" would be a better term for the outcome than "agreement".[8]

15–02   The terms settled upon in what are called Minutes of Agreement may be made at any time, whether prior to the marriage ("ante-nuptial agreements"), during it, or on or after divorce. In the past, marriage contracts were important when married women did not have the right to administer their own property[9] for they represented a device whereby parties could create their own property regime during marriage.[10] However, with changes in the law conferring rights on both husbands and wives to enjoy their own property regardless of marriage[11] much of the traditional rationale for their existence disappeared and they fell into disuse.[12] However, there has been a revival, as a means of protecting the property of the very wealthy (mainly men) against the kind of claims their spouses might make on them on divorce. While prenuptial marriage contracts ware generally recognised in Scotland, their status in England has been somewhat uncertain. In the English case of *F v F*[13] the court opined that such contracts were of limited significance because it was undesirable for standards that are intended to be of universal significance to be limited by private contracts. Then in *K v K*[14] the court took the prenuptial contract into account in so far as making an award of capital to the wife. English law has moved some distance towards respecting pre-nuptial agreements by virtue of *Radmacher v Granatino*,[15] although the English position is still some way short of the robust way in which Scots courts hold the parties to the terms of a prenuptial agreement in the absence of grounds of attack

---

[7] F. Wasoff, "Mutual Consent: Separation Agreements and the Outcomes of Private Ordering in Divorce", 2005 JSWFL 27, Nos 3–4, pp.237–250.

[8] F. Wasoff, "Mutual Consent: Separation Agreements and the Outcomes of Private Ordering in Divorce", 2005 JSWFL 27, Nos 3–4, p.247.

[9] See Ch.10.

[10] According to E. Clive, *The Law of Husband and Wife in Scotland*, 4th edn (Edinburgh: W.Green, 1997): "In the nineteenth century the marriage contract was widely used among the propertied classes. Its general purpose was to alter the normal property consequences of marriage" (para.17.001).

[11] Family Law (Scotland) Act 1985, s.24(1) as amended by s.261(2), Sch.28, para.27 of the Civil Partnership Act 2004 to extend to civil partnerships.

[12] In the first edition of E. Clive, *The Law of Husband and Wife in Scotland* (Edinburgh: Greens, 1974) it was observed that, "marriage contracts are now comparatively rare": p.345.

[13] [1995] 2 F.L.R. 45, CA.

[14] [2003] 1 F.L.R. 120, Fam Div.

[15] *Radmcher v Granatino*, 2010 UKSC 42.

at common law or under s.16 of FLSA 2006.[16] One major consideration for entering into a prenuptial agreement, which is common in the USA,[17] is to preserve property as inheritance for the children of a previous marriage where the proposed marriage is a second or third marriage.

Agreements regulating issues on breakdown of the relationship are also sometimes known as separation agreements, but will be referred to formally throughout this chapter as minutes of agreement. MoAs are usually registered with the consent of both parties in the Books of Council and Session for preservation and execution, or in the Sheriff Court Books. The purpose of this is not only to maintain a record of the agreement, but to enable either party to enforce the terms of the deed when the other is in default, by means of summary diligence.[18]When MoAs are registered for execution they become public documents open for examination. MoAs are binding legal contracts[19] and as such can only be varied or withdrawn from under very special circumstances (discussed below). Around 3,000 MoAs are made in Scotland each year.[20]   **15–03**

Sometimes, parties will reach agreement only after the divorce is already underway in the courts. Disputes about financial provision, in particular, often commence as defended actions in court, but end up being settled by agreement between the parties. In such cases, settlement can be reached in the form of a Joint Minute. It is usual to ask the court to interpone authority to a Jonint Minute and to grant decree in terms of the arrangements in the agreement. This has the effect of transforming the parties' private agreement into a binding decree of the court. Thus, as with MoAs, neither party may unilaterally withdraw from the Joint Minute[21] unless the special circumstances set out below apply. A Joint Minute cannot, however, deal with the ground of the divorce because that is a matter on which the court must consider evidence.[22] The Joint Minute is lodged with the court as part of the process rather than being publicly registered.   **15–04**

It can be estimated that MoAs and Joint Minutes are used to resolve disputes in a larger proportion of the total number of divorces in any year.[23]   **15–05**

---

[16] In the wake of *Radmacher* the English Courts have tended to disregard the terms of any agreement which prejudices the interests of children (*Kremen v Agrest* [2012] EWHC 45 (Fam)) and has considered the extent to which parties to an agreement may be assumed to have had in contemplation of the possibility that their case may be addressed by a court in a discretionary jurisdiction (*B v S* [2012] EWHC 265 (Fam)).

[17] See D. Weisberg and S. Appleton, *Modern Family Law: Cases and Materials*, 2nd edn (New York: Aspen, 2002), pp.145–146.

[18] This saves time and money as a party can act immediately on the warrant contained in the document, without having to go to court to enforce the terms of the deed. When the agreement is registered for execution in the Books of Council and Session, diligence may take place anywhere in Scotland. For this reason, most MoAs are registered there rather than in Sheriff Court Books.

[19] *Anderson v Anderson*, 1991 S.L.T. (Sh. Ct.) 11.

[20] Wasoff, McGuckin and Edwards, *Mutual Consent: Written Agreements in Family Law* (Edinburgh: Scottish Central Research Unit, 1997).

[21] See *Horton v Horton*, 1992 S.L.T. (Sh. Ct.) 37; *Milne v Milne*, 1987 S.L.T. 45; *Elder v Elder*, 1985 S.L.T. 471.

[22] This will usually take the form of affidavit evidence: see also para.14–04.

[23] In 1992, there were approximately 3,000 MoAs and at least 1,443 JMs made as compared with a total divorce figure of 12,479 for that year (see Civil Courts Administration, *Civil Judicial*

This shows that in a significant proportion of divorces it is the couple themselves who decide on the terms on which their marriage will be dissolved, rather than leaving the decision to the discretion of the courts.

15–06   Once reached, such agreements, whether MoAs or Joint Minutes, are binding and cannot be extra-judicially varied or reduced without the consent of both parties, except in certain limited circumstances.[24] This serves to prevent reappraisal and re-negotiation of matters that have already been dealt with and provides another type of "clean break". Thus parties are free to set their own terms, which may be quite different from the kind of settlement that would be reached under the 1985 Act. Once made, agreements are binding and enforceable in law[25] except with regards to children.

CIRCUMSTANCES ALLOWING FOR VARIATION OR REDUCTION

Children

15–07   Under s.12 of the Children (Scotland) Act 1995, the court is directed in any matrimonial proceeding or such between civil partners where there are children under 16, to consider whether any s.11 order should be granted, such as a residence or contact order.[26] Its paramount concern in so doing must be the welfare of the child.[27] Thus, agreements reached by parents concerning their childcare arrangements are not binding on the court and, indeed, any person may apply at any time for a s.11 order notwithstanding that an agreement has already been signed about residence or contact.[28] In most cases where agreements about children have been reached, the court rubber stamps them.[29] However, it has to be satisfied that the proposed arrangements are the best that can be achieved, for which weight is given to affidavit evidence such as from relatives, neighbours or others who know the children well.

Contractual Grounds for Reduction

15–08   Agreements may, exceptionally, be set aside or reduced under the general law of contract where one party can establish that his or her consent was

---

Statistics Scotland 1992, p.12). Civil Judicial Statistics no longer records this information.

[24] Note that where one of the parties is in material breach it may be open to the other party to rescind the agreement without the other's consent. See *Morrison v Morrison*, 2000 Fam. L.B. 42–6.

[25] However, where parties make a separation agreement and then reconcile, their actings may be held to be consistent with an intention to revoke the agreement and the principles of financial provision under the 1985 Act may be applied. See *Methven v Methven*, 1999 S.L.T. 117.

[26] 1995 Act s.12 as amended by s.291(2), Sch.28, para.60 of the 2004 Act where there is a child who has been accepted by both partners as a child of the family which their partnership constitutes.

[27] 1995 Act s.11(7)(a).

[28] See *Norton v Horton*, 1992 S.L.T. (Sh. Ct) 37.

[29] See Royal Commission on Legal Services, Cmnd. 7846 (1980), Vol.1, p.157.

vitiated by force and fear, fraud or misrepresentation, undue influence, or facility and circumvention.[30]

There is a heavy onus of proof on the party seeking to challenge the valid- **15–09** ity of a formal written agreement. If the challenge is successful, the agreement will be set aside. However, the longer an agreement remains in force after the divorce, the more difficult it is to challenge. A contract may also be set aside for mutual or common error, but only very rarely indeed for unilateral error, e.g. where one party thought the other had no assets and this was not due in any way to misrepresentations by that party.[31] However, if both parties agreed that a written agreement does not correctly implement what was informally or orally agreed, the court has power to rectify the agreement.[32]

Variation of Periodical Allowance and Aliment Elements

Terms as to capital payments or transfer of property cannot, in principle, **15–10** be varied once an agreement has been concluded. Terms in MoAs allowing for a periodical allowance *can* be set aside or varied by the court but only if the parties have expressly provided that this should be allowed.[33] In contrast, if a JM is incorporated into a decree which contains a periodical allowance element, it may be varied or recalled like any other decree, i.e. if there has been, since the date of the decree, a material change of circumstances.[34] This applies whether or not the parties contemplated variation at the time the agreement was made. It is also important to note that a material change in circumstances must be actual and not based on a deemed or hypothetical change of circumstances brought about, for example, by the granting of decree on the basis of erroneous information.[35] The court may also vary or set aside any term relating to a periodical allowance where the payer has become bankrupt.[36]

Agreements frequently provide for the payment of aliment to children. **15–12** Provision in both MoAs and Joint Minutes can be varied by application to the court if there had been a material change of circumstances since the date of the agreement.[37] When a maintenance calculation under the Child Support Act 1991 is made in respect of a child for whom aliment is payable under an agreement then the part of the alimentary provision which could have been part of a Child Support claim becomes void and is superseded by the maintenance calculation. Such an application to the statutory child support system cannot be made within 12 months of the date of the agreement.[38]

Statutory Challenge—s.16

---

[30] See further, McBryde, *The Law of Contract in Scotland*, 3rd edn (Edinburgh: W.Green, 2007), Chs 13–17.
[31] McBryde, *The Law of Contract in Scotland*, p.364–365.
[32] Law Reform (Miscellaneous Provisions) (Scotland) Act 1985 ss.8 and 9.
[33] Family Law (Scotland) Act 1985 s.16(1)(a) as amended by s.261(2), Sch.28, para.22 of the 2004 Act for civil partners.
[34] 1985 Act s.13(4).
[35] See *Bye v Bye*, 1999 G.W.D. 33–1591.
[36] 1985 Act s.16(3) as amended by s.261(2), Sch.28, para.22 of the 2004 Act for civil partners.
[37] See ss.7(2) and 5(1) respectively of the 1985 Act.
[38] Child Support Act 1991 as amended, s.4(10)(aa). For further discussion see Ch.5.

15–11   Any term in an agreement relating to financial provision which was not "fair and reasonable at the time it was entered into" may be set aside or varied by the court under s.16(1)(b) of the 1985 Act. This will apply to any term of the agreement whether it relates to capital, income or transfer of property. The jurisdiction of the court to alter agreements under s.16 cannot be ousted and any term of the agreement purporting to do this will be void.[39] The power applies in respect of both MoAs and Joint Minutes[40] The test of unfairness must be applied as at the time agreement was reached, and not at any other date. This means that changes in the parties' circumstances *after* agreement has been reached cannot be taken into account, e.g. if one spouse acquires unforeseen financial burdens in the shape of a new family after separation.[41] An "agreement" must be a bilateral obligation and so does not include a gift.[42]

15–12   In *Mackay v Mackay*[43] the wife successfully sought to vary an agreement entered into some time after she and her husband had separated. The husband had failed to disclose significant pension interests before the deed had been executed and these interests came to light much later. The Sheriff Principal said that, since the pension interests were significant in the context of the parties' wealth, the sheriff had been right to regard the agreement as having been unfair and uinreasonable at the date it was entered into.

15–13   In *Clarkson v Clarkson*[44] the couple had entered into an agreement which gave the house to the wife while the husband retained his business interest, resulting, it had been thought, in a more or less equal split of the matrimonial property. Later it was discovered that there was a large VAT liability rendering the husband's business interests valueless. The sheriff decided that the agreement had to be set aside in order "to do substantial justice" in the light of information which should have been available at the time of the agreement.

15–14   At one point it was argued that, since an agreement to be challenged under s.16 could not have been between parties who were about to be married—a pre-nuptial agreement—because the section refers to "parties to a marriage" and the parties in such a case were clearly not yet parties to a marriage. The court took a different, and more purposive view, in *Kibble v Kibble*[45] and it is now clear that pre-nuptial agreements are vulnerable to attack under s.16.

15–15   One of the major issues the court will consider is whether the parties had independent legal advice when drawing up the agreement. If such advice was obtained, then the courts will normally assume that each party was fully appraised of his or her legal rights and understood the consequences of entering the particular agreement. However, the presence of legal advice does not

---

[39] 1985 Act s.16(4).
[40] See *Jongejan v Jongejan*, 1993 S.L.T. 595.
[41] See *Drummond v Drummond*, 1992 S.C.L.R. 473.
[42] See dicta in *Anderson v Anderson*, 1991 S.L.T. (Sh. Ct) 11 at 13E.
[43] *Mackay v Mackay*, 2006 S.L.T. (Sh. Ct) 149.
[44] *Clarkson v Clarkson*, 2008 S.L.T. (Sh. Ct) 2.
[45] *Kibble v Kibble*, 2010 S.L.T. (Sh. Ct) 5.

necessarily mean the agreement cannot be reduced. In *McAfee v McAfee*[46] the court held that

> "the extent of a party's professional qualifications and experience and the nature of any advice received from a professional source may well be important factors to bear in mind in the judgment of what is fair and reasonable. Nevertheless, they cannot in themselves be determinative of the issue where there are other circumstances, suggesting unfair advantage or unreasonable conduct by one party to influence the other in the signing of an agreement which in its terms expressly surrenders rights which that other party would have on divorce".

This approach was upheld in *Gillon v Gillon (No.1)*.[47] In this case, the main issue was whether the *quality* of the legal advice had been substandard. The wife maintained that when she signed the agreement, it had not been made clear to her by her lawyers that she had been entitled to a share of the value of the defender's pension rights, nor had these rights been valued. These were later found to be worth about £30,000. The court held it should consider all the circumstances surrounding the making of the agreement to see whether there was some unfair advantage taken by virtue of the relationship between the parties. If relevant information, such as the value of the pension, had been withheld, this should be taken into account even if (as here) the omission was accidental rather than fraudulent. What was to be disclosed should not be restricted to what would be required in a commercial context. Accordingly, a proof of the facts was allowed.

In *Gillon v Gillon (No.3)*[48] the court held that, notwithstanding the failure to value the pension, the agreement was fair and reasonable at the time it was entered into. Under the agreement, the wife was to purchase the husband's interest in the matrimonial home at a very substantial discount in return for renouncing any further claim on any of her husband's assets, including his pension. It was clear that the wife had been anxious to reach this agreement for fear that if she waited until the case came to court, the house would rise in value, and she would be unable to buy him out. The evidence suggested this fear was well-founded and that the wife had not done badly out of the arrangement. Taking all the facts into consideration in this case, the court refused to vary the agreement. **15–16**

In *Inglis v Inglis*[49] the court endorsed the approach adopted in *Gillon (No.3)* and held that the agreement had been entered into by the wife in the full knowledge that she had a potential claim in her husband's pension rights, but that she had renounced that claim in order to achieve what had appeared to her to be the immediate and significant advantage of the husband's departure from the matrimonial home. **15–17**

---

[46] *McAfee v McAfee*, 1990 S.C.L.R. (Notes) 805 at 808. In this case, husband and wife were both solicitors in partnership together. The wife had also consulted a professional colleague. She argued that notwithstanding this, her husband had applied undue pressure by virtue of his superior business position.

[47] *Gillon v Gillon (No.1)*, 1994 S.L.T. 978 at 983.

[48] *Gillon v Gillon (No.3)*, 1995 S.L.T. 678.

[49] *Inglis v Inglis*, 1999 S.L.T. (Sh. Ct) 59.

15–18   The fact that both parties are advised by the same law agent does not automatically imply that the agreement drawn up was not fair or reasonable because of the conflict of interest.[50] In *Worth v Worth*[51] the parties drew up their own agreement and took it to the solicitor who had acted in their house purchase and was a mutual friend. They were advised that they should seek independent legal advice if they thought there might be a conflict of interest, but chose not to.[52] Several years after the agreement had taken effect, the wife learned that she might have had a claim on her husband's pension under the 1985 Act, an issue never raised or mentioned in the original agreement. She sought to have the agreement set aside under s.16. The court found that the solicitor had not acted improperly as he had raised the issue of conflict of interest, and had attempted to act as an "honest broker" between the parties. However, the court said that the agreement might still be objectively unfair even though there had been no "concealment, trickery, or pressure", and reluctantly found that the agreement did not "fairly reflect the actual value of the parties' property or the defender's fair entitlement to it, for the defender was in law, and thus presumably in fairness, entitled to a share of the value of the pursuer's pension rights".[53] As a result a term of the agreement was reduced.

15–19   The mere fact that there has been an unequal division of assets between the parties by agreement does not of itself give rise to an inference of unfairness or unreasonableness.[54] In some cases, an unequal division may be accepted by one party against their best interests because, as in *Gillon*, they prefer the certainty of knowing precisely what they are to receive on divorce, rather than the uncertainty of waiting to see what a court settlement might produce at a future date.

15–20   An agreement can be reduced or varied under s.16 only either before decree of divorce is granted, or within such time thereafter as the court may specify.[55] Thus, in most cases, if the s.16 plea is not made at the time of divorce the agreement will stand. This can be invidious, given that divorce is often a time of turbulence and disruption, and that the full effect of an agreement negotiated under the pressures of this period—which are unlikely to constitute

---

[50] But note Patterson's observations on r.3 of the Solicitors (Scotland) Practice Rules dealing with professional responsibility in this matter: *Professional Responsibility: Student Manual* (2001) at p.110. See also Lord Nicholls observation in *Royal Bank of Scotland v Etridge (No.2)* [2001] 4 All E.R. 449 at 471 where he sets out the pros and cons of acquiring independent legal advice as set against the benefits of use of the same law agent, such as, less expense.

[51] *Worth v Worth*, 1994 S.C.L.R. (Notes) 362.

[52] Note this was also an issue in *Inglis v Inglis*, 1999 S.L.T. (Sh. Ct) 59 where the court held that the wife had been given the clearest warning that it would have been in her best interests to seek separate legal representation and advice but had declined to do so without any undue pressure from her husband.

[53] *Worth v Worth*, 1994 S.C.L.R. (Notes) 362 at 365.

[54] *Gillon v Gillon (No.3)*, 1995 S.L.T. 678. In *Anderson v Anderson*, 1991 S.L.T. (Sh. Ct) 11 the husband in a fit of remorse at his conduct made a written gift of his whole share of the matrimonial property to his wife. The court held that even if this was an "agreement" under s.16(1)(b), which was dubious, it was fair and reasonable when entered into as the husband had acted voluntarily and in full knowledge of what he was doing.

[55] 1985 Act s.16(2)(b); and see *Jongejan* above, n.21. Further, note that until amended by s.45(1), Sch.2, para.5 of the FLSA 2006 s.16(2) referred to divorce only and not dissolution, whilst referring back to s.16(1)(a) and (b) which did mention civil partnerships and dissolution.

legal duress sufficient to allow reduction—may not become apparent until some time later when the action is barred.[56] Furthermore, in many cases, full details as to the financial position, e.g. the value of pension rights, may only emerge after the divorce. Even where the action is raised in time, as can be seen in cases like *Gillon* and *McAfee*, the courts are most reluctant to reopen a formal written agreement reached by the parties. This is because of the ordinary principle that parties should be bound to contracts they have entered voluntarily, in the interests of certainty for both the parties themselves and third parties.

PRIVATE ORDERING FOR COHABITANTS

The discussion of minutes and joint minutes has so far focused on married **15–21** couples and civil partners, yet unmarried couples—including same-sex couples—may, of course, also wish to enter into binding agreements about finance and property. Indeed, until the FLSA 2006 introduced a limited right to cohabitants to make a claim when their relationship terminates,[57] such cohabitants, if they could not seek a remedy in Unjustified Enrichment, had no claim upon the other in the event of relationship failure *unless* such an agreement had been made. The legal status of such agreements is even stronger than those made by married couples, because there is no equivalent of the s.16 right to seek the setting aside of an agreement as not fair and reasonable as there is for married persons and civil partners.

A key feature of the statutory cohabitation scheme under FLSA 2006 is **15–22** that it is an opt-out system. If couple are cohabiting within the meaning of s.25 of the 2006 Act then the statutory scheme applies to them unless they have specifically excluded or adjusted it by a prior agreement.

ILLEGALITY AND IMMORALITY

Under the "illegal purposes" doctrine in contract law, all contracts which **15–23** promote illegality are unenforceable. Nineteenth-century and earlier case law defined illegal contracts to include any contracts which furthered immoral purposes.

To clarify the position, the Scottish Law Commission some time ago rec- **15–24** ommended enacting a statutory provision to the effect that:

> "A contract between cohabitants or prospective cohabitants relating to property or financial matters should not be void or unenforceable solely

---

[56] Most of the sample questioned in the *Mutual Consent* study, above (n.20) reported that they felt under stress when making their agreement, and that they made compromises which they later regretted.

[57] FLSA 2006 s.28. See also ss.26 and 27 of the 2006 Act

because it was concluded between the parties in, or about to enter, this type of relationship".[58]

This was not, however, included in the FLSA 2006. It is clear, nonetheless, that unmarried couples can validly make wills in each other's favour, give each other gifts, and take title to heritable property in common. Contractual provisions will, however, be useful when attempting in advance of the event to distribute property not yet acquired, or to provide for transfer of property contingent on the breakdown of the relationship or other circumstances. While the provisions of the FLSA 2006 make some property provision for cohabitants, this is not on a par with the kind of financial provision accorded to married couples or civil partners. Despite many cohabitants' erroneous beliefs that they are "common law" spouses and entitled to a half share of each other's property, this is not the case in law and so they still need to consider regulating their relationship through the use of contract.

15–25   Unfortunately there is very little empirical evidence as to how many cohabitants enter into cohabitation contracts. In the study on *Mutual Consent*, only about five per cent of agreements were made by cohabiting couples. It appeared that lawyers had in the early 1990s relatively rarely been called on to draft such contracts in Scotland.[59] Since the coming into force of FLSA 2006 cohabitation agreements have become much more common. Guidance on the type of issues which should be covered in a cohabitation agreement is provided by *Butterworths Lexis Family Law Service*[60] and in *Family Agreements*.[61]

Content of Minutes and Joint Minutes

15–26   Where parties engage in private ordering it is useful to know what emerges from negotiations in the form of content for comparison with the framework set out for division of matrimonial property in the Family Law (Scotland) Act 1985 and its resulting case law. To what extent do such negotiations reflect bargaining "in the shadow of the law"?[62] Such considerations are important for they raise questions about the extent to which parties should be able to supplant legislative standards with their own terms which may

---

[58] See *Report on Family Law*, Scot. Law Com. No.135 (1992), Draft Bill, cl.42. For an English attempt at drafting such legislation, see German's Cohabitation (Contract Enforcement) Bill, June 11, 1991, Bill 175.

[59] See Kingdom, "Lawyers will Draft Anything: Attitudes to Cohabitation Contracts", Occasional Paper No.5 in *Issues in Sociology and Social Policy* (University of Liverpool, Department of Sociology, Social Policy and Social Work Studies, 1994). Kingdom notes that solicitors sometimes negotiate an effective cohabitation agreement when problems arise by way of a minute, or through exchange of solicitors' letters, rather than drafting a full contract in advance.

[60] See *Butterworths Family Law Service* (Lexis Nexis), Division F, Style 10 (vi, vii and viii).

[61] *Butterworths Family Law Service* (Lexis Nexis), *Family Law Agreements*, Ch.6, pp.46–48.

[62] See R. Mnookin and L. Kornhauser, "Bargaining in the shadow of the law; the case of divorce", 1979 Yale Law Journal, Vol.88, p.950–997 who were the first to coin this term.

depart radically from the established framework.[63] As Wasoff has observed, when it comes to private ordering "little is known about bargaining outcomes or the extent to which their substance is genuinely within 'the shadow of the law'".[64] While it is desirable that parties should be able to reach agreements that suit their own individual needs, when private ordering goes beyond this to substantially extinguish rights that would arise under the statutory framework, this can cause hardship. It is true that agreements may be set aside on the grounds discussed above but these are limited and can be hard to establish. Experience from the United States has shown that prenuptial agreements may be used effectively to extinguish a spouse's claim to almost all financial provision altogether and still be upheld.[65] Most jurisdictions in the United States are unwilling to get into questions of the substantive aspects of such agreements and opt instead to judge the matter on the basis of procedural safeguards such as full disclosure of assets and access to legal advice.

Unfortunately, little is known (other than anecdotally) about the actual content of MoAs and Joint Minutes. In 1992, a study was made of written agreements of both kinds entered into by separating and divorcing couples.[66] The overwhelming majority of couples in this survey made agreements while they were still married.[67] A number of important points can be distinguished. **15–27**

First, those making MoAs are disproportionately home owners.[68] It is **15–28**

---

[63] See in respect of the English position *F v F* [1995] 2 F.L.R. 45, CA where the court held that prenuptial agreements were of limited significance because it was undesirable that standards that are intended to be of universal significance should be limited by private contracts. However, see *K v K (Anicillary Relief: Prenutpial Agreement)* [2003] 1 F.L.R. 120, Fam Div where the judge took account of the prenuptial agreement when determining the amount of capital to be paid to the wife and *Wicks v Wicks* [1999] Fam 65

[64] F. Wasoff, "Mutual Consent: Separation Agreements and the Outcomes of Private Ordering in Divorce", 2005 Journal of Social Welfare and Family Law, Vol.27 (3–4), pp.237–250 at p.238.

[65] See *Simeone v Simeone*, 581 A.2d 162 (Pa. 1990) where a 39-year-old neurosurgeon with an income of $90,000 a year presented his 23-year-old bride who was unemployed with an prenuptial agreement on the eve of the parties' wedding. This agreement limited her claims on divorce to a maximum total payment of $25,000 regardless of the period of time that elapsed between the marriage and divorce. Without legal advice she signed the agreement and the court upheld its validity refusing to find that the agreement had been entered into under duress and embarrassment of postponing the wedding. It is certain that the Scottish courts would come to a different conclusion on these facts. See also *In Re Marriage of Greenwald*, 454 N.W.2d 34 (Wis. Ct. App. 1990).

[66] F. Wasoff, "Mutual Consent: Separation Agreements and the Outcomes of Private Ordering in Divorce", 2005 JSWFL 27, Nos 3–4. This study was based on 1,042 agreements including both MoAs and Joint Minutess. The MoAs studied formed a representative sample, so that the findings can be taken as an accurate picture of agreements of this type. It is important to remember that there are important differences between the old dichotomy of custody/access and the new one of residence/contact. It is the policy of teh 1995 Act that both parents should retain parental responsibilities and rights post-divorce unless there is a strong reason to deprive either parent of them.

[67] F. Wasoff, "Mutual Consent: Separation Agreements and the Outcomes of Private Ordering in Divorce", 2005 JSWFL 27, Nos 3–4. 83% were still married, compared with 8% divorced and 5% made by cohabiting couples.

[68] F. Wasoff, "Mutual Consent: Separation Agreements and the Outcomes of Private Ordering in Divorce", 2005 JSWFL 27, Nos 3–4. 77% of those who made a MoA were home owners,

therefore unsurprising that one of the principal concerns of these agreements is the distribution or transfer of the matrimonial home. The favoured option in just under two-thirds of cases was to transfer one spouse's share in the home to the other. It is interesting to compare this to the very limited use being made of property transfer orders in the courts, especially since *Wallis v Wallis*.[69] The survey found women were more than twice as likely to continue occupying the matrimonial home after separation as men, usually because the woman was the one who continued to care for the children after divorce. About two-thirds of mothers with care of the children remained in the matrimonial home after separation.

15–29   Secondly, it was found arrangements for care of the children after divorce are an important topic in separation agreements. Almost 95 per cent of agreements made by couples with children contained discussion and agreement on which parent the children should reside with after separation. Overwhelmingly, this was the mother (in 91 per cent of agreements). There was very little support for joint residence after divorce between couples, which was agreed to in only three per cent of cases.[70] This appears to mark a notable divergence between what parties choose for themselves in childcare arrangements, and the aims of the Children (Scotland) Act 1995, which introduces a presumption of joint parental responsibility after divorce.[71] Contact arrangements were considerably more hazy than those relating to residence, with precise details of access agreed in only about one-fifth of cases involving children. As in the courts, contact was more typically left to mutual arrangement between the parties. Aliment for the children was another matter commonly agreed, especially in MoAs where aliment was discussed in 90 per cent of cases. Interestingly, evidence drawn from interviews suggested that enforcement of agreed aliment payments was less of a problem than it is when payments are ordered by the court, however this is likely to be a reflection of the quality of relationship between adults who are able to cooperate with each other and reach agreement in the first place.

15–30   Thirdly, in the survey the "clean break" philosophy underlying the Family Law (Scotland) Act 1985 also appeared to be endorsed by couples making agreements. Periodical allowance was discussed in only 16 per cent of agreements and provided for in 10 per cent. This can be compared with the fact that court orders for periodical allowance were made in the same year in

---

compared with only 48% of those making Joint Minutes. This is scaceley surprising since it is the wealthier party who has assets which are particularly worth protecting.

[69] *Wallis v Wallis*, 1992 S.L.T. 676, affirmed by the House of Lords at 1993 S.L.T. 1348. For fuller discussion of this case and relevant reform of the valuation date of matrimonial property under s.16 of the FLSA 2006, see paras 13–22 *et seq*. Note: property transfer orders were made in only five % of ordinary divorce actions in 1992: see Morris, Gibson and Platts, *Untying the Knot: Characteristics of Divorce in Scotland* (Edinburgh: Scottish Central Research Unit, 1993), p.28.

[70] However, see *McKechnie v McKechnie*, 1990 S.L.T. (Sh. Ct) 75 in which the parents had put before a court a JM in which they had agreed joint custody. The court said the cases where joint custody would be in the best interests of a child must be rare and awarded custody to the mother and three consecutive residential access to the father.

[71] s.11(7)(a) of the Children (Scotland) Act 1995, as amended by s.291(2), Sch.28, para.17 of the 2004 Act to include civil partners.

about 15 per cent of divorces.[72] The most typical duration provided for a periodical allowance was three years, which echoes the maximum time limit in s.9(1)(d) of the 1985 Act for adjustment from financial dependence. In around 90 per cent of agreements then, a "clean break" was achieved, most typically by transferring one party's share in the matrimonial home to the other, and sometimes by the additional or alternative payment of a capital lump sum. Such payments were far more commonly found in agreements, especially MoAs, than capital sum orders are in the divorce courts.[73]

Finally, one of the most conspicuous features of all the agreements studied   **15–31**
was the absence to a great extent of any mention of pension rights, except by exclusion. Pensions were specifically referred to in only nine per cent of agreements, and payments specifically related to pension rights were recorded in only a mere three per cent of cases.[74] This omission may be due to a negotiated term that the wife would renounce her claims to her husband's pension in return for a transfer of his half share in the matrimonial home or in return for a lump sum.

REACHING AGREEMENT: MEDIATION AND COLLABORATIVE LAW

There are a number of ways in which agreements between parties may be   **15–32**
reached. These may involve negotiated settlement by lawyers (as discussed above), mediation or the use of collaborative law. The trend in family law over the last two decades has been to encourage parties to reach their own decisions on financial provision, and on residence and contact arrangements with respect to children, so that less reliance is placed on court intervention.

One means of achieving this goal is through mediation.[75] Mediation is   **15–33**

> "a process in which an impartial third person, the mediator, assists couples considering separation or divorce to meet together to deal with the arrangements which need to be made for the future".[76]

These include reaching agreements about childcare and financial matters. The Government's White Paper on divorce reform in England in 1995 commented that:

---

[72] Morris, Gibson and Platts, *Untying the Knot: Characteristics of Divorce in Scotland* (Edinburgh: Scottish Central Research Unit, 1993), p.32.

[73] They were found in 40% of MoAs and 17% of JMs. By comparison, capital sum orders were made in only 5% of ordinary divorce actions in 1992 (Morris, Gibson and Platts, *Untying the Knot: Characteristics of Divorce in Scotland*, p.28).

[74] It should be noted that the empirical study on which these data are based was carried out in 1992 before the Child Support Act 1991 and the Children (Scotland) Act 1995 came into force and before reform on pensions and divorce in the Welfare Reforms and Pensions Act 1999.

[75] For an account of mediation, see *The Blackwell Handbook of Mediation: Bridging Theory, Research, and Practice* (M. Herrman (ed.), Blackwell Publishing, 2005). See also Quail: *Keep CALM and Carry On*, JLSS Feb 2013. Mediation now has a substantive European dimension—see Cross-Border Mediation (EU Directive) regs 2011.

[76] *Looking to the Future: Mediation and the Ground for Divorce—the Government's Proposals*, Cm.27990 (1995), para.5.4.

"Unlike current legal processes, mediation is a flexible process which can take into account the different needs of families, and differing attitudes and positions of the parties".[77]

As such, it represents "an alternative to negotiating matters at arms length through two separate lawyers and to litigating through the courts".[78]

15–34   It has been asserted that the aim of mediation is to assist "divorcing and separating couples to reach agreements amicably, especially over the arrangements for their children".[79] There has been debate in Scotland about the various claims made on behalf of mediation as a preferable alternative to court-based dispute settlement, e.g. that it empowers individuals by allowing them to maintain control over their own affairs and assert their autonomy from the courts.[80] There has been a similarly hard fought debate in England[81] over whether the assumptions underlying mediation are justified. There are also concerns about the extent to which parties are empowered to negotiate, where one or other party is in a relatively weaker bargaining position, as well as the issue of whether mediation should be used at all in cases involving domestic abuse. Alongside these considerations is the issue of children's participation in the process.[82] This consideration is especially pertinent given the terms of s.11(7) of the Children (Scotland) Act 1995 in respect of the views of children on any major decision affecting their welfare.

---

[77] *Looking to the Future: Mediation and the Ground for Divorce—the Government's Proposals*, Cm.27990 (1995), para.7.7.

[78] *Looking to the Future: Mediation and the Ground for Divorce—the Government's Proposals*, Cm.27990 (1995), para.5.8.

[79] *The Scottish Family Conciliation Service (Lothian): Report of an Assessment of the First Two Years of the Service* (Edinburgh: Scottish Central Research Unit, 1986), p.2.19.

[80] See F. Raitt, "Mediation As A Form of Alternative Dispute Resolution: A Rejoinder", 1995 J.L.S.S. 40(5) at p.182; A. Dick, "*Lawyer Mediator—Interface or Interloper?*", 1995 S.L.T. 33 at 305; Griffiths, "The Future of Family Law: Empowerment: Rhetoric or Reality?" in *Scots Law into the 21st Century* (Edinburgh: MacQueen (ed.), W.Green, 1996), pp.193–203; M. Upton, "Mediation in Family Disputes", 1996 J.L.S.S. 41(3) at p.115; A. Oswald, "Mediation in family disputes", 1996 SCOLAG 231 at p.20; F. Raitt, "Limitation of family mediation", 1996 SCOLAG 234 at p.68; R. Ward, "CALMing the Waters—Two Years On", 1996 SCOLAG 235 at p.102; A. Oswald, "In defence of family mediation", 1996 SCOLAG 237 at p.148; F. Raitt, "Informal Justice and the Ethics of Mediating in Abusive Relationships", 1997 J.R. Vol.2 at p.76; S. Brand, "Separation and Divorce: Why Clients Should See a Solicitor Mediator", 1998 J.L.S.S. 43(2) at p.58; F. Myers and F. Wasoff. "Meeting in the Middle: Mediators' and Solicitors' Divorce Practice", 2000 S.L.T. 259; J. Scoular and C. Irvine, "A Review of 'Meeting in the Middle'", 2001 S.L.T. 125; F. Myers and F. Wasoff, "Meeting in the Middle: A Reply to Scoular and Irvine", 2001 S.L.T. 128; A. Dick and E. Malcolm, "Let Mediation take the Strain", 2001 J.L.S.S. 46(8) at p.24; J. Sturrock and D. Semple, "Mediation a Cultural Revolution", 2001 J.L.S.S. 46(8) at p.21.

[81] See, inter alia, Roberts, "Decision-Making for Life Apart", (1995) 58 M.L.R. 714; Cretney, "The Divorce White Paper—Some Reflections", 1995 Fam. Law 302; McCarthy and Walker, "Mediation and Divorce Law Reform—The Lawyer's View", 1995 Fam. Law 361; Sclater, "The Limits of Mediation", 1995 25 Fam. Law 494; and Davis, "Divorce Reform—Peering Anxiously into the Future", 1995 25 Fam. Law 564; S. Roberts, "Family Mediation After the Act", 2001 13 C.F.L.Q. 265; R. Dingwall and D. Greatbach, "Family Mediators—What Are They Doing?" [2001] Family Law 378; G. Davies, "Reflections in the Aftermath of the Family Mediation Pilot", 2001 12 C.F.L.Q. 371.

[82] For a discussion of these issues see Edward and Griffiths, *Family Law* (Edinburgh: W.Green, 1997), pp.401–414, paras 15–14 to 15–22.

Whatever the concerns, mediation should not be dismissed as failing to **15–35** provide a just and fair result simply because it fails to follow the model of legal representation and judicial supervision we are familiar with in the court system. So long as established legal norms, such as the "best interests of the child" and "fair sharing of matrimonial property", play a role in shaping agreements reached through mediation, there is no reason why such agreements cannot be as respectful of legal rights as those adjudicated by courts. Furthermore, it is disingenuous to regard the courts, in comparison with mediation, as bastions of justice and rights in the divorce process. The truth is that the great majority of ordinary divorce actions come before the courts uncontested[83] with the court required only to establish that there are grounds for divorce,[84] and that satisfactory arrangements have been made for the children.[85] Mediation, in any event, proceeds generally in the shadow of possible litigation, and a party will be unlikely to agree to any settlement after mediation which is radically worse from his or her point of view than that which would have been granted by the Court.

Mediation began in Scotland in 1984 under the auspices of a voluntary **15–36** body, the Scottish Family Conciliation Service ("Lothian") and has since expanded to cover regions throughout Scotland, under the general supervision of a national umbrella body, Family Mediation[86] Scotland ("FMS"), which was created in 1987.[87] The organisation is now Relationship Scotland following a merger between FMS and Relate Scotland. As the service has developed, so has its remit extended from providing mediation services only in relation to children in divorce, to providing "all-issues" mediation which deals with disputes relating to finance and property as well as children., although there may be problems if a mediator who is not legally qualified seeks to conduct a mediation session at which these technical matters are to be discussed.

The courts in Scotland have the power compulsorily to refer parties **15–37** involved in divorce or child-related disputes to mediation.[88] Such a referral may be made at any stage in the proceedings up until the final determination of the action.[89] However, it is important to note that only a small percentage of referrals to mediation in Scotland do come from the courts.[90] The

---

[83] Morris, Gibson and Platts, *Untying the Knot: Characteristics of Divorce in Scotland*, p.15.

[84] See also para.14–04.

[85] Children (Scotland) Act 1995 s.12.

[86] The term "mediation" has been substituted for "conciliation" in order to avoid any confusion with reconciliation which has different aims.

[87] The current title was adopted in 1992.

[88] OCR 33.22 (as substituted by the Act of Sederunt (Family Proceedings in the Sheriff Court) 1996 (SI 1996/2167) Sch., para.12); and OCR 33A.22 for civil partners. Also, RCS 49.23 (as amended by the Act of Sederunt (Rules of the Court of Session Amendment No.3) (Miscellaneous) 1996 (SI 1996/1756) para.2(17) and by the Act of Sederunt (Rules of Court of Session Amendment No.5) (Family Actions and Miscellaneous) 1996 (SI 1996/2587) para.2(16)). Compulsory referral is very little used. Sheriffs are well aware that if parties are forced against their will to attend mediation it is unlikely that the mediation process will be fruitful.

[89] See *Patterson v Patterson*, 1994 S.C.L.R. 166.

[90] See further, Garwood, *Trying To Get Us Talking, a Study of Rule of Court Referrals to Family Conciliation (Mediation) Services* (Family Conciliation Scotland, Edinburgh, 1992).

rest come from solicitors, voluntary aid agencies, or the parties themselves.[91] Agreements reached in mediation may be embodied in a MoA or Joint Minute in order to make them binding and enforceable. Statements made in mediation are confidential[92] unless, for example, they pertain to damage to property or personal injury during a mediation session, or the civil proceedings to which the mediation relates concerns the protection of a child with whom social services are involved.[93] The statement of outcomes or the fact that no agreement has been reached may, of course, be made public.

15–38   Mediation in Scotland is not at present an alternative to seeing a lawyer or going to court, but rather an optional extra. A decree of divorce or of civil partnership can be obtained only from the courts and, except in simplified divorce/dissolution, a lawyer still institutes court proceedings in almost every case. Originally, FMS mediators were not usually qualified to advise on the complicated issue of finance after divorce and, for this reason, traditionally devoted their efforts to helping parties to reach agreement on disputes concerning residence and contact with children of the marriage. However, as in England, it is rapidly becoming normal for experienced family lawyers to train as mediators, creating a hybrid profession of lawyer-mediators who are jointly accredited by the Law Society of Scotland and CALM ("Comprehensive Accredited Lawyer Mediators").[94] FMS mediators usually either work free, or are paid a nominal hourly rate, while lawyer-mediators charge for their services, though usually at a lesser rate than for ordinary work.

15–39   Whatever the advantages and disadvantages associated with mediation, it is clear that it is here to stay and that it is also being used increasingly as a form of alternative dispute resolution in non-family cases.[95] Initial debates on the subject tended to become polarised around the pros and cons of mediation, as distinct from those attributed to the formal legal system.[96] However, it is important to recognise that while mediation in Scotland does not form part of the court system in the same way as it does in England, it nonetheless cannot be divorced from it. In practical terms, whatever the parties agree to in mediation, the mediated agreement is not legally binding but must be sub-

---

[91] In 2004–2005, 71% of cases referred to FMS were self-referrals. The remainder comprised 13% of referrals from solicitors, 5% referrals from the Sheriff Court, 0% from the Court of Session and 10% from other agencies, e.g. Citizens Advice Bureaux: *2005 FMS, Annual Review 2005*

[92] Civil Evidence (Family Mediation) (Scotland) Act 1995.

[93] The exclusions are at s.2 of the Civil Evidence (Family Mediation) (Scotland) Act 1995.

[94] According to the CALM website, at June 2013 there were 53 trained and accredited lawyer-mediators in Scotland.

[95] See J. Sturrock and D. Semple, "Mediation a Cultural Revolution", 2001 J.L.S.S. 46(8), p.21; S. O'Neill, "Mediation and Non-Family Civil Disputes", 2002 SCOLAG 81; and E. Macolm, "Breakpoint", 2004 J.L.S.S. 49(7) 15 on the work of the Scottish Mediation Network who are exploring the growing range of disputes in Scotland that are moved forward by solicitors' strategic use of the mediation process. See also M. Hassock, "New Balls Please: Civil and Commercial Mediation", 2004 J.L.S.S. 49(7) 18. For England, see E. Harte on the Solicitors Family Law Association's first mediation conference in 2003 in "Comment: Mediation—Help or Hindrance, and What of its Future?" [2003] Fam. Law 33 at p.865.

[96] For a critique of the way in which the roles of lawyers and mediators have been set off against one another see C. McEwen, N. Rogers and R. Maiman, "Bring in the Lawyers: Challenging the Dominant Approaches to Ensuring Fairness in Divorce Mediation", 1994–1995 79 Minn L. Rev. 1317.

mitted to the parties' lawyers to be made into a legally binding document in the appropriate form which allows for third party scrutiny. Similarly, some sheriffs are in favour of exploring mediation as an option and alternative to the court process.[97]

What is clear is the extent to which mediation and the formal legal process **15–40** compliment one another. This is highlighted by the fact that solicitors may now take on the role of mediators. This raises questions about the extent to which the two roles may become blurred or rather lead to a change in practice on the part of their practitioners. A study on *Meeting in the Middle: a Study of Solicitors' and Mediators' Divorce Practice*[98] compared how three profession groups who assist divorcing couples in Scotland—solicitors, solicitor-mediatiors (CALM) and all-issues family mediatiors (associated with FMS)—managed disputes between the parties. While this qualitative study noted differences in approach it nonetheless found that the three groups had more common ground and were closer in practice than expected from commonly made claims about partisanship and impartiality

Collaborative Law

These developments highlight the extent to which family law as a field **15–41**

> "has undergone a sea-change over the past 20 years as bitterly contested divorce hearings have given way to a much more non-confrontational approach. This draws on lawyers' negotiation and mediation skills".[99]

In keeping with this non-confrontational approach, another process for reaching agreement has been introduced into the United Kingdom[100] from the United States in the form of collaborative law. Under this process

> "four-way meetings take place between the clients and lawyers in a search for fair, interest-based solutions, with the clients having access to legal advice throughout the process."[101]

The aim is

> "to resolve family issues by practising law in which each of the parties to a family dispute voluntarily agree to assist in resolving conflict, using co-operative strategies rather than adversarial techniques and litigation".[102]

---

[97] S. Brand, "Separation and Divorce: Why Clients Should See a Solicitor Mediator", 1998 J.L.S.S. 43(2) 58 at p.59. The Sheriff Court Rules Council set up a Mediation Committee to investigate whether the court should encourage parties to use adversarial procedures, and if so, in what circumstances.

[98] By F. Meyers and F. Wasoff for the Scottish Central Research Unit 2000.

[99] G. Langdon-Down, quoting K. Beatson, Chairwoman of Resolution (formerly the Solicitors Family Law Association) in "Family Fortunes", 2005 The Law Society's Gazette, Vol.102(08), p.20

[100] For information see the website of the UK Collaborative Family Lawyers group at *www.collabfamilylaw.org.uk* [accessed July 2013].

[101] N. Laver, "Pulling together", 2004 Solicitors Journal, Vol.148(21) at p.610.

[102] K. Fretweell, "How to Get a Good Divorce", 2003 New Law Journal, Vol.153(7108), p.1877.

It adopts a holistic approach that involves

> "considering the client and legal situation as a whole, not just consid-
> ering the issue the client brings before you but all of the surrounding
> circumstances and the people themselves".[103]

In this process each client retains their own separate, independent lawyer
for the purposes of advising, negotiating and assisting in problem-solving.
It is important to note that the lawyers may be part of a team that may also
involve counsellors, child therapists, independent financial advisers, accountants and other professionals. According to one lawyer such an approach

> "does not view the children in isolation from the finances. It does not tell
> clients that certain of their very real personal concerns are 'irrelevant',
> merely because these are matters upon which the court has no power to
> make orders".[104]

Instead, what the process offers

> "is a humanistic view of divorce, taking into account that parties are
> being asked to make decisions about their futures when they are prob-
> ably least equipped to do so and considering what other agencies may be
> used to assist with better equipping the parties, not only for their deci-
> sion making but for life after divorce".[105]

The structure allows for a first individual client/solicitor consultation covering general legal information and an explanation about the process. This
includes recognition of the fact that

> "during this period of change and uncertainty a client will experience
> personal ups and downs, and the need for the client to make a commit-
> ment to letting the problem solving and decision making come from the
> up mode."[106]

After this the two solicitors meet to discuss the setting up of a joint meeting
as the process centres on four-way settlement meetings, where the clients
meet with their collaborative lawyers to work on settlement issues. The
pattern is

> "for there to be individual client/solicitor meetings followed by a plan-
> ning solicitor/solicitor meeting, then a joint meeting lasting no more
> than two hours, then a repeat of the cycle until a mutually acceptable
> formula is identified and set out in a written agreement".[107]

---

[103] L. Hickman, "Predicting the Law", 2004 The Law Society's Gazette, Vol.101(7), p.30. For a
Scottish perspective see Anne Dick, 2009 54(1) 49.
[104] E. Da Costa, "Divorce With Dignity", [2005] Fam Law 35(Jun) 478 at p.479.
[105] E. Da Costa, "Divorce With Dignity", [2005] Fam Law 35(Jun) 478 at p.479.
[106] A. Dick (professional briefing), "Now it's Collaborative", 2004 J.L.S.S. 49(9) at p.4.
[107] A. Dick (professional briefing), "Now it's Collaborative", 2004 J.L.S.S. 49(9) at p.4.

Part of this process involves making a commitment to full and honest disclosure as well as to upholding confidentiality and other provisions. Unlike mediation, it allows the lawyer to be present during the process itself to give advice to their client and help frame the solutions. This enables the lawyer to protect their client's interests and advise their client on evaluating the consequences of any particular solution.

Discussions between a solicitor and her/his client are confidential although the negotiation arising from this is open, for key to this process is a binding agreement entered into by the two parties and their lawyers to "to engage in frank and honest negotiations to settle the issues between them without recourse to the courts."[108] This means that should the negotiations prove unsuccessful, both lawyers must withdraw and any court proceedings will have to be undertaken with new lawyers. The advantage of this provision, which is the cornerstone of the process, is that clients and their lawyers are less likely to use the threat of litigation to coerce the other party to reach an agreement. By reducing this threat it gives both the clients and their solicitors a vested interest in looking for constructive ways in which to resolve issues. It also frees the lawyers from having to think in terms of having a court strategy if negotiations fail which may inform the whole way in which they frame negotiation. **15–42**

There is a certain amount of overlapping of skills used in the mediation and collaborative law processes but the latter allows collaborative family lawyers to retain the role of legal advisor albeit in a joint problem solving context. In addition, the collaborative law model may include referrals to external mediations if an impasse is reached and referrals to external counsellors ("coaches") to help the clients through the process. Although collaborative family law is an alternative to mediation, it can be used to compliment it, e.g. where a couple might seek the help of a mediator to agree a parenting plan whilst discussing financial matters in four-way meetings. Where the parties need to engage experts such as financial advisers, accountants, pension advisers and so on, this is agreed between them and done under joint instruction. **15–43**

According to one Scots lawyer, the advantage of this form of law is that: **15–44**

> "Unlike our conventional negotiation practice, it lets us concentrate on clients' interests and gives us a vested interest in adopting a constructive approach to problem solving. Unlike mediation, it provides each client with the security of his or her own representation and lets their solicitor protect their position when solutions are being discussed".[109]

Mediation and collaborative law, however, will not work with all clients and in some cases it has to be recognised that "litigation is the only option".[110] Nonetheless, a minority of family law cases end up involving fully contested litigation in the Scottish courts.

---

[108] F. Terry, "Working together", 2003 Solicitors Journal, Vol.147(48) 1445.
[109] S. Smith, "Comment, Collaborative Family Law—A Better Divorce?", 2004 Fam. L.B. 71–2.
[110] S. Smith, "Comment, Collaborative Family Law—A Better Divorce?", 2004 Fam. L.B. 71–2.

Arbitration

15–45   Arbitration in Family Law has always been possible but it was a little-used path until the coming into force of the Arbitration (Scotland) Act 2010 and the setting up of the Family Law Arbitration Group, Scotland (FLAGS), an organisation of Scots family lawyers who have undergone specialist training as arbitrators.

15–46   The advantage of arbitration is that the parties may choose their own arbitrator rather than accept the chance that their judge or sheriff may be one with little interest or background in the sphere of family law. Parties may choose to refer their whole case to arbitration, or else limit the scope of the process to, e.g. the establishment of the relevant date, the valuation or identification of matrimonial assets and specific matters to do with the case of children. An arbitrator cannot grant decree of divorce—only a court can do that—but in some cases there is only a small number of factual matters in dispute, resolution of which will render negotiation of a settelemnt very easy. Such cases are particularly suitable for arbitration. The decision of the arbitrator is binding on the parties in respect of financial provision.

15–47   Another advantage of arbitration is privacy. A high-profile family may prefer to arbitrate in a private and confidential setting rather than litigate in the full glare of public and media attention.

15–48   The fee to be paid to the arbitrator, and the procedure to be followed is agreed between the parties and the arbitrator in advance at a case management meeting, along with the precise terms of the question or questions which are to be answered.

Looking to the Future

15–49   Overall, Scots family law has come a long way in developing processes for assisting parties to reach agreement on financial and other matters on the breakdown of their relationship involving divorce or the dissolution of a civil partnership or separation at the end of cohabitation. Such processes not only involve negotiated settlement by lawyers but also the use of mediation, collaborative law or arbitration. Working in tandem with the formal legal process they aim to provide a real alternative to litigation and resolution through the court process while respecting the dignity of the parties involved. As one commentator has noted:

> "Anything that may alleviate the distress of marriage and relationship breakdown is welcomed; if the process can help solve some of the problems, especially as they reflect on the children, it will be a great step forward".[111]

---

[111]   F. Terry, "Working Together", 2003 Solicitors Journal, Vol.147(48) 1445.

INDEX